THE GUINNESS HISTORY FACT BOOK

GUINNESS PUBLISHING

Project Editor: Tina Persaud
Project Manager: Richard Milbank
Information Systems: Alex Reid
Design: Sarah Silvé
Layout: Peters and Zabransky (UK) Ltd.
Maps: Peter Harper

1st Edition
First published 1994
Reprint 10 9 8 7 6 5 4 3 2 1 0

Published in Great Britain by Guinness Publishing Ltd.
33 London Road, Enfield, Middlesex EN2 6DJ

Printed and bound by the Bath Press

British Library Cataloguing in Publication Data:
a catalogue record is available from the British Library

ISBN 0-85112-782-7

CONTENTS

CONTENTS CONT.

List of Maps

CONTRIBUTORS

A Brief History of the World

The Ancient World: Dr Tim Cornell, Senior Lecturer in Ancient History, University College, London

The Early Middle Ages; The High Middle Ages: John Gillingham, Senior Lecturer in Medieval History, London School of Economics

The Early Modern Era: Dr Christopher Storrs

The Modern World (1789–1914); The Modern World (1914–1994): Dr John Pimlott, Head of War Studies, Royal Military Academy Sandhurst

Cartographic adviser: Dr Colin McEvedy

Factfinder

David Bell, University of Leeds

Matthew Bennett, Royal Military Academy Sandhurst

Bryan Bridges

Dr Robert Cook, University of Sheffield

Dr Tim Cornell, University College, London

Dr Virginia Davis, Queen Mary and Westfield College, University of London

Dr Malcolm Deas, St Anthony's College, Oxford

Dr Peter Denley, Queen Mary and Westfield College, University of London

Nicole Douek, British Museum, London

Dr N.R.E. Fisher, University of Wales, Cardiff

Hamish Forbes, University of Nottingham

Lin Foxhall, University College, London

John Gillingham, London School of Economics

Nick Hooper

Michael Hurst, St John's College, Oxford

Richard Jones

Dr Tim Kirk, University of Northumbria at Newcastle

Dr Colin McEvedy

Richard Milbank

Dr David Morgan, School of Oriental and African Studies, University of London

Margaret Oliphant

Neil Parsons

Dr John Pimlott, Royal Military Academy Sandhurst

Dr Gowher Rizvi, Nuffield College, Oxford

Dr S.J. Salter, University of Sheffield

Dr John Springhall, University of Ulster

Dr Christopher Storrs

Dr Francis Toase, Royal Military Academy Sandhurst

Greg Woolf, Magdalen College, Oxford

Matthew Wyman, University of Birmingham

HOW TO USE THIS BOOK

The Guinness History Fact Book aims to give an accessible overview of world history from ancient times to the present. The book is organized into three sections, each of which can be exploited in different but complementary ways.

A Brief History of the World consists of six introductory essays illustrating with broad brushstrokes the main characteristics, milestones, and innovations of the key periods of world history. Each article is accompanied by box features focusing on movements and turning-points that shaped the period in question, and is amplified by clear and informative maps. The essays provide an overview of the sweep of history, in which the people and events of the past are placed in a wider context; more detailed information about these people and events can be found in the A–Z 'factfinder' section that forms the final section of the book (see below).

Time charts from prehistory to the present provide an at-a-glance chronological guide to important dates and events. Each time chart focuses on a particular time-span and is arranged by region, enabling the user to draw enlightening comparisons between events taking place simultaneously in different parts of the world.

The last and most substantial section of the book is an A–Z **Factfinder** of some 3000 entries, providing essential information on a range of subjects of historical importance – rulers, statesmen, wars, treaties, ideologies, religions, countries and many other topics. 'Feature panels' provide chronologies of important historical events for the world's leading nation-states. Cross references to related entries in the 'factfinder' are indicated by means of small capital letters. There are also frequent cross-references from the 'factfinder' to relevant maps in the first part of the book. Cross-reference between the 'factfinder' entries for present-day European nation-states and the maps of Europe in 1360, 1659, 1715, 1848, 1922 and 1991 will be of particular help in charting boundary changes and the emergence of new states.

A BRIEF HISTORY OF THE WORLD

THE ANCIENT WORLD

In terms of human evolution, the history of mankind began relatively recently. It was the product of a series of technological revolutions which began in the 'Neolithic' (New Stone) Age. The first of these was the agricultural revolution, which occurred in the Near East and southeastern Europe between 9000 and 6000 BC. Animal husbandry and the growing of food crops led to permanent settlement, and made it possible for a given area of land to support a much larger population. Aggregated settlements are attested as early as c. 6000 BC, when Catal Hüyük (Turkey) and Jericho (Israel) became substantial towns.

The earliest historical civilizations, which are distinguished from their prehistoric antecedents by the use of writing (see box), developed along the great river valleys, in Egypt and Mesopotamia before 3000 BC, in the Indus Valley around 2300, and in China (the Yellow River) before 1500. These distinctive environments favoured the development of advanced forms of social organization because of the need to control the annual inundations of the flood plains. The potential fertility of the valleys could only be realized by artificial conservation and irrigation, which required cooperative effort and centralized systems of social control. The resulting food surpluses led to differences in wealth and status, and allowed people to developed secondary occupations, as craftsmen, merchants, scribes, administrators, priests and soldiers. Technological improvements included the invention of the wheel, monumental architecture and, above all, metallurgy – the use of bronze for tools and weapons, and of precious metals for decoration and display.

The Ancient Near East

These early civilizations took different forms. In Sumer (southern Mesopotamia) city-states emerged before 3000 BC. Their principal monuments were temples, which were important centres of culture and economic power. The cities were ruled by kings who depended on the favour of the gods. Bitter rivalry led to constant wars as individual cities attempted to dominate their neighbours; the resulting hegemonies were fragile and short-lived, until Sargon of Akkad succeeded in extending his rule over all of Mesopotamia around 2370 BC. This was the earliest of the great empires that were later to dominate the history of this region. At its height, under Sargon's grandson Naram-Sin, the Akkadian empire included parts of Syria and southeastern Iran. The empire collapsed in about 2200 BC, and was followed by a century of anarchy; then Mesopotamia was once again united under the rule of the southern Sumerian city of Ur. The empire of the so-called Third Dynasty of Ur (c. 2113–2006) was based on a strong centralized administration, whose bureaucratic activities are recorded in thousands of preserved documents.

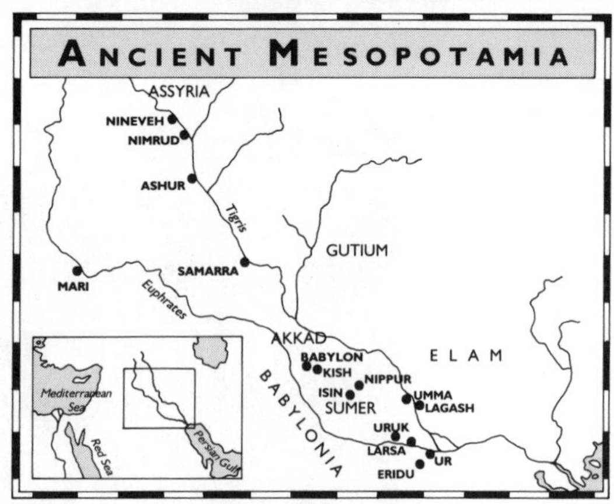

The destruction of Ur was followed by a confused period of rivalries between petty kingdoms in Mesopotamia and Syria, and the main centres of the region were gradually taken overy by the Amorites, a nomadic people from the Syrian desert. It was an Amorite dynasty ruling in Babylon that gradually emerged as the leading power, and under Hammurabi (c. 1792–1750 BC) became the centre of an empire including all of Mesopotamia. As a result Babylonian (or Akkadian) replaced Sumerian as the main language of southern Mesopotamia, and eventually became the international language of the Near East.

The other early centre of Near Eastern civilization was Egypt. Here the achievement of culture and prosperity was brought about by the unification of the country under a single ruler, the pharaoh. According to an ancient convention the history of Egypt is divided into 30 successive pharaonic dynasties. The first dynasty can be dated around 3100 BC, when Upper and Lower Egypt (the Nile Valley and the Delta, respectively) were united for the first time, and an administrative capital established at Memphis. The art of writing, using the hieroglyphic script, advanced rapidly with the development of a centralized bureaucracy. The king, who dominated the state, was himself a god and represented a tangible link between the world of men and the world of the divine. The physical symbol of the king's position was the tomb in which he resided in an eternal afterlife. Increasingly complex tomb monuments were built, and the first step pyramid appeared at Saqqara during the Early Dynastic Period (perhaps around 2700 BC). The height of Egypt's early prosperity was achieved during the Old Kingdom (c. 2575–2134 BC), the age of the Great Pyramids of Giza.

After a short interlude in which Egypt was divided, a strong centralized state was established by the kings of the 11th and 12th dynasties. During this so called 'Middle Kingdom' (2040–1640 BC) Egypt extended its power southwards into Nubia and re-established contacts with the Levant. It was at this time also that a Bronze Age urban society developed in the Indus Valley, focused on the cities of Harappa and Mohenjo-daro. This so-called Harappan civilization flourished from c. 2300 to c. 1700 BC. Further east, in China, the communities of the Yellow River valley developed into substantial bronzeworking and ceremonial centres by 2000 BC. The earliest documents, dating from around 1500 BC, reveal a civilization that prefigured classical Chinese culture, ruled by kings of the Shang dynasty (c. 1480–1100 BC).

During the later part of the Bronze Age the political centres of the Near East began to interact more closely with one another. These centres included Babylon; Assyria, a powerful state in northern Mesopotamia; the Hittites, who established an empire in Anatolia from c. 1650 to c. 1200 BC; Mitanni, a strong state in northern Syria; and a patchwork of small kingdoms and city-states in the Levant which were the target of competing hegemonies as they came under the control first of Mitanni, then of the Hittites. Both powers also conflicted with a third major power, namely Egypt. During the New Kingdom, especially under the rulers of the 18th Dynasty (c. 1550–1350 BC), Egypt established an empire extending from Nubia in the south to Lebanon in the North.

Relationships between these states were characterized by elaborate diplomacy in the form of embassies, royal correspondence, treaties of alliance, gift exchange and dynastic marriages. The ultimate instrument of policy was war, which itself became more sophisticated with the introduction of new technologies, including the horse-drawn chariot and the composite bow. Around 1350 the Hittites destroyed Mitanni and began to encroach on Egyptian possessions in the Levant. In c. 1285 BC the Hittites and Egyptians clashed at Kadesh, a chariot battle which ended indecisively and eventually led to a peace treaty.

It is not certain how far this international system included the states of Greece and the Aegean region. Our knowledge of Bronze Age Greece is based on the excavated palace centres at sites such as Pylos, Tiryns and Mycenae. Whether these sites belonged to a single political unit or were independent kingdoms is also unclear. Nevertheless they were all wealthy, and depended on a centralized economy focused on the

THE INVENTION OF WRITING

History begins with writing because only written documents can preserve the experiences, thoughts and emotions of living people. Writing allows the medium of language to transcend the narrow restrictions of human speech, and can send messages across unlimited distances of space and time. Compared with this revolution, modern developments in communications technology pale into insignificance.

Early forms of writing, such as those developed by the Sumerians and Egyptians, are based on logograms – that is, pictorial symbols that stand for whole words. An example still in use is the ancient Chinese script, consisting of over 50,000 characters. Another early development was the use of conventional symbols to represent syllables. The best known syllabic script from the ancient world is cuneiform, which used wedge-shaped marks to represent syllabic sounds in Akkadian and other languages such as Hittite. Other syllabic scripts include Linear B – used for writing early Greek – and modern Japanese.

An alphabetic script uses signs to represent individual sounds. The earliest example to be widely used was the Canaanite (Phoenician) script, dating from before 1000 BC. This script was adopted by the Greeks around 800 for their own alphabet, which introduced the novelty of using certain signs to represent vowels. Whether this step was a decisive innovation or a minor modification is disputed. In any case, it is the Latin version of the Greek alphabet that is used in the West today. The alphabet is the most efficient writing system ever devised. With a small number of simple characters it can be used to write virtually any language, and can be easily learned by the average five year old.

Written documents survive from the ancient world either because they were written on permanent materials such as clay, bronze or stone, or because they were published as literary texts in manuscript form. Copied and recopied, first as manuscripts and later in printed editions, these texts were preserved through the Middle Ages and down to modern time. Ancient books were written on long rolls of papyrus ('volumes'), with the text set out in columns. Only in late antiquity was the 'codex' invented – the book consisting of bound pages, which we are familiar with today.

palace. The work of a bureaucratic administration is revealed by thousands of clay tablets inscribed in Greek using the so-called Linear B script. The palace centres were surrounded by massive fortifications, and maintained armed forces based on chariots and archers. These features indicate a society very similar to those of the Near East, with which it had commercial and perhaps diplomatic contacts.

In c. 1450 BC the Mycenaean Greeks overran Crete, which had been the centre of a rich palace civilization going back to c. 2200 (the Minoan culture). But around 1200 the Mycenaean palaces were themselves overwhelmed in a widespread catastrophe that also engulfed the Hittite empire and many of the city-states of Syria and the Levant, Assyria and Babylonia languished in obscurity, and Egypt declined, weakened by raids on its territory from sea and land. There is at present no evidence of any large-scale migration, and the upheaval remains unexplained. It is possible that the Greek legend of the Trojan War reflects a dim memory of these troubled times.

In the unsettled conditions that followed Greece entered a 'dark age', while much of the Near East was taken over by new peoples and petty successor-states. The Philistines occupied southern Palestine (and gave it their name), while much of Syria was overrun by Aramaean tribes, whose language, Aramaic, later became the international language of the whole region. One of the most important successor states in this area was the united Israelite kingdom, which became a major regional power after c. 1000 BC under the warlike kings Saul, David and Solomon, but was irretrievably weakened by its subsequent division, between Israel in the North and Judah in the South.

The political vacuum in the Near East was eventually filled by the Assyrians, who under a series of energetic kings created a compact state in northern Mesopotamia and extended their hegemony over the small kingdoms of northern Syria. Under Tiglath-Pileser III (745–727 BC) and his successors, the Assyrians conquered a vast territory, including Babylonia, western Iran, Syria, Palestine, and (briefly) Egypt. The Assyrian empire was essentially

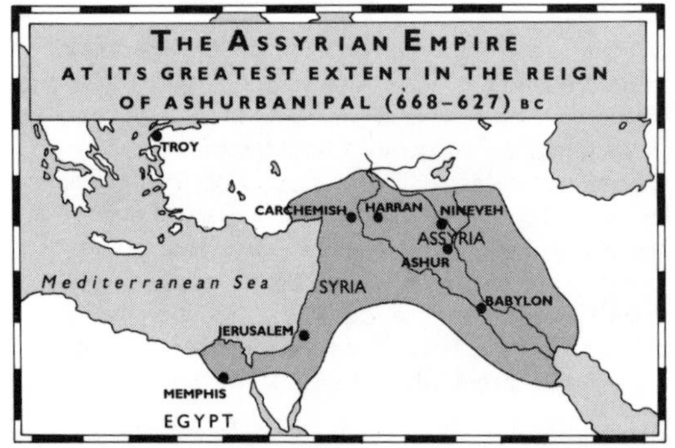

THE ASSYRIAN EMPIRE AT ITS GREATEST EXTENT IN THE REIGN OF ASHURBANIPAL (668–627) BC

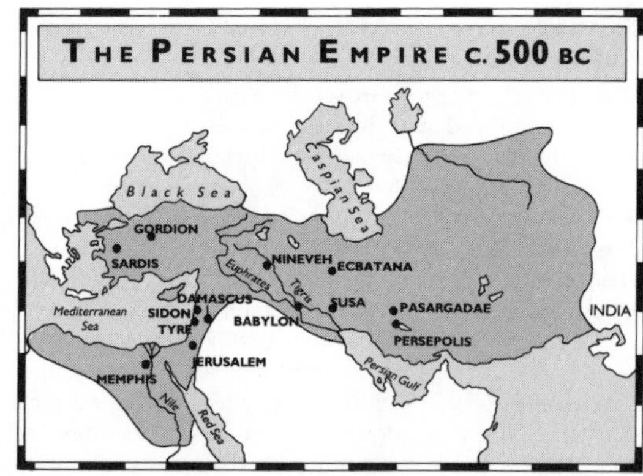

THE PERSIAN EMPIRE c. 500 BC

a military machine, using the tribute levied on subject peoples to finance annual military campaigns. Its semi-professional army used iron weapons (the use of iron had spread throughout the Near East around 1000 BC), chariots, mounted cavalry and different kinds of infantry. It was extremely mobile, capable of long-distance campaigns, and highly effective in siege warfare. In technical proficiency it remained unsurpassed until the Hellenistic period.

The Assyrian empire collapsed in 612 BC, but its place was taken by the Neo-Babylonian empire of Nebuchadnezzar (who overran Palestine and deported the Jews to Babylon); this empire was succeeded in turn by the Persians under Cyrus the Great (559–530 BC). The Persian Empire, which survived until 332 BC, was the greatest the world had seen, incorporating all of the Near East (including Anatolia and Egypt), and extending eastwards to the borders of India.

The formation of the great Near Eastern empires had a profound impact on the Mediterranean world. The Canaanites of the north Levantine coast, whom the Greeks called Phoenicians, were subjected to Assyrian rule at an early date and compelled to pay a heavy tribute. These exactions forced them to expand their trade, and to found commercial outposts along the shores of the Mediterranean. Phoenician settlements were established in Cyprus, Sicily, Sardinia, Malta, Ibiza, North Africa and Spain. The most famous was Carthage (modern Tunis), traditionally founded in 814 BC. Phoenician expansion coincided with parallel developments in the Greek world, which was emerging from a period of obscurity and relative poverty at precisely this time. Population pressures and an increasing demand for essential raw materials, especially metals, caused large numbers of Greeks to emigrate and to found colonies around the shores of the Mediterranean and the Black Sea. Contact with a wider world, and trade with the Near East, profoundly influenced Greek art, which began to imitate oriental motifs, and to incorporate naturalistic designs in place of the former geometric patterns.

Also in the 8th century the Greeks relearned the art of writing, which had been lost since the collapse of Mycenae; by adapting the Canaanite-Phoenician script they invented the alphabet that, in its Latinized form, is still used in the West today.

The Latins and their northern neighbours, the Etruscans, learned the art of writing from the Greeks in the 8th century BC. The arrival of Greek colonies on the southern coasts of Italy and Sicily stimulated the development of the native communities with whom they traded. In the 7th century city-states developed throughout the Tyrrhenian lowland zone, in Etruria, Latium and Campania. One of these was Rome, a strategic site which had been occupied since around 1000 BC, and which controlled an important crossing of the river Tiber. During the 6th century, especially under the Tarquin dynasty, Rome was the most powerful state in central Italy. She dominated Latium and maintained commercial and diplomatic links with Carthage and the Greek colonies.

Ancient Greece

Overseas expansion and increased trade undermined the traditional rule of aristocracies in the communities of Greece, and encouraged the formation of city-states. The Greek city-state (*polis*) was an autonomous political unit consisting of a town with its surrounding territory, and ruled in the interests of the independent farmers who owned the land. A strong sense of solidarity was fostered by participation in community cults, and by the need for a common defence, which was undertaken by the landowning citizens who armed themselves for combat against neighbouring cities. The heavily armed infantrymen (*hoplites*) fought together in a massed phalanx, a form of warfare that increased their political self-confidence. These developments weakened the power of hereditary aristocracies, and led to the introduction of citizen rights based on written law. In many cities these processes were hastened by tyrants – usurpers who seized power with the support of hoplites.

By the end of the Archaic Period (c. 800–500 BC) Sparta and Athens had emerged as the most powerful states in Greece. Spartan power was based on the conquest (before 600 BC) of much of the southern Peloponnese and the reduction of its native population to serfdom. The labour of the so-called *helots* supported an elite body of citizens who formed a highly disciplined hoplite army. The privileged Spartan elite was characterized by political equality and an authoritarian and regimented lifestyle. During the 6th century Sparta created a network of military alliances (the Peloponnesian League), and became the chief military power in Greece.

Athens led the way in developing democracy. The reforms of Solon (594 BC) emancipated the peasants, codified the laws and established a popular assembly for political and legal purposes. The right to hold office was from now on based on wealth, not birth. After a period of tyranny under Peisistratos and his sons, Cleisthenes in 508 BC introduced more democratic means of decision-making at local and city level, including a 'Council of Five Hundred' selected by lot from newly defined local units (*demes*).

The dominance of Athens and Sparta was reinforced as a result of the Persian invasions in 490 and 480–79 BC.

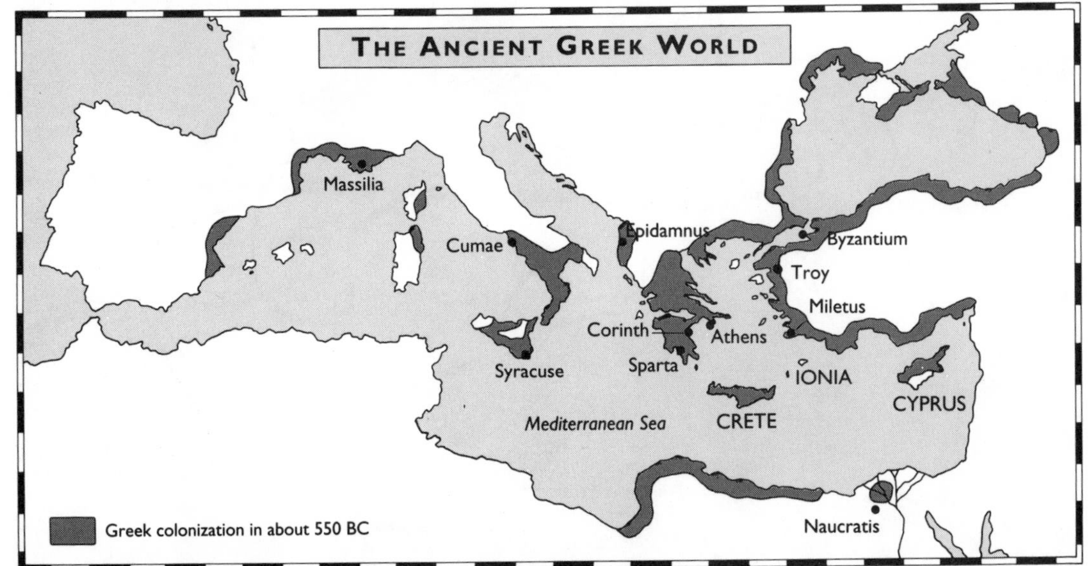

In 490 the Persians were defeated by the Athenians at Marathon, and ten years later a pan-Hellenic alliance led by Sparta prevented the forces of Xerxes from conquering Greece and annexing it to the Persian empire. For all its sophistication, which it had inherited from the Assyrians, the Persian army was no match for the disciplined Greek hoplites, and was decisively beaten at Plataea (479); meanwhile the Athenian Themistocles engineered the destruction of the Persian fleet at the Battle of Salamis (480).

The Greeks went on to liberate many Aegean cities from Persian control, and a new and successful alliance, the Delian League, was created under Athenian leadership. By 450 BC the League had become an Athenian empire, as Athens exacted tribute payments and increasingly interfered in the internal affairs of its 'allies'. During this period Athens completed the development of its democracy. Most offices were open to all, and some were chosen by lot. The assembly decided on all important matters, and lawsuits were heard by popular juries. Under Pericles, who was elected to high office every year from c. 450 to 429 BC, Athens was at its most powerful and prosperous. Drama, literature and the visual arts flourished, and the profits of the empire were used to finance building projects such as the Parthenon.

The growth of Athenian power began to alarm Sparta, and their rivalry led to the long and destructive Peloponnesian War (431–404 BC), which Sparta eventually won with financial help from Persia. The Athenian empire was dissolved, and many cities found themselves ruled once more by the Persians or by Spartan-backed oligarchies. Such an oligarchy, the 'Thirty Tyrants', ruled briefly at Athens, but was soon overthrown.

The defeat of Athens did not bring peace, Aggressive Spartan policies led to a coalition against it of former allies (Corinth and Thebes) and old enemies (Athens and Argos), supported by Persian gold. Thebes gained in military strength, and defeated Sparta in 371. Sparta failed to recover as its archaic social system gradually broke down. Although Athens regained some of its former power, in general the Greek states were weakened by wars and internal conflicts. In the end they fell victim to the aggression of Philip of Macedon (359–336 BC), who obtained mastery over Greece at the Battle of Chaeronea (338 BC). From then on, although the Greek cities continued for centuries as self-governing communities, the focus of political and military power shifted to larger power units – the Macedonian monarchy and its Hellenistic successors, and finally Rome.

When Philip was assassinated in 336 BC his son Alexander reasserted his control and forced his reluctant Greek subjects to join him in what was presented as a national crusade against Persia. The war, for which there was no pretext other than Alexander's ambition, started in 334 with an invasion of Asia Minor (Turkey); after twelve years of ruthless and destructive campaigns,

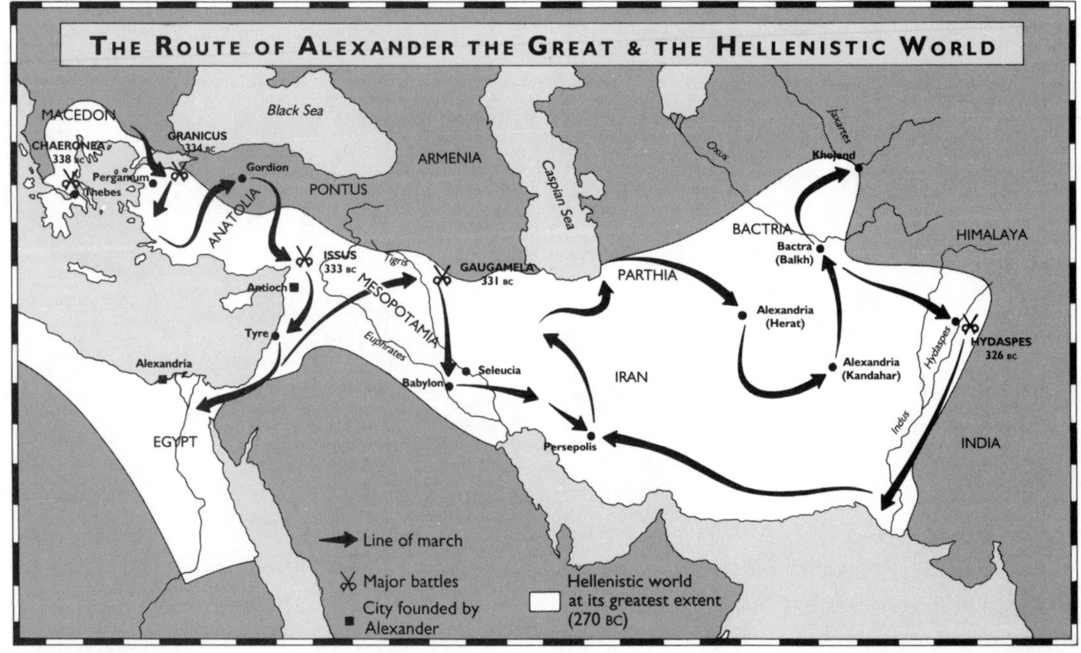

including decisive victories against the Persians at Issus (333) and Gaugamela (332), Alexander succeeded in conquering the whole of the Persian empire. But his sudden death at Babylon in 323 BC plunged the Near East into confusion; in the absence of any convincing successor from the royal family, Alexander's generals fought among themselves for the kingdom. After a generation of warfare three dynasts emerged as rulers of the different parts of the empire; Antigonus in Macedonia and Greece, Seleucus in Asia and Ptolemy in Egypt. These men and their successors established stable kingdoms which, in spite of frequent wars, managed to keep a balance of power until eventually they succumbed, one by one, to the growing power of Rome.

Ancient Rome

Around 500 BC Rome had become a republic ruled by two annual consuls advised by a council of elders (the Senate). Once the aristocratic patricians lost their exclusive privileges in the 4th century, the important distinctions in the citizen body were based on wealth. Only the well-to-do could hold office, but some political rights were extended to all land-owning citizens, who served at their own expense in the army and had a say in political assemblies. Landless proletarians were effectively disfranchised, as were women and slaves. In this respect republican Rome resembled the Greek city-states; but unlike them it was prepared to admit conquered peoples to citizenship, and to treat its allies as military partners rather than subjects.

During the Roman conquest of Italy, in a continuous series of wars from 343 to 264 BC, all the peoples of the peninsula were either incorporated as citizens or linked to Rome as military allies. The result was to give Rome vast resources of manpower that no other Mediterranean state could match. This was the main reason for her victory in the wars against Carthage (264–146 BC). In the second of these 'Punic Wars', the Romans survived an invasion of Italy (218 BC) by Hannibal, who for a time threatened to destroy them; but they emerged stronger than ever after defeating him at Zama in 202 BC, and in

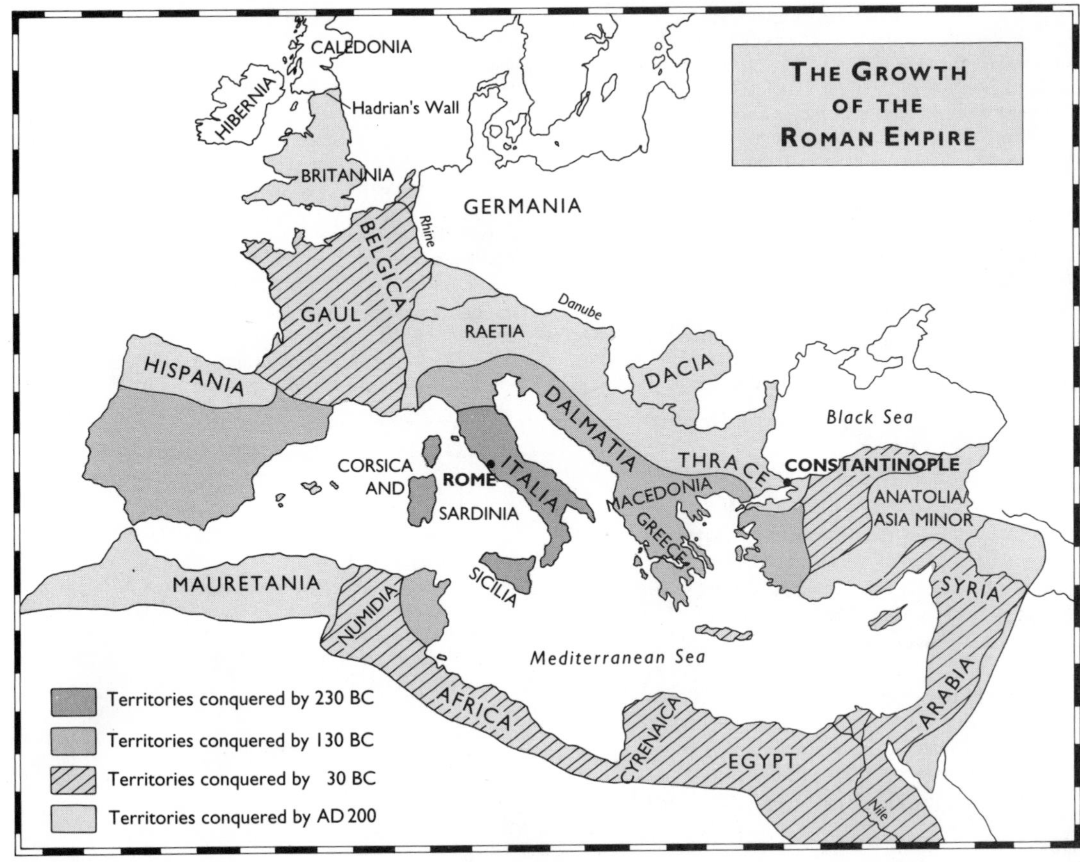

the course of less than a century conquered a Mediterranean-wide empire at the expense of the native peoples of Spain and southern France, and of the major Hellenistic monarchies.

These overseas conquests vastly increased the wealth of the upper classes, and led to the growth of large landed estates in Italy, worked by war captives imported as slaves. Slave labour replaced the small peasant proprietors, who formed the backbone of the Roman army but found that prolonged service in distant theatres made it increasingly difficult to maintain their farms. Many peasants were driven off the land to a life of penury and unemployment. Peasant displacement led not only to impoverishment and discontent, but also to growing problems of military recruitment, since the law laid down a property qualification for service in the army.

The widening gulf between rich and poor eventually gave rise to social conflict and political breakdown. Attempts at reform, for instance by the brothers Tiberius and Gaius Gracchus, ended in failure, while external attacks and internal revolts threatened the security of the empire. The government attempted to resolve the crisis by giving commands to gifted individuals and by creating a professional army from the proletariat. These measures solved the military problems, but had fatal political consequences, because they provided the poor with a means to redress their grievances, and ambitious nobles with the chance to gain personal power by means of armed force. Marius, Sulla and Pompey succeeded one another as military dynasts in the 1st century BC; but they were eclipsed in their turn by Julius Caesar (100–44 BC), who after annexing Gaul to the Roman empire led his army into Italy. After defeating Pompey at Pharsalus in 48 Caesar became consul and dictator for life.

Caesar's assassination once again plunged the empire into civil war, the main contenders being his former aide, Mark Antony (83–31) and his heir, Caesar Octavian. The issue was finally settled at the Battle of Actium (31 BC), where Octavian emerged victorious, and gained control of the empire. Under the honorary title Augustus he became the first emperor, and ruled unchallenged until his death in AD 14. Augustus' great achievement was to reconcile traditional republican opinion with the fact of personal rule. His powers, which gave him overall command of the army and the right to appoint senior officers and the governors of the major provinces, were formally conferred upon him by the votes of the senate and people.

In general the new regime, which guaranteed stability and the chance of prosperity, was welcomed by the upper classes. The provinces, which had suffered dreadfully from civil war, hailed Augustus as a saviour; he also received the adulation of the plebs, who were given free grain and lavish entertainments ('bread and circuses'). He secured the loyalty of the army by settling veterans on provincial land and establishing a permanent standing force, with fixed terms of service, regular wages, and guaranteed retirement bonuses. This reform took the army out of politics, made it dependent on the state, and ensured its loyalty to the emperor. Under Augustus the expansion of the empire continued, and its frontiers were extended to the Rhine and Danube rivers in central Europe. Victories abroad and peace at home were the hallmarks of Augustus' long reign.

However, the rule of Augustus' successors became increasingly autocratic, and some, like Caligula and Nero, were tyrants; on the other hand warlike aggression virtually ceased, and the empire enjoyed peace and prosperity for more than two centuries. During this period provincial life became sophisticated and cosmopolitan, especially in the cities, which were the centres of culture and administration.

The death of Marcus Aurelius in AD 180 was later considered the end of a golden age. The reigns of his successors saw rising taxes, increasing military pressures and political upheavals. Finally, after the fall of the Severan

THE FALL OF ROME

Historians have long puzzled over the causes of the decline and fall of the western empire, and have offered a bewildering variety of explanations. Excessive taxation, military weakness and population decline were all relevant factors, but were themselves symptoms of the condition that needs to be explained, and cannot be considered causes in their own right. The same is true of such explanations as moral corruption, while supposed environmental factors such as climatic change or poisoning from lead water pipes seem contrived and no more convincing than the theories of racial degeneracy that were fashionable before the Second World War.

Much depends on the subjective view of the historian. For instance, the 18th-century historian Edward Gibbon deeply lamented the disappearance of an enlightened and rational culture, swept away on the tide of barbarism and superstition; but Christians have not unnaturally challenged this view of the triumph of their faith. Modern academic historians are more neutral. They tend to emphasize the prosaic fact of the German invasions, which arose from external causes. Barbarian pressure on the frontiers had not existed under the early empire, but built up in the 3rd century and became irresistible in the 5th. The conclusion of this view is that the Roman empire did not fall – it was pushed.

dynasty (193–235) the empire lapsed into anarchy. Civil war, foreign invasions and rampant inflation were accompanied by political breakdown, as emperors succumbed one after another to assassination or military revolt.

In the 270s the military threat temporarily receded, and political stability returned under Diocletian (284–304) and Constantine (312–37). But the recovery was only partial, and was achieved at the price of more oppressive government and bureaucracy, heavy taxation and the reduction of the peasantry to serfdom. A notable development was the rise of the Christian Church, which gained many converts during the 3rd-century troubles, but also attracted the hostility of the state. Official persecutions were instigated, especially by Diocletian in 303; but Constantine reversed this policy and officially recognized the Church. All subsequent emperors were nominally Christians, with the exception of Julian the Apostate (361–3), who staged an abortive pagan revival. Under Theodosius I (379–95) Christianity became the official religion of the empire and other cults were banned.

Theodosius was the last emperor to rule over the whole empire. In the 5th century the eastern and western parts had separate rulers and their histories diverged. The West was menaced by foreign invaders (Rome itself was sacked by the Visigoths under Alaric in 410), and in 476 the last Roman emperor, Romulus Augustulus, was deposed by the Gothic ruler Odoacer. The Byzantine Empire (see p. 16), as the Eastern Empire became known, although steadily reduced by Arab and then Turkish conquests, was to survive until the 15th century.

THE EARLY MIDDLE AGES

During the course of the 5th century many non-Roman peoples – whom the Romans called barbarians – invaded and settled in the western half of the Roman Empire, generally adopting Christianity as they did so. By 500 the former Roman provinces of Britain, Gaul, Spain, Africa and Italy were ruled by 'barbarian' kings. Although millions of people welcomed the end of the oppressive Roman tax regime, other economic and social changes – continuing population decline, urban decay, declining levels of technology and literacy – meant that the new elites, especially north of the Alps, lived in cruder buildings, wore simpler clothing and bought fewer luxuries from the East than had their predecessors under the Roman Empire. Renaissance humanists invented the notion of the 'Dark Ages' as a period of supposed barbarism between the civilization of the ancient world and its alleged revival (by them) in their own day. Most historians today would restrict the

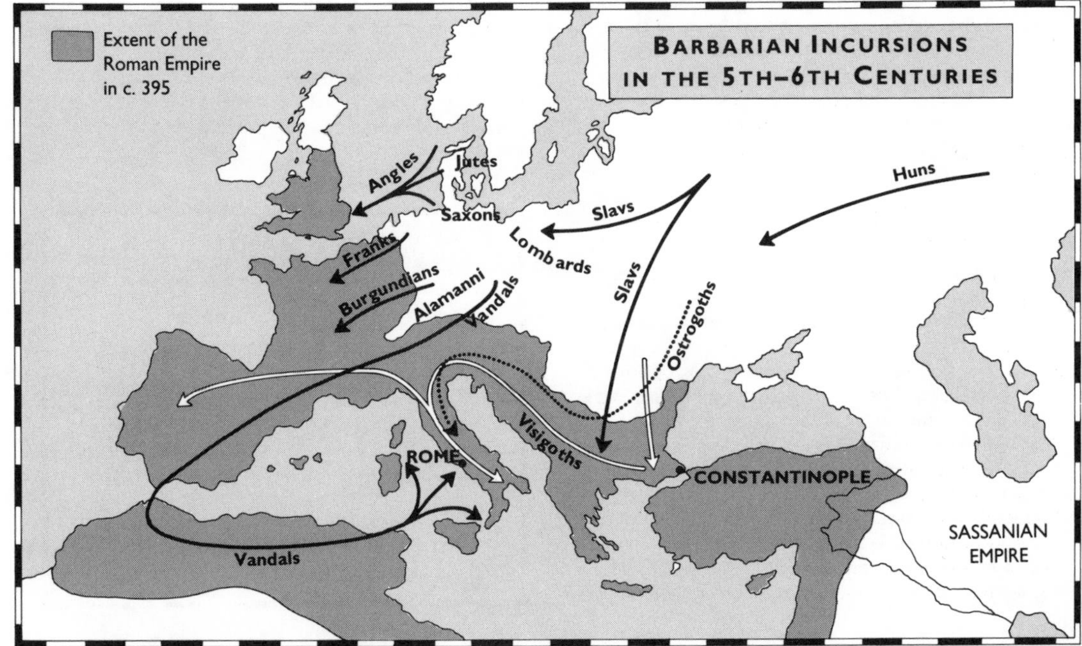

term to the first few centuries after the fall of the Western Roman Empire. Although in this period there was little formal education outside monasteries, and much of the sophisticated material culture of the ancient world was lost, the quality of surviving jewellery, metalwork and book illustration shows that the level of artistic creativity remained high.

As trade, the tax system and the volume of coin in circulation all gradually declined, so it became increasingly common for the rewards for service – both military and political – to take the form of land rather than money. Although slave labour survived on many great estates, most of the agricultural work was done by small tenant farmers (i.e. peasants), some of whom were obliged to work their lord's land as well as their own. The outcome was a social structure which historians have often called 'feudal'. In the later centuries of this period population growth, town development and the revival of a money economy were all under way.

The Franks

In the long run the most successful of the invaders of the Roman Empire were the Franks. The ruthless warlord Clovis (d. 511) established a dynasty, the Merovingians, which was to rule Gaul until the mid-8th century. However, later Merovingian kings left leadership in war to their chief ministers ('mayors of the palace') from the Carolingian family and in 751 one of them, Pepin III, took the Frankish throne. His son Charlemagne (768–814) conquered Lombard Italy, Bavaria and Saxony, stretching the Frankish dominions to their widest extent. In 800 the pope, needing Charlemagne's help, crowned him emperor at Rome. Charlemagne's descendants held on to the western part of his empire, apart from a few interludes, until 987, when the crown passed to the Capetians. But in the 10th and 11th centuries neither Carolingian nor Capetian kings were able to dominate the emerging kingdom of France. Here local powers – dukes, counts and castel-

BYZANTIUM

The wealthier and more populous eastern part of the Roman Empire, ruled from Constantinople, survived for another thousand years after the fall of Rome, as the Byzantine Empire. Its administration and its code of law was systematically overhauled on the orders of Emperor Justinian (527–65). His great church of Hagia Sophia reflected the dominant role in church matters taken by emperors as, in the tradition of Constantine, they tried with great persistence and ingenuity – though rarely with success – to impose religious uniformity on the different peoples within the Eastern Empire. In other fields Justinian's legacy was much more short-lived. His armies, under able generals such as Belisarius and Narses, succeeded in reconquering Africa from the Vandals, Italy from the Ostrogoths and parts of Spain from the Visigoths. But first bubonic plague took a heavy toll of the empire's human resources, and then an increasingly desperate war against Sassanian Persia meant that Justinian's successors were unable to prevent either Slav emigration into the Balkans or the Lombard occupation of much of northern Italy. The sudden loss of empire's richest provinces, Syria and Egypt, to the Muslims in the 630s put an end to all hopes of reconstituting the Mediterranean Roman Empire. Yet despite economic problems (population loss and decay of cities), and the religious controversies generated by the 8th-century Iconoclast movement, somehow Byzantium survived the pressure of further Arab advances. In the later 9th and 10th centuries the Empire was strong enough to go on the offensive again, both on its southern frontier against the Arabs (recapturing Crete and Cyprus for example) and in the Balkans against Bulgars and Slavs. Here (and in Russia) the work of Greek missionaries and notably the invention of the Cyrillic alphabet were to play a vital part in the establishment of Orthodox Christianity in the Slav world. However the empire was once again going through a period of domestic political difficulties when new enemies, the Seljuk Turks, moved into Asia Minor, inflicting a decisive defeat on the imperial army at Manzikert in 1071. In the face of this threat Emperor Alexius I Comnenus (1081–1118) decided to appeal to the West for aid (see p. 19).

THE BYZANTINE RECONQUEST 527–565

lans – ruled the roost. In East Francia it was a very different story. In the 10th century a new royal dynasty, the Saxons or Ottonians, defeated Magyar invaders, launched invasions of Italy and built on these military successes. They established both a powerful kingdom of Germany and the link with the Western Roman Empire which was to survive, in one form or another, until 1806. Further east, and partly in reaction to German pressure, the kingdoms of Poland, Bohemia and Hungary were created.

Anglo-Saxons, Vikings and Normans

After the Roman withdrawal from Britain (completed by 407) the island was ruled by native Britons. But pagan Germanic immigrants, whom Bede (corroborated to some extent by modern archaeology) identified as Angles, Saxons and Jutes. By 600 the Anglo-Saxons dominated lowland Britain, the natives having either fled westwards into Wales (or to Armorica, which became known as Brittany) or become culturally indistinguishable from the newcomers. During the 7th century missionaries from Rome, Francia and Iona converted them to Christianity. Politically the English were split into a fluctuating number of rival kingdoms, but gradually a big four emerged from their ferocious struggles: East Anglia, Northumbria, Wessex and Mercia. For two hundred years (c.650–c.850) Mercia was generally the most powerful of these kingdoms, but it too fell before the onslaught of the Viking 'great army' (865–880). Only Wessex, under a remarkable king, Alfred the Great, survived.

During the course of the 9th century Scandinavian raiders and traders – known as Vikings – used their highly developed seafaring skills to extend their activities from the Black Sea to the North Atlantic. Wherever they went they disrupted established cultures, causing howls of protest, some of which were written down and still survive. These protests created the one-sided – but lasting – image of the pagan Viking warrior. In fact Vikings were not militantly anti-Christian and were traders and settlers as well as pirates. In many cases there was very little difference between the Vikings and those whose lives they disrupted.

Norse and Danish raids on the Frankish, English and Irish coasts first brought them to the shocked notice of the outside world in the 790s. In the late 9th century the raids turned into campaigns of conquest and settlement. In the British Isles they overthrew most of the Anglo-Saxon kingdoms and set up coastal towns such as Dublin in Ireland. On their way to Ireland the Norse took over and settled the Western Isles, Orkneys and Shetlands and from there they sailed to Iceland, Greenland and (briefly, c.1000) to North America. In northern France they established the Viking principality that in due course became Normandy – the land of the Northmen. In eastern Europe the Swedes (known there as the Rus) began by dominating the trade routes from Novgorod to the Black Sea, and ended by carving out the Russian principality of Kiev.

The descendants of Alfred the Great attacked and defeated the recently created Viking kingdoms of East Anglia and York before they had had time to become fully established. By the later 10th century a West Saxon war of conquest had resulted in the creation of England, a kingdom with borders against the Welsh and Scots

THE RISE OF ISLAM

In 622 an Arab prophet, Muhammad, migrated from Mecca to Medina, setting in motion a train of events which within a few decades transformed the known world. By the time of his death (632) he had united the Arabs, partly by his military leadership, but chiefly by his religious teaching, Islam. By the 650s Muslim armies directed by his successors – the Caliphs – had seized the properous heartlands of the ancient civilizations of the Middle East – Egypt, Syria, Iraq and Persia. It was one of the great coups of world history. The conquerors then used their newly acquired riches to extend the rule of Islam yet further, both eastwards and westwards. They entered Spain in 711. By then the murder of Muhammad's son-in-law Ali had already led to the great split in Islam between Shiites (those who belonged to Shi'at Ali, the party of Ali) and the majority Sunnites who laid claim to the *Sunna*, the tradition of the prophet. The Sunnis were led by the Umayyad Caliphs of Damascus and then by the Abbasid Caliphs of Baghdad. Now in command of the centres of Hellenic and Persian culture, the Arabs developed their own Islamic high culture. The use of a common language, Arabic, enabled the cultural unity of the Muslim world to be preserved, but distances were simply too great for this to be replicated in the political sphere. In the 10th century Egyptian Muslims overthrew the Abbasid caliphate in favour of a local Fatimid – and Shiite – caliphate, while in Spain an Umayyad prince established the caliphate of Córdoba.

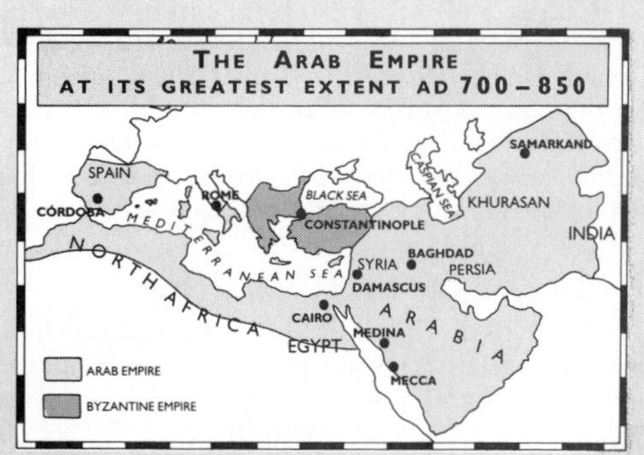

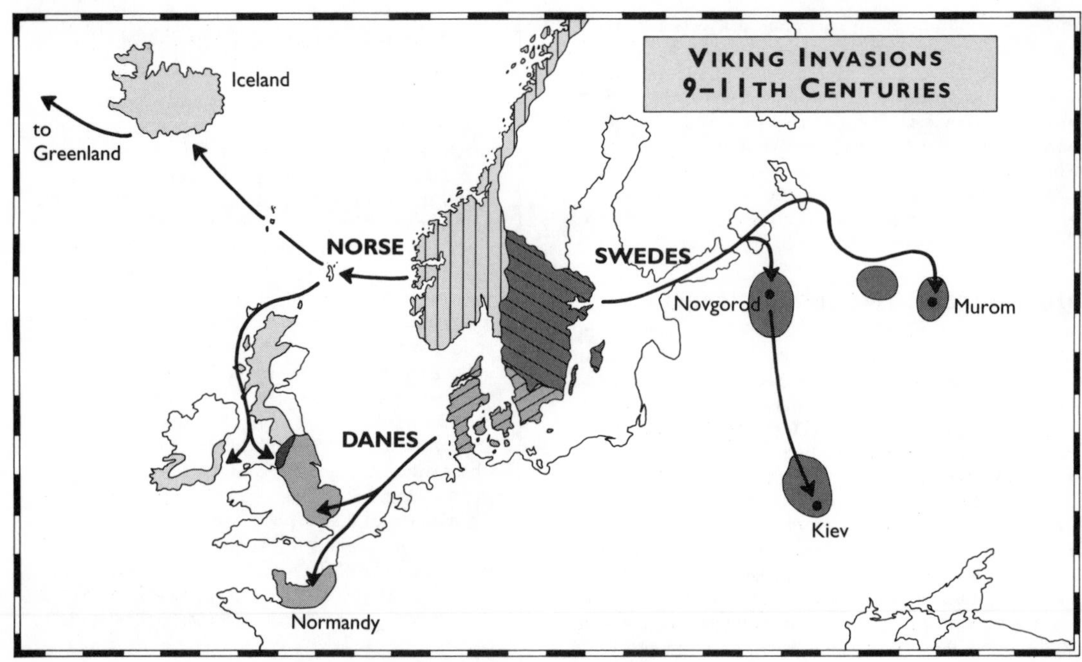

very much where today's borders are. The kingdom emerged as by far the most powerful state in the British Isles. But in the short run it was itself to prove remarkably vulnerable to invasion, falling first, in 1014–16, to the Danes under Sweyn Forkbeard and his son Cnut, and then, in 1066, to the Normans under William the Conqueror. Whereas most of the English aristocracy, by submitting to Cnut, preserved their lands and status under Danish rule, the Norman Conquest led to the virtual replacement of the native elite with a new French-speaking aristocracy. This was to have a profound effect on the development of the English language.

The Roman and Greek Churches

In the West there was no church that could match the bishop of Rome's claims to be the successor of St Peter, and by the 5th century he was claiming authority over all other Christian churches. Moreover, the fall of the Western Roman Empire meant that the pope, unlike the Patriarch of Constantinople in the East, was relatively immune to imperial power. Although popes almost entirely lacked agencies through which they could govern distant churches, the tradition of St Peter, together with Rome's role as a great storehouse of martyr's relics, gave it an unchallenged position as the spiritual centre of Western Christendom. This was enhanced by the missionary activity launched by Pope Gregory I (590–604), the first monk to become pope. He sent Augustine to Kent, and his missionary work continued when later popes lent their support to Boniface's mission to the Germans. But none of this counted for much in the great centre of Christianity in the East. When Leo III crowned Charlemagne as emperor in the West it added a political dimension to the growing differences of culture and language, but it was principally these which, in the 11th century, led to a more or less permanent schism between the Roman and Greek churches.

TANG CHINA

From the 7th to the 9th centuries the emperors of the Tang dynasty, ruling from the great capital city of Changan, successfully restored the Chinese tradition of centralized and bureaucratic government, establishing the principle of selection for office by examination. After the fall of the Tang in 907 the alternative Chinese tradition of fragmented government in the hands of regional warlords prevailed for half a century, but from 960 onwards the Song dynasty reasserted imperial rule. Under the Song – who maintained the unity of the empire until 1127 – a period of unprecedented industrial and commercial advance made China the most highly developed and prosperous state in the world, probably able to support a population of 100 million.

THE HIGH MIDDLE AGES

When Pope Urban II in 1095 urged men to help the Byzantine Emperor and to free the Eastern Christians and Jerusalem from Muslim rule, his preaching evoked an unforeseeable response. Half a dozen armies set out from Western Europe in 1096 and in 1099 after a long march, much of it through hostile territory, they captured Jerusalem. They established the crusader kingdom and the principalities of Antioch and Tripoli. The astonishing success of a papally proclaimed 'holy war' against enemies of the faith inspired not only subsequent crusades to the Middle, East but also similar wars against Muslims in Spain and Portugal, against heathens in Eastern Europe, Cathar heretics in southern France (the Albigensian Crusade), and even against the papacy's political enemies in Italy and Spain.

The success of the First Crusade had been largely due to the state of political fragmentation in the Muslim Middle East. From the 1140s on the Crusader States were thrown increasingly on the defensive as Nur Eddin and Saladin united the Syrian emirates and Egypt. Neither the Second Crusade (1146–9) nor the castles built by the newly created Military Orders, especially the Templars and Hospitallers, could stem the Muslim advance. Saladin's capture of Jerusalem (and virtually

THE MONGOLS

The Mongols were steppe nomads. They waged war as they lived, in the saddle. Steppe pony and compound bow gave them a lethal combination of mobility and firepower. In 1206 a Mongol chieftain named Temujim brought the other tribes of present-day Mongolia under his control and took the title Genghis Khan (universal lord). During the next 20 years he conquered northern China and the eastern part of the Khwarismian empire. The momentum of conquest was maintained under his successors, and by the time of Kublai Khan (1260–94) Iraq, Iran, Russia and southern China had been added to their empire. Once the motor of military expansion stopped running, so huge an empire was bound to break up. Nonetheless all of the great khanates – Russia (or the Golden Horde), Iran, Turkestan and China – were ruled by descendants of Genghis until the late 14th century. The next great steppe warlord, Tamerlane, also numbered Genghis amongst his ancestors.

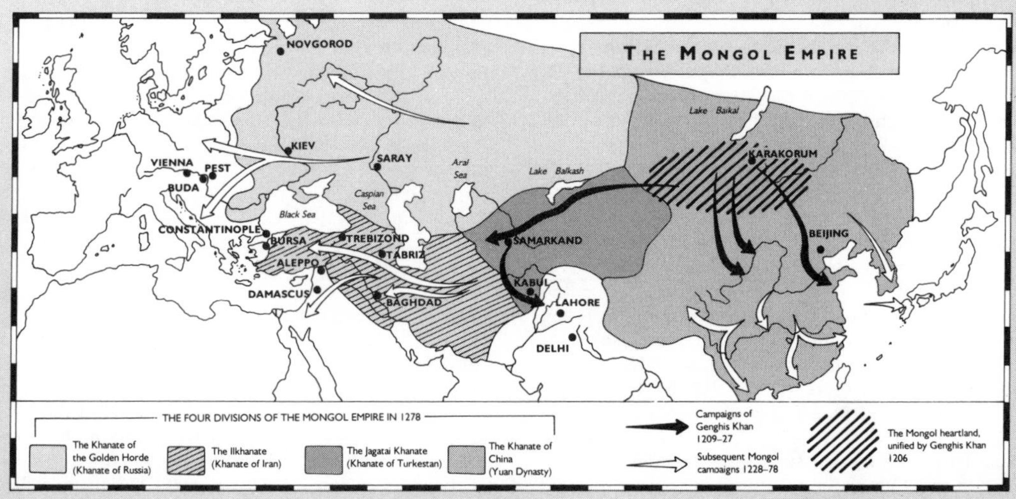

the entire crusader kingdom) in 1187 provoked the Third Crusade. By taking Cyprus (from the Greeks), and recapturing the ports of Acre and Jaffa, Richard the Lionheart gave the crusader states another hundred years of precarious existence. The need for further crusades continued to be felt as a pressing moral and political obligation in the West, but one which became increasingly impractical after the failure of Louis IX's Crusade (1250) and the Mamluks' capture of Egypt. The fall of Acre to the Mamluks in 1291 marked the end of the Crusader States and, as it transpired, of effective crusading activity – despite later attempts such as the Nicopolis Crusade of 1396. But crusading remained a generally acknowledged ideal until the 17th century.

Ironically, in the longer term the principal victim of the crusading movement was the Byzantine Empire. The Fourth Crusade, manipulated by the Venetians, captured Constantinople and established it as the capital of a new Latin empire (1204). Although the Greeks recaptured their great city in 1261, the truncated Byzantine Empire repeatedly suffered further losses at the hands of Bulgars, Serbs and a new Turkish dynasty, the Ottomans. The Ottomans moved into the Balkans, defeating the Serbs at Kosovo in 1389. Eventually in 1453 even the walls of Constantinople succumbed to their overwhelming resources and big guns. As empire-rulers the Muslim Ottomans stepped into Byzantine shoes.

Papacy and Empire

Papal leadership of the crusading movement contributed to the emergence of the papacy as the effective – rather than the notional – head of the Western Church. Another contributory factor was the radical movement often known as the Gregorian Reform after its most forceful exponent, Pope Gregory VII (1073–85). The Gregorian programme aimed at liberating the church from worldly ties by insisting on the celibacy of the clergy and on freedom from lay control; the latter led to the clash known as the Investiture Contest (c. 1075–1122). By sending out papal legates and summoning prelates to attend papal councils such as Innocent III's Fourth Lateran Council (1215), popes gradually extended their authority over the churches of the West. Except perhaps in central Italy, where Innocent III had some success in building up the papal state, laymen either ignored, resisted or found ways of circumventing papal claims which clashed with their interests. During the Investiture Contest opposition was led by German emperors, Henry IV and Henry V, who appointed alternative popes of their own – all subsequently branded 'antipopes'. In the 13th and 14th centuries conflict focused more on the question of who had the right to tax the clergy. On this issue the kings of France and England were the leaders of lay society's successful opposition to papal claims.

Papal history remained disturbed, first by its period of residence at Avignon, then by the Great Schism of 1378–1417 when rival popes, usually one at Rome and one at Avignon, competed for recognition. It required a General Council of the Church (the Council of Constance, 1414–17, called by Emperor Sigismund) to end the schism. It led many 15th-century reformers to support the idea that councils, not popes, should be supreme in ecclesiastical affairs.

One of the reasons for tense relations between popes and emperors lay in the continuing efforts made by Salian and Hohenstaufen emperors to rule Italy as well as Germany. Although the rapidly growing wealth and independence of towns made this increasingly difficult in northern Italy, the conquest of Sicily (1194) provided more than adequate compensation for Henry VI and his son Frederick II (emperor 1220–50). After the demise of the Hohenstaufen dynasty (1254), the elective character of the Holy Roman Empire – as it was now called – came increasingly to the fore, and was enshrined in Charles IV's Golden Bull of 1356. Thereafter in practice the electoral princes chose Charles IV's heirs (first from the Luxembourg dynasty, then Habsburgs) as emperors. At the same time the powers of the emperors became more clearly limited to their dynastic lands north of the Alps. In northern Italy a fiercely competitive society of rival city-states, not unlike the society of classical Greece, emerged, and became the seedbed of the Italian Renaissance.

The Western Monarchies

The early decades of the 13th century saw decisive changes in the political configuration of Western Europe. The Christian rulers of Spain, long engaged in a see-saw contest against Muslims during the Reconquista, won the upper hand after the decisive Battle of Las Navas de Tolosa (1212). With the exception of the rump state of Granada, all of the Iberian peninsula was soon held by the kings of Aragon, Castile and Portugal. In France the balance of power swung rapidly in favour of the crown. The Plantagenets, under Henry II (1154–89) and Richard I (1189–99) had ruled much of northern and western France as well as England, but Philip II Augustus (1180–1223) and his son Louis VIII (1223–6) drove John and Henry III out of Normandy, Anjou and Poitou. Hitherto the Capetian kings had governed little more than the Ile de France. From now on they were in a position to dominate their whole kingdom; even the Cathar Midi was brought to heel as a consequence of the Albigensian Crusades (1209–29). It took all the political skills of Louis IX ('Saint Louis'; 1226–70) to reconcile provincial societies to this more centralized,

Paris-based form of government. By his tax demands and his suppression of the Templars, Philip IV 'the Fair' (1285–1314) exploited the crown's new powers. But his attempts to acquire the prosperous provinces of Flanders (cloth manufacturing) and Aquitaine (wine-growing) created tensions which, after the Capetian dynasty had died out in the male line (1328), led to the formation of the Anglo-Flemish (later Anglo-Burgundian) alliance that did so much damage to the Valois kings of France during the Hundred Years War.

In England the strains of John's defeat by Philip Augustus led to rebellion and the concession of the Magna Carta (1215). English attention was increasingly focused on the British Isles, particularly when Edward I completed the conquest of Wales (1282) and then (in 1296) invaded Scotland. But the Plantagenets remained dukes of Aquitaine and could not afford to ignore French pressure on their outlying duchy. The resulting warfare took on a new aspect when Edward III challenged the Valois Philip VI's right to the French crown. Although at times the English were able to conquer substantial parts of the former Plantagenet dominions in France – particularly after the French defeats at Crécy, Poitiers and Agincourt – in the end the Valois were able to exploit both their own great resources and the inadequacy of the Lancastrian King Henry VI to bring the Hundred Years War to a rapid and triumphant conclusion (1450–3). In England the shock of this defeat was to lead to civil war. In the meantime the costs of war had led, from Edward I's reign onwards, to two major developments: the crown's highly lucrative exploitation of the wool export trade, and the summoning of representatives of town and shire to meetings of parliament to seek consent to unprecedentedly frequent taxation. The latter led to the emergence of the House of Commons.

Economy: Expansion and Crisis

As the population continued to rise throughout the 12th and 13th centuries, so more land was brought under cultivation, particularly on Europe's expanding frontiers. Ways were found to improve the processing and distribution of food, fuel and clothing. Water-mills and horizontal looms proliferated; new machines, such as windmills and spinning-wheels, were invented. Transport improved, both on sea (the cog, a bulk-carrying cargo ship) and on land, where the traditional ox cart was replaced by the much faster horse cart. New sources of silver were discovered in Germany, Sardinia and Bohemia, and a much greater volume of bullion was put into circulation. English mint records show that the weight of silver minted annually during the later 13th century was not exceeded until Victoria's reign. There was a massive rise in the number and size of towns. In many of them the leading citizens struggled, often with success, to win freedoms, notably the right to supervise their own markets and to choose their own magistrates.

Most towns functioned principally as local markets, but some, especially in Italy and Flanders, became major industrial centres and focal points of a burgeoning international trade. Some merchants, like Marco Polo's father, travelled as far as China. Other Italian businessmen employed specialist carriers and overseas agents. They invented an array of sophisticated financial practices and institutions – double entry book-keeping, negotiable paper, stocks and shares. Their development of credit finance through local and international banks such as the Bardi and Peruzzi further increased the money supply. Eventually over-optimistic lending led to a banking crash in the 1340s and to a crisis of business confidence exacerbated by the demographic shock of the Black Death.

Bubonic plague was brought to the Crimea from Asia in 1346. By 1348–9 it had spread to most of Europe. Not until 1894 was the cause of the disease established and the suggestion that this outbreak of plague – later known as the Black Death – killed a quarter of Europe's population is widely regarded as a conservative estimate. Subsequent outbreaks meant that by 1400 the population was only 60% of its pre-1348 level. The resulting labour shortage and spare land was to the advantage of those who had hitherto been the poorest members of society. Early attempts by governments and employers to circumvent the laws of supply and demand led to popular risings in the 1370s and 1380s. But economic realities were irresistible and in the late 14th and 15th centuries those rural and urban workers who escaped the plague enjoyed wage rates and living standards unmatched for centuries to come.

Renaissance

Europe in the 12th century witnessed a genuine Renaissance. It combined a recovery of much of the 'lost' learning of the ancient world, in philosophy, law and the sciences, with the creation of an entirely new architecture – Gothic – and a new flowering of vernacular literature. It also saw a tremendous expansion of educational opportunities. Whereas in previous centuries schools had been largely confined (except in Italy) to monasteries, schoolmasters now appeared all over Europe, even in some small towns and villages. By 1200 demand for higher education had led to the emergence of Europe's earliest universities (Bologna, Paris and Oxford). By 1500 more than 70 universities had been founded, among them Cambridge, Prague, Heidelberg and St Andrews. From the 12th century onwards the ferment of ideas was such that, in the minds of the ecclesiastics of Western Europe, heresy once again seemed to be a major problem.

In the earlier Middle Ages the ideas and values of secular society were rarely set down in writing and in consequence we know relatively little about them. The vernacular literature of the 12th and later centuries throws a whole new flood of light on the lay aristocracy. It shows us a courtly world in which the nobleman was expected to be not only a brave warrior and expert huntsman, but also in possession of polished manners, a fine musician, a graceful dancer, and an eloquent and shrewd speaker in several languages. As the existence of this literature suggests, in the 12th and 13th centuries it became normal for members of the upper classes, women as well as men, to be able to read – though they tended to dictate to clerks when they wanted anything written. By the 15th century there was a reading public large enough to absorb the printing industry's quantum leap in book production.

THE EARLY MODERN ERA (1450–1789)

Between the middle of the 15th and the end of the 18th centuries, the world changed fundamentally in many – if not all – respects. The key development was the change in the relationship between Europe and the rest of the world. This was both symptom and cause of striking changes within Europe itself. These included the rise of new states, and the decline of others, reflecting and reinforcing deeper shifts in economic, social and political power within the continent. The power of the state broadly increased, while the number of states contracted, a few larger states emerging to form an integrated European power system. Other major changes included the ending of the unity of medieval Christendom, the emergence of new and revitalized forms of the Christian faith (and their export overseas), a slow waning of religious belief and the power of the Church, and the emergence of new, more rational ways of thinking. By the later 18th century Europe was a visibly different place from what it had been in the mid-15th century. It was more recognizably modern, whereas the non-European world was both increasingly backward by comparison and increasingly subject to European political dominion and economic exploitation.

Europe in 1450

In 1450 Europe was by no means the world's most advanced culture, politically, economically, socially or technologically. A patchwork of some large and many smaller monarchies and city-states, Western Europe was just emerging from the Hundred Years War and the effects of the Black Death. Government and politics were still relatively primitive and personal in nature, few rulers having the bureaucracies or armed forces necessary to rule their territories as do modern governments. The Catholic Church, of which virtually all the inhabitants of Western Europe were at least notionally members, was often more visible at local level than the state. Although in some parts of Europe systems of trade, finance and industry had achieved some sophistication, they remained relatively undeveloped. The vast majority of Europe's population of about 85 million still lived on and from the land, in small communities that were often completely isolated because of poor communications. Social status (notably privileges enshrined in law) derived not only, or even primarily, from wealth, but was generally inherited.

The Rise of Spain: 1450–1560

The later 15th and early 16th centuries saw the consolidation and strengthening of princely government in much of Europe, and the emergence of new powers. Chief among these was the newly united Spain. Having completed the Reconquest of the Iberian mainland from the Moors, Spain acquired an overseas empire through participation in the voyages of discovery (see box). In Europe, too, Spain was a leading participant in and beneficiary of the Italian Wars, which soon became part of a larger Habsburg–Valois struggle. In the early 16th century Spain's possessions were inherited by the Habsburg Emperor Charles V. With Germany and Italy

THE VOYAGES OF DISCOVERY

In 1450, despite trading and other links with Asia and North Africa, Europeans were largely ignorant of most other civilizations. Earlier attempts at exploration had been tentative and without far-reaching results. However, in the 15th and 16th centuries, Europeans, particularly the Portuguese and the Spanish, took the lead in embarking on ambitious voyages overseas. Inspired by religious zeal and a desire for riches, and drawing on improvements in navigation and ship design, they not only discovered hitherto unknown lands (notably North and South America, and Africa south of the Gulf of Guinea) but also established direct links with known civilizations (such as India and the East Indies). Explorers such as Columbus, da Gama and Magellan laid the foundations of large Portuguese and Spanish empires that drew the newly discovered areas into the Christian European orbit. In the following centuries, other European explorers pushed further into the newly discovered territories and also explored new regions (such as the Pacific in the 18th century). The acquisition of overseas colonies created a global economy focused on Europe. The colonies themselves became increasingly important sources of wealth and power. Exploration, settlement and the economic exploitation of these overseas territories led to the displacement of peoples (notably from Africa to the Americas, as plantation slave labour) and to the extension of European conflicts to the wider world. The 'age of discovery' was crucial for the long-term development of a relationship between Europe and the rest of the world that has persisted almost to the present day.

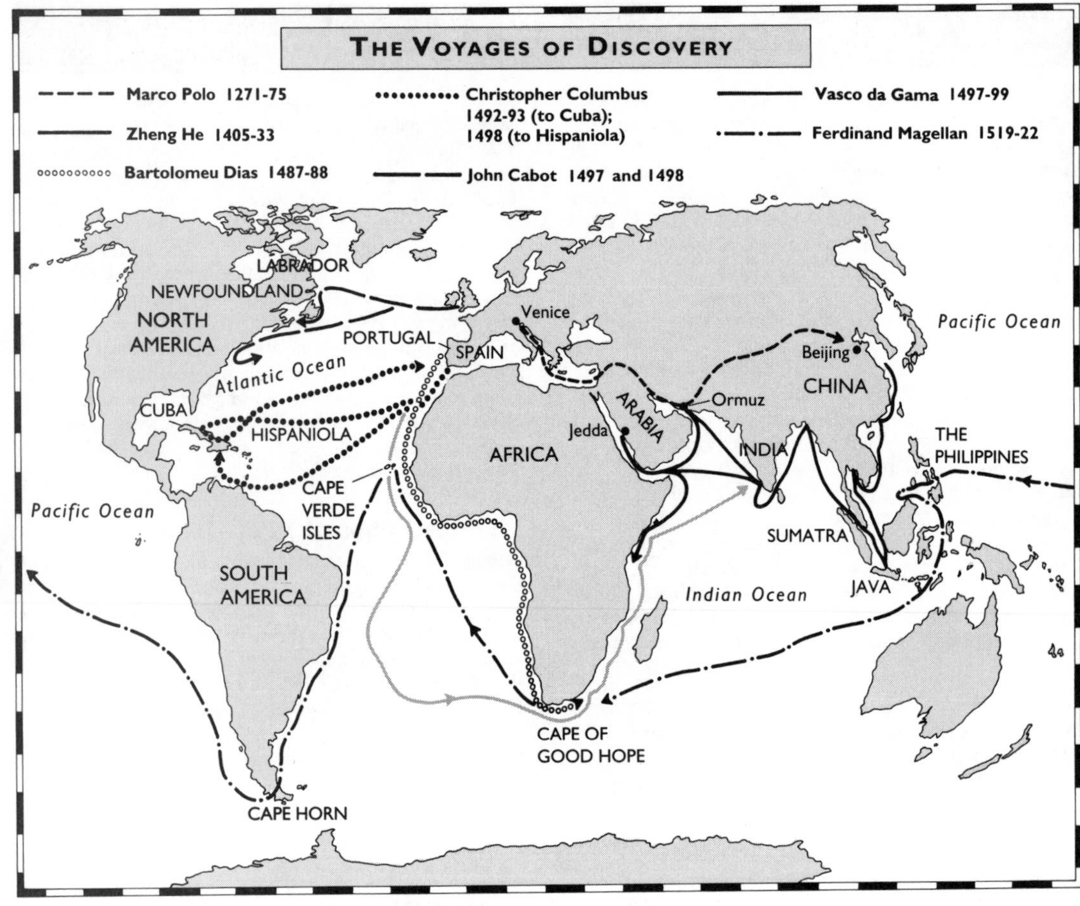

both politically fragmented, only the French (Valois) monarchs could rival the Habsburgs in Western Europe, especially as new weaponry (notably artillery) and the growth of armies made warfare much more expensive than before. In this first phase of the conflict between the Habsburgs and the French monarchy, the French were undoubtedly aided by Charles V's preoccupation with the Reformation in Germany and the struggle with the Ottoman Turks. By the middle of the 16th century, the Spanish Habsburgs were dominant in Western Europe, and were leading the Christian response to the Ottomans, who effectively dominated most of eastern Europe and the Mediterranean.

Religious Wars: 1560 – 1660

After 1560 religious divisions provoked serious domestic and foreign conflict. This was largely due to the continued success of Calvinism – particularly in France and the Dutch Republic – and to the advance of the Catholic Counter-Reformation. Even before Luther nailed his theses to the church door at Wittenberg in 1517 there had been strong reforming currents within the Catholic Church. The success of the Reformation stimulated and transformed this internal reform movement, and from the late 16th century a revitalized Catholic Church was recovering lost ground with the support of princes such as Philip II of Spain. Religious tensions contributed to the outbreak of the Thirty Years War in 1618, although that struggle increasingly focused on the traditional Habsburg–Valois (Bourbon after 1589) rivalry, reflecting France's recovery of power and influence after the trauma of the French Wars of Religion. France's entry into the war in 1635 marked the beginning of the decline of Habsburg Spain. In the course of the conflict Lutheran Sweden and the predominantly Calvinist Dutch Republic both emerged as European powers.

Religion remained a source of domestic and international dispute after 1650, but not to the same extent as in the previous century. By that time, a reinvigorated Catholicism had not only strengthened its hold where it had never been threatened, but had permanently won back areas once lost to the Reformation. The new brand of Catholicism that had emerged from the Council of Trent was carried overseas into the empires of the Catholic powers.

The Rise of the Great Powers: 1660–1789

The pressures of war produced internal upheaval in a number of European states in the mid-17th century. The following decades saw a return to stability, particularly in France, where Louis XIV's brand of absolutism became a political and cultural model throughout Europe. The international power vacuum created by the decline of Spain in the late 17th century was also largely

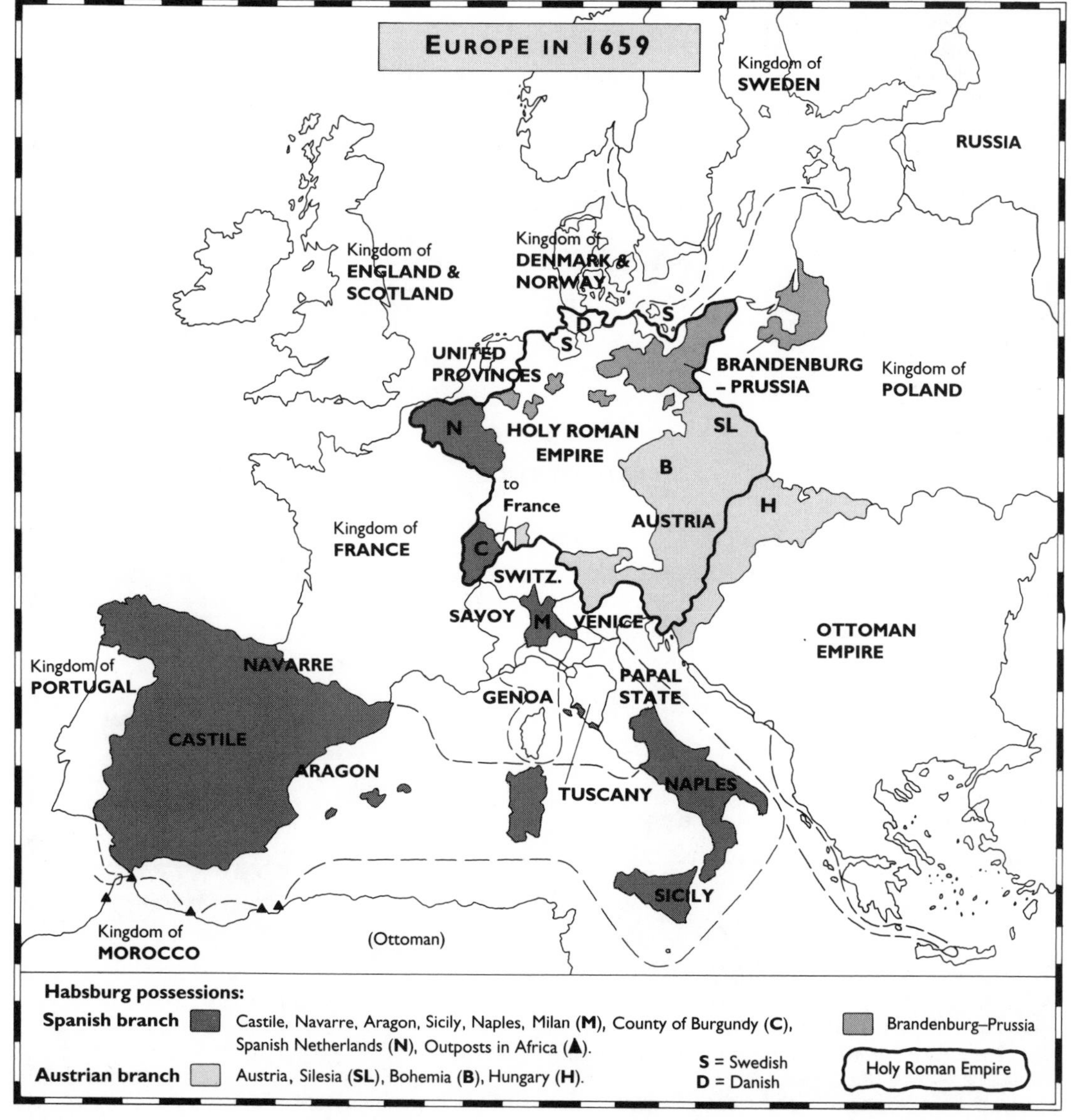

filled by France. Successful resistance to French territorial ambitions depended on co-operation between Louis' neighbours. His most persistent opponents were the Dutch Republic and the Austrian Habsburgs, who emerged from the shadow of their Spanish cousins as a major power in the late-17th century. They exploited their near-hereditary position as Holy Roman Emperors (still a source of considerable influence in Germany as late as 1789), the resources of their anti-French allies and the decline of the Ottoman Turks to supplement the meagre resources of their own relatively poor and loosely integrated territories. By the early 18th century they had established a large multi-faith, multi-ethnic empire, stretching from the Low Countries to Italy and the Balkans. During the struggle against France, Great Britain also emerged as a European power. The development of a stable parliamentary form of monarchy, combined with growing commercial and financial wealth, enabled Great Britain to emerge as a major force by the early 18th century. At the other end of Europe, another new power, Russia, exploded onto the scene in the first decades of the 18th century. There had been little contact between Russia and the West in the Middle Ages, but between the 14th and 17th centuries cultural and trading contacts had grown, and Peter the Great (1682–1725) accelerated the pace of 'westernization'. Russia's rise to European great power status in the Great Northern War was largely at the expense of Sweden, which did not have the resources to maintain the empire it had built up in the 17th century.

The Spanish colonial empire remained the largest throughout the period, but the empires of the Atlantic powers – England, France and to a lesser extent the Dutch Republic – grew significantly, contributing to the

THE OTTOMAN EMPIRE IN 1683

increasing sophistication of their economies and social structures. The commercial potential of their colonies unleashed a major colonial struggle between Britain and France. Britain emerged from the Anglo-French conflict triumphant in North America and Asia and the leading colonial power. Wealth from the colonies helped turn Britain into a major industrial power from the late 18th century (see p. 31), ensuring enormous influence for Britain in Europe itself. Yet the development of powerful navies and the acquisition of colonies were not the only means to great-power success. A small, dispersed and relatively poor German state, Brandenburg-Prussia, was catapulted to European prominence by Frederick the Great (1740–86), one of the so-called 'Enlightened Despots'. Frederick's successors had mobilized what few resources their state possessed to create a large and powerful army; in the mid-18th century Frederick built on their success to transform the international position

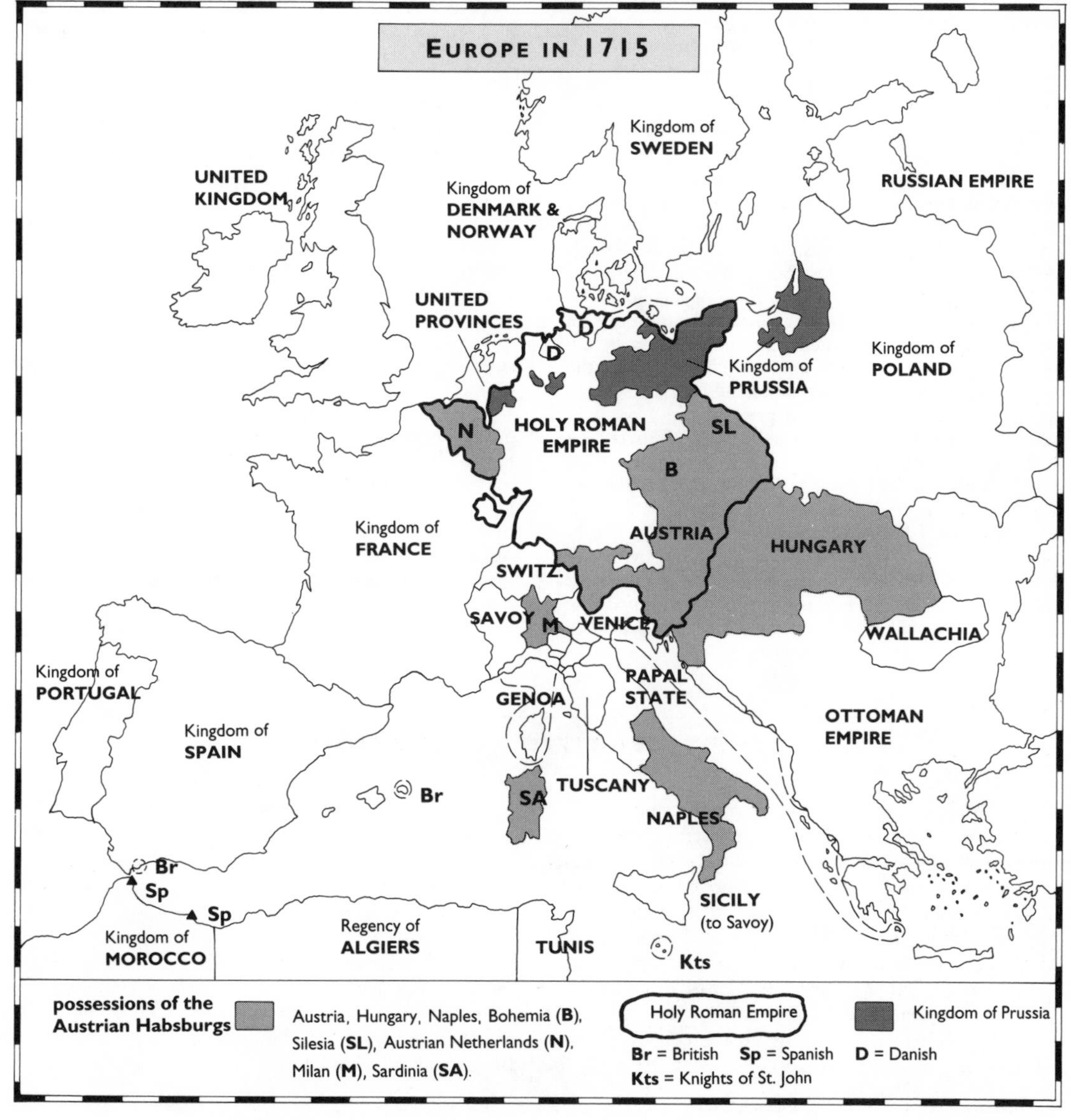

of Prussia. By 1789 Prussia was one of the major European powers, and with Austria (with whom it increasingly contested the leadership of German-speaking Europe) and Russia, dominated eastern and central Europe. These three powers cooperated in the partitions of Poland to destroy what had been one of the largest states in eastern Europe. By 1789 the Turkish Ottoman Empire had further declined, increasingly outpaced by European technology, wealth and power. The Ottoman collapse generated tensions between the potential successor states in the region – Austria and Russia – that were to dominate the politics of eastern and central Europe in the 19th century (the 'Eastern Question').

The Wider World

European dominion overseas was not established everywhere, nor at the same rate, between 1500 and 1800. Persia remained an independent power, mainly concerned with the Turkish threat, until a declining Ottoman Empire was replaced by an expansive Russia after 1700. The Indian sub-continent was dominated by the Muslim Mogul dynasty from the later 16th to the early 18th centuries. In the mid-18th century, however, it was unable to oppose the new political and territorial ambitions of European merchants and their governments, and Britain had laid the foundations of empire in India before the end of the century. Japan, still a largely feudal state and society, sought successfully to prevent the growth of European contacts and influence. In China, contact with Europeans was largely discouraged throughout this period. The Chinese empire thrived in its isolation, remaining by far the largest, most populous and wealthiest state on earth. However, by the end of the 18th century, Chinese technology was being overtaken by that of Europe. For China, as for those other parts of the world hitherto untouched by European rule or influence, the 19th century would mark the beginning of a period of political and cultural domination by the West.

European Society in 1789

In 1789 power and wealth remained very largely in the hands of a narrow elite of princes and nobles. This status represented a key element in the *ancién regime* that became one of the principal targets of the Revolutionary era after 1789. The vast bulk of the population still lived on and from the land, social differences were generally based on birth and legal privilege, the numbers of bureaucrats remained small, the churches were still entrenched, and the hold of modern rational ways of thinking was remarkably limited. Nevertheless, there had been major changes to European society. By 1789 Europe's population had doubled since 1450 to about 175 million, due not least to improvements in medicine and food supply. A larger proportion of that population lived in the increasing number of towns. Although poverty remained a major problem, Europe was far wealthier than in 1450. The emergence in Western Europe of a middle class that gained its income from trade, finance and industry created ever more complex political structures, and contributed to the emergence of consumer societies. In state policy the public good increasingly took precedence over the concerns of the monarch, in part reflecting the growth of literate public opinion. The size of bureaucracies, armies and navies and of government revenues to finance them, had all grown by 1789. Improved transport increased the sense of community both within individual states and throughout Europe as a whole. Population growth and overseas markets stimulated investment in technological improvements and industrial development. Not all parts of Europe were as advanced as the states on the Atlantic seaboard. Nevertheless, aided by its increasing technological superiority, Western Europe was consolidating its position of dominance over the non-European world, which would be strengthened yet further in the 19th century.

THE SCIENTIFIC REVOLUTION

In 1500 European understanding of the natural world and the universe was largely based upon a medieval synthesis of Christian teaching and the intellectual tradition deriving from Aristotle. Only a tiny minority questioned the traditional certainty of a universe centred upon the Earth and subject to the operation of divine power. There was little scientific thinking in the sense of a systematic investigation of reality by observation, experimentation and induction. The 16th and 17th centuries, however, marked the coming of the so-called Scientific Revolution – a period of scientific progress that emphasized experiment and resulted in a new view of the universe and the Earth's place in it. A distinction began to be made between natural science – or natural philosophy as it was known – and occult science. The new science and its practitioners acquired great prestige and contributed in the short term to the 18th century Enlightenment. In the longer term, the Scientific Revolution had a more fundamental impact on Western consciousness, contributing to the faster expansion of European technology and to the gradual secularization of European thought.

THE MODERN WORLD: 1789–1914

Towards the end of the 18th century, two revolutions rocked the known world. The first occurred in America, where discontented colonists overthrew British rule and created their own independent state, forging a constitution (ratified in 1788) that was based on a radical new doctrine of human equality. This was followed, between 1789 and 1792, by an overthrow of the existing political and social system in France, the effects of which were to be profound. Sometimes described as the first 'modern' revolution, the French upheaval began amid peasant revolts and a call for deep-rooted reform, particularly to the taxation system, but quickly escalated. In late 1792, the monarch was deposed and a republic declared. The new constitution, like that of the United States of America, emphasized the rights of citizens, based on the cry of 'liberty, fraternity and equality'.

The French Revolution

Such developments could not be ignored by neighbouring states, most of which were ruled by monarchs wary of any spread of revolutionary ideas to their own people. As early as 1792 the Austrians and Prussians invaded France, intent on nipping the revolution in the bud, but this merely exacerbated the situation. Despite panic in the streets of Paris and, in 1793, anti-revolutionary uprisings in the Vendée and Normandy, the new leadership took the opportunity to consolidate its power, appealing to the people to oppose the invasion. A revolutionary dictatorship, soon to engage in a 'Reign of Terror' against its domestic opponents, initiated a *levée en masse,* mobilizing society in a way that had not been seen before. Men were called to the defence of the revolution, helping to create enormous, ill-trained armies that overwhelmed their smaller, more professional opponents. By 1797, the 'War of the First Coalition' was over and the French, now ruled by a Directory, began to expand their influence, spreading ideas of revolution to the Netherlands, Italy and Switzerland. It was just what the major powers had feared.

The scene was therefore set for the first of the modern 'total' wars – the Revolutionary and Napoleonic Wars – fought for men's souls rather than the more limited territorial or dynastic aims of the 18th century. In the process, the nature of European society changed. Although the original ideals of the French Revolution were diluted by the 'Terror' and, more especially, by the rise of Napoleon Bonaparte, whose assumption of imperial powers in 1804 implied a return to more traditional methods of government, enough of the ideology remained to act as a focus for new aspirations. In many countries invaded by the French between 1797 and 1812, the appeal of equality was strong, leading to the acceptance of new constitutions and laws, the latter based on the *Code Napoléon,* a codification of much of the legislation enacted in France since 1789.

This ensured that the basic tenets of the Revolution survived, even after the overthrow of Napoleon in 1815, but it was not the only legacy of the conflict. In the end, the best way to defeat Napoleon was to raise large armies which could counter the effects of the *levée en masse,* something which necessitated mobilizing the people in their own defence. This was usually done through appeals to patriotism, but the process could not be entirely one-sided. Many of the soldiers who fought against French oppression, whether as part of regular armies or as guerrillas in Spain or Russia, demanded compensation for their sacrifices, usually in the form of improved rights once the war was over. Such rights may have been denied by regimes intent on a restoration of the old order, but the damage to traditional ideas of government had been done. By 1815 the people of Europe were aware that alternative systems of government and social organization existed.

Nor was Europe the only continent to be affected. In Latin America local patriots took advantage of the weakness of Spain and Portugal, devastated by French invasion and campaigns of liberation, to sever the colonial

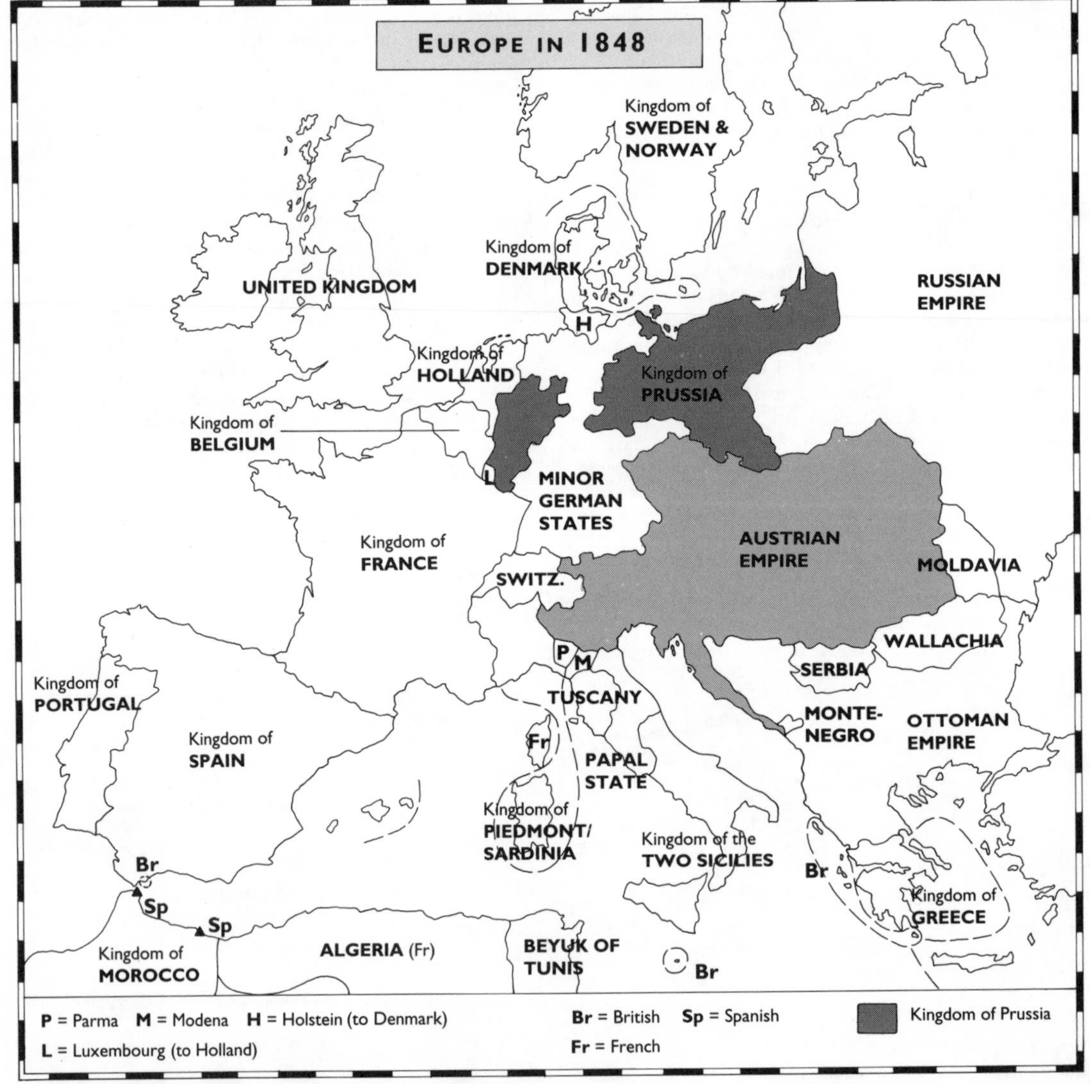

links. Led by men such as Simón Bolívar and José de San Martín, vast tracts of Latin America gained independence between 1810 and 1822. Although there was little evidence of revolutionary political thinking – most of the population of the continent merely exchanged one set of white rulers for another – the development of nationalism, based on the desire of people within a particular territorial entity to rule themselves, was a direct result of the changes that had affected both North America and Europe in the turbulent years since 1789.

The World from 1815

The European powers which had defeated Napoleon – Britain, Austria, Prussia and Russia – emerged from the war with one overriding aim: to prevent a repetition. Two decades of fighting had been costly – one estimate put French losses alone at over a million men – and the old order had been threatened by the spread of radical ideas. At the Congress of Vienna in 1814–15, territorial changes were made to the map of Europe in an effort to contain France, which was seen as the source of all the trouble. But the postwar settlement went further than this. Under the leadership of the Austrian Chancellor, Prince Metternich, the major powers (including France under a restored monarchy) agreed to meet regularly in an effort to forestall crises that might lead to war – an interesting precursor to the League of Nations and United Nations formed after the two world wars of the 20th century.

In the event, the various Congresses achieved little, falling victim to the rivalries of the participants themselves, but they did succeed in containing the early pressures of nationalism. With the exception of Greece in 1830 and Belgium a year later, no new states emerged in Europe until the 1860s; indeed, signs of nationalism in what had been Poland (divided between Austria, Prussia and Russia in the 1790s), Hungary and the Balkans were ruthlessly suppressed, not least in the Revolutions of 1848. Fears of French revolutionary resurgence, reinforced by the overthrow of the monarchy in early 1848 and the rise of Napoleon's nephew (Napoleon III from 1851), merely strengthened the resolve of the more reactionary powers. Peace may have been secured – the only major European war of the period occurred in the Crimea (1854–6) – but it was apparent that demands for change were growing.

The Industrial Revolution

Other pressures fuelled these demands. Throughout the world, populations were growing at a dramatic rate (see box) and, in Europe at least, the new numbers were sustained by the spread of industrialization. In the late 18th century, Britain had led the way in a major economic revolution, based on the discovery that power could be generated by more than just human or animal muscle. Steam was the key, powering textile looms that were capable of producing up to 20 times the output of a hand-worker. By the middle of the 19th century, this had been taken one stage further, into the realm of transport. A railway engine, for example, could transport goods more quickly and over greater distances than teams of pack-horses, while the extension of steam power to ships shortened journeys and freed sailors from the vagaries of the wind.

The result was an ability not just to mass-produce manufactured items, often at cheap prices, but also to open up new and lucrative markets at home and abroad. As these methods spread to other European countries and across the Atlantic, a fundamental transformation occurred. The wealth generated by industrialization allowed investment to take place, funding further new technology and leading to yet more wealth, while the growth of international banking allowed countries and individuals to raise the money needed for the next round of development.

States became richer, not least from their ability to tax the new wealth, and in many areas a distinct middle class emerged that was prepared to use its influence to demand a say in government. The extension of voting

POPULATION GROWTH

A major feature of the 19th century was the enormous increase in the world's population. In Europe, for example, numbers rose from about 187 million in 1800 to more than 450 million by 1913, while in Asia the corresponding figures were 500 million to well over a billion. Some states grew at an enormous rate – Russia increased its population from 51 million in 1816 to a massive 175 million by the beginning of World War I, and even Britain, covering a far smaller area, rose from 10.5 million people to 45.6 million during the same period. In some cases, such as Russia, the increase resulted principally from territorial expansion; elsewhere, increased awareness of hygiene and disease helped to create a longer life expectancy. Improvements to agriculture prevented starvation, and the absence of major wars allowed populations to flourish. This did not apply to all areas of the globe – the people of Africa and Asia were still frequently ravaged by starvation and disease – but as the wealth of certain nations grew, so did their ability to deal with the problems of public health. This did not prevent appalling slum conditions in the rapidly growing cities. By 1913, for example, over 34% of people in Britain lived in urban areas, but their chances of survival were improving.

rights to men of trade – a characteristic of most European states in the 19th century – was merely a manifestation of this pressure, although in countries where the existing government refused to respond (notably Russia), the middle classes became as vocal as the labouring classes in their demands for reform.

The Growth of Empire

But industrialization depended on the availability of raw materials. Some of these could be exploited from within Europe. Iron ore and coal, the vital ingredients in the manufacture of steel, were in relatively easy reach, but others could only be found elsewhere in the world. Control of such resources, together with the ability to transport them back to Europe, where they could be transformed into finished goods for sale across the globe, became an essential part of the power of individual states. Throughout the first half of the 19th century, Britain enjoyed a number of advantages over her European neighbours. She already had a large empire, particularly in the Caribbean and India, and her merchant marine, protected by the largest single navy in the world, could sail the oceans with virtual impunity. In addition, Britain had exploited her initial monopoly of industrialization to carve out markets in a variety of key areas, using the wealth that they produced to set up banking and lending facilities which other states needed to resort to if they were to gain a share of the new economy. Once Britain's rivals had achieved the transformation to an industrialized society, the situation changed – by about the 1860s Britain's lead was being eroded – but until then her position was pre-eminent. She used it to expand her empire, especially in Asia and Africa, ensuring that both raw materials and markets were guaranteed. The result was that by 1860 Britain, containing only 2% of the world's population, was responsible for 20% of the world's trade. Such a concentration inevitably led to rivalry with other states, envious of the wealth and power it engendered.

As European countries began to vie for shares of world trade, they did so by exploiting the weaknesses of others. Some old-established states beyond the boundaries of Europe, notably China and Turkey, had internal problems that left them vulnerable to foreign encroachment. The newly independent countries of Latin America found it hard to exploit their natural resources without European help, made available on extremely disadvantageous terms to the host nations. For most of the century, therefore, the major European colonial powers – Britain and France, with Italy and Germany emerging after 1870 – dominated world trade, forcing themselves onto weaker states or colonizing vast tracts of territory. It has been estimated, for example, that the British Empire grew at the phenomenal

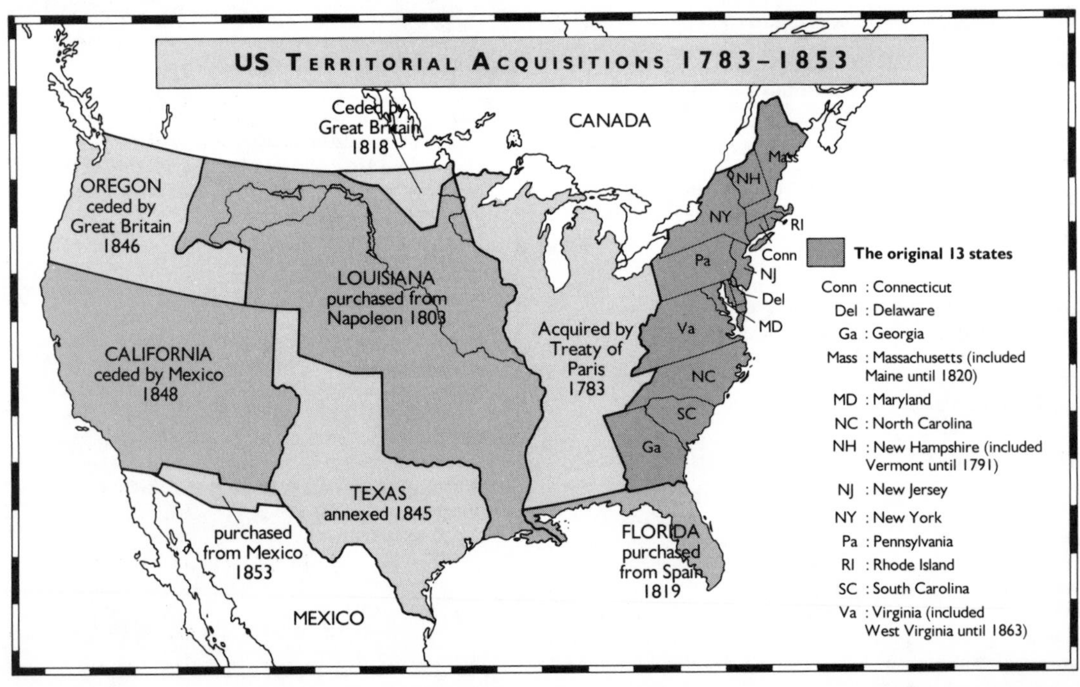

rate of 100,000 square miles a year between 1815 and 1865. In addition, Russia expanded across existing borders into Siberia and Asia Minor. By 1878 some 67% of the land surface of the globe was under the direct control of European powers, compared to only 35% in 1800. It was, without doubt, a Eurocentric world.

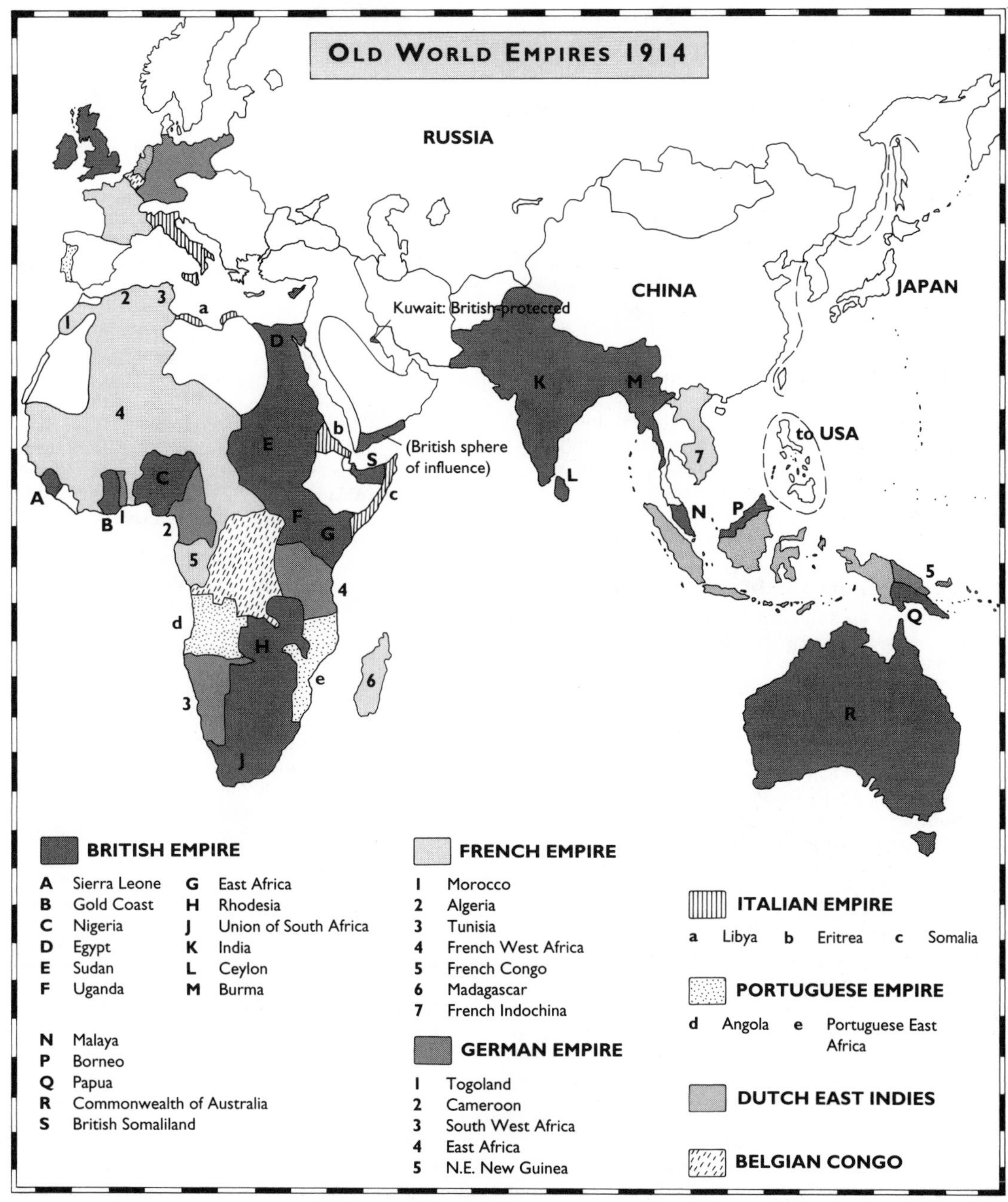

But other powers were emerging. In Japan, Western contact in the 1850s triggered a process of modernization that was to transform it into a regional power of some strength, particularly after the Meiji Restoration of 1868. Of far greater importance was the development of the USA, enjoying the advantages of isolation from the affairs of Europe and settling the extensive lands west of the Mississippi River (see p. 32). Promises of land and, in many cases, freedom from oppression, led to enormous European immigration. The US population rose from 8.5 million in 1816 to 31.4 million in 1860 – and when this coincided with the impact of new technology from Europe, opportunities for wealth and power increased. However, the Civil War (1861–5), fought between an industrialized, liberal North and an essentially agricultural, reactionary South, hindered progress. The war had many of the characteristics of totality, in that both sides were fighting for ideals, were able to mobilize their societies and take advantage of new technology (including railways, the telegraph and steam-powered warships), but its significance was ignored in Europe, where it was regarded as a conflict conducted by amateurs. The fact that the war cost the Union 360,000 men and the Confederacy 258,000 seemed to be more than cancelled out by the continuing flow of immigrants – over 800,000 into the North alone during the war years. However, it would clearly take time for the USA to recover and assume the global importance its great potential implied.

The Unification of Italy and Germany

Meanwhile, Europe had entered a new phase of development, characterized by the emergence of two new states: Italy and Germany. In 1859 Camillo di Cavour, Prime Minister of Piedmont, accepted French help in ejecting the Austrians from the northern part of Italy, prior to the creation of a unified state. A year later, Guiseppe Garibaldi and his 'Redshirt' irregulars took control of southern Italy and, by 1870, the entire peninsula (with the exception of the Vatican) was under common rule. By then, a similar process of unification was being completed in Germany, where the Prussians under prime minister Otto von Bismarck gained supremacy through a series of short, successful wars – in 1864 against Denmark, in 1866 against Austria and, most significant of all, in 1870–1 against France. The new German Empire was proclaimed on 18 January 1871, with the Prussian king declared Kaiser Wilhelm I of Germany.

The creation of both these states had far-reaching effects. Although Italy never assumed 'Great Power' status, chiefly because of the enormous imbalance of industrialization between north and south, it did pose a potential territorial threat to both France and Austria (the latter known as Austria-Hungary from 1867). Of far greater concern, however, was the strength of Germany, for what had been a collection of 39 states, each susceptible to pressure from other powers, was now a single entity intent on assuming a position of importance in both Europe and the world. Its potential was awesome. High levels of education and social provision gave it a population (66.9 million people by 1913) that was capable of making significant contributions to technological development, while the introduction of conscription ensured that it had large reserves of trained manpower in the event of war. Moreover, the creation of Germany had involved aggression, most notably against the French, and this implied a desire for further expansion, either east into Russian-controlled Poland, south into Italy or west into France and the Low Countries. Any such move, or the fear of it happening, was sure to alarm neighbouring countries, while German efforts to carve out an overseas empire, and to create a navy to protect its trade, was guaranteed to bring it into conflict with already established colonial and naval powers.

But the fears were two-sided, for Germany also felt threatened, not least by French moves to recover territory (Alsace-Lorraine) lost in 1870–1. While in power, Bismarck was able to safeguard German security by means of an elaborate series of alliances, designed to create a solid bloc of central powers in Europe (Germany, Austria-Hungary and Italy, brought together in the Triple Alliance of 1882) that would stand firm against the peripheral states (France, Russia and, possibly, Britain). Unfortunately, the system was easily undermined. Italy, aware that any war against France would leave her coastline extremely vulnerable to naval assault, slowly drifted away from the central bloc, while Austria-Hungary proved more of a burden than an asset. Riven by internal ethnic problems, not least among Slavs intent on independence, Austria-Hungary found it difficult to sustain industrial growth and could do little to avoid clashes with Russia over the future of the Balkans. At the same time, France and Russia forged a close alliance based on their common fear of Germany (the Dual Alliance of 1894), and Britain grew wary of German colonial and naval expansion. Bismarck's alliance system became a rigid confrontation between rival armed camps.

The Origins of World War I

Such a background of distrust, rivalry and fear meant that it would take little to ignite the flame of war. European diplomats, schooled in the post-1815 desire for peaceful settlement of disputes, managed to deal with a succession of international crises – over Sudan in 1898, over Morocco in 1905 and 1911 – but they could not prevent regional conflicts such as the Russo-Japanese War (1904–5) or the Balkan Wars (1912–13), which inevitably strained relations between states. Nor could they foresee the impact of public opinion on the affairs of the world. Although some states, notably Austria-Hungary and Russia, had managed to resist the growing demands from both middle and labouring classes for a greater say in domestic politics, others such as Britain, France and Germany had been more liberal. By 1914, not only had the right to vote been extended in such countries, but the press had developed as a mouthpiece of the people, exploiting the spread of rudimentary education and new printing techniques to mobilize opinion on key issues.

Thus, when the Austrian heir Archduke Ferdinand was assassinated by a Serbian nationalist on 28 June 1914, the complex balance of power in Europe quickly collapsed in the face of jingoistic demands for war. As Austria-Hungary threatened Serbia, the Russians mobilized their army in support of fellow-Slavs in the Balkans. This led to fears in Germany that the country was about to be attacked by Russia and its ally France. The Germans therefore prepared their army for a swift advance in the west to knock out France before turning east to deal with the Russians. In the process, they invaded Belgium, the neutrality of which was guaranteed by Britain, which promptly declared war on Germany. By 4 August 1914, Europe was at war.

THE MODERN WORLD: 1914–1994

When war broke out in August 1914, the general impression was that it would be 'over by Christmas'. The reality was different. Within a matter of weeks, stalemate had occurred. On the Western Front both sides had dug in, creating horrific scenes of trench warfare. Hopes for a short, decisive conflict along the lines of the Franco-Prussian War (1870–1) were soon dashed and, with mobility curtailed, a repeat of the long drawn-out American Civil War (1861–5) seemed far more likely.

There were a number of reasons for this. In terms of military capability, neither side in 1914 was strong enough to gain a decisive victory. The Germans may have enjoyed initial advantages in terms of numbers and reserves, but they were fighting on two fronts simultaneously and were shackled to the significantly weaker countries of Austria-Hungary and, from November 1914, Turkey. By comparison, on the Allied side the French were strong, but wasted enormous resources in fruitless attacks into Alsace-Lorraine and had to wait for the full strength of both the Russians and the British to be brought to bear. At the same time, the weapons available in 1914 proved to be better suited to defence than attack: machine guns and quick-firing artillery could lay down such a weight of fire that any advance was sure to be costly, made worse on the Western Front by the mud, barbed wire and defence in depth that characterized trench warfare. In such circumstances, casualties rose and this necessitated the mobilization of all available manpower reserves. In Britain, conscription had to be introduced in 1916, and in all combatant states industry had to be geared to producing the weapons of war. What began as a conflict over the future of Serbia quickly escalated into a 'total war'.

The Aftermath of World War I

The four years of war cost an estimated nine million military dead (the civilian death toll is unknown; it may have been as high as 30 million), but the impact went much deeper. Four empires had been destroyed or dismantled – the Russian, German, Austro-Hungarian and Turkish – and the victors, with the exception of the USA, had been weakened in both human and economic terms. In addition, with the establishment of Communism in Russia, a new ideology had emerged that was opposed, in its fundamental beliefs, to all the traditions of European monarchy and liberal democracy. The future stability of Europe and, by association, most of the world, clearly depended on the postwar political settlement. However, the peace treaties of 1919–21 turned out to be dangerously flawed.

An overriding concern among the victors was to prevent a repetition of the recent nightmare, and it was assumed that this could be done by deliberately weakening the Central Powers. Germany was deprived of its overseas empire and much of its industrial potential, ordered to pay enormous reparations to its erstwhile enemies and forced to disband the bulk of its army and navy. Similar conditions were imposed on Austria-Hungary, which became two separate states. In addition, territory was confiscated from both Central Powers to create new countries, the existence of which would, it was assumed, satisfy nationalist demands and defuse some of the tensions that had led to war in 1914. In central Europe, Poland was recreated to stand between Germany and Russia, Czechoslovakia was formed to drive a wedge between Germany and Austria, and Yugoslavia emerged in an attempt to settle the problems of the Balkans. In the Middle East, Turkish possessions were taken away and the majority distributed to Britain and France as 'mandates' to be prepared for eventual independence. Finally, to oversee the new arrangements and strengthen international diplomacy, a 'League of Nations' was set up in the hope that future crises could be dealt with peacefully.

Very little of the settlement worked. The stringent terms imposed on Germany led to widespread resentment in that country, while the requirement to pay reparations destroyed any hopes for economic recovery, leading to hyperinflation in the early 1920s as the German currency collapsed. Furthermore, although the new states

of central Europe had their roots in nationalism, all of them contained enclaves of people who would have preferred alternative rulers. Of much more fundamental importance was the failure of the USA to lend its support to the new arrangements. As the only country to emerge from the war with its economy enhanced and its casualties low, it could have assumed a lead in international politics, but the lure of isolationalism was strong. With Russia (known as the Soviet Union, or USSR, from 1922) weakened by civil war and distrusted by the rest of the world, Germany and Austria-Hungary dismembered, and Italy resentful at not having gained more from the postwar settlement, the onus for policing the peace lay with a toothless League of Nations. It in turn was dependent for its strength on Britain and France, neither of which had the capability or will to carry out the task.

Despite initial enthusiasm for the settlement as a means of avoiding future conflict – something that a war-weary public in Europe was demanding – it soon became clear that the system was incapable of dealing with many of the crises that emerged in the postwar period. In October 1929, for example, the New York stock exchange ceased to function, heralding a period of global economic chaos and world depression. In the continued absence of American leadership, the rest of the world found it almost impossible to cope with a combination of currency weakness, inflation and declining trade. This led in turn to widespread unemployment and poverty, helping to create conditions that were well suited to the growth of extremist political views. Communism offered the advantage of centralized financial control, but its track record in the USSR, where the civil war was followed by a prolonged period of enforced economic change that caused immense social disruption, made it unattractive elsewhere. Of far more immediate appeal was Fascism, particularly in those countries where the blame for economic collapse was laid firmly at the door of the peace settlement.

Fascism began in Italy, where Benito Mussolini gained power as early as 1922 by stressing the need to oppose the spread of Communism, but it was in Germany that the creed had its most dramatic impact. Resentment over the postwar emasculation of Germany gave Adolf Hitler and his Nazi Party a grievance to exploit; they promised a restoration of national pride combined with strong central government that would deal ruthlessly with economic problems. Hitler's appointment as Chancellor in January 1933 was swiftly followed by measures to destroy all opposition. A policy of virulent

THE DEPRESSION

World War I disrupted the world economy. Many European states that were financially strong before 1914 were forced to spend large amounts of money on armaments and to raise loans to pay for their military campaigns. Stockpiles of raw materials were run down and factories were overused, with no opportunity to replace machinery. Although there was a 'boom' in 1919–20 as countries returned to peacetime production, this merely swamped the market with goods, leading to low profits and recession. The only major power to emerge from the war with its economy enhanced was the USA – by 1918, it was owed millions of dollars by France and Britain – but the retreat into isolationalism meant that it was not prepared to exert financial leadership. Thus, when the New York stock exchange collapsed amid uncontrolled share-speculation in October 1929, the effects were felt worldwide. Less money was available for international loans, the price of commodities such as sugar, rubber and wheat fell and countries found it impossible to continue trading. The impact on the people in those countries – widespread unemployment and social unrest – made them susceptible to extremist politicians, Communist or Fascist, who used authoritarian measures to ensure recovery. It was a high price to pay.

anti-Semitism was pursued, the Jews being blamed for Germany's ills. Two years later, the Nazis began to exert pressure on other European governments to reverse some of the territorial changes of 1919. By that time it was obvious that the League of Nations was weak – in 1931 it had been unable to respond effectively to a Japanese takeover of Manchuria – and Nazi policy soon paid dividends. As German forces moved into the Rhineland (1936) and Austria (1938), France and Britain, desperate to avoid another war, tried to 'appease' Hitler. This policy culminated in the Munich Agreement of late 1938, when Hitler was permitted to dismember Czechoslovakia – ostensibly to allow Sudeten Germans to return to the Fatherland – but it was apparent that he was not going to stop there. In March 1939 he absorbed the remnants of Czechoslovakia; six months later he invaded Poland. On 3 September 1939, France and Britain declared war on Germany for the second time in 25 years.

World War II

The new conflict differed from that of 1914–18 in a number of ways. The most obvious in 1939 was that the two sides were not evenly matched. Once Poland had been defeated – something that the Allies were powerless to prevent – the Germans were free to concentrate their forces against the West, having concluded a non-aggression pact with the USSR in August. In addition, the British and French, despite desperate rearmament in the late 1930s, had neither absorbed the military lessons of the previous conflict nor recognized the potential of the German doctrine of *blitzkrieg* (lightning war), elements of which had been used during the Spanish Civil War (1936–9). Thus when Hitler took the offensive in the West, the Allies were totally unprepared for the new style of warfare. Caught by surprise, they could do little to counter German advances and the British were forced to evacuate their troops from France through Dunkirk; three weeks later the French surrendered.

To the British, the war now became a fight for survival, necessitating a full mobilization of human and industrial resources to prevent a Nazi takeover. Once that survival had been assured in 1940 by the Battle of Britain, Hitler faced a major problem. Fascism would always be opposed ideologically by Communism and, despite the pact of August 1939, Hitler had every intention of destroying the Soviet Union as the source of the rival creed. He had hoped to do so with his western flank secure, but as long as Britain remained free, this was impossible. He therefore faced the traditional German nightmare of a war on two fronts, exacerbated by Italian campaigns in North Africa and the Balkans that soon required German help to conduct. By the time the Germans invaded the USSR in June 1941, they were already seriously overstretched. When the panzers, despite stunning advances, failed to take Moscow, the Soviets were able to absorb the shock and, eventually, recover. Although it was hardly noticeable at the time, the tide was beginning to turn in favour of the Allies.

In December 1941, the war escalated dramatically when the Japanese attacked the US fleet at Pearl Harbor and began a series of sweeping advances across the western Pacific and into Asia. Although Japan, Germany and Italy were allies (known as the Axis powers), there was no co-ordination between their campaigns – Japan, for example, refused to attack the USSR – and when Hitler declared war on the USA in the aftermath of Pearl Harbor, he effectively sealed his fate. The US President,

Franklin D. Roosevelt, not only co-operated closely with the British and Soviets to ensure the 'unconditional surrender' of Germany and Italy before turning full attention to Japan, but also mobilized America for total war. US armed forces were expanded – by 1945 over 12 million Americans were in uniform – and industry was geared to producing weapons and equipment to satisfy not only American needs but also those of all the Allies (including the Chinese, at war with Japan since 1937). By 1944, America was producing a ship a day and an aircraft every 4 minutes 54 seconds. In the face of such capability, the Axis powers stood little chance.

This is not to say that Allied victory was easy. The fighting between Germany and the USSR on the Eastern Front was among the most bitter of any war in history – by the time the Soviets finally took Berlin in May 1945 they had lost an estimated 27 million civilian and military dead – and the situation was little different in the Pacific or Asia, where Japanese soldiers fought literally to the death as Allied forces moved inexorably towards

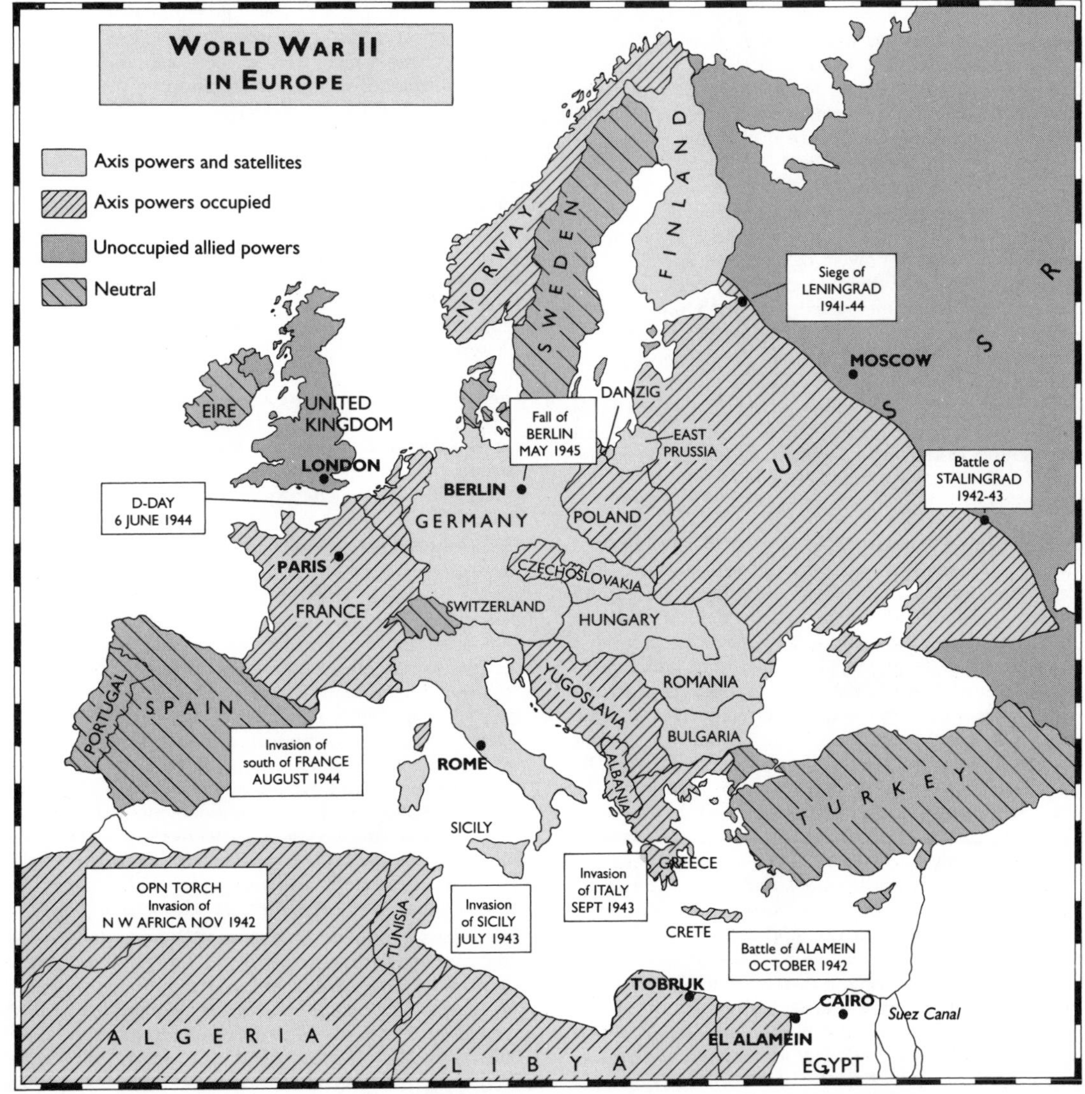

Japan. Allied campaigns in Italy (1943–5) and North-West Europe (1944–5) were equally difficult, whilst the campaigns fought at sea and in the air added to the human cost. Indeed, with the development of strategic bombing, civilian centres were deliberately destroyed from the air – in February 1945, for example, the city of Dresden was razed to the ground by Allied bombers, killing at least 50,000 people – and the search for new ways to inflict damage culminated in the use of atomic bombs against Japan in August 1945. When the war ended in September 1945, over 50 million people had been killed.

By then, the pattern of world politics had changed. Germany, Austria and most of the states of Eastern Europe were occupied by Allied troops, while those European powers that had fought the Axis were economically weakened. Britain, for example, might take pride in the fact that she had been the only major state to fight continuously from 1939 to 1945, but in the process she had expended a quarter of her national treasure, lost many of her traditional markets (notably in Latin America) and was deeply in debt. By comparison, the 'peripheral' powers of the USSR and USA had been strengthened, the former by its occupation of Eastern Europe and the latter by the mobilization of its economy and acquisition of atomic weapons. Nor was the situation very different in Asia. The defeat of Japan, the weakening of European colonial powers and the continuing civil war in China left a vacuum that was largely filled by the USA. By 1945 it was no longer a Eurocentric world but a bipolar one, spinning on the twin axes of Washington and Moscow.

The Cold War

Initially, this seemed to be a manageable situation. Both the USSR and USA had fought the same enemies and shared a common desire to destroy Fascism, but the similarities ended there. It quickly became apparent that Communism, with its emphasis on strong government control and the subordination of the individual to the state, could not co-exist with liberal democracy, characterized by free enterprise and individual liberty, that was represented by the USA and Western Europe. To Moscow, the extension of Communism to states in Eastern Europe – Poland, Czechoslovakia, Romania, Hungary, Bulgaria, Albania, Yugoslavia and Eastern Germany – may have been part of a natural desire to place 'buffers' between the USSR and possible invaders, but to Washington the process looked like dangerous expansionism that might not stop until it reached the Channel. When it coincided with a Communist takeover of North Korea, a successful revolution in China (under Mao Zedong), and a series of insurgencies in Indochina, Malaya and the Philippines, many in the West began to fear a worldwide Communist conspiracy, orchestrated by the Kremlin. In April 1949, as the Western allies struggled to maintain their hold on West Berlin, isolated 100 miles inside Communist-occupied Germany, the North Atlantic Treaty Organization (NATO) was signed by the USA, Canada and 10 European states, aimed specifically at defending those countries against perceived Communist aggression. It marked the beginning of the Cold War.

Despite the creation of the United Nations (UN) in 1945 as a forum for the defusing of international crises, the East–West split worsened as the peacetime period progressed. When South Korea was invaded by the Communist North in June 1950, America and some of her allies committed forces, under the banner of the UN, to oppose the aggession. The result was a bitter three-year war which drew in the Communist Chinese. Although it ended with a restoration of the previous border between the two Koreas – a border that was still extremely volatile in the early 1990s – an escalation to conflict elsewhere was avoided only because the Americans made a conscious decision to restrain their military capability. Nor were the problems confined to Asia; in Europe the mistrust between the power blocs deepened. In 1955, when NATO agreed to extend membership to the Federal Republic of (West) Germany, the Soviets, fearing a resurgence of German militarism, responded by setting up the Warsaw Pact to link Eastern European states (except Yugoslavia) more firmly to Moscow. Europe was divided into two rival camps, each armed to the teeth with conventional weapons. In 1961, with the building of the Berlin Wall, the division of Europe seemed to be permanent, reinforced by attempts among the western European powers to create their own economic community, the EEC.

Of far more concern was the spread of atomic (later nuclear) weapons. The Soviets test-exploded an atomic device as early as 1949, but it was not until they developed missiles with the capability of hitting US cities (first apparent during the Cuban Missile Crisis in 1962) that the world entered a situation aptly known as MAD. Standing for Mutually Assured Destruction, this was based on the belief that neither East nor West could afford to strike its enemy first, as it would be unable to destroy all its opponent's nuclear delivery systems simultaneously; some would always survive to hit back with devastating results. This undoubtedly deterred the 'superpowers' (the USA and USSR) from open war, but could only be maintained at very high cost, particularly as both sides were constantly searching for new weapons that would give them an advantage.

Attempts were made by the superpowers to control their nuclear strength – in 1972 the Strategic Arms Limitation Treaty (SALT) enjoyed some success – but any easing of tension (known as détente) invariably foundered on the ideological distrust between the rival blocs. In 1979, for example, the US Senate refused to ratify a second SALT treaty when the Soviets suddenly

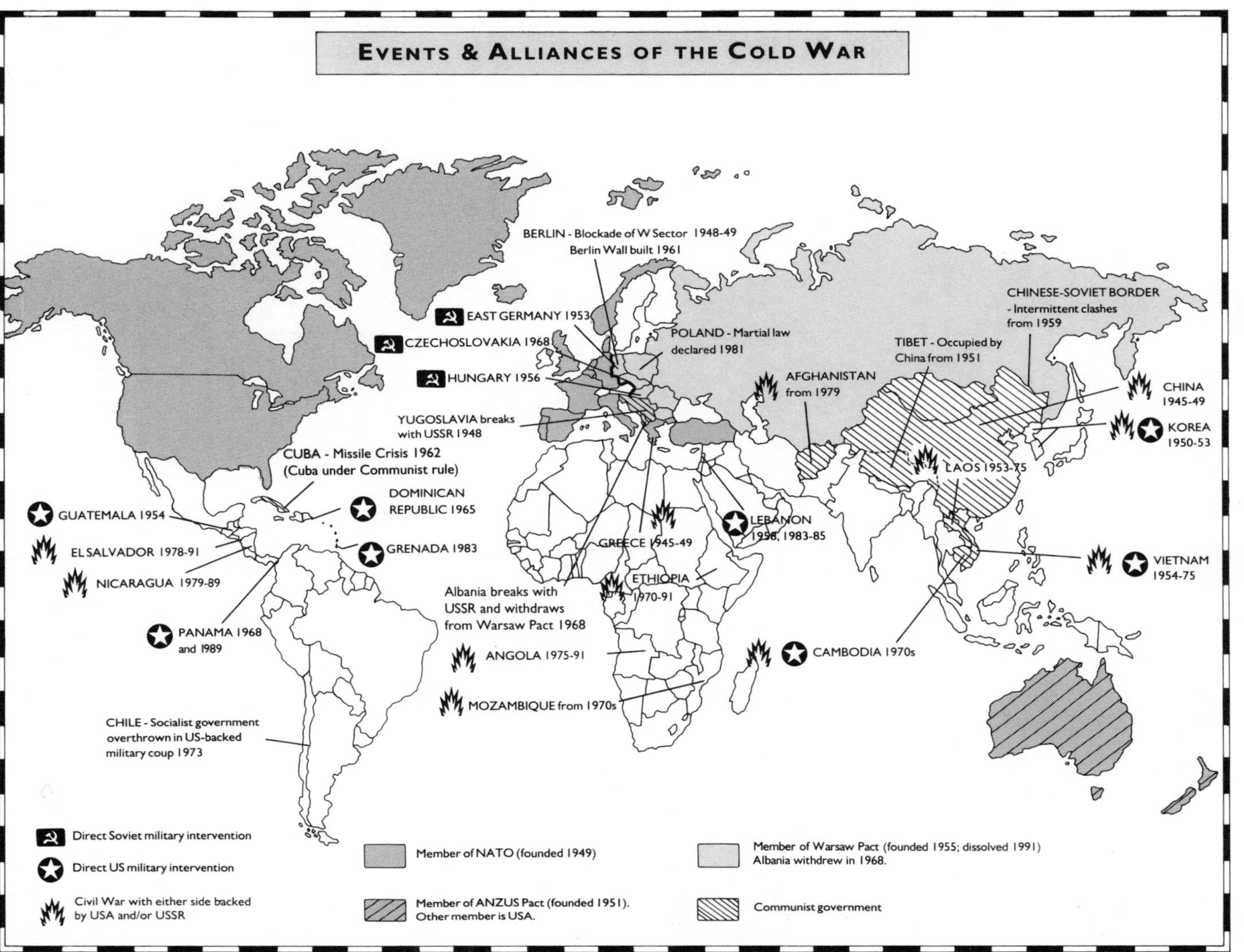
EVENTS & ALLIANCES OF THE COLD WAR
BERLIN - Blockade of W Sector 1948-49
Berlin Wall built 1961
EAST GERMANY 1953
CZECHOSLOVAKIA 1968
HUNGARY 1956
POLAND - Martial law declared 1981
YUGOSLAVIA breaks with USSR 1948
CUBA - Missile Crisis 1962 (Cuba under Communist rule)
DOMINICAN REPUBLIC 1965
GRENADA 1983
GUATEMALA 1954
EL SALVADOR 1978-91
NICARAGUA 1979-89
PANAMA 1968 and 1989
CHILE - Socialist government overthrown in US-backed military coup 1973
AFGHANISTAN from 1979
TIBET - Occupied by China from 1951
CHINESE-SOVIET BORDER - Intermittent clashes from 1959
CHINA 1945-49
KOREA 1950-53
LAOS 1953-75
VIETNAM 1954-75
CAMBODIA 1970s
LEBANON 1958, 1983-85
GREECE 1945-49
ETHIOPIA 1970-91
Albania breaks with USSR and withdraws from Warsaw Pact 1968
ANGOLA 1975-91
MOZAMBIQUE from 1970s
Direct Soviet military intervention
Direct US military intervention
Civil War with either side backed by USA and/or USSR
Member of NATO (founded 1949)
Member of ANZUS Pact (founded 1951). Other member is USA.
Member of Warsaw Pact (founded 1955; dissolved 1991) Albania withdrew in 1968.
Communist government

DECOLONIZATION

The process of decolonization in the 20th century ended the era of empire and more than doubled the number of independent states in the world. In 1945 there were 70 sovereign states and in 1975 there were 170, most of them in Africa, the Indian subcontinent, Southeast Asia and the Middle East. Some historians have explained this transformation in terms of a 'push-pull' concept – in other words, that the colonial powers abandoned their empires both because of the 'push' provided by the rise and spread of nationalism within their colonies, and because of the 'pull' provided by liberal opinion in the home countries. The 'push' – rising demand for self-government and independence – may be explained by a number of factors. One of these was the tendency of the colonial powers to provide Western-style education to their colonial subjects, albeit usually to a small elite. The result was the emergence of a group of people who understood Western ways and who were imbued with notions such as freedom, self-determination and equality, and determined to enjoy such advantages themselves.

Another equally significant factor was the development in many colonies of an economic infrastructure and even commerce and industry. This helped to stimulate 'detribalization' (the breaking down of barriers between different groups of people within a colonial area) and, allied to the spread of education, this produced groups of colonial subjects susceptible to the nationalist message.

Finally, the clash of cultures brought about by imperialism created upheaval. The imperialists were alien in terms of race and religion in most cases, and local people – often for the first time – became aware of their own unique characteristics.

The two world wars became the final catalysts for change. The struggle of World War II, especially, ended the myth of white invincibility in the colonies. Furthermore it devastated the economies of the European countries, making the burden of empire too much of a financial strain. The two factors finally combined to prompt a withdrawal from empire.

invaded Afghanistan. It was not until the 1980s, when the Americans pursued their Strategic Defense Initiative (or 'Star Wars' – a defence against missile attack that was to be stationed outside the Earth's atmosphere) that arms control began to make meaningful progress, chiefly because neither side could afford the technology involved in maintaining MAD. By then, however, countries beyond the USA and USSR had acquired nuclear weapons – Britain, France, China, India, Israel and South Africa – and many others, including North and South Korea, were close to acquiring them. Thus, regardless of any breakthrough in arms control by the superpowers, the danger of nuclear conflict remained.

East–West rivalry was also played out in the Third World, comprising those countries (principally in Asia, Africa and Latin America) that were neither industrialized nor politically sophisticated. Many were characterized by recent independence from colonial rule, reflecting a process of decolonization that was a feature of the post-1945 period (see box). Some European powers, weakened by World War II, relinquished colonial possession quickly – the British withdrew from India as early as 1947 – while others were forced out by nationalist insurgents or by a recognition that they lacked the strength to maintain their rule. The result was a dramatic growth in the number of independent states in the world – from about 70 in 1945 to 175 by 1990 – not all of which were politically or economically stable. A significant proportion remained subject to internal armed opposition or succumbed to military coups as the original civilian leaders proved incapable of ruling effectively. In addition, as the new states emerged, border disputes proliferated, leading to regional conflicts that often threatened access to important raw materials. In such volatile circumstances, the superpowers vied for influence and control, aiming to outflank the alliance stalemate in Europe or seize vital geostrategic locations.

The contest took a variety of forms. In some cases, the superpowers provided economic aid – for example, in 1956 the Soviets helped Egypt to finance the construction of the Aswan Dam – but far more frequent was the supply of military hardware, designed to strengthen their allies and, occasionally, ensure their victory in a regional conflict. This was particularly the case in the Middle East where, by the mid-1960s, the Americans were supporting the fledgling Jewish state of Israel against a number of Soviet-backed Arab powers. Sometimes the process went further, drawing one of the superpowers into a regional conflict. In 1965 the Americans committed main-force units to the defence of South Vietnam, under threat from Communist insurgents and from the North Vietnamese Army, itself

EUROPE AND ASIA SINCE 1991
1 Georgia 1991–93: Secessionist wars in Abkhazia and South Ossetia.
2 Croatia 1991–92: Serb and Croat forces fought over territory in the former Yugoslavia.
3 Bosnia-Herzegovina 1991– : Muslim, Croat and Bosnian Serb forces fought each other for territory in the region.
4 Armenia–Azerbaijan 1992: Azeri and Armenian forces fought for control of Nagorno Karabakh.
SWEDEN
FINLAND
NORWAY
RUSSIA
IRELAND
ESTONIA
DENMARK
LATVIA
LITHUANIA
THE NETHERLANDS
RUSSIA
UK
GERMANY
POLAND
BELARUS
BELGIUM
CZECH R
UKRAINE
SLOVAKIA
LUX.
KAZAKHSTAN
FRANCE
AUSTRIA
HUNGARY
MOLDOVA
ROMANIA
SWITZER-LAND
ITALY
PORTUGAL
YUGO-SLAVIA
BULGARIA
SLOVENIA
GEORGIA
UZBEKISTAN
KYRGYZSTAN
MACEDONIA
SPAIN
ARMENIA
CROATIA
GREECE
TURKEY
TURKMENISTAN
TAJIKISTAN
ALBANIA
CHINA
BOSNIA-HERZEGOVINA
AZERBAIJAN

equipped by the Soviets and Chinese. The Vietnam War continued until 1975, when the Communists finally seized power in Saigon, but by then the Americans had been forced to withdraw, having failed to defeat their enemy in a war that was both costly and domestically unpopular. Finally, the Americans, convinced that any spread of Communism was part of a global conspiracy, adopted a policy of opposing all left-wing governments in Latin America, providing military aid and even, on occasion, intervening to bolster undemocratic but anti-Communist regimes. The overall result was an extension of Cold War rivalry to many areas beyond the confines of Europe and the North Atlantic, each example of which inevitably contained the seeds of escalation to superpower (and therefore nuclear) confrontation. The UN Security Council, which should have been an instrument for controlling crises, was powerless to intervene. Because its permanent members (who enjoyed the right of veto) included the superpowers, any attempt to find a solution by one side was interpreted by the other as Cold War strategy and promptly blocked. It was a very dangerous world.

But the problems of the Third World were not just of superpower making. Many of the conflicts that occurred would have happened anyway, reflecting local rivalries. In the Middle East, for example, the creation of the Jewish state of Israel in 1948 alienated surrounding Arab powers, and although the weapons used would have been less sophisticated without US or Soviet involvement, the Arab–Israeli Wars of 1967, 1973 and 1982 would probably still have taken place. Indeed, the most destructive regional conflict of the post-1945 period – the Iran–Iraq War (1980–8), which cost an estimated one million lives – had very little superpower involvement, being largely a result of ideological and religious differences, compounded by territorial and economic rivalry. Elsewhere, Third World countries suffered internal political problems, often caused by a desire among Western-educated leaders to modernize the state regardless of traditional ways of life. The civil war that devastated Nigeria (1966–9) had elements of this within it. Even among those states that did not suffer from violence, the problems of modernization often led to a self-perpetuating spiral of borrowing, failed projects and increased debt, the results of which produced resentment against the industrialized world and created a 'North–South' divide that had the potential to be as dangerous as that between East and West.

The Post-Cold War World

In the event, the latter confrontation began to ease in the late 1980s and early 1990s as Communism collapsed in Eastern Europe. The process began in 1985, when Mikhail Gorbachov came to power in Moscow, inheriting a Soviet empire that was economically stagnant and politically corrupt. His twin policies of *glasnost* (openness) and *perestroika* (restructuring) led to a loosening of the Communist grip on the USSR, and this was soon extended to the states of Eastern Europe. As relations between Moscow and Washington improved, under the impetus of a Soviet withdrawal from Afghanistan and a series of arms control agreements (accepted by Gorbachov in an effort to save money), a wave of anti-Communist protest swept existing governments from power in Poland, Czechoslovakia, Hungary, Romania, Bulgaria and Albania, without triggering intervention by the USSR. Even more dramatically, in November 1989 local people destroyed the Berlin Wall, preparing the way for a reunification of Germany 11 months later. In 1991, following an unsuccessful anti-Gorbachov coup in Moscow, the Soviet Union broke apart, to be formally disbanded on 31 December. By then the Warsaw Pact had ceased to exist, leaving Europe seemingly free from the threat of major war for the first time since the late 1940s.

The fact that such a judgement might be premature was shown by the spread of local conflicts in Europe, any one of which could have escalated into something infinitely more dangerous. Throughout the former Soviet Union, violence was used by nationalist groups to try to gain or consolidate power, most notably in Azerbaijan and Georgia, while the success of extreme nationalists in Russian parliamentary elections in December 1993 led to deep concern in the West. Elsewhere, the fall of Communism resulted in civil wars that drew other powers in, if only to act as peacemakers: the break-up of Yugoslavia in 1991 and the ensuing bitter conflict between Serbs, Croats and Muslims was a case in point. The continuing conflicts in Eastern Europe and the Third World, no longer constrained by the pressures of Cold War fear, made the chances of peace, in reality, remote.

Nevertheless, there was cause for optimism. With the end of East–West confrontation, the UN Security Council was no longer in permanent stalemate. This was shown in the international response to the Iraqi invasion of Kuwait in August 1990. The creation (and successful use) of an American-led coalition in the Gulf War would have been impossible without Soviet backing. It was also displayed in the moves to solve a number of regional problems, ranging from the Arab–Israeli conflict to the future of South Africa. The removal of the Soviet threat meant that the power of the USA had been temporarily enhanced – Washington still had to face the growing influence of China, Japan and the European Union, as well as the developing threats of international terrorism and Muslim fundamentalism – but at least the world was in a better position to deal with the more pressing problems of hunger, population growth and regional violence.

TIME CHARTS

THE ANCIENT WORLD: 4000 BC – 600 BC

Near East

4000–3000 BC Development of the world's first known cities in Mesopotamia

c. 3300 Earliest surviving Sumerian texts

before 3000 Emergence of several city-states in Sumer

c. 3000 Rise of the Assyrian cities of Nineveh and Ashur

c. 2900–2370 Early Dynastic Period in Sumer

c. 2370 Conquest of Sumer by Sargon of Akkad

c. 2200 Akkad overrun by the Gutians

c. 2113–2006 Third dynasty of Ur

c. 2006 Elamites sacked Ur; end of Sumerian dominance of Mesopotamia

c. 1900 Amorite dynasty established in Babylon

by 1800 Amorite kingdoms established in Syria and Palestine

c. 1792–1750 Hammurabi unified Mesopotamia under the hegemony of Babylon

c. 1650 Foundation of the Hittite Empire

c. 1595 Babylon sacked by the Hittite king Mursilis I

c. 1500–c. 1157 Kassite rule in Mesopotamia

c. 1430–1350 Hurrian kingdom of Mitanni reached its greatest extent

c. 1380–1350 Under Suppiluliumas I the Hittite Empire reached its greatest extent

c. 1230 Israelite conquest of Canaan

before 1200 Collapse of the Hittite Empire

1200–1100 'Sea Peoples' raid Syria and Palestine.

c. 1000 Foundation of the kingdom of Israel

9th century BC Medes and Persians occupied western Iran

883–824 Expansion of the Assyrian Empire under Ashurnasirpal II and Shalmaneser III

after 824 Rise of the kingdom of Urartu

745–727 Major expansion of Assyrian Empire under Tiglath-Pileser III; Assyria conquered Babylon in 729

732 Aram-Damascus conquered by Assyria

721–705 The Assyrian Sargon II overthrew Urartu

704–681 Assyrian invasion of Palestine under Sennacherib; Assyrian capital moved to Nineveh

668–627 Reign of Ashurbanipal – Assyrian Empire reached its greatest extent

625–605 Babylon regained its independence under Nabopolassar

625–605 Nineveh sacked by the Medes

Egypt and North Africa

c. 3100–2725 BC Early Dynastic Period (1st–3rd dynasties) began with unification of Upper and Lower Egypt

2575–2134 Old Kingdom in Egypt (4th–8th dynasties) – a period of centralized administration; construction of the Great Pyramids at Giza

c. 2134–2040 First Intermediate Period (9th–11th dynasties)

c. 2040–1640 Middle Kingdom (11th–13th dynasties) Egypt reunited under Mentuhotep II

c. 1640–1552 Second Intermediate Period (14th–17th dynasties) – Hyksos rule; Theban dynasty liberated Egypt

1555–1070 New Kingdom (18th–20th dynasties) – Egyptian Empire extended from Syria to southern Sudan

1450–1425 The campaigns of Amenophis II against Mitanni extended the Egyptian Empire in the Near East

c. 1313 Hittite invasion of Egypt

c. 1285 Egypt clashed with the Hittites at Kadesh in Palestine

1070–712 Third Intermediate Period (21st–24th dynasties) – Egypt divided

814 Traditional date of the founding of Carthage

712–332 Late Period (25th–30th dynasties) – Egypt reunified under the 26th dynasty

675 The Assyrians under Esarhaddon attacked Egypt and took Memphis

c. 630 A Greek colony founded at Cyrene

The Ancient World: 4000 BC – 600 BC

Greece and the Hellenistic World

c. 3000 BC Neolithic settlements in Crete

c. 2220 Minoan pottery appeared in Greece; Minoan script (linear A) appeared

2200–1450 Minoan civilization in Crete reached its peak in the Middle and Late Bronze Age

from c. 1700 Construction of palace of Minos at Knossos

c. 1600 Start of Mycenaean civilization

c. 1550–1500 Minoan civilization hit by destructive earthquakes

1500–1150 Height of Mycenaean civilization on mainland Greece

1400–1300 Minoan (Linear A) script adapted as Linear B to write an early from of Greek

c. 1200–1100 Collapse of Mycenaean civilization; Greece entered a 'dark age'

c. 800 Beginning of the Archaic Period in Greece

8th century–650 Greek colonies founded around the Aegean, Adriatic and Black Seas

8th century Sparta gained control of most of the southern Peloponnese

c. 750 Reintroduction of literacy into Greece

750–700 The poems traditionally attributed to Homer were written down in their final form

mid-7th century Major revolt of the *helots* (state serfs) against Sparta

Rome and Western Europe

c. 4000 BC Neolithic culture flourished in most of Europe; earliest Neolithic sites in Britain

3000–2000 Bronze Age culture in southeastern Europe spreading to northern and western Europe; bronze artefacts

c. 2500 Burial barrows costructed in Britain; construction of Stonehenge

c. 2000 Stone circles of Carnac (Brittany) erected

2nd millennium BC Iron Age agricultural systems established in present-day France, Britain and their neighbours; construction of hillforts in much of western Europe

15th century Beginnings of Urnfield culture in eastern and central Europe

by 1000 A village settlement existed on the site of Rome

c. 800–700 Hallstatt art flourished in central Europe and then spread through much of northern and western Europe

8th century Rise of the Etruscan civilization in Italy

by 600 Rome had developed into a substantial city

6th century Etruscan colonies founded in northern and southern Italy

6th and 5th centuries Etruscan monarchies replaced by republics

THE ANCIENT WORLD: 600 BC – AD 400

Near East

605–562 BC Nebuchadnezzar II extended the Neo-Babylonian Empire, capturing Jerusalem in 597 and taking the Jews into the Babylonian Captivity

585–550 Astyages, last king of the Medes, overthrown by the Persians

549 Cyrus I united the Medes and Persians and founded the Persian Achaemenid Empire

539 Cyrus I took Babylon and acquired the Neo-Babylonian Empire

521–486 Reign of Darius I, Persian Empire reached its greatest extent

486–465 Reign of Xerxes I

333 and 332 Darius II defeated by Alexander the Great at Issus and Gaugamela

312 Foundation of Hellenistic Seleucid Empire by Alexander the Great's general Seleucus Nicator

247 Foundation of the Parthian dynasty by Arsaces

198 The Seleucid Anthiocus III took Palestine from Egypt

191 Anthiocus III defeated by the Romans at Thermopylae – decline of the Seleucid Empire began

153–63 Independent Maccabean Jewish state

133 Asia (western Anatolia) became a Roman province

120–63 Reign of Mithridates VI of Pontus

101 Cilicia (southern Anatolia) became a Roman province

AD 66–70 Jewish revolt against Rome

1st century AD Christianity spread rapidly from Palestine

226 Foundation of the Sassanian dynasty in Persia

240–272 Sassanian Empire greatly expanded by Shapur I

260 Sassanians overran Syria and captured the Roman emperor Valerian

395 Anatolia and the Roman provinces in the Near East included in the Eastern Empire when the Roman Empire was divided

Egypt and North Africa

526–525 BC Persians under Cambyses invaded Egypt

480 Carthaginian expedition to Sicily defeated by Gelon, tyrant of Syracuse, at the Battle of Himera

c. 470 Hanno of Carthage navigated down the coast of West Africa, probably as far as Sierra Leone

406 Egypt revolted against Roman rule

332 Alexander the Great invaded Egypt and founded Alexandria-in-Egypt

305 Ptolemy, Alexander the Great's general, declared himself ruler of Egypt, founding the Ptolemaic dynasty

241 Carthage defeated by Rome in the First Punic War

238 The Carthaginians under Hamilcar began the conquest of Spain

202 Hannibal defeated by Scipio at Zama

149–146 Third Punic War – Carthage was destroyed and 'Africa' became a Roman province

110–105 Jugurthian War in Numidia

96 Cyrenaica (eastern Libya) became a Roman province

41 Antony went to Egypt and ruled the Egyptian region with his mistress Cleopatra VII until defeated at the Battle of Actium (31 BC)

30 Ptolemy XVI, son of Cleopatra VII and Julius Caesar, deposed and executed; last of the pharaohs; Egypt became a Roman province

AD 41 Mauretania (Morocco) became a Roman province

395 Egypt and Cyrenaica (Libya) included in the Eastern Empire when the Roman Empire was divided; St Augustine became bishop of Hippo

5th century Vandals overran Roman provinces in North Africa

THE ANCIENT WORLD: 600 BC – AD 400

Greece and the Hellenistic World

594 BC Solon appointed 'archon' at Athens; established legal code.

6th century Sparta founded the Peloponnesian League

545–510 Athens ruled by the tyrant Peisistratos and his sons

507 The reforms of Cleisthenes in Athens

490 Battle of Marathon – defeat of the Persians by the Greeks

480 Persians defeated by the Greeks at the naval Battle of Salamis

479 Battle of Plataea – end of the Persian threat to Greece

478 Athens assumed leadership of the Delian League, which by the 440s had become an Athenian Empire

462–429 Athenian politics dominated by Pericles

431–404 The Peloponnesian War between Athens and Sparta and their allies

378/7 Athenian power re-emerged in the Aegean Confederacy

338 Defeat of the Greek city-states at Chaeronea gave Philip II of Macedon control of Greece

336–323 Alexander the Great (of Macedon) conquered the whole of the Persian Empire

from c. 240 Two federations of city-states, Aetolia and Achaea, dominated Greece

167 Macedon conquered by the Romans

147 War between Sparta and Achaea; Romans invaded Greece and destroyed Corinth

146 Most of Greece came under Roman rule

AD 123 and 128–34 Hadrian visited Greece

267 Barbarian Herulians invaded Greece, and sacked Athens, Sparta, Argos and Corinth

286 An 'Eastern' emperor established over Anatolia and Greece by Diocletian

324–37 Constantine ('the Great') reunited the Roman Empire but moved the capital to Constantinople (Byzantium)

395 Division of the Roman Empire into Eastern and Western parts – the East, based on Constantinople, became the Byzantine Empire

Rome and Western Europe

509 BC The Roman Republic established – power exercised by two anually consuls

5th–4th centuries Decline of Etruria

450 Celtic La Tène art flourished in much of Europe , reaching as far as Ireland in the west and Hungary in the east

415 Athens attempted to conquer Sicily

415 Rome sacked by the Celts

4th century BC The plebeians gained access to political office in Rome

275 The Battle of Beneventum – defeat of Pyrrhus by Romans ended Greek attempt to conquer Italy

264 Roman conquest of the Italian peninsula completed

264–241 First Punic War; Rome challenged Carthage for the control of Sicily

218–202 Second Punic War – Hannibal crossed the Alps and invaded Italy

216 Hannibal defeated the Romans at Cannae

by 167 Rome dominated the western Mediterranean

133 Tiberius Gracchus murdered after introducing land reforms

121 Southern Gaul became a Roman province

91–88 Revolt of the Italian allies

81 Sulla established himself as dictator of Rome

60 The first 'Triumvirate' – political alliance between Pompey, Caesar and Crassus

49 Caesar crossed the Rubicon and began the civil war against Pompey

48 Pompey defeated at Pharsalus; Julius Caesar became consul and dictator for life – assassinated in 44

42 Roman Empire effectively divided between Octavian and Antony (the Second Triumvirate)

31 Octavian defeated Antony at Actium

27 Octavian proclaimed emperor by the Roman Senate and given the title 'Augustus'

AD 9 loss of the Roman provinces between the rivers Rhine and Elbe

43–7 Britain became a Roman province

79 Destruction of Pompeii

98–117 Roman Empire enjoyed peace and stability under Trajan

101–6 Dacia (modern Romania) became a Roman province

122–6 Construction of Hadrian's Wall in Britain

192–7 Period of civil war after the assassination of Commodus

235 Empire entered a period of chaos at the end of the Severan dynasty

286 Diocletian reorganized the Roman Empire

313 Constantine issued the Edict of Milan tolerating Christianity

395 Division of the Roman Empire

5th century Germanic barbarians overran Gaul, Spain and Italy

OTHER WORLDS: PREHISTORY – AD 1000

China and Korea

c. 4000 BC Neolithic farming established in the Yellow River Basin

c. 2500 Farming spread to the Yangtze basin

c. 2000 Bronze working in the Yellow River valley

1480–1080 Shang dynasty ruled the first Chinese kingdom

1122–256 Zhou dynasty

551–479 Kongfuzi (Confucius) developed his social thought

481–221 BC 'Warring states'

221–210 Shi Huangdi became China's first emperor, began to build Great Wall

221–206 Qin dynasty – building of Great Wall

202 BC–AD 220 Han dynasty – invention of paper and introduction of Buddhism

AD 220–280 Northern China succumbed to warlordism and invasions by non-Chinese peoples

265–316 Jin dynasty

1st–7th centuries AD Korea divided into three kingdoms – Koryo, Paikche and Silla

383–533 Wei dynasty in the Yellow River Valley

589–618 Sui dynasty reunited China and undertook major reforms; expensive military ventures contributed to the empire's collapse

618–907 Tang dynasty extended Chinese Empire – reforms of emperor Taizong (627–649), invention of printing and gunpowder and increase in international trade

668 Korea united by the Silla kingdom as a tributary of China

755 Abortive rebellion of An Lushan; nomad invasions and revolts further weakened the empire

907–960 Disintegration of the Tang Empire; period of military dictators and warfare

918–1392 Korea united by the Koryo dynasty

960–1127 Song dynasty reunited much of northern China and restored peace

Indian subcontinent

c. 5000 BC Neolithic farming established in the Indus Valley

c. 2300–1700 Harappan civilization flourished in the Indus Valley

c. 2000 Neolithic farming spread to southern India

c. 1500 Aryan invasion of India; fall of Indus civilization; intermingling of Aryan and indigenous Dravidian cultures produced Hinduism; Bronze Age culture established in the Ganges basin

c. 800 Hindu Iron Age culture established in the Ganges basin

c. 563–463 BC Prince Gautama, the Buddha; emergence of Buddhism

543–491 Kingdom of Magdalha emerged as a major power in north India

c. 500 Indian agriculturalists colonized Sri Lanka; emergence of Jainism

326 Alexander the Great conquered the Indus Valley

c. 300 Sri Lanka converted to Buddhism

272–232 Ashoka, founder of the Mauryan Empire

185 BC–AD 320 Decline of the Mauryan dynasty; India dissolved into small kingdoms with local power struggles

2nd century BC Indo-Greek civilization in the Indus Valley

1st–5th centuries AD Indus Valley dominated by the Kushans from Central Asia

320–540 Northern India is reunited by the Gupta dynasty

c. 460–550 Northern India invaded by the Huns

606 Harsha establised a Buddhist kingdom in northern India

6th–8th centuries Calukya kingdom in the Deccan

711 Sind was conquered by an Arab army and became a province of the caliphate

c. 780–c. 927 Rastrakuta kingdom in the Deccan

c. 900 Tamils from southern India begin to settle in Sri Lanka

970–13th century Cola kingdom in southeastern India

before 1000 Dravidian kingdoms established in southern India

Other Worlds: Prehistory – AD 1000

Southeast Asia

before 7000 BC Foodgatherers settled in Indochina

c. 5000 Malay speakers moved from Taiwan into Indonesia

c. 1500 Rice farming established in Indochina

c. 900 Indian traders established links with Southeast Asia

207 Tongking conquered by a Chinese warlord

111 Tongking incorporated into the Chinese Empire

AD 39 Vietnamese revolt against Chinese rule

1st century Cambodian state of Funan founded

400–500 The Mon kingdom in Burma established

c. 590 Cambodian kingdom of Chenla overthrew Funan

c. 700–c. 850 Saliendra kingdom in Java

c. 800 Arrival of the Burmans from China – hostilities broke out with indigenous peoples; Jayavarman II expelled Japanese invaders from Khmer (Cambodia), reunited country and founded Khmer kingdom; introduction of cult of god-king and foundation of Angkor

849–1287 Burmese kingdom of Pagan founded; revolts by Mon and Shan peoples; spread of Buddhism

939 Vietnam (Annam) gained independence from China

Japan

c. 10000 BC Pottery developed in Japan

10000–c. 250 Neolithic Jomon culture – use of polished tools

c. 400 Rice farming reached Japan from Korea

c. 250 BC–AD 250 Yayoi culture – use of metals

AD 57 Japanese state of Wu sent tribute to the emperor of China

2nd century Civil war in Japan

c. 360–400 Unification of Japan

c. 538–52 Buddhism introduced

646 Centralized system of government established

710–84 Chinese-style imperial court established at Nara

794 The court moved to Kyoto

857–1160 Government dominated by the Fujiwara family

10th century Japanese script developed

OTHER WORLDS: PREHISTORY – 1000

Sub-Saharan Africa

before 3000 BC Farming spread from Egypt to the Middle Nile Valley

c. 1000–100 Village communities emerged in West Africa

c. 800 Nubian kingdom established

c. 400–100 Nok culture in West Africa

c. AD 50 Rise of the kingdom of Axum

c. 100 Negro (mainly Bantu) farmers spread east and south from West Africa

4th century Abyssinia adopted Christianity

c. 500 Bantus reached east coast of southern Africa

6th century Three separate black Christian Nubian kingdoms founded

8th century Rise of the kingdom of Kongo (Angola and Zaire); Arabs established trading links with West Africa across the Sahara

8th–12th centuries Kingdom of Ghana flourished

c. 800–1000 Takrur state controlled modern Senegal

c. 1000 Rise of Kanem Empire in northern Nigeria

Australasia

c. 40000–25000 BC Australian Aborigines arrived in the subcontinent

c. 3000 First settlement of Micronesia

c. 2500–2000 Settlement of the Solomon Islands, Vanuatu and New Caledonia

c. 1500–1250 Settlement of Fiji and Tonga

c. 300 First settlement of Samoa

c. 100 First settlement of the Marquesas

c. AD 300 First settlement of Tahiti and the Society Islands

c. 400 First settlement of the Cook Islands and Easter Island

c. 750 First settlement in New Zealand

Other Worlds: Prehistory – 1000

The Americas

c. 10000 BC First settlement of North America across the Bering Strait from Asia

c. 10000–8000 Clovis culture flourished in mid-west and SW of North America

before c. 2500 Farming established in Mexico and Central America

c. 2000 Great Plains tribes begin to hunt bison

c. 1500 Domestication of the potato in the Andes

c. 1000 Maize farming established in the North American Great Basin

1000–200 Chavin culture flourished on the Peruvian coast; improved agriculture and metallurgy

c. 300 BC–AD c. 300 Olmec civilization flourished in western Mexico

c. 100 BC Foundation of Teotihuacán in central Mexico

AD 200–1000 Migration of Arawak Indians from NE South America to the Caribbean

c. 300 Rise of the Mayan civilization (Mexico, Guatemala and the Yucatán peninsula)

c. 400–c. 700 Zapotec civilization in Mexico

c. 600 Beginning of the Ayamará civilization in modern Bolivia

c. 700 Teotihuacán abandoned by the Mayas

9th–12th centuries Huari state flourished in Peru

c. 900 Rise of the Toltec civilization based on Tula

c. 985 Viking settlements in Greenland

c. 1000 Arawak culture in the Caribbean destroyed by migrating Caribs from South America

c. 1000 Chimu state formed on the north coast of Peru

Europe

c. 2200–1450 BC Minoan civilization

c. 1500–1150 Mycenaean civilization

8th century Emergence of Greek city-states

8th–5th centuries BC Peak of Etruscan civilization in Italy

509 BC Foundation of the Roman Republic

499–479 Greek–Persian wars

336–323 Empire of Alexander the Great

27 Augustus became the first Roman emperor

AD 284 Roman Empire reorganized under Diocletian

313 Edict of Milan – Christianity tolerated in the Roman Empire

410 Rome sacked by the Visigoths

535 Byzantine conquest of much of Italy

711 Muslim invasion of Spain

800 Charlemagne crowned emperor

OTHER WORLDS: 1000 – 1900

China and Korea

11th century 'The Reformists' – Wang Anshi and Fan Zhongyan

1126 Invasion by Jin nomads split China: Jin ruled in Yellow River basin; Song ruled southern China from the Yangtze basin (1127–1279)

early 13th century Genghis Khan began conquest of Jin Empire of northern China, the first step in the creation of a pan-Eurasian Mongol Empire

1260–94 Reign of Kublai Khan as Great Khan; Kublai Khan established his capital at Beijing in the mid-1260s

1270s Kublai Khan conquered Song Empire of southern China

1271–1368 Mongol (Yuan) dynasty

1275–92/5 Marco Polo entered the service of Kublai Khan and travelled widely within the Yuan Empire

1368 Mongols fled Beijing after their overthrow by the Ming dynasty

1368–1644 Ming dynasty

1392–1910 Yi dynasty in Korea

1405–33 Voyages of Cheng He to the Spice Islands, Arabia and Africa

1517 European missionaries and traders given limited access to the Chinese Empire

1592 Unsuccessful Japanese invasion of Korea

1644 Collapse of the Ming dynasty after rebellions and attacks by the Manchu

1644–1911 Qing (Manchu) dynasty

1662–1722 Enlargement of the Chinese Empire into Central Asia and Tibet under emperor Kangxi

1682 End of civil war in southern China

1689 Chinese border with Russia defined by Treaty of Nerchinsk

1715 Christianity banned in China

1735–95 Expansion of Chinese Empire into Turkestan, Vietnam, Burma and Nepal

1839–42 First Opium War

1851 The Taiping Movement took up arms

1851–1908 Discontent grew as the dowager empress Cixi resisted reforms

1851–64 The Taiping Rebellion

1856–60 Second Opium War

1894–5 Sino-Japanese War; Taiwan annexed by Japan

1900–1 Boxer Rebellion against Western influence

1911 Army rebellion toppled the Qing dynasty

Indian Subcontinent

1001–1027 Mahmud of Ghazni raided northern India from Afghanistan

1185 Muhammad of Ghur invaded the Punjab from Afghanistan and took Lahore

1206 Islamic sultanate of Delhi founded

1336 Foundation of city and empire of Vijayanagar

1347–1518 Bahmani sultanate in the Deccan

14th century Muslim conquest of northern India completed

1398 Delhi sacked by Timur (Tamerlane)

1451–1526 Lodi kingdom in the Punjab

1494–5 Vasco da Gama reached India

1489–1686 Adil Shahi dynasty made Bijapur a major power

1518–1611 Sultanate of Golconda, the most powerful state in the Deccan

1526 Babur of Kabul overthrew the Delhi sultanate and established the Mogul Empire

1555–1605 Rule of Akbar – Moguls took Rajasthan, Gujarat, Bengal, Kashmir and the northern Deccan

1565 Muslim forces routed Vijayanagar

1658–1707 Aurangzeb made the Mogul Empire a Muslim state, discriminating against Hindus

1674–1802 Maratha empire in the Deccan

before 1700 The Mogul Empire covered all of India except the far south

c. 1700 British East India Company secured the important ports in India

18th century Provincial governors and other local rulers took power, effectively destroying the Mogul Empire

1757 Battle of Plassey – British rule firmly established in much of India

1818 The settlement of India – the subcontinent was divided between British-ruled and protected states

1845–9 Sikh Wars – British annexed the Punjab

1857–8 The Indian Mutiny; British government took direct control of India

1877 Queen Victoria became Empress of India

1885 Indian National Congress founded

OTHER WORLDS: 1000 – 1900

Southeast Asia

1150 Angkor Wat temples completed
1177 The Cambodians overthrew the empire of the Chams
1238 Thai principality of Sukhothai founded

1287 Burmese kingdom of Pagan fell to the Mongols
1290 Thai principality of Chiang Mai founded
end of 13th century Islam arrived in northern Sumatra and began to spread throughout the East Indies
1350–1400 Thai capital moved from Sukhothai to Ayutthaya; powerful Thai kingdom devastated the Khmer state
1354 Kingdom of Lanxang founded in Laos
1369 Angkor Wat sacked by the Thais
1431 Khmer rulers abandoned Angkor for Phnom Penh; decline of the Khmer empire
1471 Overthrow of the kingdom of Champa by the Viets of Tongking; kingdom of Annam founded

16th century European exploration of Southeast Asia began
1550–1700 Intermittent Thai–Burmese wars
before 1600 Burmese kingdom of Ava gained control of most of modern Burma
1620–1802 Division of Vietnam into rival states

1784 Burma conquered the kingdom of Arakan
1802 Vietnam reunited by Nguyen Anh
1819 Refoundation of Singapore
1825–30 Java War
1826–85 Burma annexed by the Britain
late 1850s–1890s French colonization of Indochina
1867 Rubber introduced into Malaya
1873–1903 Acheh War in the Dutch East Indies

Japan

by 1000 Real power passed from the emperor to the Fujiwara family
11th century Rise of the samurai
1185 Minamoto Yoritomo established the shogunate
1185–1333 Kamakura shogunate – shogunate held by the Hojo family

1274–81 Attempted invasion by the Mongols
1333–1537/8 Ashikaga shogunate
1333–92 Rival northern and southern courts
1467–77 Civil war – the Onin war
15th–16th centuries Feudal anarchy – the period of the 'Warring Country'

1540s Portuguese introduced muskets into Japan
1549 Francis Xavier, first Christian missionary to Japan
1550–60 Civil war between factions of samurai
1573 Odo Nobunaga ousted the shogun from Kyoto
1582–1600 Japan reunified by Toyotomi Hideyoshi
1592 Abortive Japanese invasion of Korea
1600–1868 Tokugawa shogunate established by Tokugawa Ieyesu
1612 Christianity banned
1630s Beginning of sakuku – policy of isolation from the rest of the world

c. 1750 Tokyo became the world's largest city
1853 US fleet under Commodore Perry forced Japan to open to trade; end of Japanese isolation
1867–9 Tokugawa shogunate toppled; Emperor Meiji gained executive power and instituted Western-style reforms
1894–5 Sino-Japanese War

Other Worlds: 1000 – 1900

Sub-Saharan Africa

11th century Islam reached the Sahel

13th–14th centuries Kingdom of Mali flourished in the Sahel

13th–15th centuries Kingdom of Zimbabwe flourished

14th century Rise of the Muslim emirate of Bornu (Nigeria)

15th century Nubian Christian states extinguished

15th–17th centuries The (Ibo) kingdom of Benin flourished in Nigeria

1441 Portuguese arrived in Guinea-Bissau

c. 1450 Sultanate of Agadès became powerful in southern Sahara

c. 1450–1550 Kongo and Ndongo kingdoms in Angola and Zaire

1460s–1591 Empire of Songhay in the Sahel

late 15th century The Portuguese explored much of the African coast; Dias rounded the Cape of Good Hope (1488)

c. 1500 Beginning of the Portuguese slave trade on the West African coast

1531 Portuguese established trading posts in Mozambique

1625 Foundation of the kingdom of Abomey

c. 1650–1750 The (Yoruba) Oyo empire flourished in West Africa

1652 Dutch colony founded at the Cape

c. 1700/50–1901 Kingdom of Ashanti flourished in West Africa

1795 Britain occupied the Cape

1835–7 The 'Great Trek' of the Boers in South Africa

1875–1900 The 'scramble for Africa' – colonial division of the continent

1885 The Mahdists took Khartoum – death of General Gordon

1896 Ethiopia resisted attempted invasion by Italian forces

1899 Beginning of the Second Boer War in South Africa

Australasia and Oceania

11th–16th centuries Easter Island statues erected

1432 Probable Chinese landing on the northern coast of Australia

c. 1500 Beginning of the Maori civil wars

1606 Willem de Janesz sighted Cape York Peninsula

1642 Abel Tasman discovered Tasmania and the south island of New Zealand

1770 Captain Cook landed at Botany Bay

1788 First British settlement in Australia

1840 New Zealand became a British colony

1860–70 Maori Wars against European settlement

1867 End of transportation of convicts to Australia

1901 The Commonwealth of Australia established

1907 New Zealand became an independent dominion

OTHER WORLDS: 1000 – 1900

The Americas

after 1000 Temple Mound Culture in North American Great Basin

11th–16th centuries Pueblo culture flourished in modern southwestern USA

12th century Toltec Empire collapsed into warring states

c. 1200 Foundation of the Inca dynasty

1345 Foundation of Tenochtitlán (modern Mexico City) by the Aztecs

before 1350–1476 Chimú empire based on Chan Chan (Peru)

c. 1440–76 Major expansion of the Inca Empire

1492 Columbus landed in the New World

1500 Peak of the Aztec Empire

1519–21 Cortez conquered the Aztec Empire

1532–5 Pizarro conquered the Inca Empire

late 16th century First permanent European settlements on the eastern seaboard of North America

1572 Last Inca state ceased to exist

1598 Pueblo culture disrupted by Spanish colonization

1607 Jamestown, Virginia, is founded by the English

1608 Québec founded by the French

1689–1763 French and Indian Wars – Britain and France vied for supremacy in North America

1750 White settlement crossed the Appalachians

1775–83 American War of Independence

1780–1 Peruvian Indians revolted against Spanish rule

1780–1 Toussaint L'Ouverture led black slave revolt in Haiti

c. 1800 White settlement west of the Mississippi

1803 The Louisiana Purchase – Mississippi Valley sold to US by France

1811–30 Full independence of Spain's South American colonies

1830 Indian Removal Act (USA)

1850–90 Indian Wars on the western Plains

1884 Araucanians defeated by Chile after 350 years' resistance

1887 US legislation on Indian reservations

Europe

1054 Schism between Roman Catholic and Greek Orthodox Churches

1066 Norman conquest of England

1096–9 First Crusade

1241 Mongols overran Eastern Europe

1337 Hundred Years War began

1340s The Black Death ravaged Europe

1450 Gutenberg's printing press

1469 Union of Aragon and Castile

1492 Moors expelled from Spain

1517 Luther's '95 Theses' – the start of the Reformatiom

1618 Start of the Thirty Years War

1700–21 The Great Northern War

1740–8 The War of the Austrian Succession

c. 1750 Start of the Industrial Revolution

1789 Start of the French Revolution

1799–1814/15 Napoleon in power in France

1861 Italian unification

1871 German unification

1878 Congress of Berlin

1914–18 World War I

THE MEDIEVAL WORLD: 400–1000

Northwestern Europe

406 Alans, Vandals and Sueves invaded Gaul across the Rhine

407 Withdrawal of the last Roman troops from Britain

412 Visigoths crossed the Alps into Gaul

418 Foundation of the Visigoth kingdom of Toulouse

5th century Anglo-Saxons settled in Britain

451 Combined force of Romans, Visigoths and Burgundians defeated Attila the Hun at the Catalaunian Fields

476 Accession of the Frankish king Clovis

c. 500 Ethelbert, king of Kent

507 Clovis defeated the Visigoths at Vouillé

613 Frankish lands reunited under Chlotar II

639 Death of Dagobert, the last powerful Merovingian king

732 Battle of Poitiers – Charles Martel defeated an Arab raiding army

751 Carolingian dynasty founded in France

757–96 Reign of Offa of Mercia in Britain

787 Viking raids on Britain began

768–814 Frankish Empire ruled by Charlemagne; Carolingian court became the centre of a cultural renaissance

9th century Viking settlements made in Ireland

9th–10th centuries Slow economic, commercial and population growth throughout Europe

800 Charlemagne crowned emperor of the West

843 Treaty of Verdun – Frankish Empire divided into three

c. 843 Kenneth MacAlpine united the Scots

874–930 Vikings settled in Iceland

878 Alfred halted Danish advance at the Battle of Edington

911 Vikings granted the Duchy of Normandy

c. 960 Unification of England by Wessex

987 Beginning of the Capetian dynasty in France

Central and Eastern Europe

375 The Huns arrived in Europe from Central Asia

378 Visigoths defeated the Romans at Adrianople

433–53 Attila the Hun conducted an offensive throughout Central Europe

453 Death of Attila the Hun

570s Slavs launched attacks on the Byzantine Empire's Balkan frontiers

7th century Slav conquest of the Balkans

8th century Moravian Empire flourished in Central Europe

772–96 Most of the German lands united under the Frankish Empire by Charlemagne, who conquered Saxony, the Avars and Bavaria

9th century Foundation of Kiev Rus

c. 900 Magyar invasion of Central Europe

924 Height of Bulgarian Empire; Simeon I threatened Constantinople

936–73 Otto the Great extended his power throughout Germany

955 Battle of Lechfeld – Germans defeated the Magyars

960–92 Reign of Mieszko I, founder of the Polish kingdom

962 Coronation of Otto I as emperor of the Romans

997–1038 Reign of Stephen, first king of Hungary

The Church

354–430 Augustine of Hippo

mid-5th century Patrick began his mission to Ireland

496 Compilation of the first Missal

c. 529 Benedict founded Monte Cassino

590–604 Pontificate of Gregory the Great

597 Augustine sent to convert the English to Christianity

7th century Lombards converted to Christianity

720s Beginning of the iconoclast movement in the Byzantine Church

c. 750 Boniface evangelized Germany

9th century Bulgars, Serbs, and Magyars converted to Christianity

910 Foundation of Cluny Abbey

960 Danes and Poles converted to Christianity

970 Christianity spread to Bohemia

988 Orthodox Christianity established in Kiev Rus

THE MEDIEVAL WORLD: 400–1000

Byzantine Empire

527–65 Reign of Emperor Justinian

530s Belisarius reconquered North Africa and Sicily for the Byzantine Empire

by 551 Belisarius recovered most of Italy for the Byzantine Empire

626 Constantinople besieged by the Persians and Avars

628 Heraclius defeated the Persians

630s and 640s Byzantines lost Syria, Palestine, Egypt and North Africa to the Muslims Arabs

678–8and 717–18 Arab sieges of Constantinople

c. 750 Byzantine Empire confined to Greece and Anatolia

811 Byzantine Empire defeated by the Bulgars

867–86 Revival of Byzantine Empire under Basil I

960s Nicephorus II destroyed the Arab fleet in the Aegean

976–1025 Reign of Basil II

Southern Europe

402–3 Visigoths invaded Italy

410 Alaric sacked Rome

411 Kingdom of Galicia founded by the Sueves

476 Romulus Augustulus, the last Roman emperor, deposed

493–526 Reign of Theoderic the Great in Italy

c. 500 Visigoth states established in Spain

563 Ostrogoth kingdom overthrown in Italy

568 Lombards invaded Italy

711 Islamic Berbers invaded Spain and soon conquered most of the Iberian Peninsula

718 Foundation of the Christian kingdom of Asturias in northern Spain

720 Muslim armies invaded Sardinia

722 Asturias defeated the Moors in the Battle of Covadonga

754–6 The pope gained temporal powers in central Italy; foundation of the papal states

774 Charlemagne conquered Lombardy

827–32 Arab conquest of Sicily

846 Rome sacked by Arabs

849 Arab fleet defeated by papal fleet at Ostia

928 Foundation of the Umayyad caliphate in Spain

951 Otto I conquered Italy (crowned emperor of the Romans in 962)

Middle East

525 Yemen conqured by Abyssinia

530–79 Period of Persian expansion and conquest

c. 570 Birth of Muhammad

622 The Hijra – Muhammad left Mecca for Medina

632 Death of Muhammad

630–50 Arabia, Syria, Egypt and Mesopotamia taken by the Muslims

661–750 Umayyad dynasty ruled from Damascus

from 8th century Reception of Classical learning by Islamic scholars

750 Beginning of the Abbasid dynasty

969 Fatimid caliphate founded in Egypt

THE MEDIEVAL WORLD: 1000–1500

Northwestern Europe

1014 Defeat of the Vikings in Ireland by Brian Boru

1016–35 Cnut's Anglo-Danish empire

1066 Norman conquest of England

12th century Rapid growth of the cloth industry in Flanders

1154 Henry II established a Plantagenet empire in England and France

1171 Henry II of England invaded Ireland and claimed sovereignty

---

c. 1200 Foundation of universities at Oxford and Paris

1215 Magna Carta in England

1283–4 English conquest of Wales completed

1302 Matins of Bruges, popular revolt in Flanders

1314 Victory at Bannockburn established Scottish independence

1327 Extinction of Capetian dynasty in France; Philip VI (Valois) challenged by Edward III of England

1337–1452 The Hundred Years War

1346 Battle of Crécy

1358 The Jacquerie, popular revolt in France

1360 The Treaty of Brétigny temporarily halted the Hundred Years War

1381 The Peasants' Revolt against the poll tax in England

late 14th century Rise of duchy of Burgundy

1397 Union of Kalmar – Eric of Pomerania crowned king of Norway, Sweden and Denmark

1399 Richard II deposed in England; House of Lancaster usurped the throne

---

1400–8 Welsh rebellion led by Owen Glendower

1415 Battle of Agincourt

1425–30 Expansion of the duchy of Burgundy under Philip the Good

1429 Joan of Arc relieved Orleans in the Hundred Years War

1439 End of Scandinavian Union

1450–3 Loss of Normandy and Gascony by the English

1455–85 Wars of the Roses in England

1477 Battle of Nancy – Charles the Bold of Burgundy killed

1485 Henry Tudor defeated Richard II of England at Bosworth Field; start of Tudor dynasty

Central and Eastern Europe

1024 First Salian king in Germany

1075–1122 The Investiture Contest between Holy Roman Empire and papacy

1152 Frederick I 'Barbarossa' established the Hohenstaufen dynasty

---

1237–41 Mongols overran Russia and Eastern Europe

1240–63 Alexander 'Nevski' established a Russian state based on Vladimir

1276 Rudolf of Habsburg became duke of Austria and established his dynasty in Vienna

1291 Independence of the Swiss cantons from Habsburg rule

1316–41 Creation of the Lithuanian empire by Gediminas

c. 1350 Foundation of the Hanseatic League

1356 The 'Golden Bull' of Charles IV regularized the election of the Holy Roman Emperor

1386 Union of the crowns of Poland and Lithuania

1389–93 Ottoman Turks annexed Serbia and Bulgaria

1399 Defeat of Poland-Lithuania by the Mongol Golden Horde

1410 Battle of Tannenberg

1419–36 Hussite Wars in Bohemia

1437 Beginning of the period of Habsburg dominance of the office of Holy Roman Emperor

1450 Gutenberg set up his printing press in Mainz

1466 Western Prussia restored to the Teutonic Knights by Poland

1478 Hungary gained Lusatia, Moravia and Silesia from Bohemia

1480 Ivan III of Moscow defeated the Mongols

The Church

1048–54 Pontificate of Leo IX; papal reformation began

1054 East–West Schism between Churches of Rome and Constantinople

11th Conversion of Sweden to Christianity completed

1096 Urban II preached crusade against Islam

1098 Citeaux, first Cistercian foundation

1209 Foundation of the Franciscan friars

1209–29 Albigensian Crusade against the Cathars

1215 Fourth Lateran Council – major pastoral reforms; foundation of the Dominican friars

1229 Teutonic Knights began to convert the Prussians to Christianity

1307–14 Destruction of the order of the Knights Templar

1309–77 Avignon papacy

late 14th century Lollard heresy in England

1378–1417 The Great Schism

1387 Lithuania accepted Christianity

1412 Jan Hus excomunicated for condemning indulgences in Bohemia

1414–17 Council of Constance ended the Great Schism

1478 Establishment of the Spanish Inquisition

THE MEDIEVAL WORLD: 1000–1500

Byzantine Empire

1040 Byzantine campaigns in Sicily

1071 Battle of Manzikert – Seljuk Turks crushed the Byzantine army

1081–1118 Revival of Byzantine power under Alexius I Comnenus

1204 Constantinople besieged and sacked by a Crusader army; foundation of the Latin Empire

1261 Restoration of the Byzantine Empire in Constantinople under the Palaeologan dynasty

by 1400 All the territories surrounding Constantinople had been conquered by the Ottoman Turks

1453 Constantinople was besieged and taken by Ottoman Sultan Mehmet II; end of the Byzantine Empire

1460 The Ottoman Turks captured Morea (the Peloponnese)

Southern Europe

1031 Caliphate of Córdoba collapsed

by 1035 Castile, Aragon and Navarre began the Reconquista in Spain

1040s The Normans began to carve out territories in southern Italy

1085 Toledo captured from the Muslims in Spain

1091 Roger Guiscard completed the Norman conquest of Sicily

1138–9 Foundation of the kingdom of Portugal

c. 1150–1200 Rise of the early Italian city-states

after 1204 Great expansion of Venetian territory and commerce in the eastern Mediterranean

1249 Moors expelled from Portugal

1266 Angevin French gained control of Sicily

1282 The Sicilian Vespers – French expelled from Italy

14th century Beginnings of humanism and the Renaissance in Italy

1346–7 The Black Death brought to Europe by Italian merchant ships from the Crimea

1378–1402 Giangaleazzo Visconti led Milan to control much of southern Italy

1380 Venetian defeat of Genoa removed Genoese influence from the eastern Mediterranean

1383 Establishment of the House of Avis in Portugal

1385 Portuguese defeat of Castile ensured Portuguese independence

1434 The Medici family came to power in Florence

1442 All of southern Italy came under Spanish rule

1454 Peace of Lodi, end of Italian Wars

1469 Marriage of Ferdinand II to Isabella I led to the unification of Spain

1492 Granada, the last Muslim state in Spain, fell to Ferdinand and Isabella

1492–3 Columbus's first voyage to the New World

1494 Treaty of Tordesillas divided the New World between Spain and Portugal

1494–5 French invasion of Italy

Middle East

1040s Seljuk Turks arrived in the Middle East

1098/1103–1268 Crusader states of Antioch and Tripoli

1099 Jerusalem taken by the Crusaders; foundation of the kingdom of Jerusalem

1187 Jerusalem recaptured by the sultan of Egypt, Saladin

1219–60 Successive Mongol attacks on Persia, Iraq and Anatolia, initially led by Genghis Khan

1250 Mamluks seized power in Egypt

1258 Last Abbasid caliph killed when the Mongols sacked Baghdad

1260 Battle of Ain Jalut – defeat of the Mongols by the Mamluks

c. 1300 Foundation of the first Ottoman Turkish state in Anatolia

1402 Tamerlane (Timur) defeated and captured the Ottoman sultan Bajezid I

1444 Timurid state established in Baghdad

1447 Persia regained independence on the breakup of the Timurid empire

1476 Timurids lost control of Mesopotamia

THE EARLY MODERN WORLD: 1500–1650

Northwestern Europe

1500 France conquered the duchy of Milan

1511 England, Aragon, the papacy and Venice formed a Holy League against France

1513 English army under Henry VIII invaded France

1513 Scottish defeated by the English at Flodden Field

1523 Gustavus Vasa elected king of Sweden

1526 Tynedale's first English translation of the Bible printed

1529 Peace of Cambrai between France and Spain temporarily halted the Habsburg–Valois Wars

1533–5 The English Reformation began – Henry VIII broke with Rome and made himself head of the Church in England

1558–1603 Elizabeth I, queen of England.

1559–98 French Wars of Religion

1567 Revolt of Protestant Dutch against Spanish rule began

1572 St Bartholemew's Day Massacre of French Huguenots

1581 Dutch declared independence from Spain

1584 Assassination of William the Silent

1587 Execution of Mary, Queen of Scots

1588 Spanish Armada attempted to invade England

1589 Henry of Navarre became the first Bourbon king of France

1603 James VI of Scotland became James I of England

1605 Catholic Gunpowder Plot against James I

1611–32 Gustavus Adolphus, king of Sweden

1620–c. 1670 Period of economic recession in Europe

1624–42 Cardinal Richelieu, chief minister of France

1635 Outbreak of Franco-Spanish War

1641–9 Catholic Irish revolt suppressed by Cromwell

1642–9 Civil war in England – Parliamentarians deposed and beheaded Charles I and declared a republic

1643 Spain defeated by France at Battle of Rocroi

1648 Dutch independence recognized

Central Europe

1510–46 Peak of prosperity of the Fugger family of German bankers

1512 Diet of Cologne established Ten Circles as basis for the government of the Holy Roman Empire

1519 Charles V became Holy Roman Emperor

1525 German Peasant's War crushed by the German princes

1529 Vienna besieged by the Turks

1531 The Protestant German states formed the Schmalkaldic League against Charles V

1534–5 Anabaptist rule in Münster, Germany

1538 Catholic German princes formed the League of Nuremberg

1543 Copernicus argued that the sun was at the centre of the universe

1552 War between Saxony and Charles V

1555 Peace of Augsburg recognized Lutheranism

1556 Abdication of Charles V

1561 Baltic lands of the Teutonic Order secularized

1597–1651 Maximilian I, elector of Bavaria, founder of the Catholic League in the Thirty Years War

1618–48 Thirty Years War; 30–60% of the population of Germany perished

1620 Bohemia reconquered by the Habsburgs at the Battle of White Mountain

1630 Swedes under Gustavus Adolphus invaded Germany

1632 Battle of Lützen – Gustavus Adolphus killed

1640–88 Frederick William (The Great Elector) created a centralized state in Brandenburg

1648 Peace of Westphalia intensified the political divisions of Germany

Eastern Europe

by 1500 Ottoman (Turkish) conquest of Bosnia, Albania and the Peloponnese completed

1512–20 Ottoman Empire doubled in size under Selim I

1520–66 Suleiman the Magnificent, Ottoman sultan

1522 Knights of St John expelled from Rhodes by the Turks

1526 Battle of Mohács – Ottoman army defeated and annexed Hungary

1533–84 Ivan IV the Terrible, tsar of Russia

1553 Chancellor reached Moscow via the North Cape

1566–74 Selim II annexed Venetian possessions in the Aegean

1571 Fleet of the Holy League defeated the Ottomans at Lepanto

1613 Romanov dynasty came to power in Russia

early 17th century Beginning of the administrative and social decay of the Ottoman Empire

1640s–60s Rapid decline and disintegration in Poland

1645–69 Crete taken from the Venetians by the Ottomans

THE EARLY MODERN WORLD: 1500–1650

The Church

1517 Luther nailed the 95 Theses to the door of the Wittenberg church

1520 Luther excommunicated

1533–5 The English Reformation began

1534 Foundation of the Jesuits

1536 Calvin's first radical Protestant treatise published

1545–63 Council of Trent launched the Counter-Reformation

1559 Church of England re-established on the basis of the Thirty-Nine Articles

1596 Catholic influence in Poland and the Ukraine extended by the Union of Brest–Litovsk

1598 Edict of Nantes recognized rights of the Huguenots in France

by 1600 Most of northern and Central Europe had become Protestant

early 17th century Roman Catholic Church sought to suppress Copernicanism

after 1605 Increase in anti-Catholic legislation in England

1611 The Authorized version of the Bible published in England

1623 Protestant worship forbidden in Bohemia

1648 Society of Friends (Quakers) founded

Southern Europe

1500 Treaty of Granada – France and Spain partitioned Italy

1508 League of Cambrai concluded between Aragon, France and the Holy Roman Empire against Venice

1508 Portuguese captured Goa

1512 France defeated at Ravenna and driven from Italy

1515 France defeated the Holy League at Marignano

1515 First circumnavigation of the world by Magellan and Del Cano

1525 Francis I defeated and captured by Charles V at Pavia

1527 Army of Charles V sacked Rome

1530 Knights of St John installed on Malta

1556 Philip II became ruler of the Spanish Empire after the abdication of his father Charles V

1565 Ottoman Turks besieged Malta

1580 Portugal annexed by Spain

1596 English force sacked Cadiz

by 1600 The Spanish Empire comprised the Iberian Peninsula, most of Latin America, parts of Italy and the Netherlands, and the East Indies

17th century Naples and Sicily came under Spanish rule

1610 Moriscos (Christian Moors) expelled from Spain

1640 Portuguese and Catalans rebelled against centralized rule from Madrid

1647–8 Revolt in Naples against Spanish rule

1652 Catalan revolt suppressed

The Americas

1500 Cabral discovered Brazil

1502 Vespucci discovered the eastern coast of South America

1519–21 Cortez overthrew the Aztec Empire in Mexico

1531–3 Pizarro subdued the Inca Empire in Peru

1534 Cartier's first voyage to the St Lawrence

late 16th century Spanish and Portuguese settlements established in many coastal areas of South and Central America

1562–7 Hawkins voyages to the West Indies

1583 Gilbert attempted to found an English colony in Newfoundland

1585–7 Unsuccessful attempts to found an English colony in Virginia

early 17th century Spanish colonies in Latin America became self-sufficient; colonial trade declined

1607 Foundation of the English settlement at Jamestown

1608 Foundation of the French colony of Québec

1625 Dutch colony of New Amsterdam (later New York)

1624–54 Dutch occupation of part of Brazil

THE EARLY MODERN WORLD: 1650–1789

Northwestern Europe

1643–1715 Louis XIV of France created an absolute monarchy and pursued an aggressive foreign policy

1652–4, 1664–7 and 1672–4 Anglo-Dutch naval wars

1653–8 Oliver Cromwell, Lord Protector of England

1659 Peace of the Pyrenees ended Franco-Spanish War

1660 Restoration of the monarchy in England under Charles II

1665 and 1666 Great Plague and Great Fire of London

1688–9 The 'Glorious Revolution' marked beginning of constitutional monarchy in England

1688–97 The Nine Years War – English-led alliance against Louis XIV

18th century Boom in colonial trade; increase in size and wealth of the middle class in Western Europe

1701–13 War of the Spanish Succession

1706 Marlborough defeated the French at Ramillies and conquered the Spanish Netherlands

1707 Act of Union between England and Scotland

1713 Treaty of Utrecht ended the War of the Spanish Succession

1714 George, elector of Hanover, succeeded to the British throne

1715 and 1745–6 Jacobite rebellions in Britain

1721–42 Sir Robert Walpole was effectively the first 'prime minister' of Britain

c. 1750 Beginning of the Industrial Revolution in Britain

1756–63 Seven Years War

1756, 1757–61 and 1766–8 Pitt the Elder in power in Britain

1770 The Parlements temporarily abolished in France

1778–83 Anglo-French War

1783–1801 Pitt the Younger, British prime minister

1785–7 Republican Dutch estates in revolt against the stadholders

1789 Beginning of the French Revolution

end of 18th century Growths in parts of Western Europe of religious and humanitarian opposition to slavery

Central Europe

1657 Brandenburg acquired duchy of Prussia

1683 Last Turkish attack on Vienna

1686 The Emperor Leopold I, Saxony, Bavaria, Spain and Sweden formed the League of Augsburg against France

1687 Battle of Mohács – Habsburgs defeated the Ottoman Turks to take control of Hungary

1704 Anglo-Austrian force defeated the French at Blenheim

1713 Pragmatic Sanction of Charles VI declared that the Habsburg lands were to pass undivided to his daughter, Maria Theresa

1713–40 Frederick William I, king of Prussia – Prussian army reformed

1740 Prussia seized Silesia from Austria – beginning of the War of the Austrian Succession

1740–86 Frederick the Great expanded Prussian territory in Germany and Poland

1740–80 Maria Theresa, ruler of Austria

1748 War of the Austrian Succession ended in the Treaty of Aix-la-Chapelle

1753–92 Kaunitz, chancellor of Austria

1756 The Diplomatic Revolution – alliance between Austria and France

1756 Prussia invaded Saxony – start of the Seven Years War

1759 France defeated by Britain and Hanover at Minden

1763 Prussia confirmed as a great power by the Treaty of Paris

1780–90 Enlightened despotism of Joseph II, ruler of Austria

1785 Prussia formed League of German Princes against Austria

Eastern Europe

1667 Romanov dynasty came to power in Russia

1674 Jan Sobieski became king of Poland

1682–1725 Peter the Great modernized Russia

1691 Habsburgs conquered Transylvania

end of 17th century Ottoman Empire ruled by Köprülü grand viziers

1700 Start of the Northern War between Russia and Sweden

1703 Peter the Great began the construction of St Petersburg

1709 Russia defeated Sweden in the Battle of Poltava

1718 Austria took northern Serbia from the Ottomans

1721 Treaty of Nystad ended the Northern War – Swedish Baltic lands ceded to Russia

1762–96 Catherine II 'the Great' reformed Russia and annexed territory from the Ottoman Turks and Poland

1772 First Partition of Poland between Austria, Prussia and Russia

1774 Russia gained an outlet to the Black Sea by the Treaty of Kuchuk Kainardji

1783–4 Russia annexed the Crimea

THE EARLY MODERN WORLD: 1650–1789

The Church

1653 Jansenism declared a heresy

1656 Pascal in his *Provincial Letters* attacked casuistry and the Jesuits

1666 Great schism in Russia

1685 Edict of Nantes revoked in France

1713 Papal Bull *Unigenitas* condemned Jansenist doctrines

1730s John and Charles Wesley began to found Methodism in England

1722–31 Expulsion of Protestants from the Archbishopric of Salzburg

1764 Jesuits expelled from France

1667 Jesuits expelled from Naples and Spain

1769 Dissolution of many monasteries in Austria

1773 Suppression of the Jesuits

1770s and 1780s Threats of schism from Catholic Church in Austria and Germany

Southern Europe

2nd half of 17th century Marked political, economic and military decline of Spain

1668 Independence of Portugal recognized

1694–1700 Venetian campaigns against the Ottomans – last period of Venetian power

1700 Philip, duke of Anjou, inherited the Spanish throne as the first Bourbon king of Spain

1704 English forces took Gibraltar

1718 Foundation of the kingdom of Sardinia

1727–8 Spanish siege of Gibraltar

1737 Tuscany came under Habsburg rule

1748 Kingdom of Sardinia made territorial gains by Aix-la-Chapelle peace settlement

1755 Beginning of Paoli's Corsican rebellion against Genoa; Lisbon earthquake

1755–77 Chief minister Pombal carried out reforms and curbed the power of the Church in Portugal

1761 Treaty of Ildefonso, Franco-Spanish Bourbon family pact

1779–82 Unsuccessful Franco-Spanish siege of Gibraltar

1780 British fleet under Rodney defeated the Spanish fleet off Cape St Vincent

1789 Accession of the last doge of Venice

The Americas

1670 Hudson's Bay Company chartered

1675–6 Indian war against New England settlers

by 1700 Chain of French forts and trading posts established from Québec to Louisiana

1689–1763 Anglo-French colonial wars in North America

1713 France ceded Nova Scotia to Britain

1729 North and South Carolina became crown colonies

1746 Britain captured Louisburg

1751 Georgia became a crown colony

1759 British force under Wolfe captured Québec from France

1760s–80s Significant growth of French West Indian trade

1763 Britain acquired Canada and Louisiana east of the Mississippi

1772 Boston Assembly threatened secession from Britain

17774 Continental Congress issued Declaration of Rights

1776 American Declaration of Independence

1776–83 American War of Independence

1783 Peace of Paris recognized American independence

1787–9 American Constitution

THE MODERN WORLD: 1789–1850

Northwestern Europe

1789 French Third Estate declared itself to be the National Assembly; fall of the Bastille; start of the French Revolution

1792 France became a republic; France defeated Prussia at Valmy; start of the French Revolutionary Wars

1793 Execution of Louis XVI

1794 The Terror; execution of Robespierre

1795 Speenhamland Poor Law Relief began in England

1795 Batavian Republic, a French puppet state, established in the Netherlands

1795–9 France ruled by the Directory

1798 Wolfe Tone's rebellion in Ireland

1799 Napoleon Bonaparte seized power in France

end of 18th century Large increase in enclosures in England

c. 1800 Major growth in religious non-conformism in Britain

1801 Act of Union between Britain and Ireland

1805 British fleet defeated French and Spanish at Trafalgar

1806–10 Louis Bonaparte, king of Holland

1814 Napoleon defeated and exiled to Elba

1815 Napoleon defeated at Waterloo by Britain and Prussia and exiled to St Helena

1814–15 Bourbons restored in France; kingdom of the Netherlands founded; Sweden gained Norway from Denmark

1829 Catholic Emancipation in the UK

1830 'July Revolution' in France – Bourbons overthrown; liberal Orleans monarchy established

1830–1 Successful Belgian revolt against Dutch rule

1832 British Great Reform Act – rotten boroughs suppressed

1832 Tolpuddle Martyrs transported to Australia

From c. 1840 Increase in emigration from USA to Europe

1845–51 Irish famine

1846 Repeal of the Corn Laws in the UK

1848 Orleans monarchy overthrown in France; Second Republic established

Central Europe

1795 French army under Napoleon Bonaparte invaded Austria

1798 France invaded Switzerland and established the Helvetic republic

1800 France defeated Austria at Marengo and Hohenlinden

1805 France defeated Austria at Ulm, and Russia and Austria at Austerlitz

1806 France defeated Prussia at Auerstadt and Jena; Confederation of the Rhine established; Holy Roman Empire abolished

1809–48 Metternich, foreign minister of Austria (chancellor after 1821)

1814–15 Congress of Vienna – Austria and Prussia enlarged; Germany reorganized

1833 German states formed a customs union (Zollverein), the first step towards German unification

1847–8 Swiss civil war – new federal constitution in 1848

1848 Marx and Engels – *The Communist Party Manifesto*

1848–9 Liberal revolts in many German states; Frankfurt Assembly attempted to unite Germany with a liberal constitution

1848–9 Habsburg monarchy shaken by revolts in Budapest (under Kossuth), Vienna and Prague

Eastern Europe

1793 Second Partition of Poland between Prussia and Russia

1795 Third Partition of Poland between Austria, Prussia and Russia

1804–13 Serbian revolt against Turkish Ottoman rule

1808 France defeated Russia at Eylau and Friedland

1812 Napoleon invaded Russia and defeated Russians at Borodino – campaign ended with retreat from Moscow

1815 Russian-ruled kingdom of Poland established

1825 Decembrist Revolt in Russia

1830 Polish revolt against Russian rule

1832 Poland annexed by Russia

1833 Russo-Turkish Treaty of Unkiar-Skelessi

1841 Straits Convention closed the Dardanelles to non-Ottoman warships

THE MODERN WORLD: 1789–1850

Southern Europe

1796–7 Napoleon Bonaparte campaigned against Sardinia and Austria in Italy

1797 French-controlled Cisalpine and Ligurian republics founded in northern Italy; France occupied Venice

1805 Napoleonic kingdoms established in Italy, Naples and Spain

1807–14 Wellesley (Wellington) defeated the French in the Peninsular War

1808 France annexed the Papal States – restored 1814

1820 Liberal revolts throughout southern Europe

1821 Greek revolt aginst the Turks

1827 Turkish power in Greece ended at the Battle of Navarino

1829 Greek independence

1830–1 Liberal revolts in Italian states suppressed by Austria

1833–8 Carlist civil war in Spain

1848–9 Liberal revolts in Italian states; Austria defeated Sardinia-Piedmont at Novara

The Americas

1787 Washington became first US president

1791 Toussaint l'Ouverture's black revolt against French rule in Haiti

1791 Division of Canada into English- and French-speaking provinces – Upper and Lower Canada

1803 Louisiana Purchase: USA bought Louisiana from France

1810 Revolts against Spanish rule in Colombia, Mexico and Argentina

1811 Venezuela in revolt against Spain

1812–14 Anglo-US War of 1812

1816 Argentine independence

1817 Independent Venezuelan government set up by Bolívar

1818 Chilean independence

1821 Peruvian independence declared

1822 Brazilian independence from Portugal

1823 Monroe Doctrine warned European powers against further New World colonization

1828 Uruguayan independence

1836–45 Independent republic of Texas

1837 Mackenzie's Rebellion and Papineau's Rebellion (1837–8) in Canada

1846–8 Mexican–American War – USA gained Arizona, California and New Mexico

1846 US–Canadian frontier defined by the Oregon Treaty

1848 Gold discovered in California

Rest of the World

1794 Foundation of Qajar dynasty in Persia

1795 Britain took Ceylon and the Cape from the Dutch

1797 Bonaparte's campaign in Egypt

1798 Tipu Sultan defeated by Britain

1799 Discovery in Egypt of the Rosetta Stone

1815 At Congress of Vienna, UK gained the Cape, Ceylon, Ionian Islands, Mauritius, Tobago and St Lucia

1818 Zulu empire founded by Shaka

1819 Refoundation of Singapore

1820 Foundation of Liberia

1822 Gold Coast became a British colony

1830 France annexed Algeria

1833 Slavery abolished throughout the British Empire

1835–7 The 'Great Trek' of Boers in South Africa

1839–42 First Opium War in China

1840 New Zealand became a British colony

1841 Mehemet Ali recognized as hereditary ruler of Egypt

THE MODERN WORLD: 1850–1914

Northwestern Europe

1851 Louis Napoleon came to power in France

1852 Second Empire established in France – Louis Napoleon became Napoleon III

1867 Second Reform Act in UK doubled the electorate

1868 Trades Union Congress formed in Britain

1868 and 1874–80 Premierships of Disraeli

1870 Gladstone's Irish Land Act

1870 Napoleon III defeated at Sedan in Franco-Prussian War; Second Empire overthrown; Commune of Paris set up in French capital besieged by Prussian forces

1871 End of Franco-Prussian War; France ceded Alsace-Lorraine to Germany; French Third Republic established

1879 Irish Land League formed with Parnell as president

1880 Anti-clericalism in France – Benedictines, Carmelites and Jesuits expelled

1881–2 Parnell imprisoned; Phoenix Park murders sparked off Anglo-Irish crisis (1882)

1884 Third Reform Bill in UK

1886 and 1893 Irish Home Rule Bills failed

1892 Keir Hardie became first independent British Labour MP

1894–1906 Dreyfus Affair in France

by end of 19th century Major improvements had been made in industrial working conditions, housing, public health and free education for children in most industrialized countries

1901 Death of Queen Victoria

1904 Entente Cordiale between UK and France

1905 Norway gained independence from Sweden

1906 Foundation of the British Labour Party

1907 Anglo-Russian entente

1909 Lloyd George's 'People's Budget' introduced social security measures and caused a constitutional crisis

1913 Third Irish Home Rule Bill rejected

1914 Militant suffragette demonstrations in London; British Expeditionary Force sent to France at outbreak of World War I

Central Europe

1862 Bismarck became chancellor of Prussia

1863–4 Schleswig-Holstein crisis – Prussia and Austria annexed the Danish duchies

1866 Austro-Prussian War – Prussia defeated Austria at Sadowa (Königgrätz) – end of Austrian influence in Europe; Prussia annexed Hanover, Nassau and Hesse-Cassel

1867 North German Conferation and Austro-Hungarian Empire established

1871 German unification – German Second Empire founded with Wilhelm I of Prussia as emperor (Kaiser)

1878 Congress of Berlin

1879 Bismarck abandoned free trade

1880 Church–state conflict in Germany ended with repeal of May Laws

1882 Germany, Austria and Italy formed the Triple Alliance

1888 William II became emperor (Kaiser) of Germany

1890 Fall of Bismarck

1897 First Zionist Congress at Basel

1907 Germany opposed arms limitations at the Hague Peace Conference

1908 Austria annexed Bosnia and Herzegovina

1914 Assassination of Austrian heir Archduke Franz Ferdinand led to declaration of war against Serbia; general mobilization; Germany declared war on Russia and France; outbreak of World War I

Eastern Europe

1853 Russia conquered Romania during Russo-Turkish War

1854–6 Crimean War – UK, France, Turkey and Sardinia-Piedmont confronted Russia; Battles of Balaclava and Inkerman (1854); siege of Sevastopol (1854–5)

1859 Romania united

1861 Emancipation of Russian serfs

1863 Revolt by Poles and Lithuanians against Russian rule

1867 Turkey withdrew from Serbia

1876 The Bulgarian massacres – Turkey savagely repressed a revolt in Bulgaria

1878 Congress of Berlin – Romania, Serbia and Montenegro independent, Bulgaria autonomous

1891 Launch of the reformist Young Turk movement

1894 Franco-Russian alliance

1903 Bolshevik/Menshevik split in Russia

1905 'Bloody Sunday' revolt in Russia – Duma established with limited powers

1912 First Balkan War – Balkan states defeated Turkey, which lost most of its European territory; Albania independent

1913 Second Balkan War – Balkan states and Turkey defeated Bulgaria

THE MODERN WORLD: 1850–1914

Southern Europe

1859–61 Unification of Italy – French and Piedmontese defeated Austria at Magenta and Solferino (1859); Lombardy, central duchies and Papal States (except Rome) united with Sardinia-Piedmont (1860); Victor Emanuel II became first king of Italy

1868 Liberal revolt in Spain; Isabella II deposed

1870 Rome occupied by Italian forces

1875 Carlists expelled from Catalonia and Valencia

1875 Liberal constitution granted in restored Spanish Bourbon monarchy

1876 End of Spanish Carlist Wars

1900 Assassination of Umberto I, king of Italy

1908 Assassination of Carlos, king of Portugal

1910 Establishment of a republic in Portugal

1912 Italy seized the Dodecanese from Turkey

The Americas

1850 Compromise of 1850 on slavery

1850–90 Indian Wars on the western US plains

1854 Kansas–Nebraska Act; formation of US Republican Party

1861 Confederate States of America formed by 11 southern secessionist 'slave' states; start of the American Civil War

1863 Union forces defeated the Confederates at Gettysburg, turning-point of the American Civil War; US emancipation of slaves

1864–7 French military involvement in Mexico – Habsburg prince Maximilian emperor of Mexico

1865 Surrender of Confederate forces at Appomattox – end of American Civil War; US president Lincoln assassinated

1867 Confederation of Canada established

1867–8 US Reconstruction Acts

1876 The Sioux massacred Custer's cavalry at Little Big Horn

1879–94 Chile defeated Peru and Bolivia in the War of the Pacific

1889 Brazil became a republic

1890 Indian Wars ended in defeat of the Sioux at Wounded Knee

1893 US settlers overthrew the Hawaiian monarchy – formal annexation of the islands 1898

1898 Spanish–American War – USA acquired Cuba, Puerto Rico, Guam and the Philippines

1901 US President McKinley assassinated; Theodore Roosevelt became president

1902 Cuba became independent republic

1903 USA gained control of Panama Canal Zone

1903 Panama seceded from Colombia

1910–40 Mexican Revolution

1914 Panama Canal completed

Rest of the World

1853 US fleet under Perry forced Japan to open to Western trade

1856–60 Second Opium War in China

1857–8 The Indian Mutiny

1860–70 Maori Wars against European settlement in New Zealand

1860s–70s Russia conquered Central Asia

1867–9 Tokugawa shogunate toppled in Japan; Meiji reforms began

1869 Opening of Suez Canal

1875–1900 The 'scramble for Africa' intensified after the 1884 Berlin Conference

1877 Queen Victoria became Empress of India

1885 Khartoum fell to the Mahdi; General Gordon killed

1895 The Jameson Raid

1898 The Fashoda Incident

1899 Start of the Second Boer War

1900–1 Boxer rebellion against Western influence in China

1901 Commonwealth of Australia founded

1902 End of Second Boer War

1910 Union of South Africa founded

1911 Army rebellion toppled the Chinese Qing dynasty; a republic established

THE MODERN WORLD: 1914–45

Western Europe

1914 Outbreak of World War I – Germany declared war on France and invaded Belgium; UK declared war on Germany; First Battle of the Marne

1915 Italy joined the Allies

1916 Battle of Verdun; naval Battle of Jutland; Battle of the Somme; Easter Rising in Dublin against British rule

1917 Battle of Passchendaele; Italy defeated at Caporetto

1918 German defeat in Second Battle of the Marne; revolution in Germany – abdication of the Kaiser; Germany signed armistice on 11 November

1919–23 Versailles Peace Settlement – France regained Alsace-Lorraine; Rhineland demilitarized

1921 Partition of Ireland

1922 Irish Free State proclaimed; Fascists under Mussolini took power in Italy

1923 Hitler attempted coup in Munich

1923–5 Franco-Belgian occupation of the Ruhr when Germany defaulted on reparations; rampant German inflation

1930 French forces left the Rhineland

1930–4 Collapse of German monetary system (1930); rise of the German Nazi Party; Hitler became chancellor in 1933

1936–9 Spanish Civil War

1938 Munich Pact allowed Germany to annex German-speaking areas of Bohemia; Germany annexed Austria; Irish Free State became Republic of Eire

1939 Britain and France declared war on Germany

1940 German invasion of Denmark, Norway, the Low Countries; British evacuation of Dunkirk; Italy entered war as ally of Germany; fall of France – establishment of Vichy regime; Churchill became British PM; aerial Battle of Britain; beginning of the Blitz

1942 Start of massive Allied air raids on Germany

1943 Mussolini overthrown; Allied invasion of Italy

1944 Germans expelled from northern Italy; Normandy Landings; Paris liberated; failure of Allied Arnhem campaign; final German offensive – Battle of the Bulge; Allied forces entered Germany

1945 Mussolini killed by partisans; Allied defeat of Germany completed

Eastern Europe

1914 Assassination of Archduke Franz Ferdinand; Austrian ultimatum to Serbia; Austria declared war on Serbia; Austria and Germany declared war on Russia; Turkey entered war allied to Central Powers

1915 Abortive Allied campaign at Gallipoli

1916 Failure of Russian offensive

1917 February Revolution in Russia – abdication of the tsar; October Revolution – Bolsheviks under Lenin seized power

1918 Russia withdrew from war; Russian imperial family murdered; Austria-Hungary surrendered – Habsburgs deposed

1918–21 Russian Civil War – Bolshevik Red Army defeated anti-Communist 'Whites'

1919 Czechoslovakia, Hungary, Poland and Yugoslavia established as independent states

1920 Independence of Baltic states recognized

1922 Foundation of the Soviet Union (USSR)

1924 Death of Lenin; Stalin became Soviet leader

1928–38 Land taken from peasants in USSR to create collectives – destruction of the kulak class

1930s Gradul elimination of democracy in many East European states as virtual dictatorships were established in Poland, Yugoslavia, Romania, Hungary, Albania, Lithuania, Estonia and Latvia

from 1934 Stalin's purges in the USSR

1939 Nazi–Soviet Pact; Germany invaded Poland – outbreak of World War II

1939–40 Russo-Finnish 'Winter War'

1940 USSR annexed Baltic states

1941 German invasions of Greece, Yugoslavia and USSR; Romania and Bulgaria joined the Axis; extermination of Jews began in German concentration camps

1942 Battle of Stalingrad (to January 1943)

1943 German retreat from USSR began; extermination of Jews intensified

1944 Yugoslavia liberated by the Allies; Soviet offensive in Eastern Europe – Germans pushed back in Poland, Hungary, Romania and Bulgaria

1945 Yalta Conference – Allies decided future division of Europe; Berlin surrendered to Soviets; Hitler committed suicide

Africa

1910 South Africa became independent dominion

1914 Foundation of the African National Congress

1914 South Africa entered the war on the side of the Allied Powers; German Togo occupied by Franco-British forces

1915 German Southwest Africa (Namibia) occupied by South Africa

1916 German Cameroon occupied by Franco-British forces; German East Africa occupied by Anglo-Belgian forces

1919 Former German colonies became League of Nations mandates – Cameroon and Togo (UK and France), Ruanda-Urundi (Belgium), Southwest Africa (South Africa) and Tanganyika (UK)

1923 Southern Rhodesia became a British crown colony

1930s Growth of Afrikaner nationalism in South Africa

1935 Italian invasion of Ethiopia

1936 Italian forces occupied Addis Ababa, Emperor Haile Selassie deposed; Ethiopia annexed

1939–45 White South African opinion divided upon participation in World War II on the Allied side

1940–2 Administration of most of French West Africa by Vichy sympathizers

1940–5 Cameroon and French Equatorial Africa held for the Free French

1942 French West Africa held for the Free French

THE MODERN WORLD: 1914–45

Asia and the Pacific

1914 Australia and New Zealand entered the war against the Central Powers; German territories in the Pacific occupied – Western Samoa by New Zealand, Nauru by Australia, Micronesia and the Marshall Islands by Japan

1923 Sun Yat-sen established Nationalist Chinese government

1927–8 Civil War in China between Nationalists and Communists

1928 Nationalists under Jiang Jie Shi (Chiang Kai-shek) reunited China

1930s Congress Party under Gandhi encouraged a campaign of civil disobedience against British rule in India

1931 Japan invaded Manchuria and established a puppet state

1934 Mao Zedong led Chinese Communists on the Long March

1937 Beginning of Sino-Japanese War – Japanese occupied Beijing and Shanghai

1940 Japan invaded Indochina

1941 Japan invaded the Philippines

1942 Japan invaded Malaya, Singapore, East Indies and Burma; Japan defeated by USA in naval Battle of Midway

1943 USA forced Japanese to retreat in Pacific

1944 US naval victory over Japan at Leyte Gulf

1945 USA dropped atomic bombs on Hiroshima and Nagasaki; Japan surrendered

The Americas

1914 Canada entered the war against the Central Powers

1915 *Lusitania* sunk by German U-boat

1916 US forces occupied Haiti

1916–17 American expedition under 'Black Jack' Pershing into Mexico against Pancho Villa

1917 USA entered war against Germany

1920 US Senate overrode President Wilson's support for the League of Nations – USA entered a period of isolationism

1920 Prohibition of alcohol in USA

1924–30 Persecution of the Church in Mexico

1928–35 Chaco War between Bolivia and Paraguay

1929 Wall Steet Crash – beginning of the Depression

1930 President Hoover adopted protectionist policies to protect US industry in the Depression

1930s Order restored in Mexico by Institutional Revolutionary Party

1930–45 Vargas's dictatorship (the 'New State') in Brazil

1933–45 F.D. Roosevelt, US president – instituted the 'New Deal' to relieve economic distress and promote recovery

1937 *Hindenburg* airship destroyed by fire

1935–9 US Neutrality Acts preventing US involvement in non-American wars

1941 US 'Lend-Lease' scheme agreed, supplying equipment to UK and its allies; Japanese attack on Pearl Harbor – USA entered the war on the Allied side

1942 US troops arrived in theatres of war in Europe, North Africa and the Pacific

Middle East

1914 British forces began Mesopotamian campaign against Turkey

1915–16 Siege of Kut – British defeated by Turks

1916–18 T.E. Lawrence played major role in encouraging Arab revolt against Turkish rule

1917 British forces took Baghdad and Jerusalem

1920 Syria mandated to France; Palestine, Transjordan and Iraq mandated to Britain

1921–2 Turkey repulsed Greek forces; Atatürk deposed the last Ottoman and laid foundations of modern Turkey

1921–7 Saudis united Arabia

1922 Egyptian independence

1919 Punjab riots; Amritsar Massacre by British troops fuelled Indian nationalist sentiment

1930s Jewish settlement in Palestine increased

1932 Iraqi independence

1936 Anglo-Egyptian Treaty – Britain retained control of the Suez Canal

1941 Start of Allied campaign in North Africa

1942 Montgomery defeated German-Italian forces at El Alamein; Allies captured Tripoli and Tunis

1943 Axis troops evacuated North Africa

The Modern World since 1945

Western Europe

1945–51 Attlee's Labour government established Welfare State in UK

1945 Germany divided into four zones of occupation; beginnings of Cold War confrontation

1948 Marshall Plan adopted to provide US aid for Europe; Berlin airlift to West Berlin

1949 Foundation of NATO, Western military alliance; foundation of Federal Republic of (West) Germany

1956 Emergence of mass disarmament movements in the West

1957 Treaty of Rome established Common Market (EEC)

1958 De Gaulle established French Fifth Republic

1964 Election of Wilson's Labour government in UK

1967 Balance of payments crisis in UK led to devaluation of pound

1967–74 Military junta in Greece – the 'Colonels'

1968 Student unrest in much of the West

1969 Start of the 'Troubles' in Northern Ireland – British troops deployed; resignation of de Gaulle as French president following the events of May 1968

1972 'Bloody Sunday' – 13 Catholics killed during a civil rights march in Derry; UK imposed direct rule on Northern Ireland

1973 UK, Ireland and Denmark joined EC

1974 Portuguese revolution – authoritarian regime deposed

1975 Death of Franco; democracy restored in Spain

1979–90 Right-wing Conservative premiership of Margaret Thatcher in UK

1981 Mitterrand became French president

1982 Helmut Kohl became West German chancellor

1986 Spain and Portugal joined EC

1990 German reunification

1991 Treaty of Maastricht on European union

1992 Conservatives in UK won fourth consecutive term of office

Eastern Europe

1945 Beginning of the Cold War – Soviet-imposed Communist regimes began to be established in Eastern Europe

1946 Greek civil war

1948 Communist takeover of Czechoslovakia

1949 Foundation of German Democratic Republic (East Germany)

1952–7 Campaign by Greek Cypriots to end British rule

1953 Stalin died; Khrushchev came to power in USSR

1955 Warsaw Pact formed

1956 Hungarian Rising put down by Soviet forces

1957 USSR launched first satellite in space – *Sputnik I*

1960s Arms race between USSR and USA intensified despite Nuclear Test Ban Treaty in 1963

1961 Berlin Wall constructed; Soviet cosmonaut Yuri Gagarin became the first man in space

1964–87 Brezhnev, Soviet Communist Party leader – Brezhnev Doctrine defined as right of USSR to intervene in affairs of Communist states

1968 Dubček's attempt to reform Communism in Czechoslovakia crushed by USSR

1970 Unrest in Poland – riots in Gdansk

1974 Turkish invasion and partition of Cyprus

1980 Solidarity trade union suppressed in Poland

1981 Greece joined EC

1985 Gorbachov came to power in USSR and began reforms

1986 Chernobyl nuclear disaster in USSR (Ukraine)

1989–91 Collapse of Communism in Eastern Europe; former Soviet satellites became multi-party democracies

1991 Attempted coup by Communist hardliners in Moscow; dissolution of USSR into 15 independent republics; Gorbachov resigned

1991–2 Civil war led to breakup of Yugoslavia

Africa

1948 National Party won power in South Africa – imposition of apartheid

1956 Morocco, Tunisia and Sudan independent

1957 Ghana became the first British black African colony to gain independence

1960 Sharpeville massacre in South Africa

1960–1 Belgian Congo independent; Katanga attempted secession – beginning of Congo crisis

1960s Independence of majority of British and French colonies in Africa

1962 Algeria independent after eight-year uprising

1965 White settler government in Rhodesia declared UDI, leading to guerrilla war

1967–70 Nigerian civil war

1975 Completion of Portuguese decolonization in Africa

1977 Crackdown on anti-apartheid activity in South Africa

1980s Increase in relative poverty of the Third World; Western aid to counter famine increased

1980 Rhodesia independent as Zimbabwe

1990–2 Dismantling of apartheid in South Africa

1994 African National Congress won South Africa's first universal suffrage general election

The Modern World since 1945

Asia and the Pacific

1946–9 Chinese Civil War; Communist victory in 1949 brought Mao Zedong to power

1947 India and Pakistan independent

1949 Indonesia independent

1950–1 Chinese invasion of Tibet

1950–3 Korean War

1954 French defeated by Communist Vietnamese at Dien Bien Phu

1964–73 US military support for South Vietnam against Communist North

1966–76 Cultural Revolution in China

1969 Sino-Soviet border dispute

1971 Pakistan civil war; secession of East Pakistan as Bangladesh; Vietnam War spread to Laos and Cambodia

1975 South Vietnam surrendered; end of Vietnam War

1975–9 Khmer Rouge in power in Cambodia – ousted by Vietnamese invasion

1979–89 Soviet intervention in Afghanistan

1989 Pro-democracy movement suppressed in China – Tiananmen Square massacre

The Americas

1946–55 Juan Perón in power in Argentina

1949 Escalation of Cold War between USA and USSR after explosion of first Soviet atomic bomb

1950–4 McCarthy's witchhunt against alleged Communists in USA

1952 USA exploded first H-bomb

mid–1950s Growth of Civil Rights Movement in Southern states of USA led by Martin Luther King

1958 First US space satellite

1959 Castro seized power in Cuba and gradually imposed a Marxist regime

1960s Race riots in many US cities

1961 Abortive 'Bay of Pigs' invasion by Cuban exiles

1962 Cuban Missile Crisis

1963 Assassination of President Kennedy

late 1960s Growth of French-Canadian separatism

1968 Martin Luther King assassinated

1968–70 Opposition to US involvement in Vietnam intensified

1969 USA landed the first man on the moon

1973 Left-wing Allende government in Chile overthrown by General Pinochet with indirect US support

1979 Somoza overthrown by Sandinistas in Nicaragua

1981–9 Two-term right-wing Republican presidency of Ronald Reagan in the US

1982 Falklands (*Malvinas*) War between Britain and Argentina following Argentine invasion of the Falkland Islands

1983 US-led forces invaded Grenada

1980–90 Spread of multi-party democracy to most Latin American countries

late 1980s Colombia destabilized by drug trade; 'Shining Path' Maoist terrorists active in Peru

1989 US intervention in Panama

1993 Democrat Bill Clinton became US president

The Middle East

1948 Foundation of state of Israel; First Arab–Israeli War

1952 Monarchy toppled in Egypt; Nasser came to power in 1954

1956–7 Nasser nationalized Suez Canal; UK and France invaded Suez Canal Zone; Israel invaded Sinai

1958 Iraqi revolution – fall of the Hashemite monarchy

1964 Foundation of the Palestine Liberation Organization (PLO)

1967 Arab–Israeli Six Day War; Israel captured Sinai, West Bank, Gaza and the Golan Heights

1970 Jordanian civil war, Palestinians expelled

1973 Arab–Israeli 'Yom Kippur' War; Arab oil embargo of the West

1975 Start of civil war in Lebanon

1979 Islamic Revolution in Iran toppled the Shah and brought the Ayatollah Khomeini to power; rise of Islamic fundamentalism

1979–81 Iran hostage crisis

1980–8 Iran–Iraq War

1982 Israel invaded Lebanon

1986 Palestinian intifada (uprising) began in occupied territories

1990 Iraqi invasion of Kuwait

1991 Gulf War – US-led coalition defeated Iraq and liberated Kuwait

1993 Israeli–Palestinian Peace Accord

FACT FINDER

Abbasid, a dynasty of SUNNI Muslim CALIPHS who replaced the UMAYYAD Caliphate, ruling from Baghdad (750–1258). They claimed descent from MUHAMMAD'S uncle, Abbas. Their political power began to wane in the 9th century, and in the 10th century the Shiite FATIMID Caliphate took power in North Africa. The Abbasids retained nominal power until 1258, when Baghdad was sacked by the Mongols.

Abdul Hamid II (1842–1918), Ottoman sultan (1876–1909). Internal disorder and foreign-policy crises disrupted his reign. He was deposed in the YOUNG TURK revolution of 1908.

Aberdeen, George Hamilton Gordon, 4th Earl of (1784–1860), British Conservative statesman. He became prime minister of a coalition government of WHIGS and PEELITE Conservatives in 1852, but resigned in 1855 over his mismanagement of the Crimean War.

Aborigines, the original inhabitants of Australia and Tasmania. A hunting and gathering people, the Aborigines reacted in a variety of sophisticated ways to a wide range of environments. Owing to their nomadic lifestyle and the destructive impact of European settlement, few physical relics of the Aborigines' rich cultural traditions remain. Their numbers were decimated within the first hundred years of white settlement, falling from around 300,000 in 1788 to 50,000 in 1888. In the 1930s Aborigine reserves were created in central and N Australia, but since World War II many Aboriginal groups have emerged to campaign for Aborigine rights and the preservation of their cultural heritage.

Aboukir bay, Battle of, see NILE, BATTLE OF THE.

Abraham, Old Testament patriarch whose migration from UR to Harran in Upper Mesopotamia and thence to CANAAN is described in the book of Genesis.

absolutism, a political system in which the monarch attempted to centralize power in his own person. The archetype of the absolute monarch was LOUIS XIV, king of France (1643–1715). He believed that kings ruled by divine right, receiving their power from God, and so must rule justly and in person.

Abu Bakr (c. 573–634), first CALIPH of Islam (632–4). On the death of his son-in-law, the Prophet MUHAMMAD, in 632, he succeeded him as head of the Muslim community.

Abyssinia, a former name for ETHIOPIA.

Achaea, a region of ancient Greece in the NW Peloponnese. Its cities were first formed into the Achaean League in the 5th century BC. From the early 3rd century BC this was reborn in a greatly extended form as a federal state.

Achaemenid, a dynasty that ruled the Persian Empire from the mid-6th to the late-4th century BC. The empire was founded by CYRUS II (d. 530 BC), who overthrew Astyages, last king of the MEDES, to become ruler of the Medes and Persians in 549 BC. Cyrus conquered Anatolia and the Babylonian Empire, while his son, Cambyses II (530–522 BC) made further gains in Egypt. The campaigns of DARIUS I (521–486 BC) brought the empire to its greatest extent. Darius reorganized the administration and finances of the empire, but neither he nor his son XERXES (486–465 BC) succeeded in conquering GREECE. Rebellion and conspiracy weakened the empire in the 4th century BC. Darius III, the last Achaemenid, was defeated by ALEXANDER the Great at ISSUS (355 BC) and GAUGAMELA (332 BC). See map, p. 10.

Actium, Battle of (31 BC), a naval battle ending the ROMAN CIVIL WARS, fought between the rival fleets of MARK ANTONY and OCTAVIAN, who were struggling for supremacy in the Roman world. Antony was defeated and went on to commit suicide with his mistress CLEOPATRA. Octavian's victory left him in complete control of the ROMAN EMPIRE.

Adams, John (1735–1826), second president of the USA (1797–1801). He pursued a pro-British foreign policy as president and head of the ruling FEDERALIST party in the 1790s.

Adams, John Quincy (1767–1848), sixth president of the USA (1825–9) and eldest son of John ADAMS. His attempts to extend federal powers were opposed by Andrew JACKSON.

Addington, Henry, 1st Viscount Sidmouth (1757–1844), British statesman. He succeeded the Younger PITT as prime minister (1801–4). As home secretary (1812–21) he used stern measures against political and economic dissidents.

Aden, a port at the entrance to the Red Sea (see map, p. 26). A British protectorate until 1957, and a crown colony until 1963, in 1967 Aden became part of the state of South Yemen, which merged with North Yemen to form YEMEN in 1990.

Adenauer, Konrad (1876–1976), German statesman. A founder of the West German CHRISTIAN DEMOCRATIC Party, he was the first chancellor of the Federal Republic of (West) GERMANY (1949–63). A staunch supporter of the Western Alliance, he helped restore the reputation of Germany after World War II.

Adrianople, Battle of (9 August 378), the defeat of a Roman army by VISIGOTH forces W of Constantinople. The Eastern Roman Emperor, Valens, was killed in the battle.

Adrianople, Treaty of (1829), a treaty ending the RUSSO-TURKISH WAR of 1828–9. The treaty confirmed the autonomy of Serbia and promised autonomy for Greece. Russia made territorial gains in Europe and Asia Minor.

Aegospotami, Battle of (405 BC), the final naval victory of the Spartans over the Athenians at the end of the PELOPONNESIAN WAR.

Aeolians, the third cultural and linguistic grouping of the ancient Greeks, comprising the Boeotians and Thessalians, and a group of cities on the N coast of Asia Minor (Turkey). See also DORIANS, IONIANS.

Aetolia, an ancient region of NW Greece. From c. 370 BC its tribes combined into a federal state, the Aetolian League.

Afghanistan, a country in S Central Asia. Afghanistan was ruled by the Persians until the 4th century BC when Alexander the Great invaded, but Greek control was short-lived as Afghanistan fell to barbarians from the N. In the 7th century AD Arabs reached the borders, bringing Islam. Various Muslim empires followed until 1222, when the country fell under the harsh control of the Mongol Genghis Khan. The rule of Tamerlane (Timur) in the 14th century was equally devastating. In the 18th century, the Persians united the country. In the 19th century, rivalry between Russia and Britain, who regarded Afghanistan as the key to

India, led to instability. Britain attempted to assert control in two disastrous ANGLO-AFGHAN WARS (1839–42 and 1878–80). Independence was only achieved in 1921 after a third war with the British. A period of unrest followed until a more stable monarchy was established in 1933. A coup in 1973 overthrew the monarchy. A close relationship with the USSR resulted from the 1978 Saur Revolution, but the Soviet invasion (1979) led to civil war. In 1989 the Soviets withdrew, leaving the cities in the hands of the government and Muslim fundamentalist guerrillas controlling the countryside. In 1992 fundamentalists took Kabul and formed a provisional government, but factional – largely ethnic – fighting continues.

African National Congress (ANC), a black South African political party founded in 1912. Uniting with Indian representatives in 1926, the ANC aimed to create a democratic and racially integrated SOUTH AFRICA. Banned and exiled in 1960, the ANC abandoned its policy of passive resistance, acquired a military wing and embarked on a campaign of violence. Its leader, Nelson MANDELA, was arrested and sentenced to life imprisonment in 1962. The ANC became a non-racial party in 1969. After a period of guerrilla warfare, Mandela was freed, the ANC was legalized and began negotiations with the South African government for a democratic non-racial state in 1990. The ANC emerged victorious in South Africa's first universal suffrage elections in April 1994, forming a government of national unity with the defeated NATIONAL PARTY.

Afrikaners, speakers of the Dutch-derived Afrikaans language in SOUTH AFRICA, also known as Boers. Afrikaners are descendants of families that emigrated from the Netherlands, Germany and France before 1806.

Agadir crisis (1911), a dispute that erupted when Kaiser WILHELM II sent a German gunboat to Agadir in SW Morocco to stop French expansion in the area and protect German interests. War was narrowly averted, but the incident strengthened Anglo–French suspicions of Germany's ambitions.

Aga Khan (1936–), see ISMAILI.

Agincourt, Battle of (25 October 1415), an English victory over the French in N France during the HUNDRED YEARS WAR. Marching N from Honfleur, HENRY V's army encountered a French force three times its size, but defeated it through the discipline of massed longbowmen. Henry went on to conquer NORMANDY.

Agricola, Gnaeus Julius (AD 40–93), Roman governor of Britain (78–c. 84). He extended Roman military power into the Highlands of Scotland.

Agricultural Revolution, the major changes in agricultural practices that began in Britain in the 18th century. Medieval strip farming was superseded by the system of ENCLOSURE of land, large-scale farming, the extension of arable farming over heaths and commons, intensive livestock husbandry and the introduction of crop rotation and new varieties of crops. Previously self-sufficient peasants became agricultural labourers.

Agrippa, Marcus Vipsanius (c. 64–12 BC), Roman general, lifelong friend and adviser of the emperor Augustus. At the time of his death he was virtually co-ruler of the empire.

Ahab, king of Israel (c. 869–c. 850 BC) and son of OMRI. He married Jezebel and fought in alliance with the ARAMAEANS against the ASSYRIANS.

Ain Jalut, Battle of (1260), the destruction of a MONGOL army by Egyptian MAMLUK forces S of Damascus, thwarting an attempted Mongol invasion of Syria and Palestine.

Aix-la-Chapelle, Treaty of (1748), the treaty concluding the War of the AUSTRIAN SUCCESSION. Maria Theresa of Austria relinquished Silesia to Frederick the Great of Prussia, the kingdom of Sardinia made gains in N Italy, while in N America the British returned the fortress of Louisburg to the French in exchange for the return of Madras in India.

Akbar ('the Great', 1542–1605), MOGUL emperor of India (1555–1605). Akbar extended Mogul rule over the whole of N India and established uniform administration and laws within the empire. He attempted to bring unity to an empire of diverse faiths through pursuit of religious toleration.

Akhenaten (Amenophis IV; d. c. 1362 BC), pharaoh of Egypt (c. 1379–1362 BC). He abandoned the worship of the state-god Amun and claimed divine guidance from Aten, the sun disc. He moved the capital from Thebes to a place named Akhenaten ('the horizon of the sun disc'). His reforms proved unpopular, however, and were overturned when TUTANKHAMUN began his reign.

Akkad, a region of central MESOPOTAMIA, centred on the city of Akkad. Founded by SARGON I c. 2350 BC, Akkad enjoyed a century and a half of dominance in Mesopotamia before it was overrun by invaders from the E around 2200 BC.

Alamo, the, a mission in San Antonio, TEXAS, besieged by Mexican troops during the Texan Revolution against Mexico (1836). The American defenders (led by Jim Bowie and Davy Crockett) were finally overwhelmed and massacred in the assault of 6 March 1836.

Alans, groups of mounted warriors who spread across Europe with the Barbarian migrations, settling in Italy, Gaul and N Africa in the 5th century.

Alaric I (c. 370–410) king of the VISIGOTHS (395–410). A former commander of Gothic troops in the Roman army, his fluctuating relations with the declining Western Empire led him to invade Italy on three occasions, culminating in his sack of Rome in 410.

Alba, Fernando Alvarez de Toledo, Duke of (1507–82), Spanish general. His brutal suppression of Protestant unrest in the Netherlands fuelled the DUTCH REVOLT against Spanish rule in the late 16th century.

Albania, a country in SE Europe. The revolt (1444–68) by Skenderbeg (?1403–68) against the Ottoman Turks – who invaded in the 14th century – is celebrated by Albanians as their national epic. Because most Albanians converted to Islam, they were able to secure autonomy and gain access to high positions in Ottoman service. By 1900, Ottoman enfeeblement encouraged Albanian nationalism, and in 1912 independence was declared. The country was occupied in both the BALKAN WARS and World War I, and the formation of a stable government within recognized frontiers did not occur until the 1920s. Interwar Albania was dominated by Ahmed Zogu, who made himself king (as Zog I) in 1928. He fled when Mussolini invaded in 1939.

Communist-led partisans took power when the Germans withdrew (1944). Under Enver Hoxha (1908–85), the regime pursued rapid modernization on Stalinist lines, allied, in turn, to Yugoslavia, the USSR and China, before opting (in 1978) for self-sufficiency and isolation. The liberal wing of the Communist Party won a power struggle (1990), instituted social and economic reforms, and held multi-party elections (1991). After the Socialists (former Communists) were defeated in 1992, a new government faced severe economic problems. Large numbers of Albanians have left the country in an attempt to find employment abroad.

Albigensians, see CATHARS.

Albuquerque, Alfonso de (1453–1515), Portuguese navigator and founder of the Portuguese empire in the E. His conquests of Goa (1510), Malacca (1511) and Hormuz (1515), laid the basis of Portugal's control of eastern trade routes.

Alcibiades (c. 450–404 BC), Athenian statesman and soldier. After being charged with desecrating sacred statues in 415, Alcibiades defected to the Spartans, supplying them with military advice that contributed to a calamitous Athenian defeat. See PELOPONNESIAN WAR.

Aleuts, a native people inhabiting the islands of the Bering Sea and adjacent Alaskan coast, related to the ESKIMO.

Alexander I (1777–1825), tsar of Russia (1801–25). The early part of his reign saw widespread reforms, but its later phases were marked by reactionary policies. Between 1805 and 1815 he was mainly preoccupied with the Napoleonic Wars, and in the following decade with upholding the conservative principles of the VIENNA settlement. His 'Holy Alliance' of the Christian monarchs of Europe was short-lived and ineffective.

Alexander II (1818–81), tsar of Russia (1855–81). His reign witnessed the emancipation of the SERFS (1861), reforms of local and provincial government, the legal system and the army, and Russian expansion into Central Asia. He was assassinated by an anarchist.

Alexander III (1845–94), tsar of Russia (1881–94). Domestically, his reign was characterized by internal repression and attempts by his ministers to promote economic modernization. In foreign affairs, it saw the conclusion of the Franco-Russian alliance (1892–4) and the consolidation of Russian gains in Asia.

Alexander III (the Great) (356–323 BC), king of MACEDON (336–323 BC). The son of PHILIP II of Macedon, Alexander was educated by ARISTOTLE. His conquests brought the whole of the ACHAEMENID Persian Empire under the control of Greek-speaking rulers (see map, p. 12). Alexander crossed into Asia Minor in 334 BC. His defeat of the western Persian provinces at GRANICUS was followed by further victories at ISSUS and GAUGAMELA. He then led his army across Asia to the edge of the Himalaya and the N provinces of India. As he moved further away from Greece Alexander used Persian soldiers and appointed Persian nobles to positions of authority, to the dismay of the Macedonians. After his exhausted army mutinied in 324 BC he turned back towards the West, but fell ill and died at Babylon.

Alexandria, the name of six cities founded by ALEXANDER THE GREAT, the most successful of which was Alexandria-in-Egypt (see map, p. 12). It became the capital of Egypt under the PTOLEMIES, and flourished as a centre of the arts and sciences and as a commercial city. Under the Romans it was acknowledged as the second city of the empire.

Alexius I (Comnenus; 1048–1118), Byzantine emperor (1081–1118) and father of the historian Anna Comnena. His request for papal help in fighting the SELJUK Turks was one of the causes of the First CRUSADE.

Alfred ('the Great'; 849–99), king of WESSEX (871–99), who successfully withstood VIKING attacks and helped revive English ecclesiastical learning. In 886 he and the Dane GUTHRUM agreed the boundaries between Wessex and the DANELAW. Building on his achievement, his successors united England. See ANGLO-SAXONS.

Algeria, a country in NW Africa. After the fall of CARTHAGE in 146 BC, coastal Algeria became Roman. In the 7th century the Arabs brought Islam despite initial BERBER resistance. Several Berber empires flourished in the Middle Ages. In the 16th century, Turkish corsairs defended Algiers against the Spanish, and placed the region under Ottoman control. During the 18th century, Algeria became a centre for piracy and in 1830 the French invaded on the pretext of protecting trade. Colonization followed, and coastal Algeria was attached to metropolitan France. By 1860 much of the best land was in French hands. Nationalist riots in Sétif were ruthlessly suppressed in 1945, and in 1954 the Front de Libération Nationale (FLN) initiated a revolt that became a bitter war. A rising by French settlers, in favour of the integration of Algeria with France, led to the crisis that returned de Gaulle to power in France (1958). Despite two further risings by the settlers, and the activities of the colonists' terrorist organization, the OAS, Algeria gained independence in 1962. The first president, Ahmed BEN BELLA, was overthrown in 1965 by Colonel Houari Boumédienne (1932–78), who established a one-party socialist state under the FLN. After his successor, Colonel Chadli Benjedid (1929–) introduced multi-party democracy (1990), Islamic fundamentalism became a political force. In 1992 the second round of multi-party elections was cancelled when fundamentalists gained a large lead in the first round. The military took power and suspended political activity. Tension increased when military-appointed President Boudiaf was assassinated in June 1992.

Algonquin, a native North American people, formerly living in the area N of the Great Lakes. The name Algonquin is also used for a wider linguistic grouping.

Ali (?600–61), fourth CALIPH of Islam (656–61) and son-in-law of MUHAMMAD. Ali and his descendants are regarded by SHIITE Muslims as the only true heirs of the authority of Muhammad.

Allende, Salvatore (1908–73), Chilean Marxist politician, president of CHILE (1970–3). He died in a military coup led by General PINOCHET.

Allied Powers or **Allies, 1.** the countries that fought against the CENTRAL Powers in World War I. The main Allied Powers were France, Britain, Russia, and the USA after 1917. **2.** the countries that fought against the AXIS Powers in World War II. The main Allied Powers were Britain, the Commonwealth countries, the USA, the Soviet Union, France, China and Poland.

Almohads, a Muslim dynasty of BERBERS who ruled in N Africa and S Spain in the 12th and 13th centuries, displacing the ALMORAVIDS.

Almoravids, a Muslim dynasty of BERBERS who ruled in N Africa from the second half of the 11th century. In the 1080s they were called into Spain to rescue the Muslim kings from Christian attack. They were overthrown by the ALMOHADS in the mid-12th century.

Alsace-Lorraine, territories in E France annexed after the FRANCO-PRUSSIAN war by the victorious Germans, who claimed that they were historically and ethnically German. They were returned to France by the Treaty of VERSAILLES at the end of World War I.

American Civil War (1861–5), a war fought between the Federal government of the USA and the 11 CONFEDERATE states of the South. The Civil War had its roots in the emergence of two distinct systems of labour in the northern and southern parts of the USA. While commercial farming and industry took root in the North on a free labour basis, the South found itself increasingly dependent on the labour of black slaves. Despite the growth of domestic abolition movement in the 1830s, most northerners were reluctant to endanger the Union by agitating the slavery question. However, US gains in the MEXICAN–AMERICAN WAR unleashed a bitter debate on the question of whether slavery should be excluded from the new territories. In 1854 the KANSAS–NEBRASKA ACT repealed a ban on slavery in the N part of the LOUISIANA purchase. The crisis deepened as Northerners perceived the South as a threat to their own freedoms and began voting for the newly formed REPUBLICAN Party, which demanded a Federal government ban on the future expansion of slavery. Southerners saw their slave-based society as under attack from abolitionists. When the northern and southern Democrats split on the slavery issue, the Republican candidate Abraham LINCOLN won the 1860 presidential election. The seven Deep South states seceded and formed a pro-slavery Confederacy under Jefferson DAVIES, and were joined later by the Upper South states of Virginia, Carolina, Tennessee and Arkansas. War broke out when Confederate forces bombarded FORT SUMTER, a Federal fort in South Carolina. For most of 1861–3 the Northern cause looked bleak. Union armies suffered a string of serious reversals. President Abraham LINCOLN was initially reluctant to tackle the slavery question, but in January 1863 he signed the famous Emancipation Proclamation declaring that all slaves outside the Union lines were free. The tide turned in the favour of Union forces in July 1863, when the Confederate forces of Robert E. LEE were repulsed at GETTYSBURG, Pennsylvania, and the Union army of General Ulysses S. GRANT finally broke through in the W by taking the Confederate stronghold of VICKSBURG. Over the next two years the armies of Grant and William T. SHERMAN ground down the rebels, and on 9 April 1865 Lee surrendered at APPOMATTOX. The war had cost over 600,000 lives, but it preserved the Union intact and set free 4 million black slaves. See also RECONSTRUCTION.

American Federation of Labor (AFL), a federation of North American labour unions, founded in 1886. By 1914 the AFL was a loose alliance of national craft unions with a membership of over two million skilled workers which avoided politics and worked for specific practical objectives.

American Revolution, see INDEPENDENCE, AMERICAN WAR OF.

Amin, Idi (1926–), Ugandan head of state (1971–9). See UGANDA.

Amorites, a Semitic people who settled in MESOPOTAMIA in the early part of the 2nd millennium BC.

Amritsar massacre (13 April 1919), a massacre of Indians gathered in Amritsar in N INDIA to protest against repressive British legislation. Gurkha troops under Brigadier R.M. Dyer fired on an unarmed crowd, killing 379 and injuring 1200.

Anabaptist, a member of a radical 16th-century Protestant sect. They took biblical fundamentalism to its limits, insisted that the true Church consisted only of those who freely entered it, and believed that only adult baptism was valid. Originating in Zürich, Anabaptist sects spread across central and N Europe in the 1520s. The theocratic 'kingdom' of Münster, founded by the Dutch Anabaptist John of Leiden, was bloodily crushed by Lutheran and Catholic princes in 1535.

anarchism, a political theory, first outlined by PROUDHON, advocating the abolition of formal government and the state. Anarchists such as BAKUNIN were particularly influential in Russia during the 1860s and 70s and were hostile to MARXISM. A number of European heads of state were assassinated by anarchists in the 1890s, but the influence of anarchism declined after the Russian Revolutions of 1917.

Anatolia, the Asian part of Turkey, formerly known as Asia Minor.

ancien régime, the social and political system in France, and sometimes by extension elsewhere in Europe, before the FRENCH REVOLUTION of 1789. The France of the *ancien régime* was a centralized absolute monarchy ruled by LOUIS XVI from Versailles. It was a society based on privilege, with the mass of taxation being paid by the unprivileged urban poor and by the peasantry, who had the additional burden of feudal dues. The wealthiest non-nobles (the bourgeois) had some privileges but had fewer legal and social rights than the aristocracy.

ANC, see AFRICAN NATIONAL CONGRESS.

Andorra, a co-principality in SW Europe, between France and Spain. Since 1278 Andorra has been under the joint sovereignty of a temporal 'prince' (since 1589 the French head of state) and a spiritual 'prince', the Spanish bishop of Urgel. Because of its peculiar constitution, Andorra has found difficulties in obtaining international recognition. In the 1970s and 1980s, however, it has achieved some constitutional and financial reform.

Andrassy, Julius, Count (1823–90), Hungarian statesman. Main negotiator of the AUSTRO-HUNGARIAN Ausgleich ('compromise') of 1867, he was prime minister of Hungary (1867–71). As Austro-Hungarian foreign minister (1871–9), he was a creator of the THREE EMPERORS' LEAGUE (1873) and a key architect of the Balkan settlement agreed at the Congress of BERLIN in 1878.

Andropov, Yuri (1914–84), Soviet politician, general secretary of the Communist Party (1982–4), president of the Soviet Union (1983–4). He was succeeded by Konstantin CHERNENKO.

Angevin, the name given by historians to two dynasties: **1.** the descendants of the early 10th-century Count Fulk of ANJOU, notably HENRY II, RICHARD I and JOHN, who ruled Normandy, England and AQUITAINE as well as ANJOU (the Angevin Empire); **2.** the descendants of CHARLES of Anjou, conqueror of the kingdom of Sicily in 1266, whose successors ruled S Italy (the kingdom of NAPLES) until 1442.

Angles, a Germanic people related to the JUTES and the SAXONS, and originating in S Denmark and its islands (see map, p. 15). In the early 5th century they settled in East Anglia and NORTHUMBRIA as auxiliaries of Britain's sub-Roman rulers.

Anglican Church or **Church of England,** the established state Church in England. In 1534 HENRY VIII renounced the supremacy of the pope, founding the Church of England with the monarch at its head. Protestant reforms were instituted during the reign of EDWARD VI. After the reign of the Catholic MARY I, the independent Church of England was re-established by ELIZABETH I on the basis of the Thirty-Nine Articles. Conflict between PURITANS (who wished for a purer Protestant Church) and the followers of 'catholicizing' Archbishop LAUD was a contributory factor in the outbreak of the ENGLISH CIVIL WAR. The Church of England was disestablished during the COMMONWEALTH and the PROTECTORATE, but restored at the RESTORATION. The Anglican Church retains many of the Catholic liturgical traditions, but holds most of the tenets of the reformed faith of Protestantism. Its doctrine is based upon the Thirty-Nine Articles (1559), while its liturgy is based upon The Book of Common Prayer (1552 and 1662) and its successors. The 18th-century Evangelical Movement emphasized the Protestant tradition (John WESLEY established an independent METHODIST Church in 1791), while the 19th-century Oxford Movement emphasized the Catholic tradition. These two movements continue in the Church of England as the Low Church and the High Church. The General Synod of the Church of England voted in favour of the ordination of women priests in 1993, prompting the defection of some conservative Anglicans to the Roman Catholic Church.

Anglo-Afghan Wars (1839–42, 1878–80 and 1919), a series of wars between Afghan rulers and British India. Fears of a Russian threat to the Indian subcontinent led to the ill-fated British expeditions of 1839 and 1878. In the final war, the Afghan amir, Amanullah, made an unsuccessful attack on British India, but secured Afghan independence by the Treaty of Rawalpindi.

Anglo-Burmese Wars (1824–6, 1852, 1885), a series of wars fought between British India and Burma (MYANMAR), during which most of Burma was annexed to British India.

Anglo-Dutch Wars (1652–4, 1665–7, 1672–4), three naval wars fought between England and the United Provinces of the NETHERLANDS for commercial and maritime supremacy. A prime cause of the conflicts was the English NAVIGATION ACTS, aimed at destroying the lucrative Dutch carrying-trade. England eventually ousted the Dutch from N America and the W Indies, and gradually excluded them from its foreign and colonial trades.

Anglo-Maori Wars, a series of conflicts between MAORIS and British colonial forces in the 1840s, 50s and 60s, fought mainly on the North Island of New Zealand. As white settlers sought more land in the 1850s, Maori chiefs increasingly refused to sell it. War broke out when troops attempted to evict Maoris from disputed lands in Waitara (1860), and continued for most of the 1860s. Maori guerrilla activity was not finally suppressed until 1872. See WAITANGI, TREATY OF.

Anglo-Saxons, the collective term used to describe the pagan Germanic invaders – principally ANGLES, SAXONS and JUTES but also FRISIANS and FRANKS – who invaded and conquered Britain between the 5th and 7th centuries. Only Scotland, Wales and the SW (Cornwall) remained in the hands of native Britons. Throughout the 7th and 8th centuries there was a fluctuating number of Anglo-Saxon kingdoms, but gradually a 'big three' emerged: NORTHUMBRIA, MERCIA and WESSEX. Hegemony passed successively from Northumbria to Mercia and finally to Wessex, which under ALFRED the Great led resistance to the VIKING invasions of the 9th century. By 960 Alfred's successors had conquered the rest of England, forming one kingdom for the first time. After a period of Anglo-Danish rule under CNUT, the West Saxon royal line was restored with EDWARD the Confessor in 1042, but ended with the NORMAN CONQUEST of 1066.

Angola, a republic in SW Africa. The Kongo and Ndongo kingdoms ruled much of the area when the Portuguese arrived in the late 15th century and developed a major slave trade. In the 20th century forced labour, heavy taxation and discrimination from white settlers helped to stimulate nationalism. Portugal's repression of all political protest led to the outbreak of guerrilla war in 1961. When independence was finally conceded (1975), three rival guerrilla movements fought for control of Angola. With Soviet and Cuban support, the (Marxist-Leninist) MPLA, under Dr Agostinho Neto (1922–79), gained the upper hand and repulsed an invasion from South Africa. In the 1980s, Cuban troops continued to support the MPLA government against the South African-aided UNITA movement in the S. Foreign involvement in the civil war ended in 1990. Following a ceasefire (1991), multi-party elections were held in 1992. However, UNITA forces resumed the conflict after rejecting the election results.

Anjou, a historic province (or county) of W France. It was ruled by an independent princely house (the ANGEVINS) from the 10th century until conquered by PHILIP II Augustus of France in 1203–5.

Annam, a former kingdom and empire of E Indochina. It became a French protectorate in 1884 and now forms part of VIETNAM.

Anne (1665–1714), queen of England, Scotland and Ireland (1702–7), queen of Great Britain and Ireland (1707–14), the last STUART monarch. She was the daughter of the Catholic JAMES II, but was raised as a Protestant and married the Protestant Prince George of Denmark. Her reign saw England's UNION with Scotland and British success in the War of the SPANISH SUCCESSION. After the death of her last surviving child, the Act of SETTLEMENT (1701) recognized the Protestant HANOVERIANS as successors to the English throne, excluding the Catholic Stuarts.

Anschluss (German, 'connection'), Hitler's annexation of Austria in 1938. In February 1938 the Austrian chancellor,

Kurt von SCHUSCHNIGG, refused HITLER's demand to include Nazis in his cabinet and called for a plebiscite on Austrian independence from Germany. Hitler, fearing an unfavourable outcome, sent German troops into Vienna on 12 March 1938, and proclaimed the Anschluss the following day.

anticlericalism, hostility towards the influence of the Christian clergy in political affairs. In the late medieval period anticlericalism set the scene for the Protestant REFORMATION. Attacks on the Church gained a new momentum during the 18th-century ENLIGHTENMENT, when scientific and rational thinking was encouraged.

Anti-Comintern Pact (25 November 1936), an agreement between Germany and Japan, declaring their hostility to international communism. Italy signed in 1937, and between 1939 and 1941 other states, including Bulgaria, Finland, Hungary, Romania, Slovakia and Spain, also signed.

Antietam (Sharpsburg), Battle of (17 September 1862), a battle during the AMERICAN CIVIL WAR in which the North's Army of the Potomac under General George McCLELLAN stalled General LEE'S Confederate drive into Pennsylvania. Over 20,000 men died in fighting on 17 September, the bloodiest day of the war.

Antigonid dynasty, a dynasty descended from Antigonus (c. 382–301 BC), one of ALEXANDER THE GREAT'S generals. The Antigonid dynasty ruled MACEDON and Greece after the fragmentation of the empire established by Alexander the Great. Antigonid control of Macedon was secure, but their hold on central and S Greece was not always so firm, being threatened by ACHAEA and AETOLIA from c. 240 BC.

Antioch, a city formerly in N Syria (now Antakiyah in Turkey). Founded by SELEUCUS I in 300 BC (see map, p. 12), it rose to prominence in the later Roman and Byzantine periods, and fell to the Arabs in 637. It was taken by CRUSADERS in 1098 and remained in Christian hands for half a century.

antipope, a rival bishop of Rome, in opposition to the lawfully elected pope. In the Middle Ages antipopes were often supported for reasons of political gain by the HOLY ROMAN EMPEROR, and in the 14th century several antipopes were elected following the GREAT SCHISM.

anti-Semitism, antagonism towards JEWS. Anti-Semitism was prominent in France, Germany, Poland and Russia in the late 19th and early 20th centuries. Pogroms and persecution forced many European Jews to Britain, the USA and later Israel. Nazi propaganda in 1930s Germany encouraged anti-Semitism, and Hitler's 'final solution' – the extermination of European Jewry – led to the death of some six million Jews in the HOLOCAUST between 1941 and 1945.

Antonescu, General Ion (1882–1946), Romanian Fascist dictator who allied ROMANIA with the AXIS Powers in World War II. His regime fell when the Red Army entered Romania in 1944, and he was executed as a war criminal.

Antonine Wall, Roman frontier barrier built in AD 142 under the emperor Antoninus Pius (ruled 138–161). It stretched between the Clyde and the Firth of Forth in Scotland. It was abandoned in AD 196.

Antony, Mark (Marcus Antonius; c. 82–30 BC), Roman general and chief aide to CAESAR. After Caesar's murder in 44 BC he seized the initiative from the assassins and in 43 formed the Second TRIUMVIRATE with Octavian and Lepidus, defeating Brutus and Cassius at PHILIPPI. Lepidus was soon pushed aside and for over a decade the Roman world was uneasily divided between Octavian and Antony. The issue was decided in Octavian's favour at the battle of ACTIUM in 31 BC, and soon after Antony committed suicide with CLEOPATRA. See ROMAN CIVIL WARS.

ANZAC, an acronym for the Australian and New Zealand Army Corps, which fought in World War I. Originally used to denote the Corps which fought in the GALLIPOLI campaign, ANZAC was later applied to all Australian and New Zealand servicemen who served together in joint forces.

Anzio, the site of an amphibious landing by Allied forces in January 1944 during the ITALIAN CAMPAIGN in World War II.

ANZUS, a Pacific security treaty between Australia, New Zealand and the USA, signed in 1951. The parties agreed to respond to any attack in the Pacific region on any of the signed parties. When New Zealand adopted an anti-nuclear policy in the mid-1980s, the USA suspended its defence obligations to New Zealand (1986).

Apache, a native North American people, predominantly nomadic hunter-gatherers. ATHAPASKAN-speakers, they moved S from the far N c. AD 1000, many eventually arriving in the SW, where they came into conflict with the PUEBLO Indians.

Apartheid (Afrikaans, *rasse-apartheid,* 'race-apartness'), a doctrine developed by AFRIKANER nationalists in SOUTH AFRICA to reinforce racial segregation after 1948. Apartheid laws defined racial groups and enforced the strict separation of blacks and whites in work, housing, education, religion, marriage, sport and other areas of social life. After 1959 South Africa was partitioned into large white areas and small black African homelands or BANTUSTANS. In 1991 the South African government repealed basic apartheid laws as part of a process towards a new constitution and democracy.

appeasement, a term now used in a pejorative sense to describe the attempts by the British PM CHAMBERLAIN and his French counterpart DALADIER to satisfy the demands of the AXIS POWERS from 1936 to 1939. Appeasement allowed Hitler to occupy the RHINELAND, and to annex Austria and the SUDETENLAND. The policy was abandoned after Hitler invaded Bohemia–Moravia in March 1939 in contravention of the MUNICH agreement.

Appomattox, a village in Virginia, USA, where LEE's Confederate Army of Northern Virginia surrendered to GRANT's Union Army of the Potomac on 9 April 1865, marking the effective end of the AMERICAN CIVIL WAR.

Aquinas, St Thomas (c. 1225–74), Italian DOMINICAN theologian, canonized in 1323. He integrated the ideas of the Greek philosopher ARISTOTLE into Catholic theological thought, making the important distinction between faith and reason.

Aquino, Corazon (1933–), president of the Philippines (1985–92). The widow of an opposition leader murdered by the security forces of Ferdinand MARCOS, she came to power after a bloodless uprising that ended the latter's repressive 20-year rule.

Aquitaine, a former province in SW France. Originally the Roman province of Aquitania, it was occupied by VISIGOTHS, then conquered by CLOVIS I, and subsequently retained a strong separate identity under its own rulers, initially kings (until the 9th century) then dukes (until the 15th century). From 1154 to 1453 the duke of Aquitaine was also king of England.

Arab conquests, the wars of conquest fought by Muslim Arabs in the century following the death of MUHAMMAD in 632, which created an empire – and spread the Islamic faith – from Spain in the W to Central Asia in the E (see map, p. 17). The 'Rightly guided' Caliphs seized Syria and Egypt from the BYZANTINES and Iraq and Persia from the SASSANIANS. The UMAYYADS continued expansion into Central Asia in the E, and N Africa and Spain in the W. The appearance of rival CALIPHATES in Spain and N Africa in the 9th and 10th centuries destroyed the political unity of the empire.

Arab–Israeli Wars (1948–9, 1956, 1967 and 1973), the wars fought between ISRAEL and its Arab neighbours. In November 1947 the UN passed a resolution in favour of the partition of PALESTINE between Jews and Arabs. When Israel proclaimed itself a state in 1948 the surrounding Arab states – Egypt, Jordan, Lebanon and Syria – declared war in support of the Palestinian Arabs. Following fierce fighting a UN armistice was declared, but Israel had made substantial territorial gains at the expense of the proposed Arab (Palestinian) state. In 1956 Israeli forces briefly occupied Sinai during the SUEZ CRISIS. As a result of the SIX DAY (1967) and YOM KIPPUR Wars (1973) Israel made further territorial gains at the expense of EGYPT and SYRIA. The 1978 CAMP DAVID ACCORD between Israel and Egypt was denounced by the rest of the Arab world and failed to tackle the Palestinian question. In 1981 Israel annexed the GOLAN HEIGHTS and the following year invaded LEBANON in retaliation for Palestinian guerrilla attacks on Israel. After withdrawal from Lebanon in 1985 Israel maintained a 'security zone' in S Lebanon as a buffer against guerrilla incursions. The ISRAELI–PALESTINIAN PEACE ACCORD of 1993 raised hopes of a lasting Arab–Israeli peace.

Arab League, an organization formed in 1945 to promote economic and cultural links and to minimize conflict between, Arab states. It includes all Arab states as well as the PALESTINE LIBERATION ORGANIZATION, which the League regards as the representative of a legitimate and independent state.

Arafat, Yasser (1920–), Egyptian-Palestinian politician, chairman of the PALESTINE LIBERATION ORGANIZATION since 1969 and leader of the al-FATAH movement. Despite challenges to his authority from radical Palestinian factions in the late 1980s and early 1990s, he was a signatory to the ISRAELI–PALESTINIAN PEACE ACCORD of November 1993.

Aragon, a kingdom that emerged from a nucleus around the River Aragon during the course of 11th-century wars against the Muslims in N SPAIN. The marriage of FERDINAND II of Aragon to ISABELLA of CASTILE in 1469 effectively created a single Spanish monarchy. See map, p. 21.

Arakan, the W coastal area of Burma (MYANMAR). A powerful kingdom in the 15th century, it was annexed by Burma in 1784 and was ceded to the British in 1826.

Aramaeans, a group of Semitic-speaking tribes who settled in Syria and along the Euphrates from the 10th century BC. They formed numerous small kingdoms and frequently fought the Assyrians and the Israelites. Their language, Aramaic, became the international language of the Ancient Near East, and was the original language of parts of the Old Testament.

Arcadia, a mountainous region in the centre of the Peloponnese, Greece. Its CITY-STATES were mostly dominated by Sparta until the latter's defeat at LEUCTRA, after which Thebes founded in 368 BC a new Arcadian Confederacy. This soon lost cohesion, and by 250 BC most of the Arcadians joined the ACHAEAN LEAGUE.

Archaic period, in ancient Greece, the period c. 800–500 BC. The period witnessed the establishment of independent CITY-STATES and Greek colonization around the Mediterranean. It was followed by the CLASSICAL PERIOD.

Ardennes Offensive ('Battle of the Bulge'; December 1944), the last major German advance of World War II. The Germans attempted to capture the Belgian cities of Antwerp and Brussels by splitting the Allied armies. It took the Allies until mid-January 1945 to prevail in bitter fighting, but by then the Germans – under heavy attack from the Soviets in the E – were close to defeat. See NORTHWEST EUROPE CAMPAIGN.

Areopagus, the earliest council of ancient ATHENS, with judicial and governing powers. Appointed from a fixed set of aristocratic families, it gradually lost powers to other, more democratic, bodies.

Argentina, a republic in S South America. See panel.

ARGENTINA

15th century: NW Argentina became part of the INCA Empire, while Patagonia and the pampas were home to nomadic Indians. **1516:** The Spanish arrived in the La Plata estuary but early colonization was slow. **1776:** Argentina became a Spanish viceroyalty. **1810–16:** Rebellion against Spanish rule led by revolutionary José de SAN MARTÍN. **1816–26:** Independence achieved (1816) but the war of liberation continued until 1820, and the first national government was only formed in 1826. **Until 1853:** Argentina wracked by disunity until the powers of provincial governments were curbed and a stable national government was formed (1853). **From 1880:** Large-scale European immigration. **1930–45:** Period of economic decline and military rule. **1946–55:** Rule of the populist leader Juan PERÓN. His wife Eva was a powerful and popular figure until her death (1952). **1966–73:** Argentina under military rule. **1973–6:** An unstable period of civilian rule including Perón's brief second presidency. **1976–83:** Argentina again under military rule; thousands of opponents of the regime were arrested or 'disappeared'. **1982:** President Galtieri ordered the invasion of the Falkland Islands, precipitating the FALKLANDS WAR. **1983:** Constitutional rule restored. **1990s:** Financial reforms improved the prospects of the economy.

Argos, an ancient CITY-STATE in the NE Peloponnese, Greece. It was repeatedly defeated by Sparta, and in the 5th century BC often allied itself with Athens. In the 390s Argos formed a brief union with CORINTH, which was broken up by Sparta, and was itself greatly weakened by civil war c. 370.

Arianism, a heretical form of Christianity practised in the late Roman Empire and in parts of Western Europe until the 8th century. It was based on the teachings of the Libyan priest Arius (250–336), who denied the divinity of Christ.

Aristides (c. 520–c. 467 BC), Athenian politician, who was ostracized in 483/2, probably after opposing THEMISTOCLES' proposal to develop the Athenian navy. He returned to fight in the Persian Wars, and was responsible from 477 onwards for the first assessment of tribute that the cities of the DELIAN LEAGUE were to pay.

Aristotle (384–322 BC), Greek philosopher, taught by PLATO. What survives of his works are full lecture-notes on his courses, which survey systematically, and develop subtly and profoundly, all known areas of intellectual enquiry, including logic and metaphysics, zoology and physics, politics, ethics, poetics and rhetoric. He tutored ALEXANDER THE GREAT and opened a school in the Lyceum in Athens.

Armada, see SPANISH ARMADA.

Armenia, a country in the Caucasus Mountains of W Asia. Ancient Armenia was incorporated, in turn, into the Persian Empire, the empire of Alexander the Great and the Seleucid Empire. Independent Armenian states appeared in the 2nd century BC and a united Armenian kingdom was established c. 55 BC. Christianity was adopted c. AD 300. In the 4th and 5th centuries Armenia was divided between the BYZANTINE Empire and Persia. An independent kingdom (Greater Armenia) emerged in the 9th century, but was constantly threatened by invasion from the Arabs, Byzantines, Persians and Seljuks. When Greater Armenia fell to the Mongols (1236–42), many Armenians fled to Cilicia (modern SE Turkey) where a second Armenian kingdom (Little Armenia) flourished until the 14th century, when it was overrun by MAMLUK armies from Egypt. In the 16th century Armenia was fought over by Persia and the OTTOMAN Turks. After 1620 W and central Armenia was ruled by the Turks and E Armenia (the present state) was annexed by Persia. Russia took Persian Armenia between 1813 and 1828. The Armenians under Ottoman rule suffered persecution and, in 1896 and again in 1915, large-scale massacres. During World War I Turkey deported nearly 2,000,000 Armenians (suspected of pro-Russian sympathies) to Syria and Mesopotamia. The survivors contributed to an Armenian diaspora in Europe and the USA. Following the collapse of tsarist Russia, an independent Armenian state emerged briefly (1918–22), but faced territorial wars with all its neighbours. Armenia became part of the Transcaucasian Soviet Republic in 1922 and a separate Union Republic within the USSR in 1936. After the abortive coup by Communist hardliners in Moscow (September 1991), Armenia declared independence and received international recognition when the USSR was dissolved (December 1991). Since 1990 Azeri and Armenian forces have been involved in a violent dispute concerning the status of NAGORNO KARABAKH, an enclave of Orthodox Christian Armenians surrounded by the Shiite Muslim Azeris – although Armenia maintains that it has no territorial claims on Azerbaijan.

Arminius (c. 18 BC–AD 19), chieftain of the Cherusci, a Germanic tribe, and leader of German resistance to Roman efforts to create a province E of the Rhine. He achieved his aim in AD 9, when his forces annihilated three Roman legions in the TEUTOBURGER FOREST.

arms control, attempts by the superpowers to restrict and control weapons and armed forces. See NUCLEAR TEST-BAN TREATY, SALT, START and INF TREATY.

Arnhem, Battle of (September 1944), an attempt by the 1st British Airborne Division to secure a bridgehead over the Rhine at Arnhem in the Netherlands to facilitate the Allied advance into Germany in World War II. The attempt failed when German units blocked the path of Allied divisions who were sent to reinforce the airborne troops. See NORTH-WEST EUROPE CAMPAIGN.

Artaxerxes II (c. 436–358 BC), ACHAEMENID king of Persia (404–358 BC); he defeated the revolt of his brother CYRUS the Younger at the Battle of Cunaxa in 401 BC. His son Artaxerxes III (ruled 358–338 BC) was ousted by DARIUS III.

Arthur, a legendary 6th-century king of Britain. Historically, Arthur may have held back the SAXONS for a generation. 'Rediscovered' by the 12th-century chronicler Geoffrey of Monmouth in his *History of the Kings of Britain* (1136), he became the model of the chivalrous warrior-king for the Middle Ages.

Arthur, Chester A. (1830–86), 21st president of the USA (1881–5). A Republican, he attempted to reform the SPOILS SYSTEM.

Aryans, an Indo-European-speaking people of the Iranian steppe who invaded the Indian subcontinent in 2000–1200 BC, conquering the native DRAVIDIANS. The term was also used in Nazi Germany to describe Caucasians of non-Jewish descent.

Ashanti, a former African kingdom ruling the inland part of modern GHANA. From the mid-18th century it became a major force in W Africa until annexed by Britain in 1901.

Ashikaga, a Japanese noble family, whose members filled the office of SHOGUN based at Kyoto 1338–1578. They were driven from Kyoto by ODO NOBUNAGA.

Ashoka, the last MAURYAN emperor of India (272–232 BC). A Buddhist, he consciously moulded the domains he inherited from his grandfather CHANDRAGUPTA into an empire. He developed a centralized bureaucracy and taxation system and promulgated the philosophy of 'State-dhamma', emphasizing the ruler's moral and social responsibility for the welfare of his subjects. His empire disintegrated soon after his death.

Ashurbanipal, king of ASSYRIA (668–627 BC). His conquest of Egypt in the E and Elam in the W took the Assyrian empire to its greatest limits, but within 20 years of his death it had fallen apart. See map, p. 10.

Ashurnasirpal II, king of ASSYRIA (883–859 BC). Under his rule Assyria reclaimed lost territory from the ARAMAEANS and began its imperial expansion.

Asquith, Herbert Henry (1852–1928), British Liberal statesman, prime minister (1908–16). He backed LLOYD GEORGE over the controversial 'PEOPLE'S BUDGET', and supported the passing of important social legislation, including the introduction of a national insurance scheme in 1911. His HOME RULE Bill provoked violence in the N of Ireland. Asquith formed a coalition with the Conservatives in 1915, but his conduct of World War I was criticized, and he was ousted in 1916 by Lloyd George.

Assad, Hafiz al- (1928–), president of SYRIA since 1971. A former air force officer and leading member of the Syrian BA'ATH Party, his rule has often been repressive. In the early 1990s he attempted to improve relations with the West, aligning Syria with the American-dominated coalition during the GULF WAR.

Association of Southeast Asian Nations (ASEAN), an organization established in 1967 by Indonesia, Malaysia, the Philippines, Singapore and Thailand to promote their mutual economic development.

Assyria, originally a small area in N Mesopotamia, centred on the ancient capital of Ashur on the Tigris, it expanded from the 9th century BC to become the first Near Eastern empire. Assyrian control over N Mesopotamia was first established by Shamshi-Adad I (c. 1813–1781 BC), but was broken by HAMMURABI of BABYLON. Assyria was later dominated by MITANNI, but reasserted its power in the 14th and 13th centuries BC. During the reigns of ASHURNASIRPAL II and his successor Shalmaneser III (858–824 BC), Assyria made gains in N Syria and the boundary was established at the Euphrates. The usurper TIGLATH-PILESER III (745–727) began the imperial expansion of Assyria, taking Babylon (729 BC), the Syrian states and outlying parts of Israel. SENNACHERIB (704–681 BC) campaigned in Palestine and overran JUDAH. His son Esarhaddon (c. 681–668 BC) defeated the Chaldaeans and conquered Egypt. The Assyrian empire reached its greatest extent, and its height of splendour in art and learning under ASHURBANIPAL (668–627 BC). However, a combination of external pressure and internal strife rendered Assyria too weak to resist an alliance of the Babylonians and the MEDES, whose forces sacked Nineveh in 612 BC, ushering in a period of Neo-Babylonian hegemony. See map, p. 10.

Astyages, the last king of the MEDES (585–550 BC). He was overthrown by CYRUS II ('the Great') of the ACHAEMENID dynasty.

Atahualpa (d. 1533), the last INCA emperor of Peru. Having defeated his half-brother and co-ruler Huáscar in a civil war, he marched against the conquistadore PIZARRO, but was imprisoned and held to ransom. On hearing that another Inca army was marching to free Atahualpa, Pizarro had him strangled. Within a few years of his death all Inca land was under Spanish rule.

Atatürk, Mustafa Kemal (1881–1938), Turkish soldier and statesman, president (1923–38). The founder of modern TURKEY, Atatürk opposed the VERSAILLES settlement for the Ottoman Empire and successfully led Turkish nationalists against Greek forces in 1922. In 1923 the Republic of Turkey was proclaimed with Atatürk as its first president. He embarked upon a policy of secular modernization, including the separation of state and religion, the abolition of the caliphate and the introduction of Western law in the place of Islamic.

Athapaskan, a group of North American languages spoken by peoples such as the APACHE and the NAVAJO.

Athelstan (895–939), king of England (925–39). The illegitimate grandson of ALFRED the Great, he consolidated the power of WESSEX, campaigning in NORTHUMBRIA, Cornwall and Wales.

Athens, one of the leading city-states of ancient GREECE (see map, p. 11). The first steps towards Athenian democracy came with the reforms of SOLON in the early 5th century BC, and a form of popular government was established by CLEISTHENES in the late 6th century BC. After success in the PERSIAN WARS in 490 and 480–79 BC, its rulers created an Athenian empire that dominated the Aegean area. However, Athens was defeated by Sparta in the PELOPONNESIAN WAR. From the mid-5th century Athens became a major centre for intellectual debate and philosophy, though relations between the democracy and thinkers such as SOCRATES, PLATO and ARISTOTLE were often ambivalent.

Atlantic, Battle of the, the struggle for control of the sea routes around the UK and to the USA during World War II. Attacks from German U-BOATS and aircraft on Allied shipping resulted in the loss of over 2500 ships. By 1943 the situation had eased with the introduction of better radar, the breaking of German codes and long-distance aircraft. The efficiency of U-boats, however, also increased, and Allied ships were only safe after Axis bases were captured in 1944.

Atlantic Charter, a joint statement of liberal-democratic principles for the postwar world signed by CHURCHILL and F.D. ROOSEVELT in 1941. It formed the ideological basis of the UNITED NATIONS Organization (UN). It stipulated the rights of all peoples to choose their own government and to live free from fear and want, and condemned territorial changes made against the wishes of local populations.

Attica, an area of SW central Greece that became the territory of the city-state of ATHENS in the 8th century BC or earlier.

Attila (c. 406–53), king of the HUNS (433–53). He forced the Hun tribes into a united horde based in Hungary, which rampaged from the Rhine to the Caspian Sea. Despite his defeat in 451 at the CATALAUNIAN FIELDS near Châlons by Roman, Frankish and Visigoth forces led by the Roman general Aetius, Attila went on to plunder Italy in 452. His kingdom collapsed soon after his death.

Attlee, Clement Richard, 1st Earl (1883–1969), British LABOUR statesman. He served under Ramsay MACDONALD but resigned when the latter formed a coalition government in 1931. Attlee became Labour Party leader in 1935 and served as deputy PM (1942–5) in CHURCHILL's wartime government. As PM (1945–51) he presided over the extension of the WELFARE STATE and a sweeping programme of nationalization.

Auchinleck, Sir John Claude Eyre (1884–1981), British field marshal who commanded the British forces in N Africa 1941–2. He established the crucial defensive line at EL ALAMEIN.

Augustine of Canterbury, St (d. 604/5), the first archbishop of Canterbury, who helped to convert the Anglo-Saxons to

Christianity. Sent by Pope GREGORY the Great, he arrived in Kent in 597, converted King Ethelbert, and was consecrated archbishop in the same year.

Augustine of Hippo, St (354–430), theologian and bishop of Hippo in N Africa. Many of his theological writings were written to defend Christianity against contemporary heresies. His best-known works are the *Confessions* and *The City of God*.

Augustinians, an order of canons that followed a code of conduct laid down by AUGUSTINE of Hippo. Augustinian canons lived together like monks, but were more outward-looking than other orders, serving the community in direct ways by preaching, teaching and running hospitals.

Augustus, the title conferred on Octavian (Gaius Julius Caesar Octavianus; 63 BC–AD 14), who was effectively if not technically the first Roman emperor (27 BC–AD 14). CAESAR's nephew and heir, Augustus gained supremacy in the Roman world after his defeat of Mark ANTONY at ACTIUM. Victories abroad and peace at home were the hallmarks of Augustus's long reign. NW Spain, the Alpine region and the Balkans were overrun by his generals. At home agriculture and trade benefited, city life prospered and literature and the arts flourished. On the negative side, political debate was suppressed and freedom of thought was discouraged, a trend that intensified under Augustus's successors. See ROMAN EMPIRE.

Aurangzeb (1618–1707), MOGUL emperor of India (1659–1707). He continued the territorial expansion of his predecessors and by 1700 the Mogul Empire covered all the subcontinent except its southernmost tip. Under Aurangzeb the Empire became a much more exclusively Muslim state, discriminating against its Hindu majority. The unity and administrative efficiency of the empire were replaced by a looser structure embracing a hierarchy of local powers.

Aurelian (Lucius Aurelius Aurelianus; AD 215–75), Roman emperor (271–5), who began the revival continued under DIOCLETIAN.

Aurelius, Marcus (AD 121–180), Roman emperor (161–180). His reign was dominated by wars against PARTHIA (161–6) and against invading German tribes from across the Danube.

Auschwitz (Polish, *Oswiecim*), a town in S Poland and site of the largest and most notorious NAZI extermination camp during WORLD WAR II. Up to 4,000,000 million Jews (and other political and social minorities) may have died there in the HOLOCAUST. The camp was liberated by the Soviets in January 1945.

Austerlitz, Battle of (2 December 1805), a battle fought near the town of Austerlitz in Moravia, in which NAPOLEON defeated larger Austrian and Russian forces, ending the military threat posed to him by the Third Coalition (Austria, Russia and Naples). See map, p. 29.

Australia, an island-continent between the Indian Ocean and the Pacific. See panel.

australopithecines, hominids of the earliest stage of human evolution, dating from over five million to nearly one million years ago.

Austria, a country in central Europe. See panel.

Austrian Empire (1806–67), a state created in 1804 by the last Holy Roman Emperor FRANCIS II (Francis I of Austria) in anticipation of the end of the HOLY ROMAN EMPIRE (1806). Its boundaries, fixed in 1815, included all the HABSBURG territories and at least 11 nationalities. Under Chancellor METTERNICH the empire was a bastion of the new European conservatism and a pillar of the system established by the Congress of VIENNA. Uprisings in Vienna, Prague and Budapest in 1848 forced Metternich to resign. Independence movements sprang up throughout the empire from Serbia to Slovakia. The new emperor FRANZ JOSEF and his minister Schwarzenberg used force to reassert Austrian control in Vienna, Prague, Budapest and N Italy. A period of neo-absolutism brought some stability in the 1850s, but defeats by French and Piedmontese at MAGENTA and SOLFERINO ended Austrian rule in Italy. Defeat by

AUSTRALIA

50,000 BC: ABORIGINES came to Australia, settling along the N and E coasts and in the Murray Basin. **AD 1606:** Willem de Janesz sighted Cape York Peninsula, the first European sighting of Australia. **1642–4:** Dutchman Abel TASMAN explored the coasts of Australia. **1770:** Captain COOK landed at BOTANY BAY and claimed NEW SOUTH WALES for Britain. **1788:** The first settlement was made at Port Jackson (Sydney), with over 700 British convicts and 250 free settlers. **1800–37:** Penal settlements established at Hobart and Launceston in Tasmania, and Newcastle (NSW) (both 1803–4), Moreton Bay (Brisbane; 1824), Port Phillip (Melbourne; 1826), and Albany (Western Australia; 1827); Adelaide (South Australia), a settlement without convicts, was founded in 1837. **From 1840:** Migration increased with the spread of sheep farming and the discovery of copper (1840s) and gold (1851). **1867:** Last convicts transported to Australia. **1855–70:** Following the rebellion at the EUREKA STOCKADE (1854) all six colonies gained self-government. **By 1900:** The population reached 3,700,000, made up largely of people of British and Irish ancestry. **1901:** Commonwealth of Australia established by the federation of the six colonies. **1914–18:** Australian contribution to ALLIED cause in World War I included the heroic landing at GALLIPOLI. **1931:** Australian independence confirmed by the Statute of WESTMINSTER. **1939–45:** World War II – N Australia threatened by Japan. **Since 1945:** Migrants from all over Europe and many parts of Asia have diluted the British connection; trading partnershps have been formed with Asian countries. **Early 1990s:** Increased domestic pressure for Australia to become a republic.

Prussia at SADOWA (Königgrätz) in 1866 ended Austrian dominance of central Europe and the following year the emperor agreed to the creation of the AUSTRO-HUNGARIAN EMPIRE.

Austrian Succession, War of the, (1740–8), a complex European conflict, fought mainly in Central Europe. The war's central issue was the right of MARIA THERESA of Austria to succeed to the lands of her father, Emperor Charles VI. This was challenged by FREDERICK II of Prussia and the Elector Charles Albert of Bavaria (Holy Roman Emperor 1742–5) who was supported by Louis XV of France and Philip V of Spain. The conflict was complicated by a number of related disputes, notably Spanish–Austrian rivalry in Italy and the continuing colonial struggle between Britain and France. Despite early reverses, the support of Britain (ruled by the Electors of Hanover since 1714 and closely involved in German affairs) and the loyalty of Hungary enabled Austria to survive intact except for the loss of SILESIA. The war was ended by the Treaty of AIX-LA-CHAPELLE (1748).

Austro-Hungarian Empire, the HABSBURG Dual Monarchy created after Austria's defeat by Prussia and Italy in 1866. The Ausgleich (Compromise) of 1867 conceded effective home rule to Hungary. The empire covered areas of what was to become Czechoslovakia, parts of Poland, the Ukraine, Romania and Yugoslavia. It was undermined by the aspirations of its minorities for national independence. The failure to resolve these aspirations was a prime cause of WORLD WAR I. The empire was partitioned by the Treaty of ST GERMAIN (1919) after World War I.

Austro-Prussian War (Seven Weeks War; June–August 1866), a conflict arising from the problematic joint administration of SCHLESWIG-HOLSTEIN after the German-Danish war of 1864 and Prussian proposals to reform the GERMAN CONFEDERATION. The war culminated in a decisive Prussian victory over Austria at SADOWA (Königgrätz) in Bohemia. Austria was excluded from German affairs and Prussia became pre-eminent amongst N German states.

Avars, a nomadic people found in the Eurasian steppe from the late 6th century (see map, p. 16). They besieged Constantinople in alliance with the Persians in 626 and went on to found a state in Hungary. After their conquest by Charlemagne in 796 they vanished from history.

Averroës (Ibn Rushd; 1126–98), Islamic philosopher whose commentaries on the works of Aristotle had a significant influence on Christian SCHOLASTICISM.

Avignon period, a period during which the popes resided at Avignon in S France (1309–77). Feuds among the Italian cardinals and their allies in Rome persuaded Pope Clement V (1305–14) to stay in S France. Strong French influence in the College of Cardinals ensured a line of French popes resident at Avignon. Their policies became increasingly influenced by the interests of the French crown. The papal court did not return to Rome until 1377.

Awami League, a political party in East PAKISTAN, founded in opposition to the ruling MUSLIM LEAGUE. Under Sheikh MUJIBUR Rahman it led the Bengali movement for independence from Pakistan that culminated in the creation of BANGLADESH.

AWB (Afrikaans, *Afrikaner Weerstansbeweging,* 'Afrikaner Resistance Movement'), a South African neo-Nazi group founded in 1973, advocating violence to maintain APARTHEID or a separate whites-only territory.

Axis Powers, the coalition of Fascist states fighting with Germany against the ALLIED POWERS in World War II. An agreement between Germany and Italy signed in 1936 established a Berlin–Rome 'Axis'. They were joined by Japan after the ANTI-COMINTERN PACT, and later by the Nazi-aligned states of Hungary, Slovakia, Croatia, Romania and Bulgaria.

Axum, an ancient city in N ETHIOPIA, capital of a kingdom that flourished from the 1st to the 6th centuries AD.

Ayub Khan, Mohammed (1907–74), president of PAKISTAN (1958–69). He came to power in a coup, subsequently

AUSTRIA

Late 10th century to 1250: The region now known as Austria was ruled by the Babenberg family. **1276:** Austria became the heartland of the Holy Roman Empire after Rudolf of HABSBURG, the Holy Roman Emperor, defeated the Babenberg successor. **1529** and **1683:** Austria repelled the OTTOMAN Turks from the walls of Vienna and halted their advance across Europe. **Mid-16th century:** CHARLES V divided the HABSBURG lands, separating Spain from the empire in Central Europe. **18th century:** MARIA THERESA and her son JOSEPH II reformed Austria and strengthened the multilingual HABSBURG state; this was based on Austria, Hungary and Czech-speaking Bohemia, but it also included Polish, Croat, Slovak, Slovene and Italian areas. **1806:** Napoleon I abolished the Holy Roman Empire, but FRANCIS II took the title emperor of Austria (1804). **Early 19th century:** The Austrian Chancellor METTERNICH shaped the fortunes of the AUSTRIAN EMPIRE with repressive conservative policies; he attempted to maintain the boundaries drawn by the Congress of VIENNA (1814–15), but the empire was bedevilled by national and ethnic divisions. **1866:** Austrian defeat in the AUSTRO-PRUSSIAN WAR excluded Austrian influence from the German-speaking part of Europe; the Habsburgs were left to dominate unstable S Central Europe. **1867:** Creation of the AUSTRO-HUNGARIAN EMPIRE. **1914:** A Bosnian Serb assassinated the heir to the Austro-Hungarian throne, precipitating WORLD WAR I. **1918–19:** The Habsburg empire was dismembered; a separate Austrian republic was established. **1938:** Austria was annexed by Germany (the ANSCHLUSS). **1945:** Austria was liberated by Allied forces. **1955:** Withdrawal of Allied occupation forces; neutral Austria regained independence. **1989–91:** Renewal of traditional economic links with Hungary, Croatia and Slovenia.

attempting to perpetuate his rule through so-called 'basic democracy' which denied the adult franchise. He was overthrown by a popular uprising.

Ayutthaya, the capital of the kingdom of Thailand from the mid-14th century until 1767, when it was destroyed by the Burmese.

Azerbaijan, a republic in western Asia. The Azeris were conquered by the Arabs in 632, but, although the region remained under Arab rule until the 11th century, Turkic rather than Arabic language and culture prevailed after the 9th century. The Mongols controlled Azerbaijan from 1236 to 1498, when the Azeris came under Persian rule. In the 18th century tsarist Russia gradually expanded into the Caucasus. Russia took N Azerbaijan in 1813, and Nakhichevan and the rest of the present state in 1828. However, the greater part of the land of the Azeris remained under Persian rule. During World War I, a nationalist Azeri movement became allied with the Turks. An independent Azeri state was founded with Turkish assistance (1918), but was invaded by the Soviet Red Army in 1920. Azerbaijan was part of the Transcaucasian Soviet Republic from 1922 until 1936 when it became a separate Union Republic within the USSR. Independence was declared following the abortive coup in Moscow by Communist hardliners (September 1991) and was internationally recognized when the USSR was dissolved (December 1991). Since 1990 Azeri and Armenian forces have been involved in a violent dispute concerning the status of NAGORNO KARABAKH, an enclave of Orthodox Christian Armenians surrounded by the Shiite Muslim Azeris. Azerbaijan withdrew from the COMMONWEALTH OF INDEPENDENT STATES in 1992 and established close links with Turkey.

Aztecs, a native people of Central America. From the mid-14th century the Aztecs, based at TENOCHTITLÁN in Lake Texcoco (modern Mexico City), brought a large part of Meso-America under their rule. The Aztec empire was founded on the subjugation of neighbouring tribes, who rendered tribute and sacrificial victims to the victorious Aztecs. By the 16th century Tenochtitlán had become a magnificent city of temples and palaces. The still evolving Aztec empire was destroyed by the Spanish under CORTEZ (1519–21), who captured Tenochtitlán and killed the emperor MONTEZUMA II.

Baader-Meinhof Gang, a terrorist group also known as the Red Army Faction. Led by Ulrike Meinhof and Andreas Baader (both of whom committed suicide after their arrest in 1972), the group was responsible for many bomb outrages and assassinations in the late 1960s and early 1970s.

Ba'athism, a pan-Arab movement, founded in April 1947, and dedicated to the unity and freedom of the Arab Nation. Ba'athist governments are currently in power in IRAQ and SYRIA.

Babi Yar, the scene of a massacre of Jews in the Ukraine by the Nazis in 1941. Nearly 33,000 Jews were machine-gunned by *Einsatzgruppen* and their bodies thrown into a ravine. See also HOLOCAUST.

Babur (1483–1530), the first MOGUL emperor of India (1526–30). A descendant of TIMUR, in 1526 he invaded N India and overthrew the DELHI SULTANATE. His attempt to carve out a wider Indian empire was incomplete at his death. He was succeeded by his son HUMAYUN.

Babylon, a city of ancient Mesopotamia to the S of modern Baghdad. It was the centre of two major Near Eastern empires. The first was under an AMORITE dynasty (c. 1900–c. 1595 BC), whose power and prosperity were at their height under the reign of HAMMURABI (c. 1792–1750 BC). Four hundred years of KASSITE rule were followed by an extended period of instability before the ASSYRIAN conquest of the 8th century BC. The second great Babylonian empire, extending as far as Syria and Palestine, was established by a dynasty of CHALDAEAN kings (c. 625–539 BC). During the reign of NEBUCHADNEZZAR II Babylon was the largest and most magnificent city of the ancient world. In 539 BC the city fell to CYRUS the ACHAEMENID. See map, p. 10.

Bactria, a satrapy (province) of the ACHAEMENID Persian Empire, now largely within N Afghanistan (see map, p. 12).

Baden-Powell, Robert Stephenson Smyth, 1st Baron (1857–1941), British soldier who defended Mafeking during the Second BOER WAR and later founded the Boy Scout (1907) and Girl Guide (1910) movements.

Baghdad Pact, see CENTRAL TREATY ORGANIZATION.

Bahamas, a group of islands off the coast of Florida. Columbus landed in the Bahamas when he reached the New World (1492). English colonists began to settle in the 17th century and slave plantations were established in the 18th century, but the abolition of slavery (1834) ended this activity. Independence was granted in 1973.

Bahrain, an independent emirate in the Gulf. Bahrain – part of the Arab Islamic world since the 7th century – was Persian from 1602 until 1783, when rule by the Sunni al-Khalifa family began. In the 19th century Bahrain became a British protectorate. Bahrain was the first Gulf state to develop its petroleum industry (from 1932). Since independence in 1971, there has been tension between the SUNNI and SHIITE communities.

Bajezid I (1347–1403), Ottoman sultan (1389–1402) and son of MURAD I. He brought rival Turkish principalities in W Anatolia into the Ottoman Empire, blockaded CONSTANTINOPLE, and humiliated a crusading army at NICOPOLIS in 1396. Defeated and captured by TAMERLANE in 1402, he died in captivity.

Bakunin, Mikhail (1814–76), Russian anarchist, revolutionary and founder of the Russian Populist Movement. Hostile to MARX, he advocated the destruction of the centralized state and insurrection by workers and peasants to create a social order based on liberty and equality.

Balaklava, Battle of (25 October 1854), an indecisive battle between Russian and British troops during the CRIMEAN WAR. A mistaken British order led the Light Brigade to charge straight at a Russian artillery position at the end of a long narrow valley. Out of a force of 673 some 247 were killed.

Baldwin, Stanley, 1st Earl (1867–1947), British Conservative statesman, prime minister (1923–4, 1924–9, 1935–7). He replaced Bonar LAW as PM in 1923. His terms of office witnessed the General Strike (1926), the crisis over the abdication of EDWARD VIII (1936) and the deterioration of international relations with the rise of the Nazis. He was succeeded as PM by Neville CHAMBERLAIN.

Balfour, Arthur James, 1st Earl (1848–1930), British Conservative statesman, prime minister (1902–3). As foreign secretary (1916–17) under Lloyd George, he issued the BALFOUR DECLARATION (November 1917).

Balfour Declaration, a letter to the World ZIONIST Organization from the British foreign secretary, Arthur BALFOUR, in November 1917. It promised that Britain would 'view with favour' the creation of a Jewish 'homeland' in PALESTINE after World War I.

Balkans, a region of SE Europe comprising ALBANIA, GREECE, BULGARIA, European Turkey, ROMANIA, SLOVENIA, CROATIA, BOSNIA-HERZEGOVINA and YUGOSLAVIA.

Balkan League, a league formed in 1912 by the BALKAN states of Greece, Serbia, Bulgaria and Montenegro to counter Turkish rule in the region.

Balkan Wars (1912–13), two wars fought between Serbia, Montenegro, Greece, Romania, Bulgaria and Turkey over the remaining Balkan territories of the OTTOMAN Empire. In 1912 the member states of the BALKAN LEAGUE declared war on and defeated Turkey in the First Balkan War (1912–13), but fell out over the spoils, with Bulgaria demanding more territory than Greece and Serbia would give. In the Second Balkan War (1913) Bulgaria was defeated and stripped of its earlier gains. Macedonia was partitioned between Greece and Serbia, Romania gained part of Bulgaria, and Albania gained its independence. The establishment of a 'big' Serbia was a factor in the outbreak of WORLD WAR I.

Ball, John (d. 1381), English priest and rebel. He attacked the wealth of the Church and nobility from the 1360s, and was executed for his role in the 1381 PEASANTS' REVOLT.

Balliol, John (c. 1250–1313), king of Scotland (1292–6). He was awarded the throne of Scotland by EDWARD I in 1292. When he objected to the English king's high-handed actions, EDWARD I invaded Scotland, and defeated and captured him. In Balliol's absence others, notably William WALLACE, took over the leadership of the Scottish War of Independence.

Baltic States, the republics of ESTONIA, LATVIA and LITHUANIA.

Banda, Hastings Kamuzu (c. 1902–), prime minister of MALAWI (1963–6), president (1966–). Banda's rule has been authoritarian, and – despite criticism – he has maintained close relations with South Africa. In 1993 he resisted calls for multi-party elections.

Bandaranaike, Solomon West Ridgeway Dias (1899–1959), Sri Lankan politician, prime minister (1956–9). He was succeeded on his death by his wife **Sirimavo Bandaranaike** (1916–), prime minister (1960–5 and 1970–7).

Bandung Conference (18–24 April 1955), the first international gathering of the newly decolonized Afro-Asian states, and the precursor of the NON-ALIGNED MOVEMENT.

Bangladesh, a republic in S Asia. A part of the Mogul Empire from the 16th century, the area came under British rule within India after 1757. On partition in 1947, as the majority of its inhabitants were Muslim, the area became the E province of PAKISTAN. Separated by 1600 km (1000 mi) from the Urdu-speaking, politically dominant W province, East Pakistan saw itself as a victim of economic and ethnic injustice. Resentment led to civil war in 1971 when Indian aid to Bengali irregulars gave birth to an independent People's Republic of Bangladesh ('Free Bengal') under Sheik MUJIBUR RAHMAN. Mujibur's assassination in 1975 led eventually to a takeover by General Zia-ur-Rahman, who amended the constitution to create an 'Islamic state'. Zia in turn was assassinated in 1981 and General Ershad took power in 1982. After Ershad was deposed (1990), a parliamentary system was reintroduced.

Bannockburn, Battle of (24 June 1314), the defeat near Stirling of the army of EDWARD II of England by a smaller Scottish army under ROBERT the Bruce. The English defeat helped secure Scottish independence.

Bantu, a group of Negroid peoples originating in W Africa. Around AD 100 the Bantu began to spread E and S out of W Africa, settling areas previously roamed by hunter-gatherers. By AD 500 they had reached as far as the E coast of southern Africa.

Bantustans, an unofficial term used after 1948 for black territories in South Africa, reserved for Bantu-speaking Africans and given a measure of self-government under APARTHEID. Four Bantustans were declared 'independent' – Transkei (1976), Bophuthatswana (1977), Venda (1979) and Ciskei (1981) – but none were recognized internationally. Bophuthatswana was reintegrated into South Africa in March 1994 following the ousting of President Lucas Mangope, who had refused to participate in South Africa's first democratic elections.

Baptists, a Protestant sect taking its name from the practice of baptism by immersion of adult believers – a ritual established by the ANABAPTISTS during the REFORMATION. Baptist Churches developed within the English and American PURITAN movements in the 17th century. The Church made great strides in the S states of America in the 18th century, where they retain their strongest influence.

Barbados, an island state in the Caribbean. Barbados was claimed and settled by the English in the 1620s. Black slaves were imported to work the sugar plantations in the 17th and 18th centuries. SLAVERY was abolished in 1834, but economic and political power remained with a small white minority. Riots in 1937 led to reforms. Barbados became independent in 1966.

barbarians, a name used by the Romans to describe the peoples outside their empire whose languages they considered uncivilized. Among them were the Germanic peoples who lived N and E of the Rhine–Danube frontier – OSTROGOTHS, VISIGOTHS, VANDALS, FRANKS and so on – whose incursions in the 5th century brought the Western Roman Empire to ruin.

Barbarossa, Khayr ad-Din (c. 1483–1546), Turkish corsair. He drove the Spanish from Algiers in 1516, and became grand admiral of the Ottoman fleet in 1533.

Barbarossa, Operation, the name used by the German High Command for the German invasion of the Soviet Union in 1941. See EASTERN FRONT CAMPAIGNS.

Barons' Wars, the name given to two civil wars in 13th-century England: **1.** the wars fought between King JOHN and his barons after the former had failed to honour the pledges given in MAGNA CARTA; **2.** the war between HENRY III and baronial opposition led by Simon de MONTFORT.

Basil II ('the Bulgar-Slayer'; c. 958–1025), Byzantine emperor (976–1025). He conquered Bulgaria and added parts of Georgia and Armenia to the Empire.

Basques, a people of the W Pyrenees living in SW France and N Spain. The Basques of Spain enjoyed virtual independence from the 9th to the 19th centuries, and their provinces have gained limited autonomy within the modern Spanish state. The separatist organization ETA has led an often violent campaign to gain independence for the Basque provinces.

Bastille, a fortress prison in Paris, whose storming by the mob on 14 July 1789 marked the beginning of the FRENCH REVOLUTION.

Basutoland, see LESOTHO.

Batista, Fulgencio (1901–73), Cuban politician, president (1933–44 and 1952–9). The dictatorial excesses of his rule ended with his overthrow by Fidel CASTRO.

Bavaria, a S German state with strong independent traditions, created an ELECTORATE in 1623 and a kingdom in 1805, a status which it retained within the GERMAN EMPIRE after 1871. Its capital, Munich, became a focus for radical right-wing politics after the suppression of a short-lived soviet republic in 1918.

Bay of Pigs, an unsuccessful attempt by CIA-trained Cuban exiles to overthrow the Communist regime of Fidel CASTRO in CUBA in April 1961. Of the 1500 troops that invaded 1173 were captured.

Beaker cultures, prehistoric cultures named after a characteristic form of drinking vessel found in early BRONZE AGE burial sites in Central, W and S Europe.

Beaufort, the family name of descendants of John of GAUNT and Katherine Swynford. Several of them played a prominent role in 15th-century English politics. Margaret Beaufort (1443–1509) – who married Edmund TUDOR – was the mother of HENRY VII.

Bechuanaland, see BOTSWANA.

Becket, St Thomas (1118–70), archbishop of Canterbury (1161–70). He clashed with HENRY II of England over the rights of the English Church, and was murdered in Canterbury Cathedral.

Bede (673–735), English monk and historian, based at Jarrow in NORTHUMBRIA. From 680 he devoted his life to writing the *Ecclesiastical History of the English Peoples* (finished 731).

Begin, Menachem (1913–92), Polish-born Israeli politician, hard-line leader of the right-wing Likud Party and prime minister of Israel (1977–83). He is best remembered for the Israeli–Egyptian peace accord he negotiated with Anwar el-SADAT at CAMP DAVID in 1978. The two men shared a Nobel Peace Prize.

Belarus, a republic of E Europe (see map, p. 43). The Belarussian Slavs arrived in the region between the 6th and 8th centuries AD. A number of small Belarussian states flourished after c. 700 but were soon conquered by KIEV RUS. When the Tatars overran Kiev Rus (1240), the Belarussian lands came under Lithuanian rule. After 1569, when Lithuania and Poland became one state, the area was dominated by a Polish Roman Catholic aristocracy. In 1648–54 the Orthodox Belarussians, who had been reduced to serfdom, rose in revolt against a resented Polish elite that controlled the land, administration and trade. The Belarussians came under Russian rule as a result of the three partitions of POLAND (1772, 1793 and 1795). The region suffered some of the fiercest fighting between Russia and Germany during World War I. Following the Russian Revolution, a Byelorussian Soviet republic was proclaimed (1919). The republic was invaded by the Poles in the same year and divided between Poland and the Soviet Union in 1921. Byelorussia was devastated during World War II. In 1945 the Belarussians were reunited in a single Soviet republic. A perceived lack of Soviet concern for the republic at the time of the accident at the Chernobyl nuclear power station (just over the Ukrainian border) in 1986 strengthened a reawakening Belarussian national identity. Contamination from Chernobyl affected about 20% of the republic, causing some areas to be sealed off and necessitating the eventual resettlement of up to 2,000,000 people. Byelorussia declared independence following the abortive coup by Communist hardliners in Moscow (September 1991) and – as Belarus – received international recognition when the USSR was dissolved (December 1991).

Belgae, a people of NW Gaul, inhabiting the region between the Seine and the Rhine, including modern Belgium. They were conquered by Julius Caesar in 57 BC. SE England was also occupied by groups of Belgae, who migrated there around 100 BC.

Belgium, a country in NW Europe. See panel.

Belisarius (505–65), Byzantine general (AD 505–65). In the 530s, during the reign of JUSTINIAN, Belisarius reconquered Vandal North Africa, Sicily and most of Ostrogothic Italy. He was dismissed by a jealous Justinian but later reinstated.

Belize, a country of CENTRAL AMERICA. Mayan settlements flourished in Belize until the 15th century. It was colonized by the English in the 17th century, formally becoming the colony of British Honduras in 1862. The colony gained independence – as Belize – in 1981, but Guatemala continued to claim it as part of its territory until 1991.

Ben Bella, Ahmed (1916–), Algerian nationalist who led his country to independence after a bloody war against France. He was prime minister of ALGERIA (1962–5) and president (1963–5), but was overthrown and imprisoned (1965–79). He returned to Algerian politics in 1990 after nine years in exile.

Benedictine, a monastic order. The Benedictine monastic rule – laid down by St Benedict of Nursia in the 6th century and reformed by Benedict of Aniane in the 9th century – reached its peak of influence in the 10th and 11th centuries. The Benedictine monk divided his day into periods of work and devotion. Benedictine monasteries were repositories of books and learning, institutions of great wealth and considerable artistic patronage.

Benedict of Nursia, St (c. 480–c. 550), Italian monk and founder of the BENEDICTINE Order.

BENELUX, a customs union created by Belgium, the Netherlands and Luxembourg in 1948. All three states are now members of the EUROPEAN COMMUNITY.

Beneš, Eduard (1884–1948), Czechoslovak statesman, president (1935–8 and 1946–8). He worked with Tomáš MASARYK for Czech independence during World War I. He succeeded Masaryk as president in 1935 but resigned over the partition of CZECHOSLOVAKIA in the MUNICH agreement. He returned to his homeland as president in 1945 but resigned after the 1948 Communist takeover.

Benevento, Battle of (1266), a battle in which CHARLES I of Anjou defeated and killed Manfred, the last HOHENSTAUFEN and illegitimate son of the emperor Frederick II.

Bengal, the NE region of the Indian subcontinent, now divided between BANGLADESH and INDIA. A productive lowland area with a distinctive regional culture, it was the first major part of India to be governed by the English EAST INDIA COMPANY.

Ben-Gurion, David (1886–1973), Russian-born Israeli politician, prime minister of Israel (1948–53 and 1955–63). A founder-member of the Labour Party (Mapai) in 1930, he led the struggle for Israeli independence against the British in the 1940s.

BELGIUM

By the 11th century: The area known as Belgium was divided into counties and duchies subject to the Holy Roman Emperor. **12th–14th centuries:** Bruges, Ghent and other Flemish textile centres were among the most prosperous cities in Europe. **From 1384:** Most of modern Belgium was controlled by the rulers of the Duchy of BURGUNDY, whose territories were inherited by the Spanish HABSBURGS in 1504. **Late 16th century:** The Protestant Dutch UNITED PROVINCES rebelled and gained independence; the Catholic south of the Low Countries ('Belgium') remained under Spanish rule. **1713:** The Spanish Netherlands passed to AUSTRIA by the Treaty of UTRECHT. **1791:** The Belgians expelled the Austrians during the French Revolutionary Wars. **1793:** Belgium was annexed by France. **1815:** The Low Countries were reunited as the Kingdom of the Netherlands. **1830:** The Belgians rebelled against Dutch rule and proclaimed their independence. **1879:** Belgian CONGO acquired as personal possession by LEOPOLD II. **1914–18:** Belgian neutrality violated by the German invasion, leading to Britain's declaration of war; brave resistance of King Albert during World War I earned international admiration. **1940–5:** Germany again occupied Belgium. **1957:** Belgium a founder member of the EUROPEAN ECONOMIC COMMUNITY. **1960:** Belgian withdrawal from the Congo (ZAIRE) was followed by a bloody civil war in that country (see CONGO CRISIS). **Since 1970:** Increased tension between Flemish and French speakers; gradual movement towards a federal system.

Benin, a country of W Africa (known as Dahomey until 1975). From the 17th century to the 19th century the kingdom of Dahomey was one of the principal slave-trading states of W Africa. In the 1890s the region was conquered by the French. Political turmoil followed independence in 1960, and five army coups took place between 1963 and 1972 when the Marxist-Leninist government of Colonel Kérékou came to power. A multi-party system was restored in 1991.

Benin, kingdom of, a former W African kingdom, based on a city in the S of modern Nigeria. It was the major power among the YORUBA peoples in the 16th and 17th centuries.

Bentham, Jeremy (1748–1832), British UTILITARIAN philosopher, economist, and legal theorist. His attempts to solve social problems on a scientific basis had a profound influence on political and social reform in 19th-century Britain.

Berbers, an indigenous people of the N African hinterland who converted to Islam after the Arab conquests of the 7th century AD. They were unusual in that they retained their own language, which was not superseded by Arabic. The most important Berber dynasties were the ALMOHADS and ALMORAVIDS.

Berlin Airlift (1948–9), the supplying by aircraft of food and other necessities to the W sectors of Berlin by the US and British governments. In June 1948 Soviet forces blocked off land links to West Berlin to prevent the unification of the Allied sectors of western Germany. However, the USA and the UK organized an airlift, and the blockade was lifted in May 1949.

Berlin, Congress of (1878), a conference attended by representatives of Russia, Turkey, Austria-Hungary, the UK, France, Italy and Germany to determine the boundaries of the Balkan states after the RUSSO-TURKISH WAR of 1877–8. The Congress was presided over by BISMARCK. Serbia, Montenegro and Romania gained their independence, Bosnia and Herzegovina passed to Austria-Hungary, Bulgaria was reduced by two-thirds and Cyprus came under temporary British occupation. It did not settle the EASTERN QUESTION and left many, particularly the Russians and the PAN-SLAVS, dissatisfied, sowing the seeds for future conflict.

Berlin Wall, a former barrier between East and West Berlin, built by the German Democratic Republic in 1961 to prevent East Germans leaving for West GERMANY. East German guards shot dead over 80 people trying to escape over the wall between 1961 and 1989, when it was opened and then demolished.

Bernard of Clairvaux, St (c. 1090–1153), French CISTERCIAN monk and abbot of Clairvaux. He turned the Cistercian order into a successful mass movement with about 500 houses by the time of his death. He was also involved in the foundation of the Order of TEMPLARS and the preaching of the Second CRUSADE.

Bessarabia, a region of E Europe, most of which forms the present-day republic of MOLDOVA.

Bevan, Aneurin (1897–1960), British LABOUR politician. As Minister of Health (1945–51) 'Nye' Bevan introduced the

NATIONAL HEALTH SERVICE. During Labour's period in opposition in the 1950s he conducted a left-wing campaign against the leadership of Hugh GAITSKELL.

Beveridge, William Henry, 1st Baron (1879–1963), British economist and civil servant. His report *Social Insurance and Allied Services* (1942; often called the Beveridge Report) formed the basis of British WELFARE STATE legislation.

Bevin, Ernest (1881–1951), British trade union leader and Labour statesman. He created, and was general secretary of, the Transport and General Worker's Union (1921–1940). He served as Minister of Labour in Churchill's wartime cabinet (1940–5), and as ATTLEE's foreign secretary (1945–51) was a staunch advocate of US involvement in Europe.

Bhutan, a kingdom in the Himalaya in S Asia. Tibetan influence over Bhutan from the 16th century was followed by Chinese overlordship (1720). It was partially annexed by British-dominated India in 1865. The monarchy was established in 1907 under British protection. India returned the annexed area in 1949 but assumed influence over Bhutan's external affairs.

Bhutto, Zulfiqar Ali (1928–79), Pakistani politician. He came to prominence as a protégé of AYUB KHAN, but later formed his own Pakistan People's Party and led the movement for Ayub's overthrow. He went on to become PM after the secession of BANGLADESH in 1971. He was overthrown by the military in 1977 and later hanged (1979) in dubious circumstances. His daughter Benazir was prime minister of PAKISTAN 1988–90 and from 1993.

Biafra, a province of NIGERIA inhabited mainly by the Ibo people. It seceded as an independent republic in 1967, but was defeated by government forces in 1970 after a bloody civil war.

Biko, Steve (1947–77), the main leader of 'black consciousness' among students and young intelligentsia in SOUTH AFRICA in the 1960s and 70s and an opponent of APARTHEID. His murder by secret police shocked the world.

Bill of Rights (1689), an act passed by the English PARLIAMENT guaranteeing the rights of the individual subject – one of the most important instruments of British constitutional law. It incorporated by statute the Declaration of Rights, which stated the terms on which WILLIAM III and Mary II were to become joint sovereigns of England, Scotland and Ireland. It stipulated that the king must have the consent of Parliament to levy taxes and organize a peacetime army. The king also lost the right to suspend or dispense with parliamentary legislation.

Bill of Rights (1791), the first 10 amendments to the CONSTITUTION of the USA. These ruled against: **1.** Abridgement of freedom of religion, speech, the press, petition, and peaceful assembly. **2.** The infringement of the right to bear arms. **3.** The illegal quartering of troops. **4.** Unreasonable searches and seizures. **5.** The capital trial of any person for the same offence; deprivation of life, liberty or property 'without due process of law'; self-incrimination; uncompensated seizure of property. **6.** Infringement of an accused person's right to a speedy and public trial before an impartial jury. **7.** Depriving persons of the right to trial by jury in common-law suits where the value in question exceeded $20. **8.** Excessive bail and punishments. Amendments **9** and **10** declared that the listing of certain rights in the Constitution should not be taken to deny other rights retained by the people, and reserved to the states all powers not delegated to the Federal government by the Constitution. Several of the amendments have been enshrined in the constitutions of other democratic countries.

Bismarck, Otto von (1815–98), Prussian chancellor (1862–90), German chancellor (1871–90), known as the 'Iron Chancellor'. He united GERMANY under his Prussian master, WILHELM I, in 1871 after skilfully exploiting pan-German feelings in a series of wars against Denmark, Austria and France. His successful foreign policy balanced the great powers and he acted as 'honest broker' in the 1878 Balkan Crisis. Stealing the political clothes of the SOCIAL DEMOCRATS, he created Europe's first social security system. He was forced to resign by WILHELM II in 1890. See also EMS TELEGRAM, FRANCO-PRUSSIAN WAR, and BERLIN, CONGRESS OF.

Black and Tans, an armed auxiliary force sent to IRELAND by the British government (1920–1). Faced with guerrilla attacks by the IRISH REPUBLICAN ARMY, the Black and Tans reacted with great brutality. They were named after the distinctive colours of their uniforms.

Black Death, the name given to the bubonic plague that originated in the Far East and was brought to Europe in 1346–7 by Italian merchant ships from the ports of the Crimea. It reached France, Spain and England in 1348 and Russia, Germany and Scandinavia the following year. Victims developed fever and swollen lymph nodes in the groin and armpits. Contemporary medicine knew no treatment for the disease, and more than half of those infected died. It is estimated that one quarter of the European population perished in the epidemic of 1348–9. The long-term effects of the Black Death were considerable. Within a few decades acute labour shortages meant that serfdom had to be abandoned, and real wages and living standards for peasants increased significantly. Outbreaks of plague continued in Europe until the 17th century.

Blackfoot Indians, a native North American people, living in the N of the Great Plains. Nomads dependent on the hunting of buffalo, their economy and society was transformed by the use of the horse in the 18th century. See also NORTH AMERICAN INDIANS.

Black Hole of Calcutta, a small dungeon in which the Nawab of Bengal incarcerated 146 British prisoners in 1756, most of whom suffocated. Inflated accounts of the incident ensured it a place in British imperial mythology.

Black Panthers, a militant BLACK POWER organization founded in 1966 to campaign for a separate black state in the USA.

Black Power, a movement of black people in the USA during the 1960s aiming to achieve economic, political, and social equality with whites. It stressed the need for a more militant approach to the campaign for CIVIL RIGHTS and for action by blacks alone. Groups involved with Black Power included the BLACK PANTHERS and the Black Muslim Movement led by MALCOLM X.

Black Prince, see EDWARD, THE BLACK PRINCE.

Black September, an ad hoc Palestinian terrorist group, recruited from al-FATAH and named after the events of September 1971, when Palestinian militants were forcibly ejected from JORDAN. Black September's most notorious action was the assassination of 11 Israeli athletes at the Munich Olympics in 1972.

Blackshirt, the name applied to members of the Italian FASCIST Party before and during World War II. The term was also used to describe Nazi SS in Germany and members of the British Union of Fascists (BUF).

Blenheim, Battle of (13 August 1704), a military engagement during the War of the SPANISH SUCCESSION in which Anglo-Austrian troops under the Duke of MARLBOROUGH and Prince EUGÈNE of Savoy defeated a Franco-Bavarian force marching on Vienna.

Bligh, William, see BOUNTY MUTINY.

Blitz, the systematic night-time bombing of British cities by the German air force (1940–1) intended to bomb Britain into submission during WORLD WAR II. However, although substantial damage was inflicted on cities such as London, Coventry, Liverpool, Glasgow, Southampton and Belfast, public morale did not crack.

Blitzkrieg (German 'lightning war'), a style of attack used successfully by German generals in the early years of WORLD WAR II, in which attacks were spearheaded by dive bombers and fast-moving tank units. It was particularly successful in the campaigns against Poland, France and Greece.

Bloody Assizes (1685), the trial and punishment of those who had taken part in MONMOUTH'S rebellion. Judge Jeffreys (1645–89), who presided over the trials, sentenced 300 to death, and 800 to be transported.

Bloody Sunday (22 January 1905), a massacre by tsarist troops of about 1000 protesters, including women and children, in St Petersburg during the RUSSIAN REVOLUTION of 1905.

Blücher, Gebhart Leberecht von (1742–1819), Prussian field marshal, whose appearance on Napoleon's flank during the Battle of WATERLOO was a major factor in the Allied victory.

Blum, Léon (1872–1950), French socialist statesman, prime minister (1936–7, 1938, 1946–7). He brought together the anti-Fascist coalition of left-wing parties that came to power in France in 1936. Blum's government lacked the parliamentary support necessary to put through his reforms, and collapsed in 1938.

Boeotia, an ancient region of central Greece, consisting of a number of city-states, of which THEBES was always the biggest and most powerful. The Boeotian Confederacy was at its most powerful between c. 378 and 338 BC, when it was defeated by PHILIP II of Macedon.

Boers, see AFRIKANERS.

Boer Wars, two wars fought by British forces in SOUTH AFRICA, the first against the TRANSVAAL (1880–1) and the second against the Transvaal and the ORANGE FREE STATE (1899–1902). When Britain annexed Transvaal in 1877, the Boers organized resistance and declared their independence (1880). British troops sent to the region were humiliated at Laing's Nek, Ingogo and Majuba Hill. The Pretoria Convention of August 1881 restored independence to the Transvaal. Tension grew as Britain continued its expansion in S Africa, carving out new territory in Bechuanaland and Rhodesia. Anglo-Boer relations were further damaged by the question of political rights for the UITLANDERS and the JAMESON RAID of 1895, which the Boers interpreted as a British plot to seize gold-rich Transvaal. In October 1899 KRUGER demanded a British guarantee of Boer independence. When this was not forthcoming, Boer forces invaded Natal and Cape Colony. The Boers enjoyed early successes, laying siege to Ladysmith, Mafeking and Kimberley, and defeating the British at Colenso, Magersfontein and Stormberg between 10 and 17 December. The tide turned with the arrival of British reinforcements under Lord Roberts and KITCHENER, who defeated the Boers at Paardeberg Drift in February 1900. British forces took the Transvaal capital of Pretoria in June and formally annexed the Boer republics. Thereafter Kitchener used scorched-earth tactics to quash the Boers' effective guerrilla campaign, burning farmhouses and the detaining Boer families in concentration camps. The Second Boer War ended officially with the Treaty of VEREENIGING on 31 May 1902.

Bohemia, a former kingdom in Central Europe. Settled by Slavs in the 9th century, it was ruled successively by the Premyslids (10th–14th centuries), the house of Luxemburg (1306–1437) – during which time the HUSSITE Reformation took hold – the Czech noble George of Podiebrady (1458–71), the Polish JAGELLION dynasty (1471–1526) and the HABSBURGS (1526–1918). The Bohemian Revolt (1618–21), which marked the opening phase of the THIRTY YEARS WAR, was suppressed with Spanish help, and was followed by the establishment of greater Habsburg control. After the breakup of AUSTRIA-HUNGARY following World War I, it formed part of CZECHOSLOVAKIA (1918–93) and since 1993 has been part of the Czech Republic.

Bohemond of Tarando (c. 1056–1111), Italo-Norman leader of the First CRUSADE and son of Robert GUISCARD. He established himself as prince of ANTIOCH (1098).

Bokassa, Jean Bédel (1921–), ruler of the CENTRAL AFRICAN REPUBLIC (1965–79), president for life from 1972 and self-proclaimed 'emperor' from 1976. He was overthrown in 1979 and sentenced to forced labour for life for murder, cannibalism and embezzlement of public funds.

Boleyn, Anne (1507–36), the second wife of HENRY VIII of England and mother of ELIZABETH I. She was executed on a charge of adultery.

Bolingbroke, Henry of, see HENRY IV of England.

Bolívar, Simón (1783–1830), South American soldier and statesman who played a key role in the liberation of Venezuela, Colombia, Ecuador, Peru and Bolivia from Spanish rule in the early 19th century. The modern state of Bolivia (formerly Upper Peru) is named after him.

Bolivia, a republic of central S America. Until conquered by Spain in 1535, Bolivia was part of the INCA empire. As Upper Peru, Bolivia was ruled from Lima until 1776, when it became part of a viceroyalty based on Buenos Aires. A revolt against Spanish rule (1809) led to a power struggle between loyalists and nationalists, ending in independence in 1825.

The remainder of the 19th century was characterized by political instability. In three devastating wars – the War of the PACIFIC (1879–83), alongside Peru against Chile, and the CHACO Wars (1928–30 and 1933–5) against Paraguay – Bolivia sustained great human and territorial losses. After 1935, political instability continued with a succession of military and civilian governments. Since 1982, however, Bolivia has had democratically elected governments.

Bolshevik (Russian, 'member of the majority'), the faction of the SOCIAL DEMOCRATIC Party in Russia that pursued revolutionary tactics from 1903 under the leadership of LENIN. The Bolsheviks believed in leadership by a well-educated, dedicated revolutionary elite and were the driving force of the RUSSIAN REVOLUTIONS of 1917. They changed their name to the Russian Communist Party in 1918. See also MENSHEVIK.

Bonaparte, see NAPOLEON I.

Boniface VIII (1235–1303), pope (1294–1303). His capture by PHILIP IV of France in 1303 after he had challenged the king's right to tax the clergy was part of the long-running struggle between the papacy and those secular rulers who resented papal attempts to assert the supremacy of spiritual over temporal power in medieval Europe. See also AVIGNON PERIOD.

Borgia, Cesare (c. 1475–1507), Italian cardinal and politician. During the career of his father, Rodrigo Borgia, as Pope Alexander VI (1492–1503), he carved out a power base in the PAPAL STATES. Anti-Spanish propaganda, together with his immortalization by Machiavelli as the model for *The Prince,* have made him a byword for cruelty and ruthlessness. His sister Lucrezia (1480–1519) was married four times, largely to further family ambitions.

Borneo, an island of the East Indies divided between INDONESIA, BRUNEI and the MALAYSIAN states of Sabah and Sarawak.

Bornu, see KANEM-BORNU.

Borodino, Battle of (7 December 1812), an engagement fought W of Moscow between Russia and Napoleon's *grande armée.* The Russians failed to prevent Napoleon's advance on Moscow, but remained strong enough to harass the French on their later retreat from Moscow. See map, p. 29.

Borromeo, St Charles (1538–84), Italian COUNTER-REFORMATION churchman who worked tirelessly to implement the reforms of the Council of TRENT.

Bosnia-Herzegovina, a republic of SE Europe. The SLAV ancestors of the Bosnians arrived in the region in the 7th century AD. From the middle of the 12th century Bosnia came under Hungarian rule. In the 13th century, the local representative of the Hungarian crown in Bosnia founded the autonomous Kotromanić dynasty. Kotromanić rulers conquered Hum (modern Herzegovina) and in the late 14th century established a powerful Bosnian kingdom. In the 1390s a disputed succession and Hungarian and (Turkish) OTTOMAN invasions led to the decline of Bosnia, which became a Turkish province in the 15th century. Under Ottoman rule – during which many Bosnians became Muslims – the region entered a long period of economic stagnation. During the 19th century, several revolts against Turkish rule were put down with ferocity. A major revolt (1875–6) attracted international concern, but the great powers overrode Bosnia's PAN-SLAVIC aspirations at the Congress of BERLIN (1877–8) and assigned an autonomous Bosnia-Herzegovina to Austro-Hungarian rule. In 1908 Austria formally annexed Bosnia to the HABSBURG Empire. In the Bosnian capital Sarajevo in 1914, Gavrilo Princip, a Bosnian student (ethnically a Serb), assassinated Archduke FRANZ FERDINAND, the heir to the Habsburg Empire – an event that helped precipitate WORLD WAR I. In 1918, Bosnia became part of the new Kingdom of Serbs, Croats and Slovenes, which was renamed YUGOSLAVIA in 1929. Following the German invasion (1941), Bosnia was included in the Axis-controlled puppet state of CROATIA. In 1945, when Yugoslavia was reorganized by Marshal TITO on Soviet lines, Bosnia-Herzegovina became a republic within the Communist federation. After the secession of SLOVENIA and Croatia and the beginning of the Yugoslav civil war (1991), tension grew between Serbs and Croats in Bosnia. The Bosnian Muslims – the largest ethnic group – reasserted their separate identity. In 1992, a referendum – which was boycotted by the Serbs – gave a majority in favour of Bosnian independence. International recognition of Bosnia-Herzegovina was gained in April 1992, but the Yugoslav civil war spread to Bosnia when Serbs attempted to secure a broad swathe of the republic, expelling Muslims and Croats in a campaign of 'ethnic cleansing'. International peace and humanitarian efforts were made, and in an attempt to control the Bosnian Serbs strict UN sanctions were were imposed on Serbia and Montenegro. UN peace envoys attempted to negotiate a partition of Bosnia acceptable to all parties, but bitter fighting between all three ethnic groups continued throughout 1993. In 1994 attempts were made to create a joint Muslim-Croat administration in those areas of Bosnia occupied by Muslims and Croats.

Boston Tea Party (1773), an incident in which a group of American radicals threw a cargo of tea into Boston harbour. In 1773 Britain allowed the struggling East India Company to dump cheap tea – on which a controversial tax was payable – on the American market. When the tea reached Boston a group of radicals, disguised as Indians, threw the tea chests into the harbour. The incident fuelled the campaign that led to the American War of INDEPENDENCE.

Bosworth Field, Battle of (22 August 1485), the final battle of the Wars of the ROSES, in which Henry Tudor's Lancastrian army defeated RICHARD III. Richard was killed, and Henry became HENRY VII, founding the TUDOR dynasty.

Botany Bay, an inlet on the SE coast of AUSTRALIA, visited by Captain COOK in 1770. Australia's first penal colony was known as Botany Bay, but it was in fact established at Port Jackson, further up the coast of New South Wales.

Botha, Louis, (1862–1919), an AFRIKANER general in the Second BOER WAR and first prime minister of the Union of South Africa (1910–19). He championed the reconciliation of Afrikaner land-owners with British gold-mining capitalists.

Botha, Pieter Willem (1916–), prime minister of SOUTH AFRICA (1978–84), president (1984–9). He used force at home and abroad to block ANC guerrilla activity, but baulked at radical constitutional reform. He was succeeded by F.W. DE KLERK.

Botswana, a republic of southern Africa. The area became a British protectorate – as Bechuanaland – in 1885. Development was slow, and many Africans had to seek work in South Africa. Nationalism was late to develop, and independence – as Botswana – was granted without a struggle in 1966. Under the first president, Sir Seretse KHAMA, and his successor, Botswana has succeeded in remaining a democracy.

Boudicca ('Boadicea'), queen of the ICENI. After the death of her husband in AD 60 she was maltreated by the Romans, and organized a revolt. She and her followers destroyed London, St Albans and Colchester before suffering a crushing defeat somewhere in the Midlands.

Boumédienne, Houari (1927–78), Algerian politician. He overthrew BEN BELLA in 1965, becoming both prime minister and chairman of the revolutionary council until his death.

Bounty Mutiny (April 1789), a mutiny that occurred near Tonga aboard HMS Bounty, a British naval ship carrying breadfruit trees from Tahiti to the West Indies. Led by Fletcher Christian, the mutineers – resentful of Captain William Bligh's harsh discipline – cast Bligh and 18 others adrift without maps, but Bligh's navigational skill allowed them to reach Timor six weeks later. The mutineers settled on Pitcairn Island with a number of Tahitian men and women.

Bourguiba, Habib Ben Ali (1903–), Tunisian nationalist politician. After independence he became prime minister (1956) and president (1957). He was elected president for life in 1975, but was overthrown in 1987.

Boxer Rising (1900), a bloody anti-Western uprising in China, so called because its members belonged to a secret society called the Righteous Harmonious Fists. With the connivance of the court of the dowager empress CIXI, its members attacked westerners and westernized Chinese. The rising was suppressed by the Western powers, who imposed a crippling annual indemnity on China and exacted further trade and diplomatic concessions.

Boyacá, Battle of (August 1819), a battle in which Simón BOLÍVAR, having crossed the Andes in an epic march, defeated a Spanish force, thereby clinching Colombian independence.

boyars, the highest order of the Russian nobility in the Middle Ages, ranking immediately below the princes. Their rank and title was abolished by PETER the Great.

Boyne, Battle of the (1 July 1690), a battle fought near Drogheda in Ireland between the Protestant forces of WILLIAM III of England, and Irish and French forces under the recently deposed JAMES II. William's victory – a major defeat for the STUART cause – ensured the triumph of the GLORIOUS REVOLUTION in England and of English Protestant rule in Ireland.

Brandenburg, a former state in NE Germany. The margrave of Brandenburg became an Elector of the Holy Roman Empire in 1356. Under the HOHENZOLLERNS it became the nucleus of the kingdom of PRUSSIA (1701).

Brandt, Willy (Karl Ernst Herbert Frahm; 1913–92), German statesman, SOCIAL DEMOCRAT chancellor of the Federal Republic of (West) Germany (1969–74). As a young man he fled Nazi Germany, taking refuge in Norway. As chancellor he adopted a policy of détente towards East Germany known as OSTPOLITIK. He resigned in 1974 when one of his associates was unmasked as an East German spy. He later chaired an international commission on development issues whose findings were published in the BRANDT REPORT.

Brandt Report, the report of the 'North–South Commission' on the state of the world economy, chaired by Willy BRANDT. It put forward a comprehensive plan for confronting the problems of Third World debt and slow development.

Brazil, a country of E South America. See panel.

Brest-Litovsk, Treaty of (3 March 1918), an agreement between Soviet Russia, Germany and Austria-Hungary, ending Russian involvement in WORLD WAR I. Russia, weakened by revolution, accepted harsh terms, including the loss of the Baltic provinces, Russian Poland, and the Ukraine.

Brétigny, Treaty of (1360), a treaty between England and France during the HUNDRED YEARS WAR. The French agreed to hand over no less than one-third of the land of France (including AQUITAINE) in full sovereignty. In return EDWARD III was to renounce his claim to the French throne. The Treaty was never ratified in full, war breaking out again in 1369.

Bretton Woods Conference, a United Nations Conference, held in New Hampshire, USA, in July 1944. Representatives discussed the establishment of the INTERNATIONAL MONETARY FUND (IMF) and the International Bank for Reconstruction and Development (World Bank).

Brezhnev, Leonid Ilyich (1906–82), Soviet statesman. He succeeded KHRUSHCHEV to become general secretary of the

BRAZIL

1500: Pedro CABRAL claimed Brazil for Portugal. **1532:** Sugar was introduced and plantations were established, first using native Indian slaves, then replacing them with Africans. **17th and 18th centuries:** Expansion S and W in search of gold and diamonds brought the Portuguese into conflict with the Spanish. **1808:** Threatened by a French invasion, the Portuguese royal family fled to Brazil; Brazil's equality with Portugal under the crown was recognized. **1821:** King JOHN VI returned to Portugal leaving his son Dom Pedro as regent. **1822:** Pedro proclaimed Brazilian independence with himself as emperor. **1831–89:** Reign of PEDRO II; relative stability and economic growth from 1840. **1889:** Deposition of Pedro II; republic established. **1930:** Getúlio VARGAS seized power in the face of mounting social unrest. **1945:** Vargas overthrown by the military. **1950:** Vargas elected president again, but committed suicide rather than face impeachment (1954). **1964–84:** Short-lived civilian governments preceded a further period of military rule during which political and social rights were restricted. **1985:** Brazil returned to civilian rule.

Communist Party (1964–82), and was president of the Soviet Union (1977–82). After crushing the Czechoslovakian PRAGUE SPRING (1968), Brezhnev formulated the 'Brezhnev Doctrine' – the right of the USSR to intervene militarily in the affairs of Communist countries to maintain ideological and political supremacy. The latter stages of his rule saw a deterioration in the Soviet economy and an intensification of the COLD WAR following the Soviet invasion of Afghanistan (1979). He was succeeded as Soviet leader by Yuri ANDROPOV.

Brian Boru (?941–1014), king of Munster. His death at the battle of Clontarf (1014), fighting a rebellion by Leinster and its Scandinavian allies, led to the collapse of Munster's overlordship of IRELAND.

Briand, Aristide (1862–1932), French socialist politician, eleven times prime minister of France. A strong advocate of peace and international cooperation in the 1920s, he was an architect of the LOCARNO Treaty and the KELLOGG–BRIAND Pact.

Brigantes, an ancient British people inhabiting the Pennine region of N England. They formed a Roman client state and remained nominally independent until AD 69, but were subsequently incorporated into the Roman province under AGRICOLA.

Britain, Battle of, the air battle fought during WORLD WAR II between the Royal Air Force and the German air force (Luftwaffe) over S England in late summer 1940. The Luftwaffe attacked factories, installations and airfields in S England in preparation for an invasion of the British Isles, but were repulsed by Spitfires and Hurricanes of RAF Fighter Command.

British Empire, a former empire comprising the UNITED KINGDOM and the overseas territories controlled by it. It reached its greatest extent in the late 19th and early 20th centuries, when it accounted for 25% of the world's population and area. The colonies increased trade and produced raw materials for Britain's expanding industrial base. Decolonization began in the years before World War II, gathering pace in the 1960s.

British Expeditionary Force (BEF), a force consisting of four infantry divisions and a cavalry brigade, sent to Belgium in 1914 to counter the German advance. It was virtually wiped out in the early battles of WORLD WAR I. The British force sent to France 1939–40 was known by the same name.

British North America Act (1867), legislation passed by the British Parliament uniting the colonies of New Brunswick, Nova Scotia, Canada East (now Quebec) and Canada West (now Ontario) as the DOMINION of Canada.

British Raj, the administration and territories of British INDIA during the period of direct rule by the crown (1858–1947).

Bronze Age, the period of human prehistory, following the NEOLITHIC period, when bronze, an alloy of copper and tin, was used for tools and weapons. The discovery of metallurgy probably occurred independently in several places, including the Near East and SE Europe. In parts of Europe and the Near East copper objects were in use centuries before the beginning of the Bronze Age: this transitional period is called the Chalcolithic ('copper-stone') Age. In Eurasia, the Bronze Age saw the development of trade, literacy and the wheel. Social distinctions increased as more powerful individuals – for example in MYCENAEAN Greece – displayed their status via bronze weapons and gold jewellery. Late Bronze Age societies of Greece and Crete had contacts with the civilizations of the Near East such as the HITTITES and EGYPTIANS, and may have influenced the neighbouring regions of Europe. Late Bronze Age societies N of the Alps were far more sophisticated than their Neolithic predecessors, with production and distribution of materials such as salt and copper carried out on an industrial scale. Dates for the Bronze Age vary according to locality. In parts of the Near East it began c. 6500 BC, giving way to the IRON AGE c. 1000 BC.

Brownshirt, a member of an early NAZI paramilitary organization, the Sturmabteilung (SA). Under their leader Ernst Röhm they murdered and intimidated opponents. The Brownshirt leadership was liquidated by Hitler in the NIGHT OF THE LONG KNIVES (1934).

Brunei, a sultanate in SE Asia. In the 16th century the sultans of Brunei ruled all of Borneo; by the 19th century they held a vastly reduced territory that had become a pirates' paradise. The British established a protectorate from 1888 to 1971. Oil was discovered in 1929. Independence was restored in 1984 under the absolute rule of Sultan Hassanal Bolkiah, allegedly the world's richest man.

Brüning, Heinrich (1885–1970), German chancellor (1930–2). He governed by decree from 1930 to 1932, but was forced to resign by HINDENBURG, paving the way for the Nazis. See WEIMAR REPUBLIC.

Brutus, Marcus Junius (c. 85–42 BC), Roman aristocrat noted for his personal integrity and staunch republicanism. With CASSIUS he plotted the assassination of Julius CAESAR. He committed suicide after his defeat by Mark ANTONY and OCTAVIAN at PHILIPPI in 42 BC.

Buchanan, James (1791–1868), 15th president of the USA (1857–61). His term of office as a Democrat president was dominated by the growing dispute over the slavery issue. His attempts at compromise between slave-holding and free states led to a split in the Democratic Party, whose Southern candidate lost the 1860 election to LINCOLN.

Buddha ('the Enlightened One'), Prince Siddhartha Gautama (c. 563–c. 483 BC), Indian religious teacher and founder of Buddhism. Born into a Nepalese princely family, he renounced family, wealth and power before experiencing enlightenment at Bodh Gaya c. 528 BC. He spent the rest of his life preaching a message of release from human suffering through right thought and conduct. His religious teaching exerted a powerful influence on Indian society up to c. AD 500 and in that time spread throughout Central and E Asia.

Bulganin, Nicolai Alexandrovich (1895–1975), Soviet politician. He became prime minister in 1955 after the resignation of Georgii MALENKOV, sharing power with KHRUSHCHEV until his removal in 1958.

Bulgaria, a country of SE Europe. See panel.

Bulge, Battle of the, see ARDENNES OFFENSIVE.

Bunker Hill, Battle of (17 June 1775), the first major engagement of the American War of INDEPENDENCE, fought on the heights commanding Boston harbour. Although the Americans were defeated by the British, their heroic defence and low casualties raised American morale.

Burgundy, a former duchy in E France, named after the Germanic people – the Burgundians – who settled there in the 5th century (see map, p. 15). Burgundy was conquered by the Merovingian FRANKS in the 6th century. In the late Middle Ages, under a series of strong dukes, it became a powerful state in its own right, and the most affluent in Europe. The territorial gains (1384) brought about by the marriage (1369) of Duke Philip 'the Bold' (1363–1404) to Margaret, heiress of Flanders and Artois, marked the beginning of a century of Burgundian power and prestige. The Anglo-Burgundian alliance during the HUNDRED YEARS WAR allowed Philip 'the Good' (1419–67) to make further advantageous gains in the prosperous Low Countries. However, the continued attempts of his son CHARLES 'the Bold' (1467–77) to extend Burgundian power ended in defeat by the Swiss at the Battle of Nancy (1477). After his death the Burgundian state broke up: Burgundy itself was annexed by the French crown, while the former Burgundian Low Countries passed to the HABSBURGS, later becoming part of the empire of CHARLES V.

Burke, Edmund (1729–97), British WHIG politician and political theorist, born in Ireland. An advocate of gradual reform, he contributed greatly to the evolution of modern Conservative thought. He split with his associate Charles James FOX over the French Revolution, which Burke considered a threat to the Christian social order of Europe.

BULGARIA

7th century: The Bulgars, a non-Indo-European people, invade the area, gradually adopting the language and culture of the conquered Slavs. **7th–10th centuries:** The Bulgar Khanate grew to dominate the Balkans, periodically threatening the BYZANTINE Empire. **1014:** Defeat of the Bulgars by the Byzantine emperor BASIL II. **12th century:** Bulgars regained their independence. **1362–93:** Bulgarian Empire succumbed gradually to the OTTOMAN advance. **1396–1878:** Bulgaria under Turkish rule, though most Bulgarians remained Christian. **1870:** Bulgarian Church established as first step towards restoration of nationhood. **1878:** Under the terms of the Congress of BERLIN Bulgaria became an autonomous principality within the Turkish empire. **1908:** Bulgaria became an independent kingdom. **1912–13:** Bulgaria lost territory to Greece in the Second BALKAN WAR. **1915–18:** Bulgaria was allied to Germany in WORLD WAR I. **1941–4:** Bulgaria allied to the AXIS powers in WORLD WAR II. **1944:** (Soviet) Red Army invasion. **1946:** The Bulgarian king was exiled and a Communist republic established. **1971–89:** Presidency of Todor ZHIVKOV. **1989:** Popular demonstrations against Communist rule. **1990:** Free elections held. **Since 1991:** Short-lived coalitions involving various combinations of the three main political parties.

Burkina Faso, a republic of the Sahel in W Africa. Mossi kingdoms dominated the area for centuries before French rule began in the 1890s. Since independence in 1960, the country – which kept its French name of Upper Volta until 1984 – has had a turbulent political history, with a succession of military coups.

Burma, see MYANMAR.

Burundi, a country of E central Africa. Burundi was a semi-feudal kingdom in which the minority Tutsi tribe dominated the Hutu majority. Colonized by Germany in 1890, it was taken over by Belgium after World War I. Independence came in 1962, after much conflict throughout the country. Following a military coup in 1966, a republic was established. The killing of the deposed king in 1972 led to a massacre of the Hutu. There have since been further coups and ethnic unrest, including a coup in 1993 during which the president was killed and thousands of Tutsis fled or were killed.

Bushmen, African racial group formerly inhabiting most of Africa S of the Equator. They were mainly confined to the less fertile lands of SW Africa by BANTU expansion in the 1st millennium AD.

Bush, George (1924–), 41st president of the USA (1989–92). A World War II veteran and Texas oil magnate, Bush served as director of the CIA and as Ronald REAGAN's vice-president before his election win in November 1988. The Allied victory in the GULF WAR won him many plaudits, but he came under increasing criticism for paying insufficient attention to domestic issues. He was defeated by Democratic challenger Bill CLINTON in the 1992 presidential elections.

Bute, John Stuart, 3rd Earl of (1713–92), British statesman, prime minister (1762–3).

Buthelezi, Mangosuthu Gatsha (1928–), prime minister of the 'non-independent' Zulu BANTUSTAN of Kwazulu in South Africa since 1972. He is also leader of the Inkatha cultural movement for Zulu revival, which became a political party in 1989.

Buyids, a Persian dynasty of N Iran that ruled in Iraq and W Persia (945–1055). Although they were SHIITE Muslims, they maintained the SUNNI caliphate in Baghdad, introducing elements of pre-Islamic Persian imperial tradition into their style of government. They were driven from Baghdad by the SELJUK Turks.

Byzantine Empire, the name by which the Eastern ROMAN EMPIRE came to be known, especially after the deposition of the last Western emperor in 476. Centred on its capital CONSTANTINOPLE (built on the site of the Greek city of Byzantium), the Eastern Empire was ruled separately from the late 4th century onwards. The Empire was attacked by GOTHS and HUNS in the 5th century, but survived to enjoy a military and cultural revival under JUSTINIAN in the 6th. Justinian's general, BELISARIUS, reconquered Africa, Sicily and much of OSTROGOTHIC Italy (see map, p. 16). The late 6th century saw SLAV advances in the Balkans, but a long war with SASSANID Persia was turned in the Byzantines' favour by the soldier-emperor HERACLIUS in the 620s. After the loss of its Near Eastern and African provinces to the ARABS in the 630s and 40s, and further losses to the LOMBARDS in Italy and to the Slavs in the Balkans, the Empire was forced to retrench. In the 8th and 9th centuries the Empire was wracked by the ICONOCLASTIC controversy, which split the ORTHODOX Church into factions and soured relations with Rome. However, the second half of the 9th century saw a revitalization of the Orthodox Church, with successful missions among the Bulgars, Slavs and Russians spreading Christianity and literacy. The period from the mid-9th to the early 11th centuries was a golden age for Byzantine military leadership and Christianizing colonization; the campaigns of John I Tzimiskes (969–76) thrust deep into Syria and Palestine, while BASIL II (976–1025) brought BULGARIA within Orthodox Christian jurisdiction. In 1054 tension between the churches of Rome and Constantinople culminated in the EAST–WEST SCHISM. A disastrous Byzantine defeat by the SELJUK Turks at MANZIKERT in 1071 reversed the regional balance of power. Emperor ALEXIUS I repulsed fresh barbarian assaults in the N and checked a NORMAN challenge in the Mediterranean, but his successes relied in part on help from outside, notably Venice, which exacted a heavy price in trading concessions. In 1204 Constantinople was besieged and sacked by a CRUSADER army and a LATIN EMPIRE was established. The Byzantine Empire re-established in 1261 was a shadow of its former self. The OTTOMAN Turks slowly closed in on Constantinople, conquering all the surrounding territory by the end of the 14th century. In 1453 the city fell to the Ottoman Sultan MEHMET II, marking the Empire's final demise.

Byzantium, see CONSTANTINOPLE.

Cabot, John (c. 1450–?98), an Italian navigator in the service of HENRY VII of England, Cabot discovered Cape Breton Island in 1497, and is sometimes credited with the discovery of North America – though the Vikings had reached there, via Iceland and Greenland, five hundred years earlier. See map, p. 24.

Cabral, Pedro Alvares (1467–1520), Portuguese navigator. He made landfall on BRAZIL en route to India in April 1500, and claimed the territory for Portugal.

Caesar, Gaius Julius (c. 100–44 BC), Roman general and politician. In 60 BC he formed the First TRIUMVIRATE with POMPEY and CRASSUS. Following his conquest of Gaul (58–50) and invasion of Britain (55), he crossed the RUBICON to invade Italy in 49 and plunged the Empire into the ROMAN CIVIL WARS. After defeating Pompey at PHARSALUS in 48 BC Caesar became consul and dictator for life, carrying out wide-ranging reforms including the introduction of the Julian Calendar. However, Caesar's monarchical tendencies went against Roman Republican tradition and offended the nobles. He was assassinated in the Senate on 15 March (the 'Ides of March') by a group of republican senators led by BRUTUS and CASSIUS.

Caetano, Marcello (1904–81), Portuguese prime minister (1968–74). SALAZAR'S chosen successor, he decided to maintain the dictatorship and fight to retain the Portuguese empire in Africa, but was overthrown by a left-wing military coup in April 1974.

Cairo Conference (November 1943), an ALLIED conference at which ROOSEVELT, CHURCHILL and JIANG JIE SHI discussed strategy against both Germany and Japan and decided on a postwar policy for the Far East.

Caledonia, an ancient name for that part of Scotland outside Roman control.

Caligula, Gaius (AD 12–41), Roman emperor (37–41) who succeeded his great-uncle TIBERIUS. After a brief honeymoon period his rule degenerated into outright despotism, and he was eventually murdered. Reports of his cruelty and megalomania, if true, suggest that he was a psychopath.

caliphate, the governing institution of the Islamic community after the death of MUHAMMAD. 'Caliph' (Arabic, *khalifa)* means 'representative' or 'successor'. Theoretically elective, the caliphate was in practice hereditary. The caliph was both religious and secular head of Islam, but had no power to define Islamic doctrine. The main caliphal dynasties were the UMAYYADS and the ABBASIDS (who were SUNNIS) and the FATIMIDS (who were SHIITES). The caliphate was later claimed by the OTTOMAN sultans, but was abolished by Turkish President Kemal ATATÜRK in 1924.

Callaghan, (Leonard) James (1912–), British Labour statesman, chancellor of the exchequer (1964–7), home secretary (1967–70), foreign secretary (1974–6), prime minister (1976–9). As PM he faced crises over inflation and British EC membership, and was forced to enter into a pact with the LIBERALS when the slim majority he inherited from Harold WILSON was whittled away. His government, weakened by industrial unrest during the 'Winter of Discontent' (1978–9), was defeated by Margaret THATCHER in the 1979 election. He was succeeded as Labour leader by Michael Foot.

Calvin, John (1509–56), French theologian and leader of the Protestant REFORMATION in France and Switzerland. Like LUTHERANISM, Calvinism was based firmly on Scripture, but differed in believing that only those predestined or chosen by God would be saved and that the efforts of individuals could play no part in their salvation. Calvin went further than Luther in rejecting religious ceremonial and imagery. Calvin reformed both the Church and government of Geneva, establishing a strict theocratic state, involving close supervision of the religious and moral life of its citizens, between 1536 and 1564. Calvinism was particularly influential in France, the Netherlands and Scotland.

Cambodia, a country of SE Asia. In the early 9th century, the Khmer king Jayavarman II established the Angkorian dynasty, with a new state religion. By the 12th century, Cambodia dominated mainland SE Asia, but, by the 15th century, Thai and Vietnamese expansion had constricted Cambodia to the Phnom Penh area. A French protectorate was established in 1863 and continued, apart from Japanese occupation during World War II, until independence in 1953. Throughout this period, the monarchy remained in nominal control. In 1955, King (now Prince) Norodom SIHANOUK abdicated to lead a broad coalition government, but he could not prevent Cambodia's involvement in the VIETNAM WAR or allay US fears of his sympathies for the Communists. In 1970 he was overthrown in by a pro-USA military junta, which, in turn, was attacked by Communist KHMER ROUGE guerrillas, who sought to create a self-sufficient workers' utopia. The Khmer Rouge were finally victorious in 1975. Under Pol Pot, they forcibly evacuated the towns and massacred up to 2,000,000 of their compatriots. In 1978 Vietnam – Cambodia's traditional foe – invaded, overthrowing the Khmer Rouge. The hostility between the two countries was sharpened by the Sino-Soviet split in which they took different sides. After Vietnamese troops withdrew in 1989, forces of the exiled government coalition invaded. In 1991 the country's warring factions agreed a peace plan that included free elections and UN supervision, and reduction of all Cambodian forces. A large UN peacekeeping force was deployed (1992) and UN participation in the administration of Cambodia was agreed. However, the Khmer Rouge subsequently withdrew from the peace plan.

Cambyses II, king of Persia (530–522 BC) and son of CYRUS II. He conquered Egypt in 526.

Cameroon, a republic of W central Africa. The area fell victim to Portuguese slave traders in the late 15th century. Germany declared a protectorate over Kamerun in 1884. After World War I, Cameroon was divided between the UK and France. The French Cameroons became independent in 1960. In 1961 the N of the British Cameroons merged with Nigeria, while the S federated with the former French territory. A single-party state was established in 1966 and a unitary system replaced the federation in 1972. Political pluralism returned in 1992, when multi-party elections were held.

Campaign for Nuclear Disarmament (CND), a British pressure group founded in 1958 to mobilize public opinion in favour of the unilateral abandonment of British nuclear weapons.

Campbell-Bannerman, Sir Henry (1836–1908), British Liberal politician, prime minister (1905–8). His premiership saw the granting of 'responsible government' to the BOER Republics, and the extension of the ENTENTE CORDIALE to include Russia (1907).

Camp David Accord (1978), a peace agreement between EGYPT and ISRAEL mediated by US president CARTER and signed by Egypt's President SADAT and Israeli PM Menachem BEGIN. By the terms of the Accord Israel agreed to evacuate all Egyptian territory captured in the SIX DAY WAR in return for the normalization of relations between the two states. Sadat was denounced by the rest of the Arab world and Egypt was expelled from the Arab League.

Canaan, the ancient name for the Semitic-speaking region roughly corresponding to PALESTINE.

Canada, a country of North America. See panel.

Cannae, Battle of (2 August 216 BC), Rome's worst military defeat, suffered during the Second PUNIC WAR in Apulia (S Italy). HANNIBAL'S Carthaginian army surrounded and annihilated the Roman forces under the consuls Aemilius Paulus and Terentius Varro. Estimates of Roman losses range from 50,000 to over 70,000 men.

Canning, George (1770–1827), British TORY statesman, foreign secretary (1807–9; 1822–7), prime minister (1827). As leader of the progressive Tories he promoted liberal policies at home and abroad. He was head of an administration formed with WHIG assistance for only a few months until his death.

CANADA

Before 20,000 BC: The ancestors of the Indians came to Canada from Asia. **c. 6000–5000 BC:** The Eskimos (INUIT) arrived. **c. 1000 AD:** Short-lived Norse settlements were established in Newfoundland (see VINLAND). **1497:** John Cabot explored the Atlantic coast for England, but did not claim it. **1534:** Canada claimed for France by Cartier. **1583:** England claimed Newfoundland. **1605:** First French colonists settled on the E coast. **1608:** Foundation of QUÉBEC. **1627:** Company of NEW FRANCE was established and encouraged settlement. **1670:** HUDSON'S BAY Company was founded to assert English control of the vast area around Hudson's Bay. **1701–63:** French and English fought in Canada; France lost Acadia (1713) and – after WOLFE took Québec in the battle of the Plains of Abraham (1759) – surrendered the rest of French Canada. **After 1783:** After the AMERICAN WAR OF INDEPENDENCE many of the loyalists in the USA settled in Upper Canada (Ontario). **1791:** Canada was divided into English-speaking Upper Canada and French-speaking Lower Canada. **1837:** Severe economic problems and a lack of political rights led to PAPINEAU'S REBELLION. **1841:** Ontario and Québec were united and granted self-government. **1867:** Ontario, Québec, New Brunswick and Nova Scotia formed the DOMINION of Canada. **1870–1905:** All the other provinces joined the Dominion except Newfoundland. **Late 19th century:** Large-scale emigration from Europe; settlements spread rapidly W; important mineral finds, including the Klondike gold rush. **1914–18:** Canadian forces distinguished themselves during WORLD WAR I, notably at VIMY RIDGE. **1931:** The Statute of WESTMINSTER recognized Canadian independence. **1939–45:** Canada played an important role in WORLD WAR II. **1949:** Newfoundland joined Canada. **1970s and 80s:** Friction over use and status of French language; increase in separatist feeling in Québec. **Since 1992:** Attempts to redefine Québec's constitutional status.

Canossa, the castle in N Italy where German emperor HENRY IV did penance before Pope GREGORY VII during the INVESTITURE CONTEST.

Canute, see CNUT.

Cape Province, a province on the S coast of the Republic of SOUTH AFRICA, formerly Cape Colony, under British rule until 1910. Under its 'colour-blind' franchise limited numbers of blacks (until 1936) and 'coloureds' (until 1955) had the vote.

Capetian, the name of a French royal dynasty founded by Hugh Capet (king of France 987–96) in succession to the CAROLINGIANS and reigning from 987 to 1328. Until c. 1200 their authority was restricted to the area of the 'royal principality' around Paris; only from the reign of PHILIP II

Augustus did they really dominate their kingdom. The Capetians were succeeded by the VALOIS dynasty.

capitalism, an economic system based on private ownership of the means of production, to which workers sell their wage-labour. Capitalism is usually seen as a product of a developing urban-industrial society. The word capitalism only began to appear in English from the early 19th century (and almost simultaneously in French and German), but the terms 'capital' and 'capitalist' were present much earlier, along with primitive kinds of capitalist production. However, capitalism as an economic system – MARX'S 'capitalist era' – dates only from the 16th century and did not reach the stage of 'industrial capitalism' until the late 18th and early 19th centuries.

Caporetto, Battle of (24 Oct–4 Nov 1917), a battle in which Austro-German forces overwhelmed the Italian army N of Trieste. The defeat effectively took Italy out of WORLD WAR I. See map, p. 36.

Caratacus ('Caractacus'; d. AD 51), British chieftain who led a war of resistance against the Roman occupation in the West Country and Wales. After his defeat he took refuge among the BRIGANTES, but was betrayed and taken to Rome in triumph, where he died.

Carbonari (Italian, 'charcoal burners'), a revolutionary secret society in early 19th-century Italy dedicated to freeing the country from foreign (Austrian) rule and establishing constitutional government. The Carbonari led the Neopolitan revolution of 1820. They were eclipsed by the radical YOUNG ITALY sect.

Carchemish, Battle of (605 BC), a battle in which the Babylonians defeated the Egyptians and the remnants of the Assyrians, extending the rule of NEBUCHADNEZZAR II.

Caribbean Community and Common Market (CARICOM), an organization of former British colonies in the Caribbean founded in 1973 with the aim of coordinating foreign policy and promoting cooperation in economic, cultural and technological matters.

Carlists, conservative and aristocratic supporters of the claim of Don Carlos (1788–1855) and his descendants to the throne of SPAIN. Defeated in the First Carlist War (1834–7) against Isabella II (reigned 1833–70), the Carlists persisted in their opposition to Spanish liberalism until their defeat in a further period of unrest and civil war (1870–6). After 1876 Carlism became a narrower movement espousing extreme right-wing principles.

Carlowitz, Treaty of (1699), a treaty between the OTTOMAN Turks and HABSBURG Austria after the defeat of the Turks at Zenta (1697). The Treaty ceded Hungary and Transylvania to Austria.

Carolingian dynasty, a Frankish dynasty founded by PEPIN the Short (who ousted the last MEROVINGIAN king in 751) and named after Pepin's son CHARLEMAGNE ('Charles the Great'), king of the Franks (768–814). Charlemagne built on the political and military achievements of his father and grandfather (CHARLES MARTEL), expanding the Frankish Empire to take in most of Christian Western Europe. He also did much to strengthen the administration of the empire. In the next two generations the Frankish system of partible inheritance (dividing land among all male heirs) greatly weakened the empire. Charlemagne's son LOUIS the Pious (814–840) divided the empire between his three sons and quarrels between these three led to the formalization of the division in the Treaty of VERDUN. In the late 9th century, the imperial leadership proved ineffective against Muslim, Viking and Magyar (Hungarian) raids, and power slipped into the hands of regional aristocracies.

Carson, Edward Henry, 1st Baron (1854–1935), Anglo-Irish lawyer and Conservative politician. A strong opponent of HOME RULE for Ireland, he raised the ULSTER VOLUNTEERS in 1914.

Carter, Jimmy (James Earl) (1924–), 39th president of the USA (1977–81). A southern Democrat and committed Baptist who cultivated an informal leadership style, he was a moving spirit behind the CAMP DAVID Accord (1978). Difficulties over the IRAN HOSTAGE CRISIS contributed to his defeat by Ronald REAGAN in the 1980 election.

Carthage, an ancient city on the coast of N Africa (near the site of modern Tunis). Traditionally founded in 814 BC by the PHOENICIANS, Carthage provided anchorage and supplies for ships trading in the W for minerals. The city became a powerful and prosperous colony and gained control of the sea routes to the W. It came into conflict with the Greek colonies of Sicily and later with Rome, with whom it fought the three PUNIC WARS from 264 BC. Carthage was destroyed after the Third Punic War, and the area became the Roman province of 'Africa'.

Carthusians, a strict contemplative order, founded by St Bruno of Cologne at Chartreuse in E central France in 1084.

Casablanca Conference (14–23 January 1943), an Anglo-US conference at which F.D. ROOSEVELT and CHURCHILL agreed that the ALLIED war aim was the 'unconditional surrender' of the AXIS powers.

Casement, Roger (David) (1864–1916), British diplomat and Irish nationalist sympathizer. He was hanged by the British for treason after attempting to gain German support for Irish independence.

Cassius (Gaius Cassius Longinus; d. 42 BC), Roman senator and soldier who, with BRUTUS, played a leading role in the assassination of Julius CAESAR. In 42 Cassius and Brutus were defeated by OCTAVIAN and Mark ANTONY at PHILIPPI in Macedonia, and committed suicide.

Castile, a kingdom that emerged in central SPAIN in the 11th century. It acquired the lion's share of the lands conquered from the Muslims in the 12th and 13th centuries, though not until after the marriage of ISABELLA of Castile to FERDINAND II of ARAGON had effectively created a single Spanish monarchy, did the conquest of GRANADA (1492) complete the RECONQUISTA. See map, p. 21.

Castlereagh, Robert Stewart, Viscount (1769–1822), British statesman. His duel with CANNING was a contributory factor in the demise of PORTLAND'S premiership. As foreign secretary (1812–22) under Lord LIVERPOOL he sought lasting peace in Europe through the post-Napoleonic 'Congress system' of diplomacy.

Castro (Ruz), Fidel (1927–), Cuban revolutionary, president of CUBA (1959–). An opponent of the repressive rule of Fulgencio BATISTA, Castro was imprisoned in 1953.

Released and exiled in 1955, he raised a guerrilla force and, in 1956, landed secretly in the SE of Cuba. By January 1959 Batista had fled, and Castro declared the Cuban revolution. Opposed by the USA, Castro increasingly established diplomatic, economic and military links with the USSR. His defeat of the abortive BAY OF PIGS invasion (1961), and survival of the CUBAN MISSILE CRISIS (1962), increased his popularity. The collapse of the Soviet Union in the early 1990s left Castro's regime isolated.

Catalaunian Fields, Battle of the (451), the defeat of ATTILA the Hun by an alliance of Romans and VISIGOTHS under the Roman general Aetius. The battle was no more than a check for Attila, who went on to ravage Italy the following year.

Catalonia, that part of NE Spain inhabited by Catalan speakers. The area was part of the county of Barcelona from the 8th century until 1137, when it became part of the kingdom of ARAGON. Catalonia is now an 'autonomous community' of Spain.

Cathars, a heretical medieval sect of the late 12th and early 13th centuries, also known as Albigensians. Catharism was a dualist heresy, whose adherents believed that the material world was evil, and that only the spiritual was good. The Cathars of S France were devastated by the crusade sent against them by Pope INNOCENT III in 1209, which also largely destroyed the distinctive culture of medieval Provence.

Catherine II ('the Great'; 1729–96), empress of Russia (1762–96). Catherine extended the Russian empire S to the Black Sea following success against the Ottomans in the RUSSO-TURKISH WARS of 1768–74 and 1787–92. Russia was also the main beneficiary of the three partitions of POLAND. After suppressing the Pugachev rebellion (1773–5) Catherine strengthened central government control by reform of the provincial administration.

Catherine of Aragon (1485–1536), first wife of HENRY VIII and mother of MARY I. Her marriage to Henry was annulled in 1533 against the authority of the Pope, marking the beginning of the English REFORMATION.

Catholic emancipation (1829), the concession of full civil and political rights for British and Irish Roman Catholics, including the right to sit in the British Parliament, by the Tory cabinet of the Duke of WELLINGTON, following agitation in Ireland led by Daniel O'CONNELL.

Cato the Elder (Marcus Porcius Cato; 234–149 BC), Roman politician who became an outspoken champion of traditional and conservative values. At the end of his life he urged the Romans to destroy CARTHAGE. His great-grandson of the same name, Cato the Younger (95–46 BC), tried to follow his political and moral example. A leading opponent of Julius Caesar, he committed suicide after hearing of the Republican defeat at Thapsus.

Cavaliers (from the French *chevalier,* 'horseman'), the name adopted in the ENGLISH CIVIL WAR by supporters of CHARLES I (who contemptuously applied the term ROUNDHEADS to their Parliamentary opponents).

Cavour, Camillo Bensodi, Count (1810–61), Italian politician, prime minister of Sardinia-PIEDMONT (1852–9 and 1860–1), and leader of the movement for the unification of ITALY. As Piedmontese PM he instituted political and economic reforms, and solicited the help of NAPOLEON III to drive the Austrians from most of N Italy in 1859. Cavour, who was working towards a liberal constitutional monarchy, was alarmed by the successes enjoyed by the radical Mazzinian nationalist GARIBALDI in S Italy in 1861, and sent an army to the Papal States to assert Piedmontese authority over the newly united Italy. In the event, Garibaldi was persuaded to accept VICTOR EMMANUEL II as king of Italy.

Caxton, William (c. 1422–91), English printer, who learned the art of printing in Cologne, Germany, and set up the first printing-press in England (1476).

Ceausescu, Nicolae (1918–89), Romanian politician, general secretary of the Romanian Communist Party (1969–89), president (1974–89). He distanced ROMANIA from Soviet foreign policy while maintaining strict Communist orthodoxy at home. The harsh, corrupt and nepotistic rule of Ceausescu and his wife Elena was overthrown in 1989, when they were executed on charges of genocide and corruption after elements of the army joined a popular revolt.

Cecil, William, 1st Baron Burghley (1520–98), English lawyer and statesman, chief adviser to ELIZABETH I. As secretary of state (1558–72) and Lord High Treasurer (1572–98) he dominated English political life for most of her reign, shaping an anti-Catholic foreign policy, and securing the execution of MARY, Queen of Scots.

Celtic Church, a Christian Church that existed in Britain from the Roman period. With the Saxon invasions of the 5th century it was driven out of England to Celtic areas such as Ireland. Members of the Celtic Church were influential in the conversion of NORTHUMBRIA. Some practices of the Celtic Church remained at odds with those of the Roman Church until the late 7th century, when they were resolved at the Synod of WHITBY.

Celts, the name given to a group of peoples inhabiting most parts of Europe in ancient times, identifiable chiefly by a shared language and cultural characteristics. The earliest known Celtic settlements – dating from about 1200 BC – were in central Europe in the basin of the upper Danube, the Alps and parts of France and S Germany. They spread to Spain and Portugal in the 6th century, and to the British Isles, N Italy, Greece, the Balkans and parts of Asia Minor over the next 300 years. In the 1st century BC they were defeated by Romans and Germanic tribes and eventually confined to the British Isles and N France. Celtic artefacts are divided into the URNFIELD, HALLSTATT (900–500 BC) and LA TÈNE periods. After the Roman conquest of much of Europe, Iron Age cultures were largely absorbed into the Romanized culture of the empire. Modern scholars have also used the term 'Celtic' to refer to the early medieval groups who inhabited present-day Scotland, Wales, Ireland, Cornwall and Brittany. Many contemporary inhabitants of these areas also think of themselves as 'Celtic'.

CENTO, see CENTRAL TREATY ORGANIZATION.

Central African Federation, (1953–63), a federation joining Southern Rhodesia, Northern Rhodesia and Nyasaland in an uneasy 'multi-racial' partnership. Designed as a counterweight to AFRIKANER-dominated South Africa, it was dissolved when Britain agreed to separate independence for MALAWI (Nyasaland) and ZAMBIA (Northern Rhodesia).

Central African Republic, a country in central Africa. French influence began in 1889, and the region became the French colony of Oubangi-Chari in 1903. It suffered greatly from the activities of colonial companies. Independence – as the Central African Republic – was gained in 1960. Jean-Bédel BOKASSA took power in a coup in 1965. Revolts by students and schoolchildren helped to end his murderous regime in 1979. Multi-party elections were held in October 1993.

Central America, the isthmus linking North and South America, extending from Mexico's S border to the NW border of Colombia. Under Spanish colonial rule, much of the area belonged to the Captaincy-General of Guatemala. After independence (1821), no region managed to dominate the isthmus and the five provinces emerged as GUATEMALA, EL SALVADOR, HONDURAS, NICARAGUA and COSTA RICA. (PANAMA remained part of COLOMBIA until 1903.) The 19th century saw frequent conflicts between the states and mutual interference in their domestic affairs. US interest in the region increased after the SPANISH–AMERICAN WAR of 1898 and the independence of Panama, with the USA constructing and controlling the PANAMA CANAL. With the exception of Costa Rica, Central America has been long dominated by dictatorships. These have begun to disappear since the 1970s.

Central Intelligence Agency (CIA), the principal intelligence and counterintelligence agency of the USA, established in 1947. A spearhead of America's COLD WAR effort, the CIA launched covert operations against a wide range of left-wing governments.

Central Powers, Germany, Austria-Hungary and their allies Turkey and Bulgaria during WORLD WAR I. See also ALLIED POWERS.

Central Treaty Organization (CENTO), a mutual security organization formed by Britain, Iran, Turkey and Pakistan in 1959. CENTO was based on the Baghdad Pact (formed in 1955 to counter Soviet influence in the Middle East), which was renamed when Iraq withdrew in 1959. The organization became inoperative with the withdrawal of Iran, Turkey and Pakistan in 1979.

Cetewayo (Cetshwayo; c. 1826–84), king of the ZULUS (1872–9). He defeated the British at ISANDHLWANA in 1879, but his capital of Ulundi fell to the British later that year. Restored by the British in 1885, he was driven out by his own people.

Chaco War (1932–5), a conflict fought between PARAGUAY and BOLIVIA over disputed territory in the Chaco desert. Both sides suffered heavy casualties, especially Bolivia, whose defeat contributed to the radical revolution of 1952.

Chad, a republic in the Sahel of W Africa. Part of the medieval African empire of KANEM-BORNU, the area around Lake Chad became French in the late 19th century. French conquest was complete by 1916. After independence in 1960, Chad was torn apart by a bitter civil war between the Muslim Arab N and the Christian and animist Black African S. Libya and France intervened forcefully on several occasions, but neither was able to achieve its aims. In 1987, an uneasy ceasefire was declared, but, following another civil war, military regimes took power in 1990 and 1991 and unrest continues.

Chaeronea, a city in central Greece, where in 338 BC PHILIP II of Macedon defeated an alliance of Greek city-states, resulting in Macedonian domination of Greece (see map, p. 12).

Chalcis, the largest city-state on the island of Euboea in central Greece. During the 'dark ages' (1100–700 BC) Chalcis, with the other chief Euboean city Eretria, was the most prosperous and developed of Greek cities; a war between Chalcis and Eretria c. 730 led to the destruction of the latter.

Chaldaea, a region of S Babylonia inhabited by wealthy tribes of Chaldaeans; the original homeland of a line of Babylonian kings of the 8th century BC. The Neo-Babylonian Chaldaean dynasty (625–539 BC) also had its origins there. See also BABYLON.

Chamberlain, Arthur Neville (1869–1940), British Conservative statesman. He succeeded BALDWIN as prime minister (1937), pursued a policy of APPEASEMENT towards Hitler, and negotiated the MUNICH AGREEMENT (1938) which led to the dismemberment of CZECHOSLOVAKIA. In its aftermath, he recognized the need for war preparation. He resigned in favour of CHURCHILL in 1940.

Champa, a former kingdom of Cambodia and central VIETNAM. The kingdom dates from the 2nd century AD and was frequently at war with the KHMERS. Champa succumbed to the Kingdom of ANNAM in the 15th century.

Champlain, Samuel de (1567–1635), French explorer who founded the colony of QUÉBEC (1608) and later played a key administrative role in consolidating his country's North American empire as governor of NEW FRANCE.

Chandragupta, ruler of N India (c. 321–c. 297 BC) and founder of the MAURYAN dynasty. He exercised control over most of the kingdoms of N and central India.

Charlemagne (c. 742–814), king of the FRANKS (768–814) and emperor of the West (800–14). The eldest son of PEPIN the Short, during a long and vigorous reign he organized and directed a remarkably sustained series of campaigns of aggression against neighbouring peoples. His defeat of the Saxons, Avars, Bavarians and Lombards gave him control of most of Western Europe, while his campaigns against the Arabs in Spain made him a champion of Christianity. He was crowned emperor of the West by LEO III in 800. His palace at Aachen (Aix-la-Chapelle) became the focal point of a CAROLINGIAN court culture that did much to preserve classical learning.

Charles I (1600–49), king of Great Britain and Ireland (1625–49), son of JAMES I. The 11 years (1629–40) during which he ruled without Parliament, raising money on his own authority and relying on advisers such as Thomas Strafford, created widespread antagonism. Equally unpopular were the religious policies of Archbishop LAUD, which seemed to threaten the return of Catholicism. In 1639 Presbyterian Scotland rebelled over Charles' attempts to impose an English-style Church. When Scotland invaded England Charles' need for money obliged him to call the LONG PARLIAMENT, his conflict with which led to the ENGLISH CIVIL WAR. After his trial and execution in 1649, the COMMONWEALTH was established.

Charles I of Anjou (1226–85), king of Sicily (1266–85). He was given the kingdom of SICILY by Pope Urban IV, who wished to restrict HOHENSTAUFEN influence in the area.

However, having defeated the last Hohenstaufen at BENEVENTO, he went on to take Naples and most of N ITALY, becoming a threat to the papacy himself. His ambitions were ended by the SICILIAN VESPERS uprising, after which the Angevins were expelled from Italy.

Charles II ('the Bald'; 823–77), king of the West Franks (843–77), emperor of the West (875–77). The son of LOUIS the Pious, he gained the title by the Treaty of VERDUN after fighting a series of wars with his brothers. He organized effective resistance to VIKING incursions in N France.

Charles II (1630–85), king of Great Britain and Ireland (1660–85) following the RESTORATION. The son of CHARLES I, his amorous adventures have perhaps obscured his achievements in promoting science, commerce and the English navy. His Catholic sympathies – he was secretly converted to Catholicism, married a Catholic and resisted attempts to exclude his Catholic brother James (later JAMES II) from the succession – provoked widespread distrust.

Charles IV (1316–78), king of Bohemia (1346–78), Holy Roman Emperor (1347–78). In 1356 Charles issued the Golden Bull, which formalized the election of the Holy Roman Emperor by the votes of a college of seven electors. This was to remain the *Grundgesetz* ('fundamental law') of the Empire till its dissolution in 1806. He was succeeded by his son Wenceslas IV (ruled 1378–1400).

Charles V ('the Wise'; 1337–80), king of France (1364–80), and son of JOHN II. He put down the JACQUERIE and regained much of the territory lost to the English in the HUNDRED YEARS WAR.

Charles V (1500–58), HABSBURG king of Spain (1516–56), Holy Roman Emperor (1519–56), by far the most powerful ruler of his day. In America his dominions were extended by the brutal conquests of CORTEZ and PIZARRO. In Europe he organized Christendom against the Turks and successfully defended Spanish and imperial rights in Italy against French aggression. His troops captured FRANCIS I in 1525, sacked Rome in 1527 and Tunis in 1530. After confronting LUTHER at the Diet of WORMS (1521), he was unable to prevent the spread of Protestantism in Germany and the Netherlands, though he did defeat the forces of the SCHMALKALDIC LEAGUE at Mühlberg in 1547. Worn down by the extent of his responsibilities, he retired to a monastery in 1556, dividing the Empire between his son PHILIP II of Spain and his brother Ferdinand I of Austria.

Charles VI ('the Mad'; 1368–1422), king of France (1380–1422). His mental illness left France without government for long periods and his reign witnessed defeat at AGINCOURT and English occupation N of the Loire. He married his daughter to HENRY V, declaring the English king to be his heir.

Charles VI (1685–1740), Holy Roman Emperor (1711–40). Lacking a male heir, he sought to prevent the destruction of the Austrian empire after his death by devising the PRAGMATIC SANCTION to ensure that all HABSBURG lands would pass undivided to his daughter MARIA THERESA. His reign saw Austrian defeat in the War of the POLISH SUCCESSION.

Charles VII ('the Victorious'; 1403–61), king of France (1422–61). During his reign, with the aid of Joan of Arc, much of the territory in N France lost to the English was regained, bringing the HUNDRED YEARS WAR to a successful conclusion for the French.

Charles X (1757–1836), king of France (1824–30). Brother of LOUIS XVI, he fled to Scotland in 1789, returning to France in 1814 as leader of the ultra-royalists. He succeeded his brother LOUIS XVIII, but his reactionary, pro-clerical and repressive reign provoked the REVOLUTION OF 1830 after which he was forced to abdicate.

Charles XII (1682–1718), king of Sweden (1697–1718) and son of Charles XI (ruled 1660–97). His reign was dominated by the NORTHERN WAR, which was to lead to the collapse of Sweden's Baltic empire.

Charles XIV (Jean-Baptiste Jules Bernadotte; 1763–1844), king of SWEDEN and NORWAY (1818–44). A veteran of Napoleon's Italian campaign, and marshal of France (1804), he was elected crown prince of Sweden (1810), in which capacity he allied his adopted country with Britain and Prussia and fought against Napoleon at the battle of LEIPZIG (1813). He succeeded the childless Charles XIII (ruled 1814–18) in 1818.

Charles Edward Stuart, see PRETENDER.

Charles Martel (c. 688–741), MAYOR OF THE PALACE under the last MEROVINGIAN kings of France, and grandfather of CHARLEMAGNE. He stopped the Muslim advance near Poitiers in 732, marking the end of northward Arab expansion. He was succeeded by his son PEPIN the Short, who established the CAROLINGIAN dynasty.

Charles the Bold (1433–77), duke of BURGUNDY (1467–77). His wars with LOUIS XI failed to make Burgundy a kingdom independent of France. He conquered Lorraine in 1475 and invaded Switzerland, but suffered defeats at Grandson and Morat and was killed at the Battle of Nancy (1477).

Charter 77, a petition signed by a group of Czech dissidents in 1977, outlining their criticisms of the Communist regime of Gustav Husak. Many of the group, including future President Vaclav HAVEL, were persecuted as a result.

Chartism, a British working-class mass movement for political reform, taking its name from the People's Charter (1838) and active between 1838 and 1849. The Charter's six demands were for annual parliaments, universal male suffrage, equal electoral districts, an end to property qualifications for MPs, voting by ballot, and payment of MPs. The two Chartist petitions presented to Parliament failed to force reforms.

Chattanooga Campaign (Aug–Nov 1863), a series of operations in the AMERICAN CIVIL WAR. Consisting principally of the battles of Chickamauga and Chattanooga (the latter won by Northern forces under Ulysses S. GRANT), the campaign secured Tennessee for the Union and paved the way for SHERMAN'S decisive thrust towards Atlanta.

Cheka, Soviet secret police agency established by the Bolsheviks (1917–22). See also NKVD, OGPU and KGB.

chemical warfare, the use of toxic or asphyxiating agents in war. Chlorine and mustard gas were first used in WORLD WAR I, but international disgust at their use led to the prohibition of poison and nerve gases in 1925. A UN Conference on Disarmament in 1989 voted to ban chemical weapons, and both the USA and the former Soviet Union have agreed to reduce their large stockpiles. Many other countries, however, maintain secret arsenals of chemical weapons. Iraq used its chemical weapons during the IRAN–IRAQ WAR and against its Kurdish population at Halabja in March 1988.

Chernenko, Konstantin (1911–85), Soviet politician, general secretary of the Communist Party and president of the Soviet Union (1984–5). He was succeeded by GORBACHOV.

Chernobyl, the site of a Soviet nuclear power station in the UKRAINE. Its explosion in 1986 caused widespread radioactive pollution.

CHILE

15th century: The INCA moved into Chile, but were halted by the Araucanian Indians. **1541:** The Spaniard Pedro de Valdivia founded Santiago. **1810:** A revolt led by Bernardo O'HIGGINS broke out against Spain. **1817:** Troops led by José de SAN MARTÍN crossed from Argentina to aid O'Higgins. **1818:** Chile was liberated. **mid-19th–early 20th centuries:** Power held by conservative landowners. **1879–84:** Chile gained territory in two wars against Peru and Bolivia. **Late 1920s–1940s:** Chile was governed by liberal and radical regimes, but social and economic change was slow. **1970:** Salvatore ALLENDE's Marxist government was elected and introduced major changes, including land reform. **1973:** General PINOCHET seized power in a US-backed military coup; tens of thousands of his left-wing opponents were killed, imprisoned or exiled. **1990:** Multi-party rule restored.

CHINA (TAIWAN)

7th century: The first settlers from CHINA came to Taiwan. **1590:** The Portuguese name Taiwan Formosa ('beautiful'). **16th and 17th centuries:** The island was the object of Spanish–Portuguese rivalry. **1662–83:** Taiwan was briefly independent under the Chinese general Koxinga. **18th and 19th centuries:** A period of Chinese rule and renewed migration lasted until a Japanese takeover (1895). **1949:** The Nationalist forces of JIANG JIE SHI (Chiang Kai-shek) were driven onto Taiwan by the Communist victory on the mainland. **1950–71:** Under US protection, the authoritarian regime on Taiwan declared itself the Republic of China, and claimed to be the legitimate government of all China. **1971:** America's rapprochement with the mainland People's Republic of China lost Taiwan its UN seat. **1978:** The USA ceased to recognize Taiwan as the legitimate government of China. **1991:** A new constitution marked the transition to a more Taiwanese, less Chinese, identity. **1993:** Taiwan effectively recognized Communist China, and entered into unofficial talks on trade and communications.

Cherokee, a native North American people, maize farmers living in a region covering the W Carolinas, Georgia and E Tennessee. One of the 'Five Civilized Indian Nations', they adapted to colonial culture but were forced out of their lands in the 1830s and re-established in Oklahoma. See also NORTH AMERICAN INDIANS.

Cheyenne, a native North American people, living in the central Great Plains. They abandoned settled village life in the 18th century and became nomads dependent on hunting buffalo from horseback. See also NORTH AMERICAN INDIANS

Chiang Kai-shek, see JIANG JIE SHI.

Chickasaw, a native North American people, maize farmers living in the region of modern Alabama and N Mississippi. One of the 'Five Civilized Indian Nations', they were removed to Oklahoma in the 1830s. See also NORTH AMERICAN INDIANS.

Chile, a republic on the Pacific coast of S America. See panel.

Chimu, a powerful state centred on the N coast of Peru during the 14th and 15th centuries. It was conquered by the INCAS in 1476.

China, a country of E Asia. See panel.

China, Republic of (Taiwan), an island republic off the coast of mainland China. See panel.

Chindits, Allied forces fighting behind Japanese lines in Burma in WORLD WAR II. The Chindits were led by Orde Wingate (1903–44), an exponent of guerrilla warfare.

Chinese Civil War (1927–37 and 1946–9), conflicts between KUOMINTANG (Nationalist) and Communist forces in CHINA (1927–37 and 1946–49). In 1927 the Nationalist leader JIANG JIE SHI (Chiang Kai-shek) suppressed a series of Communist uprisings in urban areas. The Communists – under MAO ZEDONG – now concentrated on setting up 'safe bases' among the peasantry as the foundation for future action against the Nationalists. When Jiang attacked Mao's JIANGXI base in 1934 Mao was forced to withdraw, leading his followers on the LONG MARCH from Jiangxi to Shaanxi province. The two sides agreed an uneasy alliance to counter the Japanese invasion of 1937, but the Nationalists bore the brunt of the fighting. During the SINO-JAPANESE WAR Mao extended his influence and gathered strength, waiting for a chance to attack the weakened Nationalists. With the defeat of the Japanese the civil war began again in earnest in 1946 and the Nationalists gradually lost their grip in the face of guerrilla attacks. By 1948 Manchuria was in Communist hands and, after attacks on Beijing, Jiang's forces began to collapse. On 1 October 1949 Mao proclaimed a People's Republic in Beijing, while Jiang fled to the offshore island of Taiwan, where a Nationalist government was set up.

Chinese Communist Party (CCP), a Chinese political party, the ruling party in CHINA since the defeat of JIANG JIE SHI'S Nationalists at the end of the CHINESE CIVIL WAR in 1949. It was led by MAO ZEDONG from 1921 until 1976.

Ch'ing dynasty, see QING.

Chinook, a native North American people, hunters and traders living on the NW coast of modern Oregon and Washington.

CHINA

c. 1480–c. 1050 BC: China ruled by the SHANG, the first historically documented Chinese dynasty. **c. 1122–256 BC:** The ZHOU displaced the Shang as overlords of the Chinese heartland. **481–221 BC:** China divided into small kingdoms known as the 'WARRING STATES'. **221–206 BC:** The QIN (Ch'in) emerged as the final victor of the Warring States, and established the first imperial dynasty of China under the rule of SHI HUANGDI. **202 BC–AD 220:** The succeeding HAN dynasty expanded the Chinese empire and saw the arrival of BUDDHISM. **c. 220–265:** China was divided between three kingdoms – Wei, Shu and Wu. **265–316:** The Wei became the most powerful kingdom and restored the empire under the Western JIN dynasty. **316:** China overrun by TARTAR invaders from the N. **386–533:** Yellow River valley ruled by the NORTHERN WEI; the surviving Jin ruled in the S until 420. **589–618:** The short-lived SUI dynasty reunited China. **618–907:** The TANG dynasty took power and established a strong empire. **908–960:** After the fall of the Tang the Chinese empire disintegrated with internal wars and economic depression. **960–1127:** The SONG (Sung) reunited China and brought prosperity, moving the centre of imperial China from the Yellow River to the S. **1127–1279:** The Song dynasty was reduced to the S, the N being overrun by JIN nomads; MARCO POLO visited the court of the Khan in 1275. **1271–1368:** The invading MONGOLS established the YUAN dynasty. **1368–1644:** The Mongol rulers of China were expelled by the first MING emperor who re-established a Chinese dynasty and expanded the empire; Portuguese traders and missionaries entered China (1516). **1644:** Nomads from Manchuria (the MANCHU) took advantage of instability in the Ming Empire to seize N China. **From 1682:** The Manchu gained control of the entire Chinese empire and established the QING dynasty. **1839–42:** Pressure from the West to increase trade between China and Europe led to the First OPIUM WAR; European powers gained control of the 'Treaty Ports' which imposed unequal trading terms on the Chinese. **1850–64:** The TAIPING REBELLION gained control of a large part of the S; millions died when the rebellion was brutally suppressed by the government with Western aid. **1856–60:** The second OPIUM WAR led to further unequal trading treaties for China. **1894–5:** Japan seized control of Korea and Taiwan in the First SINO-JAPANESE WAR. **1851–1908:** The Empress Dowager CIXI, who had control of the imperial court, resisted attempts to reform and reconstruct China in the face of Western expansion. **1900–1:** The xenophobic BOXER REBELLION led to an increase in European intervention in China. **1911–12:** The Qing dynasty was overthrown by the KUOMINTANG (Nationalists), and SUN YAT-SEN became the first president of the Chinese republic (1912). **1920s:** Foundation of CHINESE COMMUNIST PARTY (1921); rise of Nationalist leader JIANG JIE SHI (Chiang Kai-shek). **1927–37:** Civil war between Jiang Jie Shi's Nationalists and Communists led by MAO ZEDONG. **1931:** The Japanese annexed MANCHURIA. **1937–45:** Nationalists and Communists suspended the civil war to fight the Japanese in the Second SINO-JAPANESE WAR. **1945:** Japanese surrender. **1946–9:** CHINESE CIVIL WAR ended in Communist victory and establishment of the People's Republic of China under Mao Zedong; Nationalists forced to retreat to Taiwan. **1966–76:** The CULTURAL REVOLUTION plunged China into economic and political turmoil. **1977:** DENG XIAOPING recalled to office after death of Mao (1976). **1990:** The peaceful pro-democracy movement, led by students, was bloodily crushed in TIANANMEN SQUARE.

Chin dynasty, see JIN.

Ch'in dynasty, see QIN.

Chipewyan, a native North American people, living as nomadic caribou hunters SW of Hudson Bay.

Choctaw, a native North American people, maize farmers inhabiting modern SE Mississippi. One of the 'Five Civilized Indian Nations', they were removed to Oklahoma in the 1830s. See also NORTH AMERICAN INDIANS.

Chou dynasty, see ZHOU.

Chou En-lai, see ZHOU ENLAI.

Christian Democrats, the term used to describe a number of conservative European political parties of the centre right, especially the Christian Democratic Parties of Germany and Italy. Christian Democracy – emphasizing Christian values, a community ethic and social reform – developed after 1945 and remains one of the main political forces in Western Europe.

Christianity, the religion of those who believe that JESUS Christ is the son of God, and in his teaching; the largest religion in the world. From its beginnings in Palestine in the early 1st century AD Christianity spread rapidly through the efforts of missionaries such as St PAUL. By the 2nd century the new faith had won adherents in every part of the ROMAN EMPIRE. At this stage most people were hostile to Christianity, which was seen as a weird and irrational cult. However, the government made no attempt to stamp out the cult – early persecutions were spontaneous outbreaks of popular hatred. The 3rd-century troubles swelled the membership of the Church, but also fuelled popular hostility. Official persecutions began at this time and were intensified under DIOCLETIAN in 303. These persecutions were ruthless and bloody, but the courage of the martyrs increased the prestige and strength of the Church. CONSTANTINE issued an edict of toleration in 313. All subsequent Roman emperors were nominally Christians – with the exception of JULIAN THE APOSTATE, who staged an abortive pagan revival – and Christianity became the officially established religion of the empire in 380. The final selection of writings for the New Testament of the Christian Bible was made in 382, and a statement of Christian beliefs was issued by the First

Council of Nicaea (325). As the Church grew, however, disputes arose over questions of doctrine and Church organization. These were to lead to the emergence of different forms of Christianity in the centuries that followed. See also PAPACY, ROMAN CATHOLICISM, ORTHODOX CHURCH, HERESY, EAST–WEST SCHISM, REFORMATION, PROTESTANTISM, ANGLICAN CHURCH.

Churchill, Sir Winston Leonard Spencer (1874–1965), British conservative politician, prime minister (1940–5 and 1951–5). Elected to Parliament in 1900 as a Unionist, he switched to the Liberals in 1904 and served in ASQUITH'S and LLOYD GEORGE'S governments. As First Lord of the Admiralty in WORLD WAR I he became a scapegoat for the débâcle at GALLIPOLI. A Conservative again from 1925, he supported rearmament against Nazi Germany during the 1930s and later served in CHAMBERLAIN's wartime government. He became PM of the wartime coalition in 1940, his morale-boosting oratory and steely resolve making him an immensely popular wartime leader. He lost office to Labour in the 1945 general election, but returned in 1951.

Church of England, see ANGLICAN CHURCH.

CIA, see CENTRAL INTELLIGENCE AGENCY.

Cicero, Marcus Tullius (106–43 BC), Roman statesman and orator. He joined POMPEY's side in the ROMAN CIVIL WAR, but was pardoned by CAESAR. After delivering speeches critical of Mark ANTONY he was murdered by the latter's soldiers in 43 BC.

Cid, El, the name given to Rodrigo Díaz de Vivar (c. 1043–99), whose role in fighting the MOORS made him a Spanish national hero. In fact, he was also involved in fighting rival Spanish Christians and at one point was in the service of the Muslim ruler of Saragossa.

Cimon (d. 499 BC), Athenian commander who led the forces of the DELIAN LEAGUE to a number of victories against the Persians from 476 BC.

CIS, see COMMONWEALTH OF INDEPENDENT STATES.

Cistercians, a monastic order named after its first foundation at Citeaux in central France (1098). They built their houses in remote areas and placed great emphasis on the importance of physical labour. BERNARD of Clairvaux inspired recruitment to the order, and by 1153 there were hundreds of Cistercian monasteries all over Europe.

city-state, the typical unit of political and social organization in ancient GREECE, and also in medieval and Renaissance Italy.

Civil Rights Acts, US legislation extending the civil rights of American blacks. Although the first Civil Rights Act of 1866, later reinforced by the FOURTEENTH AMENDMENT to the Constitution, gave citizenship to all people born in the USA, Southern blacks remained persecuted second-class citizens until the mid-20th century. The Civil Rights Acts of 1957 and 1964 and the Voting Rights Act of 1965 – campaigned for by Martin Luther KING – outlawed racial discrimination in all important areas of life and gave federal agencies power to enforce black rights.

Civil Rights Movement, a US protest movement to end racial segregation and inequality in the Southern states of the USA. Its campaign – led by Martin Luther KING – culminated in the passing by Congress of the 1964 CIVIL RIGHTS ACT and the 1965 Voting Rights Act. In the mid-1960s more militant 'Black power' groups were established, including the BLACK PANTHERS and followers of MALCOLM X. Although legal protection has been gained for black Americans, they are still campaigning against informal racism in the USA.

Cixi (Tz'u-hsi; 1835–1908), empress dowager and effective ruler of China (1862–1908). Cixi entered imperial life as the concubine of the emperor Xianfeng (1851–62). Between 1862 and her death in 1908 her control of the imperial court kept China locked in a largely negative and conservative reaction to Western expansion. She supported the BOXER movement in its bloody and violent campaign against westerners and westernized Chinese.

Classical period, in ancient GREECE, the period c. 500–338 BC. See also ARCHAIC PERIOD.

Claudius (10 BC–AD 54), Roman emperor (41–54), nephew of TIBERIUS and uncle of CALIGULA. Claudius was unexpectedly made emperor by the PRAETORIANS after the murder of Caligula. A conscientious administrator, Claudius was unpopular with the Senate. In AD 43 he organized the conquest of Britain.

Clausewitz, Karl von (1780–1831), Prussian general and philosopher of war. He believed that war was a rational instrument of policy and that it must be conducted ruthlessly to ensure swift victory. His theories presaged the modern concept of 'total war'.

Clay, Henry (1777–1852), US politician, secretary of state under John Quincy ADAMS (1825–9), and later a founder of the WHIG party. He is known as 'The Great Compromiser' because of his efforts at compromise to keep the Union intact on the slavery question.

Cleisthenes (6th century BC), Athenian statesman, seen as the founder of Athenian democracy. He introduced democratic means of decision-making at local and city level (508–7 BC), dividing Athenian citizens into 10 'tribes' (each comprising citizens from all three regions of ATTICA), from which representatives were selected to serve in the COUNCIL OF FIVE HUNDRED. He also created the institution of OSTRACISM, whereby Athenians could vote for a politician to be banished from the city for ten years.

Clemençeau, Georges Benjamin (1849–1929), French socialist statesman, prime minister (1906–9; 1917–20). He was a strong supporter of DREYFUS (1897), and turned back a tide of French defeatism during the later years of WORLD WAR I. As president of the PARIS PEACE CONFERENCE (1919), he imposed harsh terms on the defeated Central Powers.

Clement V (1264–1314), pope (1305–14). Feuds among the Italian cardinals and their aristocratic allies in Rome persuaded him to move the seat of the papacy to Avignon, marking the beginning of the AVIGNON PERIOD.

Cleopatra VII (69–30 BC), queen of Egypt. Cleopatra became queen in 51 BC, but was ousted by her co-ruler, Ptolemy XIII, in 48. She was restored in 47 by CAESAR, who became her lover and (she claimed) father of her son Ptolemy Caesar. Her affair with Mark ANTONY began in 41 and continued until their suicides after ACTIUM.

Cleveland, (Stephen) Grover (1837–1908), US Democratic politician, 22nd (1885–9) and 24th (1893–7) president of the USA. He was an economic conservative and advocate of free trade. He was succeeded after a depression-wracked second term by MCKINLEY.

Clinton, William (Bill) Jefferson (1946–), US Democratic politician and 42nd president (1993–) of the USA. He won a liberal and progressive reputation as governor of Arkansas (1979–81 and 1983–93), and defeated George BUSH to become the first Democrat in the White House for 13 years in the 1992 presidential election.

Clive of Plassey, Robert, Baron (1725–74), British general and first governor of Bengal (1757–60 and 1765–7). His defeat of the Indian forces at PLASSEY (1757) and conquest and administration of Bengal laid the foundations of British rule in India. He committed suicide in 1774 after being censured by Parliament.

Clovis I (c. 466–511), MEROVINGIAN king of the FRANKS (482–511) and founder of the Frankish kingdom. He conquered all of N Gaul by 494, defeated the VISIGOTHS at Vouillé in 507, and went on to extend his territories as far as the Pyrenees. On his death his kingdom was divided between his four sons, following Frankish tradition. He was converted to Catholicism in 493.

Clovis culture, the earliest clearly defined prehistoric culture of America (c. 10 000–8000 BC), characterized by the distinctively shaped points of the stone weapons used in big-game hunting.

Cluny, Abbey of, the mother house of a reformed BENEDICTINE order, founded in 910 under papal protection.

Cnut (Canute; c. 994–1035), king of England (1016–35). He completed his father SWEYN Forkbeard's conquest of England when he defeated Edmund Ironside in 1016. He acquired Denmark (1019), and briefly held Norway (see OLAF II). His 'North Sea empire' collapsed on his death.

Cochin China, a former name for the S of VIETNAM. It formed a separate French colony from 1867 to 1949.

Cochrane, Thomas, 10th Earl of Dundonald (1775–1860), British admiral and adventurer, one of the most successful of the British and Irish mercenaries who fought in the wars for South American Independence.

Coercive Acts, repressive legislation passed by the British Parliament against the American colony of MASSACHUSETTS in the wake of the BOSTON TEA PARTY. They became known as the 'Intolerable Acts' and led to the CONTINENTAL CONGRESS.

Colbert, Jean Baptiste (1619–83), French statesman. He passed from the service of Cardinal MAZARIN into that of LOUIS XIV, becoming his chief financial minister (1661). He sought to promote French arts, trade and industry, and to develop a French navy.

Cold War, the term given to the confrontation between the superpowers – the USA and the USSR – and their respective allies from 1945 to 1990 (see map, p. 41). The term derives from the fact that the superpowers were never in direct military conflict, partly for fear of nuclear war. Instead, there was a conflict of ideologies – Western capitalism versus Eastern Communism – exacerbated by what each side believed was the other's desire for economic and political domination of the world. The division of the Communist world and the West was formalized by the creation of the military alliances of NATO and the WARSAW PACT. US intervention in the KOREAN WAR and the VIETNAM WAR, the CUBAN MISSILE CRISIS and the crisis over the status of Berlin heightened Cold War tensions, but there were also attempts to achieve DÉTENTE. The Soviet invasion of AFGHANISTAN (1979) led to a 'hotting up' of the Cold War in the early 1980s. Arms reduction treaties in the late 1980s, together with the decline of Soviet influence in Eastern Europe – culminating in the opening of the BERLIN WALL (1989) – helped bring an official end to the Cold War in November 1990.

collectivization, the creation of collective farms imposed in the USSR by STALIN after 1929. Collectivization forced peasants into communal forms that were seen as a means of accumulating capital, securing spare manpower for industry and promoting revolutionary fervour. The process led to massive casualties among the KULAK class. Collectivization was ultimately inefficient, agriculture becoming a weak point of the Soviet economy.

Collins, Michael (1890–1922), Irish nationalist, a leader of SINN FEIN and first commander of the IRISH REPUBLICAN ARMY. He helped to negotiate the Treaty with Britain that established the Irish Free State (1921). He commanded the Free State forces in the Irish Civil War, but was assassinated by republican enemies in 1922.

Colombia, a republic of NE South America. The Spanish reached Colombia's N coast in 1500, and founded their first settlement in 1525. Meeting little resistance from the Indians, the conquistadores advanced inland, reaching Bogotá in 1538. In 1718 the Viceroyalty of Nueva Granada was established at Bogotá. The struggle for independence from Spain (1809–19) was fierce and bloody. Almost from that time, the centralizing pro-clerical conservatives and the federalizing anti-clerical liberals have struggled for control, leading to civil wars (1899–1902 and 1948–1957) in which 400,000 people died. From 1957 to 1974 there were agreements between the liberals and conservatives to protect a fragile democracy threatened by left-wing guerrillas and right-wing death squads. In the early 1990s, a combination of security measures and amnesties curbed the activities of powerful drug-trafficking cartels, and left-wing guerrillas abandoned their armed struggle in favour of legitimate political activity.

Columba, St (St Columcille; c. 521–97), Irish monk and missionary. Iona, the monastery he founded off the W coast of Scotland, became an important centre of the CELTIC CHURCH, and from there the PICTS were converted to Christianity.

Columbus, Christopher (1451–1506), Italian navigator. Because Columbus believed that the world was much smaller than it is, he was confident that he could reach the East by sailing W. It had been known for centuries that the world was round, but for a long time Columbus's schemes were rejected by experts who had a much more accurate idea of the actual size of the globe. Not until 1492 was he given the support of the Spanish crown. His flotilla of three ships led by the *Santa Maria* reached the Bahamas in 33 days. On subsequent voyages he reached the American mainland. He died convinced that he had reached the East, or the Indies, hence the name 'West Indies'. See map, p. 24.

Comanche, a native North American people, nomads dependent after c. 1700 on hunting buffalo from horseback in the Great Plains. They had previously lived in the Great Basin as hunter-gatherers.

Combination Acts, legislation passed by the British Parliament (1799–1800) outlawing the 'combining' of two or more craftsmen for the purpose of bargaining for better wages and working conditions. The Acts were repealed in 1824 and TRADE UNION activity was permitted, although strikes were still outlawed.

COMECON (Council for Mutual Economic Assistance), an economic organization of the former Soviet bloc, founded in 1948 by Bulgaria, Czechoslovakia, Hungary, Poland, Romania and the USSR. They were later joined by Albania (which left the organization in 1961), East Germany, Mongolia, Cuba and Vietnam. The fall of Communist governments in Eastern Europe in 1989–90 undermined the principles on which COMECON had been created, and with the establishment of free-market economies in East European countries it was disbanded in March 1991.

Comintern (Communist INTERNATIONAL), international Communist organization formed by LENIN (1919) with the aim of spreading Communist doctrine. Largely a tool for Soviet control over Communist parties in other countries, the Comintern was dissolved by STALIN in order to reassure his non-Communist allies.

Commodus (AD 161–193), Roman emperor (180–192) and son of MARCUS AURELIUS. A maniac, he ruled with tyrannical savagery until his strangulation by a champion athlete at the behest of his mistress and advisers.

Common Agricultural Policy (CAP), the most important single common policy of the EUROPEAN COMMUNITY, absorbing about a third of the EC's budget. It supports agricultural prices and protects some products with tariffs. Although CAP has increased productivity, guaranteed supplies and stabilized markets, it remains controversial and is a cause of disagreement between the EC and other industrial states.

Commons, House of, the lower chamber of the English PARLIAMENT. Representatives of the shires and towns were summoned from the 13th century onwards (and elected on a very narrow franchise before the electoral reforms of the 19th and 20th centuries) to give the consent to national taxation that the nobles alone could not grant. This 'power of the purse', enshrined in the Parliament Act (1911), ensured the gradual eclipse of the House of LORDS by the Commons (who only began to meet separately in the 16th century).

Commonwealth, 1. the English republic established after the execution of CHARLES I and abolition of the monarchy (1649), which lasted until the RESTORATION (1660). Executive power lay with a Council of State and – from 1653 – with the Lord Protector, Oliver CROMWELL, while legislative power was vested in the RUMP Parliament (until 1653), and thereafter in a number of shortlived Parliaments. **2.** an informal grouping of the UK and the majority of its former dependencies. Its roots lie in the 1926 Imperial Conference, which defined the DOMINIONS of the British Empire as 'freely associated . . . members of the British Commonwealth of Nations'. From being a club of Western states, it has been transformed by an influx of newly independent former British colonies in Africa, Asia and the Caribbean into a predominantly Third World association. Its member-states, while independent in every respect, recognize the British sovereign as head of the Commonwealth.

Commonwealth of Independent States (CIS), an organization of former members of the SOVIET UNION. Formally established in 1992, the CIS comprises Russia, Belarus, Ukraine, Moldava, Tajikistan, Armenia, Turkmenistan, Kazakhstan, Kyrgyzstan and Uzbekistan. Azerbaijan withdrew in 1992. The organization maintains some elements of the economic, military and political coordination that existed within the former USSR, although it has no charter or constitution.

Commune of Paris (15 March–26 May 1871), a radical socialist administration set up in Paris in the aftermath of the FRANCO-PRUSSIAN WAR. After the fall of Paris, peace terms were accepted by the recently elected royalist-dominated National Assembly of Adolphe THIERS. These were bitterly opposed by the Parisian left, which favoured a continuation of the war with Prussia and a return to the principles of the First Republic. Troops sent by the French government to disarm the National Guard were met by fierce local resistance. The Parisians set up a city administration which they called the Commune – a reference to the JACOBIN Commune of 1793. The city fell to government troops after street fighting (21–28 May) which led to the deaths of 20,000 people.

communism, a political ideology – perhaps the most influential of the 20th century – aiming at the overthrow of CAPITALISM, the ownership by the community of the means of production and subsistence, and the creation of a classless society. The primary source of the social and economic doctrine of communism is the COMMUNIST MANIFESTO (1848) written by MARX and ENGELS. Marx's theories, adapted by LENIN as MARXISM-LENINISM, were the guiding force behind the RUSSIAN REVOLUTIONS of 1917, and the basis of the political system in the SOVIET UNION from 1917 to 1985. The ideas of Marx and Lenin were adapted to Chinese conditions by MAO ZEDONG.

Communist Manifesto, a key document of modern SOCIALISM and COMMUNISM, written by MARX and ENGELS and published in 1848.

Comoros, a republic comprising an archipelago between Africa and Madagascar. The four Comoran islands became a French colony in 1912. In a referendum in 1974, three islands voted unilaterally to become independent. The fourth island, Mayotte, voted against independence, and remains under French rule. From 1978 to 1990 the republic was an Islamic single-party state. Multi-party rule was restored in 1990.

Compromise of 1850, a compromise between the Northern and Southern states of the USA on the slavery issue. Promoted by Henry CLAY, it provided for California's admission to the Union as a free state and for a referendum on the slavery question in New Mexico and Utah.

concentration camp, a guarded prison camp for non-military (usually political) prisoners. Concentration camps were first used by the British for the internment of Boer families during the Second BOER WAR, but the most notorious were those established in Germany by the Nazis after 1933 for the detention and persecution of their political opponents. The HOLOCAUST saw the setting up of a number of vast extermination camps in E Europe – most notably AUSCHWITZ, Belzec, Chelmno, Majdanek, Sobibor and Treblinka – where some 6 million Jews were murdered.

Condé, a French princely family, the junior branch of the house of BOURBON. The name originated with Louis I of Bourbon (1530–69), a Huguenot leader in the FRENCH WARS OF RELIGION. His great-grandson, Louis II of Bourbon (1621–86), known as the 'Great Condé', won notable victories at Rocroi and Lens in the THIRTY YEARS WAR, and fought first for Louis XIV, then against him, in the FRONDES. A royalist 'army of émigrés', commanded (1796–9) by Louis Antoine Henri de Bourbon-Condé, duc d'Enghien (1772–1804), fought against French Revolutionary forces in Europe from 1793 to 1801.

condottiere, the name given to leaders of bands of mercenaries in the medieval period. Italian city-states were particularly reliant on hired troops to fight their wars. By the 15th century several *condottiere* had ambitions of their own and some became rulers of small territories in central Italy. Francesco SFORZA, for instance, became duke of MILAN.

Confederacy, the 11 Southern states of the USA (Alabama, Arkansas, Florida, Georgia, Louisiana, Mississippi, North Carolina, South Carolina, Tennessee, Texas and Virginia) that seceded from the Union (1860–1). They were reincorporated into the USA after their defeat by the Union in the AMERICAN CIVIL WAR.

Confederate States of America, see CONFEDERACY.

Confederation of the Rhine, an association of German states with a French constitution and Napoleonic legal system established in W Germany by Napoleon in 1806 as a pro-French buffer state. The Confederation failed to survive the withdrawal of the French after Napoleon's defeat at LEIPZIG in 1813. See map, p. 29.

Conference on Security and Cooperation in Europe (CSCE), an international conference established in 1975 under the Final Act of a security conference held in Helsinki, Finland, in 1975. In the Charter of Paris, which officially ended the COLD WAR (November 1990), the 34 member-states affirmed 'a commitment to settle disputes by peaceful means' and 'a common adherence to democratic values and to human rights and fundamental freedoms'.

Confucius, see KONGFUZI.

Congo, a republic of W central Africa. Portuguese slave traders were active in the region from the 15th century. In the 1880s, the kingdom of the Teke people came under French protection, and in 1905 the region became the colony of Middle Congo. Independence was gained in 1960. A Marxist-Leninist state was established in 1963, but a multi-party system was restored in 1991.

Congo Crisis, the political unrest in the former Belgian Congo (now ZAIRE) following independence from Belgium in 1960. Within weeks of independence the army had mutinied, Belgium colonists had fled and the mineral-rich province of Katanga had seceded (with Belgian and white mercenary backing) under the 'presidency' of Moise TSHOMBE. After an appeal from PM Patrice LUMUMBA, the UN despatched a 20,000-strong peace-keeping force which expelled the Belgians but failed to deal with the Katangan secession. Colonel MOBUTU seized power in a coup in September 1960, arresting Lumumba (who was later to be murdered). The Congo now dissolved into a confused and bloody civil war, which saw independent regimes set up at different times in Stanleyville and Kasai as well as Katanga. Katanga finally fell to UN forces in December 1962, but elsewhere chaos continued. Mobutu staged a second coup in November 1965 and imposed his authority by force.

Congress, Indian National, the main political party in INDIA, formed in 1885. In 1907 divisions emerged with a temporary split between moderates under G.K. Gokhale and militants led by B.K. Tilak. After 1920, under leaders such as M.K. GANDHI and Jawaharlal NEHRU, Congress president from 1929, Congress acquired a more sophisticated administrative structure, a mass membership and embarked on a coordinated campaign for Indian independence. Congress negotiated with Britain for Indian independence in 1945–7, Nehru becoming the first PM of independent India in 1947. The party continued to dominate Indian politics under Indira GANDHI and her son Rajiv. Indira Gandhi led a splinter group Congress I in 1978 and it remained the dominant element after the party divisions were healed.

Congress of the USA, the supreme legislative assembly of the USA. Originating as a unicameral body during the American War of INDEPENDENCE, the Congress became a two-chamber legislature after the ratification of the US Constitution (1788) – the SENATE (or upper house) comprising two delegates from each state, the HOUSE OF REPRESENTATIVES (or lower chamber) made up of Congressmen elected on the basis of a state's population strength.

Connaught (Connacht), a former kingdom of W Ireland whose rulers were kings of Ireland in the 12th century. Connaught's independence was extinguished from the 13th century.

Connolly, James (1868–1916), Irish Marxist trade unionist who was, with Joseph Plunkett, the principal architect of the EASTER RISING (1916). He was captured and shot by the British.

conquistadores (from the Spanish *conquistar,* 'conquer'), the Spanish adventurers (notably CORTEZ and PIZARRO) who conquered the indigenous empires of Central and South America in the early 16th century, and laid the foundations of Spanish power there.

Conservative Party, a right-wing political party in Britain, descended from the TORY Party. Sir Robert PEEL'S Tamworth Manifesto of 1834 is considered to mark the beginning of the move from old-style Toryism to moderate reforming Conservatism, though the name Conservative was not formally adopted until later. The split over the repeal of the CORN LAWS kept the Conservatives out of power for much of the period 1846–73, but under DISRAELI they developed into a successful mass party, claiming to represent the 'national tradition'. After 1945 the party tended towards pragmatism in its policies, accepting essentially socialist concepts such as the WELFARE STATE and a measure of state intervention in the economy, but with the accession to the leadership of Margaret THATCHER (1975–90) it embraced a philosophy of economic liberalism and the free market. Electorally it has been the most successful British political party of the 20th century.

Constance, Council of (1414–17), a council of the Christian Church convened to address the problem of the HUSSITE heresy and the GREAT SCHISM.

Constantine ('the Great'; AD ?285–337), Roman emperor in the West (312–324), and sole emperor (324–337). With the Eastern Emperor Licinius, he issued the Edict of Milan (313) tolerating Christianity throughout the Empire. Constantine's personal attitude to Christianity is uncertain, since he endorsed pagan cults and was only baptized on his deathbed. He defeated and killed Licinius in 323 and the following year became sole emperor. In 330 he inaugurated a new capital at Byzantium which he called CONSTANTINOPLE.

Constantinople, a city in Turkey, standing on the BOSPHORUS between the Black Sea and the Mediterranean, and now known as Istanbul (see map, p. 16). It began life as the Greek city of Byzantium. It took its new name from the emperor CONSTANTINE in 330, who designed the city as a new Rome and capital of the Eastern Roman (later BYZANTINE) Empire. The city's massive walls defied sieges for centuries until the city fell briefly to the Franks (1204–61), and permanently to the OTTOMAN Turks (1453).

constitutional monarchy, a monarchy in which the power of the sovereign is restrained by institutional checks (for example by a written constitution), in contrast with ABSOLUTE monarchy in which royal authority is theoretically unlimited. The UK, Sweden and the Netherlands are present-day examples of constitutional monarchies.

Constitution of the USA, the written statement of the laws and principles by which the USA is governed, ratified in 1788. Its main provisions were a stronger central government divided into three branches – a president chosen by an electoral college; a federal judiciary; and a popularly elected HOUSE OF REPRESENTATIVES and a SENATE chosen by the state legislatures. While representation in the House was based on population, each state sent two delegates to the Senate. Congress was given full power to levy import duties and taxes. The BILL OF RIGHTS, intended to balance the power of central government, formed the first 10 amendments to the Constitution.

Consul, one of two annually elected officials who held the highest authority in the ROMAN REPUBLIC. Under the emperors their power became nominal.

Consulate (1799–1804), the regime, under the first consul NAPOLEON BONAPARTE, that ruled France from the dissolution of the DIRECTORY to Napoleon's coronation as emperor in 1804.

Continental Congress (1774–89), the assembly composed of representatives of the American colonies that first met in response to the COERCIVE ACTS in 1774. The second Continental Congress (1775–6) proclaimed the DECLARATION OF INDEPENDENCE and declared itself the provisional government of the USA.

Continental System, an embargo against the import of British goods to those parts of Europe under French Napoleonic rule, aimed at crippling Britain financially by ruining its lucrative export trade. The blockade created serious difficulties for Britain, including the inconclusive WAR OF 1812 with the USA. However, the System was not effective. Its unpopularity contributed to growing disillusionment with and resentment of French occupation in many parts of Europe.

Cook, Captain James (1729–79), British naval commander. Cook visited Tahiti on the first (1768–71) of three Pacific voyages. He also charted the New Zealand coasts and landed on the coast of Australia at BOTANY BAY. On his second voyage (1772–5) Cook revisited Tahiti, charted Easter Island, the Marquesas and Society Islands, the Friendly Islands (Tonga), and the New Hebrides (Vanuatu), and discovered New Caledonia and Norfolk Island. On his last voyage, in search of a NW passage from the Pacific to the Atlantic (1775–9), he discovered the Hawaiian Islands, but was killed in a skirmish with islanders on Hawaii on his return journey.

Coolidge, Calvin (1872–1933), US Republican politician, 30th president of the USA (1923–9). A vice-presidential nominee, he succeeded to the presidency on the death of HARDING and was a keen supporter of US business interests.

Cooperative Movement, trading and social organizations, established from the early 19th century, distributing profits to their membership. Influenced in Britain by Robert OWEN, and in France by Fourier, cooperatives in Europe have generally supported SOCIALIST parties.

Coptic Church, the Egyptian Church, which survived in Upper Egypt after the ARAB CONQUESTS and persists to this day, with a liturgy and numerous patristic writings in the ancient Coptic language.

Coral Sea, Battle of the (7/8 May 1942), a naval battle fought between Australian, US and Japanese forces in WORLD WAR II in which a Japanese invasion fleet approaching Port Moresby (Papua) was intercepted and turned back. See PACIFIC CAMPAIGNS.

Corinth, an ancient Greek city-state on the isthmus joining the Peloponnese to the mainland (see map, p. 11). Initially ruled by 'tyrants' and then as a moderate oligarchy, it was a powerful and prosperous state, usually allied to SPARTA. Its union with ARGOS in the 390s was short-lived. In 338 it was defeated, along with its allies ATHENS and THEBES, by PHILIP II of Macedon, who based at Corinth his organization for the domination of Greece (the 'League of Corinth').

Cornwallis, Charles (1738–1805), British soldier and politician who led British forces during the American War of INDEPENDENCE. His defeat at YORKTOWN led to the British surrender. He went on to serve as governor-general of India (1786–93 and 1805) and viceroy of Ireland (1798–1801).

Corn Laws, legislation passed in 1815 which aimed to protect British agriculture by banning the import of foreign grain until the home price had reached 80 shillings a quarter. Opposition to the Laws increased as prices were forced up. The effects of the IRISH FAMINE and the influence of the middle-class Anti-Corn Law League led to their repeal by PEEL'S government in 1846.

Cortez, Hernán (1485–1547), Spanish CONQUISTADOR and conqueror of Mexico. In 1519 he led a private expedition to Mexico, accompanied by 600 volunteers, and marched on the AZTEC capital of TENOCHTITLÁN. They were reluctantly received by the Aztec ruler MONTEZUMA, but the Aztecs revolted, forcing the Spaniards to retreat. Cortez returned and laid siege to Tenochtitlán the following year. On 21 August 1521 the Aztecs, already weakened by smallpox brought by the Spanish from Cuba, surrendered.

Cossacks, peasant-soldiers living chiefly in the Ukraine, originally renegade TARTARS employed by the grand dukes of Muscovy to guard their frontiers against the Crimean Tartars from the 15th century. By 1600 the term was also applied to Slavs who fled serfdom in Muscovy, Poland and Lithuania and settled in the Ukraine. Although used as troops by the tsars, they remained independent and troublesome until subjected to Russian rule by PETER I and CATHERINE II.

Costa Rica, a republic of CENTRAL AMERICA. Columbus reached Costa Rica in 1502. The area was under Spanish rule – as part of the captaincy-general of Guatemala – until 1821. Although it was part of the Central American Federation (1823–38), Costa Rica developed largely in isolation from its neighbours. Dominated by small farms, Costa Rica prospered, attracted European immigrants and developed a stable democracy. Following a brief civil war in 1948, the army was disbanded. Costa Rica has since adopted the role of peacemaker in Central America.

Côte d'Ivoire, a republic of W Africa (known in the English-speaking world as the Ivory Coast). In the 16th century, Europeans established posts in the area for trading in ivory and slaves. Colonized by France in the 19th century, the Ivory Coast became a relatively prosperous part of FRENCH WEST AFRICA. Independence was achieved in 1960 under the presidency of Félix HOUPHOUËT-BOIGNY, who kept close links with France in return for aid and military assistance until his death in 1993. After over a decade of single-party rule, multi-party elections were held in 1990, but the opposition parties made claims of electoral fraud. Houphouët-Boigny died in 1993.

Council of Europe, an association of mainly West European states. Created in May 1949, it aims to foster greater unity between member-states, and to safeguard their common heritage. It established the European Convention for the Protection of Human Rights in 1950. With 25 member-states it is the largest organization of the European democracies.

Council of Five Hundred, a representative body in ancient Athens established by CLEISTHENES (508–7 BC). The Council prepared business for the assembly and performed an increasing number of administrative activities.

Counter-Reformation, the revival of the Roman Catholic Church in response to the Protestant REFORMATION between the mid-16th and mid-17th centuries. The Council of TRENT (1545–63) was established to reform the Catholic Church from within, but made few concessions to PROTESTANT criticisms. A missionary effort to recover the areas lost to Protestantism was led by the JESUITS (the Society of Jesus), and the revival of Catholic spiritualism reactivated the SPANISH INQUISITION. The Counter-Reformation was ultimately dependent on the support of monarchs such as MARY I of England, who tried to recatholicize her kingdom, and PHILIP II of Spain, who sought to re-establish Catholicism by force. The religious tensions engendered by the Reformation and Counter-Reformation eventually erupted in the THIRTY YEARS WAR. The stalemate between Catholics and Protestants was effectively recognized by the Treaty of WESTPHALIA, which ended that conflict.

Courtrai, Battle of (11 July 1302), a battle in which the French cavalry of PHILIP IV was defeated by Flemish rebel infantry.

Cranmer, Thomas (1489–1555), English cleric and founding father of the ANGLICAN Church. As archbishop of Canterbury (1533–55), he helped mould the liturgy of the new Anglican Church, revising the Book of Common Prayer in 1552. He was tried for treason and burnt as a heretic following the accession of the Catholic MARY I.

Crassus, Marcus (112–53 BC), Roman politician. In 60 BC he formed the First TRIUMVIRATE with CAESAR and POMPEY, but his attempt to match their military achievements by a war against PARTHIA ended in disaster at Carrhae in Mesopotamia in 53 BC.

Crazy Horse (1849–1877), chief of the Oglala SIOUX Indians who tried to prevent white settlement of Sioux territory. He led Plains Indian forces in their successful assault on CUSTER'S troops at the battle of LITTLE BIG HORN (1876).

Crécy, Battle of (26 August 1346), a decisive English victory in the HUNDRED YEARS WAR, fought in N France. A smaller English army, led by EDWARD III and his son EDWARD, THE BLACK PRINCE, used its archers to shoot to pieces the ill-coordinated assaults of the French. Edward went on to take Calais the following year.

Cree, a native North American people, living as nomadic hunters S of Hudson Bay.

Creek (Muskogi), a native N American people, maize farmers living in the Alabama and Georgia flatlands. One of the 'Five Civilized Indian Nations', they were removed to Oklahoma in the 1830s. See also NORTH AMERICAN INDIANS.

Creole, a native-born descendant of Spanish or other European settlers in the West Indies or Latin America.

Crimean War (1854–6), a war fought on a peninsula in the Black Sea between Russia on one side and Britain, France, Turkey, Austria and Sardinia-Piedmont on the other. In 1853 Russia, having failed to gain equal rights with France in the Christian 'Holy Places' of Palestine, occupied the Danubian principalities of the Ottoman Empire. Turkey declared war on Russia, only to see her fleet destroyed in the Black Sea. Britain and France, concerned at the upset in the regional balance of power, also declared war on Russia and sent an Anglo-French expeditionary force to capture the Russian port and naval base of SEVASTOPOL. Following the battles of the ALMA and BALAKLAVA, the Russians retreated into the fortress of Sevastopol, which the Allies subjected to a gruelling 11-month siege. The war cost the lives of half a million men. On the Allied side thousands died of disease in the squalor of the barracks hospital in Scutari. The Russians finally evacuated Sevastopol in September 1855 and peace was concluded at the Congress of PARIS in 1856. See also RUSSO-TURKISH WARS.

Critias (c. 460–403 BC), leader of the THIRTY TYRANTS set up by the Spartans following their defeat of Athens in the PELOPONNESIAN WAR.

Croatia, a country of S central Europe. By the 10th century the Croat kingdom occupied most of modern Croatia. In 1102 Croatia passed to the Hungarian crown. After Slavonia was conquered by the Ottoman Turks (1526), the rump of Croatia came under the rule of the (Austrian) Habsburgs, who established a Serb military frontier zone (Krajina) against further Ottoman expansion. Dalmatia came under Venetian rule in the 15th century, was annexed by Napoleon I in 1808, and was ceded to Austria in 1815. Ragusa (Dubrovnik) was an independent city-state from the 9th century to 1808. The Croats strove to preserve their identity within Habsburg Hungary and attempted secession during the 1848–9 Hungarian revolt. By 1900 a Croat national revival looked increasingly to independent Serbia to create a South ('Yugo') Slav state. After World War I, when the Habsburg Empire was dissolved (1918), the Croats joined the Serbs, Slovenes and Montenegrins in the state that was to become YUGOSLAVIA in 1929. However, the Croats soon resented the highly centralized Serb-dominated kingdom. Following the German invasion (1941), the occupying Axis powers set up an 'independent' Croat puppet state that adopted anti-Serb policies. In 1945 Croatia was reintegrated into a federal Communist Yugoslav state by Marshal TITO, but after Tito's death (1980), the Yugoslav experiment faltered in economic and nationalist crises. Separatists came to power in Croatia in free elections (1990) and declared independence (June 1991). Serb insurgents, backed by the Yugoslav federal army, occupied 30% of Croatia including those areas with an ethnic Serb majority – Krajina and parts of Slavonia. The fierce Serb–Croat war came to an uneasy halt in 1992 after Croatian independence had gained widespread diplomatic recognition, and a UN peace-keeping force was agreed. Fighting in Krajina recommenced in 1993. By mid-1993 Croats also controlled about 20% of BOSNIA-HERZEGOVINA, where an embryo Croat state was effectively established.

Croesus, king of LYDIA (c. 560–546 BC). Famed for his wealth, Croesus extended his territory to include all the Greek cities on the coast of Asia Minor. In 546 BC Sardis, the capital of Lydia, was attacked and captured by CYRUS the Great.

Cro-Magnons, see HOMO SAPIENS SAPIENS.

Cromwell, Oliver (1599–1658), English general and statesman, Lord Protector of England (1653–8). A PURITAN country gentleman and opposition member of the LONG PARLIAMENT, he came to prominence as a military leader on the Parliamentary side in the ENGLISH CIVIL WAR, and signed CHARLES I'S death warrant. He managed the commanders of the NEW MODEL ARMY, crushed the LEVELLERS, and extended the authority of the COMMONWEALTH to Scotland and Ireland. In 1653 he expelled the RUMP Parliament and, as Lord Protector (see PROTECTORATE), effectively became a dictator. He refused Parliament's offer of the crown in 1657. He was succeeded as Lord Protector (1658–9) by his son Richard (1626–1712).

Cromwell, Thomas, Earl of Essex (1485–1540), English statesman. He became HENRY VIII'S chief adviser after WOLSEY'S downfall. A Protestant sympathizer, he played a leading part in Henry's breach with Rome and the Dissolution of the MONASTERIES, and also reformed the central administration. He was executed after losing favour.

Crow, a native North American people, living in the central Great Plains. They abandoned settled village life in the 18th century and became nomads dependent on hunting buffalo from horseback. See also NORTH AMERICAN INDIANS.

Crusader states, the short-lived Christian kingdoms established along the coastal strip of the Levant during the First CRUSADE. They comprised the Kingdom of JERUSALEM (taken by the Crusaders in 1099), and its three fiefdoms – the counties of Antioch, Tripoli and Edessa. The Turks took Edessa in 1144, and SALADIN recaptured Jerusalem in 1187.

Crusades, a series of expeditions between the 11th and 14th centuries to recover the Muslim-controlled holy places of Palestine for Christendom. The First Crusade (1096–9) was called by Pope URBAN II, ostensibly in response to Byzantine emperor ALEXIUS I'S request for help in fighting the SELJUK Turks. In 1096 several huge armies, prominent among whose leaders were GODFREY of Bouillon and BOHEMOND of Tarando, set out for the Holy Land. The Crusaders took JERUSALEM in 1099, massacring its Jewish and Muslim populations and establishing a handful of CRUSADER STATES along the coast of the Levant. The Second Crusade (1147–9) laid seige to Damascus, but was marred by the internal squabbling between the Crusader kingdoms and the Byzantines. Saladin's recapture of Jerusalem (1187) sparked off the Third Crusade (1189–92) during which only Acre and Joppa were recaptured. At Venetian instigation the Fourth Crusade was diverted to CONSTANTINOPLE, which was sacked by the Crusaders who established a short-lived LATIN EMPIRE (1204–60). Later crusades directed towards Egypt and N Africa were unsuccessful, though the peaceful Sixth Crusade (1228) brought about the temporary recovery of Jerusalem through diplomatic means (1228–44). During the 13th century the coast of Palestine and Syria was gradually lost to the MAMLUK sultans of Egypt. The crusaders lost their last base in the Holy Land with the fall of Acre in 1291. The misbegotten crusade of 1396 was crushed by the Ottoman sultan at NICOPOLIS on the Danube.

CSCE, see CONFERENCE ON SECURITY AND COOPERATION IN EUROPE.

Cuba, an island-republic in the Caribbean. Indian tribes inhabited Cuba when Columbus claimed the island for Spain (1492). Development was slow until the 18th century, when black slaves were imported to work the sugar plantations. The first war for independence (1868–78) was unsuccessful. The USA intervened in a second uprising (1895–98), forcing Spain to relinquish the island, but independence was not confirmed until after two periods of American administration (1899–1901 and 1906–9). Under a succession of corrupt governments, the majority of Cubans suffered abject poverty. In 1959, the dictatorship of Fulgencio BATISTA was overthrown by the guerrilla leader Fidel CASTRO, whose revolutionary movement merged with the Communist Party to remodel Cuba on Soviet lines. In 1961, US-backed Cuban exiles attempted to invade at the BAY OF PIGS, and relations with America deteriorated further in 1962 when the installation of Soviet missiles on Cuba almost led to world war (see CUBAN MISSILE CRISIS). Castro encouraged revolutionary movements throughout Latin America, and his troops bolstered Marxist governments in Africa. The upheavals in the USSR and Eastern Europe

(1989–91) left Cuba increasingly isolated as a hardline Marxist state.

Cuban Missile Crisis (1962), a COLD WAR crisis involving the USA and the USSR. In 1962 Cuba's Fidel CASTRO allowed the USSR to build missile bases on the island. The USA saw this as a direct threat to its security, and President KENNEDY told the Soviets to withdraw the missiles or face a nuclear attack. His brinkmanship succeeded, and the missiles were removed.

Cuéllar, Javier Pérez de, (1920–), Peruvian diplomat, Secretary-General of the United Nations (1982–91).

Culloden, Battle of (16 April 1746), the last pitched battle on British soil, fought E of Inverness, Scotland, in which the JACOBITE forces of CHARLES EDWARD STUART were defeated by an English army under the Duke of Cumberland.

Cultural Revolution (1966–1976), a mass movement in CHINA initiated by Communist Party Chairman MAO ZEDONG. It was aimed at purging Chinese Communism of supposedly reactionary elements, but was also an attempt by Mao to strengthen his own position. Militant students formed groups of RED GUARDS to attack the existing hierarchy of local and central party officials which they regarded as bourgeois, over-westernized and technocratic. Thousands died, and thousands more bureaucrats, artists and intellectuals were sent to work in the fields. Mao himself was fortunate to survive, having to turn to the army for support against the Red Guards when they went out of control. The power struggle that ensued between the militants and the army was still being played out when Mao died in 1976.

Curzon, George Nathaniel, 1st Marquis Curzon of Kedleston (1859–1925), British Conservative statesman, viceroy of India (1899–1905). He later served as foreign secretary under LLOYD GEORGE and Bonar LAW.

Cush, see NUBIA.

Custer, George Armstrong (1839–76), US soldier who served with Union forces during the AMERICAN CIVIL WAR and subsequently commanded troops on the western frontier. Flamboyant and arrogant, he led his men to disaster against the SIOUX Indians at the battle of the LITTLE BIG HORN in 1876.

Cyprus, an island-republic in the E Mediterranean. Greek settlements were established on Cyprus in the middle of the second millenium BC. The island was ruled by the Egyptians (from 323 BC) and was part of the Roman and Byzantine Empires. Captured by Crusaders (1191), Cyprus was an independent kingdom until 1489, when VENICE acquired the island. In 1571, the OTTOMAN Turks took Cyprus. British administration was established in 1878. During the 1950s, Greek Cypriots, led by Archbishop (later President) MAKARIOS III (1913–77), campaigned for ENOSIS (union with Greece). The Turkish Cypriots advocated partition, but following a terrorist campaign by the Greek Cypriot EOKA movement, a compromise was agreed. In 1960, Cyprus became an independent republic. Power was shared by the two communities, but the agreement broke down in 1963. UN forces intervened to stop intercommunal fighting. The Turkish Cypriots set up their own administration. When pro-Enosis officers staged a coup (1974), Turkey invaded the N. Cyprus was effectively partitioned. Over 200,000 Greek Cypriots were displaced from the N, into which settlers arrived from Turkey. Since then, UN forces have manned the 'Attila Line' between the Greek S and Turkish N. Attempts have been made to reunite Cyprus as a federal state.

Cyril, St (c. 827–69), Greek monk, missionary and Bible translator. With his brother St Methodius, he spread literacy and Christianity in Slavic lands. They were probably the inventors of the Cyrillic alphabet.

Cyrus II ('the Great'; d. 530 BC), the founder of the ACHAEMENID Persian Empire. Cyrus overthrew the rule of the MEDES in 549 BC when he defeated ASTYAGES. He conquered Lydia (546 BC) and BABYLON (539 BC) and created a Persian empire stretching from the Mediterranean to Central Asia. In Babylon he ruled according to local custom and repatriated foreign exiles, including the Jews of Jerusalem. Returning to Iran, he was killed in battle on the NE frontier.

Cyrus the Younger (d. 401 BC), Persian prince, the brother of ARTAXERXES II. He hired 10,000 Greek mercenaries to help him depose his brother and seize the throne, but was killed in battle at Cunaxa.

Czechoslovakia, a former republic in Central Europe from 1918 to 1993. See CZECH REPUBLIC and SLOVAKIA.

Czech Republic, a republic in Central Europe. See panel.

CZECH REPUBLIC

5th century: SLAVS first populated the region. **9th century:** A Moravian empire flourished. **11th century:** The Moravian empire was replaced by the kingdom of BOHEMIA. **14th century:** The greatest of the Czech kings, CHARLES IV, became Holy Roman Emperor; his support of Church reform eventually led to the HUSSITE rebellion. **1526:** Bohemia fell under HABSBURG rule, and SLOVAKIA was joined to Hungary. **1618:** The determination of the Catholic Habsburgs to control the mainly Protestant Czech nobility was a cause of the THIRTY YEARS WAR. **1620:** The Czechs were defeated at the Battle of WHITE MOUNTAIN, remaining under Austrian rule until 1918. **19th century:** Growth of Czech nationalism. **1918:** On the collapse of the AUSTRO-HUNGARIAN EMPIRE, the Czechs and Slovaks united in an independent state, CZECHOSLOVAKIA – largely due to the efforts of Tomáš MASARYK. **1938:** HITLER demanded that Germany be granted the SUDETENLAND; Czechoslovakia effectively dismembered by the MUNICH Agreement. **1939–45:** The Germans established a 'protectorate' of Bohemia and Moravia. **1945:** Czechoslovakian independence restored. **1948:** The Communists staged a takeover. **1968:** Party Secretary Alexander DUBČEK's attempts to introduce political reforms led to the invasion of Warsaw Pact troops in the PRAGUE SPRING. **1989:** The peaceful 'Velvet Revolution', led by the Civic Forum movement, forced the Communists to renounce their leading role. **1990:** Free multi-party elections were held. **1993:** SLOVAKIA seceded from Czechoslovakia.

Dacia, an ancient region N of the lower Danube, roughly corresponding to Romania (see map, p. 13). It was conquered by the Roman emperor TRAJAN (AD 101–6) and became a Roman province.

da Gama, Vasco (1469–1524), Portuguese navigator. Setting out from Portugal in 1497, da Gama followed a slightly different course to that of DIAS and reached Calicut on the southwest coast of India, returning home in 1499. The route from Portugal to the East was now confirmed. See map, p. 24.

Dáil Éirann (or Dáil), the lower house of the parliament of the Irish Republic.

daimyos (Japanese, 'great names'), the provincial barons who dominated Japan from the 10th to the 19th centuries. At their most powerful during the nominal rule of the ASHIKAGA family, their activity was strictly controlled by the TOKUGAWA shoganate.

Dakota Indians, see SIOUX.

Daladier, Edouard (1884–1970), French socialist politician, prime minister (1934 and 1938–40). With CHAMBERLAIN he negotiated the MUNICH AGREEMENT (1938), then took France into WORLD WAR II in September 1939.

Danegeld, a term generally used to refer to the individual tributes raised by ETHELRED II to pay off invading Viking armies. Strictly it refers to the 'army tax' levied 1012–51 to pay for the squadron of Danish ships maintained by the English government. The Norman kings revived the tax.

Danelaw, the name given to those parts of E and N England that experienced Scandinavian rule and settlement in the 9th and 10th centuries.

Danton, Georges (1759–94), French revolutionary leader and orator. He dominated the Committee of Public Safety created by the CONVENTION, and was minister of justice (1792–4). His opposition to the TERROR led to his downfall and execution.

Danzig, the German name for the Polish city of Gdansk, a free city under the auspices of the LEAGUE OF NATIONS from 1919 to 1939.

Daoism or Taoism, a Chinese religious and philosophical system, traditionally set out by Lao Zi in the 4th century BC. Tao – 'the Way' – emphasized the individual's pursuit of the good life and the quiet acceptance of fate.

Dardanelles, the W end of the Bosphorus Straits, linking the Mediterranean to the Black Sea (see map, p. 36). The 1841 London Convention closed the Straits to warships in peacetime. In April 1915 Anglo-French forces landed at GALLIPOLI on its N edge in an unsuccessful attempt to seize the Straits. A new system established at the Paris Peace Conference placed the Straits under an international commission. The Montreux Commission of 1936 restored control of the Straits to Turkey.

Darius I ('the Great'; d. 486 BC), ACHAEMENID king of Persia (521–486 BC). He succeeded CAMBYSES II and spent the first years of his reign putting down rebellions in the empire, then campaigning in NW India. He fought unsuccessfully against the nomadic Scythians, N of the Black Sea, and was defeated by the Greeks at MARATHON in 490 BC. His reign saw the Achaemenid Empire reach its greatest extent, stretching from the Nile to the Indus. The empire was also strengthened by his administrative reforms, including the establishment of SATRAPS to rule the provinces, the reorganization of the army, an extensive road-building programme, and a new fleet. He was succeeded by his son XERXES I.

Darius III (d. 330 BC), the last Achaemenid king of Persia. He was defeated by ALEXANDER THE GREAT at ISSUS in 333 BC and again at GAUGAMELA the following year. After the defeat Darius fled but was eventually murdered by his own nobles.

Dark Ages, the period of European history from the 7th to the 10th centuries, supposed by the Renaissance HUMANISTS to be an age of barbarism.

David (d. c. 961 BC), king of Israel (c. 1000–c. 961 BC). A king of the House of JUDAH, he captured JERUSALEM from the Jebusites around 1005 BC and went on to defeat the Philistines. He was anointed at Hebron, but later moved the capital to Jerusalem. During his reign the kingdom of ISRAEL briefly became an empire dominating Syria and Palestine.

David I (c. 1082–1153), king of Scotland (1124–53). The youngest son of MALCOLM III, he welcomed Englishmen and Frenchmen to his court and adopted a consciously 'modernizing' policy. While he controlled NORTHUMBRIA and Cumbria (1139–53) he was able to face the kings of England on equal terms.

David, St (c. 520–c. 601), the patron saint of Wales. He was revered as a founder of monasteries and for his austere lifestyle.

Davis, Jefferson (1808–89), US politician. He was elected president of the CONFEDERACY in 1861. During the AMERICAN CIVIL WAR he became increasingly unpopular in the South, and narrowly escaped execution for treason when hostilities ended in 1865.

Dawes Plan (1924), a plan for German reparations payments after WORLD WAR I devised by the US financier Charles G. Dawes. The initial reparations debt after the war proved too large a burden for an economically crippled Germany. The Dawes Plan introduced a more manageable schedule of annual payments. It also established a new Reichsmark and raised a substantial loan for Germany. The economic problems in Germany, however, proved too difficult to surmount, and the Dawes Plan was replaced with the YOUNG PLAN.

Dayan, Moshe (1915–81), Israeli soldier and politician, recognizable by his black eye-patch. Active in the campaign against the British in PALESTINE in the 1940s, he led Israeli forces against Egypt in 1956 and was Minister of Defence during the SIX DAY WAR (1967).

D-Day (6 June 1944), the first day of the Allied invasion of Western Europe in WORLD WAR II. See NORMANDY LANDINGS.

Dead Sea Scrolls, a collection of ancient religious texts discovered between 1947 and 1956 in desert caves near the Dead Sea in Israel. They include fragments of nearly every book in the Old Testament and a complete text of the Book of Isaiah.

Decembrists, an early 19th-century Russian revolutionary movement, seeking emancipation of the serfs and a constitutional monarchy. In 1825, when Tsar ALEXANDER I died, a group of officers – known as 'Decembrists' from the date of their revolt – tried unsuccessfully to use the army to force the new tsar, NICHOLAS I, to introduce reforms. Their rebellion was quickly and ruthlessly suppressed.

Declaration of Independence (4 July 1776), the declaration of independence from Great Britain by the 13 colonies of North America, drafted by Thomas JEFFERSON and others. The document, approved by the CONTINENTAL CONGRESS, also announced the potentially revolutionary new doctrine: 'that all men are created equal, that they are endowed by their Creator with certain unalienable rights, that among these are life, liberty and the pursuit of happiness'.

Defence of the Realm Acts (DORA; 1914, 1915 and 1916), legislation passed by the British Parliament in WORLD WAR I to control all aspects of the war effort. It became illegal for war-workers to move away from their place of employment and left-wing activists on Clydeside were forcibly transferred to other parts of the country. The government also placed restrictions on opening hours in public houses and introduced the concept of 'summer time'. Restrictions on press reporting and other forms of censorship were also introduced.

de Gasperi, Alcide (1881–1954), Italian statesman and co-founder of the Italian CHRISTIAN DEMOCRATIC Party, prime minister (1945–53).

de Gaulle, Charles (1890–1970), French general and statesman. The leader of the FREE FRENCH during WORLD WAR II, he was head of the provisional government (1944–6), but resigned over disagreements on the constitution. He re-entered politics in 1958 during the Algerian Crisis, and became president of the Fifth Republic (see FRANCE) in 1959. He granted independence to ALGERIA, led France in the direction of an independent foreign policy, and resisted Britain's entry into the EEC (now the EC). His reputation was shaken by the student rebellions of 1968 and he resigned in 1969.

de Klerk, Fredrik Willem (1936–), South African president (1989–94). Succeeding P.W. BOTHA, he negotiated peace with the AFRICAN NATIONAL CONGRESS, released Nelson MANDELA from prison, and initiated constitutional negotiations for a non-racial 'New South Africa'. He was succeeded as president by Nelson Mandela following the ANC's victory in South Africa's first democratic elections in April 1994.

Delaware Indians, a native North American people, living as maize farmers in the Eastern Woodlands (New Jersey and adjoining areas). They were forced W in the early 18th century following early contact with European settlers. See also NORTH AMERICAN INDIANS.

Delhi Sultanate (1206–1526), the dominant N Indian Muslim kingdom between the 13th and 16th centuries. Centred on Delhi, it was ruled by a succession of dynasties, including the MAMLUKS and the TUGHLUQS. It was overthrown by BABUR of Kabul, the founder of the MOGUL dynasty, in 1526.

Delian League, an anti-Persian alliance of the 5th century BC under Athenian leadership from 478. Cities in the League were forced to pay tribute to ATHENS, either in money or ships, and any who tried to leave were forcibly brought into line. Athens also increasingly interfered in the politics and economies of its allies. By the 440s the League had virtually become an Athenian empire.

Delphic oracle, the most important ORACLE in ancient Greece. The god Apollo supposedly spoke through the voice of his priestess, the Pythia, at Delphi. Representatives of Greek city-states often came with questions, and the oracle seems to have ratified many overseas colonizing ventures.

deme, a geographical unit of local government in ancient Athens and its surroundings, created by CLEISTHENES. Demes were local villages or divisions of the city – which were run by an open assembly and annually elected officers.

Democratic Party, US political party dating back to the late 18th century when it was known as the Democratic-Republican Party. A vehicle for expansionist and laissez-faire sentiment during the presidency of Andrew JACKSON, it was the dominant political force in the republic before the AMERICAN CIVIL WAR. Traditionally racist and southern-dominated, it emerged as a powerful liberal force in American politics during the 1930s, largely through the growth of its ethnically diverse northern constituency. The party reached its zenith under the guidance of F.D. ROOSEVELT, but its strength as a national force was eroded by the defection of southern whites and blue-collar workers in the 1960s and 1970s. The election of President CLINTON in 1992 brought a Democrat to the White House after 12 years of Republican control.

Demosthenes (c. 383–322 BC), Athenian statesman and orator. He inspired resistance to PHILIP II of Macedon, and was forced to commit suicide after the unsuccessful Athenian revolt following the death of ALEXANDER THE GREAT.

Deng Xiaoping (1904–), Chinese Communist statesman. A supporter of MAO ZEDONG, he took part in the LONG MARCH (1934–5) and was General Secretary of the Chinese Communist Party (1956–67). He was denounced during the CULTURAL REVOLUTION (1967), but reinstated in 1973. Denounced for a second time in 1976, he was reinstated in 1977, and remains effective leader of China despite not holding an official government post. Although he has encouraged modernization, trade and relations with the international community, he was responsible for the violent repression of the pro-democracy demonstration at TIANANMEN SQUARE in 1989.

Denmark, a kingdom of Western Europe. See panel, p. 114.

Depression, the Great, the world economic crisis (1929–33) following the WALL STREET CRASH, the roots of which lay in the economic disruption caused by World War I and its aftermath. The apparent prosperity of the 1920s was terminated on 24 October 1929, when confidence in the New York Stock Exchange collapsed, leading to panic selling of shares. The Crash threw first the US and then the world economy into recession. As world trade suffered, unemployment rose steeply, leading to poverty, homelessness and misery for millions. The Depression placed enormous strains on democratic political systems. The British Labour government of Ramsay MACDONALD resigned in 1931 after it failed to agree a cut in public spending. The NEW DEAL policies of President F.D.ROOSEVELT helped tackle some of the social problems of the Depression in the USA. However, the economic difficulties in Germany allowed HITLER to come to power.

DENMARK

8th–10th centuries: The Danes participated in the VIKING invasions. **10th century:** Denmark became a distinct state. **1014–35:** Under the rule of CNUT Denmark was part of a short-lived Anglo-Danish empire. **12th–14th centuries:** Denmark was beset by territorial wars and dynastic difficulties. **1380:** Denmark acquired Norway. **1397:** Under the KALMAR Agreement Denmark, Norway and Sweden were united under one sovereign – Queen Margrethe I. **1534–6:** Lutheranism became the state religion after the Roman Catholic faction was defeated in a civil war. **1583:** Sweden reasserted its independence. **1626:** The Danes were defeated by imperial forces in the THIRTY YEARS WAR. **1660:** A decline in Swedish power allowed Denmark to reassert itself. **18th century:** Colonial ventures brought prosperity. **1815:** Denmark lost Norway to Sweden. **1864:** After a short war with Prussia and Austria (1864), Denmark surrendered the duchies of SCHLESWIG and HOLSTEIN (N Schleswig was returned to Denmark in 1920). **20th century:** Denmark's last colonial possessions were either sold (Virgin Islands) or given independence (Iceland) or autonomy (GREENLAND). **1940–5:** The country was occupied by Nazi Germany. **1973:** Denmark joined the EUROPEAN COMMUNITY.

Derby, Edward Stanley, 14th Earl of (1799–1869), British Conservative statesman, prime minister (1852, 1858–9 and 1866–8). The REFORM ACT of 1867 was carried in his last premiership.

Desai, Morarji (1896–), Indian statesman, prime minister (1977–9). He led the newly created Janata party to victory against Indira GANDHI in 1977.

desegregation, the process by which legal barriers to black equality in the USA (e.g. separate schools and transportation facilities) were broken down by civil rights activists and federal policymakers after World War II. Although de jure segregation in the southern states was outlawed by the CIVIL RIGHTS ACT of 1964, de facto segregation (i.e. separate housing and schooling produced by economic and social factors) remains a significant issue in American politics.

Desmoulins, Camille (1760–94), French journalist and revolutionary. A supporter of DANTON and his more moderate policies during the Reign of TERROR, he was executed in April 1794.

Dessalines, Jean Jacques (1758–1806), black emperor of HAITI (1804–6). He achieved the final declaration of Haiti's independence in 1803.

détente (French, 'relaxation'), the term applied to the reduction in COLD WAR tension between the USSR and the USA during the 1970s. Attempts to achieve a measure of 'peaceful coexistence' began in 1968 during the VIETNAM WAR peace talks. President NIXON re-established friendly relations between the USA and Communist China, which had broken with the USSR in the 1950s. The Sino–US rapprochement spurred the USSR to improve its relations with the USA. The results of détente included the SALT and ABM agreements in the 1970s at which the USA and the USSR agreed to limitations in the nuclear arms race. The Soviet invasion of AFGHANISTAN in 1979 was a major setback to détente. East–West relations became extremely frosty, with both sides accelerating the arms race. However, the liberalizing reforms and arms-control initiatives of Mikhail GORBACHOV in the USSR radically changed the international climate, paving the way for the formal end of the Cold War in 1990.

de Valera, Eamon (1882–1975), Irish statesman, prime minister (1932–48, 1951–4 and 1957–9), president (1959–73). He was sentenced to death by the British for his part in the EASTER RISING (1916), but later reprieved. He fought for Irish independence from Britain in the guerrilla war of 1919–21 as a member of the IRISH REPUBLICAN ARMY. An opponent of the Anglo-Irish Treaty which founded the Irish Free State (1921), he led his republicans to defeat in the Irish Civil War. He founded FÍANNA FÁIL in 1926 and won the 1932 election, after which he gradually severed Ireland's remaining constitutional links with Britain.

Devolution, War of (1667–8), one of the wars of LOUIS XIV. When Louis invaded the Spanish Netherlands, invoking a dubious legal claim that it was part of his wife's inheritance, England, the United Provinces and Sweden formed a defensive alliance, obliging Louis to retreat. In the Treaty of Aix-La-Chapelle (1668) Louis was forced to restore the land he had seized, and retained only a small number of towns in the Spanish Low Countries.

Dias, Bartholemeu (?1450–1500), Portuguese explorer. In 1488 he rounded the Cape of Good Hope and reported that a sea route to the spices and other wealth of the East now lay open. See map, p. 24.

Diaspora, the 'dispersal' of the 10 tribes of Israel in the aftermath of the unsuccessful Jewish revolt against the Romans in AD 135. Since 1948, the same word has sometimes been used to denote the movement of Palestinians from the new state of ISRAEL.

Díaz, Porfirio (1830–1915), dictator who governed MEXICO for all but four years (1880–4) between 1876 and 1910. The benefits of his programme of modernization through industrialization and foreign investment were unevenly distributed. Discontent at his dictatorial methods led to the outbreak of the MEXICAN REVOLUTION in 1910.

dictator, 1. under the Roman Republic, a single leader exercising supreme power appointed for a maximum of six months during an emergency. **2.** in modern times, any authoritarian ruler unconstrained by legal or constitutional restrictions, for example HITLER, STALIN and MUSSOLINI.

Dien Bien Phu, Battle of (1954), a battle in which VIET MINH forces inflicted a major defeat on the French in the FRENCH INDOCHINA WAR. The Viet Minh laid siege to French airborne forces in the isolated valley of Dien Bien Phu and after 55 days forced a French surrender (May 1954). The French defeat helped secure independence for LAOS, CAMBODIA and VIETNAM.

Dieppe Raid (19 August 1942), a failed assault on German installations in Normandy by Anglo-Canadian forces in WORLD WAR II, which led to heavy Canadian casualties.

diet, the name formerly given to the representative assemblies of a number of European states. In the HOLY ROMAN EMPIRE the diet was a meeting of representatives of the German states of the Empire with the emperor himself; it was abolished in 1806. In the 19th century a federal diet was set up in Frankfurt under the GERMAN CONFEDERATION.

Diocletian (AD 245–316), Roman emperor (284–305). After a period of decline Diocletian restored political stability and brought about an upturn in the economy. He introduced important military, financial and administrative reforms and successfully put down rebellions in the Empire, including those in Britain and Egypt. Recognizing that he could not rule the Empire on his own, he chose a colleague, Maximian, to manage the western provinces, while he took charge of the east. Diocletian and Maximian (the Augusti) each took on an assistant (Caesar), establishing the TETRARCHY ('rule of four'). Diocletian abdicated in 305.

Directory, French (1795–9), the regime that ruled France from the end of the JACOBIN Convention to the CONSULATE. It followed the end of the Reign of TERROR, and was overthrown by the coup of 18 Brumaire (8 November).

Disraeli, Benjamin, 1st Earl of Beaconsfield (1804–81), British Conservative politician and novelist, born the son of a Spanish Jew but baptized a Christian. As a flamboyant young MP his romantic Toryism was expressed through leadership of the Young England group and in political novels. Disraeli served as chancellor of the exchequer (1852, 1858–9, 1866–8) under Lord DERBY and was largely responsible for the Second REFORM ACT (1867). 'Dizzy' held the premiership briefly in 1868, then again from 1874 to 1880, when his main interest was in foreign affairs, making Queen VICTORIA Empress of India (1876) and achieving some diplomatic success at the Congress of BERLIN (1878).

Dissolution of the Monasteries, see MONASTERIES.

Djibouti, a republic in E Africa. The area became the colony of French Somaliland in 1888. In 1977 the territory became the Republic of Djibouti, but the new state has suffered ethnic unrest and drought.

dollar diplomacy, a US foreign policy of the early 20th century, aiming to serve US business interests abroad. The policy began under the presidency of William TAFT, who gained federal action to secure investments and loans to finance the building of railways in China in 1909.

Dollfuss, Engelbert (1892–1934), Austrian chancellor (1932–4). His period in office was unsettled by his antagonism towards both socialists and nationalists. His alienation of the working class deprived him of support against the growing power of the NAZIS, who assassinated him in July 1934.

Domesday Book (1086–7), a record of the possessions of all major landowners in England and their economic resources. The Book provides a unique insight into the society and economy of 11th-century England and the almost complete replacement of Anglo-Saxon by Norman land-holders. See NORMAN CONQUEST.

Dominicans, an order of friars founded by St Dominic (1170–1221). Like the FRANCISCANS, the Dominicans lived a life of devout poverty, living and preaching among the people. Originally formed to preach against heresy, the Dominicans enjoyed great popularity in Europe in the 13th century.

Dominican Republic, a republic occupying the E part of HISPANIOLA in the Caribbean. Hispaniola was discovered in 1492 by Christopher COLUMBUS, and in 1795 Spain ceded the island to France. Returned to Spanish rule in 1809, the E declared independence as the Dominican Republic in 1821, but was annexed by Haiti (1822–44). The 19th century witnessed a succession of tyrants, and by 1900 the republic was bankrupt and in chaos. The USA intervened between 1916 and 1924, and Rafael TRUJILLO (1891–1961) became president in 1930, ruthlessly suppressing opposition. Civil war in 1965 ended after intervention by US and Latin American troops. Since then, an infant democracy has faced grave economic problems.

Dominion, the name given to a territory within the BRITISH EMPIRE which, while owing allegiance to the crown, had been granted a measure of self-government.

Domitian (AD 51–96), the last Roman emperor (81–96) of the Flavian dynasty and younger son of VESPASIAN. His reign of terror ended with his assassination.

Donatism, a breakaway movement of fanatical Christians in North Africa in the 4th century. Although repeatedly condemned by Rome, the Donatist Church survived until the end of the 6th century.

Dönitz, Karl (1891–1980), German admiral, commander-in-chief of the German navy (1943–5). As head of state after HITLER'S death he surrendered to the ALLIES. He was sentenced to 10 years' imprisonment for war crimes at the NUREMBERG TRIALS.

Don Pacifico affair (1847), an international incident between Greece and Britain. Don Pacifico – a Portuguese Jew – and his family were attacked by an angry crowd in Athens. He had been born in Gibraltar and claimed British citizenship before demanding compensation from the Greek government. The British foreign minister, PALMERSTON, took up his case in 1850, insisting on Pacifico's rights as a British subject. Palmerston reinforced his claims for compensation for Pacifico by blockading Greece with the British fleet. His actions nearly led to war with France.

Dorians, one of the main cultural and linguistic groupings of the ancient Greeks. The Doric dialect was mainly spoken in the S and E of the Peloponnese, in small parts of mainland Greece, and in Crete, Rhodes and the SW coast of Asia Minor (Turkey). The Greeks believed that the 'Dorians' originally invaded from the N, and destroyed what we call MYCENAEAN civilization; it is not certain how much truth there is in this account. See also AEOLIANS, IONIANS.

Dowding, Hugh Caswell Tremenheere, 1st Baron (1882–1970), British air chief marshal. A pilot in World War I, he rose through the ranks of the RAF to become commander-in-chief of Fighter Command in 1936, contributing much to British success in the Battle of BRITAIN in 1940.

Draco, the first lawgiver of ancient Athens. In 621/620 BC he produced a set of written laws, which were afterwards thought to have been over-severe ('Draconian'), and which, except for the laws on homicide, were replaced in 594/593 by the laws of SOLON.

Drake, Sir Francis (1540–96), English sailor and pirate. He was the first Englishman to sail round the world (1577–80), combining exploration with profitable attacks on Spanish shipping and settlements in the New World. He was one of the commanders of the English naval force that defeated the SPANISH ARMADA.

Dravidians, the people originally inhabiting the Indian subcontinent. They were pushed S by the arrival of the ARYANS in the period 2000–1200 BC. The Aryans imposed themselves on the native Dravidians, and the resulting amalgam became the majority HINDU society of India.

Dreadnought, a class of heavily armed battleship first launched by Britain in 1906. The Germans built their own class of dreadnoughts, fuelling the naval rivalry between the two countries in the years before World War I.

Dresden raids (13/14 February 1945), heavy bombing raids by British and US planes on the German city of Dresden during WORLD WAR II. The action, which almost totally destroyed the beautiful baroque city and killed 135,000 people, has come under increasing criticism.

Dreyfus, Alfred (1859–1935), French army officer of Jewish parentage. He was falsely accused of passing secrets to the Germans in 1894 and sentenced to life imprisonment on Devil's Island. Fresh evidence presented in 1896 suggested his innocence, but ANTI-SEMITISM within the French army prevented a retrial. The ensuing controversy pitted nationalists, militarists and royalists against republicans and socialists. Dreyfus was finally pardoned in 1906.

Druids, a priestly order of the CELTS. Knowledge of the Druids comes largely from the critical accounts of Roman authors, who claimed that they exercised judicial and priestly functions. Their religion was stamped out by the Romans, who feared that it could become a focus for resistance to Roman rule.

Druze, an unorthodox Muslim sect, centred chiefly in LEBANON. Its followers practise a secret faith, open to men only. Although they revere the Prophet MUHAMMAD, they do not observe Ramadan or go on pilgrimage to MECCA. Druze militias occupied parts of Lebanon during the civil war of the 1970s and 80s.

Dual Alliance (1879), an alliance between Germany and Austria-Hungary, aimed at mutual protection against France and Russia respectively. Italy joined in 1882 to produce the TRIPLE ALLIANCE.

Dubček, Alexander (1921–92), Czechoslovak statesman. He became leader of the Communist Party in 1968 and launched the reforms of the PRAGUE SPRING. Removed after the Soviet invasion, he became a clerk in a lumber yard, but was to play a crucial role in the 1989 revolution that removed the Communists from power.

Dulles, John Foster (1888–1959), US Republican politician and diplomat. As President EISENHOWER'S anti-Communist secretary of state (1953–9), he was influential in formulating US foreign policy during the COLD WAR.

Duma, an elected assembly established by NICHOLAS II of Russia after the RUSSIAN REVOLUTION of 1905. Four Dumas met between 1905 and 1917, when the institution was abolished.

Dumbarton Oaks Conference (1944), an international conference held in Washington, DC, at which proposals for the foundation of the UNITED NATIONS were drawn up by representatives from the USA, UK, China and the USSR.

Dunkirk evacuation (June 1940), the rescue by sea of British and French troops from the N French port of Dunkirk during WORLD WAR II. German forces advancing into N France cut off 330,000 British and French troops, who were forced to withdraw onto warships and small boats to escape.

Dutch East India Company, a chartered company founded in 1602 by the STATES GENERAL of the DUTCH REPUBLIC. It broke the Portuguese monopoly of trade with the East Indies and then conquered most of Portugal's East Indian and African trading empire. By the 18th century it had become a large colonial power – but at the expense of its trading competitiveness. It was liquidated in 1799 and its possessions taken over by the Dutch state.

Dutch Republic, the popular name for the United Provinces of the Netherlands, a small, predominantly Calvinist state that occupied most of the area of the present-day NETHERLANDS and lasted from 1579 to 1795 (see map, p. 25). The Dutch Republic first emerged during the DUTCH REVOLTS when the northern provinces of the Netherlands formed the Union of Utrecht (1579), declaring their independence from Spain two years later. The Republic was recognized by Spain as an independent state at the Peace of WESTPHALIA (1648). In the 17th century the Dutch Republic became Europe's leading commercial power and played an important international role. The Low Countries were well placed to act as a channel of trade between the Baltic and the rest of Europe, and the DUTCH EAST INDIA COMPANY built up a colonial trading empire in Africa and the East Indies. The Republic fought off England's attempts to destroy their European and colonial trade during the ANGLO-DUTCH WARS. Under WILLIAM III OF ORANGE the Dutch played a leading role in the wars against the France of LOUIS XIV. The Republic went into economic and political decline in the 18th century, and collapsed in 1795 after the invasion of French Revolutionary forces in 1794–5.

Dutch Revolts (1568–1648), a series of rebellions by the Dutch provinces against Spanish rule, provoked by the reforming and strongly Catholic policies of PHILIP II of Spain. One of Philip's most prominent opponents was the Lutheran prince of Orange, WILLIAM THE SILENT. With such opposition it became difficult for Philip to enforce anti-heresy laws, and after the widespread destruction of images in churches in 1567, he ordered Spanish troops to the Low Countries to restore order. Their commander, the Duke of ALBA, began a notoriously brutal reign of terror. In 1572 the Sea Beggars – a well-organized force of privateers licensed by William the Silent – seized control of most of the towns of Zeeland and Holland. They wrested power from the royalists and imposed a Calvinist reformation. The sack of Antwerp by unpaid Spanish troops in 1576 led to the temporary union of the whole Netherlands, the southern provinces making their own peace with Holland and Zeeland (the Pacification of Ghent) and obliging Philip to withdraw his troops from the Low Countries in 1577. Following disturbances in the south, the Catholic nobles of the southern provinces still loyal to Philip welcomed the Spaniards back to restore order. Philip pledged to respect their privileges in the Union of Arras (1579) and incorporated the provinces of Maas and Lek into the Spanish empire. The northern provinces formed their own league, the Union of Utrecht, in 1579, and declared their independence of Spain in 1581. Philip's forces renewed their offensive in the 1580s and the rebels began to lose ground. The Dutch were saved from defeat by supplies of men and money from England (from 1585), and the diversion of Spanish efforts against England. Using new tactics, Count Maurice of Nassau cleared the Spaniards from the northern provinces. An exhausted Spain was unable to take advantage of peace with France (1598) and England (1605) to crush the Dutch. In 1609 both sides agreed a truce, but war was resumed in 1621. Fighting on many front in the THIRTY YEARS WAR, Spain again could not defeat the Dutch. At the Peace of WESTPHALIA in 1648 Spain recognized the independence of the seven United Provinces, popularly known as the DUTCH REPUBLIC.

Duvalier, François (1907–71), dictator of HAITI (1957–71), known as 'Papa Doc'. His cruel and repressive regime was based on the Tontons Macoutes, a police and spy organization. His son Jean-Claude Duvalier, or 'Baby Doc' (1951–), was president from 1971 until his overthrow in 1986.

Eastern Front campaigns, the series of campaigns fought in Eastern Europe during WORLD WAR II. In September 1939, following the NAZI–SOVIET PACT, Poland was invaded by Germany from the W and by the USSR from the E, and had collapsed by the end of the month. The Finns were defeated by the Red Army in the FINNISH–RUSSIAN WAR (1939–40). Despite the Nazi–Soviet Pact, it was inevitable that traditional enmity and ideological differences between Germany and the USSR would lead to war. On 22 June 1941 Hitler invaded the Soviet Union (Operation Barbarossa). By the end of 1941 a three-pronged German attack had overrun Byelorussia and much of the Ukraine, and laid siege to LENINGRAD. However, bad weather conditions and stiff Soviet resistance stalled the German drive on Moscow. In 1942 Hitler shifted German forces S to take oilfields in the Caucasus. The German Sixth Army reached STALINGRAD in late August, but was forced to surrender January 1943 after being trapped in the city by a Soviet counterattack masterminded by ZHUKOV. German defeat in the massive tank battle of KURSK confirmed that the tide had turned. By the end of 1943 the Soviets had reached the Dnieper, liberated Kiev and trapped an entire German army in the Crimea. Between January and May 1944 the Soviets relieved Leningrad, recaptured the Crimea and Odessa and re-entered Poland. Their advance continued through the rest of the year, thrusting through Byelorussia towards Warsaw in the N, and deep into the Balkans in the S. Romania and Bulgaria switched sides away from the crumbling Axis, while Yugoslavia, Albania and Greece were liberated by their own RESISTANCE fighters. Warsaw fell in January 1945, Budapest in February, and Vienna two months later. By now the Soviets were linking up with Allied armies approaching from the W. Berlin fell to the Soviets on 4 May, the war ending with Germany's surrender on 8 May. The war in the east cost the Soviet Union some 27 million dead.

Eastern Question, the name given to the complex series of struggles for control of the strategically important lands and seas in the Near East and the Balkans that lasted from the 18th to the early 20th centuries. At its root was the decline of the Turkish OTTOMAN Empire, and the rivalry of European powers – particularly Austria and Russia – seeking to benefit from its collapse, compounded by the emergent problem of BALKAN nationalism. The first crisis was the GREEK WAR OF INDEPENDENCE against the Turks, which finally led to Greek independence in 1830. In 1829, by the Treaty of ADRIANOPLE, Russia had gained some territory and considerable rights and privileges in the Balkans from Turkey. The Russians also turned nationalist sentiments in the region to their advantage with the doctrine of 'PAN-SLAVISM'. Help to Balkan nationalists tended to coincide with Russian foreign-policy aims, particularly for power in the E Mediterranean, and control of the strategically vital entrance to the Black Sea. In other areas, where Russia's own interests were not likely to be furthered by the promotion of local nationalist aspirations, any such stirrings were quickly and firmly crushed – as happened in Russian-ruled Poland in 1830 and 1863. British and French fears of Russian ambitions were confirmed when Russia occupied the E Balkan territories of MOLDAVIA and WALACHIA in 1853. The following year the Russians sank a Turkish fleet, precipitating Franco-British involvement in the CRIMEAN WAR (1854–6). Further Russian encroachments into Turkish territory in the Balkans were halted at the Congress of BERLIN in 1878. In return, Turkey recognized Serbia, which became the largest independent Slav state in the region. However, Slav nationalists – encouraged by Russia and Serbia – greatly resented having to exchange Turkish for Austro-Hungarian control, as happened in BOSNIA-HERZEGOVINA. The BALKAN WARS of 1912 and 1913 led to success for Slav nationalist aspirations: the territory of the Ottoman Empire was much reduced, and Serbia increased its size and strength. Austria was their next target. It was a Slav nationalist who assassinated the Austrian Archduke Franz Ferdinand in Sarajevo in 1914 – an event which precipitated the outbreak of World War I and the final break-up of the Austro-Hungarian Empire into independent nation-states following its defeat in the war. See also RUSSO-TURKISH WARS.

Easter Rising (24 April 1916), an Irish rebellion in which nationalists led by Patrick PEARSE seized a number of buildings in Dublin and issued a Proclamation of Irish Independence from British rule. Based in the General Post Office in Sackville Street, they held out against superior British forces until 29 April. Sixteen of the leaders were subsequently executed by the British, fuelling the growth of nationalist sentiment in IRELAND.

East Germany, a former Communist state in E Europe (1949–89). See GERMANY.

East India Company, English, a chartered company formed by London merchants in 1600 as a monopoly trading company. In defence of its trade in INDIA the Company established a territorial empire there in the 18th century, fighting off French competition with the help of Robert CLIVE. Complete control of its territories passed to the British government after the INDIAN MUTINY (1857).

East Prussia, a former province of Germany on the Baltic Sea. It was separated from the rest of Germany by the POLISH CORRIDOR in 1919. In 1945 the S part went to Poland and the N part to the USSR. See map, p. 37.

East Timor, a Portuguese colony from 1586 until 1975 when it was claimed and annexed by INDONESIA. Pro-independence demonstrations by the East Timorese have been brutally suppressed.

East–West Schism, the schism between the Western (Roman) Christian Church and the Eastern (ORTHODOX) Christian Church in 1054, a turning point in East–West relations. Tensions between the Eastern and Western Churches had existed since the demise of the Western ROMAN EMPIRE, and were exacerbated by doctrinal disputes and by the fact that the papacy tended to seek the support of the HOLY ROMAN EMPIRE rather than the BYZANTINE EMPIRE.

ECU (European Currency Unit), a unit of account, based upon a basket of European currencies, used as a reserve asset in the European Monetary System (the system that enables the member-states of the EC to coordinate their exchange rate through the EXCHANGE RATE MECHANISM).

Ecuador, a republic on the Pacific coast of S America. By the mid-15th century much of Ecuador had been incorporated into the INCA Empire. After being conquered by Spain (1532–3), the area was ruled as part of the vice-royalty of Peru. In 1822 Ecuador was liberated by the armies of Antonio José de Sucre (1795–1830) and Simón BOLÍVAR. Initially federated with Colombia and Venezuela, Ecuador became completely independent in 1830. Throughout the 19th century there were struggles between liberals and conservatives. Since 1895 there have been long periods of military rule, but democratically elected governments have been in power since 1978. Relations with neighbouring Peru have long been tense – war broke out in 1941, when Ecuador lost most of its Amazonian region.

Eden, Robert Anthony, 1st Earl of Avon (1897–1977), British Conservative statesman, foreign secretary (1935–8, 1940–5 and 1951–5), prime minister (1955–7). He resigned after the controversy provoked by the Anglo-French invasion of the SUEZ CANAL zone in 1956.

Edgehill, Battle of (23 October 1642), the first battle of the ENGLISH CIVIL WAR, a bloody and indecisive clash fought at Edgehill near Warwick between CHARLES I's royalists under Prince RUPERT, and Parliamentary forces under the Earl of Essex.

Edo, the capital of the TOKUGAWA shogunate from 1601, now Tokyo.

Edward I (1239–1307), king of England (1272–1307). A masterful ruler, he had a profound effect on the development of English government. He conquered the principality of Wales, but his attempts to dominate SCOTLAND only provoked the Scottish War of Independence.

Edward II (1284–1327), king of England (1307–27). An incompetent ruler, he was discredited by his defeat at BANNOCKBURN and damaged by the excessive confidence he placed in friends such as Piers Gaveston and the Despensers. In 1326 his estranged wife, ISABELLA of France, led the rising which led to his dethronement and murder.

Edward III (1312–77), king of England (1327–77). In the early years of his reign he ruled in name only, power resting with his mother ISABELLA and her lover Roger MORTIMER. His personal rule began after Mortimer's arrest in 1330. He claimed the French throne through his mother, provoking the HUNDRED YEARS WAR. Noted for his military prowess, his victories, including the battles of CRÉCY and POITIERS, won him vast tracts of France.

Edward IV (1442–83), king of England (1461–60, 1471–83). As the son of RICHARD Duke of York, he inherited the YORKIST claim to the throne, and with WARWICK'S help overthrew the LANCASTRIAN HENRY VI. Disagreements with Warwick led to him losing the throne in 1470, but through brilliant generalship he won it back again (1471).

Edward V (1470–?1483), king of England (9 April–25 June 1482). Arrangements for his coronation were in hand when his uncle (later RICHARD III) had him declared illegitimate, deposed and placed in the Tower of London. Since there is no record of him being seen again, he was probably murdered.

Edward VI (1533–53), king of England (1547–53). The son of HENRY VIII and Jane SEYMOUR, he succeeded as a minor. Effective power lay first with his uncle, the Duke of Somerset, and then with the latter's rival, the Duke of Northumberland, both of whom continued the Protestant REFORMATION. He died of tuberculosis at the age of 16.

Edward VII (1841–1910), king of Great Britain and Ireland, the eldest son of Queen VICTORIA. As Prince of Wales he was virtually excluded from royal duties, partly owing to his leadership of the rakish 'Marlborough House' set, until his long-delayed accession in 1901. He was a popular king but had little political influence.

Edward VIII (1894–1972), king of Great Britain and Ireland (1936), the eldest son of GEORGE V and brother of GEORGE VI. He abdicated in order to marry an American divorcée, Mrs Wallis Simpson, causing a constitutional crisis.

Edward, the Black Prince (1330–76), eldest son of EDWARD III (whom he predeceased), and father of the future RICHARD II. His military achievements in the HUNDRED YEARS WAR, notably at the battles of CRÉCY and POITIERS, won him a considerable reputation.

Edward the Confessor, St (c. 1003–66), king of England (1042–66), son of ETHELRED II, and founder of Westminster Abbey. The succession of HAROLD Godwinson after Edward's death led to the NORMAN CONQUEST of England. He was canonized in 1161.

EEC, see EUROPEAN COMMUNITY.

EFTA, see EUROPEAN FREE TRADE ASSOCIATION.

Egypt, a country of NE Africa. See panel.

Eichmann, (Karl) Adolf (1902–62), Austrian Nazi official who organized the sending of Jews to CONCENTRATION CAMPS. He was abducted from Argentina by the Israelis and executed (1962).

Eisenhower, Dwight D. (1890–1969), US soldier and 34th president of the USA (1953–61). Known universally as 'Ike' after his successful career as Allied Commander in Europe during WORLD WAR II, he was elected president as a Republican in 1952 and served two terms. 'The Eisenhower

EGYPT

3100–2725 BC: Early Dynastic Period: MENES united Upper and Lower Egypt; city of MEMPHIS founded; building of Step Pyramid. **2575–2134 BC:** Old Kingdom: Egyptian administration centralized; building of Great Pyramids at Giza. **2134–2030 BC:** First Intermediate Period: Egypt divided; political fragmentation as rival princes claimed the Kingship of Upper and Lower Egypt. **2040–1640 BC:** Middle Kingdom: Egypt reunified under MENTUHOTEP II; establishment of new capital, Itj-towy, and administrative reforms; co-regency introduced; conquest of NUBIA. **1640–1552 BC:** Second Intermediate Period: political fragmentation; rule of the HYKSOS kings; Theban dynasty liberated Egypt. **1552–1070 BC:** New Kingdom: Egypt became an imperial power, extending its empire from Syria to S Sudan; capital moved to Thebes; AKHENATEN moved the capital to el-Amarna and abandoned the worship of Amun; TUTANKHAMUN restored worship of Amun; great building programme undertaken; RAMESSES II came into conflict with the HITTITES in Syria. **1070–712 BC:** Third Intermediate Period: Egypt divided; priesthood of Amun ruled in Thebes, while the Pharaohs ruled in the new capital of Tanis. **712–332 BC:** Late Period: reunification of Egypt. **525 BC:** Egypt invaded by ACHAEMENID Persians under CAMBYSES II and became a Persian province. **332 BC:** Invasion by ALEXANDER the Great. **304 BC–AD 30:** On the death of Alexander, PTOLEMY took control, founding a line of Macedonian kings and queens which lasted until the death of CLEOPATRA. **AD 30:** Egypt conquered by AUGUSTUS and became a Roman province. **641:** Arab conquest of Egypt; Christianity replaced by Islam. **Until 1250:** Egypt ruled by successive Arab dynasties, including the FATIMID dynasty. **1250–1517:** Egypt prospered under the MAMLUKS. **1517:** Egypt fell to the OTTOMANS, although Mamluks retained local power. **1798–1801:** Short-lived occupation by French forces under NAPOLEON. **1805:** Ottoman viceroy MEHEMET ALI assumed control of Egypt, establishing a dynasty. **1860s:** Construction of SUEZ CANAL. **1882:** Britain occupied Egypt to secure control of canal. **1914:** Britain declared a protectorate over Egypt. **1922:** Nominal independence granted to Egypt under King Fuad I; Britain retained control of Egypt's defence and communications. **1936:** King FAROUK succeeded to the throne; Britain agreed to grant full independence. **1946:** Withdrawal of British troops. **1952:** Farouk overthrown in coup. **1953:** Republic proclaimed with General Neguib as president. **1954:** NASSER became president and encouraged Arab nationalism. **1956:** Nationalization of SUEZ CANAL led to the SUEZ CRISIS. **1958–61:** Union with Syria in UNITED ARAB REPUBLIC. **1967:** Israel defeated Egypt in the SIX DAY WAR, occupying Sinai. **1970:** Death of Nasser; succeeded by SADAT. **1973:** Further defeat in YOM KIPPUR WAR. **1979:** Sadat concluded a peace treaty with Israel. **1980–2:** Sinai regained. **1981:** Sadat assassinated by Islamic fundamentalists. **From 1980s:** Egypt regained its role as a leader of the Arab world. **1990s:** Resurgence of Islamic fundamentalism. **1991:** Egypt took part in the GULF WAR on coalition side.

Doctrine' (1957) offered US economic or military aid to any state in the Middle East threatened by Communist aggression.

Elamites, an ancient people of SW Iran (modern Khuzistan). See map, p. 8.

ELAS, a Communist guerrilla group in GREECE. ELAS fought against German occupation during WORLD WAR II, and afterwards fought to replace the monarchy with a Communist state in a bitter civil war (1946–9), but was defeated.

Eleanor of Aquitaine (1122–1204), the most powerful woman of her age. Duchess of AQUITAINE in her own right, she married the CAPETIAN Louis VII, and then – after their 1152 divorce – the ANGEVIN HENRY II. After bearing him eight children, she instigated a revolt against him (1173–4) and was imprisoned until his death (1189), after which she was once again influential.

elector, a prince of the HOLY ROMAN EMPIRE with the right to participate in the election of the emperor. The system whereby the emperor was elected by a college of seven electors was formalized by the Golden Bull of CHARLES IV (1356).

Elizabeth I (1533–1603), queen of England and Ireland (1558–1603), the daughter of HENRY VIII and Anne BOLEYN. Her reign was notable for commercial and maritime expansion and high achievement in literature, art and music. She re-established the ANGLICAN Church on the basis of the Thirty-Nine Articles, disappointing both PURITANS and Catholics. Following the discovery of plots against her life by PHILIP II and MARY, QUEEN OF SCOTS, she had the latter executed (1587). Philip II's attempt to invade Britain with the SPANISH ARMADA in 1588 failed, but he continued to threaten Elizabeth, aiding the rebellion of the Catholic Irish chiefs in 1599. She died without issue and left the Crown to her STUART relative, James VI of Scotland, who became JAMES I of England.

Elizabeth II (1926–), queen of Great Britain and Northern Ireland, and head of the COMMONWEALTH since 1952. The elder daughter of GEORGE VI, she married her distant cousin Philip Mountbatten in 1947. Since her coronation in 1953, she has visited many countries of the world, particularly those of the COMMONWEALTH.

El Alamein, Second Battle of (October 1942), a major ALLIED victory over German forces in Egypt during WORLD WAR II. The 8th Army under General MONTGOMERY defeated an overstretched Afrika Korps led by General ROMMEL. Rommel's defeat marked the beginning of the end of Germany's NORTH AFRICAN CAMPAIGN. See map, p. 39.

El Dorado (Spanish, 'the golden one'), a fabled city, rich in gold, sought by the CONQUISTADORES in the early 16th century.

El Salvador, a republic in CENTRAL AMERICA. Spain conquered the area in 1524 and governed it as part of Guatemala. El Salvador was liberated in 1821, but remained in the CENTRAL AMERICAN FEDERATION until 1838. The country has suffered frequent coups and political violence. In 1932 a peasant uprising was harshly suppressed. Political and economic power is concentrated into the hands of a few families, and this has led to social tension. A state of virtual civil war existed from the late 1970s with the US-backed military, assisted by extreme right-wing death squads, combating left-wing guerrillas. The government and guerrillas signed a peace agreement in 1992 and multi-party rule was restored.

emirate, a Muslim governorate or principality, from the Arabic *amir*, meaning 'commander'.

Ems Telegram (1870), a dispatch recording a meeting between the French ambassador and WILHELM I of Prussia, sent by the latter to BISMARCK. Bismarck altered the dispatch, inserting a supposed exchange of insults between monarch and diplomat. He released the amended text to the press, in order to exacerbate tensions between France and Prussia and provoke France into declaring war in 1870. See FRANCO-PRUSSIAN WAR.

enclosures, the enclosing by landlords of open fields, commons and wastelands. In England it was accelerated by private acts of Parliament in the late 18th and early 19th centuries following the commercial farming improvements of the AGRICULTURAL REVOLUTION.

Engels, Friedrich (1820–95), German political philosopher who collaborated with Karl MARX on the COMMUNIST MANIFESTO.

England, a country in NW Europe, part of the UNITED KINGDOM, occupying the larger part of the island of Great Britain. Unified in the 10th century, England was united with WALES in 1536, and with SCOTLAND in 1707.

English Civil War (1642–9), the conflict between the supporters of CHARLES I and the Parliamentarians, arising from disagreements on constitutional, religious and economic matters between Charles and members of the LONG PARLIAMENT. Charles claimed to rule by divine right, while Parliament asserted its constitutional rights against those of the monarch. Hostilities opened when the king raised his standard at Nottingham in 1642. Parliament's alliance with the Scots enabled it to defeat Charles' forces at MARSTON MOOR (1644), while the creation of the NEW MODEL ARMY – dominated by FAIRFAX and CROMWELL – was followed by decisive Parliamentary victories at NASEBY (1645) and elsewhere. The king's surrender in 1645 ended the first phase of the war, but his escape in 1647 prompted a brief resumption of hostilities, with Charles now in alliance with the Scots. However, Charles was soon defeated and captured (1648), and his public execution in 1649 was followed by the establishment of a republican COMMONWEALTH.

Enlightenment, a movement in 18th-century thought that applied rational and critical thinking to existing ideas and social institutions, advocating religious tolerance and freedom from superstition. Enlightenment ideas were pursued in England by LOCKE and PAINE, and in France by Voltaire and Rousseau, as well as in Germany and Scotland. Although the practical influence of the Enlightenment was never great, and its intellectual impact declined in the later 18th century, it provided some of the ideas and language of the American War of INDEPENDENCE and the FRENCH REVOLUTION.

Enosis (Greek, 'Union'), a campaign for the union of CYPRUS with GREECE, launched by the EOKA movement of Greek Cypriots in the 1950s.

entente cordiale (1904), an 'understanding' between Britain and France which aimed to counter what was seen as a growing German threat. A further 'entente' was signed between London and St Petersburg in 1907, consolidating Britain's entry into the Franco–Russian sphere in the years leading up to WORLD WAR I.

Enver Pasha (1881–1922), Turkish politician and leader of the YOUNG TURKS who seized power in 1909. He took power for himself in 1913 and led Turkey into WORLD WAR I on the side of the CENTRAL POWERS. After the war he fled Turkey and was killed fighting the Bolsheviks in Turkestan.

Epaminondas (4th century BC), Theban general who broke the military power of SPARTA at LEUCTRA (371 BC) and temporarily made THEBES the dominant power in Greece. See also PELOPIDAS.

Ephesus, an important IONIAN city on the coast of Turkey. It remained a major and prosperous city in Hellenistic and Roman times, best known for its temple of Artemis.

Ephialtes (assassinated 461 BC), Athenian politician, primarily responsible for the reforms that reduced the powers of the aristocratic council (the AREOPAGOS) and brought more democracy to Athens.

Epirus, a region of NW Greece and S Albania, inhabited in Classical times by various tribal groups. They were formed into a kingdom under Alexander I (342–330 BC), supported by PHILIP II of Macedon. Under PYRRHUS Epirus expanded its power and fought wars in Italy and Sicily.

Equatorial Guinea, a republic of W Africa. The island of Fernando Pó was acquired by Spain in 1778. Río Muni was added in 1856 to create Spanish Guinea. Independence in 1968 began under the dictatorship of Francisco Nguema, who was overthrown by a military coup in 1979. One-party rule has been in force since 1987, but the return of political pluralism is expected.

Erasmus, Desiderius (1466–1536), Dutch HUMANIST. His edition of the New Testament (1516) earned him the reputation as the first New Testament scholar. He attempted to act as a mediator between Rome and LUTHER but finally repudiated the Protestant REFORMATION.

Erhard, Ludwig (1897–1977), German CHRISTIAN DEMOCRAT statesman, chancellor of the Federal Republic of (West) GERMANY (1963–6). As economics minister (1949–63) he presided over West Germany's postwar 'economic miracle'.

Eric the Red (?940–?1010), Viking explorer who colonized GREENLAND c. 985–6. His son LEIF ERICSSON discovered land W of Greenland c. 1001, and he and his crew were the first Europeans to land on the American continent.

Eritrea, a country on the Red Sea coast of NE Africa. The region was part of ETHIOPIA from the 10th century, but was disputed by the Ottoman Empire from the 16th century. Eritrea became an Italian colony in 1890 and was the main base for Italian aggression against Ethiopia (1935–9). It was under British administration (1941–52), and was federated with (1952) and then absorbed by (1962) Ethiopia. Eritrean Muslims fought for independence from 1961 to 1991, when the Ethiopian authorities recognized Eritrea's right to secede. A referendum in April 1993 produced an overwhelming majority in favour of independence.

ERM see EXCHANGE RATE MECHANISM.

Eskimo, a group of peoples inhabiting northern N America, Greenland and E Siberia. They emigrated from Siberia about 2000 years ago. Initially a nomadic and hunting people, they began to build settlements and exploit the coastal and marine environment in the first millennium AD. See also INUIT, ALEUT.

Estates-General, see STATES-GENERAL.

Estonia, a republic on the Baltic Sea in NE Europe. Estonia was ruled by Denmark (1227–1346), the (German) TEUTONIC KNIGHTS (1346–1558) and by Sweden (1558–1712) before becoming part of Russia. Estonian national consciousness increased throughout the 19th century. When the Communists took power in Russia (1917), Estonia seceded, but a German occupation and two Russian invasions delayed independence until 1919. Estonia's fragile democracy was replaced by a dictatorship in 1934. The NAZI–SOVIET PACT (1939) assigned Estonia to the USSR, which invaded and annexed the republic (1940). Estonia was occupied by Nazi Germany (1941–4). When Soviet rule was reimposed (1945), large-scale Russian settlement replaced over 120,000 Estonians who had been killed or deported to Siberia. In 1988, reforms in the USSR allowed Estonian nationalists to operate openly. Nationalists won a majority in the republic's parliament, gradually assumed greater autonomy, and seceded following the failed coup by Communist hardliners in Moscow (August 1991). The USSR recognized Estonia's independence in September 1991. The introduction of strict Estonian citizenship laws (1992) that denied full rights to most Russian-speakers increased tension with Russia.

ETA (Basque, *Euzkadi ta Azkatasuna*, 'Homeland and Liberty'), a terrorist organization fighting for a BASQUE state independent of SPAIN.

Ethelred II ('the Unready'; c. 968–1016), king of England (978–1016). When renewed Scandinavian raids became a serious threat after 1000, he attempted to buy the Danes off with DANEGELD. In 1013 he was temporarily deposed by SWEYN FORKBEARD, king of Denmark, but was reinstated on the latter's death in 1014. His nickname means 'without counsel'.

Ethiopia, a country of NE Africa. The kingdom of AXUM flourished in the first millennium AD, accepting Christianity in the 4th century. Later, Islam also entered the country. Under MENELIK II, Ethiopia survived the European scramble for empire and defeated an Italian invasion (1896). However, the Italians occupied Ethiopia from 1936 to 1941. Emperor HAILE SELASSIE played a prominent part in African affairs, but – failing to modernize Ethiopia or overcome its extreme poverty – he was overthrown in 1974. Allied to the USSR, a left-wing military regime instituted revolutionary change, but, even with Cuban help, it was unable to overcome secessionist guerrilla movements in ERITREA and Tigray. Drought, soil erosion and civil war brought severe famine in the 1980s and 1990s. The Marxist-Leninist regime was toppled by Tigrayan forces in 1991. The interim authorities recognized the right of Eritrea to secede. Following a referendum in favour of independence, Eritrea assumed sovereignty on 24 May 1993.

Etruscans, a people of obscure origin who inhabited the W coast of Italy (modern day Tuscany) in ancient times. Etruscan civilization reached its zenith in the Archaic Period (8th to 5th centuries BC) when a number of powerful city-states emerged. In the 6th century BC the Etruscans colonized other parts of Italy, but did not attempt to unify the country. In the 5th and 4th centuries BC Etruria was hit by economic recession and social crisis and gradually fell victim to the growing power of ROME, but some Etruscan cities managed to preserve much of their ancient culture and distinctive social organization well into the Roman period. Their language was spoken until the 1st century BC, when it gave way to Latin.

EU, see EUROPEAN UNION.

Eugène of Savoy (1666–1736), French-born Austrian soldier and prince of the house of Savoy. In the service of the Austrian HABSBURG emperors he gained major military successes against the OTTOMAN Turks, and against LOUIS XIV's forces in the War of the SPANISH SUCCESSION, fighting with MARLBOROUGH at BLENHEIM, OUDENARDE and Malplaquet.

Euphrates, a river of SW Asia, on whose banks a number of important cities of ancient MESOPOTAMIA were built.

Eureka Stockade (1854), an armed rebellion by Australian gold miners at Ballarat (Eureka Stockade) over the lack of representative government. The conflict hastened reform, and between 1855 and 1870 all six colonies gained self-government.

European Coal and Steel Community, see EUROPEAN COMMUNITY.

European Commission, see EUROPEAN COMMUNITY.

European Community (EC), an organization of mainly West European states. The signing on 1 March 1957 of the Treaties of ROME by Belgium, France, West Germany, Italy, Luxembourg and the Netherlands (all members of the European Coal and Steel Community; 1951) brought into being the European Economic Community (EEC) and the European Atomic Energy Community (Euratom). These three Communities merged their executives and decision-making bodies into a single European Community (EC) in 1967. The EC's principal constituent bodies are: the Council of Ministers, the main decision-making body of the EC; the European Commission, which makes legislative proposals to the Council of Ministers and executes its decisions; the European Parliament, to which the Commission is answerable; and the European Court of Justice, which settles disputes arising out of the application of Community law. Closer economic and political union between member-states have been agreed with the formation of the European Monetary System (including the EXCHANGE RATE MECHANISM), the signing of the MAASTRICHT Treaty in 1991, and the establishment of the Single European Market in 1992. There are, however, elements in many of the member-states who oppose greater European political and economic integration.

From 1 November 1993 the EC became one of the three 'pillars' of the EUROPEAN UNION.

European Economic Community (EEC), see EUROPEAN COMMUNITY.

European Free Trade Association (EFTA), an association of West European states formed in 1960 by Austria, Denmark, Norway, Portugal, Sweden, Switzerland and Britain to achieve free trade in industrial products between member-states. EFTA was to lose Denmark, Portugal and the UK to the EC, but it gained Iceland in 1970 and Finland in 1986. Tariffs on industrial goods between EFTA and EC countries were abolished in April 1984. The EC and EFTA are scheduled to create a single European trading area.

European Parliament, see EUROPEAN COMMUNITY.

European Union (EU), a body that came into being following the ratification of the Treaty of MAASTRICHT. From 1 November 1993 the EUROPEAN COMMUNITY was absorbed into the European Union. Its bodies and structure now form one of the three 'pillars' that comprise the EU. The other two pillars – operating at inter-governmental rather than EC level – encompass foreign and security matters and cooperation in fields such as immigration, asylum and law enforcement. As defined in the Treaty of Maastricht, the EU is an expression of 'an ever closer union among the people of Europe'. The governments of the 12 EC member-states that ratified the Treaty of Maastricht agreed to a series of objectives including (eventually) a single currency and a commitment that the EU should 'assert its identity on the international scene'. Every citizen of the 12 EC member-states is also a citizen of the EU with the right to vote and to stand for elections for local and regional government authorities in any country of the EU.

evolution, human, the gradual development of modern humans from their ape-like ancestors. The earliest hominids, alive around 4 million years ago and found in Africa, are classed in the genus *Australopithecus.* About 2 million years ago, one line of the *Australopithecines* began to develop a larger brain, and are classed in their own genus of *Homo.* The best-known specimens of this line are the *Homo habilis* ('handy man'), who along with other species in the *Homo* genus used stone tools. By 1.7 million years ago a variety of *Homo* rapidly achieved the stature of modern human beings, and had even larger brains. *Homo erectus* is the principal species of this age and remains have been found in Africa, Asia and Europe. Between 1.6 million to 10,000 years ago the trend towards large brains continued. *Homo sapiens* ('wise man') appeared about 300,000 years ago as the successor to *Homo erectus,* and appeared in Africa and Europe. NEANDERTHAL man (*Homo sapiens neanderthalensis*) is the best-known variety of early *Homo sapiens,* and appears to have evolved gradually from about 200,000 years ago. Neanderthals seem to have disappeared about 40,000 or 30,000 years ago, when they were replaced by modern humans (*Homo sapiens sapiens*), exemplified by Cro-Magnon man. There is some debate as to whether Neanderthals evolved into modern humans, and some experts suggest that modern humans obtained some genes from them through interbreeding before they died out.

Exchange Rate Mechanism (ERM), a system agreed between 10 of the 12 members of the EUROPEAN COMMUNITY, whereby they limit movement in the value of their currencies. The ERM is not a fixed system; ERM members agree a set of exchange rates against each others' currencies and a margin on either side of these central rates to allow for some daily movement in the markets. In 1993 fault lines in the system forced a number of the countries out of the Mechanism and the system has since become ineffective.

Exodus, the departure of the Israelites from Egypt under MOSES, as related in the Old Testament.

Fabians, members of the Fabian Society established in Britain in 1884, and one of the groups responsible for the foundation of the LABOUR Party. Fabians rejected revolutionary methods and believed that socialism would be brought about by universal suffrage, legislation and reasoned debate.

Fabius Maximus, Quintus (c. 260–203 BC), Roman senator appointed dictator after HANNIBAL'S victory at TRASIMENE (217 BC). His strategy of avoiding pitched battles earned him the contemptuous nickname *Cunctator* ('the delayer'), which became an honour when his policy was vindicated by the Roman defeat at CANNAE in 216 BC.

Fairfax, Thomas, 3rd Baron (1612–71), English general. The commander of the Parliamentary forces (1645–50) in the ENGLISH CIVIL WAR, he was later instrumental in the restoration to the throne of CHARLES II.

Faisal I (1885–1933), king of Iraq (1921–33). The son of King HUSSEIN of the Hejaz, he campaigned with T.E. LAWRENCE in the Arab Revolt of 1917. He was made king of SYRIA in 1920 but was expelled by the French. The following year Britain made him king of IRAQ.

Faisal, Ibn Abdul Aziz (1905–75), king of SAUDI ARABIA (1964–75). Pro-Western in his sympathies, he opposed NASSER'S brand of Arab nationalism.

Falange, a Spanish Fascist movement founded in 1933 by José Antonio PRIMO DE RIVERA, and adopted by General FRANCO in 1937. The Falange was the only legal political party in Spain under his régime.

Falkenhayn, Erich von (1861–1922), German soldier. He launched the German offensive at VERDUN (1916) during World War I. He was replaced by HINDENBURG and LUDENDORFF in 1917.

Falklands War (April–June 1982), a conflict between the UK and Argentina over the Falkland Islands (Spanish, *Islas Malvinas*) – a small group of islands in the S Atlantic 12,800 km (8000 mi) from the UK and peopled by 1800 inhabitants of British descent. The islands became a crown colony in 1882 but had long been claimed by ARGENTINA, whose military leader General Galtieri launched a full-scale invasion of the islands on 2 April 1982. After the failure of peace initiatives by the USA and UN, the British government of Margaret THATCHER sent a large naval task force to recover the islands. The ensuing war, which cost the lives of 1000 servicemen, ended in the liberation of the Falkland Islands and defeat for Argentina.

Farouk (1920–65), king of Egypt (1936–52). Unable to cope with the rising tide of Arab nationalism in EGYPT, he was overthrown in a coup led by General Mohammed Neguib and Colonel Gamal Abdel NASSER.

Fascism, an extreme right-wing political system or ideology, nationalist or militarist in character and opposed to democracy, liberalism and Communism. Fascism grew out of the unstable political conditions that followed World War I. Its mass appeal derived from its promises to replace weak democratic governments with strong leadership, restore national pride and rectify the grievances of individuals and states arising out of the VERSAILLES settlement. Inspired by the success of MUSSOLINI'S *Fasci di Combattimento* in 1922, Fascist movements – with authoritarian and hierarchical structures – sprang up throughout Europe in the 1920s and 30s, most significantly in Germany, where HITLER'S NAZIS seized power in 1933, and Spain, where FRANCO established a dictatorship in 1939.

Fashoda Incident (September 1898). An Anglo-French diplomatic crisis. When French forces under Colonel Jean-Baptiste Marchand raised the French flag over the fortress of Fashoda in SE Sudan, the British – who under KITCHENER were in the process of taking the strategically vital Upper Nile region – issued an ultimatum. The French government, anxious to avoid war, ordered Marchand to withdraw on 4 November.

Fatah, al-, a Palestinian organization formed in the late 1950s and early 1960s to fight for the return of Palestinian Arabs to what is now the state of Israel. It is a dominant element in the PALESTINE LIBERATION ORGANIZATION.

Fatimids, a dynasty of SHIITE Muslim caliphs of the ISMAILI sect who ruled first in N Africa (from 909) and then in EGYPT (969–1171), where they founded Cairo as their capital. Egypt prospered greatly under their rule, though they later declined in power. The Fatimid caliphate was abolished by SALADIN, and Egypt then reverted to its allegiance to the Sunni ABBASID caliphs.

Fawkes, Guy, see GUNPOWDER PLOT.

Federal Bureau of Investigation (FBI), the chief investigative agency of the US government, established in 1908 with headquarters in Washington, DC. After the appointment of J. Edgar HOOVER as director in 1924 the FBI developed as a highly professional agency with wider powers to investigate cases involving infringement of federal laws.

Federalist Party, an early US political party that evolved in the 1790s under the leadership of George WASHINGTON and Alexander HAMILTON. Conservative and Anglophile, the party lost the watershed election of 1800 to the rival Democratic-Republicans (led by Thomas JEFFERSON) and had disappeared by 1825.

Fenian, a member of an Irish revolutionary organization founded in the USA in the 1850s to fight for Irish independence from Britain. In Ireland it was known as the Irish Republican Brotherhood. In 1867 an attempt to rescue some its members from prisons in Manchester and London failed and ended in the deaths of 12 people. The subsequent execution and imprisonment of Fenians drew attention to the campaign for Irish HOME RULE.

Ferdinand II ('the Catholic'; 1452–1516), king of CASTILE (1474–1504), king of ARAGON (as Ferdinand II; 1479–1516), king of Sicily (1468–1516) and king of NAPLES (1502–16). His marriage to ISABELLA of Castile (1469) laid the foundations of a united modern Spain. He restored royal authority in Aragon after the disorders of the 15th century and used the resources of Castile to intervene in the Italian wars and in Africa.

Ferdinand II (1578–1637), Holy Roman Emperor (1619–37), king of Bohemia (1617–27) and of Hungary (1618–26). A vigorous proponent of COUNTER-REFORMATION Catholicism, he crushed the revolt in BOHEMIA (1618) and restored Catholicism there. Despite early successes in the THIRTY YEARS WAR, he failed to restore imperial power or to eradicate Lutheranism and Calvinism in Germany.

Ferdinand VII (1784–1833), king of SPAIN (1808–33). An arbitrary and inept ruler, his abdication at Bayonne in 1810, forced on him by NAPOLEON, precipitated the wars for Spanish American Independence. His reign saw the loss of Spain's Latin American empire.

feudal system, the social and economic system that dominated Western Europe from the 8th to the 13th centuries. Throughout these centuries most of Europe was dominated by landlords. Small local landlords owed rent or service or both to greater landlords, and so on all the way up to the monarch. At each level tenants owed the kind of service – financial, administrative or military – appropriate to their status. Tenants of knightly status might be expected to perform 'knight service' in return for 'fiefs', estates granted them by their lords. At the bottom of the hierarchy were the SERFS. From the 12th and 13th centuries onwards lords increasingly secured men's services by paying them in cash. The term 'feudal' (from Latin, feudum, meaning a 'fief') is a modern one, neither the word nor the concept existing in the Middle Ages.

Fíanna Fáil (Gaelic, 'soldiers of destiny'), an Irish political party founded by Eamon DE VALERA in 1926 with the aim of creating a united republican IRELAND entirely independent of Britain. It gained power for the first time in 1932 and has held power for long periods since then. It is one of the two most important Irish political parties, along with FINE GAEL.

Field of the Cloth of Gold (1520), the site of a meeting in N France between HENRY VIII and FRANCIS I of France, marked by lavish entertainments and pageantry.

Fifteen, the (1715), a JACOBITE rebellion in favour of James II's son, the Old PRETENDER James Edward STUART, which sought to exploit English and Scottish grievances regarding the Act of UNION and the new HANOVERIAN dynasty. It ended in defeat at the battle of Sheriffmuir.

Fiji, a republic comprising a group of islands in the SW Pacific. Fiji was settled by Melanesians and Polynesians in around 1500 BC. TASMAN reached Fiji in 1643, but Europeans did not settle until the early 1800s. Chief Cakobau requested British assistance to quell civil unrest and ceded Fiji to Britain (1874). Indian labourers arrived to work on sugar plantations, reducing the Fijians to a minority. Since independence (1970), racial tension and land disputes have brought instability. A military takeover in 1987 overthrew an Indian-led government and established a Fijian-dominated republic outside the COMMONWEALTH.

Fillmore, Millard (1800–74), US WHIG politician, 13th president of the USA (1850–3). He supported the COMPROMISE OF 1850 which attempted to resolve North–South antagonism on the slavery question, but failed to achieve renomination in 1852 when his party split on the same issue.

Fine Gael (Gaelic, 'United Ireland'), an Irish political party founded in 1923 by supporters of the Anglo-Irish Treaty (which had established the Irish Free State in 1921). The Fine Gael government of 1948–51 severed the last links with Britain by declaring IRELAND to be a republic, but since then the party has held power only intermittently.

Finland, a republic of N Europe. See panel.

Finnish–Russian War (or 'Winter War'; 1939–40), a conflict between Finland and the Soviet Union that broke out when the Finns refused to accede to STALIN'S demands for Soviet military bases on their soil. The Finns were forced to accept peace on Stalin's terms and to cede their E territories.

Fire of London, a fire that devastated London in 1666. A number of churches and public buildings – notably St Paul's Cathedral – were rebuilt after the fire by Sir Christopher Wren.

First World War, see WORLD WAR I.

Fitzgerald, Garrett (1926–), Irish FINE GAEL statesman and economist, prime minister (1981–2 and 1982–7).

Flanders, a region of NW Europe that is now an autonomous region of BELGIUM. The autonomous county of Flanders rose to prominence in the 10th century and became a major centre of the cloth industry in the Middle Ages. Flanders was ruled by Burgundy (1384–1477), Spain (1477–1714), Austria (1714–90), France (1793–1814) and the Netherlands (1814–31) before becoming part of BELGIUM.

Flodden Field, Battle of (9 September 1513), a battle between the English and Scots following the invasion of England by James IV of Scotland in support of his French allies. The Scots were defeated and James killed. The victory ensured English security in the N.

FINLAND

12th century–1634: Swedish conquest of Finland. **17th century:** At the REFORMATION most Finns became Lutheran. **18th century:** Russia conquered much of the area. **19th century:** Russia gained complete control (1809), Finland becoming a grand duchy ruled by the Russian tsar; growth of tension as Russia sought to increase its political and cultural domination. **1906:** Finland was allowed to call its own Duma (Parliament), but repression followed again (1910). **1917–18:** Civil war between nationalists ('Whites') led by MANNERHEIM, and pro-Russian Bolshevik forces. **1919:** Independence secured; independent republican constitution established. **1939:** Soviet forces invaded: Finland forced to cede territory to USSR after defeat in the FINNISH-RUSSIAN War. **1941–4:** Finland briefly allied with Germany; war against USSR led to further territorial losses. **1945–91:** Finland maintained a policy of neutrality during the COLD WAR. **1992:** Finland applied for EC membership.

Florence, a former city-state in central Italy. It became economically and then politically predominant in the 13th century. Its alliance with France and the papacy kept it centre-stage during the late Middle Ages. Florence had a series of republican governments until coming under the rule of the MEDICI. In the early 15th century Florence was the first important focus of HUMANISM and the RENAISSANCE.

Foch, Ferdinand (1851–1929), marshal of France. His victory in the first Battle of the MARNE (1914) saved Paris. He commanded French forces at the Battle of the SOMME, and thereafter concentrated on ensuring Allied cooperation in the war. In March 1918 he was made Allied commander-in-chief, and received the German surrender at Compiègne on 1 November.

Ford, Gerald (1913–), 38th president of the USA (1974–7). A conservative Ohio Republican who succeeded to the presidency after the resignation of Richard NIXON, he proved a stabilizing force in the aftermath of the WATERGATE scandal. He was defeated by the Democratic candidate Jimmy CARTER in 1976.

Fort Sumter, a federal military post in Charleston harbour, South Carolina. Its bombardment by Confederate troops in April 1861 marked the opening of the AMERICAN CIVIL WAR.

Forty-five, the (1745–6), the last JACOBITE rebellion. JAMES II'S grandson, the Young PRETENDER Charles Edward Stuart, led an army of Highland Scots into England, but was obliged to retreat to Scotland, where his forces were destroyed at CULLODEN (1746).

Founding Fathers, the nickname given to the 55 delegates to the Constitutional Convention of 1787 who drafted the CONSTITUTION OF THE USA.

Fouquet, Nicholas, marquis de Belle-Isle (1615–80), French politician. He was superintendent of finance (1653–61) under LOUIS XIV, who later had him imprisoned for embezzlement.

Fourteen Points (8 January 1918), a programme for the maintenance of peace after WORLD WAR I, proposed by President WILSON in a speech to Congress. Wilson was forced by Britain and France to give way on some of the points at the PARIS PEACE CONFERENCE. The points included: the removal of international trade barriers, the impartial settlement of conflicting colonial claims, taking into account the interests of the colonial populations; self-determination for all nationalities within the Austro-Hungarian Empire; and the establishment of a 'general association of nations' (later to become the LEAGUE OF NATIONS).

Fourteenth Amendment (1868), an important amendment to the CONSTITUTION OF THE USA passed by CONGRESS in 1866 and ratified by the states two years later. Designed to protect black rights in the Southern states, it was the basis for congressional RECONSTRUCTION after the AMERICAN CIVIL WAR, and was also used for the legal assault on segregation in the 1950s and 1960s during the CIVIL RIGHTS campaign.

Fox, Charles James (1749–1806), British WHIG politician. He criticized Lord NORTH'S policy towards the American colonies, opposed the Younger PITT'S hostility towards the French Revolution and split with BURKE on the same issue. He was an advocate of parliamentary reform and the abolition of SLAVERY.

France, a country in Western Europe. See panel.

Franche-Comté, a former province of E France. It was part of the duchy of BURGUNDY (1384–1477) and passed to the Spanish HABSBURGS (1493–1674). It was acquired by France in the Peace of NIJMEGEN (1678–9).

Francis I (1494–1547), king of France (1515–47). His reign was dominated by a prolonged but inconclusive series of wars (1521–6, 1528–9, 1536–8 and 1542–4) with the emperor CHARLES V for control of Italy. A patron of the arts and scholarship, who presided over a lavishly extravagant court, he is often seen as the archetype of the RENAISSANCE prince. He became increasingly hostile to Protestantism after 1534.

Francis II, the last Holy Roman Emperor (1792–1806) and first emperor of AUSTRIA (as Francis I; 1804–35). His reign marked the end of enlightened reform in favour of the repressive conservative policies of his chancellor METTERNICH.

Franciscans, an order of mendicant friars that emerged in the 13th century. They followed the teachings of FRANCIS OF ASSISI, living a life of devout poverty among the sick and needy.

Francis of Assisi, St (1181–1226), founder of the FRANCISCAN order of friars. He renounced his wealthy family and material possessions to embrace a life of poverty, prayer and care for the needy. The teachings of St Francis reflect his deep

FRANCE

c. 1500 BC: The GAULS gradually spread over France from the E. **From 7th century BC:** The ancient Greeks established settlements on the Mediterranean coast. **From 123 BC:** The Romans conquered Gaul. **5th century AD:** Invasion of Germanic tribes; the FRANKS became dominant. **6th–8th centuries:** Rule of the MEROVINGIAN dynasty. **8th–9th centuries:** The CAROLINGIANs built an empire under CHARLEMAGNE; on Charlemagne's death in 814 his realm was divided, the W part becoming the ancestor of modern France. **987:** Accession of Hugh Capet, first CAPETIAN king of France. **1108–37:** Louis VI established control of territories around Paris. **1180–1223:** PHILIP II AUGUSTUS seized NORMANDY and recovered areas occupied by the ANGEVIN kings of England. **1328:** Accession of Philip VI, first VALOIS king of France. 1337: The English king EDWARD III claimed the French throne, precipitating the HUNDRED YEARS WAR. **1453:** English finally expelled from France, ending the Hundred Years War. **1477:** Burgundy annexed by France. **16th century:** Protestantism spread across France. **1559–98:** France ravaged by the FRENCH WARS OF RELIGION. **1572:** Some 3000 HUGUENOTS (Protestants) murdered in the ST BARTHOLOMEW'S DAY MASSACRE. **1589:** BOURBON dynasty established with the accession of HENRY IV. **1598:** Henry IV embraced Catholicism and issued the EDICT OF NANTES, granting religious toleration and ending the French Wars of Religion. **17th century:** RICHELIEU and MAZARIN helped restore the power of France within Europe. Under LOUIS XIV – France achieved a high degree of centralization. **18th century:** At the end of the War of the SPANISH SUCCESSION (1701–14) France lost its colonies in Canada and India, and was further weakened by involvement in the War of the AUSTRIAN SUCCESSION (1756–58), the SEVEN YEARS WAR (1756–63), and the AMERICAN WAR OF INDEPENDENCE. **1789–99:** Political and social institutions that had characterized France in the previous century overthrown in the FRENCH REVOLUTION; establishment of the First Republic (1792); Prussia and Austria invaded France, start of the REVOLUTIONARY WARS (1792–1802). **1799:** NAPOLEON Bonaparte began military dictatorship and embarked on aggressive foreign wars (see NAPOLEONIC WARS). **1815:** Napoleon's rule ended with defeat at WATERLOO; restoration of the Bourbon monarchy (1815–30). **1830:** French throne usurped by LOUIS PHILIPPE. **1848:** Louis Philippe overthrown in the REVOLUTION OF 1848; establishment of Second Republic. **1852:** Coup of Louis Napoleon established the SECOND EMPIRE, with himself as NAPOLEON II. **1870–71:** Reign of Napoleon III brought to an end by defeat in the FRANCO-PRUSSIAN WAR; foundation of the Third Republic. **1871:** Paris COMMUNE crushed. **1894–1906:** DREYFUS affair divided France. **End of 19th century:** French colonial empire reached its greatest extent, incorporating Indochina, N Africa and parts of S Pacific. **1905:** Separation of church and state. **1914:** France entered WORLD WAR I. **1918:** End of World War I; France regained ALSACE-LORRAINE. **1940–4:** N France occupied by the Germans during WORLD WAR II; Marshal PÉTAIN led a collaborationist French government from VICHY, but resistance was maintained by the FREE FRENCH under DE GAULLE. **1947:** A new constitution and government marked the establishment of the Fourth Republic. **1950–4:** French colonial forces defeated in INDOCHINA. **1954–8:** Political and military crisis over ALGERIA led to the fall of the Fourth Republic (1958). **1959:** Accession to power of de Gaulle as first president of the Fifth Republic. **1959–69:** Under de Gaulle, France dissolved its colonial empire, strengthened its position in W Europe through membership of the European Community and pursued a foreign policy independent of the USA. **1968:** Student and workers' demonstrations paralysed nation and led to de Gaulle's resignation and accession of POMPIDOU (1969). **1974:** GISCARD D'ESTAING elected president. **1981:** Election of François MITTERRAND, France's first Socialist president. **1993:** Electoral gains by the Right ended Socialist dominance of government.

love of the natural world, which he saw as the mirror of God.

Franco, Francisco (1892–1975), Spanish general and head of state (1939–75). He led the Nationalist forces against the elected Republican government in the SPANISH CIVIL WAR (1936–9), emerging victorious. In 1937 he adopted the FALANGE party and became dictator in 1939, banning all political opposition. Franco maintained Spanish neutrality during World War II. He was succeeded in 1975 by King JUAN CARLOS, whom he had declared his successor.

Franco-Prussian War (1870–1), a conflict between France and Prussia, skilfully engineered by BISMARCK by means of the EMS TELEGRAM. French defeats at SEDAN and Metz were followed by the siege and surrender of Paris in January 1871. The French National Assembly agreed to peace with Prussia, but Parisian radical socialists refused to lay down their arms and established the rebel COMMUNE of Paris. The war culminated in the declaration of the German SECOND EMPIRE.

Frankfurt, Treaty of (10 May 1871), the treaty ending the FRANC–PRUSSIAN WAR. By its terms France ceded ALSACE and much of Lorraine to the Germans, and paid an indemnity of five billion francs.

Franklin, Benjamin (1706–90), American statesman, author and scientist. A tireless promoter of self-improvement, material values and rational thought, he served as a Pennsylvania delegate to the CONTINENTAL CONGRESS, and helped negotiate the alliance with France during the AMERICAN WAR OF INDEPENDENCE and the Peace of Paris with Great Britain. At the age of 81 he sat in the Constitutional Convention of 1787 to help draft the CONSTITUTION OF THE USA.

Franks, a Germanic people originating on the lower Rhine (see map, p. 15). In the 5th century they controlled N Gaul. Charles MARTEL'S son PEPIN THE SHORT ousted the last Merovingian king in 751 and was crowned king of the Franks. The CAROLINGIAN dynasty that he established created the largest political unit in the West since the Roman Empire. Pepin's son CHARLEMAGNE carved out a Frankish empire in the late 8th century. The word Frank continued to denote a Western European of French culture (though not necessarily language) throughout the Middle Ages.

Franz Ferdinand (1863–1914), archduke of Austria and heir apparent of the Emperor FRANZ JOSEF I. His assassination by a Serb nationalist at Sarajevo in Bosnia on 28 June 1914 was a contributory factor in the outbreak of WORLD WAR I.

Franz Josef I (1830–1916), emperor of Austria (1848–1916) and king of Hungary (1867–1916). He succeeded to the throne following the abdication of Ferdinand I during the REVOLUTION OF 1848. His attempts to prevent the political modernization and eventual disintegration of the HABSBURG monarchy were ultimately in vain. His annexation of BOSNIA-HERZEGOVINA in 1908 increased tensions in Europe, while his government's attack on SERBIA in 1914 precipitated WORLD WAR I.

Fraser, (John) Malcolm (1930–), Australian Liberal statesman, prime minister (1975–83).

Frederick I ('Barbarossa'; c. 1122–90), king in Germany from 1152, crowned emperor at Rome in 1155. Initially Italy was his prime concern, and this led to conflict with both the papacy and the towns of LOMBARDY. However, after 1177 he successfully strengthened royal power in Germany, and firmly established his HOHENSTAUFEN family on the throne. He drowned while crossing a river during the Third CRUSADE.

Frederick II (1194–1250), Holy Roman Emperor (1220–50). He inherited the kingdom of Sicily while still a child, and was crowned king in Germany in 1215 and emperor at Rome in 1220. His marriage (1225) to the heiress to Jerusalem added the CRUSADER STATES to his dominions. His attempts to strengthen his authority in Italy led to bitter quarrels with the papacy.

Frederick II ('the Great'; 1712–86), king of Prussia (1740–86), the son of FREDERICK WILLIAM I. One of the more successful 'Enlightened Despots', he transformed the international standing of Prussia. His annexation of the Austrian province of Silesia precipitated the War of the AUSTRIAN SUCCESSION; his continuing rivalry with MARIA THERESA'S Austria was one of the causes of the SEVEN YEARS WAR. Frederick believed that foreign policy should be based upon the interests of the state rather than on morality and dynastic right, and that war should be an instrument of this policy. A military pragmatist, he fought only when necessary and sought the rapid defeat of his opponents (even if they outnumbered his own forces). At home, he established religious toleration, freed the serfs on his own estates, abolished torture and administered fair taxes.

Frederick William (1620–88), known as the 'Great Elector', HOHENZOLLERN elector of Brandenburg-PRUSSIA (1640–80). He restored the fortunes of Brandenburg after the THIRTY YEARS WAR, encouraging foreign – including HUGUENOT – settlement as part of its reconstruction. He also established a standing army and efficient bureaucracy, and eroded the power of the representative assemblies in his territories.

Frederick William I (1688–1740), king of PRUSSIA (1713–40). The son of Frederick I of Prussia (reigned 1701–13), his reforms established a disciplined and efficient Prussian army and administration.

Frederick William IV (1795–1861), king of PRUSSIA (1840–61). Demonstrations during the REVOLUTIONS OF 1848 forced him to appoint a liberal ministry and promise a national assembly, a constitution and support for German national unity. However, Frederick later refused to accept the crown of the putative German state. He was succeeded by WILHELM I.

Free French, an organization of French exiles in WORLD WAR II, led by DE GAULLE. Based in London, it continued the war against the AXIS powers after the surrender of France in 1940. They assumed the name 'Fighting French' in 1942.

free trade, an economic doctrine advocated by the economist Adam SMITH (1723–90), who argued for a system of international trade without the imposition of tariffs and import quotas by governments. British free-trade landmarks were Huskisson's reduction of tariffs in the 1820s, PEEL'S repeal of the CORN LAWS in 1846 and GLADSTONE'S virtual removal of tariffs by 1860. Free trade was not abandoned in Britain until 1932, with the introduction of 'imperial preference' for the DOMINIONS and a general tariff.

French, John Denston Pinkstone, 1st Earl of Ypres (1852–1925), British field marshal and commander of the British Expeditionary Force (1914–15) on the WESTERN FRONT in the early years of WORLD WAR I. The BEF sustained heavy losses at the battles of MONS, 1st YPRES and Loos, and French was recalled in autumn 1915 to be replaced by HAIG.

French and Indian Wars (1689–1763), the struggle between Britain and France for colonial supremacy in North America, the final stage of which (1755–63) formed part of the SEVEN YEARS WAR. Naval superiority and an alliance with PRUSSIA gave the English the advantage in terms of supplies and reinforcements. WOLFE'S victory at the PLAINS OF ABRAHAM led to the surrender of QUÉBEC (1759), and the expulsion of the French from CANADA a year later. Britain acquired Canada and LOUISIANA E of the Mississippi in the Treaty of PARIS (1763).

French East India Company, a company chartered by LOUIS XIV in 1664 to compete with the DUTCH and English EAST INDIA COMPANIES. Under Dupleix (governor-general; 1742–54) it attempted to challenge growing British influence in INDIA, but was dissolved after defeat at the hands of Robert CLIVE.

French Equatorial Africa, a former confederation of French colonies in W central Africa, comprising present-day CHAD, GABON, CONGO and the CENTRAL AFRICAN REPUBLIC.

French Indochina, the former French empire in SE Asia, comprising the protectorates of CAMBODIA, LAOS and ANNAM and the colonies of COCHIN CHINA and Tonkin, all of which were colonized between the late 1850s and 1890s (see map, p. 33). After the FRENCH INDOCHINA WAR, the French withdrew from Cambodia, Laos and Vietnam (1954).

French Indochina War (1946–54), a war fought between French colonial forces and nationalists in VIETNAM, LAOS and CAMBODIA. Under the leadership of HO CHI MINH, the VIET MINH launched guerrilla attacks against isolated French outposts. The Viet Minh victory at the decisive battle at DIEN BIEN PHU in May 1954 brought the conflict, and French rule in the region, to an end.

French Revolution (1789), the political upheaval that swept the BOURBON dynasty from power in France. The revolution had its origins in the unpopularity of the ANCIEN RÉGIME. With the government facing bankruptcy following French intervention in the American War of Independence, and discontent growing among the poor, LOUIS XVI was obliged to call the STATES-GENERAL to consider reform of the tax system. The Third Estate (the commoners) of the States-General declared itself a National Assembly, intending to introduce reform. Louis ordered troops to Paris and Versailles. On 14 July, fearing an attack on Paris and the Assembly, the Paris mob stormed the BASTILLE to obtain arms. An independent municipal government (commune) and National Guard were established in Paris and other towns as royal authority collapsed. Following a wave of peasant revolts, the Assembly abolished feudal and other privileges. This abolition was confirmed in the DECLARATION OF THE RIGHTS OF MAN. The Assembly prepared a 'modern' constitutional government, in which legislative power lay with a new elected assembly, and local government and the legal system were completely reorganized. Religious toleration for Protestants and Jews ended the privileges of the Catholic Church. After a failed attempt to flee the country in 1791, Louis XVI was obliged to approve the new constitution. In 1792 foreign powers invaded France, marking the beginning of the REVOLUTIONARY WARS, and stimulating suspicions of plots to betray the Revolution. A thousand suspected counter-revolutionaries were massacred in the prisons of Paris in September 1792, and France was declared a republic. In 1793 Louis XVI and MARIE ANTOINETTE were tried for treason and guillotined. Against a background of growing foreign and domestic opposition to the Revolution, the JACOBINS expelled the moderate GIRONDIN deputies from the Convention, and established a revolutionary dictatorship in the summer of 1793, promising to safeguard the Revolution. The Committee of Public Safety, whose most prominent member was ROBESPIERRE, unleashed a Reign of TERROR against suspected counter-revolutionaries. Robespierre and the Committee fell from power in 1794 and a group of five, known as the DIRECTORY, assumed power. However, frequent military interventions in politics culminated in a coup on 8 November 1799 (the coup of 18 Brumaire), bringing NAPOLEON Bonaparte to power.

French Wars of Religion (1559–98), a series of religious and political conflicts in France. The clash between Protestant HUGUENOTS and Catholics was caught up in the struggle of noble factions for control of the declining VALOIS dynasty. A more tolerant Catholic tendency emerged after the ST BARTHOLOMEW'S DAY MASSACRE, but from 1576 it was opposed by the extremist Catholic HOLY LEAGUE, led by Henry of GUISE, which was hostile to the conciliatory policies of HENRY III. The League's opposition to the succession of the BOURBON Henry of Navarre – a Huguenot – who became heir to the throne in 1584, led to the so-called 'War of the Three Henrys'. After Henry III's assassination in 1589, Henry of Navarre defeated the League and its Spanish allies. As HENRY IV he converted to Catholicism (1593) and established a tolerant religious settlement with the EDICT OF NANTES (1598).

French West Africa, a former confederation of French territories in W Africa, dissolved in 1959. It comprised present-day BENIN, BURKINA FASO, GUINEA, CÔTE D'IVOIRE, MALI, MAURITANIA, NIGER and SENEGAL.

Frisians, a Germanic people from what is now the Netherlands and NW Germany. They were absorbed by the FRANKS c. 800.

Frondes (1648–53), a series of revolts in France during the minority of LOUIS XIV. They were primarily a reaction by privileged officials against measures introduced by the king's minister, Jules MAZARIN, to finance France's war against Spain, but aristocratic resentment of the king's monopoly of government also played a part.

Front de Libération Nationale (FLN), a radical Muslim independence movement formed in ALGERIA in 1954, led by BEN BELLA. It was supported not only in Algeria but also by nationalists in Morocco and Tunisia. The FLN continued its campaign of violence until independence from France was gained in 1962.

Fuchs, Klaus (1911–88), German-born British nuclear physicist. He passed nuclear secrets to the Soviet Union from

1943. He was exposed in 1950 and sentenced to a long term of imprisonment.

Fugger, a wealthy S German mercantile family that developed a vast business empire based on trade, silver and copper mining and banking in the late 15th and early 16th centuries. Lending vast sums to MAXIMILIAN I, and financing CHARLES V's candidacy as Holy Roman Emperor in 1519, they enjoyed considerable political influence.

Fujiwara, a Japanese noble family, dominant from the late 9th to the late 12th centuries. In the 9th century it became traditional for the imperial court to have a Fujiwara regent, and the family's dominance was secured by the marriage of Fujiwara daughters into the imperial family. The Fujiwara ascendancy ended with the establishment of the KAMAKURA shogunate.

Fulani, nomads of the W African Sahel, originating in the far W, who spread E in the 14th–16th centuries. Strongly influenced by Islam, they undertook JIHADS to establish powerful Muslim states in Senegal and N Nigeria in the 18th and 19th centuries.

Funan, a former state in CAMBODIA.

Gabon, a republic of W central Africa. The slave trade developed after the Portuguese arrived in the late 15th century. The French colonized Gabon towards the end of the 19th century. Pro-French Léon M'Ba (1902–67) led the country to independence in 1960. Deposed in a coup (1964), he was restored to power by French troops. Under his successor, Albert-Bernard Bongo, Gabon has continued its pro-Western policies.

Gaddafi, see QADDAFI.

Gaiseric (Genseric; 390–477), king of the VANDALS (428–477). He led his people from Spain to Africa in 429, and by 439 had taken Carthage and its hinterland. They went on to capture the Balearic Islands, Sardinia and Corsica, and established a bridgehead in Sicily. In 455 his forces sacked Rome itself. Gaiseric embraced the ARIAN form of Christianity.

Gaitskell, Hugh Todd Naylor (1906–63), leader of the British LABOUR Party (1955–63). On the right wing of his party, he clashed with the left over unilateral nuclear disarmament. He bitterly opposed EDEN's action over SUEZ. After his unexpected death he was replaced by Harold WILSON.

Galatia, a region of central Asia Minor (Turkey) inhabited by CELTS who migrated there in the 3rd century BC. In AD 25 it became a Roman province.

Gallic Wars (58–51 BC), the wars waged by Julius CAESAR to establish Roman rule in N and central Europe. After crossing into GAUL Caesar defeated German tribes in the S and E, the VENETI in the W and the BELGAE in the N. He took advantage of inter-tribal disunity to subdue the N and W coasts, and twice invaded Britain (55 and 54 BC). In 53–52 VERCINGETORIX led a united force of Gallic tribes against Rome but was defeated and later executed.

Gallipoli campaign (1915–16), an abortive attempt by the Allies to seize the DARDANELLES during WORLD WAR I, with the aim of forcing Turkey out of the war and opening a sea route to Russia. After the failure of a naval expedition in February 1915, a military expedition was sent to the Gallipoli Peninsula in April. It too proved a costly débâcle, with ANZAC and British troops sustaining heavy losses. See map, p. 36.

Gambia, a republic of W Africa. Once part of the MALI empire, the area became involved in the slave trade following the arrival of the Portuguese in the mid-15th century. British traders later supplanted the Portuguese, and the region became a British colony in 1843. The Gambia achieved independence in 1965 under Sir Dawda K. Jawara. In 1981 an attempted coup against his rule encouraged the campaign to merge with SENEGAL, but the confederation was dissolved in 1989. The Gambia remains a democracy.

Gandhi, Indira (1917–84), Indian prime minister (1966–77 and 1980–4). The only daughter of Jawaharlal NEHRU, she joined the Indian National CONGRESS and the Indian struggle for independence when still a schoolgirl. She succeeded Lal Bahadur SHASTRI as prime minister in 1964. Her finest hour was the liberation of BANGLADESH in 1971; her worst when she declared a state of emergency and ruled autocratically (1975–7). She was assassinated by her SIKH bodyguards following her decision to storm the Sikh Golden Temple in Amritsar. Her son Rajiv (1944–91) succeeded her as prime minister (1984–9). He looked set to return to power in the 1991 general election but he was assassinated by TAMIL terrorists during the campaign.

Gandhi, Mohandas Karamchand (1869–1948), Indian religious and political leader, known as Mahatma ('Great Soul'). He played a major role in the Indian struggle against British rule, and was imprisoned on a number of occasions for civil disobedience. As president of the Indian National CONGRESS (from 1928) he helped negotiate Indian independence in 1947. He was assassinated by a Hindu extremist on 30 January 1948. Gandhi favoured 'non-cooperation', non-violent resistance (satyagraha) and hunger strikes as means of achieving reform. He campaigned for the rights of 'untouchables' and tried to unite Hindus and Muslims.

'Gang of Four', a group of radical Chinese politicians, including MAO ZEDONG'S widow, Jiang Qing, who allegedly plotted to seize power on Mao's death in 1976. Arrested and put on trial, the group was found guilty of plotting against the state in 1980.

Garfield, James Abram (1831–81), 20th president of the USA (1881). A Republican, he was assassinated within months of taking office.

Garibaldi, Giuseppe (1807–82), Italian nationalist and hero of the wars for the unification of Italy. In 1860 he landed in Sicily with an army of 1000 volunteers – his famous 'Redshirts' – and swiftly took control. He crossed to the mainland and swept aside minimal Bourbon resistance in Italy. Garibaldi's southern nationalists were radically democratic in the tradition of MAZZINI, and opposed the supremacy of PIEDMONT. However, in the face of pressure from CAVOUR, he and his followers accepted VICTOR EMMANUEL II as king of the newly united Italy.

Gascony, a former duchy of SW France. It was taken by the Vascones in the 6th century and enjoyed a considerable amount of independence until it came under the control of LOUIS THE PIOUS in 819. HENRY II of England acquired the duchy on his marriage to Eleanor of AQUITAINE, but it was lost to the French in the HUNDRED YEARS WAR. It was regained by the English under EDWARD III and was recognized as an English possession by the Treaty of BRÉTIGNY in 1360. CHARLES VII of France drove the English out, but the duchy only became joined to the crown of France under HENRY IV.

GATT, see GENERAL AGREEMENT ON TARIFFS AND TRADE.

Gaugamela, Battle of (332 BC), ALEXANDER THE GREAT's final victory over the Persians, near the Tigris. Beaten at ISSUS the previous year, the Persian king DARIUS III made a final stand at Gaugamela but was defeated. The fleeing king was murdered by his own nobles, only hours before Alexander caught up with him (see map, p. 12).

Gaul, the area covered by modern France and Belgium and extending to the W bank of the Rhine, inhabited in ancient times by CELTIC tribes (see map, p. 13). The S of France became a Roman province in 121 BC; the rest was conquered by Caesar in the GALLIC WARS. Gaul was sometimes referred to as 'Transalpine Gaul', and the area between the Alps and the Apennines (conquered by the Romans in 201–191 BC) as 'Cisalpine Gaul'.

Gaunt, John of (1340–99), duke of Lancaster, and a powerful figure in English politics during the reigns of his father EDWARD III and his nephew RICHARD II. Through his first wife Blanche he acquired the Lancaster estates. His third wife was Katherine Swynford, mother of the BEAUFORTS.

Gaveston, Piers (c. 1284–1312), see EDWARD II.

Gaza, a city and territory – the Gaza Strip – on the Mediterranean coast of SW Asia. Part of PALESTINE, Gaza was occupied by Egypt when the state of Israel was established (1948), and taken by Israel at the end of the SIX DAY WAR in 1967. The territory has a tradition of militant opposition to Israel.

General Agreement on Tariffs and Trade (GATT), an international trade agreement established by the UN in 1948, aiming to promote international trade by removing trade barriers, lowering tariffs, and by providing a forum for discussion of trade relations. GATT talks in the 1990s faltered over issues including the agricultural policies of the EUROPEAN COMMUNITY. However, an accord was reached in 1993 on a new round of tariff cuts and on the establishment of a new international authority to oversee further tariff agreements.

General Assembly of the United Nations, the assembly composed of all member-states of the UNITED NATIONS.

General Strike, a strike called by the British TRADES UNION CONGRESS on 5 May 1926 in support of the coalminers, who were threatened with longer hours and lower wages. The strike lasted nine days, during which the government gradually assumed control of key sectors of the economy to ensure food supplies and transport.

Geneva Conference (July 1954), a conference held in Switzerland to negotiate the end of the FRENCH INDOCHINA and KOREAN WARS. It granted independence to LAOS, CAMBODIA and VIETNAM, partitioning the latter.

Geneva Conventions, a series of agreements signed by many countries between 1864 and 1940, providing for the humane treatment of the victims of warfare.

Genghis Khan (c. 1162–1227), the founder of the MONGOL Empire. Formerly known as Temujim, he took the title of Genghis Khan in 1206 after uniting the tribes of Mongolia. He then turned his attention to conquests outside Mongolia. His first campaigns were against the Tangut kingdom of Gansu in the upper Yellow River valley and the JIN empire. By 1215 he had brought them to their knees and become the effective ruler of N China. In 1219 he overwhelmed the forces of the local Shah ruler of Afghanistan and Iran, and the E half of the domain was incorporated into the Mongol khanate. On his death he allocated fiefs to each of his sons, but made provision for one of them, OGODEI, to succeed him as Great Khan.

Genoa, a port in NW Italy (see maps, pp. 21 and 25). An independent republic from the 10th century, by the 13th century it controlled much of the W Mediterranean trade and some in the E Mediterranean, where it engaged in prolonged rivalry with VENICE, culminating in Genoese defeat in 1380. Politically Genoa was unstable, and repeatedly came under outside rule.

George I (1660–1727), first Hanoverian king of Great Britain and Ireland (1714–27), elector of HANOVER (1698–1727). Great-grandson of JAMES II, he became king on the death of the childless Queen ANNE. Never at home in England and always more interested in Hanover, he was content to give his support to WALPOLE, and thereby contributed to the rise to power of the WHIGS.

George II (1683–1760), king of Great Britain and Ireland and elector of HANOVER (1727–60). The son of GEORGE I, he supported MARIA THERESA in the War of the AUSTRIAN SUCCESSION, fighting at the Battle of Dettingen (1743). The later part of his reign was marked by British victories in Canada, the Caribbean and India during the SEVEN YEARS WAR.

George III (1738–1820), king of Great Britain and Ireland, (1760–1820) and of HANOVER (1815–20). The grandson of GEORGE II, 'Farmer George' opposed the demands of the American colonists for independence but saw the American colonies lost during his reign. He became insane in 1811, after which his son, later GEORGE IV, acted as regent.

George IV (1762–1830), king of Great Britain and Ireland, and of Hanover (1820–30). The eldest son of GEORGE III, he formed a close association with the WHIG opposition in the 1780s. As regent (1811–20) and as king his dissolute lifestyle undermined the prestige of the crown. A leader of taste and fashion, he gave his name to the REGENCY period.

George V (1865–1936), king of Great Britain and Ireland and emperor of India (1910–36), second son of EDWARD VII. Crises relating to Irish HOME RULE and reform of the House of LORDS, followed closely by WORLD WAR I, forced him to adapt to fast-changing circumstances. He was succeeded by EDWARD VIII.

George VI (1895–1952), king of Great Britain and Northern Ireland (1936–52), emperor of India (1936–47). The second son of GEORGE V, succeeding to the throne on the abdication of his brother EDWARD VIII, he is chiefly remembered for helping to sustain public morale during the BLITZ. He was succeeded by his elder daughter, ELIZABETH II.

Georgia, a republic in the Caucasus Mountains of W Asia. Georgia is the home of an ancient civilization established in the 3rd millennium BC. Georgian states, including Colchis and Iberia, flourished in the 1st millennium BC. Colchis fell to the Greeks before being ruled by Pontus and then Rome (65 BC). Christianity was adopted c. AD 330. From the 4th to the 7th centuries Georgia was fought over by the BYZANTINE Empire, the Persians and, later, the Arabs. In the 8th century the Bagratid family established several Georgian kingdoms. Bagrat III (975–1014) reunited Georgia. His descendant Queen Tamara (1184–1213) established an empire that included most of the Caucasian region, but national unity was destroyed by Mongol invasions, and dynastic quarrels. From the 16th to the 18th centuries Georgia was disputed by the OTTOMAN Turks and the Persians. An independent Georgia was reunited in 1762 and sought Russian protection against Turkey and Persia. Russia deposed the Bagratids (1801) and annexed Georgia by degrees (1801–78). Following the Russian Revolution (1918), a Georgian republic, allied to Germany, was proclaimed. A British occupation (1918–20) in favour of the WHITE Russians failed to win local support, and Georgia was invaded by the Soviet Red Army (1921). Georgia became part of the Transcaucasian Soviet Republic in 1921 and a separate Union Republic of the USSR in 1936. Following the abortive coup by Communist hardliners in Moscow (September 1991), Georgia declared independence. Locked into a fierce civil war, Georgia remained outside the CIS (the defence and economic community founded when the USSR was dissolved in December 1991). A temporary state council – led by Eduard SHEVARDNADZE, the former Soviet Foreign Minister – replaced a military council in March 1992. The Abkhazian Muslims attempted secession (1992–3).

German Confederation (1815–66), an alliance of 39 German states formed at the Congress of VIENNA. Ambassadors of member-states met regularly at the Federal DIET in Frankfurt. The confederation was conceived by the Austrian chancellor METTERNICH. Although the Confederation contained such important ancient states as BAVARIA, HANOVER, Saxony, Württemberg, Hesse, Oldenburg, Baden and Mecklenburg, none could match PRUSSIA or Austria for size or influence. The Confederation did not satisfy the longings of the German people for unity. The Confederation preserved the vested interests of minor princes, and above all those of the Austrian Habsburgs.

Germany, a country of Central Europe. See panel.

Geronimo (c. 1829–1909), APACHE Indian chief who led resistance to white settlement of Arizona.

Gestapo (German, *Geheime Staatspolizei*), Nazi Germany's secret state police founded by GOERING in 1933. Headed by HIMMLER as SS chief from 1936, it was notorious for its ruthless methods employed to eradicate anti-Nazi resistance.

Gettysburg, Battle of (1–3 July 1863), a decisive battle of the AMERICAN CIVIL WAR. The three-day engagement, which cost the Union 23,000 casualties and the Confederacy over 20,000, put a halt to Southern commander Robert E. LEE's invasion of the North. From then on the CONFEDERACY was on the defensive.

Ghali, Boutros Boutros (1922–), Egyptian statesman and diplomat, Secretary-General of the UNITED NATIONS (1992–).

Ghana, a republic in W Africa. Trade for gold, ivory and slaves led to the establishment of European coastal stations from around 1600. Britain ousted the Danes (1850) and the Dutch (1872) to establish the Gold Coast colony in 1874. The great inland kingdom of ASHANTI was finally conquered in 1898. After World War II, the Gold Coast set the pace for decolonization in Black Africa. After independence in 1957 – as Ghana – Dr Kwame NKRUMAH'S grandiose policies and increasingly dictatorial rule led to his overthrow in a military coup in 1966. Ghana has since struggled to overcome its economic and political problems. There were six coups in 20 years, including two by Flight Lieutenant Jerry Rawlings (1979 and 1982). A multi-party system was restored in 1992.

Ghana, kingdom of, a former African kingdom located in modern MALI that flourished in the 8th–12th centuries. With the kingdom of MALI, it dominated the routes between the goldfields and desert trails to North Africa.

Ghent, Treaty of (1814), the treaty ending the WAR OF 1812 between Britain and the USA.

Ghibellines, the pro-imperial faction in Italian politics from the mid-13th century. See GUELPHS.

Ghurid, a Muslim dynasty ruling in Afghanistan. under Muhammad of Ghur it established Muslim rule over large parts of N India in the late 12th century. The empire did not survive the assassination of Muhammad in 1206, though independent rulers of Turkish and Afghan origin continued to rule in N India.

Gibraltar, a rocky peninsula on the S coast of Spain commanding the entrance to the Mediterranean from the Atlantic. Ruled by Britain since the Treaty of UTRECHT in 1714, it is claimed by Spain as sovereign territory.

Gierek, Edward (1913–), Polish statesman, First Secretary of the Communist Party and de facto ruler of POLAND (1970–80).

'Gilded Age', a term coined by Mark Twain and Charles Dudley Warner to describe the decade following the AMERICAN CIVIL WAR, characterized by economic expansion, unrestricted speculation and financial and political corruption.

Girondin, a member of a party of moderate republicans during the FRENCH REVOLUTION. In 1793 they were expelled from the Convention by the SANS CULOTTES, and many of their members were executed during the TERROR.

Giscard d'Estaing, Valery (1926–), French independent republican statesman, president of France (1974–81). He was defeated by MITTERRAND in his bid for re-election in 1981. He founded the Union pour la Démocratie Française (UDF) in 1978.

Gladstone, William Ewart (1809–98), British Liberal statesman, prime minister (1868–74, 1880–5, 1886 and 1892–4). He was a Peelite TORY until 1865, serving as chancellor of the exchequer (1852–5, 1859–65, 1865–6) under ABERDEEN, PALMERSTON and RUSSELL. In 1867 he succeeded Russell as leader of the LIBERAL Party. Gladstone's first and second premierships were notable for important reform legislation, but his third (1886) was dominated by an unsuccessful bid for Irish HOME RULE which split the Liberals. His last term saw the passage of a Home Rule Bill through the Commons (1893), but he resigned when it was defeated in the Lords.

GERMANY

4th–5th centuries AD: Germanic peoples – who displaced Celts in the area that was to become Germany – helped to destroy the Western ROMAN EMPIRE. **5th–9th centuries:** Most of the German lands were united under the empire of the FRANKS. **814:** After the death of CHARLEMAGNE the Frankish empire was divided up. **9th–10th centuries:** The Saxon kings – in particular OTTO I – unsuccessfully attempted to reunite the Germans, although most of Germany was nominally within the HOLY ROMAN EMPIRE. **12th–13th centuries:** The HOHENSTAUFEN Emperors tried to make their mark in Italy as well as N of the Alps; this diversion allowed dozens of German princes, dukes, bishops and counts to assert their independence. **1437:** The HABSBURGS succeeded to the imperial title. Although they were to hold the title for almost the entire period to 1806, they were too concerned with the fortunes of their lands in AUSTRIA, HUNGARY and BOHEMIA to control their subordinate German electorates, principalities and bishoprics. **16th century:** The independence of local rulers was reinforced during the REFORMATION, when a number of princes followed the lead of the Protestant reformer Martin LUTHER. **1555:** The Peace of AUGSBURG established the principle that a state's religion followed that of its prince. **17th century:** Disputes over the Augsburg settlement contributed to the outbreak of the THIRTY YEARS WAR (1618–48), and exacerbated Germany's disunity. **1648:** The Peace of WESTPHALIA recognized the sovereignty of over 300 German states; these were to form an astonishing jigsaw on the map of Europe until the 19th century. **18th century:** Some small German states (notably Saxe-Weimar) became centres of enlightened government and culture; others – notably HANOVER from 1714 – became involved in the power politics of the major states. **1740–86:** BRANDENBURG-PRUSSIA emerged as a powerful military power under the HOHENZOLLERN family of electors (kings after 1701), achieving great power status under FREDERICK II, who greatly enlarged his kingdom at the expense of Austria and Poland. **1796–1815:** Map of Germany redrawn by France during the NAPOLEONIC WARS; foundation of the CONFEDERATION OF THE RHINE (1806); upsurge of romantically inspired German nationalist sentiment. **1815:** Formation by METTERNICH of the GERMAN CONFEDERATION under the terms of the Congress of VIENNA. **1830:** Beginnings of industrialization in Germany. **1834:** Formation of Prussian-led ZOLLVEREIN (customs union) established Prussian dominance of the German Confederation. **1848:** Liberal nationalist movements swept Germany, extracting short-lived liberal constitutions from autocratic princes. **1862:** BISMARCK became Prussian chancellor. **1864:** Prussia invaded and defeated Denmark and took control of SCHLESWIG (1866). **1866–67:** The German Confederation collapsed after the AUSTRO-PRUSSIAN WAR, and a new North German Confederation was established under Prussian domination. **1870–71:** Bismarck instigated the FRANCO-PRUSSIAN WAR: gaining ALSACE-LORRAINE from France; establishment of the German SECOND EMPIRE with WILHELM I of Prussia as emperor (Kaiser). **From 1871:** Expansionist unified Germany attempted to extend its influence in Europe. **1879:** DUAL ALLIANCE with Austria-Hungary. **1888:** Accession of the mercurial Kaiser WILHELM II, who dismissed Bismarck (1890) and embarked on an aggressive foreign policy that led to naval and commercial rivalry with Britain. **Late 19th century:** German colonization in Africa. **1914:** Germany joined Austro-Hungary in launching WORLD WAR I after the assassination of FRANZ FERDINAND. **1918:** Germany defeated. **1919:** Under the terms of the VERSAILLES TREATY Germany was stripped of its colonial empire, made to disarm and forced to pay REPARATIONS. **1919–33:** The liberal WEIMAR REPUBLIC failed to bring economic or political stability. **Early 1930s:** The NAZI Party gained popularity under Adolf HITLER. **1933:** Hitler became chancellor and then president (1934). **1935:** German Jews denied citizen rights under the NUREMBERG LAWS. **1938–9:** Hitler annexed Austria in the ANSCHLUSS and dismembered CZECHOSLOVAKIA. **1939:** The German invasion of POLAND launched WORLD WAR II. **1945:** German defeat: Germany lost substantial territories to Poland and was divided into four zones of occupation by Britain, France, the USA and the USSR. **1948–9:** The USSR blockaded West Berlin, leading to the BERLIN AIRLIFT. **1949:** The W zones of Germany merged to form the Federal Republic of (West) Germany, while the German Democratic Republic (GDR; East Germany) was proclaimed in the Soviet zone. **1950s:** West Germany experienced an 'economic miracle' under Konrad ADENAUER. **1953:** Food shortages and repressive Communist rule led to an abortive uprising in the GDR. **1955:** West Germany gained sovereignty as a member of the Western Alliance. **1957:** West Germany joined the EUROPEAN COMMUNITY. **1961:** GDR leader ULBRICHT ordered the building of the BERLIN WALL to stem the flow of East Germans to West Germany. **1972:** Willy BRANDT's policy of OSTPOLITIK normalized relations between East and West Germany. **From 1982:** Under Helmut KOHL West Germany continued its impressive economic growth and enthusiastic membership of the EC. **1989:** Massive public demonstrations in favour of reform resulted in the fall of Communist leader Erich HONECKER and the opening of the Berlin Wall. **1990:** Germany reunified. **Since 1991:** Germany has been plagued by mass unemployment in the E and the rise of neo-Nazi groups.

glasnost (Russian 'openness'), the policy of greater freedom of discussion introduced by GORBACHOV in the Soviet Union from 1985. In the mass media all past leaders were criticized, social problems examined truthfully, and previously banned literature was published. See also PERESTROIKA.

Glencoe, Massacre of (1692), the murder by English troops and members of the Campbell clan of members of the Catholic MacDonald clan in the Scottish Highlands, following the Macdonald chief's failure to meet a deadline for declaring his loyalty to WILLIAM III and MARY II.

Glendower, Owen (Owain Glyndŵr; c. 1355–c. 1417), self-styled Prince of Wales whose rebellion against HENRY IV, although unsuccessful, made him a national hero in Wales.

Glorious Revolution, the political events in England in 1688–9, which replaced JAMES II with WILLIAM III and MARY II as joint monarchs. The efforts of James II to recatholicize England led supporters of the Anglican Church to invite William of Orange, husband of James's daughter Mary, to come to their aid. William and his army landed in England in November 1688 and James fled to France. The BILL OF RIGHTS of 1689 increased the role of the English Parliament in government.

Gnosticism, a religious movement within the early Christian Church, probably with pre-Christian roots. It emphasized esoteric spiritual truths, the knowledge of which could lead to a freeing of the spirit from the body. It came to be regarded as a heresy. Its sects included MANICHAEISM.

Goa, a former Portuguese colony in India. Captured by Alfonso de ALBUQUERQUE in 1510, it became the administrative centre of Portugal's East Indian empire.

Godfrey of Bouillon (c. 1060–1100), a prominent leader of the First CRUSADE. After the capture of JERUSALEM he became first ruler of the Latin Kingdom of Jerusalem.

Goebbels, Josef (1897–1945), German NAZI politician. From 1933 to 1945 he was HITLER'S Minister of Enlightenment and Propaganda, and his control of the press, radio and cinema contributed enormously to the establishment of the totalitarian Nazi state. He committed suicide with his family in Hitler's bunker in 1945.

Goering, Hermann (1893–1945), German Nazi politician. He founded the GESTAPO, and as commander of the German air force built up the Luftwaffe into a formidable fighting force. He was named HITLER'S deputy in the early stages of WORLD WAR II, but lost influence after Germany's defeat in the Battle of BRITAIN. He was sentenced to death for war crimes at the NUREMBERG TRIALS, but committed suicide in prison.

Golan Heights, a region of SW Syria that was occupied by Israel in 1967 during the SIX DAY WAR. Israel's annexation of the Golan Heights (1981) is not recognized internationally.

Golden Horde, the W part of the MONGOL Empire (see map, p. 19). In 1278 the Empire was divided up between the Mongol princes, a line descending from Genghis Khan's eldest son becoming Khans of the Golden Horde on the Russian steppe. The khanate disintegrated at the end of the 15th century.

gold rushes, the name given to historic movements of prospectors into recently discovered gold fields. The most famous gold rushes took place in the 19th century: California 1848, Australia 1851–3, Witwatersrand (South Africa) 1884, and Klondike (Canada) 1897–8.

gold standard, a monetary system in which a country's unit of currency was defined in terms of a fixed amount of gold. By 1900 most major countries had adopted it, but could not maintain it during World War I, because of difficulties in the international movement of gold. Britain returned to the gold standard in 1925, abandoning it again in 1931 because of the DEPRESSION.

Gomulka, Wladyslaw (1905–82), Polish statesman, First Secretary of the Communist Party and de facto ruler of POLAND (1956–70).

Gonzalez, Felipe (1942–), Spanish socialist statesman. As prime minister (1982–) he dismantled the last remnants of FRANCO'S system, took Spain into the EC and modernized the economy.

Gorbachov, Mikhail Sergeyevich (1931–), Soviet statesman, general secretary of the Communist Party (1985–91), president of the Soviet Union (1989–91). His liberal reforms of GLASNOST and later PERESTROIKA led to far-reaching changes in the economic and political life of the USSR. His liberal credentials were undermined by his suppression of the nationalist movements in the BALTIC REPUBLICS, but he moved back towards the reformers during 1991. Gorbachov resigned on Christmas Day 1991 following the failure of a coup by Communist hardliners and the international recognition of the independence of the former Soviet republics.

Gordon, Charles George (1833–85), British soldier and colonial administrator. His defence of Shanghai against the TAIPING rebels earned him the nickname 'Chinese Gordon'. In 1884 he was sent by the British government to help evacuate Egyptian forces from Khartoum, which was threatened by the MAHDI, but was killed only days before the relief of the city from a ten-month siege.

Goths, the Germanic peoples who invaded large parts of the Western ROMAN EMPIRE from the 3rd to the 5th centuries. The eastern Goths were known as the OSTROGOTHS, while the western group were known as the VISIGOTHS.

Gowon, Yakubu (1934–), see NIGERIA.

Gracchus, Tiberius (c. 168–133 BC) and Gaius (c. 159–121) (often collectively known as the Gracchi), Roman politicians. In 133 Tiberius Gracchus introduced a land reform to redistribute land to the poor, but there was immense opposition, and he was murdered in an outbreak of political violence. Ten years later his brother, Gaius, attempted to bring in a series of popular reforms and suffered the same fate.

Granada, Emirate of, the last Muslim state in Spain. It survived the RECONQUISTA and did not fall to FERDINAND of Aragon and ISABELLA of Castile until 1492. See map, p. 21.

Granicus, Battle of the River (334 BC), a victory of ALEXANDER THE GREAT over the Persians. Alexander's army of 32,000 infantry and 5000 cavalry engaged the massed forces of the Western Persian provinces at the River Granicus in NW Anatolia and defeated them (see map, p. 12).

Grant, Ulysses S. (1822–85), US soldier and 18th president of the USA (1869–77). He rose quickly through Union army ranks during the AMERICAN CIVIL WAR, capturing VICKSBURG in 1863 and defeating the CONFEDERACY at CHATTANOOGA. He eventually assumed supreme command of federal operations, and accepted LEE'S surrender at APPOMATTOX. An obvious choice for president in 1868, he served two undistinguished terms as a Republican.

Gravettian culture, a phase of the Upper PALAEOLITHIC period of Eurasian prehistory, named after a cave in the Dordogne, France.

Great Exhibition (1851), an exhibition of industrial products from Britain and the continent, planned and opened by Prince Albert. Held in Joseph Paxton's specially constructed Crystal Palace in Hyde Park, London, it marked the apogee of Britain's supremacy as an urban-industrial, free-trade nation.

Great Leap Forward (1958–9), an ambitious programme of industrial and agricultural expansion launched in Communist CHINA by MAO ZEDONG. High quotas were set for the production of materials, and agriculture was organized into communes. The programme failed, but Mao again tried to introduce radical ideas in the CULTURAL REVOLUTION.

Great Plague (1664–5), the last of the great bubonic plagues to hit England; it killed about 70,000 people in London alone.

Great Schism (1378–1417), a period of upheaval in the Western Christian Church during which rival popes claimed the papacy. In 1378 Urban VI (1378–89) was elected pope, the first in Rome after the end of the AVIGNON PERIOD. His obstinacy and unwillingness to compromise alienated many non-Italian cardinals, who responded by electing a rival pope. The reputation of the papacy plummeted further as two (and, from 1409, three) rival popes vied for political support from the rulers and peoples of Europe. At the Council of CONSTANCE (1414–17), with the backing of Emperor SIGISMUND, the rivals were deposed and Martin V (1417–31) elected as unopposed pope.

Great Trek, the northward migration of Afrikaner VOORTREKKERS away from British-administered CAPE COLONY in the 1830s. Many settled in Natal but, after Natal became a British colony in 1843, crossed the Drakensberg Mountains to create the independent republics of the ORANGE FREE STATE and the TRANSVAAL.

Great Wall of China, a series of defensive structures designed to protect China from attack by Central Asian nomads. It was erected under the reign of the QIN emperor SHI HUANGDI (221–210 BC).

Greece, a country of SE Europe. See panel, p. 134.

Greek–Persian Wars, see PERSIAN WARS.

Greek War of Independence (1821–32), the revolt of the Greeks against OTTOMAN rule, resulting in Greek independence. Many individuals from Western Europe, such as the poet Byron, fought alongside the Greeks, who declared their independence in 1822 after some striking military successes. However, four years later MEHEMET ALI of Egypt reopened the war in an attempt to restore Turkish rule. Foreign intervention defeated the Egyptian fleet at NAVARINO in 1827, and the following year Russia – as an ally of Greece – seized Adrianople. The Turks made peace in 1829 and confirmed Greek independence in 1832.

Greenland, an island mostly within the Arctic Circle, first settled by INUIT by the 10th century AD. It was colonized by Norse from Iceland, Norway and the British Isles in the 980s. Worsening climatic conditions after 1200 and the effects of the BLACK DEATH led to the abandonment of the Norse settlements by c. 1500. Resettled by Danes from the 1720s, it is now an autonomous dependency of DENMARK.

Greens, the name used by a number of political parties dedicated to environmental protection and opposed to nuclear power. 'Green' parties enjoyed some electoral success in Europe, especially in West Germany in the 1980s.

Gregorian Reform, the period of reform in the Roman Catholic Church instigated by pope GREGORY VII in the late 11th century.

Gregory I, St ('the Great'; 540–604), the first monk to occupy the position of pope (590–604). A successful administrator, monastic founder and theologian, he helped to defend Rome against the invading LOMBARDS and relieved social distress caused by floods and famine. His work laid the foundations for the future PAPAL STATE. He also encouraged missionary activity, including AUGUSTINE'S mission to England.

Gregory VII (Hildebrand; c. 1021–85), pope (1073–85), a leading exponent of the papal reform movement. 'Gregorian Reform' aimed to enhance the status of the priesthood and to increase the power of the papacy over Western Christendom. His aims caused bitter conflict with the Emperor HENRY IV in the INVESTITURE CONTEST after 1075. Henry seized Rome in 1084, leaving Gregory to die in exile.

Grenada, an island in the E Caribbean. Grenada was discovered by COLUMBUS in 1498, colonized by France in 1650 and ceded to Britain in 1783. Independence was gained in 1974. The left-wing New Jewel Movement seized power in a coup in 1979. In 1983 the PM Maurice Bishop was killed in a further coup in which more extreme members of the government seized power. Acting upon a request from E Caribbean islands to intervene, US and Caribbean forces landed in Grenada. After several days' fighting, the coup leaders were detained. Constitutional rule was restored in 1984.

Grenville, George (1712–1770), British statesman, prime minister (1763–5). His STAMP ACT (1765) provoked the American colonists. His son, William Wyndham, 1st Baron Grenville (1759–1834), was prime minister (1806–7) of a coalition 'ministry of all the talents', whose most important Act outlawed the slave trade.

Grey, Charles, 2nd Earl (1764–1845), Brtitish WHIG statesman, prime minister (1830–4). His government passed the first great REFORM ACT (1832) and legislation abolishing slavery throughout the British Empire.

Grey, Lady Jane (1537–54), queen of England (10–19 July 1553), great-granddaughter of HENRY VII. Her father-in-law, the Duke of Northumberland, persuaded EDWARD VI to name her his successor to ensure a Protestant succession. The 'Nine Days' Queen' was toppled by the Catholic MARY I, and executed after a rising in her favour led by Sir Thomas Wyatt.

GREECE

c. 2200–1450 BC: The Bronze Age MINOAN civilization was based in Crete. **c. 1500–1150 BC:** The MYCENAEAN civilization flourished on the Greek mainland. **1100–800 BC:** 'Dark age' of poverty following the collapse of Mycenaean civilization. **8th century BC:** City-states began to emerge in what is known as the ARCHAIC PERIOD (c. 800–500); SPARTA gained control of the S Peloponnese. **c. 750 BC:** Reintroduction of literacy into Greece. **594 BC:** Reforms of SOLON in ATHENS – beginnings of Athenian democracy. **508–7 BC:** Reforms of CLEISTHENES made Athens a more effective military power. **490–479 BC:** PERSIAN WARS; defeat of the Persians at Marathon (490), Salamis (480) and Plataea (479). **478 BC:** Athens assumed leadership of the DELIAN LEAGUE. **c. 462–429 BC:** PERICLES played a dominant role in Athenian politics. **431–404 BC:** PELOPONNESIAN WAR ended in victory for Sparta over Athens. **4th century BC:** Opposition of a coalition of city-states to the harsh policies of Sparta led to a succession of wars; decline of Sparta after defeat at LEUCTRA (371 BC); main Greek states weakened by civil war. **359 BC:** PHILIP II became king of MACEDON and defeated the city-states to achieve dominance in mainland Greece (338). **336–323 BC:** The conquests of ALEXANDER THE GREAT brought the whole of the former Persian Empire under the control of Greek-speaking rulers (see HELLENISTIC AGE). **From 146 BC:** Greece formed part of the ROMAN EMPIRE. **5th century AD–1204:** On the division of the Roman Empire, Greece formed part of the Eastern (BYZANTINE) Empire based in Constantinople. **1204–15th century:** Greece was divided into four states – the Greek kingdoms of Salonika and Epirus in the N, and the Frankish monarchies of Athens and Achaea in the S; VENICE gained the majority of the Greek islands. **Early 15th century:** The OTTOMAN Turks gradually asserted control over the region. However, the continuing vitality of the ORTHODOX CHURCH helped maintain a strong Greek national identity. **18th century:** European powers, notably Russia, attempted to use Greece in their quarrels with the Ottoman Turks. **1821:** The GREEK WAR OF INDEPENDENCE against Ottoman rule attracted support throughout Europe. **1827:** Turkish fleet destroyed at NAVARINO by European forces. **1830:** Greek independent state established. **1832:** Monarchy established under Prince Otto of Bavaria. **1862:** Otto ousted by revolution. **1863:** Prince George of Denmark became king (George I), and Greece gained extra territory from the Turks. **1912–13:** Greece won most of the areas disputed with Turkey, including half of MACEDONIA, in the BALKAN WARS. **1920–1:** The seizure of Anatolia on the orders of King Constantine I led to military defeat by Turkey and the establishment of a republic (1924). **1935:** Monarchy restored; General Ionnis Metaxas ruled Greece as a virtual dictator (1936–41). **1941–5:** The German invasion and occupation during WORLD WAR II was met by rival resistance groups of Communists and monarchists. **1945–9:** Civil war between Communists and monarchists, finally won by the monarchists with US and British aid. **1967:** Military coup. **1967–74:** Greece ruled by military junta of the 'Colonels', headed by Colonel George Papadopoulos. **1973:** Republic proclaimed. **1974:** Dictatorship of the Colonels ended when their encouragement of a Greek Cypriot coup in CYPRUS brought Greece to the verge of war with TURKEY; restoration of multi-party civilian rule. **1981:** Greece became full member of EUROPEAN COMMUNITY. **1981–9:** Socialist prime minister Andreas Papandreou in power. **1993:** Papandreou re-elected.

Griffith, Arthur (1872–1922), Irish journalist and nationalist. A co-founder of SINN FEIN, he was the (unwilling) leader of the Irish delegation in the talks that led to the 1921 Anglo-Irish Treaty, establishing the Irish Free State. See IRELAND.

Gromyko, Andrei Andreyevich (1909–89), Soviet statesman. Appointed foreign minister in 1957, he held the post for 28 years until his replacement by Eduard SHEVARDNADZE in 1985. He was also president of the Soviet Union (1985–8).

Group of Seven (G7), an informal grouping of major Western economic powers – Canada, France, Germany, Japan, Italy, UK and the USA. Since 1975 their leaders have met regularly to discuss major economic, monetary and political problems.

Guadalcanal, Battle of (1942), a battle fought in the SW Pacific during WORLD WAR II. US marines landed on the island of Guadalcanal in the Solomon Islands in August 1942, and forced the Japanese to evacuate the island in February 1943, after six months of bitter fighting. See PACIFIC CAMPAIGNS.

Guatemala, a republic in CENTRAL AMERICA. The area was the centre of the MAYAN civilization between the 4th and 9th centuries AD. After 1524, Guatemala was the administrative centre of Spanish Central America. Independence was proclaimed in 1821, but the country was part of the Central American Federation until 1839. Guatemala has a history of being ruled by dictators allied to landowners. However, in the 1950s President Jacobo Arbenz expropriated large estates, dividing them among the peasantry. Accused of being a Communist, he was deposed by the army with US military aid (1954). For over 30 years, the left was suppressed, leading to the emergence of guerrilla armies. Thousands of dissidents were killed or disappeared. Civilian government was restored in 1986, but after mounting unrest the military took over in 1993.

Guelph, a term derived from the faction (originally the Welf family) opposed to the HOHENSTAUFEN in Germany during the High Middle Ages. In the 13th century it was exported to Italian politics where it became associated with the propapal faction. See GHIBELLINE.

Guernica, a town in the BASQUE region of Spain, razed by German bombers of the Condor Legion on 26 April 1937 during the SPANISH CIVIL WAR.

Guesclin, Bertrand du (c. 1320–80), French military commander. Under Charles V (1364–80) he helped recapture French territory from the English during the HUNDRED YEARS WAR.

Guevara, Ernesto 'Che' (1928–67), Argentinian-born revolutionary leader. He fought as a guerrilla with CASTRO in the Cuban Revolution, and was rewarded with ministerial rank in Castro's government. In 1967 he led an abortive revolution in Bolivia, during which he was killed. Guevara became a cult figure for radical students in the 1960s and 1970s.

Guinea, a republic in W Africa. Portuguese slave traders visited the coast from the 15th century. The colony of French Guinea was established in 1890. Guinea voted for a complete separation from France in 1958, suffering severe French reprisals as a result. The authoritarian radical leader Sékou TOURÉ isolated Guinea, but he became reconciled with France in 1978. The leaders of a military coup (1984) have achieved some economic reforms.

Guinea-Bissau, a republic in W Africa. The Portuguese were involved in the slave trade in the area from 1441, but did not establish the colony of Portuguese Guinea until 1879. Failing to secure reform by peaceful means, the PAIGC movement mounted a liberation war (1961–74). Independence was proclaimed in 1973 and recognized by Portugal in 1974. Democratic reforms introduced a multiparty system in 1991.

Guiscard, Robert (c. 1015–85), Norman conqueror. The son of Tancred de Hauteville, with his brother Roger he conquered the BYZANTINE provinces of Apulia and Calabria by 1071. In 1091 Roger Guiscard completed the conquest of Sicily from the Arabs. His son ROGER II later took control of all the Norman possessions in S Italy. Norman control of the region ended at the end of the 12th century. See SICILIES, KINGDOM OF THE TWO.

Guise, one of the leading noble families of 16th-century France. Their power was based on influence at court, estates in E France and military exploits in the service of the crown. Henry (1550–88), the third duke of Guise, was one of the organizers of the ST BARTHOLOMEW'S DAY MASSACRE, and led the militant Catholic HOLY LEAGUE in the FRENCH WARS OF RELIGION until his assassination at the behest of HENRY III in 1588.

Guizot, François-Pierre Guillaume (1787–1874), French politician. He held important ministerial posts under LOUIS PHILIPPE, presiding over a golden age of French industrial capitalism. He was briefly premier (1847–8) before his resignation during the REVOLUTIONS OF 1848.

Gujarat, a region in W India. Its ports developed important trading and cultural links in both westerly and easterly directions. Ruled by Muslims from the late 13th century, it was conquered by the MARATHAS in the mid-18th century before being absorbed by the English EAST INDIA COMPANY.

Gulag, Russian acronym for Chief Administration of Corrective Labour Camps. It was responsible for supervising an elaborate system of detention, torture and imprisonment of dissidents – 'enemies of the state' – inside the Soviet Union, chiefly under STALIN (1924–53). Many dissidents served their sentences in one of a huge network of camps – the 'Gulag archipelago' – in northern Siberia. Many of the worst excesses of the Gulag system were mitigated under KHRUSHCHEV, but dissidents – of whom the most celebrated were the novelist Alexander Solzhenitsyn and the physicist Andrei Sakharov – continued to be imprisoned under Brezhnev. Intellectual dissidents were released as GORBACHOV'S policy of GLASNOST came to have effect from 1987.

Gulf War (1991), a conflict in the Middle East between IRAQ and a multinational force led by the USA. In August 1990 Iraqi president Saddam HUSSEIN invaded and annexed oil-rich KUWAIT. When Iraq ignored UN demands for an Iraqi withdrawal, a US-dominated international force was despatched to the Gulf to prevent an Iraqi invasion of Saudi Arabia. A massive aerial bombardment of Baghdad and military targets in Iraq and Kuwait ('Operation Desert Storm') in January 1991 wore down Iraq's fighting capability, and on 24 February coalition forces entered Kuwaiti and Iraqi territory, routing the Iraqis in a brief ground campaign. Despite his defeat Saddam Hussein remained in power with his military capacity largely intact, enabling him to suppress revolts by KURDS in the N of Iraq and Shiites in the S.

Gunpowder Plot (1605), an English Catholic conspiracy to murder JAMES I and his ministers by blowing up the palace of Westminster during the state opening of Parliament on 5 November 1605. One of the plotters, Guy Fawkes (1570–1606), was discovered and arrested in the cellars beneath Parliament, and later hanged, drawn and quartered along with seven other conspirators.

Guptas, a Magdahlan dynasty that ruled most of N and central India from a base in NE India between the mid-4th and 6th centuries. Early Gupta rulers presided over a 'golden age' in religion and the arts during which both Buddhism and Hinduism flourished. Attacks by the HUNS brought about a collapse of Gupta power in the 6th century.

Gustavus II Adolphus (1594–1632), king of Sweden (1611–32). His reform of Sweden's administration and armed forces, together with his development of mobile field artillery, contributed decisively to Sweden's successes against Poland and in Germany in the THIRTY YEARS WAR. Most of N Germany came under the control of the Swedes and their allies after Gustavus' successful invasion of Germany in 1630. Only his death at LÜTZEN (1632) halted his further progress.

Gutenberg, Johannes (c. 1398–1468), German printer. In 1450 he set up the first printing press at Mainz in Germany, and the technique spread rapidly through urbanized Europe.

Guthrum (d. 890), the leader of a major Danish invasion of Anglo-Saxon England (871–8). Only WESSEX, under ALFRED the Great, survived the Danish onslaught, and in 886 Guthrum and Alfred agreed on the boundaries between Wessex and the DANELAW.

Guyana, a republic of NE South America. Dutch colonies on the Guyanese coast – established since the 1620s – were captured by the British in 1796 and merged to form British Guiana in 1831. From the 1840s large numbers of Indian and Chinese labourers were imported from Asia to work on sugar plantations. Racial tension between their descendants – now the majority – and the black community (descended from imported African slaves) led to violence in 1964 and 1978. Guyana has been independent since 1966.

Habsburg, a German princely family that became a leading European royal dynasty from the 15th to the 20th centuries. From 1440 to 1806 members of the family held the office of Emperor of the HOLY ROMAN EMPIRE almost without interruption. Its power was established by Rudolf I (king of the Romans, 1273–91), who extended the family's rule over Austria. The real growth of Habsburg power began in the late 15th century when MAXIMILIAN I married the heiress of BURGUNDY and the Netherlands. Spain was acquired when the Spanish crown passed to Maximilian's grandson, CHARLES V, and a marriage between the Habsburgs and the Polish JAGIELLON dynasty brought Bohemia and Hungary within the Habsburg orbit in 1526. Combining in his hands the Habsburg, Burgundian and Spanish inheritances, Charles V ruled over the largest European empire since Charlemagne. After his abdication in 1555 the Habsburg dominions were divided between the Spanish line (which died out in 1700) and the Austrian line. After the demise of the Holy Roman Empire the Habsburgs ruled in AUSTRIA (1806–67) and AUSTRIA-HUNGARY (1867–1918).

Hadrian (AD 76–138), Roman emperor (117–138). His reign was marked by prosperity at home and peace abroad. He initiated the building of HADRIAN'S WALL in Britain.

Hadrian's Wall, the wall marking the N limit of the Roman province of Britain. It was erected in AD 122–6 after a visit to Britain by the Roman emperor HADRIAN.

Haig, Douglas, 1st Earl (1861–1928), British field marshal, commander of British forces on the Western Front (1915–18) during WORLD WAR I. His attritional strategy at the Battles of the SOMME (1916) and PASSCHENDAELE (1917), which led to massive casualties, has been much criticized.

Haile Selassie (1892–1975), Ethiopian monarch and the last of its feudal rulers. Exiled in 1935, he returned to ETHIOPIA in 1941 after leading successful resistance against the occupying Italians. In 1955 he introduced a constitution, but his failure to introduce economic reforms and reduce his own political power estranged many of his supporters. The military seized power in 1974 and the emperor, stripped of his power and wealth, died in his palace in 1975.

Haiti, a republic comprising the E of the island of HISPANIOLA in the Caribbean. Columbus discovered Hispaniola in 1492, and in the 17th century the French settled Haiti, which formally became a colony in 1697. Black slaves – who were imported to work plantations – revolted in 1791 and were freed in 1794. TOUSSAINT L'OUVERTURE – a former slave – became governor general (1801), but was unable to defeat a French force sent to restore the old order. Independence was proclaimed in 1804 during a revolt led by Jean-Jacques DESSALINES and Henri Christophe, both of whom reigned as monarchs of Haiti. A united republic was achieved in 1820. Coups, instability and tension between blacks and mulattos wracked Haiti until the US intervened (1915–35). President François DUVALIER – 'Papa Doc' – (in office 1956–71) and his son Jean-Claude (1971–86) cowed the country into submission by means of their infamous private militia, the Tontons Macoutes. Several coups have followed the violent end to the Duvalier era. A free multi-party election – the first in Haiti's history – took place in 1991, but constitutional government was suspended following a military coup nine months later.

Hallstatt, a burial site in N Austria that has given its name to a Celtic culture of the early Iron Age (900–500 BC). During the Hallstatt period cremation and interment became the standard form of burial, but they were later replaced by the tumulus or raised barrow grave. The Hallstatt culture was superseded by the LA TÈNE culture.

Hamilcar Barca (c. 270–228 BC), Carthaginian general. After Carthage lost Sicily to the Romans in the First PUNIC WAR Hamilcar conquered S and E Spain. He was the father of HANNIBAL and HASDRUBAL.

Hamilton, Alexander (1755–1804), US politician. An aide to General WASHINGTON in the American War of INDEPENDENCE, he served as a New York delegate to the 1787 Convention on the CONSTITUTION OF THE USA. An advocate of strong central government, he went on to become secretary of the treasury and a leading figure in FEDERALIST party ranks. He was killed in a duel by his political rival Aaron Burr (1756–1836).

Hamites, a group of N African peoples supposedly descended from Ham, the son of Noah.

Hammarskjöld, Dag (1915–61), Swedish diplomat, Secretary-General of the UNITED NATIONS (1953–61). He was killed in a plane crash during the CONGO CRISIS.

Hammurabi (d. 1750 BC), Amorite king of BABYLON (1792–1750 BC). He unified Mesopotamia for a short time under the hegemony of Babylon, extending the territory of Babylon from the Persian Gulf to parts of ASSYRIA. He is best known for his law code which specified individual rights as well as punishments.

Han, a dynasty that ruled CHINA from 202 BC to AD 220. Founded by the general Liu Bang, who overthrew the QIN dynasty, its power was consolidated by the emperor Wu Di, who vastly extended the size of the Chinese Empire which spread W into Central Asia, S into Vietnam and E into Korea. The Han years also saw the arrival of BUDDHISM, and set the pattern of Chinese government through a rigorously educated bureaucracy. The period of Han rule to AD 8 (from a capital at Chang'an) is known as the Western Han, the period from AD 25 to 220 (from a capital at Luoyang) is referred to as the Eastern Han.

Hannibal (247–183 BC), Carthaginian general, son of HAMILCAR BARCA, who according to legend made his son swear eternal enmity to Rome. He precipitated the Second PUNIC WAR in 218 when he crossed the Alps and invaded Italy with an army of 26,000 men and several war elephants. In spite of spectacular victories at TRASIMENE and CANNAE (216), he failed to win over Rome's Italian allies and was gradually worn down by the 'Fabian' tactics of Quintus FABIUS Maximus. Hannibal withdrew from Italy in 204, and was finally defeated by SCIPIO AFRICANUS at ZAMA (202).

Hanover, a former imperial electorate and kingdom in Germany. Briefly part of the kingdom of Westphalia during the Napoleonic Wars, Hanover – whose ELECTOR had succeeded to the British crown as GEORGE I in 1714 – was returned to Britain in 1815, when it also became a kingdom within the GERMAN CONFEDERATION. With the accession to the British throne of VICTORIA in 1837, the crowns of Britain and Hanover were separated, since the laws of succession in Hanover did not allow a woman to inherit the title. It was annexed by Prussia after the AUSTRO-PRUSSIAN WAR in 1866.

Hanover, House of, a British royal dynasty (1714–1901) that took its name from the German princely family that ruled the electorate of HANOVER from 1692 to 1815. In 1714 the elector of Hanover, having married Sophia of the Palatinate, granddaughter of JAMES I, succeeded to the English throne as GEORGE I, in accordance with the Act of SETTLEMENT (1701). The Hanoverian connection ended with the accession of Queen VICTORIA (1837).

Hanseatic League, a former association of towns in N Germany, which was established as a trading alliance in 1241 to protect their economic interests overseas. By the 14th century the League, comprising over 100 towns, had become a powerful independent political force. At times of crisis, when its dominance of Baltic trade was threatened, the League proved capable of organizing naval campaigns as well as economic boycotts and blockades. Changing patterns of trade led to the demise of the Hanseatic League, which was finally dissolved in 1669.

Harappa, the site in present-day Pakistan of a major city of the INDUS VALLEY CIVILIZATION.

Hardie, James Keir (1856–1915), British socialist leader, trade unionist, and founding member of the INDEPENDENT LABOUR PARTY. He took a strongly pacifist stance during World War I.

Harding, Warren G. (1865–1923), 29th president of the USA (1921–3). A conservative product of the small-town Republican Midwest, he proved a weak and vacillating president. After he died in office, investigations revealed that he had presided over one of the most corrupt administrations in US history.

Harold II (c. 1020–66), king of England (1066). Harold Godwinson, earl of Wessex, succeeded the English throne on the death of EDWARD THE CONFESSOR despite the claim from the Norman Duke WILLIAM that Edward had designated him his successor. Harold's defence of his crown was complicated by the need to repel a Norwegian invasion under Harold Hardrada, which he crushed at STAMFORD BRIDGE near York. However, Harold was subsequently defeated and killed (traditionally shot through the eye by an arrow) at the Battle of HASTINGS by Norman forces.

Harrison, Benjamin (1833–1901), US Republican politician, 23rd president of the USA (1889–93). The Sherman Anti-Trust Act (1890) restricting business monopolies was passed during his presidency.

Harrison, William Henry (1773–1841), US WHIG politician, ninth president of the USA (1841). A veteran of the WAR OF 1812, he died within a month of taking office.

Harsha (c. 590–647), Buddhist ruler of an empire in N India. His empire covered the Gangetic plain and also parts of the Punjab and Rajasthan. His enlightened reign saw the establishment of charitable institutions and the patronage of learning.

Harun al-Rashid (c. 763–809), fifth CALIPH of the Muslim ABBASID dynasty, ruling in Baghdad (786–809). An enthusiastic patron of the arts, he owes much of his disproportionate fame to his association with the much later stories of the *Thousand and One Nights.*

Hasdrubal (d. 207 BC), Carthaginian general and son of HAMILCAR BARCA. In the Second PUNIC WAR he fought the Romans in Spain (218–208), then went to the aid of his brother HANNIBAL in Italy, but died in the Battle of the River Metaurus.

Hastings, Battle of (14 October 1066), one of the most decisive battles in English history, fought between HAROLD II and Duke William of Normandy. After defeating the Norwegians at STAMFORD BRIDGE, Harold marched his army 250 mi south to face the Norman invasion threat, meeting Duke William's army at Senlac Hill, near Hastings. Norman archers and cavalry overcame fierce resistance from the English footsoldiers, whose morale collapsed with Harold's death. Victory paved the way for William's coronation as WILLIAM I and the NORMAN CONQUEST of England.

Hastings, Warren (1732–1818), first governor-general of BENGAL (1772–85). He consolidated CLIVE'S gains in INDIA, and further extended British rule there, pursuing a robust policy of reform.

Hatshepsut (c. 1540–c. 1481 BC), daughter of THUTMOSE I and wife of Thutmose II. She was effective ruler of Egypt in the first 20 years of the reign of THUTMOSE III. Her mortuary temple at Dayr al-Bahri is decorated with reliefs recording the events of her reign.

Hattin, Battle of (1187), the defeat of a Crusader army by SALADIN, leading to the latter's capture of Jerusalem and the collapse of the CRUSADER STATES of the Levant.

Haughey, Charles James (1925–), Irish FÍANNA FÁIL statesman, prime minister (1979–81, 1982 and 1989–92). He was succeeded after his final term by Albert REYNOLDS.

Hausa, a W African people of mixed pastoral-agricultural origins, living in N Nigeria. The Muslim cities of Hausaland had major commercial and political influence in W Africa from the 17th century – particularly Sokoto in the first half of the 19th century.

Haussman, Georges Eugène, Baron (1809–91), French civil servant and town planner. He was responsible for an extensive rebuilding programme in Paris under NAPOLEON III, widening streets and laying out parks and boulevards.

Havel, Vaclav (1936–), Czechoslovak statesman and dramatist, president of Czechoslovakia (1989–93). A human rights activist, he led peaceful demonstrations against the Communist regime in 1989, and after the fall of the Communist regime became president of Czechoslovakia. He remained president of the CZECH REPUBLIC after its split from SLOVAKIA in 1993.

Hawke, Robert James Lee (1929–), Australian Labor statesman. 'Bob' Hawke was a successful trade union leader before becoming prime minister of Australia in 1983. He was succeeded by Paul KEATING in 1991.

Hawkins, Sir John (1532–95), English naval commander. As treasurer of the navy (1577–89), he played a crucial role in creating the fleet that defeated the SPANISH ARMADA.

Hayes, Rutherford B. (1822–93), US Republican politician, 19th president of the USA (1877–81). He ended the process of RECONSTRUCTION that followed the AMERICAN CIVIL WAR, and withdrew Federal troops from the Southern states.

Heath, Edward Richard George (1916–), British Conservative statesman. He became the first elected Conservative leader in 1965, and as prime minister

(1970–4) took Britain into the EUROPEAN COMMUNITY, but ran into economic difficulties and lost the 1974 election to Labour. He was savagely critical of Margaret THATCHER's hostility to closer European integration in the late 1980s and early 90s.

Heian, the capital of JAPAN AD 794–1192 (modern Kyoto).

Hejaz, a region of SW Asia that contains the main centres of Islamic pilgrimage, MECCA and MEDINA (see maps, pp. 17 and 26). The area was under OTTOMAN Turkish rule, nominally from 1517 and definitely from 1845. Hussein, Grand Sharif of Mecca, led a revolt against Turkish rule (1916) and declared himself king of Hejaz, but was defeated by ibn SA'UD in 1924.

Heligoland, a tiny island in the German Bight of the North Sea. Originally part of SCHLESWIG-HOLSTEIN, it was seized by Britain (1807) and ceded to Germany (1890) in return for Zanzibar. The island became a major German imperial naval base.

Hellenistic Age, the period from the death of ALEXANDER THE GREAT (323 BC) to the death of CLEOPATRA VII (30 BC), during which Greek dynasties ruled the area from Greece to N India. After Alexander's death Macedonian generals fought among themselves over who should govern his vast empire. Three main dynasties were eventually established, by PTOLEMY (Egypt), SELEUCUS (Asia) and ANTIGONUS (Macedonia and Greece). The HELLENISTIC Age was marked by a highly competitive spirit. Kings constantly fought, or negotiated, with each other for territory, wealth and glory. Frequent wars came to weaken the kingdoms, and they were all absorbed by the Roman or PARTHIAN Empires in the 2nd and 1st centuries BC.

Hellespont, the ancient name for the DARDANELLES.

helots, the 'state serfs' of ancient SPARTA. Around 700 BC the Spartans conquered the territory of their neighbour, Messenia, in the S PELOPONNESE, and forced the Messenians to work the land as state-serfs or 'helots' under brutal conditions. Helots did not have the political rights of Spartan citizens, and, since they outnumbered the Spartans themselves, were kept under tight military control.

Helsinki Conference (1972–5), a series of meetings of the CONFERENCE ON SECURITY AND COOPERATION IN EUROPE (CSCE), held in Helsinki and Geneva and attended by the leaders of 35 nations. The Helsinki Final Act, whose signatories included the Soviet bloc countries, contained agreements on trade and human rights.

Hengist and Horsa (fl. 449–88), the semi-legendary leaders of the first ANGLO-SAXON invasion of Britain, and joint kings of Kent.

Henry I ('the Fowler'; c. 876–936), duke of Saxony (912–36), king of Germany (919–36) and father of OTTO I. His power barely extended beyond SE Saxony, but he laid a strong foundation for expansion under his son.

Henry I (1068–1135), king of England (1100–35), duke of NORMANDY (1106–35), the youngest son of WILLIAM I, the Conqueror. A war of succession lasted until 1106, when he captured his brother Robert of Normandy and imprisoned him for life. The death of his only legitimate son in the White Ship disaster (1120) meant that his last 15 years were darkened by the prospect of an uncertain succession.

Henry II (1133–89), count of ANJOU and duke of NORMANDY from 1151, duke of AQUITAINE from 1152, king of England (1154–89). His marriage to ELEANOR of Aquitaine made him the most powerful ruler of his day in W Europe. He pursued expansionist policies, notably against the Bretons, Welsh and Irish, and curbed the power of the barons, but his attempt to control the Church was abandoned after the murder of Thomas BECKET.

Henry III (1206–72), king of England (1216–72). His personal rule began in 1227 but proved grossly incompetent. His mishandling of domestic politics led to a series of crises from 1258, culminating in civil war and his temporary dethronement by Simon de MONTFORT in 1264.

Henry III (1551–89), king of France (1574–89). Elected king of Poland, he fled that country when the death of Charles IX (1560–74) made him king of France. Although he revoked past edicts that had granted toleration to the HUGUENOTS, the Catholic HOLY LEAGUE found him too conciliatory and Paris rebelled. He was assassinated by a fanatical friar, but acknowledged Henry of Navarre (later HENRY IV) as his heir before he died. See FRENCH WARS OF RELIGION.

Henry IV (1050–1106), SALIAN king of Germany (1056–1106). His reign witnessed a bitter struggle with Pope GREGORY VII over the question of lay INVESTITURE, culminating in Henry's excommunication and penance at CANOSSA.

Henry IV (Bolingbroke; 1366–1413), king of England (1399–1413). His banishment by RICHARD II prevented him from inheriting the vast estates of his father John of GAUNT. In 1399 he invaded England and deposed Richard. His position as king was never secure, and his reign was marked by war and rebellion, notably the revolt of Owen GLENDOWER in Wales.

Henry IV (1557–1610), king of NAVARRE (as Henry III, 1563–1610) and first BOURBON king of France (1589–1610). A leader of the HUGUENOTS, he ended the FRENCH WARS OF RELIGION by converting to Catholicism (1593), and granted religious and political privileges to the Huguenots in the Edict of NANTES (1598). He obtained peace with Spain by the Treaty of Vervins (1598) and, with his chief minister, SULLY, sought to revive the French economy and royal revenues. He was stabbed to death by a Catholic fanatic.

Henry V (1387–1422), king of England (1413–22) and eldest son of HENRY IV. He conquered Normandy by his daring generalship at AGINCOURT (1415) and by ruthless exploitation of the troubles of the French court. His marriage to Catherine of Valois (1420) gained him recognition as heir to the French throne. At Troyes he dictated the treaty which, had it not been for a fatal attack of dysentery, would have made him king of France.

Henry VI (1165–97), Holy Roman Emperor (1191–97) and father of FREDERICK II. He acquired the kingdom of Sicily through his marriage to the daughter of ROGER II.

Henry VI (1422–71), king of England (1422–61 and 1470–1). The son of HENRY V, he succeeded to the throne at nine months, and suffered from mental illness from 1453. The Wars of the ROSES broke out when RICHARD Duke of York, who had a better claim to the throne than Henry, was displaced in the order of succession by the birth of an heir to Henry's queen, MARGARET of Anjou. Deposed by EDWARD IV in 1461, he was briefly restored by WARWICK, but was murdered on Edward's return to the throne in 1471.

Henry VII (1457–1509), the first TUDOR king of England (1485–1509). He gained the throne after defeating RICHARD III at BOSWORTH, although his claim to the throne through his mother Margaret BEAUFORT (who was descended from John of GAUNT) was a tenuous one. He married Elizabeth, daughter of EDWARD IV, ensuring that their children were heirs of both Lancaster and York. He defeated a number of YORKIST plots to seize his throne (notably those of SIMNEL and WARBECK) and gained foreign support by a policy of marriage alliances and peace. Thanks to Henry's careful exploitation of the crown's extensive landed estates, his son HENRY VIII succeeded to a rich and powerful crown.

Henry VIII (1491–1547), king of England (1509–47), and son of HENRY VII. He invaded France in 1513 as part of a European alliance against France, and defeated the Scots at FLODDEN in the same year. Thomas WOLSEY, the organizer of the French expedition, became Henry's chief minister. When the pope refused to allow Henry to divorce CATHERINE of Aragon (who had failed to provide him with a son and heir), Henry declared himself Supreme Head of the Church in England, which then granted him a divorce. This step marked the beginning of the English REFORMATION. With his new chief minister, Thomas CROMWELL, he dissolved the MONASTERIES and reformed the Church. Opposition to his policies was brutally suppressed. In the interests of security, Wales was incorporated into the English crown (1536, 1543), he was declared king of Ireland (1541), and efforts were made in the 1540s to subject the Scots. After the execution of his second wife Anne BOLEYN, he subsequently married Jane Seymour, Anne of Cleves, Catherine Howard and Catherine Parr.

Henry the Navigator (1394–1460), Portuguese prince, the son of JOHN I. He was patron to a series of voyages down the coast of Africa, which paved the way for the discovery of a sea route to India after his death.

Heraclius (575–641), Byzantine emperor (610–41). He seized the throne after leading a revolt against the emperor Phocas. His generalship turned a long and debilitating war with Persia in the Byzantines favour. After the Persian siege of Constantinople in 626 he launched a stunning counter-attack on the Persian heartlands, leading to a Persian collapse. However, in the 630s and 640s his exhausted empire was unable to prevent the loss of Syria, Egypt, Mesopotamia and then Africa in the ARAB CONQUESTS. Heraclius presided over a militarization of Byzantine society. The provinces of Asia Minor were organized into military zones or 'themes', each headed by a 'strategos' as military governor.

Herculaneum, a Roman town destroyed along with POMPEII in the eruption of Vesuvius in AD 79.

heresy, doctrines or opinions at variance with the orthodox beliefs of the Christian Church (see ARIANISM, DONATISM, GNOSTICISM, MANICHAEISM, CATHARS, LOLLARDS, HUSSITES). In the Middle Ages the Church tried to eradicate heresy by extensive preaching, the use of the INQUISITION, the invocation of military aid from secular rulers, and eventually by CRUSADES. Disillusionment with the wealth and worldliness of the established church led ultimately to the Protestant REFORMATION.

Herod, a Jewish dynasty ruling as Roman clients in Palestine (47 BC–AD 93). The cruelty of Herod the Great (reigned 37–4 BC) is described in the New Testament account of the Massacre of the Innocents.

Hertzog, James Barry Munnik (1866–1942), South African prime minister (1924–39). He was founder of the (Afrikaner) NATIONAL PARTY, and an architect of racial segregation in the 1920s and 30s through his 'Hertzog Bills'.

Herzen, Alexander Ivanovich (1812–70), Russian political thinker. In the 1840s he was a prominent spokesman of the 'Westernizers' but, living abroad after 1847, came to believe that Russia could evolve towards socialism without following the path of Western development.

Herzl, Theodor (1860–1904), Hungarian Zionist leader. An advocate of ZIONISM, he founded the World Zionist Organization, which first met in 1897 and had as its aim the establishment of a Jewish national home in Palestine.

Hezekiah (d. 687 BC), king of JUDAH (715–687 BC). He revolted against Assyria, ignoring the advice of the prophet Isaiah, and was defeated by SENNACHERIB in 701 BC.

Hidalgo y Costilla, Miguel (1753–1811), Mexican priest and rebel leader. He led a revolt against the Spanish in 1810 with native American support, but was defeated and executed in 1811.

hijra (Arabic, 'migration'), the flight of MUHAMMAD from MECCA to MEDINA in 622. The event marks the starting point of the Islamic calendar.

Himmler, Heinrich (1900–45), German Nazi politician. Leader of the SS from 1929, he became head of all German police forces, including the GESTAPO, in 1936. He supervised the deportation and systematic extermination of the Jews in E Europe in the HOLOCAUST. Captured by the Allies at the end of World War II, he committed suicide.

Hindenburg, Paul von (1847–1934), German field marshal. A veteran of the FRANCO-PRUSSIAN WAR, he was recalled at the outbreak of WORLD WAR I and, with LUDENDORFF, crushed the Russians at TANNENBERG. As chief of the general staff he conducted an effective, but doomed, campaign on the Western Front. As president of Germany (1925–34), he appointed HITLER as chancellor in 1933.

Hinduism, the system of religious beliefs and social customs that developed in INDIA from 1500 BC onwards, evolving from an amalgam of native DRAVIDIAN and ARYAN cultures. Hindu expansionism was mercantile and cultural rather than imperial. First the relatively backward tribal areas of S India were brought into contact with the centre and N, then overseas trading links were developed to the E. Trade planted the seeds of Indian culture far and wide. By the 3rd century AD, Hindu kingdoms were springing up all over previously tribal SE Asia, in Burma, Thailand, Cambodia, Java and Sumatra. The basic political units of Hindu India in the first millennium AD were regional kingdoms, few of which aspired to wider power. This localization of power explains the ease with which Muslim invaders were able to overcome the Hindus of the N half of the subcontinent between the 11th and 14th centuries. The southern Indian empire of VIJAYANAGAR fared better, sustaining the Hindu cause for nearly 200 years until its conquest in 1565. With the decline of the MOGUL EMPIRE in the 18th century, resurgent Hindus – notably the MARATHAS and the RAJPUTS – began to reassert their independence.

Hirohito (1901–89), emperor of JAPAN (1926–89). His reign was marked by militarization and a series of aggressive wars against CHINA (1931–3 and 1937–45) and the Allies in WORLD WAR II. Hirohito encouraged the military to accept unconditional surrender after the dropping of atomic bombs on HIROSHIMA and NAGASAKI. After the war the emperor renounced his mythical divinity and most of his powers, and became a constitutional monarch. He was succeeded by his son, Akihito.

Hiroshima, Japanese port on the Inland Sea. On 6 August 1945 it was hit by an atomic bomb – the first to be used in warfare – dropped by the US air force, which killed over 75,000 of its inhabitants. A second bomb was dropped on NAGASAKI three days later. Japan surrendered officially on 2 September, bringing the Pacific War to an end.

Hispaniola, an island in the Caribbean, first discovered by COLUMBUS in 1492. It is now divided between HAITI and the DOMINICAN REPUBLIC.

Hitler, Adolf (1889–1945), Austrian-born German Nazi dictator (1933–45). After leaving the army at the end of World War I, he joined the National Socialist German Worker's (NAZI) Party (1919), which opposed the embattled WEIMAR REPUBLIC. In 1923 he was arrested and imprisoned for his role in the MUNICH BEER-HALL PUTSCH. In prison he wrote *Mein Kampf* ('My Struggle'), setting out his beliefs on race: that 'Aryan' Germanic peoples were superior to Slavs, Negroes and, above all, Jews, and that Germany must conquer territory in the E to achieve *Lebensraum* ('living space'). In 1930 and 1932 the Nazis made considerable gains in parliamentary elections, and in 1933 Hitler was made chancellor by HINDENBURG. In the same year Hitler used the burning of the REICHSTAG as an excuse to assume dictatorial powers. After 1934 he became 'Führer' ('Leader') and outlawed all other political parties, banned trade unions, and used censorship to control information. His regime was enforced by the SS and the GESTAPO, and rivals within the party were purged in the 'NIGHT OF THE LONG KNIVES' (1934). His social policies both reduced unemployment and restored national pride, but at the cost of political rights. The persecution of Jews was legalized by the NUREMBERG LAWS of 1935. Hitler openly rearmed Germany and pursued an aggressive foreign policy, occupying the RHINELAND in 1936, annexing Austria in the *Anschluss* (1938) and then invading CZECHOSLOVAKIA and POLAND, thereby precipitating the outbreak of WORLD WAR II. Hitler enjoyed early successes in the war, but increasingly ignored military advice and fatally created a second front in the E after invading the USSR in 1941. The German grip on the war began to slip after defeats at EL ALAMEIN and STALINGRAD in 1942. When Germany was invaded in 1945 Hitler retired to his bunker beneath the Chancellery in Berlin. It is presumed that he committed suicide, along with his mistress Eva Braun, shortly after the Soviets entered the city.

Hitler Youth, a Nazi youth organization, formed in 1933. From 1936, membership of the Hitler Youth was compulsory for all children aged 10–18. The organization instilled semi-military discipline and Nazi political ideas.

Hittites, an Indo-European people of ancient ANATOLIA, who created a substantial Near Eastern empire in the 2nd millennium BC. The Hittite empire was founded in about 1650 BC with its capital at Hattusas (modern Boghazköy), and gradually extended its territory throughout Anatolia and into Syria, where it eclipsed the power of MITANNI. The empire reached its peak under SUPPILULIUMAS I (c. 1380–1350 BC), who extended its frontiers and clashed with the Egyptian empire in Syria. In c. 1283 the Hittite king, Hattusilis III, signed a treaty with RAMESSES II of Egypt after an indecisive battle at KADESH. The collapse of the empire c. 1200 BC is probably connected with the appearance of the SEA PEOPLES, and with internal disturbances.

Hobbes, Thomas (1588–1679), English political philosopher. Hobbes described the chaos in which he believed people lived when they did not have a proper government. He claimed in his most important treaise, *Leviathan* (1651), that the life of man in his natural, ungoverned state is 'solitary, poor, nasty, brutish and short'. Hobbes's doctrine is that men can only live together in peace if they agree to obey an absolute sovereign, and this agreement he called 'the social contract'. Hobbes's concern about what happened when government broke down, as in the ENGLISH CIVIL WAR during his lifetime, led him to suggest that considerable power should be placed in the hands of the sovereign.

Ho Chi Minh (1892–1969), Vietnamese nationalist and revolutionary leader, president of the Democratic Republic of (North) Vietnam (1954–69). A long-term Communist, he led the VIET MINH in the FRENCH INDOCHINA WAR. After independence he ruled in Hanoi, building up the country's industries and fighting against US-aided South Vietnam in the VIETNAM WAR.

Hohenstaufen, a German dynasty that ruled the HOLY ROMAN EMPIRE from 1138 to 1254. Hohenstaufen control of the throne was secured by FREDERICK I 'Barbarossa' (1152–90), who attempted to build up German power in Italy. The empire expanded to include Germany, N Italy and Sicily. Hohenstaufen attempts to retain control of Italy led to a series of quarrels with the wealthy and independent city-states of N Italy. Feuds with the papacy over claims to land and personal powers in Sicily culminated in the defeat and death of Manfred, the last Hohenstaufen, at the hands of CHARLES OF ANJOU at the Battle of BENEVENTO (1266).

Hohenzollern, a German dynasty that ruled BRANDENBURG from 1417, PRUSSIA from 1618, and the newly unified German Reich from 1871 to 1918. The Hohenzollerns pursued an expansionist policy after the THIRTY YEARS WAR, leading to rivalry with the Austrian HABSBURGS in the 18th and 19th centuries. The efforts of BISMARCK ensured that the Hohenzollerns emerged with the German imperial title in 1871. The last Hohenzollern emperor, WILHELM II, was forced to abdicate after German defeat in World War I.

Hojo, the dominant noble family in 13th-century Japan. During most of the years of the KAMAKURA SHOGUNATE (1192–1333) members of the family acted as regents and effectively ruled Japan. The family committed ritual suicide after the overthrow of the Kamakura Shogunate in 1333.

Holocaust, the term used to describe the systematic attempt by the German NAZIS to destroy European Jewry between 1933 and 1945. HITLER'S hatred of the Jews was expressed in the NUREMBERG LAWS of 1935, which stripped German Jews of their rights as citizens, and by 1938 open attacks against Jewish property and persons were being condoned. After Hitler's invasion of the USSR, special squads of SS *Einsatzgruppen* rooted out and shot 500,000 Soviet Jews in areas seized by the German Army in 1941–2. However, after 1941 the Nazis forced European Jews into CONCENTRATION CAMPS, and using a new gas, Zyklon B, began a programme of extermination of the prison camp population. Some of the prisoners were not killed immediately, but were used as slave labour or as guinea-pigs in horrific medical experiments. From January 1942, in a deliberate policy of extermination known as the 'Final Solution', European Jews were systematically gassed in a network of concentration camps in the east. By the time Germany was defeated in 1945, 5.4 million Jews, 400,000 Gypsies and untold thousands of Slavs had been killed in the death camps. In addition, many others had perished at the hands of *Einsatzgruppen* elsewhere. Altogether 5.9 million Jews – 67% of Europe's pre-war Jewish population – had been murdered, the population of Poland had been cut by 15%, and 10% of the world gypsy population had ceased to exist. See also AUSCHWITZ.

Holy League, the name given to a number of alliances and organizations in 15th-, 16th- and 17th-century Europe. Some of the most notable were: the League of 1511, which allied the Pope, Henry VIII, the Swiss, Venice and Ferdinand of Aragon in an attempt to expel the French from Italy (1511); that of 1526, directed by the pope, France, Milan, Florence and Venice against Emperor CHARLES V (1526); that of 1570, which allied the pope, Venice and Spain against the OTTOMANS; the French Catholic League of 1576, which confronted the HUGUENOTS in the FRENCH WARS OF RELIGION; and the alliance (1684) of Poland, the Habsburg Emperor, Venice and Pope Innocent XI against the Ottoman Turks.

Holyoake, Keith Jacka (1904–83), New Zealand National Party statesman, prime minister (1957 and 1960–72).

Holy Roman Empire (962–1806), the Western empire created in imitation of the Roman Empire during the medieval period. The term 'Holy Roman Empire' was not coined until the 13th century, but the imperial dignity to which it referred was much older, being established by the coronation of CHARLEMAGNE as emperor of the West in 800. For the next 1000 years those rulers who saw themselves as Charlemagne's successors clung to the imperial title. Centred on GERMANY and Austria, the empire came to comprise much of W and Central Europe, and included parts of E France and N Italy. From the coronation of OTTO I in 962, the empire was always associated with the German crown. When the Ottonian dynasty died out in 1024, another German princely dynasty, the SALIANS, took over. Friction between the Salian kings and the papacy came to a head in the INVESTITURE CONTEST (1075–1122), which weakened the German monarchy in favour of the princes. Despite the fact that from the 12th century the German king owed his crown to election rather than hereditary right, FREDERICK I was able to establish his HOHENSTAUFEN dynasty so firmly on the throne that they remained there until 1254. In the century that followed the German crown circulated among a number of princely houses. The empire became more clearly a German institution, and in the 15th century came to be known as the 'Holy Roman Empire of the German Nation'. When CHARLES IV's Luxembourg dynasty died out in 1437, it was succeeded by the HABSBURGS, of which dynasty the most prominent emperor by far was CHARLES V (1519–56). The Catholic Habsburgs, however, were challenged during the REFORMATION and the THIRTY YEARS WAR. Their power was diminished by a series of wars against LOUIS XIV of France, and by the emergence of PRUSSIA under FREDERICK II. In 1806 NAPOLEON abolished the Holy Roman Empire, and it was not restored in the general peace settlement of 1815. See maps, pp. 21, 25 and 27, and box, p. 142.

Home of the Hirsel, Alec Douglas-Home, Baron (1903–), British Conservative prime minister (1963–4), foreign secretary (1970–4). Chosen by MACMILLAN to succeed him, he resigned his earldom to become PM, but lost the 1964 election to Harold WILSON. He was replaced as Conservative leader in 1965 by Edward HEATH.

Homestead Act (1862), US legislation to promote westward expansion, allowing the purchase of public land for a nominal fee.

Home Rule, the campaign to repeal the Act of UNION (1801) between Britain and IRELAND and give the Irish their own parliament responsible for domestic affairs. GLADSTONE'S conversion to Home Rule in 1885 led to Joseph Chamberlain's defection to the Conservatives as a Liberal-Unionist and the splitting of the LIBERAL Party. The Home Rule bills of 1886 and 1893 were both defeated. A third Home Rule bill was passed in 1914, but suspended for the duration of World War I. Legislation in 1920 provided for parliaments for both northern and southern Ireland, but was rejected by the south, which achieved DOMINION status as the Irish Free State in 1922.

Homo erectus ('upright man'), an early human type, dating from between 1.6 million and 300,000 years ago. Originating in Africa, they were the first humans to colonize Africa and Asia. See EVOLUTION.

Homo sapiens neanderthalensis ('wise Neanderthal man'), the human type inhabiting Europe and Asia before modern humans (HOMO SAPIENS SAPIENS). They evolved some time before 100,000 years ago, lasting until 30,000 years ago in Europe. See EVOLUTION.

Homo sapiens sapiens ('wise man'), the modern human type, an early example of which came from the Cro-Magnon cave in France. The time of their first appearance is hotly debated. Although HOMO SAPIENS NEANDERTHALENSIS lasted until 30,000 years ago in Europe, recent research shows that modern humans already existed in the Near East 100,000 years ago. See EVOLUTION.

Honduras, a republic in CENTRAL AMERICA. In 1502 COLUMBUS reached Honduras and in 1523 the first Spanish settlement was established. Honduras gained freedom from Spain in 1821, but was part of the Central American Federation until 1839. Between independence and the early 20th century,

HOLY ROMAN EMPERORS

Karl I (*Charlemagne*)	800–814	Albrecht I (*Albert I*)	1298–1308
Ludwig I (*Louis I*)	814–840	Heinrich VII (*Henry VII*)	1308–13
Lothar I	840–855	Ludwig IV (*Louis IV*)	1314–47
Ludwig II (*Louis II*)	855–875	Karl IV (*Charles IV*)	1347–78
Karl II (*Charles II*)	875–877	Wenzel	1378–1400
Karl III (*Charles III*)	877–887	Rupprecht Klem*	1400–10
Arnulf	887–898	Sigismund	1410–37
Ludwig III* (*Louis III*)	899–911	Albrecht II* (*Albert II*)	1438–39
Konrad I*	911–918	Friedrich III (*Frederick III*)	1440–93
Heinrich I* (*Henry I*)	919–936	Maximilian I	1493–1519
Otto I	936–973	Karl V (*Charles V*)	1519–55
Otto II	973–983	Ferdinand I	1556–64
Otto III	983–1002	Maximilian II	1564–76
Heinrich II (*Henry II*)	1002–24	Rudolf II	1576–1612
Konrad II	1024–39	Matthias	1612–19
Heinrich III (*Henry III*)	1039–56	Ferdinand II	1619–37
Heinrich IV (*Henry IV*)	1056–1105	Ferdinand III	1637–57
Heinrich V (*Henry V*)	1105–25	Leopold I	1658–1705
Lothar II	1125–37	Joseph I	1705–11
Konrad III*	1138–52	Karl VI (*Charles*)	1711–40
Friedrich I (*Frederick Barbarossa*)	1152–90	Karl III (*Charles*)	1742–45
Heinrich VI (*Henry VI*)	1190–97	Franz I Stephan (*Francis I*)	1745–65
Philipp*	1198–1208	Joseph II	1765–90
Otto IV	1198–1215	Leopold II	1790–92
Friedrich II (*Frederick II*)	1215–50	Franz II (*Francis II*)	1792–1806
Konrad IV*	1250–54		
Konrad V	1254 (claimant)		
Richard*	1257		
Alfons*	1267		
Rudolf I*	1273–91		
Adolf*	1292–98		

In 1806 Francis II abdicated and abolished the Holy Roman Empire; see AUSTRIA

Key:
* = emperor-elect. Frederick III was the last emperor to go to Rome for coronation; all succeeding emperors assumed the imperial title upon election.

Honduras experienced constant political upheaval and wars with neighbouring countries. US influence was immense, largely owing to the substantial investments of the powerful United Fruit Company in banana production. After a short civil war in 1925, a succession of military dictators governed Honduras until 1980. Since then the country has had democratically elected pro-US centre-right civilian governments.

Honecker, Erich (1912–), East German Communist politician, general secretary of the Communist Party from 1971, and president from 1976. He was replaced during the anti-Communist Revolution of 1989.

Hong Kong, a British colony off the coast of China. Hong Kong island was occupied by the British in 1841 during the first OPIUM WAR, at the end of which it was ceded to Britain in perpetuity. The tip of the mainland Kowloon peninsula was added to the colony at the end of the second Opium War (1860), and in 1898 Britain negotiated a 99-year lease over the rest of the New Territories. The population of the colony has mushroomed, from fewer than 5000 in 1841 to over six million today. The strain on social and housing services has been exacerbated by illegal immigration from China and an influx of 'Boat People' from Vietnam. In 1984

Britain negotiated with China over the future of Hong Kong. The lease in the New Territories runs out in 1997 and, although Hong Kong island would theoretically remain British, its position would clearly be untenable. China is scheduled to take over the whole colony in 1997 – a prospect that worries many of Hong Kong's inhabitants.

Hongwu (1328–98), first emperor (1368–98) of the MING dynasty in CHINA. A beggar turned bandit, he led a rebel army to seize Nanjing from the ruling MONGOLS in 1356, and gradually extended his power over China until the Mongols fled from Beijing in 1368. As emperor, he invaded Mongolia, brought Yunnan temporarily under Ming rule, and forced Korea to pay tribute. Conquests in Asia were continued by his son and successor, YONGLE.

Hoover, Herbert (1874–1964), US Republican politician, 31st president of the USA (1929–33). Renowned for his humanitarian work in Europe after World War I, he sought to streamline American bureaucracy and industry during the 1920s. His failure to solve the problems of the DEPRESSION resulted in his crushing defeat by F.D. ROOSEVELT in the election of 1932.

Hoover, J(ohn) Edgar (1895–1972), head of the US Federal Bureau of Investigation (FBI; 1924–72). Finding the agency in disrepute after scandals during the HARDING administration, he instituted professional standards of selection and training for staff and agents. During the 1960s he was much criticized for his antipathy towards the CIVIL RIGHTS MOVEMENT.

Hopi, a native North American people of the SW, living in NE Arizona. See also NORTH AMERICAN INDIANS.

Hospitallers, a military and religious order of knights, founded in the 11th century. They were converted from a purely medical role in Jerusalem to a military order after the Holy City fell to the Christians in 1099 during the First CRUSADE. In 1320 they established themselves on Rhodes. From there they harried Muslim coasts and shipping for two centuries. Chased off the island by the OTTOMAN Turks in 1522, they defended Malta against the same enemy in 1565. There they survived, although with declining military significance, until overrun by Napoleon's forces on their way to Egypt in 1798.

Houphouët-Boigny, Félix (1905–94), first president of CÔTE D'IVOIRE (1960–93). After independence he maintained close links with France, presided over a thriving economy and maintained diplomatic relations with South Africa in the face of criticisms.

House of Representatives, the lower chamber of the US CONGRESS, which first met in 1789. With delegates apportioned according to the population strength of each state, the House tends to be a more accurate barometer of American public opinion than the SENATE. The CONSTITUTION invests it with the sole right to originate revenue bills.

Howard, Charles, Lord of Effingham (1536–1624), Lord High Admiral of England (1585–1618), commander of the fleet that defeated the SPANISH ARMADA in 1588.

Hoxha, Enver (1908–85), Albanian Communist politician, prime minister (1946–54), First Secretary of the Communist Party (1954–85). See ALBANIA.

Hua Guofeng (Hua Kuo-feng; 1920–), Chinese Communist politician, prime minister (1976–80). He survived the upheavals of the CULTURAL REVOLUTION to hold a number of key government posts from 1968 to 1975. He became PM on the death of ZHOU ENLAI, but DENG XIAOPING was the real power behind his administration.

Hudson's Bay Company, a British trading company founded by royal charter (1670) to monopolize the valuable fur trade of the Canadian NW. It annexed its main competitor, the North West Company, in 1821. It sold its territories to Canada in 1870.

Huguenot, a French Protestant, particularly a follower of CALVIN. Their numbers declined during and after the FRENCH WARS OF RELIGION, though they were granted toleration by HENRY IV in the Edict of NANTES (1598). Their political privileges were abolished by LOUIS XIII, and their religious rights by Louis XIV in the revocation of the Edict of Nantes (1685), after which many Huguenots fled abroad.

Hulagu (1217–65), MONGOL prince, a grandson of GENGHIS KHAN. He conquered Iran and Iraq but his westward advance was checked by the MAMLUKS at the Battle of AIN JALUT. His descendants became sovereigns of the division of the Mongol Empire known as the ILKHANATE.

humanism, an important cultural movement during the 15th-century Renaissance, based on the study of classical (Greek and Roman) texts, which were seen as models for public speaking, writing and conduct. Initially based in N Italy, by 1500 humanist ideas began to spread to N Europe, where ERASMUS was the most important scholar. Although humanism did not involve a rejection of Christian doctrine, it did undoubtedly focus on man's – as opposed to God's – role in the world.

Humayun (1508–56), second MOGUL emperor of INDIA (1530–40, 1554–5). The son of BABUR, he introduced Persian cultural influences into India. He was exiled after 10 years of rule but regained the throne just before his death.

'Hundred Days' (March 20–June 29 1815), the period between NAPOLEON'S return to France from Elba and his abdication after the Battle of Waterloo. Napoleon exploited the unpopularity of the new Bourbon king, LOUIS XVIII, to return to France, seize power and renew the war. After his defeat at WATERLOO he was exiled to St Helena in the South Atlantic.

Hundred Years War (1337–1453), an irregular series of wars fought between France and England over the claim of the English king to the French throne. From the accession of William I in 1066, the Norman kings of England and their successors had continued to hold vast territories in France. By the 1330s, however, only GASCONY in the SW of France was retained by the English king. When the French CAPETIAN dynasty died out in the direct male line in 1328, EDWARD III of England had an excellent claim to the French throne. But the crown went to his cousin, Philip of VALOIS, who became Philip VI (1328–50). Fighting broke out in Scotland and Flanders, with the Scottish siding with the French in the 'Auld Alliance', and the Flemish cloth towns being drawn to the English side for reasons of economic self-interest. The English won the naval Battle of SLUYS off the Flemish coast in 1340 to put paid to a threatened French invasion. At

CRÉCY (1346) and POITIERS (1356) the over-confident French knights were routed by the firepower of the English archers. The Treaty of BRÉTIGNY (1360) gave England large tracts of French land in return for Edward renouncing his claim to the French throne (see map, p. 21). In 1369, however, Edward formally resumed his claim; in renewed hostilities the French regained much of their lost territory, thanks to the efforts of captains such as Bertrand du GUESCLIN. RICHARD II agreed to a 28-year truce in 1396, but English claims to France were revived by the warrior-king HENRY V. Taking advantage of the domestic unrest caused by the mental illness of CHARLES VI of France, he invaded Normandy and won a stunning victory at AGINCOURT (1415). By 1419 Charles had named Henry his successor and an Anglo-BURGUNDIAN regime was in control of Paris and much of France. As it turned out, however, Henry died two months before Charles VI. In 1429 a French revival, in part inspired by JOAN OF ARC, recaptured the initiative. By 1435 England's Burgundian allies had swung back to the French side, and between 1450 and 1453 Normandy, Gascony and Bordeaux were lost forever. However, England retained Calais until 1558.

Hungarian Revolution (Oct–Nov 1956), the first major uprising against Communist rule in Eastern Europe. Its leader Imre NAGY denounced the WARSAW PACT and declared Hungary neutral. The revolution was crushed by a Soviet invasion and its leaders executed. The leader of the opposition to Nagy, János KADAR, became effective Hungarian leader.

Hungary, a country in Central Europe. See panel.

Huns, a nomadic people of the Volga steppe whose westward movements pushed many Germanic peoples into the ROMAN EMPIRE in the late 4th century and themselves invaded the Empire in the 4th and 5th centuries (see map, p. 15). Their leader, ATTILA (433–53), brought all German tribes E of the Rhine under the rule of the Huns, but his raid on Gaul in 451 was defeated at the CATALAUNIAN FIELDS. Attila went on to plunder Italy the following year, but his authority was undermined and his German subjects rebelled. Attila's death in 453 generated a succession dispute that enabled the subject Germans to overthrow the Huns.

Huron (Wyandot), a native North American people, maize farmers living NE of the Great Lakes. Early allies of the French settlers in the area, they suffered a shattering defeat by the IROQUOIS in the mid-17th century. See also NORTH AMERICAN INDIANS.

Hurrians, a non-Semitic people (possibly from E Anatolia) who settled in Syria in the 2nd millennium BC. Later the Hurrian kingdom of MITANNI was formed in N Syria and absorbed part of the territory of the AMORITE kingdom of Aleppo.

Hus, Jan (?1372–1415), Bohemian religious reformer. Influenced by John WYCLIF, he led a revolution in Bohemia in the early 15th century, but was condemned and burnt for refusing to recant his beliefs. His ideas became a considerable threat owing to their connection with Bohemian nationalism. Under the able command of John ZIZKA, the Hussites defeated crusaders from Germany, Austria and Hungary. In 1436 many of their distinctive beliefs were recognized and their demands granted in the Compact of Prague.

Hussein (ibn Talal) (1935–), king of JORDAN since 1952. He has pursued moderate, pragmatic policies in the face of political upheavals within and outside his country, maintaining friendly relations with Western powers, and at the same time pacifying Arab nationalist opinion.

Hussein ibn Ali (1856–1931), Arabian politician and founder of the Hashemite dynasty. He was recognized by the Allies as ruler of the HEJAZ (1916–24), but was driven from Hejaz following a power struggle with Abd al-Aziz ibn SAUD of the NAJD. His sons FAISAL and Abdullah became, respectively, kings of IRAQ and TRANSJORDAN.

Hussein, Saddam al-Takriti (1937–), president of IRAQ since 1976. Leader of the Iraqi BA'ATH Party, he has ruled repressively and embroiled his country in two disastrous wars, the IRAN–IRAQ WAR (1980–8) and the GULF WAR (1991) that followed the invasion of KUWAIT. His position was undermined by defeat in the Gulf War, which was followed by rebellions by KURDS in the N and Shiites in the S.

HUNGARY

9th century: The MAGYARS colonized the area from the E. **11th century:** The first Magyar king, STEPHEN (reigned 1001–38), encouraged Christianity and West European culture. **15th century:** MATTHIAS CORVINUS (reigned 1458–90) made Hungary a major power. **16th century:** Hungary was dismembered by the Austrian HABSBURGS and the Turkish OTTOMAN Empire. **1686:** The Habsburgs liberated Buda, the capital, from the Turks. **By the 18th century:** All the Hungarian lands were within the Habsburg Empire. **1848–9:** Lajos KOSSUTH led a nationalist revolt against Austrian rule, but fled when Austria regained control with Russian aid. **1867:** Austria granted Hungary considerable autonomy in the Dual Monarchy (AUSTRO-HUNGARIAN EMPIRE). **1919:** After Austro-Hungarian defeat in World War I, Hungary was stripped of two thirds of its territory in the Treaty of TRIANON; brief period of Communist rule under Béla KUN, terminated by Romanian invasion. **1920–44:** Hungary ruled by the Regent Admiral Miklás Horthy (1868–1957). **1941:** Horthy cooperated with Hitler in WORLD WAR II in an attempt to regain territory. **1945:** Hungarian defeat resulted in occupation by the Soviet RED ARMY, and the establishment of the Communist People's Republic (1949). **1956**: The HUNGARIAN REVOLUTION attempted to overthrow Communist rule, but was quickly suppressed by Soviet forces. **1956–88:** János KÁDÁR – Party Secretary – tried to win support through economic progress. **Late 1980s:** Reformers in the Communist Party gained the upper hand, and introduced political and economic reforms. **1990:** Democratic, multi-party state established; Soviet troops left Hungary.

Indiscriminate Iraqi bombing, particularly in the S, led to the imposition of a UN 'no-fly zone' in 1992. In 1993 the USA ordered bombing raids on strategic targets to force Saddam to comply with UN inspection of arms facilities.

Hussites, followers of Jan HUS.

Hyderabad, the largest PRINCELY STATE of India. It attempted to regain its independence when India became independent. However, it bowed to political pressure and joined the Indian Federation in 1949.

Hyder Ali (1721–82), Muslim ruler of the Indian state of MYSORE (1761–82), and father of TIPU SULTAN. He won a number of victories against the English EAST INDIA COMPANY.

Hyksos, the 15th- and 16th-dynasty rulers of EGYPT, probably originating in the Levant. They ruled from Avaris in the eastern delta in the 17th and 16th centuries BC. Later tradition claims that there was anarchy during their rule, but there is no evidence to support this. They appear to have adopted and respected Egyptian culture and introduced several innovations, including the vertical loom, the lyre, the horse-drawn chariot and new weapons. They were expelled by a new dynasty ruling from THEBES in Upper Egypt.

Ice Ages, a series of colder and warmer phases in prehistory during which almost all of the PALAEOLITHIC developments in Asia and Europe occurred. During cold phases the polar ice sheets extended as far S as Central Europe and the N American Great Plains. Some of the warmer phases (interglacials) were warmer than at present. The last cold phase ended about 10,000 BC.

Iceland, an island republic in NW Europe. Norwegians settled in Iceland in the 9th century. From 930 Iceland was an independent republic, but Norwegian sovereignty was accepted in 1264 to end a civil war. When Denmark and Norway were united (1381), Iceland became Danish. Nationalism grew in the 19th century, and in 1918 Iceland gained independence, linked to Denmark only by their shared monarchy. In World War II the Danish link was severed and a republic was declared (1944). Disputes over fishing rights in Icelandic territorial waters led to clashes with British naval vessels in the 1950s and 1970s (the 'Cod War').

Iceni, an ancient British tribe of East Anglia. The Iceni were at first allies of Rome, but in AD 60 they rebelled under BOUDICCA.

Iconoclastic controversy, a dispute about the role of icons in the Eastern (ORTHODOX) Church. In the early 8th century the Byzantines began a radical questioning of religious practices, notably the veneration of icons. This resulted in an iconoclast ('icon-breaker') movement which disturbed BYZANTINE society from the 720s until the final restoration of the icons in 843. The controversy split the Eastern Church into factions and worsened relations with Rome.

Idris I (1890–1983), king of LIBYA (1951–69). As head of the Sanusi sect in Cyrenaica (E Libya), he led resistance to Italian colonial rule. Elected king at independence, Idris was deposed by Colonel QADDAFI in 1969.

Ife, a holy city of the YORUBA people in SW Nigeria.

Ilkhanate, the division of the MONGOL Empire including Anatolia, Iran and Iraq (see map, p. 19). It emerged in 1278 after KUBLAI KHAN became an exclusively Chinese emperor and left the control of the western regions of the Mongol Empire to other descendants of Genghis Khan. The Ilkhanate disintegrated in the mid-14th century.

Illyria, an ancient region of the NW Balkans. Its non-Greek tribes fought regularly with the Macedonians, and formed a strong, often piratical kingdom in the 3rd century BC, which was gradually absorbed into the Roman Empire.

ILO, see INTERNATIONAL LABOUR ORGANIZATION.

IMF, see INTERNATIONAL MONETARY FUND.

imperialism, the process whereby one country establishes its rule over other less powerful countries, regions or peoples. Imperialism reached its height in the 19th century and by 1914 about one quarter of the globe had been taken over as colonies by half a dozen mostly European states, notably Britain, France, Germany and Italy (see map, p. 33). At the time it was argued that imperialism was needed to increase trade and find new materials for the economies of Europe. Others wanted to gain more territories to increase their strategic power in relation to other states. In the 19th century the various motives of the imperialists – economic, political and strategic – came together and encouraged the drive for empire (see SCRAMBLE FOR AFRICA). Imperialism was increasingly criticized in the 20th century, particularly by liberal and left-wing political parties, and by the 1950s and 60s many European powers were dismantling their empires. However, despite the technical independence of Third World states, many of them continue to be influenced strongly – politically and economically – by either the superpowers or a former colonial power – a situation sometimes described as neo-imperialism or economic imperialism.

Incas, a pre-Columbian native people of W South America. The Inca dynasty was founded c. AD 1200 by Manco Capac, but expansion did not take place until the 15th century. Inca conquests under Pachacuti (1438–71), Topa Inca (1471–93) and Huayna Capac (1493–1525) extended the empire from N Ecuador, across Peru, to Bolivia and parts of N Argentina and Chile. Although Inca rule was based on the military dominance of a warrior elite over many tribes and regional powers, the empire became the most unified of the American states. Central power was reinforced by a system of excellently built roads and forts and efficient administration and accountancy. From 1525 the empire was divided by the civil war between the two heirs, ATAHUALPA and his brother Huáscar. Atahualpa defeated his brother in 1532, but his own reign was cut short by the arrival of the Spanish conquistadores under PIZARRO. In 1533 Atahualpa was executed by Pizarro, and by 1535 the Spanish had subjugated the Inca empire.

Independence, American War of (1776–83), the revolutionary war fought by the American colonists against England for their independence. During the first half of the 18th century Americans increasingly became resentful of their lack of representation in the British Parliament and their economic subordination within the British Empire (particularly restrictions on their ability to trade). The imposition by Parliament in of a STAMP duty (1765) unleashed the cry of 'no taxation without representation'. Although the stamp duty was repealed, a tax on tea remained, and provoked the BOSTON TEA PARTY in 1773. When Britain instituted repressive measures against MASSACHUSETTS, the Americans reacted by sending delegates to the First CONTINENTAL CONGRESS in September 1774, which banned imported British goods. In April 1775 British soldiers were denied access to a store of arms in Boston by armed farmers at LEXINGTON. King GEORGE III retaliated by sending British troops and mercenaries across the Atlantic. In 1776 Thomas JEFFERSON drafted the DECLARATION OF INDEPENDENCE, which was approved by Congress on 4 July. In the eight-year-long struggle the Americans had a number of crucial advantages: they were fighting in conditions familiar to them but not to the British, and they had interior lines of communication, whereas England was dependent on a long supply route from Europe. The guerrilla tactics of the Americans paid off in the SARATOGA campaign of 1777. The rebels owed much to the leadership of George WASHINGTON, and France's decision to support the Americans after 1777, which diverted much of Britain's resources and threatened the Royal Navy's mastery of the seas. The British surrender at YORKTOWN in 1781 proved decisive. Two years later, in 1783, Britain recognized American independence.

Independent Labour Party (ILP), a British socialist party, founded in 1893. It helped establish the Labour Representation Committee in 1900. Affiliated to the LABOUR Party until 1932, it nevertheless put up its own parliamentary candidates and was often critical of Labour policies.

India, a republic of S Asia. See panel.

India Acts, British legislation relating to the administration of INDIA. The first India Act (1858) transferred rule of the subcontinent from the English EAST INDIA COMPANY to the crown. The Acts of 1919 and 1935 granted limited autonomy and created an Indian federation.

Indian Mutiny (1857–8), a rebellion by Indian troops (sepoys) of the English EAST INDIA COMPANY. One of the causes of the revolt was Indian outrage at the issue of

INDIA

c. 2300–1700 BC: Flourishing of the INDUS VALLEY CIVILIZATION focused on the city-states of MOHENJO-DARO and HARAPPA in the NW of the subcontinent. **c. 1500 BC:** entry of the nomadic ARYANS into the subcontinent; the amalgamation of Dravidian and Aryan cultures produced the early beliefs of HINDUISM. **6th century BC:** Rise of the kingdom of MAGDALHA; beginnings of JAINISM; emergence of BUDDHISM. **c. 325–185 BC:** CHANDRAGUPTA (321–297 BC) founded the MAURYAN dynasty, which established the first Indian empire. **272–232 BC:** The Mauryan empire embraced two thirds of the subcontinent. **From 185 BC:** Fragmentation of the Mauryan empire. **4th–5th centuries AD:** The GUPTAS created an empire that united northern and central India. **From 6th century:** Fragmented rule by local rulers. **711:** First Muslim invasion of India by Arabs who conquered the NW province of Sind. **Early 11th century:** Invasions of N India by MAHMUD of Ghazni. **Late 12th century:** Muhammad of GHUR overthrew the kingdom of Delhi. **1206:** DELHI SULTANATE established. **1324–51** Muhammed ibn TUGHLUQ expanded the Delhi Sultanate. **14th–15th centuries:** The Hindu VIJAYANAGAR kingdom flourished in the S. **1526:** The Muslim MOGUL EMPIRE was founded when BABUR invaded N India and overthrew the Delhi Sultanate. **1542–1605:** Under AKBAR the Mogul Empire expanded to cover all of N India. **1565:** Vijayanagar fell to the Moguls. **1600:** Formation of the English EAST INDIA COMPANY. **1658–1707:** Reign of AURANGZEB. **By 1700:** The Mogul Empire covered all the subcontinent except its southernmost tip. **18th century:** The Mogul Empire fell into decline. **1740s:** Increased Anglo-French rivalry in the subcontinent. **1757:** CLIVE'S victory at PLASSEY established him as governor of Bengal and made the EAST INDIA COMPANY the dominant power in India. **1857–8:** The INDIAN MUTINY was suppressed; the East India Company ceded its rights in India to the British Crown. **1877:** The Indian Empire (including present-day PAKISTAN and BANGLADESH, and comprising the Crown Territories of British India and over 620 British-protected PRINCELY STATES) was proclaimed with Queen VICTORIA as Empress. **From the mid-19th century:** The British cautiously encouraged Indian participation in the administration of British India. **1885:** INDIAN NATIONAL CONGRESS was founded and became a focus for growing Indian nationalism. **1906:** The MUSLIM LEAGUE met for the first time. **1919:** Nationalist demands grew after the AMRITSAR MASSACRE. **1919** and **1935:** The INDIA ACTS granted limited autonomy and created an Indian federation, but the pace of reform did not satisfy Indian expectations. **1920:** Congress – led by Mohandas K. GANDHI – began a campaign of non-violence and non-cooperation with the British authorities. **1940:** The Muslim League under JINNAH demanded a separate Muslim state. **1947:** India gained independence and was partitioned into mainly Hindu India and predominantly Muslim PAKISTAN: over 70 million Hindus and Muslims became refugees and many were killed in communal fighting as they crossed the new boundaries. **1947–9:** Border war with Pakistan. **1947–64:** Under PM Jawaharlal NEHRU, India became a leader of the NON-ALIGNED MOVEMENT. **1962:** Border clashes with China. **1965:** War with Pakistan over KASHMIR. **1966–77:** Premiership of Indira GANDHI. **1971:** Indian intervention in civil war in Pakistan led to the succession of E Pakistan as BANGLADESH. **Since 1984:** Indian Sikhs have waged an often violent campaign for an independent homeland. **1984:** Mrs Gandhi ordered the storming of the Golden Temple of Amritsar; assassination of Mrs Gandhi by a Sikh bodyguard. **Since 1990:** Increase in Hindu–Muslim violence, aggravated by a dispute over a holy site in Ayodhya. **1991:** Assassination of PM Rajiv Gandhi; P.V. Narasimha Rao became PM.

cartridges coated in beef and pork fat – offensive to Hindus and Muslims respectively. The rebellion revealed deep-seated resentment over growing British interference in Indian customs and culture. Economic tensions such as those arising out of the increased payment of land tax also played their part. The British brutally ended the revolt in 1858 after 14 months of bitter struggle. See also LUCKNOW, SIEGE OF.

Indian National Congress, see CONGRESS, INDIAN NATIONAL.

Indochina, the area of SE Asia between India and China, consisting of LAOS, CAMBODIA and VIETNAM. The region was under French colonial rule from the late 19th century until the end of the FRENCH INDOCHINA WAR.

Indonesia, a republic comprising a major archipelago (the East Indies) in SE Asia. See panel.

Indo–Pakistan War (September 1965), a border war between INDIA and PAKISTAN which broke out when Pakistan tried to give military assistance to Muslims opposing Indian rule in KASHMIR. The war was ended by a UN ceasefire. Further fighting occurred in 1971, Indian victory leading to the creation of BANGLADESH.

Industrial Revolution, the revolution in the manufacturing industry that began in Britain during the 18th century and spread to much of the northern hemisphere throughout the 19th and early 20th centuries. The advent of mechanized mass production transformed predominantly agricultural countries into industrial nations with increased urban populations. Britain became the first industrial nation because of a combination of social, economic and political factors, notably political stability, the availability of coal and iron ore, and surplus capital generated by British domination of world trade. The use of steam power was crucial to many of the developments of the Industrial Revolution, steam engines eventually being used to power all kinds of factory machinery, as well as railway locomotives and ships. Mechanization of the textile industry gave rise to the factory system, which increased the division and specialization of labour. The need for reliable and cheap access to raw materials and markets made improvements in transport an essential part of the Industrial Revolution. Programmes of road- and canal-building in the 18th century were followed by the advent of the railways in the early 19th century. The Industrial Revolution made Britain the world's richest and most powerful nation by the mid-19th century.

Indus Valley civilization, an early urban culture in what is now PAKISTAN that flourished c. 2500–1500 BC. The civilization evolved in much the same way as the civilization of ancient MESOPOTAMIA, from which direction the region had acquired Neolithic farming techniques by around 5000 BC. Settlements became larger, bronze working was introduced and ruling elites emerged. The high point was reached with the HARAPPAN civilization, which flourished between 2300 and 1700 BC, and was centred on the two cities of Harappa and Mohenjo-Daro. In these cities the full repertoire of Bronze Age urban society was displayed: a literate elite, carefully organized and controlled water and food supplies, and densely packed artisan quarters. This urban civilization flourished for 600 years, collapsing for reasons that remain unclear.

INF Agreement, see INTERMEDIATE NUCLEAR FORCES.

Inkerman, Battle of (5 November 1854), a clash near SEVASTOPOL during the CRIMEAN WAR, in which the Russian army under Prince Menshikov was repulsed after launching a surprise attack on an Anglo-French force.

Innocent III (1160–1216), pope (1198–1216). His pontificate is seen as the high point of the secular and spiritual supremacy of Rome in the Middle Ages. He supported the Fourth CRUSADE, instigated Church reform, excommunicated the English king JOHN, and launched a crusade against the CATHAR heretics in S France. He was also an important supporter of the DOMINICAN and FRANCISCAN friars.

Inquisition, an ecclesiastical court, established around 1332 for the detection and punishment of heretics. It was reactivated during the COUNTER-REFORMATION. The Spanish Inquisition was established in 1478 by the Spanish monarchy with approval from the pope. Between 1478 and 1500 the

INDONESIA

By 3rd century AD: Hindu kingdoms had been established in Java and Sumatra; spread of BUDDHISM and HINDUISM in the Indonesian archipelago. **7th–13th centuries:** Flourishing of the powerful Buddhist kingdom of SRIVIJAYA on Sumatra. **13th–15th centuries:** Srivijaya eclipsed by the Javan Hindu kingdom of MAJAPAHIT. **By 16th century:** Islam – brought by Arab traders – had taken the place of both established religions; beginning of European incursions in the region. **1620s:** The struggle between the Portuguese, Dutch, Spanish and British for the rich East Indian spice trade ended in Dutch ascendancy. **17th century:** The East Indies became the major and most profitable part of the Dutch Empire. **1811–14:** Brief period of British occupation. **1927:** Achmed SUKARNO founded the nationalist party. **1942:** Japanese invaders were welcomed by most Indonesians as liberators from colonial rule. **1945:** Upon Japan's surrender, Sukarno declared the Dutch East Indies to be the independent republic of Indonesia. **1945–9:** War of independence against reimposed Dutch rule. **1949:** Under international pressure, the Dutch accepted Indonesian independence under Sukarno. **1950s:** Sukarno's rule became increasingly authoritarian and the country sank into economic chaos. **1962:** Sukarno seized Netherlands New Guinea, which was formally annexed as Irian Jaya in 1969. **1963–6:** Sukarno attempted to destabilize the newly created Federation of MALAYSIA by incursions into N BORNEO. **1965–6:** Suppression of abortive Communist uprising by General SUHARTO. **1967:** Suharto overthrew Sukarno in a bloody coup, reversing the latter's policy of anti-Americanism, and violently suppressing Communist activity. **1976:** Annexation of Portuguese EAST TIMOR. **Since 1986:** Large-scale resettlement on outlying islands to relieve overcrowded Java. **Since 1991:** Increased unrest in East Timor.

Spanish inquisition – under Grand Inquisitor Tomás de Torquemada – convicted and executed thousands of Christianized Jews for Jewish practices. Punishment (burning) was carried out at elaborate public spectacles known as *autos-da-fé* ('acts of faith'). About 75% of cases dealt with by the Spanish Inquisition concerned religious 'deviance': witchcraft, Protestantism, Jewish practices and blasphemy. After 1550 its activities were less spectacular, although fear of arbitrary arrest, imprisonment, torture, and confiscation of goods by the Spanish Inquisition continued.

Intermediate Nuclear Forces (INF) Agreement (December 1987), an agreement between the USA and the USSR to abolish land-based intermediate nuclear forces, namely the Soviet SS-20 and American Pershing II and GLCM (ground-launched cruise missile).

International Brigades, groups of left-wing volunteers from outside Spain who fought for the Republicans in the SPANISH CIVIL WAR. Among their numbers were the English writers W.H. Auden and George Orwell.

International Court of Justice, a judicial body established in the Hague by the UNITED NATIONS to settle disputes brought before it by member states.

International Labour Organization (ILO), an agency of the UNITED NATIONS that aims to improve labour conditions and promote social justice.

International Monetary Fund (IMF), a specialized agency of the UNITED NATIONS founded in 1946 to promote international monetary cooperation, currency stabilization and trade expansion.

Internationals, international organizations of socialist and left-wing political groupings. MARX played a key role in the First International (1864–72). The Second International (established 1889) split with the establishment of the Soviet-controlled Third International (or COMINTERN) in 1919.

Intifada, the Palestinian uprising in the occupied territories of GAZA and the WEST BANK from 1987. The campaign includes mainly peaceful demonstrations, but also stone throwing and petrol bombing by Palestinian youths. The often brutal response of the Israeli armed forces to the Intifada has attracted international condemnation. The campaign has continued despite the signing of the ISRAELI–PALESTINIAN PEACE ACCORD in 1993.

Inuit, a native North American people who have settled the Arctic coasts in North America, the E islands of the Canadian Arctic and the ice-free coasts of Greenland during the last 1000 years. They are the dominant group among the ESKIMO, although they object to the use of the latter term. Their economy depended entirely on the hunting of seals and other marine animals.

Investiture Contest (1075–1122), a conflict between the papacy and the Holy Roman Empire. Attempts to reform the Church were opposed by many secular rulers, particularly the emperor HENRY IV. The tensions between Church and state came to a head in the 11th century when many clergy began to question lay rulers' right to 'invest' bishops with their position and property, arguing that it shackled the church to the world. When Henry tried to depose Pope GREGORY VII, he was excommunicated and forced to go in penance to CANOSSA (1077). Civil war broke out in Germany and peace was only restored at the Concordat of Worms (1122) whereby the king forfeited the power of investiture, but retained some practical control over the appointment of bishops.

Ionians, one of the main cultural and linguistic groupings of the ancient Greeks. The Ionic dialect was mainly spoken in Athens, the islands of the central Aegean, and the cities in the central part of the coast of Asia Minor (Turkey). See also AEOLIANS, DORIANS.

IRA, see IRISH REPUBLICAN ARMY.

Iran, a country of SW Asia. See panel.

Iran Hostage Crisis (November 1979–January 1981), a crisis that arose when militant supporters of the Ayatollah KHOMEINI

IRAN

From 1600 BC: The MEDES and PERSIANS overran Iran. **By the 7th century BC:** The Persians were subjects of the Medes. **550 BC:** ASTYAGES, last king of the Medes, overthrown by CYRUS II of the ruling ACHAEMENID dynasty of Persia. **From 539 BC:** The Persian Achaemenid empire grew under Cyrus II. **521–465 BC:** Under DARIUS I and XERXES the Persians ruled from the Danube to the Indus, although their attempts to conquer Greece were eventually unsuccessful. **330 BC:** ALEXANDER THE GREAT finally defeated the Achaemenids, taking the capital Persepolis. **Until 247 BC:** Persia was part of the Hellenistic SELEUCID Empire. **247 BC–AD 226:** Iran ruled by the PARTHIANS. **AD 226:** The SASSANIANS – an Iranian dynasty – established an empire that lasted until 637. **7th century:** Iran conquered by Arabs who brought Islam. **661–750:** Rule of the UMAYYAD dynasty, based in Damascus. **750–1258:** Umayyads succeeded by the ABBASIDS who moved the capital to Baghdad, where Persian traditions predominated. **13th century:** MONGOL invasion. **1501–1722:** Iran flourished under the SAFAVID dynasty, who established SHIITE – rather than SUNNI – Islam as the state religion. **1796:** Rise of the Qajar dynasty, who moved the capital from Isfahan to Tehran. **19th century:** Russia and Britain became rivals for influence in the region. **1921:** An Iranian Cossack officer, Reza Khan PAHLAVI, took power. **1925:** Pahlavi deposed the Qajars and became Shah (emperor) himself as Reza I. **1941:** Because of his pro-German sentiments, Reza I was forced to abdicate by Britain and the USSR and was replaced by his son Mohammed Reza. **1951:** The radical nationalist prime minister Muhammad MOSSADEQ briefly toppled the monarchy. **1953:** The Shah regained his throne, tightened his grip and carried out pro-Western policies. **1979:** Monarchy overthrown by Islamic fundamentalists led by Ayatollah KHOMEINI; Islamic republic proclaimed; Western-educated classes fled Iran. **1979–81:** IRAN HOSTAGE CRISIS. **1980–8:** IRAN–IRAQ WAR. **1989:** Death of Khomeini; RAFSANJANI elected president. **From 1989:** Economic necessity brought a less militant phase of the Islamic revolution.

seized the US embassy in Tehran, Iran, and took 66 American hostages. President CARTER'S unsuccessful attempts to free the hostages – through diplomatic and military means – contributed to his defeat by Ronald REAGAN in the 1980 US presidential elections.

Iraq, a country of SW Asia. See panel.

Ireland, a country of NW Europe. See panel, p. 150.

Irgun Zvai Leumi (Hebrew, 'National Military Organization'), a militant Zionist organization formed in 1931 to protect Jewish settlements in Palestine from Arab attack. It was led by Menachem BEGIN from 1943. In the 1940s it conducted a terrorist campaign against the British to force their withdrawal from Palestine, one of its most notorious actions being the bombing in 1946 of the King David Hotel, the headquarters of British administration in Palestine.

Irish famine (1845–51), a period of famine in IRELAND following a blight that ruined the potato crop (1845–7), the staple diet of the Irish population. It caused the death of about one million Irish people, and led to the emigration of a further million, chiefly to the USA. An inadequate relief programme was exacerbated by absentee landlordism and procrastination by the British government.

Irish Free State, see IRELAND.

Irish Republican Army (IRA), a paramilitary organization fighting to achieve a united republican IRELAND by means of guerrilla warfare. The IRA was formed in 1919 but had roots in earlier anti-British organizations such as the FENIANS and the Irish Republican Brotherhood. After British withdrawal from southern Ireland in 1921, the IRA fought and lost a civil war with Irish Free State forces, since when it has been an underground movement. With the renewal of sectarian violence in Northern Ireland in the late 1960s, the IRA split into Official and Provisional wings (1969). The Provisional IRA continues to wage an anti-British terrorist campaign in Northern Ireland and Britain. See also SINN FEIN.

Iron Age, term used to describe the period that saw the development of iron weapons and tools. The development of iron working in the Near East and its spread, starting at about 1000 BC, had little immediate effect on late BRONZE AGE cultures. The recognizably Celtic societies of Iron Age temperate Europe developed directly out of later Bronze Age cultures. European Iron Age societies had increasing contacts with Greece and Rome, first through trade, but later through the invasion of much of Celtic Europe by the Romans. This put an end to prehistory in those areas. However, the peripheries of Europe (Ireland, Scotland, Scandinavia, northern Germany) were never colonized by the Romans. The emergence of these areas from prehistory only occurred gradually, within the last 1500 years, after their conversion to Christianity.

Iron Curtain, a term for the frontier between the former Soviet bloc and the rest of non-Communist Europe. The frontier was destroyed by the end of the COLD WAR in 1990. The term was first employed by GOEBBELS, but was popularized by its use in a speech by Winston CHURCHILL.

Ironsides, see NEW MODEL ARMY.

Iroquois, native North American peoples, maize farmers living SE of the Great Lakes. The Iroquois Confederation was formed initially of five tribes in the later 16th century and allied with the British colonists in wars against the French. After the British defeat in the American War of Independence, the bulk of the Iroquois settled in Ontario. See also NORTH AMERICAN INDIANS.

Isabella I ('the Catholic'; 1451–1504), queen of CASTILE (1474–1504). She was joint ruler of Castile and ARAGON (1479–1504) with her husband FERDINAND. Together they restored order and royal authority in Castile, and in 1492 completed the conquest of the Moorish kingdom of GRANADA, bringing to a conclusion the RECONQUISTA. She came to an agreement with Portugal over the division of the Americas in the Treaty of TORDESILLAS in 1493.

IRAQ

By 3000 BC: Iraq – ancient MESOPOTAMIA – was the cradle of the SUMERIAN civilization. **c. 2900–2370 BC:** Early Dynastic Period – Sumerian city-states (such as UR, URUK, Kish, Lagash and Umma) at war with each other. **2370 BC:** Conquest of Mesopotamia by SARGON OF AKKAD. **2200 BC:** Akkad overrun by the Gutians. **c. 2113–2006 BC:** Third Dynasty of UR brought prosperity to the region. **2006 BC:** Sack of Ur by the ELAMITES; end of Sumerian rule. **c. 1792–1750 BC:** Rise of BABYLON under HAMMURABI. **c. 1595 BC:** Sack of Babylon by the HITTITES. **c. 1570–1157 BC:** Rule of the KASSITE dynasty. **8th century BC:** ASSYRIAN encroachments on Babylonian territory culminate in the conquest of Babylon (729 BC). **625–539 BC:** A dynasty of Chaldaean kings created a Neo-Babylonian empire, sacking the Assyrian capital of Nineveh (612 BC). **539 BC:** Mesopotamia conquered by the ACHAEMENID ruler CYRUS II. **330s BC:** Mesopotamia conquered by ALEXANDER THE GREAT. **To 3rd century AD:** The region was contested by PARTHIA and Rome. **AD 266–637:** The region formed part of the Persian SASSANIAN Empire. **AD 637:** Muslim armies from Arabia defeated the Persians. **750:** The ABBASID dynasty based its caliphate in Baghdad, which became the administrative and cultural capital of the Arab world. **13th–14th centuries:** MONGOL invasions ended Abbasid power. **1534:** Iraq was absorbed by the Turkish OTTOMAN Empire. **1914–18:** During World War I the British occupied the area. **1920:** Iraq became a monarchy under a British MANDATE. **1932:** Iraq became fully independent. **1941–5:** British occupation of Iraq. **1958:** Iraqi royal family and premier murdered in the 'Free Officers' coup. **1963:** A further coup resulted in a reign of terror against the left. **1968:** BA'ATHIST regime came to power after a military coup. **1979:** Saddam HUSSEIN became president. **1980–8:** Iraq invaded IRAN, provoking the IRAN–IRAQ WAR. **1990–1:** Iraqi annexation of KUWAIT. **1991:** Iraq defeated in the GULF WAR by Sled coalition; Saddam Hussein suppressed revolts by KURDS in the N and Shiites in the S.

Isabella of France (1295–1358), queen of England (1308–27), married to EDWARD II in 1308. She became the mistress of Roger MORTIMER, with whom she launched an invasion of England (1326) that overthrew her husband. They ruled England together until EDWARD III took over in 1330, and hanged Mortimer.

Isandhlwana, Battle of (22 January 1879), a battle between the British and the ZULUS in South Africa. Taken by surprise by Cetewayo's Impis, the British lost over 1500 men in hand-to-hand fighting.

Islam, the religion of Muslims, and the second largest religion in the world. Muslims submit themselves to Allah – whom they regard as the one true God – by accepting the faith of Islam. The sacred book of Islam is the QUR'AN (Koran), the word of God revealed to the Prophet MUHAMMAD. Five basic beliefs are central in Islam. These are the Articles of Faith and consist of belief in: the oneness of God; the holy books he has revealed for the guidance of humanity; the prophets; the angels; and the hereafter. SUNNISM and SHIISM are the two main sects of Islam. Athough the majority of Muslims are Sunnis, the Shiites are dominant in IRAN. Shiism has produced a variety of subsects, including the ISMAILIS and Zaidis. Islam spread to Egypt, Syria, Iraq, Persia and N Africa through the ARAB CONQUESTS.

Ismailis, one of the branches of the SHIITE form of ISLAM, which diverged from the major (Twelver) branch, and achieved political dominance in Egypt under the FATIMIDS. A further subdivision became famous in the medieval West as the Assassins. The Aga Khan heads the modern form of that Ismaili branch of Islam.

isolationism, the advocacy of non-participation in the affairs of other nations as the basis of US foreign policy. Isolationism prevented the USA from joining the LEAGUE OF NATIONS in 1920 and through the NEUTRALITY ACTS hindered F.D. ROOSEVELT'S support for Britain and France before WORLD WAR II.

IRELAND

5th century: Christianity – traditionally brought by St PATRICK – gave a cultural unity to the kingdoms of Celtic Ireland – CONNAUGHT, Leinster, Meath, Munster and ULSTER. **End of the 8th century:** The VIKINGS invaded, settling in E Ireland. **1014:** Vikings defeated by BRIAN BORU, who became effective king of all Ireland. **1171:** Ireland's disunited kingdoms succumbed to invasion by HENRY II of England. **12th–15th centuries:** English monarchs made successive attempts to quell Irish resistance to their authority. **By 1500:** Only a small area around Dublin (the Pale) remained loyal to English administration; most Irish land was in the hands of native Irish. **16th century:** The racial and cultural hostility between English and Irish was exacerbated by the REFORMATION. **1595–1603:** Chieftains O'Neill (Earl of Tyrone) and O'Donnell led an unsuccessful Catholic Irish revolt against the British in Ulster. **17th century:** JAMES I continued the policy – begun under MARY I and ELIZABETH I – of establishing 'plantations' of mainly Protestant settlers in N Ireland; native Catholic landowners were dispossessed. **1641:** Massacre of Protestant settlers by Catholics in the N of Ireland. **1649:** Irish rebellion suppressed by Oliver CROMWELL, who embarked on a ruthless campaign against the Irish, massacring the populations of Drogheda and Wexford. **1690:** The Catholic JAMES II, having fled England in 1688, attempted to lead a revolt in Ireland; his defeat at the Battle of the BOYNE (1690) at the hands of William of Orange (WILLIAM III of England) confirmed Protestant domination and British rule in Ireland. **18th century:** Both Presbyterians and Roman Catholics pressed for civil rights that were largely denied. **1798:** Unsuccessful nationalist revolt led by Wolfe TONE. **1801:** The Act of UNION abolished the Irish parliament and gave Ireland parliamentary representation at Westminster. **1829:** CATHOLIC EMANCIPATION achieved after the campaign led by Daniel O'CONNELL. **1845–51:** The IRISH FAMINE caused massive decline in population through starvation and emigration. **1867:** The violent campaign of the Irish nationalist FENIANS drew attention to Irish discontent. **1880s:** Growth of the HOME RULE movement led by Charles Stewart PARNELL and supported by GLADSTONE in Parliament (from 1885). **1886:** First Home Rule Bill rejected. **1893:** Second Home Rule Bill defeated in House of Lords. **1905:** Foundation of SINN FEIN. **1912:** Protestant Unionists in Ulster opposed Third Home Rule Bill. **1913:** Formation of the ULSTER VOLUNTEERS. **1916:** Nationalist EASTER RISING put down by British. **1918:** Sinn Fein MPs formed a provisional government led by Eamon DE VALERA. **1919–21:** Except in the Protestant NE, British administration in Ireland crumbled and most of the Irish police were replaced by English officers – the BLACK AND TANS; fighting broke out between nationalists and British troops and police. **1921:** Anglo-Irish Treaty granted DOMINION status to Ireland, but the six (mainly Protestant) counties in Ulster opted to remain British, forming the state of NORTHERN IRELAND. **1922:** Proclamation of the Irish Free State. **1922–3:** Civil war between the provisional government – led by Arthur GRIFFITH and Michael COLLINS – and Republicans, led by de Valera, who opposed partition; although fighting ended in 1923, de Valera's campaign for a republic continued. **1937:** Irish Free State became Republic of Eire. **1939–45:** Ireland remained neutral in World War II. **1949:** As the Republic of Ireland the country left the COMMONWEALTH. **Since 1968:** Relations between S and N – and between the Republic and the UK – have often been tense during the 'troubles' in Northern Ireland. **1985:** The Anglo-Irish Agreement provided for the participation of the Republic in political, legal and security matters in Northern Ireland.

Israel, a country on the Mediterranean in the Middle East. See panel.

Israeli–Palestinian Peace Accord (1993), a peace agreement signed In Washington in September 1993 by the PALESTINE LIBERATION ORGANIZATION leader Yasser ARAFAT and the Israeli foreign minister Shimon Peres. The accord granted the Palestinians limited self-government in the GAZA STRIP and Jericho, and provided for eventual Palestinian self-government on the WEST BANK. Israel also agreed to withdraw its troops from the Gaza Strip and Jericho. Negotiations over the implementation of the accord made slow progress and were hampered by continuing violence between Arabs and Jewish settlers in the Occupied Territories.

Issus, Battle of (333 BC), a battle fought in SE Anatolia between ALEXANDER THE GREAT and a larger Persian army led by DARIUS III. Alexander won a brilliant victory, personally leading his cavalry into the heart of the battle. Darius fled, leaving his family to be captured. Alexander entered Egypt and was accepted as its new ruler by the Egyptian priests (see map, p. 12).

Italian campaign, a campaign fought by the Allies in Italy during WORLD WAR II following the NORTH AFRICAN CAMPAIGN. In July 1943 British and US troops under MONTGOMERY and PATTON invaded Sicily, and in September, S Italy. By then MUSSOLINI had been overthrown, allowing the Italians to surrender, although not before German forces had rushed S to fill the breach. The Allied advance from Salerno and Taranto soon stalled in the mountains S of Rome, especially around Monte Cassino. Despite an amphibious landing at ANZIO (January 1944), Cassino was not taken until May. Rome was liberated on 4 June. Poor weather and German resistance thwarted an Allied thrust into the Po valley in the autumn. A final Allied push towards the Alps led to the surrender of the entire German army group serving in N Italy and S Austria on 2 May 1945.

Italy, a country of S Europe. See panel, p. 152.

Ivan I (c. 1304–41), grand prince of Muscovy (1328–41). He obtained the title of grand prince from the Mongol Khan. He formed a close alliance with the metropolitan (head) of the Orthodox Church, whose seat was transferred to Moscow in 1326.

Ivan III ('the Great'; 1440–1505), grand prince of Muscovy (1462–1505). He incorporated most of the Christian Slav principalities of Russia into Muscovy, greatly expanding its territory, and laid down the foundations of the centralized Russian state. He claimed the title of 'Ruler of all Russia' in 1497.

Ivan IV ('the Terrible'; 1530–84), grand prince of Muscovy (1533–47), and first tsar (emperor) of all Russia (1547–84). His conquest of Tartar Kazan (1552) and Astrakhan (1556) extended his rule to the Caspian Sea, and opened the way for a Russian advance into Siberia in the later 16th century. Further progress to the S was blocked by the Ottoman Turks. He made a number of legal and administrative reforms, and significantly reduced the power of the BOYARS. He was succeeded by his son Theodore I (1584–98).

Iwo Jima, Battle of (February–March 1945), a prolonged battle between US and Japanese forces for control of the W Pacific island of Iwo Jima in the later stages of WORLD WAR II. US forces took the island but at the cost of 7000 casualties. See PACIFIC CAMPAIGNS.

Jackson, Andrew (1767–1845), US Democratic politician, seventh president of the USA (1829–1837). A self-made frontier aristocrat who led American troops to victory in the Battle of NEW ORLEANS, Jackson personified the democratic and aggressive spirit of the USA as it expanded westwards during the 1830s. He was responsible for introducing the SPOILS SYSTEM into US political life.

ISRAEL

c. 14th century BC: Israel (PALESTINE) was occupied by the Hebrews. **c. 1000 BC:** The kingdom of Israel was established. **11th–10th centuries BC:** King DAVID made Jerusalem his capital; under his successor, SOLOMON, the Temple was built and Israel prospered. **10th century BC:** The kingdom was divided into Israel in the N and JUDAH in the S. **722 BC:** Israel was overrun by the ASSYRIANS. **597 BC:** Judah overrun by BABYLONIANS; Jerusalem was destroyed and many of its people taken into captivity; the Persians allowed the Jews to return 50 years later. **4th–2nd centuries BC:** Palestine was ruled successively by ALEXANDER THE GREAT, the PTOLEMIES of Egypt and then the SELEUCID Empire. **141 BC:** Judas Maccabeus revolted against the Seleucids and established a Jewish state. **65 BC:** The independent state ended with Roman conquest. **AD 66–70:** The ZEALOTS led a major revolt against the Romans at MASADA; Jerusalem was destroyed when the revolt was crushed. **AD 135:** Second Jewish revolt against the Romans; the Jewish population of Palestine was dispersed – the DIASPORA. **From 330:** Palestine was part of the BYZANTINE Empire. **7th century:** Arab invasion brought the area into the Islamic world. **12th–13th centuries:** The CRUSADERS unsuccessfully attempted to retake the Holy Land. **From early 16th century:** The Turkish OTTOMAN Empire ruled the area. **1917–18:** During World War I Palestine was captured by British forces. The BALFOUR DECLARATION encouraged ZIONISTS in their hopes of a Jewish state. **1918–48:** Palestine administered as a British MANDATE. **1922–39:** Increased Jewish settlement in Palestine. **1946:** Arrival of refugees from the HOLOCAUST heightened pressure for a Jewish state; escalation of violence between Arabs and Jews in Palestine. **1947:** Resolution in favour of partition of Palestine passed by UN; civil war between Jews and Arabs. **1948:** End of British mandate; proclamation of the state of Israel with BEN-GURION as PM; new state attacked by its Arab neighbours. **1948–9, 1956, 1967 and 1973:** ARAB-ISRAELI WARS; loss of most of the Arab Palestinian land to Israel. **1979:** CAMP DAVID ACCORD between Israel and Egypt. **From 1987:** Palestinian INTIFADA (uprising) against Israeli rule in GAZA and the WEST BANK. **Since 1990:** Large-scale influx of Soviet Jews has given extra impetus to the Intifada. **1993:** Yitzhak RABIN and Yasser ARAFAT signed the ISRAELI-PALESTINIAN PEACE ACCORD.

ITALY

509 BC: The Roman Republic was established. **By 272 BC:** All of peninsular Italy had been united under the rule of Rome. **3rd century BC–3rd century AD:** The Italian peninsula was the centre of the ROMAN EMPIRE. **3rd century AD:** The Roman Empire began to decline, plagued by civil war, economic problems and foreign invasions. **410:** Sack of Rome by the VISIGOTHS. **476:** The Western Roman Empire collapsed when ODOACER established a Gothic kingdom based in Rome. **568:** LOMBARD invasion of Italy. **8th century:** Rise of the PAPACY as a temporal power. **755:** CHARLEMAGNE conquered N Italy which became part of the Carolingian empire; S Italy disputed between BYZANTINES and Arabs. **10th–13th centuries:** Power struggle between the HOLY ROMAN EMPIRE and the PAPACY. **Late 11th century:** Norman adventurers took S Italy from the Byzantines and Sicily from the Arabs. **By 12th century:** Self-governing city-states had emerged in N and central Italy. **Late 12th century to early 16th century:** S Italy successively ruled by the HOHENSTAUFEN, the ANGEVINS, the ARAGONESE and the Spanish. **By 1400:** Five powers had come to dominate Italy: MILAN, FLORENCE, VENICE, the PAPAL STATES and NAPLES. **1494:** French invasion of N Italy. **1599–1700:** Italy under Spanish HABSBURG domination. **1713:** The Peace of UTRECHT gave much of Italy to AUSTRIA; rulers of PIEDMONT-Savoy gained Sicily. **1796–1814:** Italy temporarily united under French Napoleonic rule. **1815:** The 'old order' was essentially restored by the Congress of VIENNA – with the kingdom of Sardinia-PIEDMONT and the Austrian provinces of Lombardy-Venetia in the N, the kingdom of the Two SICILIES (Naples) in the S, and the Papal States and minor duchies in the centre. **1830–61:** The RISORGIMENTO, culminating in the campaigns of CAVOUR and GARIBALDI, led to a united Italy. **1880:** ERITREA became an Italian colony. **1895–6:** Unsuccessful attempt to annex Ethiopia. **1900:** King Umberto I assassinated. **1914–18:** Italian participation in WORLD WAR I on the ALLIED side; Italy gained territory from Austria by the Treaty of ST GERMAIN. **1922:** Rise of FASCISM; Benito MUSSOLINI became PM. 1936: Italy invaded ETHIOPIA. **1939:** Italy invaded Albania. **1940–3:** During WORLD WAR II Italy was allied to Nazi Germany. **1943:** Italy defeated; Mussolini dismissed; Italy joined the ALLIES. **1946:** Republic declared. **Since 1946:** Recurrent short-lived government coalitions dominated by the CHRISTIAN DEMOCRATS. **1970s:** TERRORIST movements – of both the left and the right – were active, kidnapping and assassinating senior political and industrial figures. **1990s:** State institutions weakened by corruption, political instability and the activities of the Mafia; growth of regional separatism in the N. **1993:** A non-political interim government was formed to effect constitutional changes. **1994:** First general election under new electoral law dominated by new right-wing and regional parties.

Jackson, Thomas ('Stonewall'; 1824–63), American soldier, one of the most gifted generals of the CONFEDERACY during the AMERICAN CIVIL WAR. He gained his nickname on account of his defensive stand at the First Battle of Bull Run (1861). The architect of the stunning Shenandoah Valley campaign of 1862, he was accidentally shot and killed by his own troops at Chancellorsville.

Jacobins, the most radical of the political clubs that flourished during the FRENCH REVOLUTION, named after the former Dominican monastery of St Jacques in Paris, where it met. The Jacobins ousted the moderate GIRONDINS in 1793 and, led by ROBESPIERRE, were responsible for the Reign of TERROR. The term Jacobin was subsequently used of any extreme left-wing radical.

Jacobites, supporters of the house of STUART and the claim to the thrones of England, Scotland and Ireland of JAMES II and his son James Edward Stuart (the Old PRETENDER) after James II's overthrow in the GLORIOUS REVOLUTION of 1688. They took their name from *Jacobus*, the Latin word for James. Drawing most of their support from the Highland clans of Scotland, the Jacobites exerted a significant influence on English politics in the late 17th and early 18th centuries, but their hopes were dashed by the failure of their major rebellions – the FIFTEEN and the FORTY-FIVE.

Jacquerie (May–June 1358), a short-lived peasants' revolt in N France named after 'Jacques Bonhomme', the aristocrats' contemptuous nickname for a peasant. The devastation caused by marauding English armies, and the heavy burden of taxation to pay for the HUNDRED YEARS WAR led to rebellion by peasants in the wake of the French defeat at POITIERS. Armed bands attacked the nobility and castles were demolished and looted. The threat to the existing social order caused the feuding factions of French noblemen to bury their differences, and the disorder was suppressed.

Jagatai Khanate, the division of the MONGOL Empire centred on TURKESTAN (see map, p. 19). It was founded when the Empire was divided by KUBLAI KHAN in 1278, and ruled by Genghis Khan's second son Jagatai. It lasted, in a much reduced form, until 1678.

Jagiellon, a Polish dynasty founded by Jagiello, prince of Lithuania (1377–1401) and king of Poland (as Wladislaw I; 1386–1434). His successors ruled Hungary and Bohemia (1471–1526). The dynasty became extinct on the death of Sigismund II Augustus (1548–72).

Jahangir (1569–1627), eldest son of AKBAR, and MOGUL emperor of India (1605–27). A patron of the arts, his reign was largely characterized by peace and economic expansion.

Jainism, an Indian religion founded by the ascetic Mahaviva (c. 599–527 BC) in the 6th century BC at about the same time as BUDDHISM. It remains strong in the W of India.

Jamaica, an island in the Caribbean. Jamaica – which was originally inhabited by Arawak Indians – was sighted by

COLUMBUS (1494) and claimed for Spain. It became British in 1655. Black slaves were brought from Africa to work the sugar plantations. The abolition of SLAVERY in the 1830s destroyed the plantation system. By the 1930s, severe social and economic problems led to rioting and the growth of black political awareness. Since independence in 1962, power has alternated between the radical People's National Party – led by Michael Manley – and the more conservative Jamaican Labour Party.

James I (1566–1625), the first STUART king of England (1603–25), and, as James VI, king of Scotland (1567–1625). The son of MARY, QUEEN OF SCOTS, he succeeded ELIZABETH I, with whose death the TUDOR dynasty ended. His refusal to effect PURITAN reform of the ANGLICAN CHURCH, together with his subservient attitude to Spain and insistence on the divine right of kings, contributed to difficulties with PARLIAMENT, which would come to a head under his son and successor CHARLES I.

James II (1633–1701), king of England and Scotland (1685–8), the second son of CHARLES I. He succeeded his brother CHARLES II, but his attempts to recatholicize England led supporters of the ANGLICAN Church to invite WILLIAM of Orange to come to their aid. When William and his army landed in England in November 1688 James fled to France (see GLORIOUS REVOLUTION) and was replaced by William and Mary. He later led a revolt in Ireland but was defeated at the Battle of the BOYNE.

James Francis Edward Stuart, see PRETENDER.

Jameson Raid (1895), an abortive raid into the TRANSVAAL led by the British colonial administrator Dr Leander Starr Jameson (1853–1917), who hoped to trigger an anti-Boer insurrection among the UITLANDERS (non-Afrikaner immigrants in the Transvaal). The failure of the raid prompted the German Kaiser to send a telegram of congratulations to the Transvaal president, Paul KRUGER. The incident fuelled the enmity between Britain and the Boers and contributed to the outbreak of the Second BOER WAR.

Jamestown, the site on the E coast of VIRGINIA of the first permanent English settlement in North America (1607).

Janissaries, the elite infantry corps of the OTTOMAN army. Originally recruited from prisoners of war, from the reign of BAJEZID I they were levied by conscription of the fittest youths of the empire's Christian population. They exercised a significant influence on Ottoman military and political life until their abolition after a revolt in Constantinople in 1826.

Jansen, Cornelius Otto (1585–1638), Dutch Roman Catholic theologian, the founder of the spiritual movement known as Jansenism. The beliefs of the Jansenists, based on the teachings of St AUGUSTINE on free will, salvation and predestination, in some ways resembled those of CALVIN, and brought them into conflict with the ecclesiastical and secular authorities, who condemned them.

Japan, a country comprising an archipelago in the Pacific off the coast of E Asia. See panel.

Jaruzelski, Wojciech (1927–), Polish soldier and statesman, prime minister (1981–5), president (1989–90). Faced with economic problems and the increasing influence of SOLIDARITY, he imposed martial law (1981–2). The success

JAPAN

660 BC: Legendary date of the first Japanese emperor, Jimmu. **From 6th century AD:** Japan was greatly influenced by Chinese culture; introduction of BUDDHISM. **By 7th century:** Chinese concepts of government were being implemented. **710–84:** Chinese-style emperor was established at Nara. **9th century:** The emperor became a religious figurehead and real power passed to the FUJIWARA family. **By late 12th century:** The Fujiwara lost control of Japan; power was exercised by provincial barons (daimyos) through bands of warriors (SAMURAI). **From 1185:** Yorimoto Minamoto ruled Japan from Kamakura (near Tokyo), eventually under the title of SHOGUN. **13th century:** The shogun became a figurehead; power was wielded by the regents from the HOJO family. **14th century:** The Ashikaga family instituted a new shogunate based at Kyoto, but this soon fell apart into warring provincial baronies. **16th century:** Three military leaders – ODO NOBUNAGA (1578–82), TOYATOMI HIDEYOSHI (1582–98) and TOKUGAWA IEYASU – fought their way out of the impasse of feudal anarchy and gained control of a united Japan. **1603:** Ieyasu established the TOKUGAWA shogunate at Edo (Tokyo) and diminished the powers of the daimyo. **Mid-17th–mid-19th centuries:** Tokugawa Japan remained hermetically sealed from outside influence. **1853:** The arrival of the American fleet under Commodore PERRY forced Japan into the global trading system. **1867–9:** Power was seized at Kyoto by a group representing daimyos and reforming imperial courtiers. **1869:** The MEIJI emperor overthrew the last shogun and restored power to the throne. **Late 19th century:** Emperor introduced Western-style reforms, abolishing feudalism and ending the power of the daimyos. **1894–6:** Japan defeated China in the First SINO-JAPANESE WAR. **1904–5:** Japanese victory in the RUSSO-JAPANESE WAR. **1910:** Korea annexed by Japan. **1914:** Japan entered WORLD WAR I against Germany. **1920s and 30s:** Increasing militarism and collapse of world trade led to the rise of totalitarianism and a phase of aggressive Japanese expansion. **1931:** Japanese army occupied MANCHURIA. **1937:** Full-scale Japanese invasion of China. **1941–2:** Allied to Nazi Germany, Japan attacked PEARL HARBOR (Hawaii), bringing the USA into WORLD WAR II. **1941–4:** Rapid Japanese military expansion across SE Asia and the Pacific. **1945:** Emperor HIROHITO surrendered after atomic bombs were dropped on HIROSHIMA and NAGASAKI. **1945–52:** Allied occupation of Japan democratized Japanese politics and began an astonishing economic recovery based on an aggressive export policy. **From 1955:** Japan ruled by the LIBERAL DEMOCRATIC PARTY. **1980s:** Japan became the world's second economic power. **1992:** Japanese government rocked by financial scandal. **1993:** Election of coalition government of breakaway conservative parties and socialists.

of Solidarity in the 1989 elections forced him to speed up democratic reforms, and he resigned from the presidency in 1990.

Jaurès, Jean (1859–1914), French socialist politician. He strongly supported DREYFUS and united the French socialists into a single movement. He was assassinated by a French nationalist in 1914, after advocating a strike by French and German workers against World War I.

Java, the most populous and historically important of the islands of the INDONESIAN archipelago. Indian contact with the region led to the emergence of Indian-style states from AD 700, one of the most significant of which, the Buddhist Saliendra kingdom, constructed the massive temple-mountain of Borobudur. After the demise of the Saliendra, a succession of Hindu kingdoms ruled in Java, culminating in the MAJAPAHIT (14th–15th centuries). The Dutch arrived in 1619 and by the mid-18th-century most of the island (renamed Batavia) was under Dutch control.

Jefferson, Thomas (1743–1826), third president of the USA (1801–9). A slave-owner, he played a key role in drafting the DECLARATION OF INDEPENDENCE in 1776. He later became governor of Virginia (1779–81) during the War of INDEPENDENCE and served as American minister in Paris and US secretary of state under Washington. After serving as vice-president under John ADAMS, Jefferson led his anglophobe Democratic-Republican party to victory in the election of 1800.

Jellicoe, John Rushworth, 1st Earl (1859–1935), British admiral, commander of the Grand Fleet at the Battle of JUTLAND during World War I.

Jena, Battle of (14 October 1806), NAPOLEON'S crushing defeat of a large Prussian force in E Germany. The French victory was followed by Napoleon's occupation of Berlin, and a reorganization of Germany in which Prussia lost much of its territory. See NAPOLEONIC WARS and map, p. 29.

Jenkins's Ear, War of (1739–48), a conflict between Britain and Spain, urged on the British government by merchants resentful of Spanish attempts to exclude English shipping from Spain's overseas empire. They put pressure on a reluctant WALPOLE in Parliament by exploiting Captain Robert Jenkins's claim to have had his ear cut off by Spanish coastguards. The war was later absorbed into the War of the AUSTRIAN SUCCESSION.

Jericho, an ancient city, now in the Israeli-occupied WEST BANK. Possibly the oldest city in the world, it has been inhabited since c. 8000 BC. In Old Testament tradition, the city fell to Joshua when the walls collapsed at the sound of the Israelite trumpets.

Jerusalem, a holy city for JEWS, Christians and Muslims. As the site of JESUS'S teaching and Crucifixion, Jerusalem became increasingly important as a Christian centre from the 4th century AD, and was one of the five PATRIARCHATES of Christendom. The city fell to the Arabs in 637; the Dome of the Rock, the city's holiest Muslim shrine, was built in 691 during the period of Muslim rule. Jerusalem was conquered during the CRUSADES in 1099 and became part of the Latin Kingdom of Jerusalem, until recaptured by SALADIN in 1187. The city was ruled by the Egyptian MAMLUKS, and then the OTTOMAN Turks until taken by the British in 1917, and remained the capital of the British MANDATE of Palestine until 1948, when it was split between Arabs and Jews in the first ARAB–ISRAELI WAR. Arab East Jerusalem was annexed by ISRAEL during the SIX DAY WAR (1967).

Jesuit, a missionary order established by St Ignatius LOYOLA as part of the COUNTER-REFORMATION effort to recover areas lost to Protestantism. The Jesuits worked both as missionaries and as teachers in Europe, America and Asia. Their teaching methods earned the Jesuit schools an exalted reputation, and by 1640 there were more than 500 of them throughout Europe, as well as Jesuit universities. In these institutions the Jesuits helped mould Catholic priests, and as royal confessors urged Catholic rulers to ignore Protestant rights as a limitation on their power.

Jesus Christ, religious teacher, regarded by Christians as the Son of God. For historical information about the life and teachings of Jesus we depend almost exclusively on the (late 1st-century) gospel accounts, which are based on an oral tradition preserved by the early Christians, and written by and for believers. Non-Christian sources, such as Tacitus, mention the crucifixion under Pontius Pilate. Jesus's birth is usually dated before the death of HEROD in 4 BC (the Christian era, starting with the year 1, is based on a miscalculation by a 6th-century monk) and his ministry to the period from c. 28 to 33. See also CHRISTIANITY.

Jews, people of Hebrew descent or those whose religion is JUDAISM. The word Jew is derived from the Latin *Judaeus*, that in turn is derived from the Hebrew *Yehudi*, signifying a descendant of Jacob, the grandson of ABRAHAM. The Exodus of the Jews – which is believed to have occurred c. 1250 BC – was the decisive event in early Jewish history: it resulted in the emergence of Israel as a distinct nation. (For the history of the Jews from the time of King DAVID to the DIASPORA, AD 135; see ISRAEL.) The dispersed European Jews were the victims of persecution by Christians, partly for religious and cultural reasons and partly because of commercial resentment, and were often confined to ghettos. Violent ANTI-SEMITISM was common in Europe from the Middle Ages on but reached its most extreme in NAZI Germany where millions of Jews perished in the HOLOCAUST. The idea of a Jewish homeland in PALESTINE was revived in the ZIONIST movement of the late 19th century, and found expression in the establishment of the state of ISRAEL (1948).

Jiang Jie Shi (Chiang Kai-shek; 1887–1975), Chinese general and statesman, president of China (1928–31 and 1943–9) and of the Republic of China (Taiwan) (1950–75). His nationalist (KUOMINTANG) government unified most of China, but had to fight provincial WARLORDS, Communists and the Japanese. He allied with the Communists to resist the Japanese (1937–45), but was defeated by them in the final phase of the CHINESE CIVIL WAR (1946–9). He was forced to withdraw to Taiwan, where he established the Republic of CHINA.

Jiangxi Soviet, a Chinese Communist base created in 1931. During the CHINESE CIVIL WAR the nationalist forces of JIANG JIE SHI forced MAO ZEDONG to withdraw from the base in October 1934 and embark on the LONG MARCH.

jihad, an obligation imposed on Muslims by the QUR'AN to 'strive in the way of God', generally interpreted to mean 'holy war' for the defence or extension of ISLAM, or of the Muslims' political control over their territories. Before his death MUHAMMAD urged a jihad against unbelievers, precipitating the ARAB CONQUESTS.

Jimmu, the legendary first ruler of JAPAN.

Jin, 1. a N Chinese state established by Juchen nomads from NE MANCHURIA, who first gained power over the whole of Manchuria (1119) and then seized N China from the SONG Empire (1126), ruling the N until the MONGOL invasion of 1210. **2.** see WESTERN JIN.

Jinnah, Mohammed Ali (1876–1948), Indian Muslim politician, first governor-general of PAKISTAN (1947–8). He became president of the MUSLIM LEAGUE in 1916. Initially willing to compromise with the Hindu Indian National CONGRESS, after 1919 he grew disillusioned with its leadership. By 1940, as leader of the Muslim League, he was campaigning for the partition of INDIA into separate Hindu and Muslim states. On partition in 1947 he became governor-general of PAKISTAN.

Joan of Arc (c. 1412–31), French national heroine. Born the daughter of a peasant, she claimed to have heard the voices of Saints Michael, Catherine and Margaret urging her to rid France of the English invaders during the HUNDRED YEARS WAR. She led the French army that relieved the besieged town of Orleans in 1429, and went on to crown the dauphin as CHARLES VII in Reims cathedral. Captured by the English, Joan was burnt as a heretic in 1431. She was made a saint in 1920.

Joffre, Joseph Jacques Césaire (1852–1931), marshal of France. As commander-in-chief of the French army (1914–16) he was largely responsible for the decisive Allied victory at the first Battle of the MARNE in World War I. He took responsibility for the failure at VERDUN (1916) and resigned.

John (1166–1216), king of England (1199–1216). Heir to the whole ANGEVIN empire, by singular incompetence he contrived first to lose ANJOU, NORMANDY and E Poitou in 1203–5 to PHILIP II AUGUSTUS, then to provoke his English barons to rebel. In 1215 they forced him to seal MAGNA CARTA, but by the time he died the realm was once again torn apart by civil war.

John I (1357–1433), king of Portugal (1385–1433). His victory over CASTILE in the Battle of Aljubarotta (1385) ensured Portuguese independence. He then carried the RECONQUISTA across the Strait of Gibraltar in 1415, conquering Ceuta.

John II ('the Good'; 1319–64), king of France (1350–64). In 1356 he was taken prisoner at the Battle of POITIERS by EDWARD, THE BLACK PRINCE. He returned home after the Treaty of BRÉTIGNY (1360), but left his son, the Duke of Anjou, as a hostage. When the Duke escaped, John was forced to return to London, where he died.

John VI (1769–1826), king of Portugal (1816–26). In 1808 the Portuguese royal family fled to BRAZIL, fearing a French invasion. As prince regent Dom John reformed the Brazilian administration and introduced legal, academic and educational institutions, and recognized Brazil's equality with Portugal. John did not return to Portugal until 1821, and left his son Dom Pedro (later PEDRO I) as regent in Brazil.

Johnson, Andrew (1808–75), US Republican politician, 17th president of the USA. He served as LINCOLN'S vice-president, assuming the presidency on the latter's assassination in April 1865. His attempts to veto measures for the RECONSTRUCTION of the Southern states after the Civil War led to clashes with the Republican majority in Congress.

Johnson, Lyndon B(aines) (1908–73), US Democratic politician (known as LBJ), 36th president of the USA (1963–9). As KENNEDY'S vice-president he was sworn in as president when Kennedy was assassinated, and won a sweeping victory in the presidential election of 1964. As president he embarked on the most ambitious social programme in American history. He enacted legislation providing federally subsidized medical insurance and medical care for the elderly and persons on welfare. He also oversaw the Voting Rights Act of 1965 to secure the vote for Southern blacks, and created the office of Economic Opportunity to promote ways of improving living conditions for the urban poor. His 'Great Society' programme became mired in the débâcle of the VIETNAM WAR. The war proved to be his undoing and he did not seek re-election in 1969.

John of Austria, Don (1547–78), Spanish general. The illegitimate son of Emperor CHARLES V, he commanded the fleet of the HOLY LEAGUE that defeated the Turkish fleet at LEPANTO (1571) and was governor-general of the Netherlands (1576–8) at a key phase of the DUTCH REVOLT.

John Paul II (Karol Wojtyla; 1920–), pope (1978–). A Pole, he became the first non-Italian Pope since 1522 when elected pope in 1978. Anti-Communist and doctrinally conservative, he became popular through a series of foreign journeys.

Jones, John Paul (1747–92), Scottish-born American seaman whose maritime exploits during the AMERICAN WAR OF INDEPENDENCE made him one of the founding fathers of the US Navy and a popular hero in America.

Jordan, a kingdom in the Middle East. After being incorporated into the biblical kingdoms of Solomon and David, the region was ruled, in turn, by the ASSYRIAN, BABYLONIAN, ACHAEMENID Persian and SELEUCID empires. The Nabateans – based at Petra – controlled Jordan from the 4th century BC until 64 BC, when the area came under Roman rule. Jordan was part of the BYZANTINE Empire from 394 until 636 when Muslim Arab forces were victorious in the Battle of Yarmouk. At first Jordan prospered under Muslim rule, but declined when the ABBASID caliphs moved their capital to Baghdad. In the 11th and 12th centuries, CRUSADER STATES flourished briefly in Jordan. The area was conquered by the (Turkish) OTTOMAN Empire in the 16th century. In World War I the British aided an Arab revolt against Ottoman rule. The League of Nations awarded the area east of the River Jordan – Transjordan – to Britain as part of the MANDATE of Palestine (1920), but in 1923 Transjordan became a separate emirate. In 1946 the country gained complete independence as the Kingdom of Jordan with Amir Abdullah (1880–1951) as its sovereign. The Jordanian army fought with distinction in the 1948 Arab–Israeli War, and occupied the West Bank territories, which were formally incorporated into Jordan in 1950. In 1951 Abdullah was assassinated. His grandson King HUSSEIN (reigned 1952–) was initially threatened by radicals encouraged by Egypt's President Nasser. In the 1967 ARAB–ISRAELI WAR, Jordan lost the WEST BANK, including Arab E Jerusalem, to the Israelis. In the 1970s the power of the Palestinian guerrillas in Jordan challenged the very existence of the Jordanian state. After a short bloody civil war (1971) the Palestinian leadership fled abroad. King Hussein renounced all responsibility for the West Bank in 1988. A ban on party politics ended in 1991. There has since been a major growth in support for Islamic fundamentalism.

Josephine, Empress (Marie Josephine Tascher de la Pagerie; 1763–1814), empress of the French (1804–9) and wife of NAPOLEON I.

Joseph II (1741–90), Holy Roman Emperor (1765–90), effectively joint ruler of Austria with his mother MARIA THERESA to 1780, sole ruler (1780–90). An 'enlightened despot', his edict of 1781 granted toleration to Jews and Protestants. He also curbed the privileges of nobles and abolished serfdom. His measures to establish greater centralized control over Hungary and the Low Countries provoked resistance and had to be withdrawn.

Joshua, (according to the Old Testament) MOSES' successor as leader of the Israelites. He led the Jews in the conquest of Canaan (Palestine) c. 1230 BC.

Juan Carlos I (1938–), king of Spain from 1975. Nominated by FRANCO as his successor, he became king on the latter's death and presided over Spain's transition to a democratic system.

Juárez, Benito (1806–72), Mexican liberal politician who led the resistance to the French-supported Emperor MAXIMILIAN (1862–7).

Juchen, see JIN.

Judah, the ancient southern Jewish kingdom with its capital at JERUSALEM. It was nominally independent until it became part of the Babylonian empire in 587 BC.

Judaism, the oldest of the monotheistic religions. Judaism traces its history back to ABRAHAM'S revolt against the idol-worship of his native Mesopotamia (modern Iraq), when he smashed his father's idols and fled to Canaan (modern ISRAEL). The observance of the Passover (Pesach) establishes a special relationship with the One God, whose laws Jewish people undertake to observe faithfully. Jewish scripture comprises the same books as the Christian Old Testament. Orthodox Judaism regards all authority as deriving from the Torah (the Pentateuch) and the Talmud. The Torah includes the teachings of MOSES, which provide the instruction in religious belief and moral issues. Conservative Judaism stands between Orthodoxy and Reformed and Liberal Judaism, which rejects rabbinic authority and holds that Judaism must adapt to changing circumstances. See also JEWS.

Jugurtha (c. 160–104 BC), king of Numidia, who murdered his way to the throne between 118 and 112 BC. He aroused the wrath of Rome by massacring some Italian traders resident in Cirta. The ensuing war lasted until 105 BC, when Jugurtha was defeated and captured by MARIUS.

Julian the Apostate (332–63), Roman emperor (361–3). On becoming emperor he renounced Christianity and proclaimed toleration for all religions, restoring old cults and temples and abolishing Christian privileges. After his death during a campaign against the SASSANIAN Persians, these changes were reversed.

July Revolution (1830), a revolution in FRANCE that brought about the abdication of the absolutist CHARLES X and the election of the duc d'Orléans, LOUIS PHILIPPE, as 'king of the French'. Louis became a constitutional monarch at the head of a liberal state. The 'July Revolution' was the most spectacular outbreak of a wave of unrest that swept across Europe, largely liberal in orientation in the West, and nationalist in the East.

Justinian I (482–565), Byzantine emperor (527–65). Under his reign the BYZANTINE Empire underwent an intellectual, administrative, architectural and military revival, including the establishment of a new law code and the building of the great church of Hagia Sophia. Justinian's military conquests, under his great general BELISARIUS, recaptured North Africa, Sicily and most of Ostrogothic Italy (see map, p. 16). The empire recovered from the devastating economic and financial consequences of bubonic plague (542) to regain Italy and conquer S Spain in the 560s.

Jutes, a Germanic people originating in Jutland (N Denmark; see map, p. 15) who settled in Kent and the Isle of Wight in the early 5th century during the ANGLO-SAXON invasions of England.

Jutland, Battle of (31 May 1916), a naval battle between the British Grand Fleet under JELLICOE and the German High Seas Fleet, fought off the coast of Jutland, Denmark, in the North Sea. The only major naval battle of WORLD WAR I, the engagement ended in stalemate, with Britain retaining control of the North Sea and Germany turning to a policy of unrestricted submarine warfare.

Kádár, János (1912–89), Hungarian Communist politician. He became party leader after the suppression of the HUNGARIAN REVOLUTION in 1956, dealing ruthlessly with its leaders. He followed a policy of moderate economic reform until his resignation in 1988.

Kadesh, Battle of (1285 BC), a clash between Egypt and the HITTITES in Syria, one of the earliest recorded battles. Despite RAMESSES II'S claims of victory, the battle was indecisive. Both sides withdrew and 16 years later signed a peace treaty.

Kalmar, Union of, the union of the crowns of DENMARK, SWEDEN and NORWAY from 1397 to 1523. Dominated by Denmark, the Union collapsed when Sweden, under Gustavus I (1523–60), threw off Danish rule.

Kamakura, a city SW of Tokyo, where Japan's first SHOGUNATE was set up in 1185.

kamikaze (Japanese, 'divine wind'), a suicide tactic used by the Japanese in the later stages of the PACIFIC CAMPAIGNS in WORLD WAR II, whereby pilots deliberately crashed aircraft loaded with explosives onto enemy targets.

Kampuchea, see CAMBODIA.

Kanagawa, Treaty of (1858), a treaty between JAPAN and the USA, the first to grant a Western power diplomatic and trading rights in Japan. The terms were extended in the later Treaty of Edo (1858).

Kanem-Bornu, a Central African kingdom located around Lake Chad. Kanem is recorded from the 9th century, Bornu to the W from the 14th century. Bornu annexed Kanem in the late 16th century, forming a powerful Muslim state that dominated the central Sahel.

Kangxi (1654–1722), Chinese emperor of the QING dynasty (1661–1722). During his reign, Taiwan, Tibet and Outer Mongolia were brought under effective imperial control. In the Treaty of NERCHINSK (1689) he established diplomatic relations with Russia and agreed a Sino-Russian frontier across the steppes of Central Asia.

Kansas–Nebraska Act (1854), an Act of the US Congress allowing a referendum on SLAVERY in the territories of Kansas and Nebraska. By repealing a previous ban on slavery in the N part of the LOUISIANA Purchase, the Act appeared to open up all the new territories to slave labour, and Northern and Southern hotheads became embroiled in a vicious guerrilla war (1855–7) to make Kansas a state in their own image. The conflict contributed to the creation of the REPUBLICAN Party, which opposed slavery in the new territories. See also AMERICAN CIVIL WAR.

Kapp putsch (March 1920), an attempt by right-wing paramilitaries, led by Wolfgang Kapp (1858–1922), to overthrow the WEIMAR REPUBLIC and restore the German monarchy. Kapp seized Berlin, but his putsch failed following a strike by Berlin workers and the refusal of civil servants to obey Kapp's orders.

Karageorge, Petrović (1766–1817), the leader of the first Serbian revolt against the OTTOMAN Turks (1804–13) and founder of the Karageorgevic dynasty, which ruled SERBIA 1852–8 and 1903–45 (and YUGOSLAVIA from 1929). He was appointed hereditary chief by the Serbian National Assembly (1808), but was defeated by Turkey and driven into exile (1813). He was murdered in 1817 when he re-entered Serbia to assert his authority against the new Serb leadership of Milos OBRENOVIĆ.

Karnak, the site of the temple of Amun-Ra at THEBES in ancient Egypt, built c. 1320–1237 BC by the pharaohs Seti I (1313–1292 BC) and RAMESSES II.

Kasavubu, Joseph (1910–69), Congolese politician, first president of the Republic of the Congo (1960–5; now ZAIRE). He was overthrown by MOBUTU in November 1965 at the end of the CONGO CRISIS.

Kashmir, short for Jammu and Kashmir, a former PRINCELY STATE that attempted to regain independence when India became independent (1947). The state was effectively partitioned – and is still disputed – by INDIA and PAKISTAN. War between the two countries over the status of Kashmir broke out in 1948 and the UN imposed a temporary ceasefire in 1949. Fighting flared up again in 1965 and 1971.

Kassites, a dynasty ruling at BABYLON (c. 1570–1157 BC). Their long and largely peaceful rule of the region saw considerable social change, but also increasing conflict with ASSYRIA. On the death of the last Kassite king, Babylon entered an extended period of political instability.

Kaunda, Kenneth David (1924–), Zambian statesman. After the independence of Northern Rhodesia (ZAMBIA) in 1964 he became its first prime minister and six months later its first president – an office he held until his electoral defeat in 1991. He was active in the NON-ALIGNED MOVEMENT, and coordinated the policy of the COMMONWEALTH towards the racist regime in South Africa.

Kazakhstan, a republic of Central Asia (see map, p. 43). The Kazakhs first appear in written history in the late 15th century when they established a nomadic empire in the W and centre of the present republic. Between 1488 and 1518 Kazakh khans controlled virtually all the Central Asian steppes, but before 1600 the Kazakh khanate split into three separate hordes. In the 17th century the Kazakhs were constantly raided by the Oryats from Djungaria (Xinjiang in China). In the 18th century the Russians began to penetrate the Kazakh steppes and were initially welcomed as overlords in exchange for protection from the Oryats. Revolts against Russian rule were suppressed (1792–4) and what little autonomy the khans still enjoyed was abolished between 1822 and 1848. During the tsarist period there was large-scale Russian peasant settlement on the steppes, but Russian rule was resented and there was a major Kazakh revolt during World War I. After the RUSSIAN REVOLUTION, Kazakh nationalists formed a local government and demanded autonomy (1917). The Soviet Red Army invaded in 1920 and established an Autonomous Soviet Republic. Kazakhstan did not become a full Union Republic within the USSR until 1936. Widespread immigration from other parts of the USSR became a flood in 1954–6 when the 'Virgin Lands' of N Kazakhstan were opened up for farming. By the time Kazakhstan declared independence – following the abortive coup by Communist hardliners in Moscow (September 1991) – the Kazakhs formed a minority within their own republic. When the USSR was dissolved (December 1991), Kazakhstan was internationally recognized as an independent republic. The vast new Kazakh state – in theory, a nuclear power because of former Soviet nuclear weapons on its territory – occupies a pivotal position within Central Asia.

Keating, Paul (1954–), Australian politician, prime minister (1991–). He succeeded Bob HAWKE as Labor Party leader and prime minister, and has campaigned for the creation of an Australian Republic.

Keitel, Wilhelm (1882–1946), German field marshal, chief-of-staff of the Supreme Command of the German armed forces from 1938 until the end of WORLD WAR II (1945). A faithful associate of HITLER, he was convicted at the NUREMBERG TRIALS and hanged.

Kekkonen, Urho Kaleva (1900–86), Finnish statesman. As president (1956–82) he promoted his country's neutrality, pursuing a policy of cautious friendship with the Soviet Union.

Kellogg–Briand Pact (1928), a multilateral agreement condemning war, proposed by the US secretary of state Frank B. Kellogg, and the French foreign minister Aristide BRIAND. The document – signed by 65 nations – renounced war as a means of settling disputes, but proved to be of little lasting value.

Kennedy, John Fitzgerald (1917–63), US Democratic politician, 35th president of the USA (1961–3), and the first Roman Catholic to hold that office. His domestic programme involved social reforms and civil rights proposals.

The darling of American liberals, Kennedy was in fact less liberal than many of his backers. In foreign policy he presided over the fiasco of the BAY OF PIGS invasion and confronted the USSR in the CUBAN MISSILE CRISIS. His presidency saw the start of major US military involvement in VIETNAM. He was assassinated in Dallas, Texas, apparently by Lee Harvey OSWALD. Many of Kennedy's reforms were carried through by his successor Lyndon B. JOHNSON. His brother Robert F. Kennedy (1925–68) was also assassinated when running for the Democratic presidential nomination in 1968. His brother Edward M. Kennedy (1932–) remains an influential Democratic senator.

Kenneth I (MacAlpine; d. c. 859), first king of SCOTLAND (843–58). He suppressed the kingdom of the PICTS and imposed Gaelic law and culture on Scotland.

Kenya, a republic of E Africa. Arabs established coastal settlements from the 7th century, and the Portuguese were active on the Kenyan coast from 1498 until the 17th century, when they were evicted by the Arabs. The varied black African peoples of the area were brought forcibly under British rule in 1895 in the East African Protectorate, which became the colony of Kenya in 1920. White settlement in the highlands was bitterly resented by the Africans – particularly the Kikuyu – whose land was taken. Racial discrimination and attacks on African customs also created discontent. Black protest movements emerged in the 1920s and, after 1945, developed into nationalism, led by Jomo KENYATTA, who in 1947 became the first président of the Kenya African Union. When the violent MAU MAU rising – which involved mainly Kikuyu people – broke out (1952–56), Kenyatta was held responsible and was imprisoned on doubtful evidence (1953–61). After the British had crushed the Mau Mau revolt in a bloody campaign, they negotiated with Kenyatta and the other nationalists. Independence, under Kenyatta's KANU party, followed in 1963. His moderate leadership and pro-capitalist policies were continued by his successor, Daniel arap Moi. Considerable restrictions on political activity followed an attempted military coup (1982). From 1969 to 1991, KANU was the only legal political party, but multi-party elections were held in 1993.

Kenyatta, Jomo (c. 1889–1978), first prime minister (1963–4) and president (1964–78) of independent KENYA. During his campaign for Kenyan independence he was held responsible for MAU MAU violence and imprisoned by the British (1953–61). Under his presidency Kenya enjoyed economic growth and a degree of tribal harmony.

Kerensky, Aleksandr Fyodovich (1881–1970), Russian revolutionary politician, head of the provisional government after the overthrow of NICHOLAS II in March 1917. He continued the war against Germany but failed to implement economic reforms and was ousted by Lenin's BOLSHEVIKS in the second RUSSIAN REVOLUTION of November 1917.

Keynes, John Maynard, Baron (1883–1946), British economist. He criticized the REPARATIONS imposed on Germany after World War I as damaging to the international economy. The DEPRESSION of the early 1930s led him to argue that unemployment can only be avoided by government spending on public works programmes. Keynes helped to found the INTERNATIONAL MONETARY FUND and the WORLD BANK. His views were central to the establishment of the British WELFARE STATE.

KGB (Russian abbreviation, 'Committee of State Security'), the Soviet secret police, formed in 1953 and responsible for external intelligence and internal security. By the 1980s the KGB had over 200,000 men under arms, but lost its powerful position when the Soviet Union was dissolved in 1991. See also CHEKA, NKVD and OGPU.

Khama, Seretse (1921–80), president of BOTSWANA (1966–80). He was exiled to Britain (1949–56) after South African pressure on Britain following his marriage to an Englishwoman. He led Botswana as southern Africa's first prosperous non-racial democracy.

khanate, a region ruled by a Mongol or Turkic ruler.

Khmers, a people of CAMBODIA. The Khmers of Chenla conquered Funan (in the Mekong basin) around AD 550, producing a unified Cambodian kingdom. Its Hindu kings – who ruled a Buddhist population – established the concept of rule by a semi-divine king. Their divinity was expressed through a series of grandiose 'temple cities', of which the most famous is Angkor Wat. The Khmer Empire reached its height in the 12th century when it extended into CHAMPA territory in central Vietnam. The Khmer came under pressure from the Thai from the 14th century. In 1369 and again 20 years later Thai armies sacked Angkor, forcing the Khmers to withdraw to Phnom Penh. The remnant Khmer state – which was to be further reduced by Viet encroachments – became a satellite of the Thai kingdom.

Khmer Rouge, a Cambodian Communist movement that ruled CAMBODIA 1975–9. The Khmer Rouge overthrew the military regime of Lon Nol following the withdrawal of American forces in the VIETNAM WAR. The Khmer Rouge leader POL POT initiated a 'social re-education' programme, forcibly moving city dwellers to rural areas to work the land. The policy led to the deaths of an estimated 1.4 million people. The Khmer Rouge were overthrown by a Vietnamese invasion in 1979. Since the Vietnamese retreat in 1988–9 the Khmer Rouge have continued to launch offensives in Cambodia's W and S provinces.

Khomeini, Ruhollah (c. 1900–89), SHIITE Muslim leader of the Iranian Revolution of 1979, known as the Ayatollah Khomeini. After overthrowing Shah Mohammed Reza PAHLAVI, he established an Islamic Republic in IRAN based on an all-embracing application of Islamic values. Militantly anti-Western, he supported fundamentalist – especially Shiite – Islamic movements throughout the Middle East, destabilizing secular Arab states such as Iraq and Egypt as well as the traditional monarchies of the Gulf. His sponsoring of radical Shiites in Lebanon contributed to that country's political chaos in the 1980s. On his death political power passed to the more pragmatic RAFSANJANI. See also IRAN HOSTAGE CRISIS.

Khrushchev, Nikita Sergeyevich (1894–71), Soviet statesman, First Secretary of the Communist Party (1953–64), prime minister (1958–64). Following STALIN's death he emerged as the dominant leader of the USSR. He embarked upon a policy of reform, attempted to restructure the inefficient planned economy, and in his 'secret speech' of 1956 denounced Stalin. The optimism of the first years of his rule, however, disappeared with the HUNGARIAN REVOLUTION of 1956, the CUBAN MISSILE CRISIS of 1962, and continuing economic decline. He was ousted by BREZHNEV in 1964.

kibbutz, a communal farming settlement in Palestine (later Israel) run by Jews dedicated to the socialist principles first advocated by Theodor HERZL. Self-contained and defensible locations during the early years of Jewish settlement, they are now basically agricultural centres.

Kiesinger, Kurt-Georg (1904–), German CHRISTIAN DEMOCRAT statesman, chancellor of the Federal Republic of (West) GERMANY (1966–9).

Kiev Rus, a state founded in the 9th century, centred on the city of Kiev, which later became divided into a number of principalities. Kiev Rus converted to Christianity in 988. At its height in the the 10th and 11th centuries, it extended from the Baltic to the Black Sea, but declined as trade routes shifted to the Mediterranean. Most of Kiev Rus fell to the MONGOLS in the 13th century; the W and S was later overrun by the Lithuanians. Its NE developed into the grand duchy of MUSCOVY.

Kim Il-sung (1912–), prime minister of the Democratic People's Republic of (North) KOREA (1948–72), president (1977–). He has ruled North Korea with an iron grip, pursuing a policy of socialist self-sufficiency, and campaigning for the unification of Korea.

King, Martin Luther, Jr (1929–68), US Baptist minister and CIVIL RIGHTS activist. He came to prominence when he led a grass-roots protest against segregated seating on the buses of Montgomery, Alabama. King's successful non-violent campaign resulted in the CIVIL RIGHTS ACT of 1964. His integrationist philosophy and brilliant oratory made him popular with moderates of both races, though by the 1960s more radical blacks were criticizing his policy of non-violent direct action and turning to groups such as the BLACK PANTHERS. Awarded the Nobel Peace Prize in 1964, he was assassinated in Memphis, Tennessee, by James Earl Ray on 4 April 1968.

King, William Lyon Mackenzie (1874–1950), Canadian Liberal politician, prime minister (1921–6, 1926–30 and 1935–48). An advocate of Canadian national unity, he governed with the support of Progressives and French Canadians. He promoted Canada's role in NATO after World War II.

Kinnock, Neil Gordon (1942–), leader of the British LABOUR Party (1983–92). He initiated a major policy review following the electoral defeat of 1983, and reversed the party's shift to the left. He resigned after Labour's 1992 election defeat, and was replaced by John Smith (1938–94), a pragmatic right-winger.

Kirghizia, see KYRGYZSTAN.

Kirov, Sergei Mironovich (1888–1934), Soviet politician whose murder (probably on Stalin's orders) was used by STALIN to launch his purge of the Communist Party.

Kissinger, Henry (1923–), German-born US political scientist and statesman who, as National Security Adviser (1969–73) and secretary of state (1973–7), had a major impact on American foreign policy. A one-time hardliner over the VIETNAM WAR, he won the Nobel Peace Prize (1972) for his role in ending America's involvement in Vietnam. He also helped to end the 1973 ARAB–ISRAELI WAR.

Kitchener, Horatio Herbert, 1st Earl (1850–1915), British soldier and statesman. His campaign to expel the MAHDI from Sudan ended in victory at Omdurman in 1898. His ruthless policy towards the Boers in the Second BOER WAR aroused Liberal anger in Britain. As secretary for war from 1914, he played a crucial role in recruiting manpower on a vast scale (the 'Kitchener Volunteers') during WORLD WAR I, but was drowned when HMS *Hampshire* was mined off the Orkneys in 1915.

knighthood, a cult of warrior virtues, also known as chivalry, popular in the medieval period. Knights formed a class or 'Order' within medieval society. They entered it through an arming ceremony at about 15 years of age and were expected to be able to ride, fight with lance and sword, and display courtly manners towards women and non-combatants.

Knights of Labor, a US trade union founded in 1869 by the reformer Uriah S. Stephens. For 20 years he ran a kind of modern industrial unionism, welcoming blacks, women, immigrants and unskilled workers – as well as artisans – into membership. At its height in 1886 it had almost a million members. Disenchantment with organized labour and factional fighting led to its decline and virtual extinction by 1900.

Knossos, the site of the main palace of the MINOAN CIVILIZATION of ancient Crete. It was excavated and partly restored by the British archaeologist Sir Arthur Evans between 1899 and 1935.

Knox, John (1505–72), Scottish Protestant reformer and theologian. He prepared the 'Confession of Faith' adopted by the Scottish Parliament as the foundation of the PRESBYTERIAN Church of Scotland (1560).

Kohl, Helmut (1930–), German statesman. The leader of the CHRISTIAN DEMOCRATS from 1973, he was chancellor of West Germany (1982–90). In elections following German reunification in 1990 he became chancellor of a united Federal Republic of Germany, after which he had to contend with problems arising from the integration of the formerly Communist E part of the country into the West German market economy.

Kongfuzi or **Confucius** (551–479 BC), Chinese administrator-philosopher. He set out, around 500 BC, the basis of an ethic of civilized life – based on hierarchies of family and state, culminating in the emperor. His ideas were to influence Chinese society down to the 20th century.

Königgrätz, Battle of, see SADOWA, BATTLE OF.

Köprülü, an Albanian family, several of whose members occupied the influential office of grand VIZIER in the OTTOMAN Empire in the 17th and early 18th centuries.

Koran, see QUR'AN.

Korea, Democratic People's Republic of, a republic of E Asia – popularly known as North Korea. Korea – a Japanese possession from 1910 to 1945 – was divided into zones of occupation in 1945. The USSR established a Communist republic in their zone N of the 38th parallel (1948). North

Korea launched a surprise attack on the South in June 1950, hoping to achieve reunification by force. The KOREAN WAR devastated the peninsula. At the ceasefire in 1953 the frontier was re-established close to the 38th parallel. North Korea has the world's first Communist dynasty, whose personality cult has surpassed even that of Stalin. President KIM IL-SUNG and his son – and anticipated successor – Kim Jong-Il have rejected any reform of the country's Communist system. Since the collapse of Communism in the former USSR and Eastern Europe, North Korea has become increasingly isolated. The country's nuclear ambitions have caused international concern. See KOREA, REPUBLIC OF (panel).

Korea, Republic of, a republic of E Asia – popularly known as South Korea. See panel.

Korean War (1950–53), a war between North and South KOREA. In 1950 Communist North Korea, supported by the USSR, launched a massive invasion of the South. The UN Security Council sent mainly US armed forces to intervene. UN forces under General MACARTHUR counterattacked, and by the end of October had pushed the North Koreans back over the 38th parallel. They continued to advance N, ignoring Chinese warnings. China now entered the war on the North Korean side, responding with a massive attack that drove as far S as the South Korean capital of Seoul by January 1951. The war now stabilized into stalemate along the border, where fighting continued for another two years. In 1953, after the USA threatened to use nuclear weapons, the PANMUNJOM ARMISTICE was signed, restoring the status quo. See COLD WAR.

Koryo, a former Korean kingdom (918–1392). It emerged supreme from a period of civil war, establishing a Chinese-style administration and encouraging Buddhism. It bowed to the inevitability of MONGOL overlordship from 1259. The fall of the YUAN in China enabled Yi Song-gye to seize power in 1392 with the help of the MING, ending the rule of the Koryo dynasty. See KOREA, REPUBLIC OF (panel).

KOREA, SOUTH

108 BC: NW Korea conquered by the Han Chinese. **1st century AD:** Emergence of kingdom of Koguryo in the N. **4th century:** Buddhism reached Korea. **c. 350:** Koguryo overrun by the Silla kingdom. **668–868:** Korea ruled by Silla as a tributary state of China. **918–1392:** Korea under the control of the Koryo Kingdom. **1259:** The Mongols overran Korea. **1392–1910:** Yi Song-gye established the Yi dynasty in Korea after the fall of the YUAN dynasty. **1592:** China helped the Koreans to repulse a Japanese invasion, exacting recognition of Chinese overlordship in return. **From 17th century:** Korea discouraged contact with the outside world. **1910:** Korea annexed by Japan. **1945:** After WORLD WAR II Korea was divided into US and Soviet zones of occupation. **1948:** Republic of Korea (South) founded in the American zone in the S. **1950–3:** KOREAN WAR. **Since 1953:** Astonishing economic transformation of the S; long periods of authoritarian rule, including the presidencies of Syngman RHEE and PARK CHUNG-HEE. **Since 1987:** Adoption of more democratic constitution after student unrest. **1991:** Non-aggression pact signed with North Korea.

Kossuth, Lajos (1802–94), Hungarian revolutionary and statesman, one of the leaders of the Hungarian REVOLUTION OF 1848 against Austrian Habsburg rule. He became provisional governor of an independent Hungarian republic in April 1849, ruling as a virtual dictator. His generals inflicted a series of reverses on the Austrians, practically driving them from the country, but Russian intervention brought about the collapse of the republic and drove Kossuth into exile.

Kosygin, Alexei Nikolaevich (1904–80), Soviet Communist politician. In 1964 he became prime minister following the removal of KHRUSHCHEV. He initially shared power with BREZHNEV, but was eclipsed by him from the late 1960s, resigning in 1980.

Kreisky, Bruno (1911–), Austrian Social Democrat statesman, prime minister (1970–83). In international affairs Kreisky pursued a policy of 'active neutrality'.

Kremlin, the (Russian, 'citadel'), the administrative headquarters of the Soviet government (Russian government from 1992). The term was also used to describe the central government of the USSR.

Kruger, Stephanus Johannes Paulus (1825–1904), AFRIKANER statesman, president of the TRANSVAAL (1883–1900). He thwarted the JAMESON RAID in 1895, and his refusal to grant political rights to the Uitlanders (non-Afrikaner immigrants in the Transvaal) contributed to the outbreak of the Second BOER WAR.

Kublai Khan (1214–94), founder and first emperor (1279–94) of the YUAN dynasty of China, a grandson of GENGHIS KHAN. Kublai had become Great Khan in 1260, but his concentration on eastern affairs meant that other descendants of Genghis Khan were left to manage the rest of the MONGOL EMPIRE. He moved his capital from Karakorum in Mongolia to Beijing in N China in the 1260s, and in 1271 adopted a Chinese name, Yuan, for his dynasty. His conquest of the Song Empire of S China by 1279 brought the whole of China under his control. Kublai ruled China in Chinese imperial style and maintained the traditional Chinese way of life. Buddhism was encouraged, and contacts with W Asia and Europe along the Silk Route were nurtured.

Kuchuk Kainardji, Treaty of (21 July 1774), a treaty ending the RUSSO-TURKISH War of 1768–74. The OTTOMANS ceded to Russia substantial territories N of the Black Sea. The treaty also gave Russia the right to intervene on behalf of ORTHODOX Christians in the Danubian principalities of MOLDAVIA and WALLACHIA, and in Constantinople itself.

Ku Klux Klan, the name of two historically distinct white racist organizations. The first was founded in the South in 1867 to obstruct federal RECONSTRUCTION policy. The second – anti-Catholic as well as anti-black – emerged during World War I and spread its pernicious doctrines through midwestern and southern states during the course of the 20th century.

Kulak (Russian, 'fist'), a term applied to Russian peasants who were allowed to buy medium-sized farms in STOLYPIN'S reforms of 1906. During STALIN's COLLECTIVIZATION of Soviet agriculture the Kulak class was destroyed, with perhaps 10 million deaths in 10 years.

Kulturkampf (German, 'conflict of cultures'), a dispute between BISMARCK'S German government and the Roman Catholic Church during the 1870s. In an attempt to strengthen the power of central government, in 1873 Bismark introduced the May Decrees, which secularized German education and diminished the number of parish priests.

Kun, Béla (1886–1937), Hungarian Communist politician. He overthrew the liberal government and set up a Communist republic in 1919, but was overthrown after only six months by invading Romanian forces. He returned to Russia, where he was a victim of Stalin's PURGES of the 1930s.

Kuomintang (or Guomindang, 'National People's Party'), a Chinese Nationalist movement founded in 1911 by SUN YAT SEN. Under JIANG JIE SHI it dominated China from 1928 to 1948, when it was defeated by the Communists in the CHINESE CIVIL WAR. Since 1949 it has been the ruling party of TAIWAN.

Kurdistan, the area inhabited by the Islamic Kurds, which includes parts of the modern states of Iraq, Iran, Turkey, Syria and Armenia. Kurdistan has never achieved statehood, though at the end of World War I it briefly seemed that it might. Kurdish guerrillas remain active in Iran, Iraq and Turkey. A major Kurdish rebellion in Iraq after the GULF WAR was harshly suppressed by Saddam HUSSEIN despite the creation of 'safe havens' by UN-sponsored forces.

Kursk, Battle of (1943), a tank battle between the RED ARMY and German forces in WORLD WAR II; one of the decisive battles of world history. Hitler's 'Operation Citadel' – intended to pinch out a Russian salient centred on Kursk – ran into trouble when delays allowed the Soviets to establish deep defences. The Germans were defeated in the biggest tank battle of the war, losing over 2000 armoured vehicles, 1000 guns, 1400 aircraft and 70,000 men. They also lost the initiative on the EASTERN FRONT.

Kushans, nomads of Iranian origin, who established power over an area stretching from TRANSOXIANA across Afghanistan and KASHMIR to central N INDIA between the 1st and 5th centuries AD.

Kuwait, an EMIRATE on the Persian Gulf. Islam came to Kuwait during the Prophet MUHAMMAD's lifetime. In 1760 the Sabah family created the emirate that has lasted to today, although from 1899 to 1961 Kuwait was a British-protected state. Oil was discovered in 1938 and was produced commercially from 1946. In August 1990 IRAQ invaded and annexed Kuwait. When Iraq failed to respond to repeated UN demands to withdraw, the UN authorized armed action, precipitating the GULF WAR. Kuwait was liberated by a US-led coalition in early 1991. Pressure for reform grew and the constitution, which had been suspended in 1968, was restored in 1992.

Kyrgyzstan (formerly Kirghizia), a republic of E Central Asia (see map, p. 43). The Kirghiz – a Turkic people – are thought to have migrated to the region in the 12th century. Although nominally subject to UZBEK khans, the nomadic Kirghiz retained their independence until after 1850, when the area was annexed by Russia. Opposition to the Russians found expression in a major revolt in 1916 and continuing guerrilla activity after the RUSSIAN REVOLUTIONS of 1917. A Kirghiz Soviet Republic was founded in 1926 and became a full Union Republic within the USSR in 1936. After the abortive coup by Communist hardliners in Moscow (September 1991), Kirghizia declared independence and – under its new name, Kyrgyzstan – received international recognition when the Soviet Union was dissolved (December 1991).

Labour Party, a British left-wing political party founded in 1906 to represent the interests of organized labour. Unlike corresponding socialist and SOCIAL DEMOCRAT parties in Europe, the Labour Party has been little influenced by MARXISM. Its 1918 constitution called for democratic control of industry, progressive taxation and the improvement of workers' living conditions. Minority Labour governments held office in 1923–4 and again in 1929–31 under Ramsay MACDONALD. Labour was in opposition after 1931, but entered an all-party wartime coalition in 1940. Under ATTLEE it won a landslide election victory in 1945. The Labour governments of 1945–51 undertook wide-ranging nationalization and extended the WELFARE STATE. Labour lost the 1951 election, remaining in opposition until 1964. The Labour governments of 1964–66, 1966–70 and 1974–79 under WILSON and CALLAGHAN were plagued by mounting economic problems. Since 1979, Labour has been in opposition. It was weakened by the defection of a number of leading MPs to the breakaway SOCIAL DEMOCRATIC Party in 1981. The party's sharp move to the left under the leadership of Michael Foot (1980–3) was largely reversed under Neil KINNOCK (1983–92) and his successor John Smith (1992–4).

Lafayette, Marie Joseph, marquis de (1757–1834), French aristocrat and soldier who served in America during the War of INDEPENDENCE. He initially supported the FRENCH REVOLUTION, but became disillusioned and fled to Austria in 1792, where he was imprisoned. He was later a leader of the moderates during the French JULY REVOLUTION (1830).

laissez-faire (French, 'leave alone'), an economic doctrine that championed commerce and trade without government intervention or control. Popular in the mid-19th century, it continues to inform right-wing economic thinking.

Lancastrian, the dynastic name given to the English kings from HENRY IV to HENRY VI, descendants of John of GAUNT, Duke of Lancaster. In 1460 their right to the throne was disputed by RICHARD Duke of York; in consequence they became one of the two parties in the Wars of the ROSES.

Land League, an organization founded in 1879 by the ex-FENIAN Michael Davitt (1846–1906), with PARNELL as president, to channel Irish agitation over tenant evictions by boycotting unpopular landlords. By 1882 it had given way to the Irish National League, which put HOME RULE in the forefront of its programme.

Laos, a country of SE Asia. The powerful Lao Buddhist kingdom of Lan Xang was established in the 14th century following the southward movement of the Lao people through the highlands E of the Mekong. It was divided into three in 1707. A French protectorate was established in 1893. Japanese occupation in World War II led to a declaration of independence which the French finally accepted in 1954, after the colonial war in VIETNAM spilled over into Laos. However, the kingdom was wracked by civil war, with royalist forces fighting Communist PATHET LAO. The VIET CONG used Laos as a supply route in the VIETNAM WAR, and US withdrawal from Vietnam allowed the Pathet Lao to take over Laos (1975). Since 1990 reforms have been introduced, but there is no suggestion that a multi-party system will be tolerated.

Las Navas de Tolosa, Battle of (1212), a decisive battle in the Spanish RECONQUISTA. The victory of Alfonso VIII of CASTILE over the Muslim ALMOHADS of North Africa checked the Muslim advance and paved the way for further Christian gains in the peninsula.

La Tène, a site near Lake Neuchâtel in Switzerland that has given its name to a CELTIC culture of the late Iron Age. It developed around 450 BC under the influences of civilizations of the S and E. The style first appeared in the Rhineland, but spread even further than HALLSTATT art, reaching Ireland and Spain in the W and Hungary in the E.

Lateran Council, a council of the Christian Church summoned by the pope and held at the Lateran Palace in Rome. The most important were the ecumenical or general councils, held in 1123, 1139, 1179, 1215 and 1512–17, whose decrees were binding throughout Western Christendom. The Council of 1215 set out church doctrine on theology and pastoral affairs and denounced the ALBIGENSIAN heresy.

Lateran Treaties (1929), the agreements between MUSSOLINI's Fascist government and Pope Pius XI, recognizing the VATICAN as an independent state. They ended years of hostility between the Catholic Church and the Italian state.

Latimer, Hugh (1485–1555), English Protestant reformer. He was burnt at the stake for heresy with CRANMER and Ridley during the reign of MARY I.

Latin Empire of Constantinople, the Frankish state (1204–61) established by Crusaders after the sack of Constantinople, consisting of territories in the Balkans and Asia Minor seized from the declining BYZANTINE EMPIRE.

Latvia, a republic on the Baltic Sea in NE Europe. Latvia was ruled by the (German) Teutonic Knights from 1237 until 1561. The E (Livonia) was Polish until 1629, then Swedish until 1710–21 when it was taken by Russia. The W (Courland) was an autonomous duchy until annexed by Russia in 1795. Latvian national consciousness grew throughout the 19th century. Following the Communist takeover in Russia (1917), Latvian nationalists declared independence (1918). A democratic system lasted until 1936, when General Ulmanis established a dictatorship. The NAZI–SOVIET PACT (1939) assigned Latvia to the USSR, which invaded and annexed the republic (1940). After occupation by Nazi Germany (1941–4), Soviet rule was reimposed. Large-scale Russian settlement replaced over 200,000 Latvians, who were killed or deported to Siberia. In 1988, reforms in the USSR allowed Latvian nationalists to operate openly. Nationalists won a majority in Latvia's parliament and seceded following the failed coup by Communist hardliners in Moscow (1991). The USSR recognized Latvia's independence in September 1991. Tension remains over the large Russian minority in Latvia.

Laud, William (1573–1645), archbishop of Canterbury (1633–45). He sought to reform the ANGLICAN Church of PURITAN 'corruptions' and restore the power of the clergy. His policies convinced many that he and CHARLES I wished to reintroduce Catholicism, and were a major cause of the ENGLISH CIVIL WAR, during the course of which he was executed.

Lausanne, Treaty of (1923), a postwar peace settlement between Turkey and the ALLIES. The initial settlement, the Treaty of SEVRES, had been abandoned after the Turkish defeat of Greece. By the terms of the new Treaty, Turkey retained its lands in Anatolia and Thrace, and was freed from reparation payments. Greece lost E Thrace, the Smyrna region and the islands of Imbros and Tenedos. In the exchange of Turkish and Greek territory 380,000 Turks were uprooted from Greece and 1.3 million Greeks left Anatolia. The Treaty also confirmed Britain's annexation of Cyprus.

Laval, Pierre (1883–1945), French politician, prime minister (1931–2 and 1935–6). After the collapse of France in June 1940 he supported the VICHY government of PÉTAIN, becoming effective head of government (1942–4). Arrested as a traitor in 1945, he was tried and executed.

Law, Andrew Bonar (1858–1923), British Conservative politician, prime minister (1922–3). He succeeded BALFOUR as leader of his party in 1910 and became PM in 1922, when the Conservatives brought down LLOYD GEORGE'S coalition government.

Lawrence, T(homas) E(dward) (1888–1935), British scholar and soldier, known as 'Lawrence of Arabia'. He worked for British intelligence during WORLD WAR I and played a major part in the Arab Revolt (1917–18) against the OTTOMAN Turks, leading highly successful raids against Turkish communications. He was a close associate of FAISAL I of Syria.

League of Nations, a former international organization created at the PARIS PEACE CONFERENCE of 1920 in an attempt to outlaw war. It was intended that aggressor states would be punished by economic sanctions or military action. The refusal of the US Senate to ratify the Covenant and join the League weakened it from the outset. It failed to curb the expansionism of aggressor states, such as NAZI Germany, Italy and Japan, in the 1930s, but its ideal of collective security formed the basis of its successor, the UNITED NATIONS.

Lebanon, a republic on the Mediterranean coast of the Middle East. Lebanon – the home of the ancient PHOENICIANS – came, in turn, under Egyptian, Assyrian, Persian, Seleucid, Roman and Byzantine rule. The early Islamic conquests bypassed the Lebanese mountains, leaving important Maronite Christian enclaves. From the 10th century, Shiite Islam came to Lebanon, and in the 11th century the DRUZES (a breakaway sect from the Shiites) became a significant force in the region. In the 12th and 13th centuries, the Crusader state of Tripoli flourished in Lebanon; in the 14th century the area was ruled by MAMLUKS from Egypt. In 1516 the OTTOMAN (Turkish) Empire took Lebanon, administering it as part of Syria, although Druze princes enjoyed considerable autonomy. Intercommunal friction was never far from the surface. A massacre of thousands of Maronites by the Druzes (1860) brought French intervention. After World War I, France received Syria as a League of Nations MANDATE, and created a separate Lebanese territory to protect Christian interests. The constitution under which Lebanon became independent in 1943 enshrined power-sharing between Christians and Muslims. The relative toleration between the various religious groups in Lebanon began to break down in the late 1950s, when Muslim numerical superiority failed to be matched by corresponding constitutional changes. Radical Muslim supporters of the union of Syria and Egypt in 1958 clashed with the pro-Western party of Camille Chamoun (president 1952–8). Civil war ensued, and US marines landed in Beirut to restore order. The 1967 ARAB–ISRAELI war and the exile of the Palestinian leadership to Beirut (1970–1) destabilized Lebanon. Civil war broke out in 1975 – with subsequent Syrian and Israeli interventions – and plunged the country into ungovernable chaos. In 1990 the defeat of Christian militia by Syrian troops allowed the Lebanese government to reassert its authority over the whole of Beirut. Most Lebanese sectarian militias were disarmed in 1991, when the civil war seemed to be over. However, Israeli-sponsored forces continue to occupy the S and the (Islamic fundamentalist) Hizbollah forces control the Beka'a Valley.

Lebensraum (German, 'living space'), a term used by the NAZIS from the early 1920s to describe those non-German-speaking territories to the E of Germany which they intended to settle. See HITLER, ADOLF.

Lechfeld, Battle of (955), a battle fought near Augsburg in S Germany in which a MAGYAR raiding army was decisively defeated by Saxon and Frankish forces under OTTO I and Conrad the Red. Thereafter the Magyars ended their raids and settled down as Hungarians.

Lee Kuan Yew (1923–), prime minister of SINGAPORE (1959–90). As Singapore's first PM, he took his country out of the Malaysian federation in 1965. He worked hard to protect his country's economic base and political independence, but his policies, based on the establishment of a virtual one-party state and a free-market economy, remained paternalistic and often heavy-handed.

Lee, Robert E. (1807–70), Virginian-born soldier who commanded the forces of the CONFEDERACY in the E theatre of the AMERICAN CIVIL WAR. Although one of the finest tacticians of that conflict, he was nonetheless responsible for the South's disastrous defeat at GETTYSBURG in 1863. He was forced to surrender at APPOMATTOX (1865).

Leif Eriksson (10th–11th centuries), Norse explorer and son of ERIC the Red. He reached E Canada (VINLAND) in around 1000, thus becoming the first European to reach America.

Leipzig, Battle of (also called the 'Battle of the Nations'; 16–19 October 1813), a decisive defeat of NAPOLEON by Prussia, Sweden and Austria under Schwarzenberg and BLÜCHER. Napoleon's army suffered enormous losses and was forced back across the Rhine, allowing the allies to invade France. The defeat contributed to the collapse of the Napoleonic empire and Napoleon's abdication in 1814. See map, p. 29.

Lemass, Séan Francis (1889–1971), Irish FÍANNA FÁIL statesman, prime minister (1959–66).

Lend-Lease Act (1941), US legislation introduced by F.D. ROOSEVELT authorizing the supply of equipment and services to Britain and its Allies during WORLD WAR II.

Leningrad, siege of (1941–4), the defence of Leningrad by the RED ARMY in WORLD WAR II. On 19 July 1941 Hitler diverted Panzers of Army Group North from their drive on Moscow, ordering half of them N to complete the encirclement of Leningrad (which was also under attack from Germany's Finnish allies). Soviet attacks in January 1944 relieved Leningrad from a siege that had lasted nearly 900 days and cost a million lives from starvation, cold and disease. See EASTERN FRONT CAMPAIGNS and map, p. 39.

Lenin, Vladimir Ilyich (b. Ulyanov; 1870–1924), Russian revolutionary politician, the leader of the BOLSHEVIKS (from 1903) and founder of the Soviet Union (1922). He studied the works of Karl MARX and spread the word to workers in St Petersburg before being exiled to Siberia (1897–1900). He became leader of the Bolsheviks in 1903 but spent most of the period up to 1917 abroad, developing and disseminating his political views. After the RUSSIAN REVOLUTION of March 1917, Lenin was smuggled back into Russia by the Germans, and seized power in the Revolution of November 1917. He became a virtual dictator, ending Russian involvement in WORLD WAR I and accepting the harsh terms of the Treaty of BREST-LITOVSK. Using TROTSKY'S RED ARMY Lenin defeated the counter-revolutionary 'Whites' in the RUSSIAN CIVIL WAR. He used the Red Army again between 1920 and 1921 to recapture Armenia, Georgia, Azerbaijan and the Ukraine, which were reorganized into the Union of Soviet Socialist Republics in 1922. Lenin's wholesale nationalization and state control of agriculture from 1918 led to a collapse of industrial production and food shortages, and was partially reversed in the NEW ECONOMIC POLICY of March 1921, which improved both industrial and agricultural output. His death in 1924 initiated a power struggle that was finally won by STALIN.

Leo III (c. 750–816), pope (795–816). He was expelled from Rome by rivals, but reasserted himself with the help of CHARLEMAGNE, whom he crowned emperor in 800. His links with the CAROLINGIAN Empire weakened the ties between the papacy and the BYZANTINE Empire and directed the energies of successive popes towards the West.

Leonidas I, king of Sparta (c. 490–480 BC). He commanded the Greek forces at the battle of THERMOPYLAE.

Leopold I (1640–1705), Holy Roman Emperor (1658–1705). He significantly increased Austrian HABSBURG power, exerting a tight grip over Austria, Bohemia and that part of Hungary not in Turkish hands. Although he failed to achieve much against Louis XIV in the wars of the 1670s and 1680s, the 1680s and 1690s saw a number of brilliant Habsburg success in the Danube valley. EUGÈNE of Savoy's decisive defeat of the Turks at Zenta (1697) was followed by territorial gains from the Ottomans in the Treaty of CARLOWITZ (1699).

Leopold II (1835–1909), king of the Belgians (1865–1909). His chief concern was Belgian colonial expansion. He became king of the Congo Free State (now ZAIRE) in 1885, amassing great personal wealth from its rubber and ivory trade and imposing a brutally repressive regime on its native population. An international outcry forced him to pass the territory to his parliament in 1908.

Lepanto, Battle of (7 October 1571), a naval battle off W Greece between the OTTOMANS and the combined Spanish and Venetian fleet of the HOLY LEAGUE. The Ottoman defeat prevented Turkish expansion into the W Mediterranean, and was the last great naval engagement involving oar-powered galleys.

Lepidus, Marcus (d. 13 BC), Roman politician, the third member of the Second TRIUMVIRATE. However, he was soon squeezed out of the Triumvirate and the Empire was uneasily divided between OCTAVIAN and Mark ANTONY.

Lesotho, a country in southern Africa. Lesotho was founded in the 1820s by the Sotho leader Moshoeshoe I (c. 1790–1870). The kingdom escaped incorporation into South Africa by becoming a British protectorate (Basutoland) in 1868. Since independence (1966), landlocked Lesotho remains dependent on South Africa. Chief Jonathan (PM 1966–86) attempted to limit South African influence, but was deposed in a coup. The Military Council removed the king's powers and (in 1990) placed his son on the throne. Multi-party consitutional rule was restored in 1993.

Leuctra, Battle of (371 BC), a Theban victory over the Spartans in central Greece that ended Spartan hegemony in Greece.

Levellers, a radical group that enjoyed support within the NEW MODEL ARMY during the ENGLISH CIVIL WAR. They advocated an increase in the electorate, the abolition of the monarchy and House of LORDS, law reform, religious toleration and the abolition of excise taxes and tithes. The Levellers mutinied in 1647 and 1649, but were rooted out of the army, and were a spent force by the 1650s. The 'True Levellers', or Diggers, a more radical group, favoured the communal ownership of land.

Lewis and Clark expedition (1804–6), a trail-blazing transcontinental journey by Meriwether Lewis and William Clark, which explored the territory acquired by the USA in the LOUISIANA Purchase. They were followed by trappers, traders and surveyors, and later by settlers.

Lexington and Concord, Battle of (19 April 1775), the opening skirmish of the American War of INDEPENDENCE. British forces trying to confiscate a cache of weapons N of Boston were repulsed by armed Massachusetts farmers, and retreated without achieving their objective.

Leyte Gulf, Battle of (23–25 Oct 1944), a naval battle between US and Japanese forces in WORLD WAR II. On 24/25 October the remaining Japanese fleet carriers near the island of Leyte in the Philippines were sunk. In desperation, Japanese pilots mounted KAMIKAZE (suicide) attacks on Allied shipping, but to little avail, and Leyte was secured by the end of December. See PACIFIC CAMPAIGNS.

liberalism, a political philosophy based on the values of tolerance, freedom of expression and individual liberty. The writings of John LOCKE were an early source of liberal political thought, and many of the principles of political liberalism were enshrined in the CONSTITUTION of the USA. Liberal principles were fundamental to the demands of many of the French revolutionaries of 1789, and reflected the political aspirations of a growing middle class during a period of rapid economic change and political upheaval. Early 19th-century European liberals sought to establish governmental accountability in place of the arbitrary rule of kings and their ministers. They opposed the traditional privileges of monarchy, aristocracy and clergy alike, and demanded the establishment of political rights, including freedom of conscience, expression, association and assembly. However, despite their insistence of equality before the law, liberals were opposed to the open-ended democratization of society and restricted the franchise – the vote – to the propertied and educated. It was not until later in the 19th century that some male liberals began to support the growing pressure from women for the vote. Freedom from arbitrary interference – whether by the state or traditional institutions – was also central to liberal economic philosophy, which insisted on a free market ('laissez-faire') economy. The triumph of political liberalism coincided with the extension of industrial capitalism in Western Europe. In the late 19th century the social inequalities created by unfettered industrial capitalism produced a new type of liberal thinking, given practical expression by the reforming administrations of ASQUITH and LLOYD GEORGE in Britain. Henceforth, however, the cause of political and social reform was to be more successfully championed by the emerging SOCIAL DEMOCRAT and SOCIALIST parties, and Liberal parties went into decline. Traditional 'free-market' economic liberalism enjoyed a revival of influence in the hands of right-wing conservatives such as Margaret THATCHER in Britain and Ronald REAGAN in the USA during the 1980s.

Liberal Democratic Party (LDP), the dominant political party in JAPAN since World War II. In power from 1955 to 1993, the LDP is an amalgam of conservative factions preoccupied with domestic interests. It has worked closely with a highly efficient bureaucracy and an adroit business community to chart Japan's economic successes.

Liberal Party, a British political party, the successor to the WHIG party. Associated with FREE TRADE and the growth of civil and political liberty, it flourished from the mid-19th century to the 1920s under such premiers as GLADSTONE, ASQUITH and LLOYD GEORGE. The party split between Asquith's and Lloyd George's factions after World War I, and, with the rise of the LABOUR PARTY, went into decline until the 1960s. Many of the founders of the WELFARE STATE, notably BEVERIDGE and KEYNES, were Liberals. Under David Steel (leader 1976–88) the Liberals forged a pact with CALLAGHAN'S Labour government, and in alliance with the SOCIAL DEMOCRATIC PARTY (SDP) challenged Labour as the principal opposition party in the 1980s. After their merger with the SDP in 1988, the party became the Liberal Democratic Party, with Paddy Ashdown (1941–) as leader. See also LIBERALISM.

Liberia, a republic in W Africa. Founded by the American Colonization Society in 1821–2 as a settlement for freed slaves, Liberia was declared a republic in 1847. Black American settlers dominated the local Africans and extended their control inland. From 1878 to 1980 power was held by presidents from the True Whig Party, including William Tubman (president 1944–71). Samuel Doe, the first Liberian of local ancestry to rule, took power in a military coup (1980), but was overthrown in a civil war (1990). Despite a ceasefire in 1991 fighting continues.

Libya, a country of N Africa. In the 7th century BC PHOENICIANS settled Tripolitania – which became part of the CARTHAGINIAN Empire – and the Greeks founded cities in Cyrenaica. From the 1st century BC coastal Libya came under Roman rule. By the 5th century AD Libya – then part of the BYZANTINE Empire – was largely Christian. Arab armies brought Islam to Libya in the 7th century. Tripolitania came under BERBER rule, and Cyrenaica became Egyptian, while the S – Fezzan – remained independent. In the 16th century, the whole of Libya was united under Ottoman (Turkish) rule, although autonomous local dynasties flourished. In 1911 the Italians took Libya. The British Eighth Army defeated the Italians at EL ALAMEIN in the Libyan Desert (1942), and after World War II the country was divided between British and French administrations. Libya became independent in 1951 under King IDRIS, formerly Amir of Cyrenaica. Although oil revenues made Libya prosperous, the pro-Western monarchy became increasingly unpopular. In 1969 junior army officers led by Muammar al-QADDAFI took power. Qaddafi nationalized the oil industry, but his various attempts to federate with other Arab countries proved abortive. In the 1970s he began a cultural revolution, dismantled formal government, collectivized economic activity, limited personal wealth and suppressed opposition. Libya's alleged support of terrorism provoked US air raids on Tripoli and Benghazi in 1986, and UN sanctions in 1992.

Liebknecht, Wilhelm (1826–1900), German politician, a co-founder of the SOCIAL DEMOCRATIC PARTY.

Liechtenstein, a principality in Central Europe. In 1719 the counties of Schellenberg and Vaduz were united to form a principality for the Austrian Princes of Liechtenstein. Separated from Germany by Austrian territory, Liechtenstein was the only German principality not to join the German Empire in 1871. Since 1924 the country has enjoyed a customs and monetary union with Switzerland, and since 1989 has taken a more active role internationally, for instance joining the UN and EFTA.

Lie, Trygve (1896–1968), Norwegian politician and first Secretary-General of the UNITED NATIONS (1946–53).

Lin Biao (Lin Piao; 1908–71), Chinese Communist politician and general. A close associate of MAO's during the CULTURAL REVOLUTION, he was designated Mao's successor in 1969. He was apparently killed in a plane crash while fleeing to the USSR after organizing an abortive coup against Mao.

Lincoln, Abraham (1809–65), 16th president of the USA (1861–5). His election as REPUBLICAN president on an anti-slavery programme led to the secession of the states of the CONFEDERACY and thereby to the AMERICAN CIVIL WAR. His salvation of the Union in that conflict, together with his emancipation of the slaves (1862) and his championing of American democracy, have ensured him almost legendary status in US history. He was assassinated by a Southern sympathizer, John Wilkes Booth, at Ford's Theatre in Washington, DC, on 14th April 1865.

Lithuania, a country on the Baltic Sea in NE Europe. The Lithuanians were first united c. 1250. Their 'grand princes' greatly enlarged the country, annexing Byelorussia and most of the Ukraine. The marriage of grand prince JAGIELLO to the queen of Poland (1386) united the crowns of the two countries, although Lithuania retained autonomy until 1569. Lithuania was annexed by Russia in 1795. Lithuanian national consciousness increased throughout the 19th century and Lithuanians rose with the Poles against Russian rule in 1830–1 and 1863. German forces invaded in 1915 and encouraged the establishment of a Lithuanian state. After World War I, the new republic faced invasions by the Red Army from the E and the Polish army from the W (1919–20). Internationally recognized boundaries were not established until 1923. The dictatorship of Augustinas Voldemaras (1926–9) was followed by that of Antonas Smetona (1929–40). The NAZI-SOVIET PACT (1939) assigned Lithuania to the USSR, which invaded and annexed the republic (1940). Lithuania was occupied by Nazi Germany (1941–4). When Soviet rule was reimposed (1945), large-scale Russian settlement replaced over 250,000 Lithuanians who had been killed or deported to Siberia. In 1988, reforms in the USSR allowed Lithuanian nationalists to operate openly. Nationalists won a majority in the republic's parliament, but their declaration of independence (1990) brought a crackdown by Soviet forces in Lithuania. Following the failed coup by Communist hardliners in Moscow (August 1991), the USSR recognized Lithuania's independence. After the economic collapse of Lithuania in 1992–3, the nationalists lost power to the former Communists, who slowed down the pace of reforms.

Little Big Horn, Battle of (25 June 1876), the defeat of General CUSTER'S forces by the SIOUX under CRAZY HORSE. Over 200 men of the US 7th cavalry died in Custer's last stand.

Litvinov, Maksim Maksimovich (1876–1951), Soviet politician and diplomat. He was a firm supporter of the LEAGUE OF NATIONS and an advocate of collective security against the rising tide of Fascism in the 1930s. As Commissar for Foreign Affairs (1930–9), his foreign policy emphasized the need for the USSR to cultivate possible allies abroad.

Liverpool, Robert Banks Jenkinson, 2nd Earl of (1770–1828), British TORY politician, prime minister (1812–27). His premierships witnessed the final stages of the Napoleonic Wars, the War of 1812 with the USA and a slow readjustment to peace. His government's repressive measures were mitigated after 1822 by the more liberal influence of PEEL and CANNING.

Livingstone, David (1813–73), Scottish missionary and explorer whose discoveries included the Zambezi River (1851), the Victoria Falls (1855) and Lake Malawi (1859). His famous meeting with STANLEY took place at Ujiji in 1871.

Lloyd George, David, 1st Earl of Dwyfor (1863–1945), British LIBERAL politician, prime minister (1916–22). He served as chancellor of the exchequer (1908–15) under ASQUITH, his 'PEOPLE'S BUDGET' causing a constitutional crisis. He became PM of a coalition government after Asquith's overthrow in 1916, proving an energetic leader during WORLD WAR I. He strove for a more moderate settlement at the PARIS PEACE CONFERENCE. Known as the 'Welsh wizard', he was an eloquent orator, but his perceived opportunism led to a split in the LIBERAL Party from which it never recovered. His coalition collapsed after the Conservatives withdrew their support, and he resigned in 1922 to be succeeded by Bonar LAW.

Llywelyn ('the Great'; 1195–1240), king of Gwynedd. He established a powerful Welsh principality centred on N Wales. Taking advantage of the civil war at the end of JOHN'S reign, he was able to bring the English crown to recognize his achievement.

Locarno, Treaties of (1925), a series of agreements, signed by various European powers, guaranteeing German frontiers in the W and, by treaties of mutual guarantee between France, Czechoslovakia and Poland, safeguarding borders in the E. However, the treaties failed to prevent the aggressive advance of NAZI Germany.

Locke, John (1632–1704), English philosopher and political theorist, author of Two *Treatises of Government* (1690). He opposed ABSOLUTISM, and saw the free consent of the governed as the basis of legitimate government. According to Locke, obedience depends on governments ruling for the good of the governed, who have the right to rebel if they are oppressed. His ideas were influential in the development of political LIBERALISM.

Lodi, Peace of (9 April 1454), a treaty between warring Italian states. It ended decades of wars, and heralded the formation of the Italic League (1455), to which the dominant Italian powers of Venice, Milan, Florence, Naples and the papacy were signatories.

Lollards, a derogatory term for the followers of the late 14th-century English religious reformer John WYCLIF. They stressed the importance of individual action for salvation in contrast to the Church's emphasis on the mediatory role of the priesthood. They circulated extracts from the Bible and other religious texts written in English (rather than the orthodox Latin), so they were more easily understood by the laity. Persecuted under HENRY IV and deserted by the nobles, the Lollards went into decline after their abortive uprising in 1414.

Lombardy, a region of N Italy, taking its name from the Lombards whose invasion of Italy in the 6th century finally ended JUSTINIAN'S reconquest. Independent until conquered by the FRANKS in the 8th century, the cities of the plain of the River Po developed a high material culture and became important financial centres from the 12th century. Lombardy experienced rule by Spain, France and Austria before becoming part of a united ITALY in the 19th century.

Long March (1934–5), the epic journey undertaken by Chinese Communists under MAO ZEDONG from SE to NW China. It followed repeated KUOMINTANG attacks on the JIANGXI SOVIET during the CHINESE CIVIL WAR. Over 12 months Mao led his followers on a 9000-km trek from Jiangxi to the remote NW province of Shaanxi.

Long Parliament, the Parliament called by CHARLES I in November 1640. Despite periodic purges of its members and the frequent changes of regime between 1649 and the RESTORATION, it was not legally dissolved until March 1660.

López, Francisco Solano (1827–70), Paraguayan dictator (1862–70). His devastating PARAGUAYAN WAR with Brazil, Uruguay and Argentina (1865–70) reduced the male population of Paraguay by as much as nine-tenths.

Lords, House of, the upper chamber of the English PARLIAMENT. Composed of unelected hereditary peers (until the addition of life peers in the 20th century) and the heads of a number of monastic houses (until the Reformation, after which they were replaced by a number of bishops), it was for long the more important of the two chambers. It was temporarily abolished during the COMMONWEALTH and, although restored in 1660, its power vis-à-vis the COMMONS has gradually declined since the 17th century.

Louis I ('the Pious'; 778–840), king of the FRANKS, emperor of the Romans (814–40) and son of CHARLEMAGNE. He inherited a united CAROLINGIAN Empire. In accordance with the Frankish tradition of partible inheritance he divided the empire between his four sons, quarrels between whom led to the formalization of the division in the Treaty of VERDUN.

Louis IX, St (1214–70), king of France (1226–70). His piety – he led two crusades – sense of honour and justice did much to reconcile the French people to the massive expansion of the power of central government that had characterized the reigns of both his father Louis VIII (1223–6) and grandfather PHILIP II. He was canonized in 1297.

Louis XI (1423–83), king of France (1461–83). He consolidated the remarkable territorial gains made by his father CHARLES VII. At the Treaty of Picquigny (1475) he bought off an English invasion. He later exploited the death of CHARLES THE BOLD (1477) to acquire Picardy and the duchy of BURGUNDY.

Louis XIII (1601–43), king of France (1610–43). The eldest son of HENRY IV and Marie de Médicis, he was greatly influenced by his chief minister RICHELIEU from 1624.

Louis XIV (1638–1715), king of France (1643–1715), and son of LOUIS XIII, known as *le roi soleil* (the 'sun king'). He succeeded to the throne as a child, and during his minority much power rested in the hands of Cardinal MAZARIN. Resentment of Mazarin's influence contributed to the outbreak of civil war – the FRONDES (1648–53). Louis' personal rule, which began on Mazarin's death in 1661, was defined by his belief that kings ruled by divine right, and he became the epitome of the absolute monarch (see ABSOLUTISM). The growing regulation of the economy by finance minister COLBERT stimulated the development of a centrally controlled bureaucracy. French nobles were encouraged to attend his lavish court at VERSAILLES, where Louis could keep an eye on them. In 1685 Louis revoked the EDICT OF NANTES and asserted his authority over the Church in France against the pope, although he helped the latter to suppress the anti-papal JANSENISTS. Louis' identification with the state was most evident in his foreign policy. He asserted a weak claim to the Spanish Empire, and between 1667 and 1713 fought a series of large-scale and expensive wars to strengthen French frontiers and his prestige. The War of the SPANISH SUCCESSION brought France close to collapse. On his death, Louis left a France territorially strengthened but at a heavy economic and social cost. See also DEVOLUTION, WAR OF, and NINE YEARS WAR.

Louis XV (1710–74), grandson of Louis XIV and king of France (1715–74). His reign saw disastrous defeats abroad in the SEVEN YEARS WAR, increasing political conflict with the sovereign courts (PARLEMENTS), and a loss of prestige by a monarchy increasingly seen by its opponents as despotic.

Louis XVI (1754–93), the last king of France (1774–92) before the FRENCH REVOLUTION. The opposition of his wife

MARIE ANTOINETTE and the aristocracy thwarted the attempts of his ministers NECKER and Turgot to introduce social and economic reforms. His summoning of the STATES GENERAL (1789) precipitated the Revolution. Confined to the Tuileries Palace, the royal family attempted to flee in 1791, but were recaptured. He and Marie Antoinette were tried for treason and guillotined in 1793.

Louis XVIII (1755–1824), king of France (1814–15 and 1815–24). The brother of LOUIS XVI, he assumed the title of king while in exile in 1795. He was restored to the throne after NAPOLEON's defeat at WATERLOO in 1815. He attempted to rule as a moderate constitutional monarch, retaining many of the legal, clerical and educational reforms introduced under Napoleon, but was opposed by the ultraroyalist party. He was succeeded by the reactionary CHARLES X.

Louisiana, 1. a state of the USA admitted to the Union in 1812. **2.** a former French province encompassing much of the present-day S and midwestern USA, purchased by President Thomas JEFFERSON from Napoleon in 1803. The 'Louisiana Purchase' doubled the size of the USA and made it the dominant power in N America. See map, p. 32.

Louis Philippe I (1773–1850), king of the French (1830–48), elected to that position after the JULY REVOLUTION of 1830. However, the 'citizen king' became ever more repressive as dissent, fuelled by agricultural and industrial depressions, grew. He was overthrown by the REVOLUTION OF 1848, fleeing to England as 'Mr Smith'.

Loyola, St Ignatius (1491–1556), Spanish Catholic reformer and founder of the JESUITS.

Lucknow, Siege of (1857–8), the siege of the British garrison of Lucknow in India during the INDIAN MUTINY. During the five-month siege, the British and Indian garrison together with women and children sheltered in the Residency but suffered heavy casualties. Henry Havelock led his troops to relieve the garrison, but was also besieged until he in turn was relieved by troops under Sir Colin Campbell on 16 November. The city was not restored to the British until March 1858.

Luddite, a member of a protest group of textile workers involved in the wrecking of industrial machinery in N England 1811–16 during the INDUSTRIAL REVOLUTION. Luddites feared that the faster output of the new machinery threatened the jobs of hand-loom operators. The supposed leader of the Luddites, Ned Ludd, may never have existed. Many Luddites were punished by hanging or transportation.

Ludendorff, Erich von (1865–1937), German general and politician. Chief-of-staff to HINDENBURG, he orchestrated the decisive defeat of the Russians at TANNENBERG and stabilized the German line on the Western Front after 1916. He planned the last major German offensive of World War I and fled to Sweden after Germany's defeat. A nationalist and a racist, Ludendorff took part in the KAPP PUTSCH (1920) and assisted HITLER in the abortive MUNICH BEER-HALL PUTSCH.

Lumumba, Patrice (1925–61), Congolese politician, first prime minister (1960–1) of the Democratic Republic of the Congo (now ZAIRE). During the mayhem of the CONGO CRISIS he was sacked by President KASAVUBU, later arrested by Joseph MOBUTU, and finally murdered by Katangan secessionists in February 1961.

***Lusitania*,** British transatlantic liner sunk by a German submarine on 7 May 1915 with the loss of 1195 lives, some of them citizens of the neutral USA. The attack contributed to anti-German sentiment in the USA, which entered World War I on the Allied side in 1917.

Luther, Martin (1483–1546), German monk and reformist theologian. His beliefs became the focus of the Protestant REFORMATION. In 1517 he published his opposition to indulgences and other abuses in the Church. He believed that the foundation of all faith must be the Bible, and that all people should have access to it, not just those who understood Latin. Those religious doctrines and practices not founded in Scripture he regarded as abuses; only faith in God brought salvation. Luther also denied the special status of the clergy administering the sacraments. Following his excommunication in 1520 he rejected papal authority. His protest against the Catholic Church, spread by the new printing presses and by preachers, was popular in Germany. By the middle of the 16th century Lutheran Churches had been established in a number of states in Germany and in Sweden and Denmark. The emerging ANGLICAN Church in England was also influenced by Lutheran doctrines.

Luthuli, Albert John (1898–1967), black South African politician, president of the AFRICAN NATIONAL CONGRESS (1952–67). Representing the Christian liberal element in the ANC, he advocated passive resistance to APARTHEID and received the Nobel Peace Prize in 1960.

Lützen, Battle of (1632), an engagement during the THIRTY YEARS WAR in which the Protestant forces of the Swedish king, GUSTAVUS II ADOLPHUS (who died in the battle) defeated the Catholic imperial forces under WALLENSTEIN.

Luxembourg, a country in NW Europe. Luxembourg has changed hands many times through inheritance and invasion. In 1443, it passed to the dukes of Burgundy, and was inherited by the Spanish HABSBURGS in 1555–6. In 1713 the country came under Austrian rule, but was annexed by France during the NAPOLEONIC WARS. In 1815 Luxembourg became a Grand Duchy with the Dutch king as sovereign, but in 1890 was inherited by a junior branch of the House of ORANGE. Occupied by the Germans during both World Wars, Luxembourg concluded an economic union with Belgium in 1922 and has enthusiastically supported European unity.

Luxemburg, Rosa (1870–1919), German revolutionary leader, founder (with Karl Liebknecht) of the Communist SPARTACIST Movement. She and Liebknecht were murdered by right-wing irregulars during the Spartacist Rising of 1919.

Lydia, an ancient kingdom that flourished in W Anatolia in the 1st millennium BC. Under CROESUS it became a powerful independent power, but was attacked and captured by CYRUS II in 546 BC. It was later ruled by the SELEUCIDS and PERGAMUM, before becoming part of the ROMAN EMPIRE in 133 BC.

Lynch, John Mary (1917–), Irish FÍANNA FÁIL statesman. 'Jack' Lynch – a leading Gaelic football player – was prime minister 1966–73 and 1977–9.

Lysander (c. 456–395 BC), Spartan admiral who did most to win the naval victories of Notium and AEGOSPOTAMI that sealed Spartan victory in the PELOPONNESIAN WAR.

Maastricht, Treaty of, a treaty on European union, signed by leaders of the 12 EUROPEAN COMMUNITY nations in the Dutch town of Maastricht on 10 December 1991. The Treaty regularized the EC's decision-making processes and provided for closer monetary union, as well as closer links on foreign policy. It was opposed by elements within certain EC countries, notably Britain, Denmark and France, who claimed that it was federalist in nature. The plans for monetary union under the Treaty, however, were set back by the collapse of the Exchange Rate Mechanism (ERM) in 1993. See EUROPEAN UNION.

MacArthur, Douglas (1880–1964), US general. He conducted a brilliant campaign in the SW Pacific in WORLD WAR II and was commander of the Allied occupation forces in Japan (1945–51). He commanded UN forces during the KOREAN WAR (1950–1), but was sacked for advocating attacks on China. See also PACIFIC CAMPAIGNS.

McCarthy, Joseph Raymond (1908–57), Republican senator for Wisconsin from 1946. In the 1950s, at the height of the COLD WAR, he declared that there existed an orchestrated Communist campaign to infiltrate the US government at the highest level, and embarked on a campaign to root out 'un-American' activity in all walks of life. As chairman of the Senate Permanent Subcommittee on Investigations, he conducted hearings in which people suspected of left-wing beliefs were subjected to accusations – ranging from Communist sympathies to homosexuality – often based on little evidence. Many people were found 'guilty by association' when no evidence was found. Hundreds of Americans lost their jobs as a result; others fled the USA in fear or disgust. In 1954 the Senate censured McCarthy and his influence declined.

Macbeth (d. 1057), king of Scotland (1040–54). He became king after killing his predecessor (Duncan I). In 1054 he was defeated by Earl Siward of Northumbria at Dunsinnan Hill, but was able to hold on in Moray until he was killed in 1057.

Maccabees, a Jewish family who led a revolt against the Syrian rulers of ISRAEL (168–142 BC). The semi-independent state they created lasted until the capture of Jerusalem by the Romans in 63 BC.

Maccabeus, Judas, see ISRAEL.

McClellan, George B. (1826–85), US soldier who commanded the Union Army of the Potomac during the early years of the AMERICAN CIVIL WAR. His apparent reluctance to engage the enemy after the Battle of ANTIETAM led to his dismissal in November 1862.

MacDonald, James Ramsay (1866–1937), British LABOUR statesman, prime minister (1924 – the first Labour PM – and 1929–35). His second Labour government (1929–31) collapsed over a cabinet split on employment benefit cuts. MacDonald's decision to form a coalition National Government (1931–5) split the Labour party, which expelled him in 1935.

Macdonald, Sir John Alexander (1815–91), Canadian politician, the first prime minister of the Dominion of Canada (1867–73 and 1878–91) after the passing of the BRITISH NORTH AMERICA ACT.

Macedon, a kingdom in the N of ancient Greece (see map, p. 12). It emerged as a powerful state under PHILIP II in the 4th century BC. He achieved a position of dominance in mainland Greece after his final victory at the battle of CHAERONEA (338 BC). Philip's son and successor, ALEXANDER THE GREAT, carried out his father's plan to invade Persia, and went on to establish one of the largest empires the world has seen. Macedon briefly came under the control of PYRRHUS, but was regained by Antigonus II in 276 BC. Macedon became part of the Roman Empire in 146 BC.

Macedonia, a country in S Central Europe. Ancient Macedonia – the kingdom of PHILIP II of Macedon and ALEXANDER THE GREAT – was an Hellenic state whose centre was in N Greece. The region came under Roman rule in 146 BC and became Christian in the 4th century AD. In the following centuries, the area was invaded by the Goths, Huns, Avars and Slavs. In the 8th and 9th centuries all of the present Republic was overrun by Bulgarians and as part of Bulgaria for most of the next 500 years, it became thoroughly Slavic. Serbian intervention began in the 1280s, but Serb rule was replaced by OTTOMAN rule in 1371. Muslim Albanians settled in the W and the entire region suffered political and economic stagnation. Nationalist feeling among Macedonia's neighbours emerged in the mid-19th century. A revived Bulgaria claimed the entire region, but Macedonia was partitioned following the First BALKAN WAR (1912). Those areas with a Greek-speaking majority – the S districts – were assigned to Greece and the remainder in the N was partitioned between Bulgaria and SERBIA, the latter gaining the area comprising the present republic. Macedonia was occupied by Bulgaria during World War I, but in 1918 was incorporated into the new kingdom of Serbs, Croats and Slovenes, renamed YUGOSLAVIA in 1929. When Yugoslavia was reorganized on Soviet lines by Marshal TITO in 1945 a separate Macedonian republic was formed within the Communist federation. Following the secession of Slovenia and Croatia and the outbreak of the Yugoslav civil war (1991), Macedonia declared its own sovereignty. Despite fierce opposition from Greece, which objected to the use of the name 'Macedonia' and denied the existence of a 'Macedonian' people, the republic eventually gained international recognition in 1993.

Machel, Samora (1933–86), first president of independent MOZAMBIQUE (1976–86). Continuing civil war defeated his plans for socialist transformation of his country.

Machu Picchu, a well-preserved city of the INCAS in the Andes of Peru. It escaped destruction at the hands of the conquistadores and was only rediscovered in 1911.

McKinley, William (1843–1901), 25th president of the USA (1897–1901). He was elected president as an orthodox Republican in the watershed election of 1896. The SPANISH–AMERICAN WAR was fought during his presidency. Elected to a second term in 1900, his career was cut short by an anarchist's bullet in 1901.

Macmillan, Harold, 1st Earl of Stockton (1894–1987), British Conservative politician, prime minister (1957–63). He succeeded EDEN after the SUEZ crisis. His term as PM was one of prosperity, Macmillan himself saying, 'You've never had it so good.' His government dismantled the British Empire in Africa, and strengthened Anglo-US collaboration, but failed to take Britain into the EEC when DE GAULLE vetoed British membership in 1963. His administration was undermined by an alleged sex and spy scandal involving his Secretary of State for War, John Profumo. He was succeeded by Alec Douglas-HOME.

Madagascar, an island-republic off the SE coast of Africa. The first inhabitants were POLYNESIANS from Indonesia in the early centuries AD, and were later joined by mainland Africans and by Arabs. In the early 19th century, the island was united by the Merina kingdom. The Merina sovereigns attempted to modernize Madagascar, but the island was annexed by France in 1896, although resistance continued until 1904. Strong nationalist feeling found expression in a major rising (1947–8) that was suppressed with heavy loss of life. Independence was finally achieved in 1960. Since a military coup in 1972, Madagascar has had left-wing governments. Mounting public pressure brought economic and political reforms after 1990, and multi-party elections resulted in a change of power in 1993.

Madero, Francisco Indalécio (1873–1913), a leader of the MEXICAN REVOLUTION and president of MEXICO (1911–13).

Madison, James (1751–1836), US politician, fourth president of the USA (1809–17). Initially a defender of federal power over STATES' RIGHTS, he played a major role in drafting the US CONSTITUTION and Bill of Rights. His presidency was dominated by the WAR OF 1812.

Magdalenian, the final phase of the Upper PALAEOLITHIC period of European prehistory. It produced the most accomplished art of the period in the cave art of S France and N Spain.

Magdalha, a centre of ancient kingdoms of NE India on the middle Ganges. Its first important king was Bimbisara (543–491 BC). Under the Nanda dynasty (362–321 BC), Magdalha rose to new heights and, under CHANDRAGUPTA (321–297 BC), founder of the MAURYAN dynasty, it became the centre of the first Indian empire. The empire was consolidated by ASHOKA (272–232 BC). After the decline of the Mauryan dynasty India fragmented, but in the 4th century AD another Magdalhan dynasty, the GUPTAS, created an empire centred on N and central India that lasted until the 6th century.

Magellan, Ferdinand (c. 1480–1521), Portuguese navigator. In 1519 he set out with five ships to seek a western route to the East Indies. He negotiated the strait later named after him between Tierra del Fuego and the South American mainland. The expedition crossed the Pacific and reached the East Indies in 1521, where Magellan was killed. One ship returned to Spain in 1522, completing the first circumnavigation of the world. See map, p. 24.

Magenta, Battle of (4 June 1859), Franco–Piedmontese victory over Austria during the wars for the unification of ITALY.

Maginot Line, fortifications built by the French to protect their border with Germany before WORLD WAR II. Since it was not continued along the Franco-Belgian border to the coast, the Germans were able to outflank the line and advance into France from Belgium (spring 1940).

Magna Carta, a charter that rebel barons forced the English king JOHN to seal at Runnymede (15 June 1215) – in effect the first written constitution in European history. It granted rights and liberties 'to all freemen of the realm and their heirs for ever' and by the mid-13th century was generally regarded as a fundamental statement of English liberties – hence the term 'Great Charter'. But John had no intention of abiding by its terms and civil war soon broke out again.

Magyars, nomadic raiders who occupied the area W of the Carpathians in the 890s and terrorized much of Central and S Europe in the following decades. But as they gave up nomadism so they gradually became less of a threat; the raid that ended at LECHFELD (955) was probably a last throw before they settled down as Hungarians.

Mahdi, the name given by SUNNI Muslims to a Messiah whose coming before the Last Day will bring a reign of justice on Earth. Of the many who have claimed the title, the most notable was the Sudanese Muhammad Ahmad bin Abdallah (1843–85), who revolted against Anglo-Egyptian rule and besieged General GORDON in Khartoum.

Mahican or **Mohican**, a native N American people, living as maize farmers in the Eastern Woodlands (upper New York state). They were dispersed by the Dutch in the mid-17th century. See NORTH AMERICAN INDIANS.

Mahmud of Ghazni (969–1030), Muslim ruler of the Ghaznavid dynasty of Afghanistan. He led his followers on a series of raids into N India which yielded a huge booty, but did not lead to any permanent conquests.

Majapahit, a former Hindu kingdom centred on Java. The kingdom replaced the SRIVIJAYA kingdom as the most dominant in the region in the 14th–15th centuries.

Major, John (1943–), British Conservative politician. He became prime minister in November 1990 after Margaret THATCHER was persuaded to stand down, and led the Conservatives to their fourth consecutive election victory over LABOUR in April 1992.

Makarios III (1913–77), Greek Cypriot Orthodox archbishop and politician. Originally a supporter of the union of Cyprus with Greece (ENOSIS), he became the first president of the Republic of CYPRUS (1960–74 and 1974–7).

Malacca, a former city-state on the SW coast of the Malay peninsula. Its Muslim rulers controlled the spice trade through the Straits of Malacca in the 15th century. Its capture by the Portuguese in 1511 marked the beginning of European dominance in the area.

Malan, Daniel François (1874–1959), South African National Party statesman, prime minister (1948–54). His alliance of 'purified' and 'reunited' Afrikaner nationalists defeated SMUTS in the 1948 election and initiated the policies of APARTHEID.

Malawi, a republic of central Africa. David LIVINGSTONE and other British missionaries became active in the area from the 1860s. A British protectorate, later called Nyasaland, was declared in 1891. In 1915 the Rev. John Chilembwe led a violent rising in the fertile S where Africans had lost much land to white settlers. Federation with the white-dominated CENTRAL AFRICAN FEDERATION (1953–63) was resented. The nationalist leader Hastings BANDA (later president) helped to break the Federation. Since independence as Malawi in 1964, Banda has provided strong rule and – despite criticism – maintained close relations with South Africa. Pressure for political reforms grew in 1992–3.

Malaya, a region of SE Asia, now the peninsular part of the state of MALAYSIA.

Malaysia, a country of SE Asia. Malaysia's ethnic diversity reflects its complex history and the lure of its natural wealth and prime trading position. Most of the area was part of the Buddhist Sumatran kingdom of SRIVIJAYA from the 9th century to the 14th century, when it fell to the Hindu Javanese. From the 15th century, Islam came to the region and the spice trade attracted Europeans. The trading post of Malacca was taken by the Portuguese in 1511 and then by the Dutch in 1641. The British established themselves on the island of Penang (1786), founded SINGAPORE (1819), and in 1867 established an administration for the Straits Settlements – Malacca, Penang and Singapore. Ignoring Thai claims to overlordship in the peninsula, the British took over the small sultanates as protected states. The British suppressed piracy, developed tin mining with Chinese labour and rubber plantations with Indian workers. Sarawak became a separate state under Sir James Brooke – the 'White Raja' – and his family from 1841, and was ceded to the British Crown in 1946. Sabah became British – as British North Borneo – from 1881. The Japanese occupied the whole of Malaysia during World War II. A Federation of Malaya – the peninsula – was established in 1948, but was threatened by Communist insurgency until 1960. Malaya became independent in 1957 with a constitution protecting the interests of the Malays who were fearful of the energy and acumen of the Chinese. Sabah, Sarawak and Singapore joined the Federation – renamed Malaysia – in 1963. Singapore left in 1965 but the unity of the Federation was maintained, with British armed support, in the face of an Indonesian 'confrontation' in Borneo (1965–6). Tension between Chinese and Malays led to riots and the suspension of parliamentary government (1969–71), but scarcely hindered the rapid development of a resource-rich economy. During the 1980s, the growth of Islamic fundamentalism led to a defensive re-assertion of Islamic values and practices among the Muslim Malay ruling elite.

Malcolm III (Canmore; c. 1031–93), king of Scotland (1058–93). He defeated MACBETH in 1054, and killed him in battle in 1057. After 1066 he welcomed English exiles (including Margaret – later St Margaret – whom he married) to his court. He was killed at Alnwick while raiding NORTHUMBRIA.

Malcolm X (1925–65), US militant black activist, a leading spokesman of the Black Muslim movement in the 1950s. Championing the cause of BLACK POWER, he called for violent resistance to white oppression and advocated a separate black state. He was assassinated by a rival in 1965.

Mali, a republic in the Sahel of W Africa. Mali is named after a kingdom in the area (13th–14th centuries). Conquered by France (1880–95), it became the territory of French Sudan. Mali became independent in 1960. A radical socialist government was toppled in 1968, after which Mali was ruled by military governments. A multi-party system was restored in 1992

Mali, kingdom of, a W African kingdom located in the S of modern MALI. It was the centre of a Muslim empire in the later 13th and 14th centuries, dominating the routes between the goldfields and the desert trails to North Africa.

Malta, an island-republic in the central Mediterranean Sea. Malta was ruled, in turn, by Rome (218 BC–AD 394), the BYZANTINE Empire (until 870), the Arabs (until 1091) and Sicily (until 1530). From 1530 to 1798, Malta was in the hands of the Knights of St John or HOSPITALLERS, who repelled a Turkish siege in 1565. The French held Malta from 1798 to 1800, provoking the Maltese to request British protection (1802). As a British colony (from 1814), Malta became a vital naval base, and the island received the George Cross for its valour in WORLD WAR II. Malta gained independence in 1964.

Mamluk or **Mameluke,** a word denoting a slave, specifically a military slave, in Islamic societies. Turks from beyond the E frontier of Islam in Central Asia were imported to serve in this capacity from the 9th century. They were favoured because of their fighting qualities and their (sometimes uncertain) loyalty to their masters. Military slavery was not regarded as shameful, and Mamluks were able to form regimes of their own in Egypt (the Mamluk sultanate, 1250–1517) and India (the DELHI SULTANATE, 13th–16th centuries). The Mamluk sultanate extended its rule from Egypt to Syria, Israel, Jordan, Lebanon and W Arabia. The OTTOMAN Turks overthrew the Mamluks when they captured Cairo in 1517.

Manchu, a nomad people of Altaian origin, who took over MANCHURIA and then CHINA, establishing the QING dynasty (1644–1911).

Manchukuo, the name given by the Japanese to the puppet-state they established in MANCHURIA, after occupying it in 1932. The area was placed under the nominal control of Pu Yi, the last QING emperor of China. Soviet forces liberated Manchukuo in 1945, after which it reverted to its more familiar name.

Manchuria, the NE part of modern China. The SW was sometimes incorporated in Chinese empires but the rest was under nomad control. The last of its nomad rulers, the MANCHU, brought Manchuria within the Chinese state when they took control of the empire in 1644 (and established the QING dynasty). Between 1932 and 1945 it was occupied by the Japanese as the puppet-state of MANCHUKUO.

mandate, the name given to former territories of the OTTOMAN Empire and former German colonies administered by the ALLIES under the trusteeship of the LEAGUE OF NATIONS after World War I. See Treaty of SÈVRES.

Mandela, Nelson Rolihlahla (1918–), black South African politician, president of the AFRICAN NATIONAL CONGRESS (1991–). A lawyer and ANC activist from the 1940s, he became the symbolic leader of all black South Africans during his imprisonment from 1962. He was freed by President DE KLERK in 1991 and headed ANC negotiations with the South African government. Mandela became president of South Africa following the ANC victory in South Afraca's first universal suffrage general election in April 1994. See also SOUTH AFRICA (panel, p. 223).

Manfred (1232–66), king of Sicily (1258–66), the last HOHENSTAUFEN ruler of Sicily. He was defeated and killed by CHARLES OF ANJOU at the Battle of BENEVENTO.

Manichaeism, a GNOSTIC sect started by Mani (AD 216–77), a Babylonian living in Sassanid Persia. His teachings offered redemption to a chosen few who renounced all worldly possessions, and saw the universe as a battleground for a constant struggle between good and evil. The sect spread to the West, and survived into the 10th century.

Manifest Destiny, a 19th-century slogan used to advocate US expansion across the N American continent. Employed mainly by Jacksonian Democrats (followers of Andrew JACKSON), it served to justify wars of aggression against Mexico and native American Indians in the 1840s.

Mannerheim, Baron Carl Gustav Emil von (1867–1951), Finnish soldier and politician, president (1944–6). He commanded non-Communist 'Whites' against the Communist 'Reds' in the civil war following FINLAND'S declaration of independence, and he was Finnish commander-in-chief in the FINNISH–RUSSIAN WAR (1939–40).

Manzikert, Battle of (1071), a battle in which the forces of the BYZANTINE Empire were defeated by the SELJUK Turks in E Anatolia (modern TURKEY). Turkish tribes subsequently flooded into the area, which has remained Turkish ever since.

Maoris, a POLYNESIAN people living in NEW ZEALAND. They settled late in the first millennium AD and developed their own variation of Polynesian culture. At first hunters, they later turned to horticulture and developed a warrior culture based on fortified villages. This enabled them to offer armed resistance to European advances in the 19th century. Peace between the Maoris and British colonists was only achieved in 1871, 30 years after the first colony was founded. See ANGLO–MAORI WARS.

Mao Zedong (Mao Tse-tung; 1893–1976), Chinese revolutionary politician, founder of the People's Republic of CHINA (1949) and chairman of the Chinese Communist Party until his death. He joined the Chinese Communist Party in 1919–21 and after 1927 organized the peasantry into a revolutionary force. He used guerrilla tactics against JIANG JIE SHI'S KUOMINTANG in the late 1920s, and although forced to retreat in the LONG MARCH of 1934–5, finally emerged victorious in the CHINESE CIVIL WAR (1946–9). His cult of personality was one of the most powerful of the 20th century. His radical reforms notabl – the GREAT LEAP FORWARD of the 1950s and the CULTURAL REVOLUTION of the 1960s – proved disastrous. He gave his tacit support to the radical GANG OF FOUR, who were increasingly powerful after 1973, but their bid for power after Mao's death in 1976 was blocked by HUA GUOFENG. See also JIANGXI SOVIET.

Maquis, a French underground movement that carried out RESISTANCE to German occupation after the fall of France in 1940. The Maquis harassed the German rear during the Allied landing in France in 1944.

Marathas, Hindu clan-leaders who established a powerful military position in central India (the Deccan) in the mid-17th century under the leadership of Sivaji. They ruled the area until defeated by the British in the early 19th century, when they accepted British protection of their PRINCELY STATES.

Marathon, Battle of (490 BC), a battle in E Attica in which Athens and Plataea defeated the invading Persian forces of DARIUS I during the PERSIAN WARS. Pheidippides ran 240 km to summon Spartan help, giving the name 'marathon' to the long-distance race.

Marat, Jean Paul (1743–93), French journalist and revolutionary. An advocate of revolutionary dictatorship, his opposition to the moderate GIRONDINS led to their overthrow in 1793. He was assassinated in his bath by Charlotte Corday, a Girondin sympathizer.

'March on Rome' (1922), the convergence of squads of Fascists on Rome, after which MUSSOLINI took power in Italy.

Marco Polo (c. 1254–1324), Venetian traveller. Trade between Europe and China along the SILK ROUTE had long been established, and in 1260–9 Marco Polo's father and uncle made a trading expedition there. Marco Polo accompanied them on their second expedition, reaching China in 1275. There he entered the service of the emperor, KUBLAI KHAN, and remained in China until 1292. See map, p. 24.

Marcos, Ferdinand (1917–89), president of the PHILIPPINES (1965–86). A corrupt and ruthless dictator, he presided over gross economic mismanagement. He was forced to leave the country after he lost the 1986 election to Corazon AQUINO.

Margaret of Anjou (1430–82), queen of England (1445–61). The incapacity of her husband HENRY VI meant that she played an unusually dominant political role. This contributed to the outbreak of the Wars of the ROSES, in which she took an active part on the LANCASTRIAN side until her capture after the Battle of TEWKESBURY.

Mari, a prosperous trading city of ancient MESOPOTAMIA. It was destroyed by HAMMURABI by 1750 BC.

Maria Theresa (1717–80), ruler of the HABSBURG hereditary lands and queen of Hungary (1740–80). Her right to succeed to the lands of her father – Holy Roman Emperor CHARLES VI – was the central issue of the War of the AUSTRIAN SUCCESSION, in which Austria lost SILESIA to Prussia. Her reforms after the war included greater centralized coordination of – and unity between – Austria and Bohemia, a larger army, and the 'Diplomatic Revolution' of 1756, which brought an alliance with France. Austro–Prussian rivalry continued in the SEVEN YEARS WAR. Her husband Francis of Lorraine became Holy Roman Emperor in 1745 as Francis I. She was succeeded by her son JOSEPH II.

Marie Antoinette (1755–93), queen of France, the daughter of MARIA THERESA and the Holy Roman Emperor Francis I. She enjoyed a brief period of popularity as the queen of LOUIS XVI, but soon fell from favour. She was executed along with her husband during the FRENCH REVOLUTION.

Marius, Gaius (157–86 BC), Roman general and politician. His military achievements included his defeat of JUGURTHA and important reforms of the army. He opposed SULLA in the civil war of the 80s.

Marlborough, John Churchill, 1st Duke of (1650–1722), English general and statesman. He commanded the allied forces in the War of the SPANISH SUCCESSION (1701–13), his spectacular victories at BLENHEIM, RAMILLIES, OUDENARDE and Malplaquet contributing greatly to the defeat of LOUIS XIV.

Marne, Battles of the, two battles fought on the River Marne in WORLD WAR I. In the first battle (September 1914), French and British forces turned back the German assault on Paris. The Germans fell back to the River Aisne and 'dug in', setting the pattern of trench warfare. In the second battle

(July 1918), the Allies repelled a similar assault, the last German offensive of the war. See WESTERN FRONT.

Maronite, a follower of John Maron (or Maroun), a 7th-century Christian patriarch who preached that Christ had both a human and a divine nature but a single divine will. Persecuted for heresy, the Maronites fled to what is now LEBANON, where they became the dominant sect.

Marshall Plan, US aid programme to assist recovery in Europe after WORLD WAR II. The USA injected $13 billion of aid into Western Europe between 1948 and 1951. The USSR refused to participate in the scheme and discouraged its Eastern Europe satellites from accepting aid.

Marston Moor, Battle of (2 July 1644), a key battle of the ENGLISH CIVIL WAR, fought in Yorkshire. The rout of Prince RUPERT'S Royalists by CROMWELL'S Parliamentary forces left most of the N of England in Parliamentary hands.

Marx, Karl Heinrich (1818–83), German political philosopher and founder, with Friedrich ENGELS, of modern COMMUNISM. His beliefs were published in *The Communist Party Manifesto* (1848) and *Das Kapital* (1867–94). He spent most of his life exiled in London, and inspired the First INTERNATIONAL, which lasted until 1876. MARXISM has been the source of many of the Communist revolutions of the 20th century.

Marxism, the economic and political doctrine outlined by Karl MARX and Friedrich ENGELS. According to their theory of dialectical materialism, human history has seen the existence of a number of progressive modes of production, each characterized by fundamental class division and exploitation. They believed that changes in modes of production occurred through class struggle and were always signalled by revolution. They thought that the socialist revolution would be characterized by a temporary 'dictatorship of the proletariat' (working class) – in which the means of production would be owned by the state – which would build the conditions for a classless Communist society. The means of production would be collectively owned by all members of society, and goods and services distributed justly according to people's needs. Marxism is the basis of COMMUNISM.

Marxism-Leninism, the revolutionary philosophy of LENIN and guiding doctrine of the USSR; a modification of MARXISM asserting that imperialism is the highest form of CAPITALISM.

Mary I (1516–58), queen of England (1553–58). The daughter of HENRY VIII and CATHERINE of Aragon, her marriage to her cousin PHILIP II of Spain failed to produce children. The execution of Protestants during her reign earned her the nickname 'Bloody Mary'. She was succeeded by ELIZABETH I.

Mary II (1662–94), queen of England (1689–94) with WILLIAM III. She was the Protestant eldest daughter of JAMES II by his first wife. She accepted the crown jointly with her husband after the GLORIOUS REVOLUTION of 1688.

Mary, Queen of Scots (1542–87), queen of Scotland (1542–67). The daughter of James V of Scotland and Mary of Guise, she was brought up in France as a Catholic. A rising of anti-Catholic nobles led to her deposition in favour of her son James VI (later JAMES I of England) in 1567. She fled to England where, after years of imprisonment, she was executed at Fotheringay for plotting against ELIZABETH I.

Masada, a fortress in Judaea. It was captured by the ZEALOTS at the start of the Jewish revolt in AD 66. Besieged by the Romans, the rebels held out until 73, when they destroyed the fort and committed mass suicide.

Masaryk, Tomáš Garrigue (1850–1937), Slovak politician, first president of CZECHOSLOVAKIA (1919–35). He worked with BENEŠ for Czech independence during World War I, raising a Czech Legion to fight against the CENTRAL POWERS. He gained power when the Austro-Hungarian Empire collapsed, resigning in 1935 in favour of Beneš.

Mason-Dixon line, the state boundary between Pennsylvania and Maryland surveyed by Charles Mason and Jeremiah Dixon (1763–7). It is popularly regarded as the line dividing the Northern and Southern states of the USA.

Matabele, see NDEBELE.

Matilda (or Maud; 1102–67), the daughter of HENRY I, she married the German emperor Henry V in 1114 and was subsequently known as the Empress. In 1127 HENRY I made her his heir and from 1135 she and her second husband, Geoffrey PLANTAGENET, fought STEPHEN for the throne of England. Her son HENRY II succeeded Stephen as king.

Matthias Corvinus (1440–90), king of Hungary (1458–90). It took years of struggle before his election as king was generally recognized. An active defender of his kingdom against the Turks, he was later able to take the initiative against the Holy Roman Emperor, capturing Vienna in 1485.

Mauritania, a republic in NW Africa. The French arrived on the coast in the 17th century, but did not annex the Arab emirates inland until 1903. Mauritania became independent in 1960. When Spain withdrew from the WESTERN SAHARA in 1976, Morocco and Mauritania divided the territory between them, but Mauritania could not defeat the Polisario guerrillas fighting for West Saharan independence and gave up its claim (1979). Tension between the dominant Arab N and black African S led to violence in 1989. The country was a one-party state from 1979 to 1992, when multi-party elections were held.

Mauritius, an island republic in the S Indian Ocean. Known to the Arabs and the Portuguese, the island was settled by the Dutch in 1638. Mauritius was French from 1715 until 1814, when it became British. Black slaves were imported, followed in the 19th century by Indian labourers whose descendants are the majority community. Independence was gained in 1968.

Mauryan Empire (c. 325–185 BC), the first major Indian empire. The Mauryan dynasty was founded by CHANDRAGUPTA, who exercised control over most of the kingdoms of N and central INDIA. His grandson, ASHOKA, consciously moulded them into an empire stretching from Afghanistan to the S Deccan. The Mauryan dynasty went into decline after the death of Ashoka, and finally collapsed on the assassination of Birhadratha (185 BC).

Mau Mau, a secret organization founded in KENYA in 1950. Centred on the Kikuyu tribe, it was dedicated to the expulsion of white settlers by acts of terrorism and the withdrawal of the British from the colony.

Maximian (Marcus Aurelius Valerius Maximianus; d. 310), co-emperor with DIOCLETIAN (286–305). He was entrusted with the management of the W provinces. Diocletian and Maximian each took on assistants and established a TETRARCHY ('rule of four').

Maximilian (1832–67), Austrian archduke who was installed by Mexican conservatives and NAPOLEON III of France as emperor of MEXICO (1864–7). He remained in Mexico City after falling from power but was captured and executed.

Maximilian I (1459–1519), Holy Roman Emperor (1493–1519). A HABSBURG, he created significant new prospects for the family in the Low Countries by his marriage to Mary of Burgundy, daughter of CHARLES THE BOLD (1477). He achieved a further dynastic coup by marrying his son Philip to the daughter of FERDINAND and ISABELLA, thereby uniting Spain and the Habsburgs.

Maya, the name given to a pre-Columbian culture of Meso-America, centred on the tropical lowlands of SE Mexico (Yucatán) and Guatemala. Maya culture reached its peak during the Classic phase of Meso-American prehistory (AD 300–900) and was characterized by extensive temple-cities built around stepped pyramids. The city of Mayapán was dominant from 1200, but was replaced by a number of smaller cities when it was overthrown around 1450.

Mayflower, the ship in which the PILGRIM FATHERS sailed from Plymouth to Cape Cod, Massachusetts, in 1620.

mayors of the palace, lords of the royal household under the MEROVINGIAN dynasty who came to wield effective political power after the death of Dagobert I in 639. Notable mayors included Charles MARTEL (ruled 714–41) and PEPIN III (the Short), founder of the CAROLINGIAN dynasty.

Mazarin, Jules (1601–61), Italian cardinal. He left the papal diplomatic service for that of Cardinal RICHELIEU, becoming first minister to Anne of Austria, widow of LOUIS XIII, and regent during the minority of LOUIS XIV. He secured good terms for the French at the Treaty of WESTPHALIA (ending the THIRTY YEARS WAR), but his continuation of the war with Spain led to the civil wars known as the FRONDES.

Mazzini, Giuseppe (1805–72), Italian nationalist, republican and founder of YOUNG ITALY. A supporter of the RISORGIMENTO, he was active in Italy during the REVOLUTIONS OF 1848 and briefly established a Roman republic in 1849. His nationalist uprisings in 1834, 1852 (Mantua) and 1853 (Milan) failed and he spent many years in exile in London.

Mecca, the birthplace of the prophet MUHAMMAD and holy city of ISLAM, now in Saudi Arabia (see map, p. 17). A pilgrimage to Mecca once during a lifetime – if possible – is an obligation on Muslims. The date of Muhammad's flight from Mecca to MEDINA (622) begins the Muslim calendar.

Medes, a people of ancient Iran. In the 9th century the Medes were probably a loose tribal confederation, but by the 7th century BC had united, and controlled a large area around their capital (modern Hamadan in Iran). By the end of the century, the Medes were attacking Assyrian cities. In alliance with BABYLON, they besieged and captured the Assyrian city of NINEVEH in 612 BC. The Medes received Assyria's N domains, reaching to central Anatolia. They came into conflict with the LYDIANS in Anatolia until peace was made in 585 BC. Astyages (585–550 BC), the last king of the Medes, was overthrown by CYRUS II of the Persian ACHAEMENID dynasty in 549 BC.

Medici, a family that ruled FLORENCE from the 15th to the 18th centuries. Immigrants to Florence in the 13th century, they became eminent bankers with international connections. Cosimo 'Il Vecchio' (1389–1464) ruled Florence unofficially from 1434 to 1464; he and his grandson Lorenzo 'The Magnificent' (ruled 1469–92) were famed as patrons of artists and humanists. After a period of exile the Medici returned in 1512, and ruled as dukes, then grand-dukes, from 1530 to 1737.

Medici, Catherine de (1519–89), wife of Henry II of France (1547–59). She sought to protect the interests of her sons, Francis II, Charles IX and HENRY III in the difficult circumstances of the FRENCH WARS OF RELIGION. Her alliance with the Catholic GUISE faction led to the ST BARTHOLOMEW'S DAY MASSACRE (1572).

Medina, an Arabian city about 450 km (280 mi) NE of Mecca, to which MUHAMMAD emigrated or fled (the HIJRA) in 622, and where he is buried. See map, p. 17.

Mehemet Ali (1769–1849), Albanian-born soldier in the service of the OTTOMAN Turks, and pasha of EGYPT (1805–49). He fought in the OTTOMAN army against NAPOLEON I and returned to Egypt to sweep the MAMLUKS from power in 1811. Although nominally under Ottoman suzerainty, he effectively ruled Egypt as an independent sovereign. He was defeated at NAVARINO in 1827, but went on to make Egypt the leading power in the E Mediterranean. In 1833, under French pressure, the Ottomans ceded Syria to Mehemet Ali, and by 1839 he had extended his power as far as Yemen and the Persian Gulf. However, in 1840 Britain, Russia, Austria and Prussia forced him to retreat within Egypt's borders and accept Ottoman suzerainty. As compensation his family was granted hereditary right of rule in Egypt, where they held power until the middle of the 20th century.

Mehmet II (the Conqueror; 1430–81), OTTOMAN sultan (1451–81). He greatly improved the Turkish army and navy, and used them to extend Ottoman rule in the Balkans, the Aegean and the Mediterranean. In 1453 he seized CONSTANTINOPLE, which became the capital of the Ottoman Empire.

Meiji restoration (1867–9), the restoration of imperial government in JAPAN. In 1867–8 a group representing daimyos from W Japan and reforming imperial courtiers seized power from the weak TOKUGAWA shogunate, and restored the imperial throne under MUTSUHITO. The emperor adopted 'Meiji' ('enlightened government') as his throne name, and the term is also applied to the period of his reign (1867–1912). The group of privy councillors who exercised power on behalf of the emperor then proceeded to transform Japan. Within ten years, virtually all vestiges of feudalism had been removed. The daimyos and samurai were pensioned off and the peasants given ownership of the land they worked (and then heavily taxed). Western systems of law, administration and taxation were introduced, followed in 1889 by a constitution and parliament along Western lines. The Meiji reformers saw that survival in the modern world demanded not just Western institutions but also a Western-style economy. This took longer to achieve, but industrialization, sponsored by the state, was well under way by the beginning of the 20th century.

Meir, Golda (Goldie Mabovitch; 1898–1979), Israeli politician, prime minister (1968–74) of ISRAEL. Born in Russia, she was educated in the USA and emigrated to Palestine in 1921. She founded the Israeli Labour Party in 1967.

Melbourne, William Lamb, 2nd Viscount (1779–1848), British Whig statesman, prime minister (1834 and 1835–41). He was a close adviser of Queen VICTORIA in her early years as sovereign.

Melanesians, the peoples of the SW division of Oceania. Melanesian horticulturalists had settled New Guinea, New Caledonia and the New Hebrides by 2000 BC.

Memphis, the ancient capital of EGYPT, traditionally founded by Menes during the Early Dynastic Period (3100–2725 BC).

Mendès-France, Pierre (1907–82), French socialist politician, prime minister (1954–5). He became PM after the French defeat at DIEN BIEN PHU, taking France out of INDOCHINA and granting independence to Tunisia, but was brought down by an economic crisis.

Menelik II (1844–1913), emperor of Abyssinia (ETHIOPIA) (1889–1913). He kept his country independent during the European SCRAMBLE FOR AFRICA, inflicting a humiliating defeat on the Italians at Adowa (1896).

Mennonites, a radical Protestant sect that emerged in the 16th century. They took their name from Menno Simmons (1496–1561), who became an ANABAPTIST in 1536. Large Mennonite communities in Holland and Switzerland were driven abroad by persecution, many emigrating to the USA in 1663.

Menshevik (Russian, 'member of the minority'), a member of the moderate wing of the SOCIAL DEMOCRATIC Party in Russia, which advocated gradual reform to achieve socialism. They split with the more militant BOLSHEVIKS in 1903.

Mentuhotep II, the first Theban pharaoh of EGYPT (2060–2010 BC), whose reign inaugurated the Middle Kingdom (2040–1640 BC). His accession ended 90 years of conflict (the First Intermediate Period). He took control of the whole country, restored order and consolidated the borders.

Menzies, Sir Robert Gordon (1894–1978), Australian statesman. He was prime minister as head of the United Australia Party (1939–41) and again (1949–66) as head of the Liberal Party.

mercantilism, an economic theory held during the 18th century. The theories of mercantilism assumed the amount of wealth in the world to be fixed, and therefore that individual states had to ensure that their subjects achieved the largest share possible of world trade. Since economic success depended on a favourable trade balance, governments felt that their policies should encourage manufactured exports, and discourage their import. It was thought that a country's trade should be monopolized by its own subjects, and that colonies existed only to benefit the mother country.

Merchant Adventurers, English businessmen dealing principally in general imports and the export of cloth. The associations that they formed to protect their interests both at home and abroad were especially prominent in the 15th and 16th centuries. They became the dominant force in England's foreign trade, eclipsing the HANSEATIC LEAGUE.

Mercia, the central kingdom of ANGLO-SAXON England, which achieved its greatest power in the 8th century, and was partitioned by the Danes (VIKINGS) in 878.

Meroë, the capital of the African kingdom of NUBIA (on the Nile in modern Sudan) from the 6th century BC to the 4th century AD. It was a major point of contact and trade between Mediterranean civilizations and central Africa.

Merovingians, a dynasty of Frankish kings (c. 500–751) founded by CLOVIS I. During the 6th century their territories expanded to include the whole of Gaul N of the Alps. In accordance with the Frankish system of partible inheritance (division amongst heirs), on his death in 511 Clovis' kingdom was divided between his four sons. The Frankish realms survived the vicissitudes of divided inheritance remarkably well. After the death of Dagobert I in 639, effective power in the Frankish lands passed to the MAYORS OF THE PALACE. The later Merovingians were often mere puppets in the hands of the mayors. Charles MARTEL was a member of an aristocratic Frankish family who held the post of mayor of the palace. In 751, his son and successor, PEPIN the Short, ousted the last token Merovingian, Childeric III, and created the CAROLINGIAN dynasty.

Mesolithic, the period in Near Eastern and European prehistory (from 10,000 BC) that followed the end of the PALAEOLITHIC Age and was succeeded by the NEOLITHIC Age. Humans took advantage of climatic and environment changes after the end of the ICE AGE to become hunter-gatherers.

Mesopotamia, an area of SW Asia between the TIGRIS and EUPHRATES rivers (now in IRAQ). The southernmost part of Mesopotamia was the ancient land of SUMER, where several cities had emerged by 3000 BC. Following the conquest of these cities by SARGON of AKKAD, they became part of the short-lived Akkadian Empire, which was itself succeeded by a Sumerian renaissance under a dynasty at UR. By 1894 BC a new empire had been established by Sumuabum with its centre at BABYLON. About the same time N Mesopotamia was taken by the ASSYRIANS. Although both powers lost control of the region to invaders in the 2nd millennium BC, the Assyrians established a great empire between 744 and 609 BC, incorporating Egypt. Their hegemony was destroyed by the Neo-Babylonian CHALDAEAN dynasty and empire, but that in turn was conquered by CYRUS the Great. From then on Mesopotamia was ruled by a succession of empires, the ACHAEMENIDS, the SELEUCIDS, the PARTHIANS and the SASSANIANS. Fragmentation after the ARAB CONQUESTS (635–7) was followed by the rule of the ABBASID dynasty. The region was devastated by the MONGOLS in 1258 and 1401 and eventually became part of the OTTOMAN Empire. See map, p. 8.

Methodism, English evangelical Protestant movement, originally developed by John Wesley (1703–91) and his followers in the 18th century. Methodism was hostile to liberalism and science, and emphasized religion as an emotional experience rather than a system of thought. It broke away from the ANGLICAN Church in 1791 and thereafter gained many adherents in both Britain and America.

Metternich, Clemens Wenzel Nepomuk Lothar, Prince (1773–1859), Austrian foreign minister (1809–21) and chancellor (1821–48). The arch-conservative architect of

Restoration Austria and Europe at the Congress of VIENNA after the NAPOLEONIC WARS, he attempted to suppress nationalism in the non-German-speaking parts of the AUSTRIAN EMPIRE by force, and was removed from office during the REVOLUTIONS OF 1848.

Mexican–American War (1846–8), a conflict between MEXICO and the USA, easily won by US forces under Generals Zachary TAYLOR and Winfield Scott. It was ended by the Treaty of Guadelupe Hidalgo. The USA gained California, together with the future states of New Mexico, Arizona, Nevada, Utah and Colorado. See map, p. 32.

Mexican Revolution, a period of violent upheaval and political reform in MEXICO (1910–40). In 1910 Porfirio DÍAZ's long rule was ended by a movement of democratic protest led by Francisco MADERO. However, Madero's brief presidency unleashed pent-up discontent. In the central state of Morelos, ZAPATA led an agrarian revolt of villagers deprived of their lands by the expansion of sugar estates. The N of Mexico produced a series of revolutions that brought about the collapse of the old centre. Madero was murdered by the counter-revolutionary General Huerta in 1913, but fighting during the rest of the decade saw the triumph of revolutionary forces in the N. Combining many forces besides peasants and workers, the Mexican Revolution was a genuine social revolution, achieving land and other reforms unprecedented in Latin American history. However, it also ushered in a long period of single-party rule.

Mexico, a republic in the N of Central America. See panel.

Michael VIII (Palaeologus; 1224–82), BYZANTINE emperor (1259–82). A successful soldier in the NICAEAN EMPIRE, he usurped the throne and went on to reconquer CONSTANTINOPLE from the Franks in 1261.

Micronesians, the peoples of the NW division of Oceania, including the Mariana, Marshall and Gilbert islands.

Middle Ages, the period of European history usually dated from the fall of the last Western Roman emperor in the late 5th century to the 15th-century Italian RENAISSANCE.

Midway, Battle of (3–6 June 1942), a battle fought between Japanese and US naval-air fleets in the Pacific during WORLD WAR II. The Americans lost one carrier but destroyed four Japanese equivalents in a battle that marked the end of the Japanese advance in the Pacific. See PACIFIC CAMPAIGNS.

Milan, a former Italian state ruled by the VISCONTI family from 1395 to 1535. In 1535 Milan was absorbed into HABSBURG Lombardy and was ruled by Spain (1535–1714), Austria (1714–97), the French-dominated Cisalpine Republic (1797–1805), the Napoleonic kingdom of Italy (1805–14) and Austria (1814–59), before becoming part of the kingdom of ITALY.

Miletus, the most important of the ancient IONIAN cities on the coast of Asia Minor. Miletus founded more than 60 colonies in the ARCHAIC period, most in the Black Sea area.

Minamoto Yoritomo (1147–99), military ruler of JAPAN (1185–99) and first shogun. He established the KAMAKURA shogunate.

Ming (1368–1644), an imperial dynasty of CHINA. Having ousted the MONGOLS (see YUAN dynasty), the rebel leader Zhu Yuanzhang was proclaimed HONGWU, the first emperor of the Ming dynasty. The Ming established Chinese imperial boundaries well into Central Asia and controlled the nomads of N China. Ming influence in the empire was reinforced under Hongwu's son YONGLE (1403–24). Between 1405 and 1433 Ming China moved its capital from Nanjing back to Beijing and began trading and missionary contacts with Europeans, notably Portuguese. The empire entered a period of instability in the first half of the 17th century, and the MANCHU seized N China. However, it was not until 1682 that the QING dynasty of the Manchu was able to establish an unchallenged hold over the whole empire.

Minoan civilization, an ancient civilization, named after the legendary King Minos, based on the island of Crete. It reached its peak in the Middle and Late Bronze Age between 2200 and 1450 BC. Important Minoan palace sites have been discovered at Knossos, Phaistos, Aghia Triadha and Mallia. A seafaring people, the Minoans were not Greek-speakers, using an as yet undeciphered script known as Linear A. The palace of Knossos revealed frescos and pottery of considerable beauty and intricacy. The contents of storage rooms in the palace show that the rulers who lived there had the power to collect tribute and redistribute it to their allies and friends. The Minoan civilization was destroyed, possibly by earthquake or war, around 1450 BC. The Minoans were replaced as the dominant power in the Aegean by the MYCENAEANS.

Mirabeau, Honoré Gabriel Riqueti, vicomte de (1749–91), French aristocrat and revolutionary. A leading figure in the

MEXICO

15th century: Decline of the dominant MAYAN civilization in Yucatán. **1519–21:** The AZTEC Empire was overthrown by Spanish conquistadores under CORTEZ. **16th–19th century:** Mexico was under Spanish rule, its economy largely based on silver and gold mining and the produce of large estates owned by Spanish grandees. **1810:** The first revolt against Spanish rule, led by HIDALGO and MORELOS. **1821:** Mexican independence gained after a guerrilla war led by Vicente Guerrero. **1823:** Mexico became a republic; civil war between federalists and centralists. **1836:** TEXAS rebelled against Mexico, declaring independence. **1846–8:** MEXICAN–AMERICAN WAR; Mexico lost Texas, New Mexico and California after defeat by USA. **1858–61:** Civil war between reformists and conservatives was won by the reformists under Benito JUÁREZ. **1863–4:** French invasion; Archduke MAXIMILIAN of Austria appointed emperor. **1867:** French withdrawal. **1876–80** and **1888–1910:** Dictatorship of General Porfirio DÍAZ. **1910:** Beginning of MEXICAN REVOLUTION. **1916–17:** US expeditionary force sent against the outlaw and revolutionary PANCHO VILLA. **From 1924:** The revolution became anticlerical, leading to persecution of the Church. **1929:** Order restored by Institutional Revolutionary Party (PRI). **1929–89:** PRI had a virtual monopoly of power. **From 1990:** More liberal economic and political climate.

early stages of the FRENCH REVOLUTION, his efforts to prevent the complete erosion of royal power discredited him in the eyes of the radicals.

Mississippi culture or **Temple Mound Culture**, a North American culture that predominated in the Mississippi basin, c. AD 700–1500. It was characterized by the building of large earthen mounds or pyramids supporting wooden temples, tombs and elite residences.

Missouri Compromise (1820–1), legislation passed by the US Congress to resolve disagreement over the extension of SLAVERY in the territories beyond existing state boundaries. Maine entered the Union as a free state and Missouri as a slave state, while slavery was banned in the N part of the LOUISIANA purchase.

Mitanni, a kingdom of ancient N Syria. At its greatest extent, between 1430 and 1350 BC, Mitanni reached from the Zagros to the Mediterranean. Although its population was mainly HURRIAN, the ruling aristocracy seems to have been Indo-Aryan. In the mid-14th century BC, the HITTITES defeated Mitanni and her vassals, taking control of Syria.

Mithras, a god of Persian origin who became the object of a cult among soldiers of the Roman army during the late Empire.

Mitterrand, François (1916–), French socialist statesman. He held ministerial posts under the Fourth Republic and sought to unite the parties of the left in the 1960s. He became leader of a unified Socialist Party in 1971 and president in 1981, defeating GISCARD D'ESTAING. A strong advocate of the French nuclear bomb, he weathered economic and political crises and profited from disunity on the right to secure a second term in 1988.

Mixtec, a Meso-American people who established an important regional state in central MEXICO before they were conquered by the AZTECS in the late 15th century.

Mobutu, Sese Seko (1930–), president of ZAIRE (1965–). He seized power in a military coup at the end of the CONGO CRISIS, and maintained order by imposing harsh policies. Allegations of corruption, violent opposition and rebel Angolan invasions have undermined his long rule, but Mobutu continues to oppose constitutional reform.

Moguls, a Muslim dynasty that ruled India from the 16th century. In 1526 BABUR of Kabul invaded N India and overthrew the DELHI SULTANATE. His attempts to carve out an empire were continued by his son HUMAYUN. Under AKBAR the Moguls were able to extend their power over the whole of N India. In the first half of the 17th century, under Akbar's successors, JAHANGIR and SHAH JAHAN, the empire and its economy continued to flourish, and in the second half of the 17th century AURANGZEB maintained the momentum of territorial expansion, but his harsh religious policies precipitated a decline in the unity and administrative efficiency of the empire. In the 18th century the decentralization of power, combined with a succession of weak Mogul rulers, allowed regional powers to assert themselves. Resurgent Hindus such as the MARATHAS and RAJPUTS took control of their regions. By 1800 the British EAST INDIA COMPANY had become a major political power on the subcontinent and, taking advantage of internecine quarrels in the coastal states, imposed direct control over increasing areas of India. The last nominal Mogul 'king of Delhi' was deposed by the British in 1857.

Mohács, Battle of (1526), a battle fought outside Buda, in which a Hungarian army was crushed by Ottoman forces under SULEIMAN I (see map, p. 26).

Mohammed, see MUHAMMAD.

Mohawk, a native North American people, the easternmost of the five tribes of the IROQUOIS confederation, living in the Eastern Woodlands (E New York State). See also NORTH AMERICAN INDIANS

Mohenjo-daro, the most important site of the ancient INDUS VALLEY civilization that flourished between 2300 and 1700 BC.

Mohican, see MAHICAN.

Moldavia, see MOLDOVA and ROMANIA.

Moldova, a republic of SE Europe. Known as Bessarabia, the area was ruled by KIEV RUS (10th–12th centuries) and the Tartars (13th–14th centuries) before becoming part of the Romanian principality of Moldavia – within the (Turkish) Ottoman Empire – in the 15th century. Bessarabia was intermittently occupied by Russia in the 18th century before being ceded to the Russians in 1812. Briefly restored to Moldavia (1856–78), Bessarabia remained Russian until World War I. An autonomous Bessarabian republic was proclaimed in 1917, but was suppressed by a Russian Bolshevik invasion (1918). The Russians were removed by Romanian forces and Bessarabia became part of the kingdom of Romania (1918). When Romania entered World War II as a German ally, the USSR reoccupied Bessarabia, which was reorganized as the Moldavian Soviet Republic in 1944. Following the abortive coup by Communist hardliners in Moscow (September 1991), Moldavia declared independence. As Moldova, the republic received international recognition when the Soviet Union was dissolved (December 1991). Civil war broke out in 1992 when Russian and Ukrainian minorities – fearing an eventual reunion of Moldova with Romania – attempted to secede. The intervention of CIS forces brought an uneasy peace.

Molly Maguires, a secret Irish-American organization active in the 1860s and 1870s. They campaigned – often with the use of violence – against anti-union mine-owners and managers in America. Ten of their leaders were hanged for murder and conspiracy on the evidence supplied by the Pinkerton Detective Agency.

Molotov, Vyacheslav Mikhailovich (1890–1986), Soviet politician, foreign minister (1939–41 and 1953–6), in which capacity he negotiated the NAZI–SOVIET PACT. After the death of STALIN in 1953, Molotov joined Beria and Malenkov in a ruling triumvirate, but was ousted by KHRUSHCHEV in 1957.

Moltke, Helmuth, Count von (1800–91), Prussian field marshal, chief of the imperial German general staff (1871–88). He won victories for Prussia against Denmark (1864), Austria (1866) and France (1870–1), in the latter two cases using railways for swift mobilization.

Moluccas, see SPICE ISLANDS.

Monaco, a principality on the Mediterranean coast of France, which has been ruled by the Grimaldi family since 1297. Monaco was annexed by France in 1793 but restored in 1814, under the protection of the king of Sardinia. The greater part of the principality was lost – and eventually annexed by France – in 1848. Since 1861 Monaco has been under French protection. Prince Rainier III granted a liberal constitution in 1962.

Monasteries, Dissolution of the (1536–40), the systematic abolition of MONASTICISM during the English REFORMATION, following a survey of monastic wealth organized by Thomas CROMWELL. The lesser monasteries were dissolved in 1536, the rest two years later. By 1539 more than 500 had been suppressed. The crown gained substantial lands and income, some of which was used to establish new dioceses. Successive monarchs sold off these lands, mainly to the advantage of the gentry and nobility.

monasticism, the lifestyle of monks or nuns living in secluded communities. Monasticism is found in various religions, especially Christianity, Buddhism and Jainism. The earliest Christian monks were the desert hermits who lived on top of tall pillars. Hermits continued to exist throughout the Middle Ages, but increasingly a communal lifestyle devoted to God rather than an isolated one became popular. Monasteries were founded where devout men or women lived under a 'rule' (code of conduct) that governed their daily routines. The most influential of all rules was that laid down by the 'father' of Western monasticism, St BENEDICT of Nursia.

monetarism, an economic doctrine emphasizing the role of the money supply in the functioning of an economy. Unlike KEYNESIAN economists, monetarists believe that with the exception of managing the money supply, governments should not intervene in the economy. Monetarism was at the centre of the economic policies of Margaret THATCHER in the UK and Ronald REAGAN in the USA.

Mongol Empire, an Asian nomad empire founded in the early 13th century (see map, p. 19). By 1206 the Mongol chieftain, Temujim, had united all the tribes of MONGOLIA and established himself as GENGHIS KHAN. Using his skilled horsemen and archers, he swept eastwards, defeating the nomad states of N China and the JIN empire. Turning westward, he overran parts of Afghanistan and Iran by 1215. Genghis's descendants continued the expansion of the empire, incorporating central Russia, Poland, Hungary, Bulgaria and Romania. In the 1250s HULAGU completed the conquest of Iran and Iraq. Expansion into Syria and Palestine, however, was thwarted by the Mongol defeat at AIN JALUT by MAMLUK forces. Further westward expansion was prevented by succession disputes that followed the death of Genghis Khan (1259). In 1260 KUBLAI KHAN became Great Khan, and after his conquest of the Chinese Song empire, concentrated on eastern affairs, establishing the YUAN dynasty. The rest of the empire was divided into three; the Khanate of the GOLDEN HORDE (Russia), the ILKHANATE (Anatolia, Iran and Iraq), and the JAGATAI Khanate (Turkestan). The Ilkhanate lasted until the mid-14th century, the Golden Horde until the end of the 15th, and the Jagatai Khanate, in a much reduced form, until 1678. The Yuan dynasty in China came to an end in 1368.

Mongolia, a country of E Central Asia. Mongolia was the home of the HUNS – who ravaged both the Chinese and Roman empires (1st–5th centuries AD) – and of the strong Uighur state in the 8th and 9th centuries. In the 13th century the MONGOL dynasty of GENGHIS KHAN created an immense but short-lived Asian empire. In the 17th century, Mongolia was annexed by China, but 'Outer' Mongolia – the N – retained autonomy as a BUDDHIST monarchy. In 1921, Outer Mongolia broke away from China with Soviet assistance and in 1924 the Mongolian People's Republic was established. Pro-democracy demonstrations led to a liberalization of the regime in 1990. The Communists won the first multi-party elections.

Monmouth's Rebellion (1685), the attempt by CHARLES II'S illegitimate son, James, Duke of Monmouth (1649–85), to seize the throne from JAMES II. His largely peasant army was defeated at the battle of Sedgemoor. Monmouth's supporters were savagely punished in the BLOODY ASSIZES.

Monnet, Jean (1888–1979), French economist and administrator. As author of the SCHUMAN Plan for the European Coal and Steel Community, and president of the latter (1952–5), he was a 'founding father' of the EUROPEAN COMMUNITY.

Monroe Doctrine (1823), a US foreign-policy doctrine enunciated by President MONROE, hinting at plans for an American imperial role. It warned Europeans not to seek further colonies in the New World and against interference in American affairs.

Monroe, James (1758–1831), fifth president of the USA (1817–25). The USA acquired FLORIDA from Spain during his two-term presidency. A moderate Democratic-Republican, he lacked imagination, but his warning against European involvement in American affairs (the MONROE DOCTRINE) has won him a lasting place in US history.

Mons, a people of S Burma and Thailand, related to the KHMERS of Cambodia. By 825 they ruled lower Burma and had established the city of Pegu. They were conquered by the PAGAN kingdom in the 11th century but after their demise regained some power in S Burma. They were again defeated by the Toungo in 1539, but reasserted their control of the region in 1752 before finally succumbing to the Konbaung dynasty in 1757.

Mons, Battle of (23 August 1914), a battle fought in Belgium during WORLD WAR I. The British Expeditionary Force slowed the advance of the German First Army, giving the French time to recover for their counterattack at the Battle of the MARNE.

Montenegro, a former kingdom of SE Europe that was never subjugated by the Turkish OTTOMAN Empire (see map, p. 30). It was ruled by prince-bishops (1516–1851), became a secular principality (1851), was recognized as independent at the Congress of BERLIN (1878), and became a kingdom (1910). After occupation by Austria-Hungary during World War I, Montenegro was absorbed by SERBIA (1918). In 1992, it formed – with Serbia – the new smaller Yugoslav Federation.

Montezuma (1466–1520), the last AZTEC emperor (1502–20). He was overthrown by CORTEZ, and killed either by the Spaniards or by his own people.

Montfort, Simon de, Earl of Leicester (c. 1208–65), leader of the baronial opposition to HENRY III from 1258, despite being the latter's brother-in-law. After defeating Henry at the battle of Lewes (1264), he was de facto ruler of England until killed in battle at Evesham.

Montgomery, Bernard Law, 1st Viscount of Alamein (1887–1976), commander of the British 8th army in the NORTH AFRICAN and ITALIAN campaigns during WORLD WAR II. His victory at EL ALAMEIN (1942) turned the tide in the Allies' favour. He supervised the D-DAY landings and subsequent breakout from Normandy in June–September 1944, and as commander of the Anglo-Canadian 21st army group during the NORTHWEST EUROPE CAMPAIGN accepted the surrender of all German forces facing him on 4 May 1945.

Moor, a term used by Europeans for the Muslim inhabitants (of Arab, Berber or mixed stock) of N Africa and Spain. The word derives from ancient Mauretania (roughly equivalent to modern Morocco).

More, Sir Thomas (1478–1535), lord chancellor of England (1529–32). A humanist, author of *Utopia* (1516), and critic of abuses in the Church, More nevertheless opposed the REFORMATION. Refusing to recognize HENRY VIII as head of the ANGLICAN CHURCH, he was tried and executed.

Morelos, José María (1765–1815), Mexican priest and revolutionary. He led the revolt against Spain after the death of HIDALGO (1810). He used guerrilla tactics to harry the Spanish, and in 1813 formally declared Mexican independence. His plans for administrative and economic reforms were cut short by his capture and execution by the Spanish.

Moro, Aldo (1916–78), Italian CHRISTIAN DEMOCRAT statesman, prime minister (1963–8 and 1974–6). He was kidnapped and murdered by the RED BRIGADES in 1978.

Morocco, a kingdom of NW Africa. The region became a Roman province in 46 AD. In the 7th century Morocco became Islamic. In the 11th and 12th centuries the ALMORAVID empire – which included Muslim Spain – was based in Marrakech. Morocco was ruled by the ALMOHAD dynasty who ruled a N African empire from 1147 until 1269. The Sharifian dynasty – descended from the Prophet Muhammad – rose to power in the 16th and 17th centuries, and still retains the throne. In the 19th century Spain confirmed control of several long-claimed coastal settlements. In the 'Moroccan Crises' (1905–6 and 1911), French interests in Morocco were disputed by Germany. Under the Treaty of Fez in 1912 France established a protectorate over Morocco, although the Spanish enclaves remained. The 1925 Rif rebellion stirred nationalist feelings, but independence was not gained until 1956. King Hassan II (reigned 1961–) has survived left-wing challenges through strong rule and vigorous nationalism – as in his 1975 'Green March' of unarmed peasants into the then-Spanish (Western) Sahara. Morocco still holds WESTERN SAHARA despite international pressure and the activities of the Algerian-backed Polisario guerrillas fighting for the territory's independence. A ceasefire was agreed in 1991 but a scheduled UN-sponsored referendum on Western Sahara has yet to be held.

Mortimer, Roger, 1st Earl of March (1287–1330), English nobleman. See ISABELLA OF FRANCE.

Morton, John (c. 1420–1500), English cleric. As bishop of Ely he reputedly helped to organize the overthrow of RICHARD III in 1485. HENRY VII made him archbishop of Canterbury in 1486 and chancellor in 1487.

Moses, the leader of the Israelites at the time of the EXODUS. He was responsible for the Ten Commandments and the establishment of Jewish Law.

Mosley, Sir Oswald Ernald (1896–1980), British politician, founder of the British Union of Fascists (BUF) in 1932. He had been an MP, of both the Conservative and Labour parties, between 1918 and 1931 until he created the BUF. He was interned during WORLD WAR II and never recovered political credibility.

Mossadeq, Muhammad (1880–1967), Iranian politician, leader of a nationalist-populist front that ruled IRAN 1951–3.

Mountbatten, Louis, 1st Earl Mountbatten of Burma (1900–79), British naval commander, Chief of Combined Operations (1942–3), Supreme Commander in SE Asia (1943–5) and last viceroy of INDIA (1947). He was instrumental in the Burma campaigns during WORLD WAR II, and oversaw the transference of Indian sovereignty from Britain. He was assassinated by the IRISH REPUBLICAN ARMY in 1979.

Mozambique, a republic of SE Africa. The coast attracted Arab settlements from the 9th century AD. The Portuguese founded coastal trading posts from 1531, but only gained control of the whole country at the end of the 19th century. Forced labour and minimal development fuelled nationalist feelings, and in 1964 the Frelimo movement launched a guerrilla war against Portuguese rule. Independence was achieved in 1975, and a Marxist-Leninist state was established. The pressures of poverty and the destabilization of the country by South Africa – through support for the Renamo guerrilla movement – led to renewed ties with the West, and Marxism was abandoned by Frelimo in 1989. Political pluralism has been permitted since 1990. A ceasefire – and a UN presence in Mozambique – were agreed in 1992.

Mubarak, Hosni (1928–), Egyptian politician, president (1981–). He succeeded to the presidency on the assassination of SADAT, whose moderate policies he has continued. In the 1990s he has attempted to contain the rise of radical Islamic fundamentalism.

Mugabe, Robert Gabriel (1924–), first prime minister (1980–8) and then president (1988–) of independent ZIMBABWE. As leader of the Zimbabwe African National Union (ZANU), he fought with Joshua NKOMO's Zimbabwe African People's Union (ZAPU) against the white government of Rhodesia. After securing Rhodesian (Zimbabwean) independence in 1980 he became PM. He won the fierce power struggle with Nkomo and the two parties agreed an uneasy alliance in 1976, finally merging in 1986.

Muhammad (c. 570–632), the Prophet and founder of ISLAM. From 610 he received what he believed were revelations from God which eventually formed the basis of the QUR'AN (Koran). His preaching in MECCA was not always welcome and in 622 he made his flight (HIJRA) to MEDINA, where he founded his Islamic community. Islam spread throughout the region, and by 632 he was the effective ruler of Arabia.

Mujibur Rahman, Sheikh (1920–75), first prime minister (1972–5) and president (1975) of BANGLADESH. Co-founder of the AWAMI LEAGUE, he opposed discrimination against the BENGALIS by the PUNJABI-dominated government of PAKISTAN. He was assassinated by a group of army officers.

Mukden Incident (18 September 1931), the seizure of the Manchurian city of Mukden (now Shengyang) by Japanese troops. Although ordered to stop by Tokyo, the Japanese army proceeded to occupy the whole of MANCHURIA, establishing the state of MANCHUKUO. Japan's response to the LEAGUE OF NATIONS denunciation was to leave the League and pursue its own aggressive policies. The incident strengthened further the role of the military in the government of JAPAN.

Mulroney, (Martin) Brian (1939–), Canadian Progressive Conservative statesman, prime minister (1984–92). He was succeeded by Kim Campbell, but her party suffered electoral annihilation in 1993.

Munich Agreement (29 September 1938), an agreement between Britain, France, Germany and Italy compelling Czechoslovakia to cede the SUDETENLAND to Germany. Following his policy of APPEASEMENT, Neville CHAMBERLAIN agreed to the annexation in exchange for what he called 'peace in our time'. The Agreement also guaranteed the borders of independent Czechoslovakia, but was ignored by the Germans when they invaded in 1939.

Munich 'beer-hall' putsch (8 November 1923), an abortive uprising by the NAZIS. Led by HITLER, Nazis and other right-wing groups attempted to overthrow the Bavarian government. The putsch failed and Hitler served a short prison sentence.

Müntzer, Thomas (1489–1525), a rebel leader in the German Peasants' War. He believed in a more radical REFORMATION, and preached that the poor were God's chosen, and should hasten the imminent Second Coming by violent action. He was executed after the bloody suppression of the Peasants' War by the Swabian League under PHILIP OF HESSE.

Murad I (1360–89), OTTOMAN sultan (1362–89). Through marriage and skilful financial deals he extended the Ottoman Balkan territories. He lost his life in a notable victory over the Serbs at KOSOVO in 1389.

Murat, Joachim (1767–1815), marshal of France. He was created king of Naples (1808–15) by NAPOLEON I, but deserted him during the retreat from Moscow, and conspired with the Austrians to protect his own throne. He rallied to Napoleon in 1815 during the HUNDRED DAYS, but was later captured and shot by the Austrians.

Muscovy, grand duchy of, a former Russian principality (13th–17th centuries) centred on Moscow. The town of Moscow was founded in the 12th century and formed part of KIEV RUS until it became part of the MONGOL Empire. By the middle of the 15th century Muscovy had asserted its independence from the Mongols, and IVAN III incorporated the Christian Slav principalities of Russia into Muscovy. Its expanded territory laid the foundations of the centralized Russian state. See RUSSIA.

Muslim, a follower of ISLAM.

Muslim League, a political party representing the interests of Indian Muslims during the campaign for Indian independence. Founded in 1905, the League initially worked alongside Hindus in pursuit of independence, notably in GANDHI's non-cooperation movement. In 1940, however, the leader of the League, Mohammed Ali JINNAH, demanded a separate Muslim state of PAKISTAN. The League all but disappeared after defeat in Pakistan's first elections.

Mussolini, Benito (1883–1945), Italian dictator, known as 'Il Duce' (the leader). He was appointed prime minister by King Victor Emanuel III after the 'MARCH ON ROME'. He assumed dictatorial powers in 1925, annexed Abyssinia (ETHIOPIA) in 1936 (the year in which he allied Italy with Germany) and took Italy into WORLD WAR II in 1940. He was deposed after the Allied invasion of Sicily, and was shot by Italian partisans after briefly heading a puppet regime in German-occupied N Italy. His most notable achievement was the LATERAN TREATY of 1929.

Mutsuhito (1852–1912), emperor of Japan (1867–1912). After the overthrow of the TOKUGAWA shogunate he was installed with executive power. See MEIJI RESTORATION.

Myanmar (Burma), a republic of S Asia. Burman supremacy over the Irrawaddy valley was first claimed in 1044 by King Anawratha, who adopted Buddhism from the rival MON people. Chinese conquest (1287) allowed a reassertion of Mon power until the 16th century. After 1758 the Konbaung dynasty expanded Burman territory until British counter-expansion led to total annexation (1826–85). Separated from British India in 1937, Burma became a battleground for British and Japanese forces in WORLD WAR II. In 1948, Burma left the Commonwealth as an independent republic, keeping outside contacts to a minimum, particularly following the coup of General Ne Win in 1962. Continuing armed attempts to gain autonomy by non-Burman minorities have strengthened the role of the army, which retained power following multi-party elections in 1990 and detained leaders of the winning party (including Aung San Suu Kyi, who was awarded the 1991 Nobel Peace Prize). The government has come under strong international pressure to introduce reforms but it has continued to exert military pressure on minorities including the Karen and Muslims.

Mycenaean civilization, an Ancient Greek civilization. They replaced the MINOANS as the dominant power in the Aegean from about 1450 BC. They were based in citadel cities with great palaces throughout mainland Greece, the most important of which included Mycenae, Tiryns, Pylos, Thebes, Gla and Athens. A prosperous and powerful civilization, the Mycenaeans were highly skilled artists and traders. Like those of the Minoans, Mycenaean palaces were centres of economic and political control. The Mycenaeans used a script called Linear B, which is similar to Minoan Linear A, but the language is a form of Greek. Around 1200–1100 BC many of the palaces were destroyed. The decline of the Mycenaean civilization remains a mystery, but it may be related to the invasion of the DORIANS from the N.

Mysore, a former regional state of SW India. Under HYDER ALI and his son, TIPU SULTAN, it was a major force in the area during the second half of the 18th century until defeated by the British in 1799.

Nabonidus (d. 530 BC), the last CHALDAEAN king of BABYLON (556–539 BC). He spent many years of his reign at Teima in Arabia. The Babylonian priests resented his neglect of the temple of the god Marduk and his absence from Babylon. He was ousted by the invasion of CYRUS the Achaemenid.

Nagasaki, a port on Kyushu island in Japan. It was hit by an atomic bomb dropped by the US air force on 9 August 1945, three days after the first atomic bomb attack on HIROSHIMA. Some 35,000 people were killed in the blast. The two explosions hastened the Japanese surrender and the end of WORLD WAR II. See PACIFIC CAMPAIGNS.

Nagorno Karabakh, a predominantly Armenian enclave within AZERBAIJAN, formed in 1923 on the orders of Stalin (see map, p. 43). It declared itself part of ARMENIA in 1987, leading to anti-Armenian pogroms in Azerbaijan and hostilities between the two republics.

Nagy, Imre (1896–1958), Hungarian Communist politician. He became prime minister in 1953 and introduced a programme of economic and political liberalization. When the HUNGARIAN REVOLUTION broke out in 1956 he promised free elections and an end to Soviet domination, but was overthrown by Soviet tanks and executed by the regime of János KÁDÁR in 1958.

Najd or **Nejd**, a former sultanate of central Arabia, ruled by the SA'UD family from the early 19th century. The Sa'udis extended their territory by conquest to found SAUDI ARABIA (1932).

Namibia, a republic of SW Africa. A German protectorate of South West Africa – excluding Walvis Bay, which had been British since 1878 – was declared in 1884. Seeking land for white settlement, the Germans established their rule after great bloodshed – over three-quarters of the Herero people were killed 1903–4. South Africa conquered the territory during World War I, and (after 1919) administered it under a LEAGUE OF NATIONS MANDATE. In 1966, the UN cancelled the mandate, but SOUTH AFRICA – which had refused to grant the territory independence – ignored the ruling. The main nationalist movement SWAPO began guerrilla warfare to free Namibia, the name adopted by the UN for the state. South Africa unsuccessfully attempted to exclude SWAPO's influence. After a ceasefire agreement in 1989, UN-supervised elections were held in November 1989 for a constituent assembly. Independence, under the presidency of SWAPO leader Sam NUJOMA, was achieved in March 1990.

Nanak (1469–1539), Indian religious teacher, the founder and first Guru of the SIKH faith. Coming from a Hindu background, he settled in PUNJAB and taught a faith that was neither Hindu nor Muslim, emphasizing personal devotion to God and strict personal morality.

Nanjing, Treaty of (1842), a treaty between Britain and CHINA, ending the first OPIUM WAR. China ceded HONG KONG to Britain and opened five 'Treaty Ports' – including Guangzhou (Canton) and Shanghai – to overseas traders, who were given immunity from Chinese law.

Nantes, Edict of (1598), a decree by HENRY IV terminating the FRENCH WARS OF RELIGION and defining the religious and political rights of the HUGUENOTS. The latter were granted freedom of worship and control of 200 cities. This last condition was incompatible with the centralizing policies of RICHELIEU and LOUIS XIV, the latter revoking the Edict in 1685.

Naples, kingdom of, a former state in S Italy, with Naples as its capital. Founded by Greek colonists around 600 BC, the city fell to Rome in 326 BC, but retained its Greek culture. Naples was under BYZANTINE rule from the 6th to the 8th centuries, and survived as an independent duchy until it became part of the Norman kingdom of Sicily in 1139. The kingdom passed to the HOHENSTAUFEN in the late 12th century. As part of the Kingdom of the Two SICILIES, it passed successively to the ANGEVINS, to the ARAGONESE, to Spain (from 1504), to Austria (during the War of the SPANISH SUCCESSION), to the BOURBONS in 1734, to NAPOLEON I in 1799, and to the Bourbons again in 1816. It fell to GARIBALDI in 1860, when the kingdom was united with the rest of ITALY.

Napoleon I (Napoleon Bonaparte; 1769–1821), emperor of the French (1804–14). He came to power in a military coup on 8 November 1799 (the coup of 18 Brumaire), and had himself crowned emperor of France in 1804, so ending the First Republic. He came to the country's attention in the REVOLUTIONARY WARS as a brilliant young general in the 1796–7 campaign against the Austrians in Italy, and his generalship won further plaudits during the NAPOLEONIC WARS. His military dictatorship saw the restoration of central control of local government, the end of representative assemblies and the creation of a new aristocracy. In 1810 he divorced his wife Josephine and married an Austrian princess, with the aim of producing an heir and securing peace with Austria. He abdicated in 1814, following his defeat at LEIPZIG, and was exiled to the French island of Elba. However, in March 1815 he exploited the unpopularity of the new Bourbon king, LOUIS XVIII, to return to France and seize power. His 'HUNDRED DAYS' ended with defeat at WATERLOO (June 1815) and permanent exile on St Helena. His most enduring achievements were his military reforms and the NAPOLEONIC CODE. See map, p. 29.

Napoleon III (Charles-Louis Napoléon Bonaparte; 1808–73), emperor of France (1852–70). He came to power by election to the presidency of the Second Republic (1848). He became emperor in 1852 following a coup of the previous year which established an authoritarian pseudo-democracy. Captured at SEDAN (1870) during the FRANCO-PRUSSIAN WAR, he spent the rest of his life in exile in England.

Napoleonic Code, the legal codification of the principles of the FRENCH REVOLUTION of 1789. Completed by 1804, it included religious toleration and the abolition of feudal rights, but emphasized the rights of property and stressed the rights of husbands and fathers (reducing the status of women). The 2251 articles of the code spread the basic principles of the Revolution across Europe.

Napoleonic Wars (1796–1815), the series of wars fought between France under NAPOLEON I and various coalitions of European powers (principally Britain, Prussia, Russia and Austria). France began the wars in an attempt to safeguard the Revolution, but soon went onto the offensive. In 1796–7 the young General Napoleon Bonaparte led a brilliant French campaign in Italy, forcing Austria to surrender Belgium in exchange for Venice. A Second Coalition of European powers was established to fight France, and although Napoleon was beaten by NELSON in ABOUKIR BAY (1798) he went on to achieve victory against the Austrians at Marengo (1800). Britain was forced to settle (the Treaty of Amiens, 1802), but declared war again in 1803. Napoleon's plans to invade Britain were frustrated by Nelson's defeat of the Franco-Spanish fleet at TRAFALGAR

(1805). The same year Napoleon embarked on a lightning campaign against the countries of the Third Coalition, defeating the Austrians at ULM (October) and an Austro-Russian army at AUSTERLITZ (December). Austria was forced to recognize French supremacy in Italy and Germany. Prussia decided to restrain Napoleon, but suffered a disastrous defeat at JENA (1806). In 1807 Russia too was beaten, settling with Napoleon and declaring war on Britain. Austria, defeated again in 1809, decided to join France. In 1808 Napoleon imposed his brother as king of Spain, sparking off a popular revolt. Henceforth vital French troops were held up in Spain, fighting the PENINSULAR WAR. Despite the French victory over the Russians at BORODINO in 1812, Napoleon was forced to retreat with heavy casualties. The Russian fiasco stimulated the formation of a Fourth Coalition, including Prussia and Austria and again financed by British subsidies. Fighting on two fronts – in Spain and Germany – Napoleon was defeated at LEIPZIG (1813). He abdicated and was exiled to Elba in 1814, but returned to France the following year to renew the war. His 'HUNDRED DAYS' ended with his defeat at WATERLOO by allied forces under WELLINGTON and BLÜCHER. A peace settlement was worked out at Paris and the Congress of VIENNA (1814–15).

Nara, the first capital of JAPAN (710–784).

Naseby, Battle of (1645), a decisive victory for the Parliamentary forces in the ENGLISH CIVIL WAR. The NEW MODEL ARMY under FAIRFAX and CROMWELL routed the Royalist forces under Prince RUPERT near Naseby in Northamptonshire, hastening the final defeat of CHARLES I.

Nassau Agreement (1962), an agreement between the USA and Britain in which the USA supplied Britain with Polaris missiles for its nuclear submarines. The agreement displeased DE GAULLE, who vetoed British entry into the EUROPEAN COMMUNITY, claiming Britain was not sufficiently orientated towards Europe.

Nasser, Gamal Abdel (1918–70), president of EGYPT (1956–70). He came to power following a military coup led by the Free Officers Movement in 1952, which forced the abdication of King FAROUK. In 1956 he established a republic and became president, initiating a programme of domestic reform and modernization. His nationalization of the Suez Canal precipitated the SUEZ crisis, from which he emerged as the dominant figure in the Arab world. Despite the failure of attempts at federation with SYRIA and the Egyptian defeat by Israel in the SIX DAY WAR, Nasser retained his position and reputation until his death.

Natal, a province on the E coast of the Republic of SOUTH AFRICA, a British colony until 1910. It includes numerous small areas of Zulu BANTUSTAN.

Natchez, a native North American people, maize farmers of the Southeast (SW Mississippi). They preserved many features of MISSISSIPPI CULTURE into the period of European contact until dispersed by the French in the early 18th century.

National Health Service (NHS), the system of national health care (financed by taxation) introduced in Britain by Aneurin BEVAN in 1948. The principle of totally free health care lasted only three years. See also WELFARE STATE.

nationalism, a feeling of common identity shared by a group of people with the same language, culture, ethnic origins and history. It manifests itself in a sense of loyalty to a 'mother country', particularly where that country has not yet become a state in its own right. Nationalist sentiment can lead to movements for national independence or secession. FASCISM contains elements of extreme nationalism.

National Party, an AFRIKANER-dominated political party in SOUTH AFRICA, originally founded in 1914. The 'purified' Nationalist Party of D.F. MALAN defeated SMUTS in the 1948 election, enacted the policy of APARTHEID, and has held uninterrupted power since. In 1991, under F.W. DE KLERK, the National Party removed basic Apartheid laws from the statute book, and began negotiations with the ANC for a non-racial South Africa. The party's new stance on constitutional matters led to defections to extreme right-wing parties. In 1994 the National Party was defeated by the AFRICAN NATIONAL CONGRESS in South Africa's first democratic general election.

National Socialism, see NAZI.

Nations, Battle of the, see LEIPZIG, BATTLE OF.

NATO (North Atlantic Treaty Organization), a military alliance of Western nations that came into force in August 1949. Its original members were Belgium, Canada, Denmark, France, Iceland, Italy, Luxembourg, the Netherlands, Norway, Portugal, the UK and the USA, with Greece, Turkey (1952), West Germany (1955, as reunified Germany from 1990) and Spain (1982) joining later. Members are pledged to come to each other's assistance in the event of armed aggression against them. During the COLD WAR NATO served as a guarantee of US commitment to Western Europe, particularly in the event of a Soviet attack from Eastern Europe. See also WARSAW PACT.

Navajo, a native N American people of the SW (Arizona and adjoining areas). Originally Athapascan migrants from the far N, they abandoned nomadic hunting-gathering c. 1700 and adopted farming techniques. See also NORTH AMERICAN INDIANS.

Navarino, Battle of (20 October 1827), a key battle of the GREEK WAR OF INDEPENDENCE in which a joint British, French and Russian naval force sank the Egyptian fleet in Navarino Bay.

Navarre, a former kingdom of SW France and N Spain. It was ruled by the kings of France from 1284 to 1316 and again after 1589, when Henry III of Navarre became HENRY IV of France, and united with France in 1620. The S (greater) part of Navarre was annexed by the Spanish kingdom of CASTILE in 1515. See map, p. 21.

Navigation Acts (1651, 1662 and 1696), English legislation aimed at destroying Dutch trade. They reserved the produce of England's colonies for England, and their carriage to English shipping. The Acts contributed to a series of ANGLO-DUTCH WARS.

Nazca, a pre-Columbian South American culture centred on S Peru, at its peak during the Classic phase of South American prehistory (AD 1–800).

Nazi, a member of the National Socialist German Worker's Party (NSDAP), which was founded in 1919. Adolf HITLER took over the party in 1921 and led the Nazis in the abortive MUNICH BEER-HALL PUTSCH in 1923. During his spell in prison he wrote *Mein Kampf,* which became a key document for Nazi policies. The unpopularity of the faltering

WEIMAR REPUBLIC and the hardships of the DEPRESSION were exploited by the Nazis, who made considerable electoral gains in 1932. The following year Hitler became chancellor by constitutional means, but used the burning of the REICHSTAG to claim dictatorial powers. After 1934 the move to totalitarianism was swift. The Nazis outlawed all other political parties, banned trade unions and used censorship to control information. Their regime was enforced by the SS and the GESTAPO. Rivals within the party were killed in the 'NIGHT OF THE LONG KNIVES' (1934). The persecution of Jews was legalized by the NUREMBERG LAWS, and led ultimately to the HOLOCAUST. Aggressive Nazi foreign policy – in the search for LEBENSRAUM – led to the outbreak of WORLD WAR II.

Nazi–Soviet Pact (23 August 1939), a non-aggression pact between NAZI Germany and the Soviet Union. The pact effectively partitioned POLAND between Germany and the Soviet Union; it also allowed STALIN to annex the independent Baltic republics of ESTONIA, LATVIA and LITHUANIA in 1940. However, in 1940 Germany invaded the Soviet Union, bringing the USSR into WORLD WAR II. See EASTERN FRONT CAMPAIGNS.

Ndebele or Matebele, a people of S Africa. Pushed N in the 1820s by both ZULU and BOER pressure, many eventually settled in Matebeleland (in modern ZIMBABWE) from the mid-1830s, dominating the local SHONA peoples.

Neanderthals, see HOMO SAPIENS NEANDERTHALENSIS.

Nebuchadnezzar II (d. 562 BC), CHALDAEAN king of BABYLON (604–562 BC). In 605 BC he defeated an Egyptian force at Carchemish and campaigned extensively in Syria and Palestine. In March 597 BC he captured JERUSALEM and took thousands of Jews, including the king, into exile in Babylon (the Babylonian Captivity). With his predecessor Nabopolassar, he rebuilt the city of Babylon, making it the largest and most magnificent city of the ancient world.

Necker, Jacques (1732–1804), Swiss Protestant banker and chief finance minister to LOUIS XVI (1777–81 and 1788–9). His use of loans rather than taxation to finance government contributed to his popularity at the beginning of the FRENCH REVOLUTION.

Nefertiti (14th century BC), the wife of the Egyptian pharaoh AKHENATEN.

Nehru, Jawaharlal (1889–1964), Indian statesman. He became a leader of the Indian National CONGRESS and worked with GANDHI in campaigns of civil disobedience from the 1920s, for which he was imprisoned several times by the British. As the first prime minister of independent INDIA (1947–64) he worked for a secular democratic state, embarked on a path of industrialization, and attempted to tackle the poverty problem with a series of five-year economic plans. He had to face conflicts with Pakistan over KASHMIR (1948) and with China over the N borders (1962). His daughter Indira GANDHI became Indian PM in 1966.

Nelson, Horatio, Viscount (1758–1805), the most successful British admiral of the NAPOLEONIC WARS. He abandoned the tactics of 18th-century naval warfare (mostly exchanges of broadsides between two opposing lines of ships), preferring – as at the battles of TRAFALGAR and the NILE – to break the enemy line at right angles and then engage in destructive fighting at close quarters. He was fatally wounded at Trafalgar, having lost his right eye and right arm in earlier engagements.

Neolithic, a period of prehistory that lasted from c. 9000 to 6000 BC in the Near East, and from c. 4000 to 2400 BC in Europe, the last division of the STONE AGE. Neolithic culture saw the appearance of primitive agriculture and the use of polished stone axes and pottery. Although it appeared first in the Near East, Neolithic culture developed independently in other parts of the world after the last ICE AGE. The spread of agriculture was relatively rapid: Neolithic sites in Greece start before 6000 BC and appear in Britain by 4000 BC. Farming hastened the decline of hunting societies and led to metalworking and the creation of cities, states and empires. By 6000 BC some substantial towns existed in the Near East, for instance at Çatal Hüyük in Turkey, and JERICHO in the Jordan valley. During the Neolithic period considerable social distinctions emerged along with increasingly centralized political power. These developments are associated with the building of large burial and ceremonial monuments in earth and stone that began in many parts of Europe at this time. See also BRONZE AGE.

Nepal, a Himalayan kingdom in S Asia. The Kathmandu Valley supported a Hindu-Buddhist culture by the 4th century AD. In 1768 the ruler of the principality of Gurkha in the W conquered the Valley, and began a phase of expansion that ended in defeat by the Chinese in Tibet (1792) and the British in India (1816). From 1846 to 1950 the Rana family held sway as hereditary chief ministers of a powerless monarchy. Their isolationist policy preserved Nepal's independence at the expense of its development. A brief experiment with democracy was followed by a re-assertion of royal autocracy (1960). Violent pro-democracy demonstrations (1990) forced the king to concede a democratic constitution. Multi-party elections were held in 1991.

Nerchinsk, Treaty of (1689), a treaty between Russia and QING China, fixing the Sino-Russian border to the N of the River Amur.

Nero (AD 37–68), Roman emperor (54–68), stepson of CLAUDIUS. His reign began well, but later degenerated into a catalogue of crimes (including the murder of his mother), extravagance and irresponsibility, leading to disaffection, conspiracies and revolts. Deserted by all, he committed suicide.

Nerva (c. AD 30–98), Roman emperor (96–98). A weak and ineffectual ruler, he only averted renewed civil war by adopting a popular general, TRAJAN, as his successor.

Nestorian Church, a Christian sect established by the followers of Nestorius (d. c. 451), who was ousted from the PATRIARCHATE of Constantinople for his heretical views on the nature of Christ and the Virgin Mary. The Church survived in Persia until the MONGOL invasions of the 14th century.

Netherlands, a kingdom of NW Europe (often referred to as Holland). See panel.

Neutrality Acts (1935–9), US legislation designed to prevent the USA from becoming embroiled in a European war. The first act (1935) banned loans and shipments of war materials to belligerents. The ISOLATIONIST impulse behind the legislation was undermined by F.D. ROOSEVELT's policy of LEND-LEASE.

Neville, Richard, see WARWICK, EARL OF.

New Amsterdam, see NEW YORK.

Newcastle, Thomas Pelham-Holles, Duke of (1693–1768), English WHIG prime minister (1754–6 and 1757–62). His second premiership, in coalition with the Elder PITT, was marked by English success in the SEVEN YEARS WAR.

New Deal (Works Project Administration), an economic and social programme launched in 1933 by F.D. ROOSEVELT to help the USA recover from the DEPRESSION. The Deal was characterized by a widespread extension of federal authority. It involved centralized regulation of production and prices, government-sponsored 'public works' projects for the unemployed, and large-scale federal industrial developments. With cuts to federal employees' salaries and war veterans' pensions to raise the necessary money, it was far from popular. Nonetheless, by 1934 unemployment – though still high – was falling, bank reserves were rising and bankruptcies were in decline.

New Economic Policy (NEP), a policy introduced in the USSR by LENIN in March 1921 in the aftermath of the naval mutiny at Kronstadt, permitting some private ownership of industries. It also allowed farmers to sell their crops, and led to the emergence of a class of kulaks (affluent peasant farmers). The NEP improved both industrial and agricultural output.

NETHERLANDS

Until 15th century: A patchwork of duchies, bishoprics and cities ruled the Netherlands. **15th century:** Most of the Netherlands was governed by the dukes of BURGUNDY. **16th century:** Control of the Netherlands – the present kingdom, plus BELGIUM and LUXEMBOURG – passed to the Spanish HABSBURGS. **1567–1648:** DUTCH REVOLT against Spanish rule, initially led by WILLIAM THE SILENT, became a lengthy struggle for independence. **17th century:** The Dutch dominated Europe's trade and financial life and created an overseas empire in the East Indies. **1648:** The independence of the UNITED PROVINCES of the Netherlands was recognized in the Peace of WESTPHALIA. **1652–4, 1665–7, 1672–4:** ANGLO-DUTCH WARS. **18th century:** Decline of the Dutch economy. **1795–1806:** The French invaded and ruled the country as the Batavian Republic. **1796–1815:** The Dutch lost important colonies to the British in the NAPOLEONIC WARS, but kept an empire in INDONESIA and the West Indies. **1806–10:** Netherlands ruled as the Kingdom of Holland under Louis Bonaparte. **1815:** The Congress of VIENNA united all three Low Countries in the Kingdom of the Netherlands under the House of ORANGE; Belgium broke away from the Kingdom in 1830 and Luxembourg in 1890. **1914–18:** Dutch remained neutral during World War I. **1940–5:** German occupation during World War II. **1948:** Foundation of BENELUX. **1949:** Dutch recognition of Indonesian independence after bitter colonial war. **1957:** Netherlands a founder member of the European Economic Community (EEC).

Newfoundland, an island province of CANADA. First discovered by Europeans in 1497, it was a focus for Anglo-French rivalry until sovereignty was granted to Britain in the Treaty of UTRECHT (1713–14). It did not officially join the Dominion of Canada until 1949.

New France, the collective name for the French empire in continental North America (1534–1763). Initially embracing the shores of the St Lawrence River, NEWFOUNDLAND and Acadia (NOVA SCOTIA), the territory expanded W under the impetus of the fur trade to include much of the Great Lakes region. Designated a royal province in 1663, the area became a focal point for Anglo-French rivalry in the 18th century and was ceded to Great Britain after the SEVEN YEARS WAR (1763).

New Granada, a former Spanish colony comprising present-day COLOMBIA. It became a viceroyalty in 1717.

Ne Win (1911–), Burmese soldier and statesman. After seizing power in March 1962 he abrogated the 1948 constitution, disbanding political parties and promulgating a constitution to strengthen the military's political control. He retired from the presidency in 1981 but continued to wield considerable power behind the scenes. See MYANMAR.

New Model Army, the Parliamentary army created in 1645 during the ENGLISH CIVIL WAR. The New Model Army, whose members were known as 'Ironsides', itself became a powerful – and often radical – political force until the RESTORATION.

New Orleans, Battle of (8 January 1815), a British defeat at the hands of American forces led by General Andrew JACKSON. Although the battle was fought after the Treaty of GHENT had concluded the WAR OF 1812, it catapulted Jackson to national fame and was an important factor in his 1828 presidential election victory.

New Right, an informal and diffuse conservative movement that exercised a major influence on US politics during the late 20th century. Essentially a reaction to the liberal statist reforms of the 1960s, it drew its strength from a number of sources, notably fundamentalist Christians and alienated white middle-class voters. The presidency of Ronald REAGAN in the USA and the premiership of Margaret THATCHER in the UK represented the high point of New Right influence in the 1980s.

New South Wales, the original British colony in AUSTRALIA (1788). It once included all of E Australia.

New Spain, a former Spanish viceroyalty comprising present-day MEXICO and large parts of what are now the SW states of the USA.

New York, one of the original 13 states of the USA. Originally the Dutch colony of the New Netherlands (whose capital New Amsterdam was on the site of present-day New York City), the region passed into British hands in 1664 and was the scene of important military operations during the American War of INDEPENDENCE.

New Zealand, a country in the S Pacific and an independent member of the COMMONWEALTH. See panel p.184.

Ney, Michel, duc d'Elchingen (1769–1815), marshal of France. He served with distinction in the NAPOLEONIC WARS, earning the epithet 'bravest of the brave' at BORODINO in

NEW ZEALAND

8th century: The MAORIS migrated from Polynesia to New Zealand. **1642:** The Dutch explorer Abel TASMAN discovered the W coast of South Island. **1769–70:** Captain James COOK circumnavigated both main islands; his descriptions of the country encouraged colonization. **By beginning of 19th century:** A number of whaling stations had been established in New Zealand by Australian interests. **1840:** North Island was ceded to the British Crown by Maori chiefs under the Treaty of WAITANGI (South Island was claimed by right of discovery). New Zealand governed as part of NEW SOUTH WALES. **1841:** Establishment of separate colonial government. **1840s:** Beginning of ANGLO-MAORI WARS. **1872:** Maori guerrilla activity suppressed. **Late 19th century:** The discovery of gold and introduction of refrigerated ships to export meat and dairy products stimulated the colonization and economy of South Island. **1907:** New Zealand granted DOMINION status, though the country did not formally acknowledge its independent status until 1947. **By 1911:** Population boosted by British immigrants to one million. **1914–18:** New Zealand fought as a British ally in WORLD WAR I, achieving distinction in the GALLIPOLI campaign (1915). **1939–45:** New Zealand's security threatened by Japan in WORLD WAR II. **Since 1945:** Postwar alliance with Australia and USA in ANZUS pact. **Since 1973:** New trading links with the Far and Middle East.

1812. He joined the restored Bourbon army in 1814 but defected to NAPOLEON in the WATERLOO campaign. He was shot for treason following Napoleon's defeat and abdication.

Nez Perce, a native North American people, living in the Plateau area of the West (Idaho and adjoining areas). Originally semi-nomadic hunter-gatherers, they adopted a horse-riding, buffalo-hunting way of life after c. 1750. See NORTH AMERICAN INDIANS.

Ngo Dinh Diem (1901–63), president of South VIETNAM (1955–63). He began military action against VIET CONG guerrillas, but his repressive regime was brought down, and Diem killed, in a US-backed coup in November 1963.

Nguyen Van Thieu (1923–), South Vietnamese soldier and politician, president (1967–75). Involved in the military coup that overthrew NGO DINH DIEM, he took control of South Vietnam and spent much of his energies fighting the VIET CONG in the VIETNAM WAR. He resigned in 1975 with the Communists closing in on the South Vietnamese capital.

Nicaean Empire (1204–61), a Greek empire based on Nicaea (modern Iznik in Turkey), which became a centre of BYZANTINE resistance after the capture of CONSTANTINOPLE by Frankish Crusaders (1204) and the establishment of the LATIN EMPIRE.

Nicaragua, a republic of CENTRAL AMERICA. In 1502 Columbus landed in Nicaragua, which remained a Spanish possession until independence was gained in 1821. Independent Nicaragua witnessed strife between conservatives and liberals. Early in the 20th century, the political situation deteriorated, provoking American intervention – US marines were based in Nicaragua from 1912 to 1925, and again from 1927 until 1933. General Anastasio SOMOZA became president in 1937. Employing dictatorial methods, members of the Somoza family, or their supporters, remained in power until overthrown by a popular uprising led by the SANDINISTA guerrilla army in 1979. Accusing the Sandinistas of introducing Communism, the USA imposed a trade embargo on Nicaragua, making it increasingly dependent on Cuba and the USSR. Right-wing Contra guerrillas, financed by the USA, fought the Sandinistas from bases in HONDURAS. A ceasefire between the Contras and Sandinistas was agreed in 1989. In free presidential elections in February 1990, the Sandinista incumbent Daniel Ortega was defeated by Violeta Chamorro of the opposition coalition.

Nicholas I (1796–1855), tsar of RUSSIA (1825–55). His reign was characterized by unrelenting repression of dissent. Nicholas' foreign policy was formed by his hatred of revolution and support of the Restoration settlement of 1815.

Nicholas II (1868–1918), last tsar of RUSSIA (1894–1917). Autocratic and incompetent, his loss of control of his country precipitated the RUSSIAN REVOLUTIONS of 1905 and 1917. In March 1917, when the revolution began, he abdicated, and in July 1918 he and his family were murdered by the BOLSHEVIKS, ending the ROMANOV dynasty.

Nicopolis, Battle of (23 September 1396), the defeat of a Crusader army under SIGISMUND, king of Hungary, by the OTTOMAN Turks at the town of Nicopolis on the River Danube (see map, p. 26).

Niger, a republic of the Sahel in W Africa. From the 15th century, the area was dominated in turn by the sultanate of Agadès, HAUSA kingdoms and the Nigerian empire of Sokoto. The French territory of Niger was proclaimed in 1901, but much of the country was not pacified until 1920. Independence was gained in 1960. After the economy was wracked by a prolonged drought, the military took power in a coup (1974). Civilian rule was restored in 1989. Following pro-democracy demonstrations (1990–1), free elections for a constituent assembly were held in 1993.

Nigeria, a republic in W Africa. See panel.

Nightingale, Florence (1820–1910), British nurse, popularly known as the 'Lady with the Lamp'. Her work in organizing hospitals for the British wounded during the CRIMEAN WAR (1854–6) brought her immense public acclaim.

'Night of the Long Knives' (30 June 1934), the liquidation by HITLER'S SS of the leadership of the BROWNSHIRTS. Ernst Röhm, leader of the Brownshirts and potential rival to Hitler, was murdered along with 150 of his followers.

nihilism, a doctrine rejecting all traditional values and institutions and advocating the violent overthrow of the latter, especially as held by Russian revolutionary extremists in the late 19th century.

Nijmegen, Peace of (1678–9), the series of treaties ending LOUIS XIV'S Dutch War (1672–8), in which Louis acquired FRANCHE COMTÉ from Spain.

Nile, Battle of the (also called the Battle of Aboukir Bay; 1 August 1798), a naval battle during the NAPOLEONIC WARS in

NIGERIA

11th–14th centuries: The KANEM empire flourished in N Nigeria, during which time Islam was introduced. **From the 15th century:** Various HAUSA kingdoms emerged in the NW; YORUBA kingdoms and the Kingdom of BENIN occupied the SW, and Ibo kingdoms the SE; arrival of Portuguese explorers. **From 1713:** Nigerian slave trade dominated by Britain. **Early 19th century:** Hausa kingdoms conquered by the FULANI empire. **1807:** British slave trading ended; British traders and explorers penetrated the interior. **1861:** British acquired Lagos. **1885:** British protectorate established on the coast. **1886:** The commercial Royal Niger Company colonized the interior during the SCRAMBLE FOR AFRICA. **1900:** Nigerian territories surrendered to the British crown as the protectorate of Northern Nigeria. **1914:** British coastal protectorate and inland colonies united to form Nigeria. **1960:** Independence. **1963:** Nigeria became a republic with a federal structure to accommodate different ethnic groups. **1966:** PM Tafawa Balewa assassinated in coup; counter-coup brought General GOWON to power. **1967–70:** Bitter civil war as Eastern Region – the homeland of the Ibo – attempted to secede as BIAFRA. **1975:** Gowon overthrown in coup. **1985:** Military coup brought General Ibrahim Babangida to power; further reforms to federal structure increased number of states to 30 (1991). **1993:** Scheduled return of civilian rule delayed.

which the British commander NELSON destroyed the fleet that had carried the French army to Egypt.

Nilo-Saharans, a group of black African peoples who originated in the Nile Valley and spread W into W Africa and S into present-day Kenya and Tanzania after 3000 BC.

Nimeiri, Gaafar Mohammed Al- (1930–), Sudanese soldier and statesman. He led a successful coup in May 1969 and subsequently elevated himself to the presidency. He fled to Egypt after his overthrow in a coup in 1985.

Nimitz, Chester William (1885–1966), commander of the US Pacific fleet from 1941. He played a large part in the defeat of JAPAN in WORLD WAR II, successfully leading American forces in the Battle of LEYTE GULF (1944). See PACIFIC CAMPAIGNS.

Ninety-five Theses, the criticisms of the Roman Catholic Church nailed to the door of the castle church at Wittenberg by Martin LUTHER in October 1517. Luther's action is traditionally regarded as the starting point of the REFORMATION.

Nineveh, a city of ancient ASSYRIA. It became the capital of Assyria under SENNACHERIB, who initiated a large building programme. Sacked by the MEDES in 612 BC, it never recaptured its prestige. See map, p. 10.

Nine Years War (1688–97), one of the wars of LOUIS XIV. Fearing the growing power of Austria, Louis launched a pre-emptive attack on the Rhineland in 1688. His aggression led to the formation of a 'Grand Alliance' of England, the United Provinces, Austria, Spain and Savoy. A leading role in directing the alliance was played by WILLIAM III, king of England and effective ruler of the United Provinces. The stalemate of the war was finally broken by the superior financial resources of England and the United Provinces, and a settlement was reached in the Treaty of RYSWICK.

Nixon, Richard Milhous (1913–94), 37th president of the USA (1969–74). A conservative Republican, he was vice-president to EISENHOWER but was defeated by KENNEDY in the 1960 presidential election. He took America out of the VIETNAM WAR during his second term, but is chiefly remembered for the WATERGATE scandal which led to his resignation in 1974. Watergate and the saturation bombing of CAMBODIA have perhaps obscured the foreign-policy successes of the Nixon years: agreements with the USSR aided DETENTE, while the Communist regime in the People's Republic of China was recognized by the USA as the official government of China.

Nkomo, Joshua Mqabuko Nyongolo (1917–), Zimbabwean politician. See ZIMBABWE.

Nkrumah, Kwame (1909–72), Ghanaian statesman, prime minister of the Gold Coast (1952–7) and first prime minister of independent GHANA (1957–60). He was president from 1960 until his deposition in 1966.

NKVD (Russian acronym for 'People's Commissariat of Internal Affairs'), Soviet secret police agency created in 1934 from the former OGPU. It oversaw all internal security in the USSR as well as coordinating foreign intelligence gathering, and was involved in STALIN'S purges. It merged with the MVD (Ministry of the Interior) in 1946 and finally became the KGB in 1953.

Nok culture, the earliest identifiable Iron Age culture of W African sculpture, dated to the last few centuries BC.

Non-Aligned Movement (NAM), a conference meeting every three years to promote world peace, to reject the system of world power blocs and help bring about a more even distribution of the world's wealth. Initially dominated by developing countries, such as India, it has been increasingly attended by oil-producing countries. However, with the end of the COLD WAR, the future of the movement is in doubt.

Norman Conquest (1066), the conquest of England by the Norman WILLIAM I (later known as 'the Conqueror'). William claimed that he had been made heir to the English throne by EDWARD the Confessor, and invaded England to wrest the throne from Edward's successor HAROLD II. Norman success at the Battle of HASTINGS secured the throne for William. Until 1071 the Norman grip on England was severely tested by revolts and Danish invasions, but this opposition hastened the destruction of the English ruling class and its replacement by a new Norman-French nobility. The Norman Conquest initially involved only some 10,000 newcomers. There were many things the settlers did not wish to change. The more sophisticated administrative structures of Anglo-Saxon England were taken over virtually unchanged, and these formed the framework of English government not just in the Middle Ages but down to the present day. DOMESDAY BOOK, a vast survey of property, land and tax liability, testifies to Norman efficiency and attention to detail, though it was largely based on pre-Norman administrative records.

intermarriage between Normans and Anglo-Saxons, the modification of existing institutions, and the co-existence of Norman French and the Old English language led in the long-term to a hybrid administration and culture. In addition to their cultural legacy, the establishment of Norman kings in England who still held vast possessions in France was to create conflict between the two countries, culminating in the HUNDRED YEARS WAR.

Normandy, a former independent duchy in NW FRANCE (see map, p. 18). In 911 the Viking ROLLO was granted control of the lower Seine valley by Charles the Simple. Rollo's descendants and their followers strengthened their grip on the Channel coast to create the duchy of Normandy, 'the land of the Northmen'. Under Duke WILLIAM (later known as 'the Conqueror'), it was forged into a powerful principality, William harnessing the forces of internal disorder to wage a successful war of conquest against England (see NORMAN CONQUEST). Other Normans, in acts of private enterprise, were active in Spain fighting the Muslims, and in S Italy, where they began to carve out territories for themselves from the 1040s. By 1071, Robert GUISCARD had conquered the BYZANTINE provinces of Apulia and Calabria. In 1091 his brother Roger completed the conquest of Sicily from the Arabs. Eventually Roger's son, ROGER II, ousted his kinsmen and took control of all the Norman possessions in S Italy. However, Norman control in S Italy was to be short-lived; by the end of the century it was in the hands of the HOHENSTAUFEN emperors. Normandy was conquered by PHILIP II AUGUSTUS of France in 1204, but was recaptured by HENRY V of England in the Hundred Years War. It was finally reunited with France in 1450.

Normandy Landings (June 1944), the start of the Allied invasion of Western Europe in WORLD WAR II ('Operation Overlord'). On 6 June 1944 (D-DAY) Allied forces crossed the Channel under the command of General EISENHOWER to make amphibious landings on the Normandy coast. Beachheads were seized and, although fighting was difficult, the Allied armies broke out in August, surrounding substantial German forces in a pocket near Falaise. Paris was liberated on 25 August, and, as further Allied formations moved up the Rhône valley from landing beaches in S France (secured on 15 August in Operation Dragoon), most of France, Belgium, Luxembourg and the S Netherlands was seized. See NORTHWEST EUROPE CAMPAIGN and map, p. 39.

Norsemen, see VIKINGS.

North, Frederick, Lord (1732–92), British prime minister (1770–81). His early successes were obscured by his mishandling of the American War of INDEPENDENCE. Although supported by GEORGE III, he lost the confidence of Parliament after the British defeat at YORKTOWN, and resigned.

North African campaigns, a series of military campaigns in N Africa in WORLD WAR II in which the Allies fought to gain control of the S coast of the Mediterranean as a springboard for an invasion of S Europe (see map, p. 39). Following an Italian invasion of Egypt in September 1940, the British launched a counterattack in December that developed into a successful invasion of E Libya. However, a German attack by the *Afrika Korps* under ROMMEL in February 1941 forced the British to retreat to the Egyptian border. A British offensive in November 1941 (Operation Crusader) relieved the besieged port of TOBRUK and forced Rommel back, but his riposte in early 1942 caused the British to retreat again, this time as far as Gazala. A further German attack in May 1942 pushed the British back into Egypt, but the tide was turned at EL ALAMEIN in late October, when forces under General MONTGOMERY defeated an overstretched *Afrika Korps*. Montgomery's forces pushed W and were joined by General EISENHOWER'S forces in Operation Torch. German troops finally withdrew to Italy in May 1943. See ITALIAN CAMPAIGN.

North American Indians, the native peoples of North America. On reaching the New World in 1492, COLUMBUS mistakenly believed he had reached India and referred to the natives as 'Indians'. The million or so inhabitants of North America in 1492 gained their living in a wide variety of ways. In and around the Mississippi basin and over to the E coast were well-established farmers relying largely – but not exclusively – on agriculture for their subsistence. In the SW were other farmers living in a more hostile and arid environment. Along the NW coastline were prosperous villagers who relied on the ample resources of the sea and rivers for their main food supply. Elsewhere, life was more mobile: following game on the Plains or gathering plants in the deserts and hills W of the Rockies. There were hunters in the forests beyond the Great Lakes, and up towards the Arctic were the INUIT (ESKIMO) fishers and hunters. The villagers and some of the more organized bands of hunter-gatherers were grouped into tribes. In the E and the NW tribes grouped themselves into more permanent confederations for the purpose of waging war. European settlement brought disease, war and dispossession. Disease was initially the most damaging to native society, but dispossession of land was more destructive in the longer term. As the line of settlement advanced, tribes migrated and regrouped. Remodelled tribes such as the IROQUOIS Confederation in the E fought a long rearguard action throughout the 17th and 18th centuries, waging war, negotiating concessions and exploiting divisions between the British and the French. Further W on the Great Plains the acquisition of horses and firearms gave tribes such as the BLACKFOOT the advantage over both the buffalo and neighbouring settled tribes. In the first half of the 19th century all of the remaining tribes E of the Mississippi were dispossessed and moved further W. The 'Five Civilized Indian Nations' of the SE – CREEK, CHEROKEE, CHOCTAW, CHICKASAW and SEMINOLE – were removed to Oklahoma in the 1850s. By the end of the 19th century the only native American peoples still pursuing traditional lifestyles and living in the areas they inhabited before the Europeans came were the PUEBLO farmers of the SW, and the hunters and fishers of the NW and far N.

North Atlantic Treaty Organization, see NATO.

Northern Ireland, a province of the UNITED KINGDOM in the NE of IRELAND. The kingdom of ULSTER flourished in what is now Northern Ireland before the Vikings began to raid the region about 800. The Danes founded several coastal towns but were finally defeated c. 1014. Anglo-Norman adventurers began their involvement in Ulster in the 12th century, but Ulster remained a centre of unrest and resentment of

English rule. After a major revolt at the end of the 16th century, a plantation of Scottish Protestant settlers was made in Ulster under JAMES I. These settlers were the ancestors of Ulster's large Protestant population. Ireland was united with England in 1801 in the United Kingdom, but Ulster's non-Roman Catholic majority stood apart from the growing nationalist movement throughout the 19th century. When the Irish Free State (the forerunner of the Republic of IRELAND) was established in 1922, the six counties of Northern Ireland remained part of the United Kingdom. From 1969 bitter conflict resurfaced in the province as Roman Catholics – seeking unity with the Republic of Ireland – clashed with Protestant Loyalists intent upon preserving the link with Britain. British troops were stationed in Northern Ireland to keep order and to defeat the terrorist violence of the IRISH REPUBLICAN ARMY and Protestant paramilitary groups.

Northern War (1700–21), a conflict in which SWEDEN on one side opposed Russia, Denmark, Poland and Saxony on the other. CHARLES XII of Sweden won some notable victories, defeating Peter the Great at Narva. But the war stretched Sweden's resources and Swedish forces were defeated by the Russians at POLTAVA in 1709. When Prussia and Hanover – supported by the British fleet – joined her enemies, Sweden's fate was sealed. The Swedish empire collapsed, losing Bremen and Verden to Hanover, Pomerania to Prussia, and the Baltic provinces to Russia in the Treaty of NYSTAD.

Northern Wei, a dynasty of nomad origins ruling N China (AD 386–533). The Wei were one of a number of nomad dynasties that ruled the Yellow River valley – the heartland of Chinese culture – for nearly 300 years.

North German Confederation, a Prussian-dominated association of N German states formed after the AUSTRO-PRUSSIAN WAR of 1866.

North Korea, see KOREA, DEMOCRATIC PEOPLE'S REPUBLIC OF.

Northumbria, the northern kingdom of ANGLO-SAXON England. Settled by the ANGLES during the period of Anglo-Saxon invasions, Northumbria became a kingdom and was Christianized by St Aidan and his successors in the mid-7th century. VIKING invaders overran the kingdom in 867. Although reconquered by WESSEX in the 10th century, and remaining a distinct earldom, it never regained its previous independence. It was disputed between England and Scotland for several centuries before finally becoming part of England.

Northwest Europe Campaign (1944–5), a military campaign in WORLD WAR II following the Normandy Campaign (see NORMANDY LANDINGS). In September 1944 MONTGOMERY, commanding the British-Canadian 21st Army Group, tried to maintain momentum by using a large parachute force to seize bridges in the N Netherlands (Operation Market Garden), but when this failed at ARNHEM on the lower Rhine, the Allied advance stalled. As autumn turned to winter, allied units in NW Europe fought bitterly for small gains around Aachen, in the Hurtgen Forest, and in Alsace-Lorraine, tempting the Germans to mount a counterattack in December 1944 in the ARDENNES. It took the Allies until mid-January 1945 to win the 'Battle of the Bulge', but by then the Germans – under heavy attack from the E by the Soviets – were close to defeat. Massive fleets of British and US bombers intensified their attacks on German cities – destroying DRESDEN on 13/14 February – while ground units advanced to the W bank of the Rhine in March, preparatory to assault crossings in the N and S. Berlin was left to the Soviets, allowing EISENHOWER to commit the bulk of his forces to central and S Germany. At the same time, Allied armies in Italy pushed towards the Alps (see ITALIAN CAMPAIGN), and by early May direct connections had been made between Allied and Soviet units on the Elbe. With Berlin in Soviet hands, the Germans surrendered unconditionally on 8 May.

Northwest Frontier, the strategically important mountainous region of N PAKISTAN between Afghanistan and KASHMIR, inhabited mainly by the PATHANS. It was under British control 1849–1947 and is now a province of Pakistan.

Northwest Passage, the route to Asia around the N coast of North America, proposed by Sir Humphrey Gilbert (1572), and unsuccessfully attempted by the English explorers Martin Frobisher (1576–8) and John Davis (1585–7) and others.

Norway, a kingdom of NW Europe. See panel.

Nova Scotia, a maritime province of E CANADA that was the scene of bitter Anglo-French rivalry until Great Britain's sovereignty was confirmed under the Treaty of PARIS (1763). It was the first Canadian colony to achieve 'responsible' government (1848) and acceded to confederation in 1867.

Novgorod, a city-state of medieval Russia (see map, p. 18). It bowed to MONGOL overlordship only in the later Middle Ages. After years of struggle with Muscovy, it was incorporated into the grand duchy of MUSCOVY by IVAN III in 1478.

Nubia, an ancient region of NE Africa in the N of modern Sudan, known as 'Cush' by the ancient Egyptians. By 800 BC, the Nubians had established a powerful kingdom which

NORWAY

9th–11th centuries: Expansion of the VIKINGS from their Scandinavian homelands; Norway divided into a number of warring small kingdoms. **1015–28:** Norway united under OLAF II, who converted many Norwegians to Christianity. **1028–35:** Danish rule. **From 12th century:** Civil wars brought instability and disunity. **1217–63:** Norway again united under the reign of Haakon IV. **1397–1523:** Norway, Sweden and Denmark brought together under a single monarch in the Danish-dominated Union of KALMAR; conversion to Lutheranism. **1523–1814:** After the dissolution of the Union, Norway was ruled by Danish governors. **1814:** Norway ceded to Sweden. **1884:** Norway gained 'responsible government'. **1905:** Sweden gave up its claims to Norway and allowed a peaceful separation of the two countries. **1940–5:** German occupation during World War II; puppet government of Vidkun QUISLING. **1972:** Norway rejected EUROPEAN COMMUNITY membership. **1992:** Norway reapplied to join EC.

supplied EGYPT with a dynasty, the 25th, in the century around 700 BC. The kingdom lasted until AD 350, when it was destroyed by AXUM. One of the three Christian empires that emerged was defeated by an Egyptian army in 652. The N was taken by the MAMLUKS in the 13th century and the S by the Funj kingdom in the 16th century.

Nuclear Test Ban Treaty (1963), an international agreement, signed by the USA, UK and USSR, prohibiting the testing of nuclear devices in the atmosphere or in outer space or under water. In 1974 the USA and USSR agreed not to test devices on earth larger than 150 kilotons.

Nujoma, Sam (1929–), first president of independent NAMIBIA (1990–). He helped found SWAPO in 1959, and was active as a guerrilla leader during his period in exile in Zambia and Angola until 1990.

Numidia, an ancient kingdom in N Africa to the W of Carthage (see map, p. 13). From the time of HANNIBAL it was ruled by native kings who supported Rome and enjoyed its protection. Under the empire it became a Roman province. See also JUGURTHA.

Nuremberg Laws (1935), laws passed by the NAZIS depriving Jews of citizenship rights. Jews were forbidden to practise certain professions, to marry non-Jews, or to join the armed services.

Nuremberg rallies, open-air conventions held annually by the NAZI Party in the 1930s in Nuremberg, Bavaria, used by HITLER to deliver major political speeches.

Nuremberg Trials (1945–6), the trials held in Nuremberg after World War II, in which NAZI leaders were convicted by an Allied tribunal of WAR CRIMES, and crimes against peace and humanity, several of them being sentenced to death. Japan's wartime leaders were convicted in similar trials in Tokyo.

Nyasaland, see MALAWI.

Nyerere, Julius Kambarage (1922–), Tanzanian statesman. He was first prime minister (1961) and president (1962) of independent Tanganyika (1961), and – following the union of Tanganyika and Zanzibar – president of TANZANIA (1964–85).

Nystad, Treaty of (1721), the treaty ending the NORTHERN WAR. Russia acquired the Baltic provinces (modern-day Estonia, Latvia and Lithuania) from Sweden, taking a significant step towards great-power status.

OAS, see ORGANIZATION OF AMERICAN STATES.

OAU, see ORGANIZATION OF AFRICAN UNITY.

Obote, Milton (1924–), Ugandan statesman, prime minister (1962–6), president (1966–71 and 1980–5). He was deposed by Idi AMIN in 1971, but returned from exile to take up the presidency again after Amin's downfall. He was overthrown by the military in 1985. See UGANDA.

Obrenović, a Serbian dynasty founded by Milos Obrenović I (1780–1860). It ruled SERBIA 1817–42 and 1858–1903, alternating with the rival KARAGEORGEVIĆ dynasty.

O'Connell, Daniel (1775–1847), Irish nationalist and barrister who founded the Catholic Association in 1823 to mobilize support for CATHOLIC EMANCIPATION. Although unable to take his seat as he was a Catholic, he was elected MP for Co. Clare in 1828. Catholic Emancipation was conceded in the following year. O'Connell later campaigned for the repeal of the Act of UNION of 1801.

Octavian, see AUGUSTUS.

October Revolution, the seizure of power in Russia by Lenin's BOLSHEVIKS in November (October according to the Julian calendar) 1917. See RUSSIAN REVOLUTIONS.

Oder-Neisse Line, the present-day border between Germany and Poland, formed by the Oder and Neisse rivers, agreed at the POTSDAM Conference in July 1945.

Odoacer (c. 433–93), Gothic king who became effective ruler in Italy when he overthrew the last Roman emperor in 476. His capital at Ravenna was besieged by THEODORIC, king of the Ostrogoths. He surrendered in 493 on the condition that he retain half of Italy. However, Theodoric murdered him and took control of the entire area.

Odo Nobunaga (1534–82), military ruler of JAPAN (1578–82), who fought his way to supreme power between 1559 and 1578. He was assassinated before his rule over the whole of Japan could be consolidated.

OECD, see ORGANIZATION FOR ECONOMIC COOPERATION AND DEVELOPMENT.

Offa (d. 796), king of MERCIA (757–96), who constructed the earthwork known as Offa's Dyke between England and Wales.

Ogodei (1185–1241), MONGOL ruler and son and successor of GENGHIS KHAN, whose policy of conquest he continued.

OGPU (Russian acronym for 'United State Political Administration'), the Soviet secret police agency from 1923 to 1934, when it was succeeded by the NKVD.

O'Higgins, Bernardo (1778–1842), Chilean revolutionary, born of an Irish father. He led the struggle for independence from Spain and was the first president of CHILE (1817–23). His economic and social reforms met with opposition and he resigned in 1823 before going into exile.

Okinawa, an island between Taiwan and Japan. Strategically a vital location with bases commanding the approaches to Japan, Okinawa was captured from the Japanese by US forces after fierce resistance in June 1945 at the end of WORLD WAR II. See PACIFIC CAMPAIGNS.

Olaf II, St (Haraldsson; c. 995–1028), king of NORWAY (1015–28), where he attempted to stamp out paganism. Driven out by CNUT, he died in battle attempting to regain his kingdom from the Danes.

Oldowan, the earliest stone tool-making tradition, named after the OLDUVAI GORGE, and starting contemporary with *Homo habilis* (see EVOLUTION). Simple flakes were struck from pieces of stone for cutting various materials.

Olduvai Gorge, the best-known early human fossil site in Africa, part of the Great Rift Valley System in Tanzania. It has revealed fossil remains of three types of hominid – AUSTRALOPITHECINES, *Homo habilis* and HOMO ERECTUS – as well as animal bones and stone artefacts.

Olmec, a pre-Columbian Meso-American culture, centred on lowland E Mexico. Olmec culture was a major influence during the Formative phase of Meso-American prehistory (1000 BC–AD 300).

Oman, a SULTANATE of SW Asia. Persia ruled Oman from the 4th century AD until Muslim armies invaded, bringing Islam in the 7th century. The area's flourishing trade with the E attracted the Portuguese (1507), who founded Muscat and occupied the coast until 1650. Ahmad ibn Sa'id, who became Imam in 1749, founded the present dynasty. His successors built an empire including the Kenyan coast and ZANZIBAR, but in 1861 Zanzibar and Oman separated. A British presence was established in the 19th century and Oman did not regain complete independence until 1951. Sultan Qaboos – who came to power in a palace coup in 1970 – has modernized and developed Oman. In the 1970s South YEMEN supported left-wing separatist guerrillas in the S province of Dhofar, but the revolt was suppressed with military assistance from the UK.

Omri, king of ISRAEL (c. 876–c. 869 BC) and father of AHAB. He established his capital at SAMARIA.

OPEC, see ORGANIZATION OF PETROLEUM EXPORTING COUNTRIES.

Opium Wars (1839–42 and 1856–60), two wars fought between Britain and CHINA. The first war broke out when the Chinese imperial government acted to prevent British opium imports. The war revealed the weakness of Chinese military power and enabled the British to impose the first of the 'Unequal Treaties' (the Treaty of NANJING), regulating trade on European terms and securing European control over five 'Treaty Ports'. Continuing pressure from Western powers for more trading concessions led to a second war which saw an Anglo-French army march on Beijing and occupy the seat of imperial government. Further unequal treaties followed, with Treaty Ports conceded to all Western powers.

Orange Free State, an inland province of the Republic of SOUTH AFRICA, a former independent AFRIKANER (Boer) republic (1854–1900) and, after the Second BOER WAR, a British colony (1900–10).

Orange, House of, a European princely family whose territories were originally centred on Orange in S France. William of Nassau succeeded to the title of Prince of Orange in 1544, and as WILLIAM THE SILENT played a leading role in the DUTCH REVOLT against Spain. His successors were prominent both in Dutch domestic politics and in wider European affairs, WILLIAM III of Orange becoming king of England in 1689. The Princes of Orange became hereditary monarchs of the new kingdom of the Netherlands in 1815.

Oregon Boundary Dispute (1843–6), a dispute between Britain and the USA over territory in the NW previously jointly occupied by the two states. Compromise was reached in 1846, when the USA received a large portion of the disputed territory (now the US states of Oregon, Washington, Idaho and parts of Montana and Wyoming).

Organization for Economic Cooperation and Development (OECD), an organization founded in 1961 to replace the Organization for European Economic Cooperation, which had been established in connection with the US MARSHALL PLAN in 1945. It aims to encourage economic and social welfare in member-states and to stimulate aid to Third World countries. Its membership has grown from the original 20 to 24 states.

Organization of African Unity (OAU), an organization of 32 African states founded in 1963. Chief among its objectives have been the eradication of colonialism, and the promotion of economic and political cooperation between member-states. Since foundation the OAU has grown to include all the African states except South Africa. Morocco, a founder-member, withdrew in 1985.

Organization of American States (OAS), an organization established in 1948 to promote solidarity amongst the states of the Americas. Its 32 members include the USA as well as Latin American and Caribbean states.

Organization of Petroleum Exporting Countries (OPEC), an organization founded in Baghdad, Iraq, in 1960 with the aim of coordinating the petroleum-producing and exporting policies of its 13 member-states: Algeria, Ecuador, Gabon, Indonesia, Iran, Iraq, Kuwait, Libya, Nigeria, Qatar, Saudi Arabia, the United Arab Emirates and Venezuela. It sprang to prominence during the 1973 ARAB–ISRAELI WAR, when members restricted the supply and quadrupled the price of their oil exports, causing serious economic problems for the consumer nations of the West.

Orkhan (1326–60), the son of OSMAN I and 'Bey' of the OTTOMAN Turks (1326–60). His reign saw the expulsion of the Byzantine Empire from Asia Minor.

Orléans or ***Bourbon-Orléans,*** the junior – and (after 1883) only surviving – branch of the French royal house of BOURBON. The Orléanist LOUIS-PHILIPPE reigned from 1830 to 1848.

Orthodox Church, a family of Christian churches in Eastern Europe under the general primacy of the PATRIARCHATE of Constantinople. From 1453 the Russian Church has been its largest member. The Orthodox Church developed from the Greek Church of the BYZANTINE Empire. The Greek Church finally broke with Rome in 1054 (the EAST–WEST SCHISM) after centuries of controversy over the issues of papal primacy and the wording of the Creed. Veneration of icons plays an important part in worship.

Osman I (1258–1326), the founder of the OTTOMAN Empire, a nomad leader of W Anatolia who turned from raiding to a policy of permanent conquest. In 1290 he declared his independence from the Seljuk Turks, and set about extending his territory to the NW at the expense of the declining BYZANTINE Empire.

Ostpolitik (German 'eastern policy'), the West German foreign policy introduced from 1969 by Willy BRANDT. The policy normalized relations between West and East GERMANY through direct talks, trade, treaties and mutual recognition of frontiers, and helped reduce East–West tension in the 1970s.

ostracism, an institution in ancient Athens for banishing politicians. Introduced by CLEISTHENES in the 6th century BC, it allowed Athenians to vote for a politician to be banished from the city for ten years. Its purpose was probably to avoid another tyranny, and to resolve serious political disputes by exiling an advocate of the less popular policy.

Ostrogoths, the eastern Goths, a people originating in the Don basin (see map, p. 15). They became vassals of the HUNS in Pannonia c. 375–454 after being displaced by the latter's westward movement. Under THEODERIC the Great they overthrow ODOACER in 488 and became rulers of Italy c. 493–523. They were eventually overwhelmed by JUSTINIAN'S reconquest between 536 and 552.

Oswald, Lee Harvey (1939–63), the alleged assassin of President John F. KENNEDY in 1963. Oswald himself was gunned down by a nightclub owner, Jack Ruby, before he could stand trial. The Warren Commission set up to investigate Kennedy's assassination rejected allegations of a wider conspiracy, concluding that Oswald had acted on his own.

Ottawa Agreements (1932), a series of economic agreements between Britain and its DOMINIONS, establishing a system of 'imperial preferences' to counter the effects of the DEPRESSION. The agreements imposed high tariffs on imports into Britain from countries outside the COMMONWEALTH and provided for duty-free imports of quotas of goods from the Dominions. The USA raised tariffs in response.

Otto I ('the Great'; 912–73), king of Germany (936–73), emperor (962–73). He inherited a small Saxon empire, but by determination, skill and good fortune extended his influence over the other German duchies (Bavaria, Franconia, Lorraine and Swabia). He defeated the Magyars at the Battle of LECHFELD (955) and conquered the kingdom of Italy. Otto established imperial supremacy over the papacy, and in 962 was crowned emperor in Rome.

Otto II (955–83), king of Germany (961–83), emperor (973–83) and son of OTTO I. He succeeded to his father's rights both N and S of the Alps.

Otto III (980–1002), king of Germany (983–1002), emperor (996–1002), and son of OTTO II. He hoped to re-create the power of the Roman empire in a state uniting the whole of Christendom under the emperor, but his ambitions were frustrated by rebellions in Italy and ended by his death.

Ottoman Empire, an Islamic empire that emerged from the early 14th century to become a major power in SE Europe and the Middle East. Devoted to holy war (jihad), the Ottomans became the outstanding holy warriors among the Turks of Asia Minor. From small beginnings around 1300, the Ottoman Turks, under the Empire's founder OSMAN I, made Anatolia (Asian Turkey) the centre of attacks on the BYZANTINE capital, CONSTANTINOPLE. By the end of the 14th century, Ottoman raids into the remaining Byzantine territory had reduced the Byzantine Empire to the walls of Constantinople. In 1402 the Mongol leader, TAMERLANE, defeated the Ottomans and captured the Sultan, BAJEZID I, thwarting their attack on Constantinople. However, in 1453 forces under Sultan MEHMET II overwhelmed the city. From their new capital, now named Istanbul, the Ottoman sultans embarked on campaigns of expansion spearheaded by large and efficient armies, at the core of which were the permanent infantry or JANISSARIES. In 1517 SELIM I conquered Syria and Egypt, and under his successor, SULEIMAN the Magnificent, the empire reached its peak. By Suleiman's death the empire extended from Central Europe to the Persian Gulf, dominating the E Mediterranean, Adriatic and Black Seas. The northern boundary of their conquests in Europe was marked by the failed sieges of Vienna in 1529 and 1683, but the Ottomans were to hold on to most of SE Europe until the 19th century. The naval defeat at LEPANTO in 1571 meant that Mediterranean expansion was effectively over by 1600. From as early as the middle of the 16th century the empire showed signs of administrative, social and economic decay. In addition, the conservatism of powerful Muslim institutions ensured that the Ottomans fell behind the rest of Europe in technological and industrial advances. The full implications of these defects were not immediately apparent. The empire continued to expand in the 17th century (see map, p. 26) – as far as the Caspian Sea in the E – while the KÖPRÜLÜ grand viziers provided strong leadership from the 1650s. The 18th century brought renewed domestic instability and the loss of territory around the Black Sea in disastrous wars against Russia (1768–72 and 1787–92). In the 19th century the nationalist aspirations of the various peoples under Turkish domination in Eastern Europe became linked with attempts by Austria and Russia to fill the vacuum created by Ottoman decline (see EASTERN QUESTION). The empire finally collapsed on the defeat of the Central Powers in World War I, substantial parts of the old Ottoman Empire being given to France and Britain as MANDATES by the Treaty of SÈVRES. See also TURKEY.

Ottonian dynasty, the German dynasty founded by HENRY I, duke of Saxony. He was succeeded by OTTO I, who created an empire. Otto's son (OTTO II) and grandson (OTTO III) continued the dynasty, but it died out in 1024.

Oudenarde, Battle of (July 1708), a victory of EUGÈNE of Savoy and MARLBOROUGH over the French during the War of the SPANISH SUCCESSION. The French had outflanked Marlborough and occupied Ghent and Bruges, threatening the Allies' hold on the S Netherlands and the security of the Dutch Republic.

Owen, Robert (1771–1858), British manufacturer and socialist visionary. Owen built a model environment for his workers in the New Lanark mills and put his cooperative theories into practice at various experimental communities, such as New Harmony, Indiana (1825).

Oxenstierna, Axel Gustaffson, Count (1583–1654), Swedish chancellor (1612–54). A brilliant reforming administrator under GUSTAVUS II ADOLPHUS, he directed Swedish foreign policy during the THIRTY YEARS WAR.

Oyo, kingdom of, an inland African kingdom of the 18th century; see also YORUBA.

Pacific, War of the (1879–83), a war fought between CHILE on one side and BOLIVIA and PERU on the other for control of the nitrates of the N Atacama desert. Enjoying command of the sea, Chilean forces eventually captured Lima in 1881. By the Treaty of Ancón (1883) Peru lost two S provinces, while Bolivia was deprived of access to the Pacific.

Pacific campaigns, the naval and amphibious engagements fought between Japanese and Allied forces in the central and SW Pacific during WORLD WAR II. Following their assault on PEARL HARBOR in December 1941 the Japanese proceeded to carve out an immense East Asian empire, occupying Borneo, Malaya, the Philippines, parts of New Guinea, the Dutch East Indies, French Indochina, Thailand and Burma as well as those areas of N China taken in the SINO-JAPANESE WAR. The tide turned when Japanese invasion fleets were repulsed at the Battles of the CORAL SEA and MIDWAY; further American success followed at GUADALCANAL. The Americans established a two-pronged advance under General MACARTHUR in the SW and Admiral NIMITZ in the central Pacific, while the British counterattacked in Burma. By late

1943 MacArthur had made significant gains in the Solomon Islands and New Guinea and gradually moved towards the Philippines during 1944, while Nimitz began an 'island-hopping' campaign aiming for Taiwan. After taking the Marshall and Mariana Islands, Nimitz defeated the Japanese at the Battle of the PHILIPPINE SEA. Both Macarthur and Nimitz now converged on the Philippines. Japanese naval power was effectively destroyed at the Battle of LEYTE GULF. By June 1945 the British had liberated Burma, and US forces had captured IWO JIMA and occupied OKINAWA in the face of KAMIKAZE air raids. With Japan still refusing to surrender, President TRUMAN authorized the use of the newly developed atomic bomb at HIROSHIMA and NAGASAKI, leading to a ceasefire on 15 August 1945. The Pacific War ended officially on 2 September.

Pagan, a former kingdom of BURMA based on the central Irrawaddy and founded c. AD 849. The kingdom was occupied by the MONGOLS from 1287 to 1301.

Pahlavi, Reza Khan (1877–1944), Shah of Persia (IRAN) (1926–41). Rising through the ranks of the Persian army, he led a coup in 1921 and proclaimed himself Shah five years later. His son Mohammed Reza (1919–80) became Shah on his father's abdication in 1941, ruling Iran until his overthrow in KHOMEINI'S Islamic Revolution of 1979.

Paine, Thomas (1737–1809), English radical political theorist. His pamphlet *Common Sense* (1776) defended the rights of the American colonists against Britain. *The Rights of Man* (1790) defended the FRENCH REVOLUTION against the attacks of BURKE.

Paisley, Reverend Ian R.K. (1926–), militant NORTHERN IRELAND politician and evangelical Protestant clergyman. He founded the Democratic Unionist Party in 1969 and has been an MP since 1974, and a Member of the European Parliament since 1979. He is implacably opposed to the IRISH REPUBLICAN ARMY and its goal of a united republican Ireland.

Pakistan, a republic of S Asia. See panel.

Palaeolithic, the earlier part of the STONE AGE. It is commonly divided into Lower, Middle and Upper phases. The period is characterized by its flaked stone tools and weapons. During the Lower Palaeolithic – the time of *homo habilis* and HOMO ERECTUS, beginning 1 million years ago – simple stone tools such as hand axes were developed and fire was used. During the Middle Palaeolithic phase, which started c. 100,000 years ago, NEANDERTHAL man used more specialized stone tools such as spear heads and knives. Modern man, HOMO SAPIENS SAPIENS, appeared during the Upper phase, which started around 30,000 BC, developing stone blades and bone tools and producing the first art in the form of cave paintings and small sculptures. The achievements of these early modern humans included the peopling of the previously unoccupied continents of Australasia and the Americas. A less positive achievement was the extinction of a number of large mammal species (such as mammoth) both in Eurasia and the Americas before the end of the last ICE AGE.

Palatinate, a former German state whose prince was one of the ELECTORS of the HOLY ROMAN EMPIRE, comprising the Lower Palatinate on the Rhine and the Upper Palatinate between Bavaria and Bohemia.

Pale, the area around Dublin that was the effective extent of English authority in IRELAND before ELIZABETH I and her Stuart successors imposed their rule.

Palestine, the area of land between the Jordan River in the E and the Mediterranean coast in the W, and the GOLAN HEIGHTS in the N and the borders of Egypt in the S, which has become the modern state of ISRAEL. In the process, the indigenous Arab population has been largely displaced. The PALESTINE LIBERATION ORGANIZATION has campaigned for the establishment of a Palestinian state.

Palestine Liberation Organization (PLO), a Palestinian Arab organization dedicated to bringing about an independent state of PALESTINE. Founded in 1964 virtually as an Egyptian front organization, the PLO was dominated from 1967 by al-FATAH, a guerrilla group led by Yasser ARAFAT, who advocated a policy of armed struggle against ISRAEL. In the years that followed, the PLO conducted terrorist campaigns against Israel and her alleged supporters throughout the world to promote its cause. Al-Fatah guerrillas established commando bases in Jordan from where they carried out raids on Israel. In 1970 hostilities broke out between the guerrillas – angered by the moderate stance of King HUSSEIN – and the Jordanian government, which felt threatened by their activities. Al-Fatah's military bases were

PAKISTAN

2300–1700 BC: The Indus Valley in Pakistan was the seat of the ancient HARAPPAN civilization. **By 1500 BC:** The Ganges Basin had become the driving force in the subcontinent. **From 1500 BC:** The area was ruled by a succession of kingdoms and empires along with INDIA before the colonial age. **8th century AD:** Pakistan was converted to Islam. **From the 18th century:** The region came under British rule. **1947:** Pakistan as a nation was born when British INDIA was partitioned as a result of demands by the MUSLIM LEAGUE under JINNAH. **1947–49** and **1965:** War with India over KASHMIR, which was effectively partitioned. **1958:** Imposition of military rule after a coup by General Muhammad AYUB KHAN. **1960s:** Rising tension between heavily populated East Pakistan and West Pakistan, where political and military power was concentrated. **1969:** Coup brought Muhammad Yahya Khan to power. **1970:** First elections with universal suffrage. **1971:** East Pakistan declared its independence as BANGLADESH, leading to civil war; war with India, which supported the new state, ended in defeat for Pakistan. **1977:** Zulfiqar Ali BHUTTO (PM 1972–7) was deposed (and later executed) in a military coup led by the Army Chief of Staff, Mohammed ZIA UL-HAQ. **1985:** Zia lifted martial law and began to return Pakistan to civilian life. **1988:** Zia killed in a plane crash; Benazir BHUTTO became PM (the first woman premier of an Islamic state). **1990:** Benazir Bhutto dismissed by president; subsequent elections won by the Islamic Democratic Alliance. **1993:** Benazir Bhutto re-elected to lead coalition government.

broken up by the Jordanian army, and the PLO moved its forces to LEBANON. When Israel invaded S Lebanon in 1982 the PLO was obliged to move its headquarters to Tunis. In the late 1980s Palestinians in the occupied territories of GAZA and the WEST BANK began the campaign against Israel known as the INTIFADA. The PLO recognized Israel's right to exist in 1988. However, despite hopes engendered by the ISRAELI–PALESTINIAN PEACE ACCORD of 1993, peace talks between Israel and the PLO remained hampered by deep mutual distrust. The PLO's position has been increasingly challenged by Hamas, a militant rival Palestinian organization committed to the destruction of the Israeli state.

Palme, Olaf (1916–86), Swedish SOCIAL DEMOCRAT statesman, prime minister (1969–76 and 1982–6). He was assassinated by a gunman.

Palmerston, Henry John Temple, 3rd Viscount (1784–1865), British statesman, prime minister (1855–8 and 1859–65). He entered the Commons as a TORY in 1806 but served in WHIG governments as foreign secretary (1830–41 and 1846–51). He supported British interests and liberal and national causes abroad, initiating the First OPIUM WAR and intervening against Greece in the DON PACIFICO affair. As PM he presided over the conclusion of the CRIMEAN WAR and kept Britain neutral during the AMERICAN CIVIL WAR.

Pan-Africanist Congress (PAC), a black South African political party that broke away from the AFRICAN NATIONAL CONGRESS in 1959. More militant than the ANC, it encouraged strikes and boycotts and led the demonstration at SHARPEVILLE. Along with the ANC it was banned by the South African government and forced into exile in the early 1960s. It was unbanned in 1990.

Panama, a republic of CENTRAL AMERICA. Panama was discovered in 1501, and became part of Spanish NEW GRANADA (COLOMBIA). In the 1880s a French attempt to construct a canal through Panama linking the Atlantic and Pacific Oceans proved unsuccessful. After Colombia rejected US proposals for completing the canal, Panama became independent (1903), sponsored by the USA. The PANAMA CANAL eventually opened in 1914. The USA was given land extending 8 km (5 mi) on either side of the canal – the Canal Zone – complete control of which will be handed to Panama in 2000. From 1983 to 1989 effective power was in the hands of General Manuel Noriega, who was deposed by a US invasion and taken to stand trial in the USA, accused of criminal activities.

Panama Canal, a waterway across the isthmus of PANAMA in Central America built by the USA (1904–14) on territory leased from the republic of Panama. The Canal Zone, under US control since 1903, will revert to Panama in 2000, but the Canal's perpetual neutrality is assured.

Panipat, Battles of (1526, 1556 and 1761), three battles fought NW of Delhi. In the first battle BABUR defeated the Sultan of Delhi, establishing the MOGUL Empire. In the second AKBAR consolidated Mogul power by defeating an Afghan challenge. The last battle saw an Afghan army defeat MARATHA forces, ending their attempt to fill the political vacuum left by the collapse of Mogul power.

Pankhurst, Emmeline (1858–1928), British feminist and leader of the SUFFRAGETTES. The militant methods she used in her campaign for universal WOMEN'S SUFFRAGE led to her being imprisoned on eight occasions. Her daughters Christabel (1880–1958) and Sylvia (1882–1960) were also suffragettes.

Panmunjom Armistice (27 July 1953), a ceasefire agreement signed in the demilitarized zone between North and South KOREA by representatives of the United Nations Command and the North Koreans and Chinese, ending the KOREAN WAR.

Pan-Slavism, a 19th-century movement for a confederation of all Slavic peoples under the leadership of Russia. Pan-Slavism, which aimed to overthrow the rule of the Ottoman Turks and HABSBURG Austria, intensified in the period 1867–70, when Austrian ambitions in the BALKANS increasingly confronted those of Russia. The movement also fuelled the outbreak of the RUSSO-TURKISH WAR (1877–80) and the creation of the BALKAN LEAGUE in 1912. The nationalist aspirations of the movement contributed to tensions that led to the outbreak of WORLD WAR I. See EASTERN QUESTION.

papacy, the office of, or system of government by, the pope in the ROMAN CATHOLIC CHURCH, see boxes, pp. 193 and 194. The links forged between the papacy and the CAROLINGIAN Empire weakened those between the papacy and the BYZANTINE Empire, and led ultimately to the separation of the ORTHODOX Church. Pope GREGORY VII introduced important reforms and asserted the pope's leadership of Western Christendom. A revived papacy instigated the CRUSADES, while the INVESTITURE CONTEST – which set Rome at loggerheads with the HOLY ROMAN EMPIRE – put the papacy at the storm centre of European politics and created a new style of militant Christianity. The policies of the papacy became increasingly influenced by the interests of the French crown during the AVIGNON PERIOD (1305–77). The return of the papacy to Rome, however, proved divisive and led to the GREAT SCHISM. The increasing power, secularism, and, some believed, corruption of the papacy contributed to the REFORMATION in the 16th century.

Papal States (or 'Patrimony of St Peter'), lands in central Italy under the rule of the pope. In 756 the LOMBARD king ceded territory in central and N Italy to the pope, who became a temporal as well as a spiritual ruler. The Papal States comprised the territories of Latium (the area around Rome), Umbria, Marche and Romagna (see maps, pp. 21, 25, 27 and 30). Papal control – hampered by disputes with the Holy Roman Emperors throughout the Middle Ages – remained ineffectual until the 1350s. The Papal States reached their greatest extent under Pope Julius II (reigned 1503–13), but by the 18th century the pope's temporal power was weak. During the REVOLUTIONARY and NAPOLEONIC WARS the Papal States were variously annexed by their neighbours and absorbed into the French Empire. They were restored in 1815, but were lost to the new kingdom of ITALY during Italian unification.

Papen, Franz von (1879–1969), German chancellor (1932). He made concessions to the NAZIS, and after resigning persuaded HINDENBURG to appoint HITLER chancellor in January 1933.

Papineau's Rebellion (1837), an abortive French Canadian republican uprising against British authority in CANADA.

POPES

Pope	Reign	Pope	Reign
St Peter	c. 33–67	St Boniface IV	608–15
St Linus	67–76	St Deusdedit I	615–18
St Cletus (also called Anacletus)	76–88	Boniface V	619–25
St Clement I	88–97	Honorius I	625–38
St Evaristus	97–105	Severinus	638–40
St Alexander I	105–15	John IV	640–42
St Sixtus I	115–25	Theodore I	642–49
St Telesphorus	125–36	St Martin I	649–55
St Hyginus	136–40	St Eugenius I	654–57
St Pius I	140–55	St Vitalian	657–72
St Anicetus	155–66	Deusdedit II	672–76
St Soterus	166–75	Donus	676–78
St Eleutherius	175–89	St Agatho	678–81
St Victor I	189–99	St Leo II	681–83
St Zephyrinus	199–217	St Benedict II	683–85
St Callistus I	217–22	John V	685–86
St Urban I	222–30	Conon	686–87
St Pontian	230–35	St Sergius I	687–701
St Anterus	235–36	John VI	701–05
St Fabian I	236–50	John VII	705–07
St Cornelius	251–53	Sisinnius	707
St Lucius I	253–54	Constantine	708–15
St Stephen I	254–57	St Gregory II	715–31
St Sixtus II	257–58	St Gregory III	731–41
St Dionysius	259–68	Saint Zacharias	741–52
St Felix I	269–74	Stephen 'II' (died before he could be enthroned)	752
St Eutychianus	275–83	Stephen II or III	752–57
St Caius	283–96	St Paul I	757–67
St Marcellinus	296–304	Stephen III or IV	768–72
St Marcellus I	308–09	Adrian I	772–95
St Eusebius	309–10	St Leo III	795–816
St Miltiades	311–14	Stephen IV or V	816–17
St Silvester I	314–35	St Paschal I	817–24
St Mark	336–37	Eugenius II	824–27
St Julius I	337–52	Valentine	827
Liberius	352–66	Gregory IV	827–44
St Damasus	366–84	Sergius II	844–47
St Siricius	384–99	St Leo IV	847–55
St Anastasius I	399–401	Benedict III	855–58
St Innocent I	401–17	St Nicholas I	858–67
St Zosimus	417–18	Adrian II	867–72
St Boniface I	418–22	John VIII	872–82
St Celestine I	422–32	Marinus I	882–84
St Sixtus III	432–40	Adrian III	884–85
St Leo I	440–61	Stephen V or VI	885–91
St Hilary	461–68	Formosus	891–96
St Simplicius	468–83	Boniface VI	896
St Felix II	483–92	Stephen VI or VII	896–97
St Gelasius I	492–96	Romanus	897
St Anastasius II	496–98	Theodore II	897
St Symmachus	498–514	John IX	898–900
St Hormisdas	514–23	Benedict IV	900–03
St John I	523–26	Leo V	903
St Felix III	526–30	Sergius III	904–11
Boniface II	530–32	Anastasius III	911–13
John II (Mercurius)	533–35	Lando	913–14
St Agapetus I	535–36	John X	914–28
St Silverius	536–37	Leo VI	928
Vigilius	537–55	Stephen VII or VIII	928–31
Pelagius I	556–61	John XI	931–35
John III	561–74	Leo VII	936–39
Benedict I	575–79	Stephen VIII or IX	939–42
Pelagius II	579–90	Marinus II	942–46
St Gregory I	590–604	Agapetus II	946–55
Sabinianus	604–06	John XII	955–64
Boniface III	607	Leo VIII	963–65

POPES CONT.

Benedict V	964–65
John XIII	965–72
Benedict VI	973–74
Benedict VII	974–83
John XIV (Pietro Canepanova)	983–84
John XV	985–96
Gregory V (Bruno of Carinthia)	996–99
Silvester II (Gerbert)	999–1003
John XVII (Sicco)	1003
John XVIII (Fasino)	1003–09
Sergius IV (Pietro Buccaporci)	1009–12
Benedict VIII	1012–24
John XIX	1024–32
Benedict IX	1032–44
Silvester III	1045
Benedict IX (restored)	1045
Gregory VI	1045–46
Clement II	1046–47
Benedict IX (restored)	1047–48
Damasus II (Poppo)	1048
St Leo IX	1048–54
Victor II	1055–57
Stephen IX or X	1057–58
Nicholas II	1058–61
Alexander II	1061–73
St Gregory VII (Hildebrand de Soana)	1064–85
Victor III (Desiderius, Prince of Benevento)	1086–87
Urban II (Odon de Lagery)	1088–99
Paschal II (Ranieri)	1099–1118
Gelasius II (Giovanni Gaetani)	1118–19
Callistus II (Gui de Bourgogne)	1119–24
Honorius II (Lamberto Scannabecchi)	1124–30
Innocent II (Gregorio Papareschi)	1130–43
Celestine II (Guido di Castello)	1143–44
Lucius II (Gerardo Caccianemici)	1144–45
Eugenius III (Bernardo Paganelli)	1145–53
Anastasius IV (Corrado)	1153–54
Adrian IV (Nicholas Breakspeare*)	1154–59
Alexander III (Rolando Bandinelli)	1159–81
Lucius III (Ubaldo Allucingoli)	1181–85
Urban III (Uberto Crivelli)	1185–87
Gregory VIII (Alberto di Morra)	1187
Clement III (Paolo Scolari)	1187–91
Celestine III (Giacinto Buboni)	1191–98
Innocent III (Lothario, Count of Segni)	1198–1216
Honorius III (Cencio Savelli)	1216–27
Gregory IX (Ugolino, Count of Segni)	1227–41
Celestine IV (Goffredo Castiglioni)	1241
Innocent IV (Sinibaldo Fieschi)	1243–54
Alexander IV (Rainaldo, Count of Segni)	1254–61
Urban IV (Jacques Pantaléon)	1261–64
Clement IV (Gui Faucois)	1265–68
Gregory X (Theobaldo Visconti)	1271–76
Innocent V (Pierre de Tarentaise)	1276
Adrian V (Ottobono dei Fieschi)	1276
John XXI (Pedro Juliani)	1276–77
Nicholas III (Giovanni Gaetano Orsini)	1277–80
Martin IV (Simon de Brion)	1281–85
Honorius IV (Giacomo Savelli)	1285–87
Nicholas IV (Girolamo Moschi)	1288–92
St Celestine V (Pietro del Morrone)	1294
Boniface VIII (Benedetto Gaetani)	1294–1303
Benedict XI (Nicola Boccasini)	1303–04
Clement V (Bertrand de Got)	1305–14
John XXII (Jacques Duèse)	1316–34
Benedict XII (Jacques Fournier)	1334–42
Clement VI (Pierre Roger)	1342–52
Innocent VI (Etienne Aubert)	1352–62
Urban V (Guillaume Grimoard)	1362–70
Gregory XI (Pierre Roger de Beaufort)	1370–78
Urban VI (Bartolommeo Prignano)	1378–89
Boniface IX (Pietro Tomacelli)	1389–1404
Innocent VII (Cosimo dei Migliorati)	1404–06
Gregory XII (Angelo Corrari)	1406–15
Martin V (Odo Colonna)	1417–31
Eugenius IV (Gabriele Condolmieri)	1431–47
Nicholas V (Tommaso Parentucelli)	1447–55
Callistus III (Alonso Borgia)	1455–58
Pius II (Aeneas Piccolomini)	1458–64
Paul II (Pietro Barbo)	1464–71
Sixtus IV (Francesco della Rovere)	1471–84
Innocent VIII (Giovanni Battista)	1484–92
Alexander VI (Roderigo Borgia)	1492–1503
Pius III (Francesco Todeschini)	1503
Julius II (Giuliano della Rovere)	1503–13
Leo X (Giovanni de Medici)	1513–21
Adrian VI (Adrian Florensz Boeyens**)	1522–23
Clement VII (Giulio de Medici)	1523–34
Paul III (Alessandro Farnese)	1534–49
Julius III (Giovanni Maria Ciocchi del Monte)	1550–55
Marcellus II (Marcello Cervini)	1555
Paul IV (Giovanni Pietro Carafa)	1555–59
Pius IV (Gianangelo de Medici)	1559–65
St Pius V (Antonio Michele Ghislieri)	1566–72
Gregory XIII (Ugo Buoncompagni)	1572–85
Sixtus V (Felice Perretti)	1585–90
Urban VII (Giovanni Battista Castagna)	1590
Gregory XIV (Niccolo Sfondrati)	1590–91
Innocent IX (Giovanni Antonio Facchinetti)	1591
Clement VIII (Ipollito Aldobrandini)	1592–1605
Leo XI (Alessandro Ottaviano de Medici)	1605
Paul V (Camillo Borghese)	1605–21
Gregory XV (Alessandro Ludovisi)	1621–23
Urban VIII (Maffeo Barberini)	1623–44
Innocent X (Giovanni Battista Pamfili)	1644–55
Alexander VII (Fabio Chigi)	1655–67
Clement IX (Giulio Rospigliosi)	1667–69
Clement X (Emilio Altieri)	1670–76
Innocent XI (Benedetto Odescalchi)	1676–89
Alexander VIII (Pietro Ottoboni)	1689–91
Innocent XII (Antonio Pignatelli)	1691–1700
Clement XI (Gianfrancesco Albani)	1700–21
Innocent XIII (Michelangelo de Conti)	1721–24
Benedict XIII (Pietro Francesco Orsini)	1724–30
Clement XII (Lorenzo Corsini)	1730–40
Benedict XIV (Prospero Lambertini)	1740–58
Clement XIII (Carlo della Torre Rezzonico)	1758–69
Clement XIV (Giovanni Vincenzo Antonio Ganganelli)	1769–74
Pius VI (Giovanni Angelo Braschi)	1775–99
Pius VII (Barnabo Chiaramonti)	1800–23
Leo XII (Annibale della Genga)	1823–29
Pius VIII (Francesco Xaverio Castiglioni)	1829–30
Gregory XVI (Bartolomeo Cappellari)	1831–46
Pius IX (Giovanni Maria Mastai-Ferretti)	1846–78
Leo XIII (Vincenzo Gioacchino Pecci)	1878–1903
St Pius X (Giuseppe Sarto)	1903–14
Benedict XV (Giacomo della Chiesa)	1914–22
Pius XI (Achille Ratti)	1922–39
Pius XII (Eugenio Pacelli)	1939–58
John XXIII (Angelo Giuseppe Roncalli)	1958–63
Paul VI (Giovanni Battista Montini)	1963–78
John Paul I (Albino Luciani)	1978
John Paul II (Karol Wojtyla)	1978–

Papua New Guinea, a country of the S Pacific and an independent member of the COMMONWEALTH. The first inhabitants of New Guinea came from Indonesia around 50,000 BC. European colonization began in 1828 when the Dutch claimed W New Guinea. A British protectorate, established in the SE in 1884, was transferred to Australia (1906) and renamed Papua. NE New Guinea came under German administration in 1884, but was occupied by Australian forces in 1914. From 1942 to 1945 Japanese forces occupied New Guinea and part of Papua. In 1949 Australia combined the administration of the territories, which achieved independence as Papua New Guinea in 1975. Bougainville island, a major source of copper, declared independence unilaterally in 1990, but a central government economic blockade has isolated the island. Fighting on the island diminished in 1992 and peace talks began.

Paraguay, a republic of central South America. The Spanish reached the area in the 1520s. Jesuit missionaries to the Guaraní Indians dominated the country from 1609 until 1767, when they were expelled. Since independence in 1811, Paraguay has suffered many dictators, including General José Francia, who totally isolated Paraguay (1814–40). War against Argentina, Brazil and Uruguay (1865–70) cost Paraguay over one half of its people and much territory. The CHACO Wars with Bolivia (1929–35) further weakened Paraguay. General Alfredo STROESSNER gained power in 1954, ruling with increasing disregard for human rights until his overthrow in a military coup in 1989. Free multi-party elections were held in 1993.

Paraguayan War (1864–70), a war fought by Argentina, Uruguay and Brazil against Paraguay. The ambitious diplomacy of the Paraguayan ruler Francisco Solano LÓPEZ antagonized all his neighbours at once. López led a tenacious resistance, resulting in heavy loss of life and the ruin of his country. This 'War of the Triple Alliance' was the most prolonged international conflict in Latin American history.

Paris, Congress of (1856), a conference that negotiated the end of the CRIMEAN WAR. It recognized the independence of Serbia, Romania and Montenegro, but Bosnia-Herzegovina passed under Austro-Hungarian rule. Russia was forced to relinquish part of BESSARABIA to MOLDAVIA and WALLACHIA in the Balkans.

Paris, Treaty of (1763), the treaty that ended the SEVEN YEARS WAR. It confirmed Britain's maritime and colonial supremacy at the expense of France and Spain. Britain gained French Canada and French territory E of the Mississippi. Spain ceded Florida to Britain but gained LOUISIANA from France. The settlement left Britain the dominant power in North America.

Paris Peace Conference (1919–20), the conference that followed the end of WORLD WAR I. Most of the major decisions were made by the British and French PMs, LLOYD GEORGE and CLEMENÇEAU, and the US president Woodrow WILSON. As well as concluding the Treaty of VERSAILLES with Germany, the Allies signed the Treaty of ST GERMAIN and the Treaty of TRIANON with Austria-Hungary, the Treaty of NEUILLY with Bulgaria and the Treaty of SÈVRES with Turkey.

Park Chung-Hee (1917–79), president of the Republic of (South) KOREA (1961–79). He imposed a firm discipline on the economy, which flourished under his presidency. However, his authoritarian rule led to his assassination.

Parlement, the sovereign judicial authority in ANCIEN REGIME France. Originally a single court in Paris, it spawned a number of provincial Parlements. Their power increased in the 17th century, and they challenged the monarchy during the FRONDES. Suppressed by LOUIS XIV, they were restored in 1718 and assumed the role of opposition to the monarchy, though they remained defenders of aristocratic privilege. Their resistance to the monarch culminated in the calling of the STATES-GENERAL in 1789. The Parlements were suppressed in 1792.

Parliament, a representative assembly summoned by the monarch in England from the 13th century to give advice and agree to taxation; it has since become the legislative body of the UNITED KINGDOM. Composed of the crown, the House of LORDS and the House of COMMONS, only since the GLORIOUS REVOLUTION of 1688 has the latter become the most important of the two chambers and its sessions a regular rather than occasional event. Originally drawn from very narrow social groups, the size of the electorate has greatly increased in the 19th and 20th centuries.

Parnell, Charles Stewart (1846–91), Irish nationalist leader. A Protestant Anglo-Irish landowner, he became leader of the Irish MPs supporting HOME RULE in 1878. In 1881 he was imprisoned in Kilmainham gaol for inciting agrarian violence. From 1886 Parnell supported the Liberal leader GLADSTONE, a convert to home rule, but was forced to resign the Irish party leadership in 1890, after being cited in the O'Shea divorce case. See also IRELAND.

Parthia, a satrapy in NE Iran that seceded from the Hellenistic SELEUCID kingdom in the mid-3rd century BC (see map, p. 12). The Parthian dynasty was founded by Arsaces in 247 BC. Mithridates I (171–138 BC) gained control of IRAN c. 148–147 BC, and MESOPOTAMIA in 141 BC. Under Mithridates II (124–87 BC), who campaigned as far E as the Euphrates in Syria, Parthia reached its greatest extent. In 53 BC the Parthians defeated Rome at Carrhae (Harran) in N Syria. But by the 2nd century AD, much territory had been lost to Rome, and Parthia was in decline. The last Parthian king was overthrown in AD 226 by Ardashir, the first ruler of the SASSANIAN dynasty.

Passchendaele, Battle of (31 July–21 November 1917), a British attack in Flanders (officially the third Battle of YPRES), in WORLD WAR I. The combined British, Australian and Canadian offensive became bogged down in 'a porridge of mud'. The British suffered over 240,000 casualties for no gain in a battle whose name has become synonymous with the horrors of trench warfare. See map, p. 36.

Pathan, a people living in AFGHANISTAN and NW PAKISTAN. Pathan uprisings on the NORTHWEST FRONTIER led to a British military occupation of the area in the late 1890s.

Pathet Lao, a Laotian Communist organization. From the mid-1950s until the mid-1970s they fought for control of LAOS, finally taking power in 1975 in the wake of US withdrawal from Vietnam.

Patriarchate, the title given in the early Middle Ages to the five chief bishoprics of Christendom – Rome, Alexandria, Antioch, CONSTANTINOPLE and JERUSALEM. Rome was to become pre-eminent in the Western Church, and Constantinople in the Eastern (ORTHODOX) Church.

patricians, the hereditary elite in ancient Rome. They held all the official posts until the 4th century BC, when the PLEBEIANS also obtained access to high office.

Patrick, St (c. 390–c. 460), the patron saint of IRELAND. Born in Britain, he came to Ireland as a missionary (c. 435), establishing the see of Armagh.

Patton, George Smith (1885–1945), US WORLD WAR II general. He led the 3rd Army in the invasion of France in 1944, breaching the German defences in Normandy, taking Paris and reaching the Moselle. See NORMANDY LANDINGS.

Paul, St (Saul of Tarsus; d. c. AD 65), early Christian apostle and the author of 13 Epistles in the New Testament. Formerly a persecutor of Christians, he was converted to CHRISTIANITY on the road to Damascus, and went on to carry out missionary work in Rome, Greece, Anatolia and elsewhere. He died a martyr's death under NERO.

Pawnee, a native North American people, living in the Great Plains (Nebraska). They mixed settled farming with the seasonal hunting of buffalo. See also NORTH AMERICAN INDIANS.

Pearl Harbor, a US naval base on the Hawaiian island of Oahu. A surprise Japanese attack on the US Pacific Fleet there in December 1941 took out five US battleships and brought the USA into WORLD WAR II. See PACIFIC CAMPAIGNS.

Pearse, Pádraic (1879–1916), Irish poet and nationalist who proclaimed Irish independence in the EASTER RISING (1916). He was later court-martialled and shot by the British.

Peasants' Revolt (1381), an English rebellion led by Wat TYLER and John BALL. The main revolt in Kent and Essex was sparked off by the bungled collection of the third poll tax – which hit the poor particularly – in an area that had recently suffered from French raids. Led by Tyler and Ball, the local men marched on London, attacking the property of tax collectors, burning tax records, and lynching members of the government. They demanded from RICHARD II the abolition of serfdom and the charging of moderate rents. Richard managed to defuse the riot by promises of pardons and concessions, but later took action against the rebels.

Peasants' War (1525), a revolt of the German peasantry during the REFORMATION. Believing they were supported by LUTHER'S teachings, the rebels sought the restoration of customary rights and a reduction of the demands of ecclesiastical and lay lords. The peasants were encouraged by Thomas MÜNTZER, who was executed when the revolt was bloodily crushed by the forces of the Swabian League under PHILIP of Hesse.

Pedro I (1798–1835), first emperor of BRAZIL (1822–31). He became regent of Brazil when his father, King JOHN VI, returned to Portugal in 1821. The Portuguese parliament undid John's reforms, reduced Brazil to its former colonial status and insisted that Pedro return to Portugal. Pedro refused and declared Brazil independent with himself as emperor. After a disastrous war against Argentina (1828) he abdicated in favour of his infant son (PEDRO II).

Pedro II (1812–91), emperor of BRAZIL (1831–89). Central government was weak during his minority, but during his personal rule, from 1840, Brazil enjoyed relative stability and economic growth. A coup in 1889 forced him to abdicate and a republican government was established.

Peel, Sir Robert (1788–1850), British CONSERVATIVE statesman, prime minister (1834–5 and 1841–6). As home secretary (1822–7 and 1828–30), he set up the Metropolitan Police Force (1829). His second premiership saw the passage of some significant reforms, but his repeal of the CORN LAWS in 1846 split the Conservative Party and he was compelled to resign.

Peisistratos (c. 600–527 BC), tyrant of Athens. He and his sons ruled Athens from about 545 to 510 BC. Like SOLON they helped secure the peasants on their lands, and their building and religious programme helped unify the city-states as a whole, but their regime became unpopular and cruel in its later years.

Pelham, Henry (1695–1754), British WHIG statesman, prime minister (1743–6 and 1746–54). He was succeeded by his brother and close political associate, the Duke of NEWCASTLE.

Pelopidas (c. 410–364 BC), Theban general. With EPAMINONDAS he achieved major successes against SPARTA, notably at LEUCTRA in 371 BC.

Peloponnese, the large peninsula in S Greece, dominated in the 8th–4th centuries BC by SPARTA, which formed the Peloponnesian League in the 6th century.

Peloponnesian War (431–404 BC), a conflict between SPARTA and ATHENS and their allies, whose origins lay in areas (notably CORINTH) where the interests of Athens and the Peloponnesians overlapped. In 431 BC the complaints of the Athenian allies, and the refusal of Athens to compromise, led Sparta to declare war. Sparta's more deep-seated motive for war was fear of Athenian power and the loss of its own allies. Sparta was strong on land and Athens at sea, and for long each avoided a decisive battle. Since one side tended to support democracies and the other oligarchies, and each tried to win over the other's allies, the war greatly intensified political and economic conflicts inside many Greek cities. A peace made in 421 BC did not last, once Athens had made the serious mistake – following the advice of ALCIBIADES – of committing large forces in a disastrous attempt to conquer SYRACUSE, which appealed for Spartan help. Having destroyed the Athenian forces in Sicily, Sparta then attacked the Athenian empire in the Aegean. The Persian contribution to the Spartan fleet and the tactical skill of the Spartan Admiral LYSANDER proved decisive. With the Athenian defeat at AEGOSPOTAMI in 404 BC the war ended in victory for Sparta. Most Greek cities found themselves ruled by the Persians or by Spartan-backed oligarchies.

Peninsular War (1807–14), a conflict forming part of the NAPOLEONIC WARS, fought in the Iberian Peninsula between France on one side and British, Spanish and Portuguese forces on the other. The conflict, which arose from NAPOLEON'S efforts to control Spain and Portugal, ended in defeat for France. The future duke of WELLINGTON quickly recovered Portugal, but was obliged to fight a lengthy campaign against Napoleon's generals in Spain before achieving ultimate victory at the Battle of VITORIA (1813).

Penn, William, see PENNSYLVANIA.

Pennsylvania, a colony and state of the E USA, one of the original 13 colonies. Founded by the Quaker William Penn (1644–1718) in 1681, the colony remained a fiefdom of the Penn family until the American War of INDEPENDENCE. Ethnically heterogeneous and dominated by the great commercial centre of Philadelphia (the national capital during the revolutionary period), it swiftly became one of the most politically significant states in the Union.

'People's Budget' (1909), a budget introduced in Britain by LLOYD GEORGE, introducing tax on high incomes and a land tax to finance social reforms such as pensions and national insurance. The rejection of the budget by the House of LORDS – a breach of constitutional convention – led to legislation curtailing their powers.

Pepin III ('the Short'; 715–768), king of the FRANKS (751–768). 'MAYOR OF THE PALACE' and son of CHARLES MARTEL, he overthrew the last Merovingian king, Childeric III, and was crowned king of the Franks. The CAROLINGIAN dynasty that he established created the largest political unit in the West since the last Roman emperors. His son CHARLEMAGNE continued his father's policy of expansion.

Perceval, Spencer (1762–1812), British TORY politician. He succeeded the Duke of PORTLAND as prime minister (1809–12) and remains the only British PM to have been assassinated.

Percy, a noble family of medieval England. As earls of Northumberland from 1377 to 1670, they were pre-eminent in N English society. The Percy rebellion of 1403–8 posed serious problems for HENRY IV.

perestroika (Russian, 'reconstruction'), the policy of economic and political reform instituted in the Soviet Union by GORBACHOV from 1987. It involved far-reaching changes in the Soviet political and economic systems, and in the USSR's relations with the outside world. Many abuses of human rights were ended, and political prisoners were released. Politically, the reforms meant a reduction in the power of the Communist Party, which renounced its monopoly of power in March 1990.

Pergamum or **Pergamon**, a Hellenistic city in W Asia Minor (Turkey), and the centre of a powerful independent kingdom ruled by the Attalid dynasty until 133 BC, when it became a Roman province (see map, p. 12).

Pericles (c. 495–429 BC), Athenian statesman and general under whose dominance Athens was at its most prosperous, successful and powerful. With EPHIALTES he completed the development of Athenian democracy. From 462 BC until his death he played an increasingly influential role in Athenian politics, from 443 BC exercising a degree of dominance in policy-making that was quite exceptional. He encouraged and supported the expansion of the Athenian empire and initiated a major building programme that included the Parthenon. He persuaded the Athenians to rely on their fleet when the Spartans invaded during the PELOPONNESIAN WAR.

Per-Ramesses, an ancient Egyptian capital, established in the 13th century BC under the rule of RAMESSES II.

Perry, Matthew Calbraith (1794–1858), US naval officer, the leader of an expedition to JAPAN (1853–4) that forced the shogunate to open two Japanese ports to US trade in the Treaty of KANAGAWA, ending Japan's isolation.

Persepolis, a ceremonial centre of the Persian ACHAEMENID empire (see map, p. 10).

Persia, a region of SW Asia, modern Fars in Iran; the area in which the Iranian Persian tribe settled in the 1st millennium BC. The term is also applied to the Persian ACHAEMENID Empire, and was the name used for IRAN until 1935.

Persian Wars, a series of conflicts between the ACHAEMENID Persians and the Greek city-states in the first half of the 5th century BC. Persian domination over the Greek cities of W Anatolia led to Athenian support for an unsuccessful revolt against Persian rule by these cities (500–494 BC). The Persian king, DARIUS I, responded by invading the Greek mainland for the first time in 490 BC, but was repulsed in the land battle at MARATHON. A more serious invasion followed in 480 BC under XERXES, and an anti-Persian alliance was formed under the leadership of SPARTA. After the initial heroic defeat at THERMOPYLAE, the combined Greek forces defeated the Persians at sea at SALAMIS (480), and on land at PLATAEA the following year. The Greek fleet pursued the Persians across the Aegean and 'liberated' the Greek cities from Persian rule. By c. 465 BC the Persians had been pushed back to Cyprus. Active fighting ceased by c. 450 BC.

Peru, a republic on the W coast of South America. When the Spanish arrived in Peru in 1531 the INCA Empire was at its peak. Inca resistance was quickly subdued by PIZARRO and Peru became one of Spain's most valuable possessions. Much of South America was governed from Lima as the Spanish Viceroyalty of Peru. Independence was proclaimed in 1821 after the Argentine SAN MARTÍN took Lima, but Spanish forces did not leave until 1824. Independent Peru saw political domination by large landowners. Progress was made under General Ramon Castilla (1844–62) and civilian constitutional governments at the beginning of the 20th century, but instability and military coups have been common. War (1879–83) in alliance with Bolivia against Chile resulted in the loss of nitrate deposits in the S, while victory against Ecuador (1941) added Amazonian territory. From 1968 a reformist military government instituted land reform, attempting to benefit workers and the Indians, but faced with mounting economic problems the military swung to the right in 1975. In 1980 elections were held, but owing to the economic crisis and the growth of an extreme left-wing guerrilla movement – the Sendero Luminoso ('Shining Path') – Peru's democracy remained under threat. In 1992, the president effected a coup, suspending the constitution and detaining opposition leaders. Subsequent elections were boycotted by the principal opposition parties. Guerrilla activity lessened after the capture of Abimael Guzman, the leader of the Sendero Luminoso in 1992.

Pétain, Henri-Philippe (1856–1951), French general and head of state. A hero of World War I, he was appointed PM in 1940 and concluded an armistice with the Germans, surrendering three fifths of France to German control. He set up the VICHY Government which administered unoccupied France, and collaborated with the Germans. With the ALLIED invasion of France, he retreated into Germany, but returned to be tried for treason and condemned to death. The sentence was commuted by DE GAULLE to life imprisonment.

Peter I ('the Great'; 1672–1725), joint tsar of Russia with Ivan V (1682–96) and sole tsar (1696–1725). He transformed Russia and its international position through large-scale military, fiscal, educational and ecclesiastical reforms, and encouraged the spread of Western influence in Russia. After defeat by Sweden at the Battle of Narva in 1700 he reformed the Russian army, organizing them along Western lines, and established Russia's Baltic fleet. The effectiveness of his reforms was borne out by the Russian defeat of the Swedes at POLTAVA (1709). A disastrous war against the Turks in 1711 resulted in the loss of Azov (originally gained from Turkey in 1696). But in the W Peter's armies established Russian influence in Poland, reduced the independence of the COSSACKS of the Ukraine, and conquered Estonia, Latvia and Ingria. The latter were formally ceded by Sweden at the end of the NORTHERN WAR in 1721. Peter also rebuilt St Petersburg, modelling it on Western cities. With its easy access to the Baltic and W Europe, St Petersburg became the Russian capital in 1712.

Peter, St (Simon Peter; d. c. AD 64), the leader of the apostles who followed JESUS, regarded by Roman Catholics as the first pope.

Peterloo Massacre (16 August 1819), a clash between demonstrators and the local yeomanry at a mass meeting for parliamentary reform at St Peter's Fields, Manchester. Troopers tried to arrest the chief speaker, the reformer Henry Hunt, resulting in 11 civilians dead and hundreds injured. The name given to the incident by its critics is an ironic reference to the battle of WATERLOO (1815).

Pharaoh, the title used by the kings of ancient EGYPT, derived from Per'ao, meaning 'the Great House' or palace.

Pharsalus, Battle of (9 August 48 BC), a battle in Thessaly (N Greece) where POMPEY was completely defeated by CAESAR, the latter becoming Roman consul and dictator for life.

Philby, Harold (known as 'Kim'; 1912–88), British double agent active during the COLD WAR. A Communist from his days at Cambridge, he spied for the Soviet Union while working for the British secret service. In 1963 he defected to the Soviet Union, where he was granted citizenship.

Philip II (382–336 BC), king of MACEDON (359–336), who brought all Greece under his domination. In 359 BC he became king of Macedon and immediately reorganized the army and the kingdom. By a blend of diplomacy and force he achieved a position of dominance in mainland Greece, winning a final victory at the Battle of CHAERONEA (338 BC) over a coalition of Greek states led by Athens and THEBES. Assassinated in 336, he was succeeded by his son ALEXANDER THE GREAT, who continued his conquests.

Philip II (Augustus; 1165–1223), CAPETIAN king of France (1179–1223). The most successful of all French kings, his administrative developments and his conquests, notably of NORMANDY and ANJOU, more than doubled the resources of the French monarchy.

Philip II (1527–98), king of Spain, Naples and Sicily (1556–98), and of Portugal (as Philip I, 1580–98). The son of Emperor CHARLES V, his four wives included MARY I of England. On his accession to the throne Spain dominated much of Italy, surrounded France and threatened England through its possession of the Netherlands. Spain also led the Christian fight against the OTTOMAN Turks at sea, a largely Spanish fleet defeating the Turks at LEPANTO in 1571. As a champion of Counter-Reformation Catholicism Philip attempted to suppress the DUTCH REVOLT from 1567, intervened in the FRENCH WARS OF RELIGION and launched the ARMADA against Protestant England. On his death he left a strong Spain with an extensive empire, but with an economy crippled by military expenses.

Philip IV (the Fair; 1268–1314), king of France (1285–1314), a high-handed and highly controversial ruler, he launched attacks on FLANDERS and AQUITAINE, arrested Pope BONIFACE VIII and ordered the suppression of the TEMPLARS.

Philip V (1683–1746), BOURBON king of Spain (1700–46), grandson of LOUIS XIV. He succeeded to the throne on the terms of the will of Charles II, the last Habsburg king of Spain. Louis XIV's acceptance of this will sparked off the War of the SPANISH SUCCESSION. Philip's claim to the throne was confirmed at the Peace of UTRECHT.

Philip of Hesse (1504–67), German prince who played a prominent role in establishing Protestantism in Germany during the REFORMATION. He created the SCHMALKALDIC LEAGUE to defend Lutheranism against Emperor CHARLES V, and helped suppress the PEASANTS' WAR and the ANABAPTIST experiment at Münster.

Philippi, Battle of (42 BC), a battle in which the republican forces of BRUTUS and CASSIUS were defeated by Mark ANTONY (accompanied by OCTAVIAN, who played little part in the battle).

Philippines, a republic comprising an archipelago in the Pacific off the E coast of Asia. See panel.

PHILIPPINES

1521: MAGELLAN discovered the islands, naming them after PHILIP II of Spain. **From 16th century:** Spanish rule spread through the archipelago, but was harassed by the Dutch and by Moro pirates from Mindanao. **1896:** Rising nationalism and resentment of economic injustice led to unsuccessful revolt against Spanish rule. **1898:** The islands were ceded to the USA after the SPANISH–AMERICAN WAR. **1898–1906:** Armed resistance to US rule; thereafter US policy wavered between delaying and accelerating Filipino self-rule. **1935:** Semi-independent 'Commonwealth' of the Philippines established with Manuel Quezon as president. **1941–5:** Japanese occupation during WORLD WAR II (see PACIFIC CAMPAIGNS). **1946:** Independent republic established. **1953–7:** President Ramon Magsaysay crushed Communist-dominated guerrillas. **1965–86:** Increasingly dictatorial presidency of Ferdinand MARCOS, who presided over large-scale corruption. **1986:** Marcos overthrown in a popular revolution in favour of Corazon AQUINO. **1992:** Corazon Aquino succeeded by democratically elected President Ramos; continuing insurgency by groups including Communists and Islamic nationalists remains a problem.

Philippine Sea, Battle of the (19/20 June 1944), a naval battle fought between US and Japanese forces in the Pacific during WORLD WAR II. The Japanese suffered a heavy defeat, US forces going on to take Guam and Tinian by 10 August. See PACIFIC CAMPAIGNS.

Philip the Bold (1342–1404), duke of BURGUNDY (1363–1404). By his marriage to Margaret, heiress to Flanders and Artois, he became one of the wealthiest and most powerful of the French princes.

Philip the Good (1396–1467), duke of BURGUNDY (1419–67). Between 1425 and 1430 he took advantage of the Anglo-Burgundian alliance during the HUNDRED YEARS WAR to add Hainault, Holland and Brabant to his list of territories. Prosperous centres such as Amsterdam, Antwerp, Bruges, Brussels, Ghent and Lille thereby fell under his rule. In 1435 he ended the Anglo-Burgundian alliance and, siding with France, waged war against England.

Philistines, the descendants of the Peleset, one of the 'SEA PEOPLES' who settled the area around Gaza early in the 1st millennium BC, and ultimately gave their name to the whole region of PALESTINE. Their battles against the Israelites are recorded in the Old Testament, and the remains of their iron weapons bear out the biblical accounts.

Phoenicians, a Semitic-speaking people of the Levantine coast descended from the Canaanites of the 2nd millennium BC. In the 1st millennium BC the Phoenicians became great seafaring traders. The most ancient of their coastal cities was Byblos (ancient Gubla), but Tyre became the greatest and wealthiest. As well as dye and textiles, the Phoenicians exported glassware, carved ivory, jewellery and metal goods. They founded a colony on Cyprus – the 'copper island' – sailed to Britain to obtain tin from Cornwall, and in Spain founded the colony of Gades (modern Cadiz) to extract its rich silver deposits. CARTHAGE, their most famous colony, developed into a major maritime power. The Phoenician cities remained prosperous through the various political changes wrought in the Near East, but eventually came under the influence of powers such as the Babylonians, ACHAEMENIDS, ALEXANDER THE GREAT, the SELEUCIDS and finally Rome. Their greatest legacy to posterity was the alphabetic writing system.

Phoenix Park murders, the assassination in Dublin, on 6 May 1882, of the new Chief Secretary for Ireland, Lord Frederick Cavendish, and his Permanent Undersecretary, Thomas Burke, by members of an extreme Irish nationalist group.

Phoney War, the period of inactivity between the start of WORLD WAR II and HITLER'S assault on the West in April 1940.

Picts, a Celtic people living in what is now Scotland, who conducted raids into N England in the 4th and 5th centuries. Gradually confined by pressure from the SCOTS to the NE, they were absorbed by KENNETH I MacAlpine to create the kingdom of Scotland in the 9th century.

Piedmont, a former kingdom of N ITALY (see map, p. 30). From 1718–20 its rulers – the dukes of Savoy – were also kings of Sardinia. In the 19th century Piedmont, under its prime minister CAVOUR, played a central role in the the movement for Italian unification. The Piedmontese king, VICTOR EMMANUEL II, became the first king of Italy.

Pierce, Franklin (1804–69) 14th president of the USA (1853–7). His alienation of the Northern wing of the Democratic Party through his support for the KANSAS–NEBRASKA Act cost him the chance of renomination in 1856.

Pilgrim Fathers, a 19th-century term for the original settlers of New PLYMOUTH, the first permanent British colony on the NE coast of N America. In 1620 the *Mayflower* sailed from Plymouth in England to Cape Cod, Massachusetts.

Pilsudski, Józef Klemens (1867–1935), Polish soldier and president (1918–21). He led Polish troops against Russia between 1914 and 1917. In 1919, having changed sides to support the ALLIES, he was appointed head of state of the newly recreated POLAND. He fought a successful war against the BOLSHEVIKS (1919–20), and was virtual dictator of Poland from 1926 until his death.

Pinochet, Augusto (1915–), Chilean soldier and politician. He led the CIA-backed coup that overthrew ALLENDE in 1973, becoming president himself in 1974. After 16 years of repressive rule, he allowed elections to be held in 1989, handing over to Patricio Aylwin as head of a coalition in March 1990.

Pitt, William, 1st Earl of Chatham (Pitt the Elder; 1708–78), British WHIG politician, prime minister (1756–7, 1757–61 and 1766–8). His leadership (in coalition with NEWCASTLE) took Britain to victory in the SEVEN YEARS WAR, and his vigorous foreign policy helped lay the foundations of Britain's imperial power.

Pitt, William (Pitt the Younger; 1759–1806), British politician. He became prime minister at the age of 24 in 1783 and occupied the post until 1801, carrying out important economic reforms. From 1793 his premiership was dominated by the REVOLUTIONARY and NAPOLEONIC WARS. He resigned over GEORGE III'S opposition to CATHOLIC EMANCIPATION, but was PM again from 1804 to 1806.

Pizarro, Francisco (1475–1541), Spanish CONQUISTADORE. In 1531 he arrived in PERU with one ship, 180 men and 87 horses. Under cover of a private interview, he seized the INCA Emperor, ATAHUALPA, imprisoned him and demanded a vast ransom. An advancing Inca army retreated on hearing of Pizarro's execution of the emperor. Pizarro – his force boosted to 600 men by reinforcements from Panama – advanced on the Inca capital of Cuzco and seized the city without a struggle in November 1533. Pizarro went on to found new settlements in Peru, including Lima, but was later assassinated by a partner from one of his earlier expeditions.

Plaid Cymru (Welsh 'party of Wales'), a political party, founded in 1925, seeking to achieve autonomy for Wales within the UK in cultural, linguistic and economic matters.

Plantagenet, the name by which HENRY II'S father, Geoffrey of Anjou (1113–51), was known. Since the 15th century the name has been used to identify the dynasty of kings of England descended from him, beginning with HENRY II and ending with RICHARD III. The first three Plantagenet kings are usually referred to as ANGEVINS.

Plassey, Battle of (13 June 1757), the victory in W Bengal of Robert CLIVE over Nawab Siraj ud-Daula, which established British dominance in BENGAL. Outnumbered by Indian forces, Clive gained the support of the Nawab's enemies to win the battle. See also EAST INDIA COMPANY.

Plataea, Battle of (479 BC), the final battle of the PERSIAN WARS, in which Greek infantry forces led by Pausanias the Spartan defeated the Persian forces of XERXES I, at Plataea, a Boeotian city-state in central Greece.

Plate, Battle of the River (13 December 1939), a naval battle between British and German forces in the S Atlantic early in WORLD WAR II. The German battleship *Graf Spee* sunk a number of cargo ships before being forced into Montevideo harbour by British cruisers. Her crew were later forced to scuttle the ship on Hitler's orders. It was one of the few incidents during the period of the 'PHONEY WAR'.

Plato (428/7–348/7 BC), Athenian philosopher. In his many philosophical dialogues, and his teachings in his Academy, he set out, from SOCRATES' starting position, a constantly developing range of new ideas and theories, including the so-called 'Theory of Forms', and the proposed radical reorganization of society and politics in his *Republic.*

plebeians, in ancient Rome, all citizens apart from the elite PATRICIANS. In the 4th century BC they gained the right to hold office. They formed their own assemblies and elected their own officials, called tribunes, to represent them. In 287 BC the plebeians obtained the right to pass laws in their assemblies.

Plekhanov, Georgi (1856–1918), Russian political philosopher and politician. The most influential Russian interpreter of MARXISM, he helped formulate the programme of the Russian SOCIAL DEMOCRATIC Party. When the party split, he sided with the MENSHEVIKS.

PLO, see PALESTINE LIBERATION ORGANIZATION.

Plymouth Colony, the first permanent British colony on the NE coast of N America, settled by the PILGRIM FATHERS in 1620. It joined the New England Confederation in 1643 and became part of MASSACHUSETTS in 1691.

Pocahontas (c. 1595–1617), ALGONQUIN princess. She successfully pleaded for the life of John SMITH, who was about to be sacrificed by her father and Algonquin chief, POWHATAN. She became an intermediary between her tribe and the struggling colony, and was later kidnapped, and converted to Christianity. After marrying an Englishman and bearing a child, she travelled to England only to die at 22 as she prepared to return to America.

pogrom, (Russian 'destruction'), a word used to describe organized massacres of, or attacks on, Jews which took place in Russia from the 1880s onwards. See ANTI-SEMITISM.

Poincaré, Raymond Nicolas Landry (1860–1934), French politician, prime minister (1912–13, 1922–4, 1926–9), president (1913–20). He provided strong leadership in WORLD WAR I, and supported severe reparations against Germany in 1919. As PM in the postwar years, he ordered, with Belgium, the occupation of the RUHR (1923–5).

Poitiers, Battle of (19 September 1356), a battle fought between the French and English during the HUNDRED YEARS WAR. English archers, under the command of EDWARD THE BLACK PRINCE, slaughtered the overconfident French knights. John II of France was taken prisoner.

Poland, a country of E Europe. See panel.

Poland, Partitions of (1772, 1793 and 1795), the three partitions of Poland by Russia, Prussia and Austria. FREDERICK the Great, anxious to calm Austro-Russian relations and thereby avoid a general war that might prove disastrous for Prussia, proposed that Austria, Russia and Prussia divide up considerable portions of Polish territory between them. All would gain without upsetting the balance of power between them. In the First Partition Poland lost one-third of its territory and population. In an attempt to prevent further losses, reforming Poles established a strong constitutional monarchy. However, CATHERINE II pre-empted their plans by effecting a Second Partition with Prussia, in which Poland lost half of its remaining territories. A Polish revolt against Russian rule was suppressed and a Third Partition carried out by Austria,

POLAND

11th century: Small Polish states united to form a single nation. **14th century:** Kings Wladyslaw I and Casimir III (the Great) strengthened Poland, encouraged trade and codified laws. **1386:** Queen Jadwiga married Jagiello, the grand duke of LITHUANIA, uniting the two realms. **1569:** The Union of Lublin established full political ties between the two countries. **1572:** the last of the JAGIELLONS died, leaving no heir; monarchy became elective, and the power of both sovereign and parliament declined. **16th and 17th centuries:** Wars against Muscovites, Turks, Tartars, Cossacks and Swedes. **1674–96:** John SOBIESKI expelled the Ottoman Turks from Poland. **1700–21** and **1733–8:** Poland ravaged by NORTHERN WAR and the War of the POLISH SUCCESSION. **1772, 1793** and **1795:** Russia, Prussia and Austria carve up Poland in the Partitions of POLAND. **1830, 1848** and **1863:** Unsuccessful revolts against Russian rule. **1919:** Polish statehood restored. **1926–35:** Virtual dictatorship of Józef PILSUDSKI. **1939:** Poland partitioned by Germany and USSR in the NAZI-SOVIET PACT. **1940–5:** German occupation during WORLD WAR II; Poland lost 15% of its population, including almost all its Jews, in the HOLOCAUST. **1944:** WARSAW RISING. **1945:** Liberation by Soviet Red Army; Communist state established; Poland lost 50% of its territory in the E to the USSR, but gained in the N and W from Germany. **1956:** Political crisis brought Wladyslaw GOMULKA to power. **1980:** Period of unrest led to the birth of the independent trade union SOLIDARITY (*Solidarnosč*), led by Lech WALESA. **1981:** Martial law declared by General Wojciech JARUZELSKI; Solidarity banned; unrest and economic difficulties continued throughout the 1980s. **1989:** Solidarity legalized; free elections held; Solidarity formed a government with former allies of Communists. **1990:** Walesa became President. **1990–1:** Political, economic and social reforms; first free multi-party elections. **1993:** Former Communists emerged as largest single party in elections.

Prussia and Russia. This final partition removed Poland from the map of Europe, and the Poles did not regain independence until the end of World War I.

Polish Corridor, a strip of territory ceded by Germany to Poland in the VERSAILLES Peace Settlement (1919) to allow Poland access to the Baltic. It was retaken by Germany in 1939. See map, p. 37.

Polish Succession, War of the (1733–8), a conflict arising from the rival claims to the Polish throne of Augustus of Saxony and Stanislas Leszczynski. These were used by France and Spain as an excuse to attack the Austrian HABSBURGS in Italy and the Rhineland to obtain Lorraine for France.

politburo, the most important decision-making body of the COMMUNIST party under all Marxist regimes.

Polk, James Knox (1795–1849), 11th president of the USA (1845–9), a Jacksonian Democrat and devotee of MANIFEST DESTINY. His term was marked by the acquisition of California and New Mexico after US victory in the MEXICAN-AMERICAN War, and the settlement of the OREGON BOUNDARY DISPUTE with Britain.

Pol Pot (1925–), Cambodian Communist politician, prime minister (1976–9). As leader of the KHMER ROUGE he overthrew the Cambodian military regime in 1975 and sought to create a self-sufficient workers' utopia. He forcibly moved city-dwellers to rural areas to work the land and massacred up to 2,000,000 of his compatriots. He was overthrown by the Vietnamese invasion in 1978, but remains an influential figure within the Khmer Rouge.

Polynesians, the peoples of the islands of the central Pacific, including Hawaii, Samoa, Tonga and New Zealand. Settlers had reached Fiji by 1500 BC, spreading to Tonga and Samoa. Over the next 1000 years the language and culture of the islands developed the traits we recognize as Polynesian. The Polynesians were outstanding seafarers, using their navigational skill to colonize islands all over the Pacific. Once settled, they lived in small but highly complex societies, with hereditary chiefs playing a powerful economic and social role. Major islands were divided between several chiefdoms, whose relationships gave much scope for rivalry and warfare. Religion, too, developed its own complexities. New Zealand's Polynesians – the MAORIS – developed their own variation of Polynesian culture.

Pombal, Sebastiao José de Carvalho e Mello, Marquis of (1699–1778), first minister of King José I (1750–77) of PORTUGAL. He was responsible for the rebuilding of Lisbon after the earthquake of 1755, the expulsion of the Jesuits from Portugal (1759) and efforts to improve the Portuguese economy.

Pompeii, a Roman town in Campania, destroyed by the eruption of Vesuvius in August AD 79. Excavations since the 18th century have provided a unique glimpse of the life of a 1st-century Roman town.

Pompey (Gnaeus Pompeius Magnus; 106–48 BC), Roman general and statesman who conquered much of the Middle East for Rome in the 60s BC. In 49 he led the republican forces against Caesar, his former ally, but was defeated at PHARSALUS in 48. Pompey fled to Egypt, where he was murdered. See ROMAN EMPIRE.

Pompidou, Georges (1911–74), French statesman, prime minister (1962–8), president (1968–74). As PM in DE GAULLE's government he helped negotiate an end to the war with ALGERIA. As president he lifted de Gaulle's veto on British entry into the EC.

Pontius Pilate, the Roman prefect of Judaea from AD 26 to 36 who ordered the crucifixion of JESUS.

Pontus, an ancient region of N Asia Minor, extending along the S Black Sea coast (see map, p. 12). It became a Roman province after POMPEY's victory over its king Mithridates VI in 63 BC.

Poor Laws, English legislation to provide relief for the poor. Parish relief for the rural poor had been available since the 16th century. The UTILITARIAN-influenced Poor Law Amendment Act of 1834 abolished the Speenhamland system of outdoor relief (1795); henceforth paupers were forced for relief into the deliberately harsh conditions of the workhouses.

Popish Plot (1678–81), a supposed Catholic plot to murder CHARLES II, invented by the Anglican cleric Titus Oates (1649–1705). It exploited and fuelled English fears of Catholicism and led to a major political crisis in England, with attempts to oust the king's brother, the Catholic JAMES II, from the succession.

Popular Front, the name given to various coalitions of moderate and left-wing parties committed to the defence of democratic government from FASCISM in the 1930s, especially those forming governments in Spain, Chile and France (the latter under Leon BLUM).

Populist Movement, an agrarian socialist movement in 19th-century Russia. Populists such as BAKUNIN believed that the only way to achieve reform was by mobilizing the peasant masses into socialist communes to overthrow the tsar and establish a democratic republic. However, the Russian peasantry did not respond to the imposition of ideas from an alien middle class. In 1879 the radical wing of the movement established the terrorist 'People's Will' organization, which was responsible for terrorist attacks including the assassination of ALEXANDER II in 1881.

Populist Party, a short-lived US political party that sought to articulate the views of hard-pressed farmers in the southern and midwestern states during the 1890s. The party was dissolved after agreeing to merge with the DEMOCRATS in 1896.

Portland, William Henry Cavendish Bentinck, 3rd Duke of (1738–1809), British statesman, prime minister (1783 and 1807–9). In both his ministries he was only nominal head of the government, his first term being dominated by the strange alliance of FOX and NORTH, the second by CANNING and CASTLEREAGH.

Portsmouth, Treaty of (5 September 1905), a peace treaty ending the RUSSO-JAPANESE WAR, signed at Portsmouth, New Hampshire, USA, following mediation by US President Theodore ROOSEVELT. Japan gained a protectorate over KOREA and railway rights in S Manchuria, as well as the Liaodong Peninsula (including Port Arthur, now Lüshun) and the S part of Sakhalin island.

Portugal, a country of W Europe. See panel.

Potemkin, the battleship whose crew mutinied in the Black Sea during the RUSSIAN REVOLUTION OF 1905.

Potsdam Conference (17 July–2 August 1945), a meeting of the USA, UK and USSR at Potsdam, outside Berlin. The conference confirmed the decision made at the YALTA Conference to divide Germany and Austria into zones of Allied military occupation, outlawed the NAZI Party, broke up large German business monopolies, and redistributed certain German territories to Poland and the USSR. It confirmed that the Soviet Union could retain E Poland, which would receive part of E Germany in compensation.

Powhatan (early 17th century), ALGONQUIN chief. He supplied the JAMESTOWN colonists with essential food in the early days, and in exchange received guns and swords. His daughter, POCAHONTAS, successfully pleaded with him to spare the life of JOHN SMITH.

Praetorians, the elite unit of the Roman army, established as a permanent force in the early empire. The Praetorian Guard played an important part in political events, installing CLAUDIUS on the throne, and its commander, the Praetorian Prefect, was the most powerful official in the empire.

PORTUGAL

8th century: The N of Portugal resisted the Muslim conquests in the Iberian Peninsula. **11th century:** Portuguese territory regained from the Muslims during the RECONQUISTA. **1139:** Portugal became a kingdom. **1270:** Portugal's present boundaries established. **15th century:** Portugal became a dynamic trading nation; Prince HENRY the Navigator became a leading patron of Portuguese exploration; which mapped much of the W African coast. **By mid-16th century:** Portugal had laid the foundations of a vast colonial empire in BRAZIL, Africa and Asia. **1580:** On the extinction of the Aviz dynasty the thrones of SPAIN and Portugal were united. **1640:** Revolution led to the accession of the Portuguese Braganza family. **17th–18th centuries:** Portuguese power declined, but the country retained major colonies. **1807:** The royal family fled to Brazil to escape a Napoleonic invasion. **1821:** King JOHN VI returned from Brazil (a liberal constitution had been established during his absence). **1822:** John VI's son Pedro (later PEDRO I) declared Brazil independent. **1832–4:** Portugal crippled by civil war between liberal constitutionalists supporting Queen Maria II (Pedro's daughter) and absolutists under the rival King Miguel (Pedro's brother); instability continued throughout the 19th century. **1910:** Monarchy overthrown; republic proclaimed. **1926:** Military coup. **1932–68:** Dictatorship of António SALAZAR; Portugal became a one-party state. **1961–75:** Expensive colonial wars; Portugal attempted to check independence movements in ANGOLA and MOZAMBIQUE. **1974:** Left-wing military coup. **1974–5:** Independence of Portugal's African colonies. **1976:** Constitutional multi-party elections. **1986:** Portugal joined the EUROPEAN COMMUNITY.

Pragmatic Sanction (1713), the decree promulgated by the Emperor CHARLES VI to ensure that his territories passed undivided to his children. By 1720, lacking a male heir, he feared the destruction of the Austrian empire on his death, and obtained a promise from the European powers to respect the succession of his eldest daughter, MARIA THERESA, to all her father's lands. After Charles' death, FREDERICK II of Prussia and other states reneged on their promise, precipitating the War of the AUSTRIAN SUCCESSION.

Prague, Defenestration of (1618), the ejection by Bohemian Protestant aristocrats of two imperial Catholic representatives from a window of the Royal Palace in Prague. The ensuing revolt against the anti-Protestant and centralizing policies of the Habsburg emperor FERDINAND II marked the beginning of the THIRTY YEARS WAR.

Prague Spring (1968), the name given to the period of reform in CZECHOSLOVAKIA under the Communist regime of Alexander DUBĆEK, involving greater freedom of speech and moves towards multi-party democracy. It was crushed by tanks of the WARSAW PACT in August 1968. Dubćek was replaced by hardliner Gustav Husák.

prehistory, the period of history before written records. It is divided into the STONE AGE (PALAEOLITHIC, MESOLITHIC and NEOLITHIC), the BRONZE AGE and the IRON AGE. Written records of events began in Egypt and Mesopotamia c. 3000 BC.

Presbyterians, anti-Episcopalian Protestants who – influenced by CALVIN – favoured a form of Church government in which each church was governed by its minister aided by lay elders within a national structure headed by a synod. During the REFORMATION the HUGUENOTS organized such a Church in France, while John KNOX founded the Presbyterian Church of Scotland.

pretender, any claimant to a throne from which he or his ancestors were ejected, particularly the JACOBITE 'Old Pretender', James Edward Stuart (1688–1766), son of JAMES II by his second wife, and his son the 'Young Pretender', Charles Edward Stuart (Bonnie Prince Charlie; 1720–88), who attempted to make good their claims in the FIFTEEN and the FORTY-FIVE.

Primo de Rivera y Orbaneja, Miguel (1870–1930), Spanish general and dictator (1923–30). He seized power in a military coup in 1923 and tried to unite Spain around the slogan of 'Country, Religion and Monarchy'. He failed to undertake necessary reforms, and was finally forced to resign in 1930.

princely states, the 629 British-protected states in INDIA whose rulers enjoyed varying degrees of autonomy. The principal states (in order of precedence) were HYDERABAD, MYSORE, Baroda, (Jammu and) KASHMIR, Gwalior, Bhopal, Travancore, Kolhapur, Udaipur (Mewar) and Indore. Some of the princely states were coerced into joining India at independence and three – Travancore, Hyderabad and Kashmir – seriously attempted to regain their independence. Travancore and Hyderabad succumbed to political pressure and joined the Federation, but the claims of Pakistan on KASHMIR provoked confrontation and war with India.

printing, the mass production of text and illustrations by mechanical devices. Movable type was invented in Europe around 1450, but woodblock printing dates back to 8th-century China. The printed word played a crucial role in the spread of the REFORMATION.

privateering, the activity of armed, privately owned ships commissioned for action against those of hostile states by governments or sovereign princes (particularly English, French and Dutch). It was an important component of naval warfare before the emergence of large, state-controlled navies.

Progressive Movement, a multi-faceted movement working to achieve social and economic reforms appropriate to a modern industrial economy in the USA (c. 1900–20). Committed to free trade and the control of monopolistic 'trusts', the movement drew support from a wide range of groups. Social reforms espoused included improved working conditions as well as PROHIBITION. Some of the aims of the movement were incorporated into the legislation of Presidents Theodore ROOSEVELT and Woodrow WILSON.

Progressive Parties (1912, 1924 and 1948), the label assumed by three short-lived 20th-century US political parties. The first, a vehicle for the renewed presidential ambitions of Theodore ROOSEVELT, unsuccessfully fought the election of 1912. The second sought to convince the electorate of the need for public control of natural resources and railroads, but won only 17% of the popular vote in 1924. The third represented a dissident left-liberal faction united behind the abortive presidential candidacy of former Democratic vice-president Henry Wallace in 1948.

Prohibition (1920–33), the period of prohibition of alcohol in the USA. The Eighteenth Amendment to the Constitution (1920) banned the manufacture, transport, sale or consumption of alcohol throughout the USA. Prohibition proved difficult to enforce and illegal drinking dens – 'speakeasies' – proliferated, selling illicitly distilled 'bootleg' whisky at inflated prices. Despite the actions of police and Federal Bureau of Investigation (FBI) agents the appeal of alcohol did not decline. The situation was made worse by gangsters like Al Capone (1899–1947) who made a profit from bootlegging. Their activities – including the corruption of police and local government – created an atmosphere of lawlessness in the major cities. The US legislature ended Prohibition with the Twenty-First Amendment in 1933.

Protectorate, English (1653–9), the regime established by Oliver CROMWELL after the dissolution of the RUMP Parliament, during which he ruled as Lord Protector. After his death, the Protectorate was brought to an end by army intervention, and the monarchy restored.

Protestantism, the religion of those churches that broke with the Roman Catholic Church at the REFORMATION, whose doctrines are based on the principles of reformers such as LUTHER, CALVIN, ZWINGLI and others. Movements rejecting Roman authority established reformed national forms of Christianity in the various states of N Europe, such as Lutheranism in Sweden and parts of Germany, Calvinism in Switzerland and Scotland (PRESBYTERIANS) and ANGLICANISM in parts of England. The 18th century saw movements for spiritual reform in Protestant countries – Pietism in Germany, and the Evangelical revival in Britain and North America. European emigration took all the Protestant traditions to America, Canada, Australia and elsewhere.

Proudhon, Pierre Joseph (1809–65), French political writer and revolutionary, most famous for his assertion that 'property is theft'. His belief that ANARCHY was the most just form of social organization partly inspired the Paris COMMUNE of 1871.

Prussia, a former state in N and central Germany (see maps, pp. 25, 27, 29 and 30). By the early 18th century BRANDENBURG-Prussia had developed into a powerful Protestant state. Its territories were expanded by FREDERICK the Great, under whom it became a great power. In the 19th century Prussia vied with Austria for dominance within the GERMAN CONFEDERATION. Under BISMARCK, Prussia emerged as the victor in the SEVEN WEEKS WAR (1866) and dominated the new North German Confederation. Prussian victory in the FRANCO-PRUSSIAN WAR ensured that Prussia was the nucleus of the German state created in 1871. Prussia was abolished as a distinct entity by the Allied powers after WORLD WAR II.

Ptolemy, the family name of the Macedonian dynasty that ruled EGYPT from 304 BC – when Ptolemy I Soter, one of ALEXANDER the Great's generals, proclaimed himself king – to the death of CLEOPATRA VII, the last of the line, in 30 BC. Ptolemy I extended his rule over Cyprus, Palestine and other cities in Asia Minor and the Aegean. His successors were caught up in conflicts with the SELEUCIDS over control of Syria, Asia Minor and the Aegean. Cleopatra drew the wrath of Rome over her alliance with Mark ANTONY, and after their defeat at ACTIUM, Egypt was annexed by OCTAVIAN. By taking pharaonic titles and paying honour to Egyptian gods, the Macedonian Ptolemies linked themselves to the ancient dynasties and gained the support of the priesthood. The prosperous city of ALEXANDRIA became a great centre of Hellenistic learning and culture, endowed with the world's first museum and largest library.

Punic Wars, three wars between Rome and CARTHAGE (264–241 BC, 218–202 BC and 149–146 BC). In 264 BC Rome challenged the Carthaginians for control of Sicily. In spite of immense losses the Romans finally emerged as victors in what is considered the First Punic War (from *Punicus*, 'Carthaginian'). The Second Punic War began in 218 when the Carthaginian general HANNIBAL crossed the Alps and invaded Italy. He won some spectacular victories, notably at CANNAE, but failed to win over Rome's Italian allies and withdrew from Italy in 204 BC before being defeated at ZAMA in 202 BC. Carthage was forced to yield Spain to Rome. In 149 Rome allied itself with NUMIDIA against Carthage in the Third Punic War. Carthage was completely destroyed and the area became the Roman province of 'Africa'.

Punjab, a region of S Asia that was ruled by the SIKHS until 1849 when it was annexed by the British. In 1947 it was divided between INDIA and PAKISTAN on a religious basis. However, the movement of Hindus and Sikhs from Muslim areas and Muslims from Hindu areas during partition was accompanied by violence that led to thousands of deaths. Fighting on the Punjabi border between the two countries broke out in 1965 and 1971. Despite the division of the Indian state of Punjab into Sikh and Hindu areas, the Sikhs continue to campaign for an independent state in the region (Khalistan).

purges, the execution, exile and imprisonment of thousands of people in the Soviet Union under STALIN during the 1930s. The murder of the Communist official, Kirov, in 1934 was used by Stalin to purge the party of potential rivals. Over four years Stalin's rivals were brought before show trials, convicted and shot. The victims included 1108 Communist delegates. The purges also claimed the lives of intellectuals and army officers. Altogether tens of millions of people were executed, exiled, or put in prison. See also GULAG.

Puritans, those English Protestants in the later 16th and early 17th centuries who sought to 'purify' the ANGLICAN Church of its imperfections, and who emphasized the importance of independent judgement based upon conscience and the Bible. Some Puritans emigrated to America in the 1620s. Attempts by Parliament to impose such changes on the crown contributed to the tensions that led to the ENGLISH CIVIL WAR. After the RESTORATION some Puritans were absorbed into the Anglican Church, while others joined Nonconformist denominations.

Pygmies, a racial group of central Africa, hunter-gatherers now mainly inhabiting the rainforest of the Congo basin.

Pym, John (1583–1643), English politician, one of the leaders of the opposition to CHARLES I in the LONG PARLIAMENT. His administrative and financial measures (and alliance with the Scots) helped ensure the final success of the Parliamentary forces in the ENGLISH CIVIL WAR.

pyramids, monumental tombs built by the pharaohs of the Egyptian Old Kingdom (2575–2134 BC). The sheer size of the Great Pyramids of Giza shows that the pharaoh was the dominant figure of the state, acting as an intermediary between the gods and mankind.

Pyramids, Battle of the (1798), NAPOLEON'S victory over the MAMLUKS in Egypt was intended to be the prelude to French colonization of the East and an attack on British India, but these plans were overturned by NELSON'S victory at the Battle of the NILE.

Pyrenees, Treaty of the (7 November 1659), a peace treaty concluding the Franco-Spanish War of 1648–59. France acquired Roussillon, Artois and – subject to certain conditions – Alsace-Lorraine. French conquests in Catalonia were restored to Spain. The treaty is often seen as marking the beginning of French hegemony in Europe. See map, p. 25.

Pyrrhus (c. 318–272 BC), king of EPIRUS (307–303, 297–272 BC). A cousin of ALEXANDER the Great, his ambition was to revive the latter's empire. His campaigns in Italy involved some costly ('Pyrrhic') victories, and he was finally defeated by the Romans in 275 BC.

Qaddafi, Muammar al- (1942–), Libyan politician, president of LIBYA from 1971. A Bedouin, he led a military coup to overthrow King IDRIS I in 1969. Allegations of international terrorism have left him isolated and at odds with the USA.

Qatar, an emirate in the Persian Gulf. By the 8th century AD Qatar was Islamic and had developed as a trading centre. In the 1860s Britain intervened in a dispute between Qatar and its Bahraini rulers, installing a member of the Qatari ath-Thani family as sheik. Qatar was part of the OTTOMAN Empire from 1872 until 1914. Its ruler signed protection treaties with Britain in 1916 and 1934, and did not regain complete independence until 1971.

Qianlong (1710–96), Chinese emperor of the QING dynasty (1736–96). The Chinese Empire reached its greatest extent during his reign, with conquests in TURKESTAN, Xinjiang, Nepal and Burma. He restricted trade with the West, and was troubled by financial problems, corruption and provincial revolts. He abdicated in favour of his son four years before his death.

Qin or **Ch'in**, the first imperial Chinese dynasty (221–206 BC). It emerged as the final victor from the WARRING STATES. Its ruler became SHI HUANGDI – 'the First Emperor' – and in the 11 years of his reign expanded the empire to touch the South China Sea and Central Asia. He began the erection of the Great Wall of China to mark the border with the nomads. Qin rule did not long outlast Shi Huangdi, collapsing in 206 BC, but the foundations of empire had been firmly laid for the succeeding HAN dynasty.

Qing or **Ch'ing**, the last Chinese imperial dynasty (1644–1911) established by the MANCHU who seized N China in 1644, finally bringing S China under their yoke in 1682. Under the Qing, particularly under KANGXI and QIANLONG, China rose to new heights of power and prosperity. Tibet and Turkestan were taken under effective control. In the N firearms turned the balance of power against the nomads. In the Treaty of NERCHINSK China was able to reach agreement with Russia to fix a boundary across the steppes of Central Asia. The dynasty ruled in traditional Chinese ways through old-fashioned bureaucracy, and a century and a half of peace and prosperity pushed the Chinese population to over the 400 million mark in the 18th century. The Qing dynasty began to decline in the 19th century as population pressure, official corruption and heavy taxation took their toll. The problems of the dynasty were compounded by pressure from European powers to increase trade. The conflict with the West culminated in the OPIUM WARS and the UNEQUAL TREATIES. In the middle of the century the Qing dynasty was seriously challenged by the TAIPING Movement, which was brutally suppressed with Western help. An assertive Japan took advantage of Chinese difficulties to launch the SINO-JAPANESE WAR in 1894. Attempts to modernize and reform China were thwarted by the empress dowager, CIXI, who encouraged the bloody and xenophobic BOXER REBELLION. In 1911 the Qing dynasty fell to an army rebellion.

Quadruple Alliance, the alliance of Britain, Prussia, Austria and Russia against NAPOLEON in 1813, also known as the Fourth Coalition. An army of Prussian, Austrian, Russian and Swedish troops defeated Napoleon at the Battle of LEIPZIG that year.

Quakers, a radical Christian sect – the Society of Friends – founded by George Fox (1624–91). They rejected a formal church, admitting only the authority of divine revelation, and advocated pacifism.

Québec, a Canadian province and historic centre of French-Canadian political power. First settled during the 17th century, it remained in French hands until 1763, when sovereignty was transferred to Great Britain by the Treaty of

PARIS. During the 19th century Québec was riven by tensions between the French-speaking rural majority and British merchants in Montreal, which prompted the outbreak of PAPINEAU'S REBELLION in 1837. The BRITISH NORTH AMERICA ACT of 1867 made Québec a separate province within the Dominion of CANADA. Since 1990 separatist pressure has increased in Québec, where a referendum on sovereignty is scheduled to be held.

Québec Liberation Front (FLQ), a French-Canadian terrorist organization seeking independence for the Canadian province of QUÉBEC. Its terrorist campaign of the late 1960s and early 1970s was unpopular and the constitutional Parti Québécois proved a more successful vehicle for French-Canadian separatism.

Quetzalcóatl, a legendary hero and god of pre-Columbian Meso-America, traditionally associated with the foundation of the cities of Tula and Chichén Itzá and the establishment of TOLTEC power. He allegedly sailed E, promising to return, a legend exploited by the Spanish CONQUISTADORES.

Quisling, Vidkun (1887–1945), Norwegian Fascist politician. He declared himself head of state after the German invasion of NORWAY in 1940. His name is now used pejoratively to describe a traitor who aids an occupying enemy force.

Qur'an or **Koran**, the holy book of ISLAM. Muhammad's revelations from God form the basis of the book, which Muslims hold to be the word of God.

Rabin, Yitzhak (1922–), Israeli Labour politician, prime minister (1974–7 and 1992–). His second term of office saw the signing of the ISRAELI–PALESTINIAN PEACE ACCORD.

Raffles, Sir (Thomas) Stamford (1781–1826), British colonial administrator who established a settlement at SINGAPORE.

Rafsanjani, Ali Akbar (1934–), Iranian politician and cleric, president of IRAN (1989–). Following the Islamic Revolution of 1979–80 he became Speaker of the Iranian parliament, and succeeded his teacher, Ayatollah KHOMEINI, as president in 1989.

Raglan, Fitzroy James Henry Somerset, 1st Baron (1788–1855), British soldier and diplomat. As commander-in-chief during the CRIMEAN WAR he was widely blamed for his mismanagement of the campaign.

Rajputs, members of a Hindu landowning caste who established a powerful military position in W INDIA (modern Rajasthan) in the 17th century. The various Rajput states, notably Jodhpur and Jaipur, retained a measure of autonomy as PRINCELY STATES under British rule.

Raleigh, Sir Walter (1552–1618), English explorer and courtier. A favourite of ELIZABETH I, he made the first – unsuccessful – attempt to colonize VIRGINIA (1584). Imprisoned by JAMES I on trumped-up treason charges, he was executed after an unsuccessful mission to find gold in South America.

Ramesses II, a pharaoh of the 19th dynasty of ancient EGYPT (c. 1304–1237 BC). His conflict with the HITTITES in Syria culminated in the indecisive encounter at KADESH in 1285 BC. Sixteen years later they signed a peace treaty and Ramesses married a Hittite princess. His reign was marked by prosperity and artistic creativity. He went on to found a new capital of Per-Ramesses in the Delta.

Ramillies, Battle of (23 May 1706), a victory won by MARLBOROUGH over a Franco-Spanish army during the War of the SPANISH SUCCESSION. It was followed by the virtually bloodless conquest of much of the Spanish Netherlands.

Rapallo, Treaty of (1922), a treaty of friendship between Germany and the Soviet Union, renewing diplomatic relations between the two states after their severance during World War I. It was the first international agreement to recognize the Soviet Union.

Rasputin, Grigor Efimovich (1871–1916), Russian mystic and religious fanatic, popularly known as the 'Mad Monk'. He came to wield undue influence at the Court of St Petersburg in the years before the RUSSIAN REVOLUTION, gaining a disastrous hold on the Tsarina (Empress) Alexandra Feodorovna, who believed he could cure her son's haemophilia. He was assassinated by a group of noblemen in 1916.

Rastadt, Peace of (1714), a treaty between the Emperor CHARLES VI and LOUIS XIV, putting an end to the former's attempt to continue the War of the SPANISH SUCCESSION.

Reagan, Ronald W. (1911–), 40th president of the USA (1981–9). A conservative anti-Communist Republican and champion of the economics of the NEW RIGHT, Reagan was a Hollywood actor before becoming governor of California (1966–74). He won landslide election victories against Democratic challengers Jimmy CARTER in 1980 and Walter Mondale in 1984. Reagan charmed his supporters with folksy homilies, low taxes for the rich, and a massive increase in defence spending. While he did much to restore the confidence of the nation, he failed to coordinate and lead his administration. One result of this was the 'Iran-gate' scandal, in which it was revealed that White House staff had been involved in secret talks to sell arms to Iran – the profits from which were to be channelled illegally to anti-Communist Contra guerrillas in NICARAGUA. More damaging in the long term was Reagan's economic legacy of a US budget deficit ballooning out of control despite cuts in welfare spending. Reagan was succeeded by his vice-president George BUSH in 1989.

Reconquista, the Christian reconquest of SPAIN. In the mid-11th century the small Christian kingdoms of N Spain, principally CASTILE and ARAGON, began to regain territory from the Muslim states that had long dominated the peninsula. The conquest of Toledo by Alfonso VI in 1085 was followed by further successes. The reconquest was stalled by the invasions of the ALMORAVIDS in 1086 and the ALMOHADS in 1145, but Christian forces continued to regain territory, establishing the kingdom of Portugal in 1139. The Castilian victory at Las NAVAS DE TOLOSA in 1212 set the seal on the reconquest. By the mid-13th century Muslim rule was confined to the Emirate of GRANADA. In the 14th century Aragon secured the Mediterranean coast and the Balearic islands. The Muslim defeat by Castile at Salado in 1340 and the capture of Algeçiras (1342–4) ended the threat of Islamic invasion. Granada was finally incorporated into Spain by the dual monarchy of FERDINAND of Aragon and ISABELLA of Castile.

Reconstruction Acts (1867–8), legislation passed by the US Congress reorganizing the defeated CONFEDERATE states of the South after the AMERICAN CIVIL WAR. A fierce political struggle evolved during which moderate and radical Republicans united to give the vote to American blacks. More radical measures were vetoed by President Andrew JOHNSON, an ally of the defeated planter class. Despite the founding of racist Southern organizations like the KU KLUX KLAN, Reconstruction was a period of hope for the emancipated slaves. During the 1870s Deep South states with large black populations sent black delegates to Congress for the first time in US history. However, after the onset of economic recession in 1873, Northern voters lost interest in Reconstruction and the Republicans abandoned their Southern allies to the racist white majority. During the 1890s Southern blacks were deprived of the vote by state laws, and they remained second-class citizens until the mid-20th century. See CIVIL RIGHTS MOVEMENT.

recusant, a term used for those in England (primarily Catholics) who would not attend the services of the ANGLICAN Church as laid down by the law, and who were fined for their non-attendance.

Red Army, the land forces of the USSR, originally created by TROTSKY to defend the RUSSIAN REVOLUTION during the RUSSIAN CIVIL WAR. The Red Army may have lost as many as 10 million men in World War II.

Red Brigades, Italian anarchist organization. It conducted a campaign of bombings, kidnappings and murders in the 1970s, the most notorious being that of Aldo MORO in 1978.

Red Cross Society, an international humanitarian agency established in 1863 by Henri Dunant, who was also responsible for the first of the GENEVA CONVENTIONS. Based in Switzerland, it is dedicated to caring for the victims of war. The Red Cross (known as the Red Crescent in Islamic countries) now has over 100 national societies and its work has expanded to include disaster relief.

Red Guards, militant student supporters of MAO ZEDONG during the CULTURAL REVOLUTION. Their attacks on party officials led to thousands of deaths and Mao was forced to call in the army for support when the Red Guards went out of control.

Reform Acts, three far-reaching measures for electoral reform in 19th-century Britain. In 1832 the WHIGS increased the electorate by nearly a half, enfranchising mainly prosperous middle-class voters. The Conservative administration of Lord DERBY gave the vote to many urban working men in the Reform Act of 1867. In 1884 the LIBERALS extended the household franchise to agricultural workers in the counties, increasing the total electorate from about three to about five million male voters.

Reformation, a movement that attempted to reform the practices and doctrines of the ROMAN CATHOLIC CHURCH. It culminated in the establishment of PROTESTANTISM and Protestant churches. The Reformation was the outcome of dissatisfaction with abuses within the Roman Catholic Church, which was increasingly seen as corrupt and worldly. Criticisms of the Church began with the LOLLARDS and HUSSITES of the late 14th and early 15th centuries, but the start of the Reformation is usually given as 1517, the year Martin LUTHER published his opposition to indulgences and other abuses in the Church. The Lutheran Church spread rapidly thereafter in Germany and N Europe, and influenced the emerging ANGLICAN Church in England. In 1555 the Peace of Augsburg allowed each German prince, Lutheran or Catholic, to decide the religion of his subjects. A number of rulers ordered Reformation in their states because they profited from the seizure of Church property, and increased their authority by creating a clergy subject to them and not to Rome. Reform was also effected in Switzerland by ZWINGLI and John CALVIN, who established the Calvinist Church. Their different beliefs led to conflict with other reformers as well as with Catholics. In Scotland, a successful revolt against Catholic Mary, Queen of Scots was followed by reform of the Church on Calvinist lines by John KNOX. In France the HUGUENOTS (French Calvinists) became involved in the rivalries of the noble factions in the FRENCH WARS OF RELIGION. Calvinist resistance contributed to the success of the DUTCH REVOLT against Spain. The religious tensions unleashed by the Reformation culminated in the THIRTY YEARS WAR. See also COUNTER-REFORMATION.

Regency, in general the rule of any regent during the incapacity of the legal monarch on grounds of age or health; in England, specifically, the period of government of the Prince of Wales, the future GEORGE IV, from 1811 (when GEORGE III was finally declared insane) to 1820.

Reichstag (German, 'imperial parliament'), the legislative assembly of the German SECOND EMPIRE and the WEIMAR Republic. The Reichstag building was burnt on 27/28 February 1933, probably by agents of the NAZIS, who claimed the fire was part of a Communist plot.

reparations, compensation payments exacted from a defeated enemy by the victors, especially those demanded of Germany by the ALLIES after World War I. Germany's failure to meet reparations demands led to an international crisis in 1924, when Franco-Belgian forces occupied the Ruhr to enforce their claims to debt repayment. The DAWES Plan was introduced to reschedule the payments, but Germany's economic problems proved too great and the Dawes Plan and its successor, the YOUNG Plan, both failed. In 1932 all reparations were cancelled at the Lausanne Conference.

Representatives, House of, the lower house of the US CONGRESS.

Republican Party, a US political party originating in the mid-1850s. Committed to preventing the spread of slavery into the W territories, the party was victorious in the presidential election of 1860 (under LINCOLN), which prompted the secession of the states of the CONFEDERACY. Republicans played a key role during the AMERICAN CIVIL WAR, suppressing the rebellion against federal authority and subsequently formulating a plan of RECONSTRUCTION for the conquered South. During the late 19th and early 20th centuries the party moved away from its antislavery roots to become a strong ally of American corporate capital. Long recognized as the more conservative of America's two major parties, it enjoyed a long period of success in presidential elections 1980–92, under Ronald REAGAN and George BUSH, but has failed to maintain a majority over the DEMOCRATS in CONGRESS.

resistance movements, the underground organizations that fought against the AXIS occupiers in WORLD WAR II. Their activities included helping prisoners of war and Jews to escape, sabotage, publishing underground newspapers and transmitting intelligence by secret radio. Among the resistance movements that emerged were the MAQUIS in France, the *Weerstand* in Belgium, and *Het Verzet* in the Netherlands. Partisan and resistance groups were also active in E Europe and the Far East.

Restoration (1660), the re-establishment of the English STUART monarchy after the PROTECTORATE, largely brought about by General Monck (1608–69). Few former supporters of the Protectorate were punished, although the restoration of the ANGLICAN Church meant the expulsion of some clergy. In an attempt to prevent further conflict, CHARLES II was given a fixed revenue and a small standing army.

Revere, Paul (1735–1818), an American patriot who rode from Boston on the night of 18 April 1775 to warn Concord farmers of the approach of British troops. The ensuing engagement marked the beginning of the American War of INDEPENDENCE. Although his exploits were immortalized by the 19th-century poet Henry Wadsworth Longfellow, Revere was in fact captured by the redcoats and never reached his destination.

Revolutionary Wars (1792–1802), a series of European wars following the FRENCH REVOLUTION. Urged by anti-revolutionary Frenchmen, the Austrians and Prussians invaded France in 1792, but were repulsed, and France went onto the offensive. French success, particularly the conquest of the Austrian Netherlands, led to the establishment by Britain of the First Coalition of European powers against Revolutionary France. However, the absence of an effective strategy and the power of France's conscripted army led to French victories across Europe. One by one the allies settled with France. NAPOLEON'S campaign in Italy in 1796–7 forced Austria to surrender Belgium in exchange for Venice. The French, co-operating with local enthusiasts, established 'sister republics' in the United Provinces, Italy and Switzerland. Napoleon next turned his attention to Egypt, but was defeated by NELSON at the Battle of the NILE. Having seized political power, he defeated the Austrians at Marengo (1800) in Italy and forced them to recognize French domination of the region. Britain's other allies were soon forced to settle with France, and Britain found it too expensive to carry on alone. The wars ended when Austria signed the Treaty of Lunéville (1801) and Britain signed the Treaty of Amiens (1802), but fighting resumed during the NAPOLEONIC WARS.

Revolutions of 1848, a series of nationalist revolts in Western and Central Europe, with their roots in economic grievance in large sections of the population and resentment of autocratic governments that failed to meet the demands of the middle classes for LIBERAL forms of government. Many of the revolts were also associated with NATIONALIST demands. The catalyst to revolution on a European scale was the outbreak of revolution in Paris in February 1848, which led to the overthrow of the ORLÉANS monarchy and the establishment of a republican government. In ITALY outbreaks of revolution occurred throughout the peninsula, leading to the wholesale expulsion of the Austrians ocupying the N. However, disunity among the nationalists led to the Austrians (and the Spanish Bourbons in the S) regaining control. In the vast, multilingual Austrian Empire, the revolutionaries of 1848 set their sights on overthrowing Austrian HABSBURG rule. The Hungarians, Croats and Czechs all managed to assert their independence from the Austrians and set up their own states for a brief period. However, the old rulers soon returned to power, partly by exploiting the divisions between the various national groupings. Popular uprisings also occurred in the GERMAN CONFEDERATION. A liberal 'German National Assembly' met in Frankfurt in May, but by the end of 1849 the attempt to construct a constitutional unified German state had ended. In France the initial success of the 1848 revolutions was also deceptive. Street fighting in Paris was followed by government reprisals. Louis Napoleon Bonaparte was to establish himself as dictator (later NAPOLEON III) following a coup d'état in 1851. The Habsburgs reasserted their control in Prague, and two years later Austria's constitution was suppressed, initiating a period of neo-absolutism under FRANZ JOSEF.

Reynolds, Albert (1932–), Irish politician. A FÍANNÁ FÁIL MP from 1977, he was minister for industry and commerce (1987–9) and finance (1989–91) before being dismissed by his predecessor, Charles HAUGHEY. He became party leader and prime minister in 1992.

Rhee, Syngman (1871–1965), Korean statesman. He became first president of the Republic of (South) KOREA in 1948. Popular unrest forced his resignation in 1960.

Rhineland, an area of Germany surrounding the banks of the Rhine and bordering France and the Low Countries. It was 'demilitarized' under the Treaty of VERSAILLES and occupied by Allied forces until 1930. HITLER'S troops reoccupied the area in 1936. See map, p. 37.

Rhodes, Cecil (John) (1853–1902), British colonial administrator in SOUTH AFRICA, often seen as the quintessential 19th-century British imperialist. He amassed a fortune from diamond mining and defended British interests against the BOERS, playing a key role in the acquisition of Bechuanaland and the territories that are now Zimbabwe. He was prime minister of Cape Colony (1890–6), but resigned after the JAMESON RAID.

Rhodesia, see ZIMBABWE.

Ribbentrop, Joachim von (1893–1946), German NAZI politician. As German foreign minister (1938–45), he negotiated the NAZI–SOVIET PACT and the Tripartite Pact between Germany, Italy and Japan (1940). He was executed as a war criminal.

Ricci, Matteo (1552–1610), Italian Jesuit resident at the Chinese (MING) imperial court from the beginning of the 17th century.

Richard I ('Coeur de lion' or 'the Lionheart'; 1157–99), king of England (1189–99). He spent most of his reign in the continental lands of the ANGEVIN empire and on CRUSADE, leaving England to be governed by ministers. On his return from the Crusades in 1192 he was captured by Duke Leopold of Austria and imprisoned by Emperor Henry VI until he agreed to be ransomed (1194). He spent the rest of his reign campaigning against PHILIP II in France, and died while besieging the castle of Châlus in Aquitaine. He was succeeded by his brother JOHN.

Richard II (1367–1400), king of England (1377–99). He kept his head during the PEASANTS' REVOLT (1381), but thereafter governed much less effectively, and was dethroned by Bolingbroke (HENRY IV) in 1399. He died in prison, presumably murdered.

Richard III (1452–85), king of England (1483–5). After years of loyal service to his brother EDWARD IV, he proclaimed the illegitimacy of his nephew EDWARD V and seized the throne in June 1483. It was widely believed that he had ordered the murders of Edward V and his brother in the Tower of London. Although Richard successfully suppressed the rebellion of October 1483, less than two years later he was defeated by Henry Tudor at BOSWORTH, and died in the fighting.

Richard of York, see YORK, RICHARD, 3RD DUKE OF.

Richelieu, Armand-Jean du Plessis, duc de (1585–1642), French cardinal, chief minister to LOUIS XIII (1624–42) and the effective ruler of France until 1642. He completed the political subjugation of the HUGUENOTS, and made enormous efforts – in alliance with Protestant Sweden – to defeat the Spanish Habsburgs.

Rights of Man and the Citizen (1789), the statement of the principles of the FRENCH REVOLUTION, incorporated as the preface to the French Constitution of 1791. It stated that the natural rights of man and the citizen (liberty, property, security, and the right to resist oppressión) could never be given up. All men were free and equal, and equally liable to taxation, and any individual or 'body of men' drew their authority solely from the will of the people.

Riot Act, an act passed by the English PARLIAMENT in 1714, intended in part to protect the new Hanoverian regime from JACOBITE demonstrations. It required any unlawful gathering of 12 or more people to disperse within one hour of the reading of the Act by a Justice of the Peace. The act was frequently invoked in the 19th century, notably at the PETERLOO Massacre (1819).

Rio de la Plata, a Spanish viceroyalty established in 1776, comprising present-day ARGENTINA, URUGUAY and PARAGUAY.

Risorgimento (Italian, 'resurrection'), the period of and movement for Italian unification in the 19th century. At the Congress of VIENNA in 1815, Napoleonic Italy was divided into 13 separate states, of which only two, the PAPAL STATES and the kingdom of Sardinia (including PIEDMONT), were ruled by Italians. Austria dominated the peninsula. Nationalist secret societies such as the CARBONARI ('charcoal burners') staged several risings and conspiracies during the 1820s and 30s, but none succeeded in dislodging Austrian rule. Other groups, including the YOUNG ITALY movement of Giuseppe MAZZINI, fared little better. After the failure of the REVOLUTIONS OF 1848, it was PIEDMONT, the most industrialized and economically prosperous Italian state, that moved to the forefront of the Risorgimento. Camillo di CAVOUR, Piedmont's prime minister from 1852, seized every opportunity to advance the cause of Italian unification, and successfully solicited French help in driving the Austrians out of most of N Italy in 1859 (see MAGENTA and SOLFERINO). In 1860 the nationalist guerrilla leader Giuseppe GARIBALDI landed in Sicily with an army of 1000 volunteers, and swiftly took control. He crossed to the mainland and swept aside minimal Bourbon resistance in S Italy. Cavour moved troops to the Papal States in order to assert Piedmontese control of the newly united Italy. In 1861 the 'Kingdom of Italy' comprised the entire peninsula, with the exceptions of Venetia (in the NE) and Rome. Venetia was eventually acquired from Austria after Italian help had been given to Prussia in the 1866 AUSTRO-PRUSSIAN WAR. Rome, with the exception of the Pope's own territory of the Vatican, was taken over when the French garrison left in 1870.

Roanoke Island, the site (off the coast of modern North Carolina) of the earliest English settlement in the New World (1585). Unfortunately for Walter RALEIGH, the organizer of the venture, the first settlers failed to establish a viable colony and the island was abandoned by English adventurers in favour of VIRGINIA.

'robber baron', the archetype of the ruthlessly aggressive businessman of the USA's GILDED AGE in the 1870s and 1880s.

Robert I ('the Bruce'; 1274–1329), king of Scotland (1306–29), one of the heroes of the Scottish War of Independence. After years of indecision in 1306 he had himself crowned to provide a rallying-point for the Scottish nation against English domination. Victory over EDWARD II at BANNOCKBURN (1314) enabled him to organize an invasion of Ireland and the raids on the N of England which forced MORTIMER and ISABELLA to recognize his kingship.

Robert II (1316–90), king of Scotland (1371–90), the first king of the Stewart (STUART) dynasty. He was active in the government of Scotland from the 1330s, but by the time he eventually succeeded to the throne he was a spent force.

Robespierre, Maximilien François Marie Isidore (1758–94), French revolutionary and leader of the JACOBINS. He played a crucial role in the overthrow of the GIRONDINS and, as a member of the Committee of Public Safety, helped unleash the reign of TERROR. He re-introduced religion – in the form of the 'Cult of the Supreme Being' – believing it to be necessary to social stability. Robespierre's power became so great that his enemies had him arrested and executed in the coup of 9 Thermidor (1794). See FRENCH REVOLUTION.

Rockingham, Charles Watson-Wentworth, 2nd Marquis of (1730–82), British statesman, prime minister (1765–6 and 1782). As leader of the Whig opposition (the 'Rockingham Whigs'), he opposed Britain's war against the American colonists.

Roger II (Guiscard; c. 1095–1154), Norman king of SICILY (1130–54) and son of Roger GUISCARD. He ruled a powerful centralized state, dominating the central Mediterranean, which tolerated and combined its Latin, Greek and Islamic elements.

Rokossovsky, Konstantin Konstantinovich (1896–1968), Polish-born Soviet field marshal. He played a major role in the battles of STALINGRAD and KURSK during WORLD WAR II. In 1944 his forces failed to intervene to assist the WARSAW RISING against the occupying German forces.

Rollo (c. 860–931), a Viking leader who invaded NW France and in 912 was recognized as Duke Robert of NORMANDY by Charles III of France.

Romania, a country of SE Europe. See panel.

Roman Catholic Church, the Western Church founded by the apostle St PETER, comprising Christians in communion with the PAPACY. In the early medieval period Christians from Ireland to the Carpathians came to acknowledge the bishop of Rome as pope (from the Vulgar Latin *papa*), and used Latin for worship, scripture reading and theology. The Eastern (ORTHODOX) Church finally broke with Rome in 1054. In the 16th century most of N Europe broke away from the primacy of Rome to form reformed Churches during the REFORMATION. In an attempt to claw back some of the ground lost to the reformed Churches they launched the COUNTER-REFORMATION. This division of Western Christianity led to the terms 'PROTESTANT' for these northern churches and 'Roman Catholic' for Latin Christianity. After the Reformation, the Catholic Church continued to develop new religious orders such as the JESUITS. Supreme in S Europe, Catholic Christianity was later extended to the Americas and parts of Asia and Africa.

Roman civil wars, the period of turmoil in the 1st century BC leading to the breakdown of the Roman Republic. At the beginning of the 1st century Rome was menaced by external attacks and internal revolts. The ruling oligarchy showed itself corrupt and incompetent in responding to these crises, which were only overcome by allowing able and ambitious individuals to take control of the government and by creating a professional army from the proletariat. These measures solved the military problems, but had fatal political consequences, because they provided the poor with a means to redress their grievances, and ambitious nobles with the chance to gain personal power by means of armed force. The first civil war was between Gaius MARIUS (c. 157–86) and Lucius SULLA (c. 138–78). In 81 Sulla set himself up as dictator and tried to reform the political system. His efforts were ineffectual, however, and the same lethal trends continued. New military crises in the 70s enabled the popular general POMPEY to gain a position of pre-eminence in the state, but he was unable to prevent other leaders from doing the same thing. In 49 BC Julius CAESAR, the conqueror of Gaul, invaded Italy at the head of an army (see RUBICON). After defeating Pompey at PHARSALUS in 48 he became consul and dictator for life. Caesar's assassination on 15 March, 44 BC once again plunged the empire into civil war, the main contenders being his former aide, Mark ANTONY and his heir, Caesar OCTAVIAN. The issue was finally settled at the battle of ACTIUM in 31 BC, when Octavian emerged victorious, and gained complete control of the Roman Empire. Under the honorary title Augustus he became the first emperor, and ruled unchallenged until his death in AD 14. Civil war broke out again in AD 68 in the struggle for succession after NERO's death. The war was finally ended by VESPASIAN who fought his way to power in late 69.

Roman Empire, 1. the territories ruled by ancient Rome (see map, p. 13). **2.** strictly speaking, the period when Rome and its territories were under the rule of the emperors, from 27 BC to AD 476 (see box, p. 210). ROME became a powerful city-state in the 6th century BC and dominated the Latin communities on its S borders. By 500 BC the monarchy had been replaced by a Republic dominated by the aristocratic PATRICIANS. But in the 5th and 4th centuries BC their monopoly of power was broken by the PLEBEIANS, who soon gained equal political rights. During this period the Romans were continually at war with their Italian neighbours, whom they compelled to become allies and contribute to further wars. Rome became the centre of an increasingly powerful alliance and was driven to ever greater military commitments. The first overseas war began with an assault on Sicily, where Rome clashed with CARTHAGE in the first of the PUNIC WARS. The Romans eventually emerged victorious, taking the Carthaginian provinces in Spain. In the decades that followed they defeated the HELLENISTIC kingdoms and formed the new provinces in Greece and Macedonia in 146 BC. 'Africa' (roughly modern Tunisia) was also taken in 146, Asia (W Turkey) in 133, S Gaul (Provence) in 121, Cilicia (S Turkey) in 101, and Cyrenaica (E Libya) in 96. Slaves were introduced to work the large estates in Italy and peasants were forced off the land to a life of poverty. The gulf between rich and poor gave rise to social conflict and political breakdown. Attempts at reform by Tiberius and Gaius GRACCHUS ended in the deaths of both brothers; other would-be reformers

ROMANIA

2nd and 3rd centuries AD: Romanians – possibly descended from the DACIANS, a Thracian people – were Romanized. **6th–12th centuries:** Romania overrun by Huns, Bulgars, Slavs and other invaders. **14th century:** The Romanians emerged from the highlands to found the principalities of WALLACHIA and MOLDAVIA. **15th century:** Romania came under the overlordship of the OTTOMANS , but were never subjected to direct Turkish rule. **18th century:** Oppressive rule by Greek princes imposed by the Turks stimulated Romanian nationalism. **1859–61:** Wallachia and Moldavia united under Alexander Cuza as Romania. **1878:** Romania's independence was internationally recognized at the Congress of BERLIN. **1916–18:** Romania fought on the ALLIED side against Austria and Germany during WORLD WAR I. **1919:** Romania acquired BESSARABIA (now Moldova) and TRANSYLVANIA after the collapse of the Russian and Austro-Hungarian empires at the end of World War I. **1938–41:** Dictatorship of King Carol II. **1940:** Romania forced by Germany to cede lands to Hungary; USSR retook considerable territory, including the present republic of MOLDOVA. **1941–4:** Romania – under Marshal Ion ANTONESCU – joined the AXIS powers in WORLD WAR II and fought the USSR to regain lost territories. **1944:** King Michael dismissed Antonescu and declared war on Germany; Soviet Red Army invaded. **1945:** Soviet-dominated government installed. **1947:** Monarchy abolished. **1965–89:** Dictatorship of Nicolae CEAUSESCU and his wife Elena. **1989:** Ceausescus overthrown; army took power; Communist power dissolved. **1990:** Multi-party elections (considered 'flawed' but not fraudulent by Western observers) brought the National Salvation Front to power.

ROMAN EMPERORS

Claudian Emperors

Augustus (Octavianus)	27 BC–AD 14
Tiberius	AD 14–37
Gaius Caesar (better known as Caligula)	37–41 (assassinated)
Claudius I	41–54
Nero	54–68

Later Claudian Emperors

Galba	68–69 (assassinated)
Otho	69
Vitellius	69 (assassinated)

Flavian Emperors

Vespasianus	69–79
Titus	79–81
Domitianus	81–96 (assassinated)

Antonine Emperors

Nerva	96–98
Trajanus	98–117
Hadrianus	117–38
Antoninus Pius	138–61
Lucius Verus	161–69
Marcus Aurelius	169–180
Commodus	180–192 (assassinated)

Emperors of African and Asian origin
(including co-emperors)

Pertinax	193 (assassinated)
Didius Julianus	193 (assassinated)
Septimus Severus	193–211
Marcus Aurelius Antoninus I (better known as Caracalla)	211–17 (assassinated)
Geta	209–12 (assassinated)
Macrinus	217–19 (assassinated)
Marcus Aurelius Antoninus II (better known as Elagabalus)	218–22 (assassinated)
Severus Alexander	222–35 (assassinated)
Maximinus	235–38 (assassinated)
Gordianus I	238
Gordianus II	238 (assassinated)
Pupienus Maximus	238 (assassinated)
Balbinus	238 (assassinated)
Gordianus III	238–44 (assassinated)
Philippus	244–49 (assassinated)
Decius	249–51 (assassinated)
Gallius	251–53 (assassinated)
Hostilianus	251
Aemilianus	253 (assassinated)
Valerianus	253–60
Gallienus	260–68 (assassinated)

Illyrian Emperors

Claudius II	268–70
Quintillus	270
Aurelianus	270–75 (assassinated)
Ulpia Severina (Empress)	275
Tacitus	275–76 (assassinated)
Florianus	276 (assassinated)
Probus	276–82 (assassinated)
Carus	282–83
Carinus	283–85
Numerianus	283–84 (assassinated)

Collegiate Emperors
(More than one emperor ruled at a time in a 'collegiate' system.)

Diocletianus	284–305
Maximianus	286–305
Constantius I (better known as Chlorus)	305–06
Galerius	305–11
Severus	306–07
Maximianus (restored)	307–08
Maximinus Daia	308–13
Constantinus I (Constantine the Great)	312–37
Maxentius	306–12 (assassinated)
Licinius	308–24
Constantinus II	337–40
Constans I	337–50 (assassinated)
Constantius II	337–61
Magnus Magnentius	350–53
Julianus (Julian the Apostate)	361–63
Jovianus	363–64

Collegiate Emperors
(ruling part of the Roman Empire)

Valentinianus I (Emperor in the West)	364–75
Gratianus (Emperor in the West; assassinated)	367–83
Valens (Emperor in the East)	364–78
Procopius (Emperor in the East)	365–66
Valentinianus II (Emperor in the West)	375–85
Magnus Maximus (Emperor in the West)	383–88
Flavius Victor (Emperor in the West)	386–88
Theodosius I (Emperor in the East 379–88; in the East and in the West 388–95)	379–95
Valentinianus II (restored) (Emperor in the West)	388–92
Eugenius (Emperor in the West)	392–94
Honorius (Emperor in the West; in 395 he became emperor of the Western Roman Empire)	393–95

Emperors of the Western Empire

Honorius	395–423
Constantius III	421
Valentinianus III	425–55 (assassinated)
Petronius Maximus	455 (assassinated)
Avitus	455–56
Majorianus	457–61
Libius Severus	461–65
Anthemius	467–72
Olybrius	472
Glycerius	473–74
Julius Nepos	474–75
Romulus Augustus	475–76

In 476 Romulus Augustus was expelled from Rome by the Vandals

suffered a similar fate in the decades to come. The first century BC witnessed the ROMAN CIVIL WARS, which ended the Republic and brought Rome and its overseas provinces under the rule of an emperor, AUGUSTUS, from 27 BC. His reign – often seen as the high point of Roman civilization – brought prosperity and further expansion in central Europe. However, the rule of his successors – especially that of TIBERIUS, CALIGULA, NERO and DOMITIAN – became increasingly autocratic. Wars of conquest virtually ceased apart from the invasion of Britain under CLAUDIUS, and of Dacia (Romania) under TRAJAN. The benign rule of the latter was continued by HADRIAN and ANTONIUS PIUS. Signs of strain appeared in the reign of Marcus Aurelius (169–80) and became more pronounced under his successors in the 2nd century. After the death of Alexander SEVERUS the empire lapsed into anarchy. Civil war, foreign invasions and rampant inflation were accompanied by political breakdown. Political stability returned under DIOCLETIAN and CONSTANTINE, but the recovery was only partial, and was achieved at the price of more oppressive government and bureaucracy, heavy taxation and a peasantry reduced to serfdom. The growing number of Christians were officially persecuted after 303 under Diocletian, but Constantine reversed this policy and recognized the church, which became the official religion of the Empire under THEODOSIUS I (379–95). In the 5th century the Western and Eastern parts of the empire had separate rulers and their histories diverged. The West was menaced by BARBARIAN invaders, and in 476 Romulus Augustulus, the last Western Roman Emperor, was deposed by the Gothic ruler ODOACER. The Eastern (or BYZANTINE) Empire would survive until the 15th century.

Romanov dynasty, the dynasty that ruled RUSSIA from the accession of Michael Romanov in 1613 to the abdication of NICHOLAS II during the RUSSIAN REVOLUTION of February 1917.

Roman Republic, the period (509–27 BC) when Rome was ruled as a republic. See ROMAN EMPIRE.

Rome, the capital of the ROMAN EMPIRE traditionally founded in 753 BC by ROMULUS. However, archaeology has shown that the site was occupied from at least the 10th century BC. It became the seat of the PAPACY, and capital of modern Italy from 1871.

Rome, Treaties of, see EUROPEAN COMMUNITY.

Rommel, Erwin (1891–1944), German field marshal whose brilliant command of the *Afrika Korps* in N Africa in WORLD WAR II earned him the name 'the Desert Fox'. His success in N Africa came to a halt at EL ALAMEIN. He was accused of plotting to kill HITLER in 1944 and forced to commit suicide by the GESTAPO.

Romulus, the traditional founder of ROME. According to legend the city took its name from him, a shepherd king who founded a settlement on the banks of the Tiber after killing his twin brother Remus.

Romulus Augustulus (b. c. AD 461), the last Roman emperor in the West (475–6). He was deposed and replaced in Italy by the Gothic king ODOACER.

Roosevelt, Franklin Delano (1882–1945), 32nd president of the USA (1933–45). He overcame a crippling bout of polio to become Democratic governor of New York and then leader of his country during the DEPRESSION and WORLD WAR II. Essentially a pragmatist, Roosevelt was a driving force behind the NEW DEAL and America's decisive contribution to the ALLIED cause in World War II. At times arrogant and insensitive to the plight of the powerless (notably blacks and Japanese-Americans), he was nonetheless an inspirational leader whose infectious optimism lightened the burdens of economic depression and war for a generation of Americans.

Roosevelt, Theodore (1858–1919), 26th president of the USA (1901–9). A bluff progressive Republican, he succeeded to the presidency after the assassination of MCKINLEY. He pursued an imperialistic foreign policy and sought to limit the power of the huge corporations that dominated the US economy. He fought an unsuccessful presidential campaign in 1912 on a PROGRESSIVE Party ticket.

Rosebery, Archibald Philip Primrose, 5th Earl of (1847–1929), British Liberal politician. A keen imperialist, he succeeded GLADSTONE as prime minister (1894–5).

Roses, Wars of the (1455–85), the name given to the intermittent English civil wars of the later 15th century. The wars emerged from the dynastic struggle for the throne between Edmund Beaufort, of the House of LANCASTER (whose badge was a red rose), and Richard 3rd Duke of YORK (whose badge was a white rose). HENRY VI and his wife MARGARET of Anjou were supported by Edmund, but opposed by Richard of York. Richard won control of England by defeating the Lancastrians at the first Battle of St Albans (1455) and capturing Henry VI. The rivalries and private disputes of the nobility were now absorbed into a bitter civil war. At the Battle of Wakefield (1460) Richard of York was killed, and the Lancastrians, supporting Henry VI, won a further victory at the second Battle of St Albans (1461). They failed to capitalize on their victory, however, and Richard's son Edward became the first Yorkist king (EDWARD IV). A Lancastrian invasion in 1470 restored Henry VI to the throne, although effective power was held by the Earl of WARWICK. The Yorkist victory at Barnet in April 1471 regained the throne for Edward, and most of the Lancastrian leaders were killed a month later at TEWKESBURY. The war ended in 1485 when RICHARD III was defeated by the future HENRY VII at BOSWORTH. Henry VII (of the House of Lancaster) married Edward IV's eldest daughter, Elizabeth of York, thereby ensuring that their children were heirs of both Lancaster and York.

Rosetta Stone, a bilingual inscription of 196 BC, written in three scripts – hieroglyphic, Egyptian demotic and Greek, and found at the village of Rosetta in Egypt in 1799.

Rothschild, a family of Jewish bankers. Lionel (1808–79), an Anglo-Jewish financier and politician, was one of the first Jews to serve as a British MP. In 1875 he loaned £4 million to the British government to enable it to purchase substantial shares in the SUEZ CANAL.

Roundheads, the supporters of PARLIAMENT during the ENGLISH CIVIL WAR, so called on account of their close-cropped heads.

Rousseau, Jean-Jacques (1712–78), Swiss-born French philosopher and political theorist. In his *Social Contract* (1762) he argued that it was only through the state that men reached their true potential. Rousseau (unlike his predecessors) placed sovereignty in the hands of the people as a whole, and declared that it could not be divided, separated or alienated. He believed in a 'General Will' – the good of the community – which all wished for though they might not know it. The authoritarian implications of Rousseau's political theory are evident in this, as they are in his granting the state far more responsibilities in all areas of a citizen's life than any had done before him.

Royal Society, a scientific society founded in Britain in 1660 and chartered by CHARLES II in 1662. Sir Isaac Newton (1643–1727) was a leading figure in the Society, which became an important institution in the spread of new discoveries during the SCIENTIFIC REVOLUTION.

Rubicon, a stream in N Italy flowing into the Adriatic near Rimini, important because it marked the boundary of the province of Cisalpine GAUL. When CAESAR crossed it in 49 BC he was entering Italy in arms and therefore starting a civil war. See ROMAN CIVIL WARS.

Ruhr, the principal industrial region of W GERMANY. It was occupied by France in 1921 when Germany defaulted on REPARATIONS.

Rump Parliament, the remnant of the LONG PARLIAMENT following the expulsion of some of its members by Colonel Thomas Pride of the NEW MODEL ARMY (1648). It ordered CHARLES I'S execution in 1649.

Rupert, Prince (1619–82), the son of Frederick V, elector of the PALATINATE, and the nephew of CHARLES I. He served as a royalist commander in the ENGLISH CIVIL WAR, suffering defeats at MARSTON MOOR and NASEBY.

Russell, John, 1st Earl (1792–1878), British statesman, prime minister (1846–52 and 1865–6). A WHIG MP from 1813, he was largely responsible for drafting the 1831 REFORM Bill. His first ministry was troubled by CHARTIST agitation, and failed to gain the support of the Whig aristocracy. He succeeded PALMERSTON to become PM for a second time until the defeat of his last franchise bill.

Russia, a country of E Europe and Central and N Asia. See panel.

RUSSIA

1st millennium BC: SLAVS from the Carpathians migrated towards the Dnieper valley. **9th century AD:** Foundation of the state of KIEV RUS. **13th–17th centuries:** Growth of the Grand Duchy of MUSCOVY. **13th century:** S steppes overrun by the Mongols; Kiev Rus became part of the MONGOL EMPIRE. **1326:** Seat of the ORTHODOX Church transferred to Moscow. **1462–1505:** IVAN III ('the Great') ousted the Mongols and united the NW. **1547–84:** IVAN IV ('the Terrible') became tsar of all Russia, conquering Kazan and Astrakhan, and beginning the colonization of Siberia. **1584–1605:** BOYAR families challenged Theodore I (1584–98) and Boris Godunov (1598–1605). **1605–13:** 'Time of Troubles'; upheavals in Russia as several rival candidates vied for the throne. **1613:** Election of the first ROMANOV tsar, Michael (1613–45); Muscovy recovered its stability and prosperity. **1649:** Serfdom introduced. **1667:** Alexis I (1645–76) gained much of the E UKRAINE. **1682–1725:** PETER I ('the Great') modernized the army and bureaucracy, creating a Westernized Empire stretching from the Baltic to the Pacific. **1762–96:** CATHERINE II ('the Great') gained Crimea, W Ukraine, White Russia and part of POLAND (see Partitions of POLAND). **1798–1814:** Russian involvement in the NAPOLEONIC WARS, during which Napoleon occupied Moscow (1812). **1801–25:** ALEXANDER I dabbled with constitutional ideas. **1825–55:** Under NICHOLAS I – the champion of autocracy, the Orthodox Church and Russian nationalism – a fierce reaction set in. **1853–6:** CRIMEAN WAR. **1855–81:** ALEXANDER II (the 'Tsar Liberator') emancipated the serfs, but suppressed the Polish rising of 1863–4. **1881–94:** ALEXANDER III combined repression at home with restraint abroad. **Early 20th century:** NICHOLAS II began rapid industrialization and faced increased demands for constitutional reform. **1904–5:** Russia defeated in the RUSSO-JAPANESE WAR. **1905–6:** Revolution led to limited constitutional reform; first Duma (parliament) established. **1914–17:** Russia fought the CENTRAL POWERS in WORLD WAR I. **1917:** The RUSSIAN REVOLUTIONS overthrew the monarchy and established a Communist state, bringing the BOLSHEVIKS to power under LENIN. **1918–22:** Outlying parts of the Russian empire seceded; RUSSIAN CIVIL WAR won by the RED ARMY. **1922:** SOVIET UNION formed; Red Army re-established control over most of former Russian empire. **1924–53:** Dictatorship of STALIN. **1930:** KULAKS dispossessed. **1936–8:** PURGES of Stalin's political rivals. **1939:** Stalin signed NAZI–SOVIET PACT with HITLER. **1940:** USSR invaded Poland, Finland, Romania and the Baltic states. **1941:** Germany invaded the USSR; up to 27 million Soviet citizens may have died in WORLD WAR II. **After 1945:** USSR established control of a cordon of satellite states in E Europe and confronted the West in the COLD WAR. **1953:** Death of Stalin; KHRUSHCHEV came to power. **1956:** USSR put down the HUNGARIAN REVOLUTION. **1964–82:** BREZHNEV in power. **1968:** Soviet invasion of CZECHOSLOVAKIA. **1979:** Soviet invasion of AFGHANISTAN. **1985–91:** GORBACHOV's reforms of GLASNOST and PERESTROIKA introduced. **1989–91:** Abandonment of Communism by E European Soviet satellites. **1991 (August–September):** Abortive coup by hardline Communists; Boris YELTSIN and Russian parliament led resistance; republics began to renegotiate relationship with the centre. **1991 (December):** Soviet Union dissolved; Russia – under Yeltsin – took over the international responsibilities of the USSR. **From 1991:** Ethnic disputes and severe economic and constitutional crises. **1993:** Yeltsin suspended Parliament and ruled by presidential decree after an attempted coup; multi-party elections saw the emergence of the extreme right-wing nationalist Liberal Democratic Party.

Russian Civil War (1918–21), a conflict in Russia between anti-Communist 'Whites' and the Bolshevik RED ARMY after the RUSSIAN REVOLUTION. The Whites, a loose coalition of democrats, socialists and reactionaries, were joined by armies sent by Britain, France, Japan and the USA. However, they were unable to coordinate their strategy, and were defeated piecemeal by the Red Army created by TROTSKY. During the war the Red Army reconquered most of the European non-Russian areas of the former tsarist empire that had formed their own republics in 1917–18. Transcaucasia (Armenia, Georgia and Azerbaijan) was captured in 1920 and Ukraine was finally suppressed in 1921. The recaptured territories – along with Soviet Central Asia – were reorganized into the Union of Soviet Socialist Republics, which was formally established in 1922.

Russian Revolutions (1905, March 1917 and November 1917). A series of uprisings in Russia that culminated in the establishment of a Communist state. At the turn of the century there was growing unrest in urban and rural Russia which came to a head in 1905 after Russia's humiliating defeat in the RUSSO-JAPANESE WAR. On 'BLOODY SUNDAY' (22 January 1905) troops opened fire on a peaceful demonstration in St Petersburg, killing 1000 protesters. The massacre was followed by a general strike, peasant uprisings, rioting and army mutinies. In October 1905 the Tsar agreed to elections to a DUMA (parliament). The move rallied moderate reformers who helped the government crush the revolt. The reforms of the chief minister of the conservative third Duma, STOLYPIN, had only limited success, and he was assassinated in 1911. WORLD WAR I placed Russian society under tremendous economic and political strain. Respect for the imperial government crumbled and revolutionary propaganda spread among soldiers and workers. On 8 March 1917 revolution broke out in Petrograd (or St Petersburg, as it had been renamed in 1914) and soviets (councils) of soldiers, workers and peasants were set up all over Russia. On 15 March Tsar NICHOLAS II abdicated and a moderate provisional government was established. In the summer of 1917 KERENSKI became the chief minister, but the powerful Petrograd soviet was controlled by LENIN and his followers. On 7–8 November (25–6 October in the old Russian calendar) Kerenski was ousted in a coup led by LENIN which brought the BOLSHEVIKS to power. On seizing power, Lenin moved against rival socialist groups (including the MENSHEVIKS), using the CHEKA as a weapon, and executed the deposed tsar and his family. The Bolsheviks took Russia out of World War I (see Treaty of BREST-LITOVSK), which had proved deeply unpopular, and successfully defended the Revolution in the RUSSIAN CIVIL WAR.

Russo-Japanese War (1904–5), a conflict between Russia and Japan for ascendancy in MANCHURIA and Korea. The Russian naval base of Port Arthur and the Manchurian capital, Mukden, both fell to the Japanese, while the Russian Baltic fleet was destroyed in the Straits of TSUSHIMA (May 1905) after an epic 28,000 km (18,000 mi) journey from its base. The war was ended by the Treaty of PORTSMOUTH. Russia's humiliating defeat – the first defeat of a Western power by Japan – caused unrest that led to the 1905 RUSSIAN REVOLUTION.

Russo-Turkish Wars (1768–74, 1787–92, 1806–12, 1828–9, 1853–6 and 1877–8) a series of wars fought between Russia and Turkey over disputed territories in the BALKANS, the Crimea and the Caucasus. The wars steadily reduced the European territories of the OTTOMAN Empire. Defeat in the war of 1806 forced the Turks to recognize the autonomy of Serbia and the Russian annexation of BESSARABIA. The war of 1828–9 formed part of the GREEK WAR OF INDEPENDENCE; it resulted in the effective independence of WALLACHIA and MOLDAVIA and brought part of Armenia under Russian control. At the end of the war of 1853–6 (the CRIMEAN WAR), Russia lost territory in the Balkans. In 1876 an uprising in Bulgaria was crushed by the Turks, leading to European claims of 'Bulgarian atrocities'. The following year Russian forces invaded, on the pretext of protecting Bulgarian Christians. The war was ended in 1878 by the Treaty of SAN STEFANO, later modified by the Congress of BERLIN. See also EASTERN QUESTION.

Rwanda, a country of E central Africa. The feudal kingdom of Rwanda was a German possession from 1890 until it was taken over by Belgium after World War I. The monarchy – of the dominant minority Tutsi people – was overthrown by the majority Hutu population shortly before independence in 1962. Tribal violence has continued intermittently. In 1990–1 an army of Tutsi refugees occupied much of the N. In February 1991, in an attempt to solve the problem, Rwanda's neighbours agreed to grant citizenship to Tutsi refugees, and Rwanda conceded the principle of multi-party elections. In April–May 1994 at least 200,000 Rwandans were slaughtered in political and ethnic violence.

Ryswick, Treaty of (1697), the treaty ending the NINE YEARS WAR. LOUIS XIV was obliged to recognize WILLIAM III as king of England, end his occupation of Lorraine and restore Luxembourg to Spain.

SA, see BROWNSHIRT.

Saar (Saarland), a region of GERMANY on the French border. As the Saar, it was administered by France under the auspices of the LEAGUE OF NATIONS from 1919 until 1935 when it was returned to Germany following a plebiscite. As Saarland, it was again occupied by France after 1945 – and (from 1948) part of the French customs union – until 1957 when it became a German Land. See map, p. 37.

Sabah, a state of MALAYSIA, formerly British North Borneo (1882–1963).

Sadat, Anwar el- (1918–81), Egyptian statesman. He succeeded NASSER as president in 1970. He signed a peace treaty – the CAMP DAVID ACCORD – with Israel in 1978 which earned him and Menachem BEGIN the Nobel Peace Prize. Although fêted by the West, Sadat was denounced by the rest of the Arab world and EGYPT dismissed from the ARAB LEAGUE. He was assassinated by militant Islamic fundamentalists in 1981 and was succeeded by Hosni MUBARAK.

Sadowa, Battle of (3 July 1866; also known as the Battle of Königgrätz), a battle fought near the Bohemian town of Sadowa, in which the Prussian army under MOLTKE overcame Benedek's Austrian army. The Prussian victory ended the AUSTRO-PRUSSIAN WAR (Seven Weeks War) and marked the end of Austrian dominance in the German-speaking part of Europe.

Safavids, a dynasty – probably of Kurdish descent – that ruled IRAN from 1501 to 1722. They were originally a SUFI order, founded in NW Persia in the early 14th century. Under their rule Iran became officially SHIITE. Ismail I was defeated by the Ottomans at Chaldiran in 1514. The greatest Safavid ruler, Shah Abbas I (ruled 1587–1629) introduced military and administrative reforms that strengthened the dynasty sufficiently to survive the pressure of the Ottomans and Uzbeks until 1722, when they were overthrown by the Afghans.

Saigo Takamori (1827–77), one of the leaders of the MEIJI restoration in JAPAN. He later turned against Meiji policy, particularly the destruction of SAMURAI influence, and led a rebellion (1877), committing suicide when it failed.

St Bartholemew's Day Massacre (23/4 August 1572), a massacre of Protestant HUGUENOTS by Catholic mobs during the FRENCH WARS OF RELIGION. The massacre was ordered by the French queen mother, Catherine de MEDICI, who was strongly influenced by the Catholic GUISE faction. Some 3000 Protestants were killed in Paris, and many more in the provinces.

St Germain, Treaty of (10 September 1919), a treaty between the Allied Powers and Austria, part of the PARIS PEACE CONFERENCE after WORLD WAR I. Under the terms of the treaty Austria lost Bohemia (including the SUDETENLAND) and Moravia to the newly created state of CZECHOSLOVAKIA; Galicia went to Poland; and Trieste, Istria and the South TYROL to Italy.

St John, Knights of, see the Knights HOSPITALLERS.

Saint-Just, Louis de (1767–94), French revolutionary. A member of the Committee of Public Safety during the TERROR, he denounced DANTON, and was later executed with ROBESPIERRE.

St Laurent, Louis Stephen (1882–1973), Canadian Liberal politician. As a reforming prime minister (1947–57) he promoted good relations between English- and French-speaking Canadians.

Saint-Simon, Claude (1760–1825), French nobleman and early theorist of SOCIALISM. He advocated an industrial society controlled by industrialists dedicated to ameliorating the condition of the poor, and the spiritual guidance of society by scientists.

Saite, the 26th and last great native dynasty of ancient EGYPT (664–525 BC), under whom the country was reunited and enjoyed a last period of splendour. There was an artistic renaissance and trade flourished. An invasion by CAMBYSES in 525 ended the dynasty and Egypt became a province of the ACHAEMENID Persians.

Saladin (Salah al-Din; ?1137–93), Kurdish soldier who seized power in Egypt and Syria and defeated the armies of the CRUSADER STATES at HATTIN (1187), recapturing JERUSALEM. He was the adversary of RICHARD I of England and PHILIP II AUGUSTUS of France during the Third CRUSADE.

Salamis, Battle of (480 BC), naval battle in which the Greek fleet defeated the Persian fleet in the narrows between the island of Salamis and the coast of Attica. This, crucially, gave the Greeks control of the sea, and was the decisive battle of the PERSIAN WARS.

Salazar, António de Oliveira (1889–1970), Portuguese prime minister (1932–68). Effectively a dictator, he established a neo-Fascist state in which political opposition was strictly repressed. He was succeeded by CAETANO.

Salians, 1. a group of FRANKS who settled in the Netherlands in the 4th century. **2.** a dynasty of German emperors of the 11th and 12th centuries. They succeeded the OTTONIAN dynasty in 1024, but soon became embroiled in demands for Church reform. During the reign of Salian HENRY IV the bitter dispute over the claims of Church and state erupted into the INVESTITURE CONTEST. The Salian dynasty died out in 1125.

Salic Law, the legal code of the SALIAN Franks. It was most notably invoked during the dispute between CHARLES VI of France and EDWARD III of England, the French claiming that it excluded Edward from inheriting their throne since he was a descendant in the female line.

Salisbury, Robert Arthur Talbot Gascoyne-Cecil, 3rd Marquess of (1830–1903), British Conservative statesman, prime minister (1885–6, 1886–92, 1895–1900 and 1900–2) and the last British PM to lead the government from the House of LORDS. He succeeded DISRAELI as Conservative leader in 1881. His first two premierships saw the imperialist SCRAMBLE FOR AFRICA, and his third and fourth terms were dominated by the Second BOER WAR.

SALT, see STRATEGIC ARMS LIMITATION TALKS.

Samaria, the capital of the northern kingdom of ISRAEL, founded by OMRI in the 9th century BC.

Samnite Wars, the series of conflicts between Rome and the peoples of the S central Apennines, known collectively as Samnites, between 343 and 290 BC, which led to the Roman conquest of the region. They continued to resist Roman rule until they were heavily defeated by SULLA at the Battle of Colline Gate in 82 BC.

samurai, the Japanese warrior class. The samurai gave absolute loyalty and military service to his DAIMYO, who in turn owed allegiance to the SHOGUN. The samurai combined military discipline with a knowledge of culture and the arts. Many became competent bureaucrats in the 17th century when fighting was not necessary. Their rank was abolished in the 1870s by the MEIJI reformers.

Sandinistas, the Sandinista Liberation Front, a guerrilla army of NICARAGUA named after Augusto César Sandino, a Nicaraguan guerrilla leader killed by government forces in 1934. The Sandinistas overthrew the regime of Anastasio SOMOZA in July 1979 and Daniel Ortega (1945–) became president. US-backed right-wing rebels, known as Contras, fought a guerrilla war with the Sandinista government until 1989. The following year the Sandinista government was defeated in elections.

San Francisco Conference (25 April–26 June 1945), was an international meeting held in San Francisco, USA, which established the UNITED NATIONS Organization (UN). Altogether, 51 states signed the UN Charter on 26 June.

San Marino, a small S European republic surrounded by Italian territory. Established as an independent commune by the 12th century, San Marino retained its autonomy because of its isolation and by playing off powerful neighbours against each other. Its independence was recognized by Napoleon (1797), the Congress of VIENNA (1815) and the new Kingdom of ITALY (1862). In 1957 a bloodless 'revolution' replaced the Communist-Socialist administration that had been in power since 1945.

San Martín, José de (1778–1850), South American revolutionary soldier who played a major role in the liberation of Argentina, Chile and Peru from Spanish rule. In 1817 he led an army across the Andes, liberating Chile after victory at the Battle of Maipú (1818). He invaded Peru in 1820 and was protector of Peru 1821–2, but resigned following disagreements with BOLÍVAR over the country's future.

sans culottes (French, 'without breeches'), the revolutionary Paris mob during the FRENCH REVOLUTION between 1789 and 1795, so named because working men wore trousers.

San Stefano, Treaty of (March 1878), a treaty ending the RUSSO-TURKISH WAR of 1877–8. The treaty recognized the independence of an enlarged Serbia, Romania and Montenegro, autonomy for Bosnia-Herzegovina, the creation of a large Russian-dominated Bulgaria and the cession of considerable Ottoman territory to Russia in the Caucasus. Fearing that the Ottoman Empire would not survive, the European powers overturned the Treaty and a new division of the Balkans was agreed at the Congress of BERLIN.

Santa Anna, Antonio López de (1795–1876), Mexican soldier and politician. His defeat at the battle of San Jacinto (1836) resulted in Mexico's loss of TEXAS. As commander of Mexican forces he was defeated again in the MEXICAN–AMERICAN WAR of 1846–8, which saw further loss of territory to the USA.

Saracen, a term used by medieval Europeans, especially during the CRUSADES, for Arabs and Middle Eastern Muslims. The derivation of the word is uncertain.

Sarajevo, see BOSNIA-HERZEGOVINA.

Saratoga, Battle of (7 October 1777), a decisive battle between British and American forces in the American War of INDEPENDENCE. The British defeat ended General Burgoyne's attempt to isolate NEW ENGLAND from the other American colonies, and encouraged the French to aid the Americans.

Sarawak, a state of MALAYSIA occupying the NW part of Borneo.

Sargon I (c. 2370–2315 BC), Akkadian conqueror of SUMER (2370 BC). He created the Akkadian empire, conquering Mesopotamia, parts of N Syria, and Elam to the E. He founded as his capital the city of AKKAD. During his reign Sumerian cuneiform script was adapted to write Akkadian (ancient Babylonian). His dynasty was overthrown c. 2200 BC. See MESOPOTAMIA and SUMER.

Sargon II (d. 705 BC), king of ASSYRIA (721–705 BC). A powerful king, he consolidated the empire's territories in a series of campaigns.

Sassanians, a Persian dynasty that overthrew the last PARTHIAN king in AD 226. The Sassanian Shapur I (AD 240–72) expanded the borders N and E to Central Asia and Pakistan, and SW to the E coast of Arabia. Rome and later the BYZANTINE Empire were the traditional enemies of Sassanian Persia, but in the end the Sassanians were defeated by the armies of Islam. In 637 their capital, Ctesiphon (modern Baghdad), was captured and Yazdigird III, the last Sassanian king, was murdered by his nobles.

Sa'ud, Abd al-Aziz ibn (c. 1880–1953), king of SAUDI ARABIA from 1932 until his death. Proclaimed Sultan of NAJD in 1921, he overthrew Ibn Ali HUSSEIN, king of HEJAZ, five years later to gain control of Mecca. In 1932 he created the kingdom of SAUDI ARABIA.

Saudi Arabia, a kingdom of SW Asia. See panel.

Saul, first king of the Israelites (c. 1020–1000 BC); he fought successfully against the PHILISTINES. The rise of DAVID dominated the later years of his rule.

Saxons, the name used by the Romans to describe the tribes living between the Elbe and Weser in N Germany and S Denmark (see map, p. 15). They raided Britain from before 300 and settled there in the 5th century. See ANGLO-SAXONS.

Saxony, a former duchy (9th century), electorate (1432) and kingdom (1806) in GERMANY. Because of its alliance with NAPOLEON I, Saxony lost half its area at the Congress of VIENNA. Saxony became part of the German Empire in 1871. The monarchy was overthrown in 1918.

Scapa Flow, a British naval base in the Orkney Islands, enjoying easy access to both the Atlantic and North Sea. In 1919 the German High Seas Fleet, interned at the end of WORLD WAR I, scuttled itself there.

Schleswig-Holstein, a province (Land) of N GERMANY. The duchies of Schleswig and Holstein were inherited by the

SAUDI ARABIA

7th century AD: The Prophet MUHAMMAD was born in MECCA, where he received revelations from God and proclaimed ISLAM. **From 632:** The political focus of Islam moved, first to Damascus, then to Baghdad. **8th century:** The unity of Muslim Arabia collapsed and gave way to tribal rivalries. **Early 16th century:** The OTTOMAN Turks established their authority over much of the peninsula. **1744:** A Muslim preacher – Muhammad ibn abd al-Wahhab – and the ancestor of the country's present rulers, the Sa'udis, formed an alliance that was to spearhead the Wahhabi political-religious campaign. **20th century:** The Wahhabis united most of Arabia under ibn SA'UD. **1902:** ibn Sa'ud took Riyadh. **1906:** ibn Sa'ud defeated his rivals to control central Arabia (NAJD). **1912–27:** ibn Sa'ud added the E, the SW (Asir) and the area around Mecca (HEJAZ). **1932:** The lands controlled by ibn Sa'ud became the kingdom of Saudi Arabia. **1973:** Following the 1973 ARAB-ISRAELI WAR Saudi Arabia cut oil production in an attempt to persuade the USA to encourage Israel to withdraw from the occupied territories of PALESTINE. **1980s:** Problems caused by Islamic fundamentalism and the rivalry between SUNNI and SHIITE Islam; Saudi Arabia supported Iraq in its war with Shiite Iran. **1991:** Saudi Arabia played a major role in the coalition against IRAQ in the GULF WAR.

king of DENMARK in 1460 and held by Denmark – despite their mainly German population – until 1866, when Prussia seized Schleswig and Austria took Holstein. North Schleswig – which has a Danish majority – was returned to Denmark in 1920.

Schlieffen Plan, a plan prepared in 1905 by Count Alfred von Schlieffen (1833–1913) to counter the Franco-Russian alliance in the event of war. The plan – involving violation of Belgian neutrality to outflank French defences, followed by an attack on Russia – was the basis of Germany's attack at the outbreak of WORLD WAR I.

Schmalkadic League (1531), a league established by German Protestant princes during the Reformation to resist Emperor CHARLES V's attempts to reintroduce Catholicism. Charles recognized their religious rights in 1544, but went on to defeat the League militarily at the Battle of Mühlberg (1547).

Schmidt, Helmut Heinrich Waldemar (1918–), German SOCIAL DEMOCRAT statesman. As chancellor of West Germany (1974–82) he continued BRANDT's policy of OSTPOLITIK and grappled with the economic problems of the mid-1970s. He was unseated as chancellor when the Liberal Free Democratic Party withdrew support from his coalition government. He was succeeded by Helmut KOHL.

scholasticism, a style of philosophical learning based on ARISTOTLE and his Arabic commentators combined with Christian doctrine. It was characteristic of European universities from the 13th to the 16th century. When it fell out of fashion it came to be misunderstood and despised.

Schuman, Robert (1886–1963), French politician, prime minister (1947–8). As foreign minister (1948–52) he put forward the 'Schuman Plan', proposing the creation of the EUROPEAN COAL AND STEEL COMMUNITY, which developed into the EUROPEAN ECONOMIC COMMUNITY.

Schuschnigg, Kurt von (1897–1977), Austrian chancellor (1934–8). He could do little to prevent the German takeover of AUSTRIA (the ANSCHLUSS) and resigned under pressure from HITLER in 1938.

Scientific Revolution, a period of scientific progress in the 16th and 17th centuries that emphasized experiment, and resulted in a new view of the universe and the Earth's place in it. Through the work of Copernicus, Kepler, Galileo and Newton, the Scientific Revolution advanced the study of astronomy, mathematics and mechanics. The establishment of academies under royal patronage such as Louis XIV's *Académie des Sciences* and Charles II's ROYAL SOCIETY helped spread knowledge of new discoveries. The close relationship between religious orthodoxy and discredited old scientific ideas contributed to the breakdown of respect for religious authority. In the 18th century the application of science to industry produced the steam engine and advances in textile manufacture. See INDUSTRIAL REVOLUTION.

Scipio Aemilianus, Publius Cornelius (c. 185–129 BC), adopted grandson of SCIPIO AFRICANUS, who commanded the Roman forces in the Third PUNIC WAR and destroyed CARTHAGE in 146 BC.

Scipio Africanus, Publius Cornelius (236–183 BC), Roman general who defeated the Carthaginians in Spain in the Second PUNIC WAR, and then led an expeditionary force to Africa, where he defeated HANNIBAL at Zama in 202 BC.

Scotland, a country of NW Europe, part of the UNITED KINGDOM, occupying the N of the island of Great Britain. Pre-Roman Scotland was inhabited by the CELTS. Only S Scotland was included within the ROMAN EMPIRE's sphere of influence. The N – beyond the ANTONINE WALL – was largely untouched by Romanization. The Scots from NE Ireland invaded N Britain in the 5th and 6th centuries and when their king (KENNETH I MacAlpine) also became king of the PICTS (843), the foundations of a Scottish state were laid. The early Scottish kingdom was unstable owing to the power of the nobles and a system of succession by which the king was usually succeeded by the eldest member of a collateral branch of the royal family – a system that usually produced a king of age, but which led to endless dynastic squabbles and the assassination of the majority of the early monarchs. Primogeniture cannot be said to have been established until the reign of the reforming DAVID I (reigned 1124–53), under whom English influence greatly increased. Scotland came steadily within the English sphere of influence from the 11th century, and EDWARD I of England attempted to dominate Scotland at a time of disputed succession in the 13th century. After the Battle of BANNOCKBURN (1314), Scottish independence was asserted by ROBERT the Bruce (reigned 1306–29), whose grandson was the first Stewart (STUART) king of Scotland. After 1371, Scotland suffered a succession of long minorities, weak Stewart kings, conspiracies by overmighty nobles and continuing border wars with England. Threatened by England, Scotland entered the 'Auld Alliance' with France for protection. The REFORMATION in Scotland – during the turbulent reign of MARY, Queen of Scots (reigned 1542–67) – took on a CALVINIST character. The succession of James VI of Scotland as JAMES I of England in 1603 united the crowns of the two realms, although full integration did not occur until Scotland's Parliament was abolished by the Act of UNION in 1707.

Scottish National Party (SNP), a political party dedicated to achieving Scottish independence from the UNITED KINGDOM. Originally founded in 1928, it enjoyed some electoral success in the 1970s, fell away in the 1980s, then attracted strong support in the early 1990s for its demands for an independent SCOTLAND within a federal Europe.

'Scramble for Africa', the rush by the major European powers to acquire colonial territories in Africa after 1870 (see map, p. 33). The French gained most of N and W Africa as well as Madagascar. Germany acquired an empire in the Cameroons, Togoland, South West Africa and Tanganyika. Italy obtained Libya, Eritrea and part of Somaliland, but in 1896 failed to conquer Abyssinia. The British made the greatest gains, including Egypt, Sudan, Uganda, Kenya, British Somaliland, Nigeria, Ghana, the Rhodesias and Nyasaland. They consolidated their rule in South Africa after the Second BOER WAR. The Portuguese gained Angola, Mozambique and Guinea, while the Congo became the personal property of LEOPOLD II of Belgium. See IMPERIALISM.

Scythians, a nomadic people of the STEPPES, famed for their horsemanship. By 550 BC they had developed the equipment that characterized the mature nomadic culture – compound bows, horse trappings and felt tents. This culture spread to the Huns, Turks and MONGOLS of the E half of the steppe. They adopted a scorched-earth policy after attempts by DARIUS the Great to subdue them in c. 512 BC. They defeated a Macedonian army c. 325 BC before making peace with ALEXANDER THE GREAT.

SDI, see STRATEGIC DEFENSE INITIATIVE.

Sea Peoples, marauders who laid to waste many cities of the E Mediterranean in the late 13th and early 12th centuries BC. The disturbances of c. 1200 changed the face of the Near East. The HITTITE empire was probably eclipsed by them, while Egypt, BABYLONIA and ASSYRIA lost much of their strength. One group of Sea Peoples – the Peleset – settled round Gaza in S Canaan. Known later as the PHILISTINES, they gave the region its name, PALESTINE.

SEATO, see SOUTHEAST ASIA TREATY ORGANIZATION.

Second Empire, a term variously used to describe both the regime of NAPOLEON III in France (1852–70), and the German Empire or 'Reich' created in 1871. The first German Reich implicit in the title was the HOLY ROMAN EMPIRE.

Second Front, the popular name for Anglo-American plans to attack Germany from the W in WORLD WAR II.

Security Council, a permanent organ of the UNITED NATIONS, established for the maintenance of international peace and security. It has five permanent members – China, France, Russia (the Soviet Union until 1992), the UK and the USA – and 10 other seats taken by other member-states in turn. Decisions are reached through 9 out of 15 members voting for a measure. However, any one of the permanent members has a right of veto.

Sedan, Battle of (1 September 1870), French defeat by Prussia in the FRANCO-PRUSSIAN WAR which precipitated the fall of NAPOLEON III'S Second Empire and the proclamation of the Third Republic.

Sedgemoor, Battle of, see MONMOUTH'S REBELLION.

Seleucid dynasty, the dynasty descended from Seleucus, one of ALEXANDER THE GREAT'S generals. The Seleucid kingdom covered an area stretching from Asia Minor to NW India. Much of their territory fragmented into ethnic kingdoms, such as Bactria, Armenia, Bithynia and PONTUS. The areas they did retain were controlled like the Achaemenid empire by local governors (satraps). By 63 BC all that remained of their empire was the Syrian heartland, which was suppressed by the Romans.

Selim I ('the Grim'; 1470–1520), OTTOMAN sultan (1512–20). He doubled the size of the empire by taking Syria and Egypt from the MAMLUKS. His defeat of the SAFAVID Persians at Chaldiran in 1514 strengthened Ottoman control of E Anatolia. In 1517 he occupied the HEJAZ. He was succeeded by his son SULEIMAN the Magnificent.

Seljuks, a Turkish dynasty that conquered large areas of the E part of the Middle East in the first half of the 11th century. Converted to Sunni Islam before they left their ancestral pastures in Central Asia, they swept through the E Islamic world from the 1040s. They drove the BUYIDS from Baghdad, and restored the Abbasid Caliph to a position of honour, though they retained much of the actual power in their own hands. They were unable, however, to destroy the FATIMID Caliphate. In 1071 they routed the BYZANTINES at MANZIKERT. From the end of the 11th century they were involved in fighting Western armies in the CRUSADES. The Seljuk sultanate of Rum rose to prominence in the 12th century, but suffered a crushing defeat by the MONGOLS in 1243.

Semites, peoples of the Middle East speaking one of the Semitic languages, such as Akkadian, Aramaic, Phoenician and Hebrew.

Senate, 1. (in ancient Rome) an aristocratic body of c. 300 (later 600) lifelong members whose function was to advise the CONSULS. It had immense prestige and in practice was the governing body of the Roman Republic. Under the ROMAN EMPIRE it lost its real power, but remained a repository of traditional aristocratic values, and was the main source of political opposition to the emperors. **2.** the name given to other assemblies and legislatures in various countries, notably the upper house of the US CONGRESS.

Seneca, a native North American people, the westernmost of the five tribes of the IROQUOIS Confederation, living in the Eastern Woodlands (W New York state). See NORTH AMERICAN INDIANS.

Seneca, Lucius Annaeus (c. 4 BC–AD 65), Roman senator, playwright and philosopher. Seneca was one of NERO'S chief advisers during the early years of his reign, but was later ousted and eventually forced to commit suicide on suspicion of involvement in a conspiracy.

Senegal, a republic of W Africa. The region was part of the medieval empire of MALI. The coast was explored by the Portuguese in the 15th century and gradually came under French control from the 17th century. A national political awareness developed early in the 20th century, and the country contributed substantially to the nationalist awakening throughout French Africa. After independence in 1960 – under the poet Léopold Sedar Senghor – Senegal maintained close relations with France, and received substantial aid. Attempted federations with MALI (1959–60) and GAMBIA (1981–9) were unsuccessful. Senghor retired in 1980, having reintroduced party politics.

Sennacherib (d. 681 BC), king of ASSYRIA (704–681 BC). He entered Palestine, defeated the coastal cities, repelled an Egyptian force, and overran JUDAH. In 689 BC he sacked BABYLON after a nine-month siege. He went on to rebuild his capital at NINEVEH.

Serbia, a country of SE Europe. Serbia threw off allegiance to the BYZANTINE EMPIRE c. 1180 and flourished as an independent state. In 1345 Stefan Dusan declared himself emperor of Serbia, but the Serbian empire was destroyed by (Turkish) OTTOMAN conquest, symbolized by the Battle of KOSOVO in 1389 (see map, p. 26). Led by KARAGEORGE, the Serbs rose against Turkish rule between 1804 and 1813. Under his rival Miloš OBRENOVIĆ, the Serbs rose again in 1815 and became an autonomous principality, but the country was destabilized by rivalry between the Karageorge and Obrenović dynasties. Serbia was recognized as independent in 1878. For the history of Serbia after 1878, see YUGOSLAVIA.

serf, a word deriving from the Latin *servus*, meaning a slave. However, the serf was not a slave but a property-holding VILLEIN, a characteristic figure in the FEUDAL SYSTEM of Western European society after the demise of slavery there between the 10th and 12th centuries. The long period of labour shortage following the BLACK DEATH in the 14th century led to the end of serfdom. Serfdom was a prominent feature of Russian society from the 16th to the mid-19th century.

Servius Tullius (6th century BC), semi-legendary king of Rome. He is said to have created the system by which different classes voted according to their wealth and contribution in war.

Settlement, Act of (1701), an act of the English Parliament assigning the English crown to the House of HANOVER in the event of Queen ANNE dying without children.

Sevastopol, a Russian port and naval base on the Crimean peninsula, besieged during the CRIMEAN WAR.

Seven Weeks War, see AUSTRO-PRUSSIAN WAR.

Seven Years War (1756–63), a wide-ranging conflict fought in Europe, India, and North America, in which Prussia, Britain and Hanover faced Austria, France, Russia, Sweden and Spain. The principal issues at stake were Austro-Prussian rivalry in Germany and the Anglo-French colonial struggle. FREDERICK II of PRUSSIA made the opening move with an invasion of Saxony, but he faced overwhelming odds. Despite his alliance with Britain, and victories over much larger opposing forces, Frederick's territories were severely pressed, particularly by the Russians, who devastated East Prussia. Near collapse, Prussia was saved by the accession of Tsar Peter III, whose admiration for Frederick undermined the coalition. Frederick kept SILESIA at the Peace of PARIS, which confirmed Prussia's status as a rival to Austria in Germany. While Prussia distracted France in Germany, the British navy in North America achieved domination over the French at the naval battles of Lagos and Quiberon Bay (1759). General WOLFE'S victory at QUEBEC secured Canada for Britain. In India Robert CLIVE and the British EAST INDIA COMPANY achieved military success against the French and Indians (notably at PLASSEY), and emerged as the most powerful trader in the subcontinent.

Severus, Alexander (AD 208–35), Roman emperor (222–235). He was murdered by his soldiers in 235, ending the Severan dynasty that had begun with Septimius Severus (see next entry), and plunging the empire into anarchy.

Severus, Lucius Septimius (c. AD 145–211), Roman emperor (193–211), who fought his way to the throne in the civil war (192–7). His reign was a naked military despotism, and the army became politically dominant under his successors.

Sèvres, Treaty of (August 1920), a treaty between the Allies and Turkey, part of the PARIS PEACE CONFERENCE after WORLD WAR I. It gave substantial parts of the old OTTOMAN Empire as MANDATES to France (which received 'Greater Syria') and Britain (which gained Palestine, Iraq and Transjordan). The nationalist revolt led by Kemal ATATÜRK cleared much of Turkey of foreign troops, and in 1923 he signed the Treaty of LAUSANNE, which secured better terms for Turkey.

Seychelles, an archipelago in the Indian Ocean. The islands became a French colony in the middle of the 18th century, were ceded to Britain in 1814 and gained independence in 1976. The PM – Albert René – led a coup against President James Mancham in 1977, and established a one-party socialist state. Attempts to overthrow René, including one involving South African mercenaries (1981), have been unsuccessful. The government conceded the principle of multi-party elections in 1991. These were duly held in 1992.

Seymour, Jane (1509–37), the third wife of HENRY VIII (following Anne BOLEYN), and mother of EDWARD VI.

Sforza, a family that ruled MILAN (1450–1535). Francesco Sforza (1401–66), a Romagnol mercenary, was invited by the Milanese to become their duke shortly after the end of the rule of the VISCONTIS. He and his son Lodovico 'il Moro' (1451–1508) held Milan at the centre of Italian politics and culture. Lodovico was partly instrumental in encouraging the French invasion of 1494.

Shaftesbury, Anthony Ashley Cooper, 7th Earl of (1801–85), British reformer. A prominent evangelical Christian, as Lord Ashley he was leader of the 'ten-hour movement' (1832–3) for restricting factory working hours, and an active campaigner behind successive Factory Acts.

Shah Abbas I, see SAFAVIDS.

Shah Jahan (1592–1666), MOGUL emperor of INDIA (1628–57). During his reign the boundaries of the empire continued to expand, particularly in central India. He was the patron of such major works as the Red Fort and the Taj Mahal.

Shaka, see ZULUS.

Shamir, Yitzhak (1915–), Israeli politician, leader of the right-wing Likud Party and prime minister of ISRAEL (1983–4 and 1986–92). As a member of the STERN GANG, he was involved in the campaign to oust the British from Palestine in the 1940s. During his years in office he consistently refused to enter into negotiations with the PLO.

Shan, a people of SE Asia, closely related to the Thai. They moved from SW China to their present territory in NE BURMA by the 13th century. The Shan states have belonged to the unified Burmese states since the 16th century.

Shang, the first historical Chinese dynasty (1480–1050 BC), established in the Yellow River heartland. The remains of Shang cities and tombs reveal a civilization clearly ancestral to classic Chinese culture. Its script was of the ideographic type still used today, and its capital cities were laid out on a grid system oriented to the points of the compass, as all subsequent Chinese capitals have been. Civilization gradually spread outwards from the core area ruled by the Shang. The ZHOU finally displaced the Shang as overlords of the Chinese heartland around 1000 BC.

Sharpeville, a segregated black township outside Vereeniging, S of Johannesburg. It was the scene of a massacre by police of 69 anti-APARTHEID demonstrators of the PAN-AFRICANIST CONGRESS in March 1960.

Shastri, Lal Bahadur (1904–66), Indian statesman. He was chosen to succeed NEHRU as a stop-gap prime minister in 1964, but died in Tashkent hours after signing the peace treaty ending the 1965 war with Pakistan.

Sheridan, Philip (1831–88), US soldier who served with distinction as a Union commander during the AMERICAN CIVIL WAR, noted particularly for his offensive operations in the Shenandoah valley.

Sherman, William Tecumseh (1820–91), US Union soldier renowned for his campaigns against the CONFEDERACY in the

AMERICAN CIVIL WAR. While his famous 'March to the Sea' through Georgia in 1864 presaged the onset of 'total war', his subsequent drive N to link up with GRANT effectively terminated Confederate resistance.

Shevardnadze, Eduard (1928–), Soviet foreign minister (1985–90), president of GEORGIA (1992–). As foreign minister under GORBACHOV he revolutionized Soviet foreign policy. Relations with the West were improved, a number of arms reduction treaties agreed with the USA and its NATO allies, and the Soviet Union abandoned its commitment to intervene in the affairs of WARSAW PACT countries. In 1991 he resigned from the Communist Party and as foreign minister. The following year he became president of GEORGIA.

Shi Huangdi (259–210 BC), the first ruler of all CHINA and founder of the QIN dynasty. In the 11 years of his reign he established an empire that stretched from the South China Sea to Central Asia. The N boundary with the nomads was defined by the building of the Great Wall of China. The famous terracotta army of 6000 life-size warriors and horses, found in 1974, guards the approach to his as yet unexcavated tomb.

Shiite, a follower of the smaller of the two main divisions of ISLAM, taking its name from the Shi'at 'Ali, the 'party of ALI', the son-in-law of MUHAMMAD. Shiites, unlike the majority SUNNIS, believe that Ali and his descendants are the sole true heirs to the authority of Muhammad. Shiitism has produced a variety of sects, including the ISMAILIS. The Shiites are dominant in IRAN, where they make up 93% of the population.

Shimonoseki, Treaty of (17 April 1895), the treaty ending the SINO-JAPANESE WAR of 1894–5. China was heavily defeated by Japan and was obliged to grant Korean independence in the treaty, which marked the beginning of Japanese domination in the region.

Shinto, the principal native religious philosophy of JAPAN: 'the Way of the Gods'. Its major features are worship of the spirits present in nature, loyalty to the emperor as descendant of the sun-goddess, and an emphasis on ritual purity.

ship money (1635–8), a tax levied from English seaports by CHARLES I to finance his government in England independently of PARLIAMENT. The LONG PARLIAMENT declared it illegal in 1641.

shoguns, the hereditary military dictators who ruled JAPAN from the late 12th to the 19th centuries, during which time the emperors retained a purely notional supremacy. Beneath the shogun were the ranks of the military barons, DAIMYOS, and beneath them their warriors, the SAMURAI. The first shogunate, the KAMAKURA, lasted a century and a half. The ASHIKAGA family instituted a new shogunate based at Kyoto in the 14th century. This lasted in name until 1578. The feudal anarchy that followed the end of the Ashikaga shogunate was ended by Tokugawa Ieyasu, who established the TOKUGAWA shogunate. In 1869 the last Tokugawa shogun was overthrown by Emperor Mutsuhito, who effected the MEIJI restoration.

Shona, a SE African people of BANTU origin, living in the area of modern Zimbabwe and Mozambique. From the 13th century they were ruled by powerful states controlling the export of gold to the E coast.

Shoshone, a native North American people, hunter-gatherers living in the Great Basin region (modern Nevada). See also NORTH AMERICAN INDIANS.

Sicilian Vespers (1282), a popular revolt ending ANGEVIN rule in Sicily, so called because it took place at the time of the evening service on Easter Tuesday 1282. The people of Palermo rose up against Angevin tyranny and invited Pedro III of Aragon to be their king. The ensuing war lasted 20 years and ended in the partition of Sicily into the Angevin kingdom of NAPLES and the Aragonese kingdom of Trinacria. The Angevins were ousted by the Aragonese in the mid-15th century.

Sicilies, Kingdom of the Two, a term used to describe S ITALY during the periods when NAPLES and Sicily were under common rulership. The first occasion of this was Norman rule: ROGER II styled himself king of Sicily and Italy from 1130. After periods of NORMAN, HOHENSTAUFEN and ANGEVIN rule the unity was broken by the Sicilian revolt of 1282 (the SICILIAN VESPERS), after which the island came under ARAGONESE control. Naples eventually became Aragonese in 1442, and under Alfonso the Magnanimous (ruled 1442–58) the two kingdoms were reunited. See map, p. 21.

Siegfried Line, the line of defensive fortifications built by Germany along its W frontier with France before and during WORLD WAR II. It proved incapable of stopping Allied advances in 1944–5.

Sierra Leone, a republic of W Africa. Freetown was founded by British philanthropists (1787) as a settlement for former slaves and became a British colony in 1808. The interior was added in 1896. Independence was gained in 1961. A disputed election led to army intervention (1967), and Dr Siaka Stevens – who came to power in a coup in 1968 – introduced a one-party state. The military took power in 1992.

Sigismund (1368–1437), as king of Hungary (1387–1437) he led resistance to the Turks; as Holy Roman Emperor (1411–37) he presided over the reunification of the Latin church at the Council of CONSTANCE; as king of BOHEMIA (1419–37) he had to cope with the HUSSITE rebellion.

Sihanouk, Norodom (1922–), Cambodian politician, king of CAMBODIA (1941–55), prime minister (1955–60), head of state (1960–70). After his abdication in 1955, he dominated Cambodian political life until 1970, when he was overthrown in a US-backed military coup. He was nominal head of state (1975–6) following the victory of the KHMER ROUGE in the civil war, but was finally forced into exile. He returned to Cambodia in 1989 to help broker a UN-sponsored peace settlement. Following multi-party elections in 1993, the monarchy was restored and he regained the throne.

Sikh, a follower of the Indian religious teacher NANAK. Sihkism originated in the PUNJAB, where it is still the majority religion. In recent years militant Sikhs have pursued a violent campaign for an autonomous state of 'Khalistan'. See INDIA.

Sikh Wars (1845–9), a series of wars fought between the English EAST INDIA COMPANY and the Sikhs of NW India, which resulted in British annexation of the PUNJAB.

Sikkim, a former PRINCELY STATE that retained virtual independence from British INDIA. It was an Indian protectorate until 1975, when it became part of India.

Silesia, a major industrial region in N Central Europe. Silesia was Polish (from 989/92), was settled by Germans (from the 11th century), and then passed in turn to Bohemia (1335), Hungary (1469), Bohemia (1490) and the Austrian HABSBURGS (1526). Prussia fought and won two wars for possession of Silesia in the 18th century. Silesia was partitioned between Poland, Germany and Czechoslovakia after World War I. Since 1945 most of Silesia has been in POLAND.

Silk Route, a trade route between China and the West that first flourished at the beginning of the Christian era, when it linked the Chinese HAN and ROMAN Empires at the height of their prosperity. Silk, and later porcelain, travelled from East to West; in exchange came gold, silver, gems, ivory and natural rarities unobtainable in China. The passage of technological ideas along the same route mainly benefited the West. The Silk Route carried these ideas W, where greater advantage was eventually taken of them. The Chinese developed paper, printing, gunpowder and the magnetic compass well before the West. In the 16th century the arrival in the East of Western ships steered with compasses and defended by guns marked the end of the usefulness of the Silk Route.

Simnel, Lambert (c. 1477–c. 1500), a boy coached to pose as Edward, earl of Warwick, who was imprisoned by HENRY VII as a potential rival for the throne of England. His supporters launched an unsuccessful invasion of England in 1487, and Lambert was captured and given a menial post in Henry's household.

Sind, a region occupying the lower Indus Valley, the site of one of the world's earliest urban civilizations. The area increasingly fell under Islamic influence after an Arab invasion in 711. A province of British INDIA from 1843, it became a province of SE PAKISTAN in 1947.

Singapore, a city-state of SE Asia. Singapore was a trading centre until destroyed by the Javanese in the 14th century. The city was revived by Sir Stamford RAFFLES for the British EAST INDIA COMPANY (1819), and developed rapidly as a port for shipping Malaya's tin and rubber. It acquired a cosmopolitan population and became a strategic British base. Occupied by the Japanese (1942–5), it achieved self-government (1959), and joined (1963) and left (1965) the Federation of MALAYSIA. Following independence it became wealthy under the strong rule of prime minister LEE KUAN YEW.

Sinhalese, a people of SRI LANKA who arrived by sea from N India c. 550 BC and soon adopted Buddhism. They remain the majority population of SRI LANKA, outnumbering the later Hindu arrivals, the TAMILS.

Sinn Fein (Gaelic, 'ourselves alone'), an Irish political party, founded in 1905, whose goal is a united republican IRELAND. Sinn Fein MPs won a majority of the Irish seats in the 1918 general election, and proclaimed Irish independence from Britain in 1919. The party split over the creation of the Irish Free State and the partition of Ireland in 1922. Most Sinn Fein members were absorbed into DE VALERA'S new FÍANNA FÁIL party in 1926. In 1969 it split into 'official' and 'provisional' wings, as did the IRISH REPUBLICAN ARMY, with which it is closely connected.

Sino-Japanese Wars (1894–5 and 1937), two conflicts between CHINA and JAPAN. The war of 1894–5 was fought in Korea over the future of that state, which had long been a Chinese vassal, but was increasingly a focus for Japanese expansionism. The Chinese were soon defeated by superior Japanese forces, and by the Treaty of SHIMONOSEKI agreed to Korean independence and ceded Formosa (Taiwan) to Japan. The war of 1937 arose from the Japanese army's seizure of MUKDEN (1931) and subsequent annexation of MANCHURIA. The Japanese, although opposed by JIANG JIE SHI'S Nationalists as well as the Communists, quickly overran N China. Beijing fell on 7 August 1937, closely followed by Shanghai and Nanking. With Japan's entry into WORLD WAR II, the war became absorbed into that wider conflict, at the end of which the Japanese were expelled from China.

Sioux or Dakota Indians, a group of native North American peoples living in the Great Plains. They were the first major group of Plains Indians to abandon settled agricultural village life in the 18th century to become nomads dependent on the hunting of buffalo from horseback. The western Sioux mounted fierce resistance to white encroachment on their lands under leaders such as SITTING BULL and CRAZY HORSE until the late 19th century. See also NORTH AMERICAN INDIANS.

Sitting Bull (c. 1834–90), Dakota SIOUX chief. His resistance to white encroachment on Plains Indians' hunting grounds culminated in the Sioux victory at LITTLE BIG HORN in 1876. He settled on a Dakota reservation after an amnesty (1881), but was killed in further hostilities in 1890.

Six Acts, British parliamentary statutes passed after the PETERLOO Massacre (1819), designed to suppress radical and reform agitation.

Six Day War (5–10 June 1967), the name given by the Israelis to the 1967 ARAB–ISRAELI WAR. President NASSER of Egypt precipitated the war when he formed a military alliance with Syria and Jordan and blockaded the Strait of Tiran, cutting off Israeli shipping. Israel retaliated with a devastating attack on the air forces of the Arab coalition, followed immediately by a rapid land campaign. In six days Israel defeated Egypt and captured territory from the Egyptians in Sinai, and did the same to the Jordanians on the WEST BANK, and the Syrians on the GOLAN HEIGHTS. Israel also took the whole of JERUSALEM. Israel's gains placed it behind more defendable borders but made Israel less prepared to countenance a negotiated settlement of the Palestinian question. Jewish settlement in the newly occupied territories increased Arab resentment.

Sixteen States, a period of Chinese history (317–420 AD) when the area of the Chinese empire – particularly the N – was split into small states, some ruled by dynasties of nomad origins, none of which was powerful enough to reunite China.

slavery, a system of human ownership whereby some people are treated as property belonging to other social groups or individuals. There have been many forms of slavery, even in societies considered civilized, such as those of the ancient Greeks and Romans. The slave trade to the New World colonies began in the 17th century when the Portuguese discovered that the best way to produce sugar in their new colonial possessions in Brazil was on large-scale plantations. Such plantations provided their European owners with fabulous wealth. A large labour force was needed to work these enormous estates, and initially the Portuguese in Brazil used native Indians, but the decline of the Indian population obliged them to seek an alternative source of labour: black slaves from Africa. The British and French did the same in their colonies. By 1680 the slave population of the British West Indies totalled more than 60,000, and that of the French West Indies 21,000. In the 1780s there were 100,000 black African slaves in the Spanish Caribbean, 400,000 in the British West Indies, about 500,000 in the French West Indies, 400,000 in the USA, and more than 800,000 in Brazil. This demand for labour could only be met by the continued transport of slaves across the Atlantic from Africa: 968,000 made the crossing in the later 17th century, and a further 6 million in the 18th century. While many slaves died on the Atlantic crossing, many more died on the journey from the interior of Africa to the ports. By the end of the 18th century religious and humanitarian opposition to slavery and the slave trade was growing in Western Europe (see WILBERFORCE). The British slave trade was abolished in 1807, and slavery in the British Empire in 1833. The question of slavery became a major issue of the AMERICAN CIVIL WAR.

Slavs, the peoples who settled E Europe in ancient times, first referred to by this name in the mid-6th century (see map, p. 15). They were initially subject to the AVARS, whose westward migration pushed the southern Slavs into the Balkans, but became increasingly independent. After CHARLEMAGNE'S destruction of the nomads c. 800, they converted to Christianity and became part of the BYZANTINE orbit, though they often constituted a threat to CONSTANTINOPLE. Today ethnic Slavs make up a large portion of the populations of Russia, Ukraine, Belarus, Poland, the Czech Republic, Slovakia, Bulgaria, Serbia, Croatia, Montenegro and Macedonia.

Slovakia, Slovakia was part of Hungary from the 11th century, although when most of Hungary fell to the Ottoman Turks in the 16th century, Slovakia remained in the hands of the Habsburgs. Slovak nationalism grew in the 19th century and increased Magyarization under the AUSTRO-HUNGARIAN Dual Monarchy (1867–1918) was greatly resented. On the collapse of the Habsburg Empire (1918), the Slovaks joined the Czechs to form CZECHOSLOVAKIA. When Hitler's Germany dismembered Czechoslovakia in 1938, Slovakia became an Axis puppet state. A popular revolt against German rule (the Slovak Uprising) took place in 1944. Following liberation (1945) Czechoslovakia was re-established. After the Communist takeover in 1948, heavy industry was introduced into rural Slovakia. In 1968, moves by Party Secretary Alexander DUBĆEK (a Slovak) to introduce political reforms met with Soviet disapproval, and invasion by Czechoslovakia's WARSAW PACT allies. The conservative wing of the Communist party regained control until 1989, when student demonstrations developed into a peaceful revolution. The Communist Party renounced its leading role. A new government, in which Communists were in a minority, was appointed. In 1990 free multi-party elections were held, Soviet troops were withdrawn and the foundations of a market economy were laid, but the pace of economic reform brought distress to Slovakia, whose old-fashioned industries were ill-equipped to face competition. Increased Slovak separatism led to the division of the country in 1993. Independent Slovakia faces possible tension concerning the large Hungarian minority.

Slovenia, a republic of S Central Europe. The Slovenes arrived in the W Balkans in the 6th and 7th centuries. In the 9th century, the area was divided between several German rulers and only the Slovenes in the S (Carniola) resisted Germanization. Carniola became a HABSBURG (Austrian) province in 1335 and, although it remained under Habsburg rule almost continuously until 1918, the Slovenes managed to preserve their national identity. Official encouragement of the Slovene language under Napoleonic French rule (1809–14) gave impetus to a Slovene national revival in the 19th century. When the Habsburg Empire collapsed (1918), the Slovenes joined the Serbs, Croats and Montenegrins in the new state that was renamed YUGOSLAVIA in 1929. When Yugoslavia became a Communist federal state in 1945, the Slovene lands were reorganized as the republic of Slovenia. After the death of Yugoslav President TITO (1980), the federation faltered in nationalist crises, and in free elections in 1990, nationalists gained a majority in the Slovene Assembly, which declared independence in June 1991. Following reverses in a short campaign, Yugoslav federal forces were withdrawn from Slovenia, whose independence gained widespread diplomatic recognition in 1992.

Sluys, Battle of (24 June 1340), an English naval victory over the French in the HUNDRED YEARS WAR. Massed English archers gave notice of the threat they would pose at the later battles of Crécy and Poitiers by defeating a force of French, Castilian and Genoese ships off the coast of Flanders. Victory gave England control of the English Channel.

Smith, Adam (1723–90), Scottish economist and philosopher. In his *Wealth of Nations* (1776) Smith argued that unregulated labour – whether in agriculture, trade, or industry – was the true source of wealth, and opposed MERCANTILIST regulation as inimical to wealth creation. Smith's views had few practical consequences in the 18th century, but subsequently became the foundation of free-market ideas, which were to have widespread influence in the 20th century.

Smith, Ian Douglas (1919–), prime minister of (Southern) Rhodesia (ZIMBABWE) 1964–78. He led the white settler electorate to declare independence (UDI) in 1965, finally conceding power to Robert MUGABE in 1979–80.

Smith, John (1580–1631), one of the founders of the JAMESTOWN colony in Virginia. He was captured by the Algonquin chief POWHATAN and would have been killed but for the intervention of the chief's daughter POCAHONTAS.

Smuts, Jan Christian (1870–1950), prime minister of SOUTH AFRICA (1919–24 and 1939–48). He fought in the BOER WAR before entering politics. His active support for Britain in World War II cost him the 1948 election. He was succeeded by D.F. MALAN, who campaigned on an APARTHEID ticket.

Soares, Mário Lopés (1924–), Portuguese socialist statesman, prime minister (1976–8 and 1983–5), president (1986–).

Sobieski, John III (1629–96), king of POLAND (1674–96). In response to an appeal from the pope, he joined Austrian and German forces to compel the Turks to lift their siege of Vienna in 1683, and also joined the HOLY LEAGUE of 1684 against the Turks.

social contract, a term used by political theorists such as HOBBES, LOCKE and ROUSSEAU to describe the agreement by which the individual sacrifices some of his liberty in return for the protection of the state.

Social Darwinism, a theory applying the principles of evolution to the development of human society. A pseudo-scientific creed of the late 19th century, it asserted not only the rightful duty of the 'superior' white races to dominate and exploit the 'inferior' coloured races, but also encouraged conflict between imperialist nations. These assertions were based on the principle of the 'survival of the fittest', regarded as the key to evolutionary progress.

Social Democrat, a term used to describe a number of left-of-centre political parties. Before the establishment of the Third INTERNATIONAL in 1919, the term described socialist political parties usually subscribing to a MARXIST analysis of society. Between 1919 and 1945, the label described those left-wing parties – such as the German Social Democratic Party (SDP) – which, whilst often avowedly Marxist, rejected the leadership of the SOVIET UNION. In the postwar period, the term has come to be applied to democratic left-wing parties committed to redistribution of wealth, extension of welfare and social security schemes, and limited state management of the economy. In Britain, a Social Democratic Party (SDP) was formed in 1981 by four LABOUR dissidents, who formed an alliance with the LIBERAL party. The majority of the party merged with the Liberals in 1988, but a minority persisted as the SDP until the 1992 elections.

Social Democratic and Labour Party (SDLP), a Northern Irish political party of the moderate left, seeking to achieve a united IRELAND by constitutional means. Founded in 1970, it has been led by John Hume (1937–) since 1979.

Social Democratic Party (SDP), see SOCIAL DEMOCRAT.

socialism, a political and economic theory advocating the ownership and control of the means of production, distribution and exchange by the entire community or by the state, and the equal distribution of wealth. The term was first used in France and Britain by SAINT-SIMON and Robert OWEN. Parties describing themselves as 'socialist' range from extreme left-wing COMMUNIST parties advocating political change by violent revolution, to moderate SOCIAL DEMOCRAT or LABOUR parties embracing the institutions of representative democratic government.

Society of Friends, see QUAKERS.

Socrates (470–399 BC), Athenian philosopher. He founded no formal school and wrote nothing, but spent his life debating in Athens with other philosophers and wealthy young men, some of whom stayed as devoted adherents, while others like CRITIAS and ALCIBIADES went into politics. He professed only a unique awareness of his own ignorance, and everyone else's, and sought to demonstrate the moral confusions of others, and to found ethical conduct on more satisfactory rational definitions of the virtues. He was successfully prosecuted after the end of the PELOPONNESIAN WAR for corrupting the young and introducing new gods, and was executed by the administration of hemlock.

Solferino, Battle of (25 June 1859), the second bloody battle (three weeks after MAGENTA) of the Franco-Piedmontese campaign to expel Austria from Lombardy. Although Austria was defeated, French casualties were so high that NAPOLEON III concluded a separate peace with Austria at VILLAFRANCA.

Solidarity (Polish, *Solidarnosc*), an independent trade union movement that emerged from unrest in the Lenin shipyard in Gdansk, POLAND, in 1980, under the leadership of Lech WALESA. In 1981 martial law was imposed and many of the Solidarity leaders were imprisoned, forcing the movement underground. Following the reforms of GORBACHOV, they forced the Communist Polish government to agree to free multi-party elections in August 1989. Solidarity won enough seats to form a coalition government with former allies of Communists and Walesa became president. They lost considerable support in the 1993 elections and are now in opposition.

Solomon (d. c. 922 BC), king of ISRAEL (c. 961–c. 922 BC) and son of DAVID, traditionally famous for his wisdom. His policies, which included organized tax and labour – from which his own tribe of JUDAH was omitted – led to the division of the kingdom shortly after his death.

Solomon Islands, an archipelago in the S Pacific. Settled by MELANESIANS about 2500 BC, the islands were briefly colonized by Spain (1568–1606). The islanders were exploited as a workforce for plantations in other Pacific islands before Britain established a protectorate in 1893. Occupied by the Japanese (1942–5) during World War II, the Solomons were the scene of fierce fighting, including a major battle for GUADALCANAL. Independence was gained in 1978.

Solon (7th–6th centuries BC), Athenian statesman and lawgiver who made the first steps towards democracy in Athens. He was appointed in 594 to create new laws after a period of serious unrest between rich and poor. His reforms freed many peasant-citizens from various forms of dependence on richer landowners and debts, and did much to establish the peasants in ownership of their lands. His laws encouraged all citizens to participate in the assembly, in the prosecution of legal cases, and as jurors in a new people's court of appeal. He introduced a division of all citizens based on wealth, but restricted the various offices to the better-off classes.

Somalia, a republic of E Africa. Muslim traders established trading posts along the Somali coast from the 7th century. In 1886 Britain established a protectorate in the N of the region, while the Italians took the S. In World War II the Italians briefly occupied British Somaliland. In 1960 the British and Italian territories were united as an independent Somalia. In 1969 the president was assassinated and the army – under Major-General Muhammad Siad Barre – seized control. Barre's socialist Islamic Somalia became an ally of the USSR. In 1977 Somali guerrillas – with Somali military support – drove the Ethiopians out of the largely Somali-inhabited Ogaden. Somalia's Soviet alliance was ended when the USSR supported Ethiopia to regain the Ogaden. In January 1991 Barre was overthrown by dissident troops who overran Mogadishu, while rival groups seized districts in the N and S. The infrastructure of Somalia collapsed in bitter civil war between rival factions. In 1992 a US-led UN force intervened to help famine victims.

Somme, Battle of the (July–November 1916), a 20-week Anglo-French offensive planned by HAIG and JOFFRE and intended to smash the German hold on N France in WORLD WAR I. The British lost 57,470 casualties (including 19,240 dead) on 1 July 1916, the first day of the battle. Thereafter the offensive became a grinding attritional slog, torrential rain in October turning the battlefield into a nightmare of impassable mud. By the time the British front stabilized again in November, the new Allied trenches were only 8 km (5 mi) in advance of the old front line, but 420,000 British, 450,000 German, and 200,000 French casualties had been sustained. See map, p. 36.

Somoza, a family that dominated Nicaraguan politics from the 1930s to 1979. Anastasio Somoza Garcia (1896–1956) ruled NICARAGUA 1936–56, his road to power opened by the assassination of Augusto César Sandino in 1934. On his own assassination he was succeeded by his sons Luis (1956–63) and then Anastasio (1966–79). Anastasio was ousted by the SANDINISTA revolution of 1979.

Sonderbund, an association of seven conservative Roman Catholic cantons in Switzerland, formed in 1845 in response to the liberal reforms in other cantons. They were established to protect Catholic interests and preserve the federal status of the cantons. The 'Sonderbund War' of 1847 was followed by the promulgation of a new liberal constitution that ended the virtual sovereignty of the cantons.

Song or **Sung,** an imperial dynasty of CHINA (960–1127). After a century of distintegration the Song empire reunited the old area of the TANG empire and allowed China to rise to a new peak of imperial grandeur. Song China was larger and had a more complex economic and social structure than previous empires. The new cities along the Yangtze and S and E coasts marked a drift of imperial power from the Yellow River to the S. In 1126 an invasion by JIN nomads split China, and the Song retreated to the S, ruling a reduced southern Song empire for another century and a half, before succumbing to the MONGOL invasion.

Songhay, a people and kingdom of the W African Sahel (in modern MALI). In the 15th and 16th centuries, Songhay formed a powerful Muslim empire controlling trans-Saharan trade. It was conquered by Moroccans in 1590.

South Africa, a country of southern Africa. See panel.

Southern Rhodesia, see ZIMBABWE.

South Korea, see KOREA, REPUBLIC OF.

South Sea Bubble (1720–1), a speculative boom in the stock of the South Sea Company, caused by the granting to the Company of a monopoly of the trading privileges in Spanish America ceded to Britain in 1713. The 'bubble' burst, ruining many and threatening – temporarily – the position of the House of HANOVER.

soviet (Russian, 'council'), a council elected by the workers or soldiers of a particular district in RUSSIA, created under Communist leadership to act as the basic organizational structure of the 1917 RUSSIAN REVOLUTION. Delegates from each soviet met at an all-Russian Congress in June 1917. In the Soviet Union soviets existed at local, regional and national level, the highest governing council being the Supreme Soviet.

Soviet Union, the Union of the Soviet Socialist Republics (USSR), a former Communist federal state of Eastern Europe and Central and N Asia founded by LENIN in December 1922. The RED ARMY invaded the republics surrounding Russia at the end of the RUSSIAN CIVIL WAR and incorporated them into the Union; they comprised ARMENIA, AZERBAIJAN, Byelorussia (now BELARUS), ESTONIA, GEORGIA, KAZAKHSTAN, Kirghizia (now KYRGYZSTAN), LATVIA, LITHUANIA, Moldavia

SOUTH AFRICA

By AD 500: African peoples – including the BANTU – had reached the E coast of southern Africa. **1652:** White settlement began in the Dutch colony of Cape Town. **19th century:** Conquest of the local African societies provided a source of slave labour. **1814:** Britain acquired the CAPE. **1818–28:** The ZULUS became the dominant military force in Natal under the leadership of Shaka. **1833:** Slavery abolished. **1835–7:** The Boers (or AFRIKANERS) moved inland on the GREAT TREK to found the republics of the TRANSVAAL and ORANGE FREE STATE. **1843:** NATAL annexed by the British. **1879:** Zulus defeated by the British in the Zulu War. **1880–1:** British attempts to annex Afrikaner republics led to the First BOER WAR. **1886:** Discovery of gold in the Transvaal. **1899–1902:** Second Boer War; British achieved supremacy in South Africa. **1910:** Foundation of the Union of South Africa, ruled by a white minority consisting largely of Afrikaners. **1912:** AFRICAN NATIONAL CONGRESS (ANC) founded as a protest movement against white supremacy. **1914–15:** South Africa – as a British ally in World War I – took German South West Africa (NAMIBIA). **1919–24** and **1939–48:** Premierships of Jan SMUTS; South Africa joined Allied cause in World War II despite strong Afrikaner opposition. **1948:** Afrikaner NATIONAL PARTY came to power; racial segregation increased by the policy of APARTHEID. **From 1959:** Plan for black homelands (BANTUSTANS) implemented. **1960:** SHARPEVILLE massacre of black demonstrators; ANC banned; South Africa left the COMMONWEALTH. **1960s:** International pressure against apartheid increased. **1964:** Nelson MANDELA, sentenced to life imprisonment, became symbol of black opposition to apartheid. **1970s–80s:** Black opposition revived; SOWETO uprising (1976). **1980s:** P.W. BOTHA granted limited political rights to the coloured and Indian communities and implemented minor reforms for blacks, but unrest continued. **1986:** State of emergency introduced; censorship and detentions. **1989:** F.W. DE KLERK became president. **1990:** ANC prisoners, including Nelson Mandela, released. **1991:** Legal structures of apartheid dismantled; negotiations began for constitution of a 'new' non-racial South Africa. **1994:** ANC won South Africa's first universal suffrage general election; Mandela became president.

(now MOLDOVA), the Russian Federation (RUSSIA), TAJIKISTAN, TURKMENISTAN, the UKRAINE and UZBEKISTAN. The Soviet Union was dissolved in December 1991 following the abortive coup in Moscow by Communist hardliners in September.

Soweto (South-Western Townships), a segregated black residential area SW of Johannesburg, SOUTH AFRICA, the scene of police shootings of hundreds of schoolchildren demonstrating in June 1976.

Spain, a kingdom of Western Europe. See panel.

Spanish–American War (1898), a war between Spain and the USA. CUBA'S second war of independence against Spain, begun in 1895, gradually drew in the USA. The explosion of the battleship USS *Maine* in Havana harbour precipitated direct US intervention in the conflict. Spain lost Cuba, while the USA gained Puerto Rico and the Philippines, and a quasi-protectorate over Cuba.

Spanish Armada, the large military and naval force sent by PHILIP II of SPAIN to invade England in 1588. Defeated in the English Channel by the English fleet under the Lord High Admiral, HOWARD of Effingham, it tried to escape round Scotland and Ireland, suffering further losses by storm and shipwreck. Of the 130 Spanish ships that originally set out, only 86 returned.

Spanish Civil War (1936–9), a war between Republican and Nationalist forces in SPAIN. In 1936 Spain elected a POPULAR FRONT of socialists, radicals and Communists. General FRANCO – leading a right-wing coalition of conservatives, army officers and monarchists – invaded Spain from Morocco. Franco's Nationalists had the advantages of experienced forces and German and Italian aid, although the Republicans enjoyed widespread public support. Franco seized much of N and W Spain by July 1936 and took Madrid in the autumn, but the Republicans launched a counterattack and regained the city. During this counterattack, the Republicans fielded the first of their 'INTERNATIONAL BRIGADES'. The decision by France and Britain to remain neutral (1937) cut off the Republican's main source of supply, while Fascist support for Franco continued unabated. The Nationalists' use of modern German aircraft, tanks and artillery proved decisive. Despite such disadvantages, in early 1937 the Republicans won victories at Jarama and Guadalajara. On 26 April the Nationalists launched their infamous air assault on GUERNICA, and their subsequent air and land attacks on Bilbao, Catalonia, Aragon and New Castile marked the beginning of the end for the Republicans. The last-ditch Republican attack across the Ebro in mid-1938 failed and both Madrid and Barcelona fell to the Nationalists in Franco's offensive of early 1939. On 1 April he announced that the war was over. The war cost Spain over 800,000 casualties, leaving the country exhausted and embittered by a legacy of internal hatreds.

SPAIN

8th century BC: Greek settlements were founded on the Mediterranean coast. **7th century BC:** Celtic peoples settled in the Iberian Peninsula. **6th century BC:** The Carthaginians founded colonies in Spain, including Barcelona, Cartagena and Alicante. **From 218 BC:** the Romans gradually annexed Iberia. **5th century AD:** Germanic invasions ended Roman occupation. **By 7th century:** Most of the Iberian Peninsula was controlled by the VISIGOTHS and Christianity had been introduced. **711–14:** Muslim invaders from Morocco conquered most of the peninsula, establishing a powerful emirate – later a caliphate – at Córdoba. **11th century:** Start of the Christian reconquest of Spain (RECONQUISTA). **By the 13th century:** Only GRANADA remained in Muslim hands. **1469:** Spanish unity achieved following the marriage of FERDINAND II of ARAGON to ISABELLA I of CASTILE. **1492:** Conquest of Granada concluded the Reconquista. **1500–58:** During the reign of the HABSBURG CHARLES V, Spain gained control of the Netherlands, Sicily, Naples and Milan; Spanish conquistadores – PIZARRO and CORTEZ – established an empire in the Americas. **1556–98:** Golden age under PHILIP II, who encouraged the COUNTER-REFORMATION and sent the ARMADA against Protestant ENGLAND (1588). **17th century:** Decline of Spanish power, especially after defeat by the French at Rocroi (1643). **1700:** End of the HABSBURG line. **1701–13:** War of the SPANISH SUCCESSION; by the Treaty of UTRECHT Spain lost Belgium, Luxembourg, Naples, Sicily, Milan, Gibraltar and its last possessions in the Netherlands. **From 1714:** BOURBON rulers brought a measure of reform and enlightenment to a deeply conservative Spain. **1808:** NAPOLEON placed his brother Joseph on the throne of Spain, provoking fierce Spanish resistance and the PENINSULAR WAR. **1814:** British and Spanish armies forced the evacuation of the French from the Iberian Peninsula; restoration of King FERDINAND VII. **First half of 19th century:** Struggles between liberal and monarchist elements; revolt in Latin America; Spain lost its empire in Central and South America. **1833–9, 1849** and **1872–6:** The CARLIST WARS. **1868:** Queen Isabella II deposed in a revolution which was followed by a short-lived liberal monarchy under an Italian prince (1870–3). **1873–4:** Brief period of republican rule. **1898:** Defeat in the SPANISH–AMERICAN WAR; loss of CUBA, the PHILIPPINES, Guam and PUERTO RICO. **After 1900:** Growth of republicanism, socialism and anarchism. **1914–18:** Spain remained neutral in World War I. **1923–30:** Dictatorship of General Miguel PRIMO DE RIVERA. **1931:** Alfonso XIII abdicated; republic established. **1936–9:** SPANISH CIVIL WAR ended in victory for Nationalists under General FRANCO, who restricted political expression. **From 1966:** Terrorist campaign by the BASQUE separatist movement, ETA. **1975:** Death of Franco; monarchy restored under JUAN CARLOS. **1978:** Liberal constitution established. **1981:** Attempted army coup. **1982:** Felipe GONZALEZ became prime minister; Spain joined NATO. **1986:** Spain joined the EUROPEAN COMMUNITY.

Spanish Inquisition, see INQUISITION.

Spanish Main, the area of Spanish settlement and trading activity in the Caribbean between the 16th and 18th centuries, whose wealth and trading opportunities attracted the attention of foreign pirates, PRIVATEERS and traders.

Spanish Netherlands, the S provinces of the Netherlands ceded to Philip II of Spain by the Union of Arras (1579), including modern BELGIUM, LUXEMBOURG and part of N France. On receiving the provinces, Philip renewed his offensive against the rebellious N provinces (see DUTCH REVOLT). In 1598 he gave sovereignty of the Spanish Netherlands to his daughter, Isabella, and her husband the Archduke Albert. The region was only nominally independent during the Twelve-Year Truce (1609–21) and continuation of the war against the United Provinces (1621–48). In the later 17th century Spain lost a considerable amount of the territory, including Artois and part of Flanders, to LOUIS XIV. The Spanish Habsburg dynasty ended in 1700 and the region came under French rule until 1706, when it was taken over by the British and Dutch. The region later passed to the Austrian HABSBURGS in the Treaty of UTRECHT (1713).

Spanish Succession, War of the (1701–13), a war fought over the succession to the throne of SPAIN. In 1700 the childless Charles II of Spain died, bequeathing his empire to the grandson of France's LOUIS XIV, Philip of Anjou (the future PHILIP V of Spain). Louis – who had previously agreed to divide the Spanish empire between France and Austria in the event of Charles's death – could not resist the opportunity of preventing Spain from falling into the hands of the Austrian Habsburgs (who also claimed to have inherited the right to rule the Spanish empire); he accepted Charles's will, and began to intervene in Spanish affairs. To counter the renewed threat of French domination of Europe, WILLIAM III of England formed a grand alliance of England, the UNITED PROVINCES, Austria and Savoy, with the intention of putting the rival Austrian candidate – the Archduke Charles – on the throne of Spain. In the ensuing war the resources of the allies, and the superiority of their generals – notably the Duke of MARLBOROUGH and Prince EUGÈNE of Savoy, who achieved notable victories at BLENHEIM, RAMILLIES, OUDENARDE and Malplaquet – brought France near to collapse. The war was ended by the Treaties of UTRECHT and RASTADT.

Sparta, one of the leading city-states of ancient GREECE (see map, p. 11). In the 8th century BC Sparta gained control of the S PELOPONNESE, the majority of whose defeated peoples (the Messenians) were forced to work for the Spartans as state-serfs or HELOTS. Following a revolt c. 650 BC the Spartans introduced a series of military and social reforms to prevent further rebellions. By the end of the 6th century BC it had become the leading military power in Greece. It exercised wider influence through its domination of the PELOPONNESIAN LEAGUE. Spartan victory over Athens in the PELOPONNESIAN WAR resulted in a brief naval empire. However, by the 4th century BC Spartan power had declined and they were defeated at LEUCTRA (371 BC) by the Thebans, who went on to liberate the Messenians. Spartan power collapsed thereafter.

Spartacist Rising (1919), an attempted revolutionary uprising by the German Communist Party in Berlin led by Rosa LUXEMBURG and Karl Liebknecht. The revolt was brutally crushed and Luxemburg and Liebknecht murdered.

Speer, Albert (1905–81), German NAZI politician. The official architect of the Nazi party, he designed the massive stadium at Nuremberg. Minister of armaments during WORLD WAR II, he was imprisoned at the NUREMBERG TRIALS.

Spice Islands, the Moluccas, between the Indian and Pacific Oceans, highly valued as a source of profitable spices. The Portuguese established settlements there in the 16th century but were ousted in the early 17th century by the DUTCH EAST INDIA COMPANY, which established a more complete monopoly of the local spice trade.

spoils system, a system of patronage widespread in 19th-century US politics, whereby a victorious party rewarded its backers with public appointments.

Sri Lanka, an island of S Asia. In the 6th century BC SINHALESE invaders from N India arrived in Ceylon – as Sri Lanka was known before 1972. They established a capital at Anuradhapura, which became a key centre of Buddhist learning. In the 12th century TAMIL invaders from S India established a kingdom in the N where they displaced the Sinhalese. Spices drew Arab traders. Trading settlements were founded by the Portuguese in the 16th century, and then by the Dutch, who were invited by the king of Kandy to oust the Portuguese in the 17th century. From 1796 British rule replaced the Dutch, uniting the entire island for the first time. Nationalist feeling grew from the beginning of the 20th century, leading to independence in 1948, and a republican constitution in 1972. The country has been bedevilled by Tamil–Sinhalese ethnic rivalry, which led to major disorders in 1958, 1961 and since 1977. In 1971 a Marxist rebellion was crushed after heavy fighting. Sri Lanka elected the world's first woman Prime Minister, Sirimavo BANDARANAIKE (PM 1960–5 and 1970–7). In the 1980s separatist Tamil guerrillas fought for an independent homeland (Eelam). Fighting between rival Tamil guerrilla groups, Sinhalese extremists and government forces reduced the NE to near civil war. An Indian 'peace-keeping' force intervened (1987), but this aggravated an already complex situation. The Tamil NE is scheduled to achieve autonomy under the dominant Tamil Tigers guerrillas, who registered as a political party in 1989. Indian forces withdrew in 1990, but Tamil guerrilla activity continues in the NE. Tension increased in 1993 after the assassination of President Premasada.

Srivijaya, a former empire based on S Sumatra. The Saliendras, who had earlier built the temple-mountain of Borobudur, ruled over the kingdom of Srivijaya in S Sumatra and the region of the Straits for 300 years (9th–12th centuries). Their dominant position in the region eventually passed to the Javanese kingdom of MAJAPAHIT (14th–15th centuries).

SS (abbreviation for Schutzstaffel, German, 'protection squad'), a NAZI organization run by HIMMLER as a powerful and ruthless military elite. It was used by HITLER to suppress the SA in the NIGHT OF THE LONG KNIVES (1934), and later controlled the concentration camps. The GESTAPO was one of its subdivisions.

Stalin, Josef Vissarionovich (b. Dzhugashvili; 1879–1953), Soviet Communist politician and dictator. General Secretary of the Communist Party from 1922, he became leader of the Soviet Union in 1929 following the power struggle after LENIN's death. He eased his chief rival, TROTSKY, out of power and into exile. With his slogan of 'Socialism in one Country', Stalin introduced a series of five-year plans to collectivize agriculture and policies for rapid industrialization. The former proved disastrous and led to food shortages and thousands of peasant deaths. He eliminated all opposition in the PURGES of the late 1930s, imprisoning and killing millions of members of the government, armed forces and intelligentsia. He moved closer to Britain and France in the early 1930s, but fear of isolation and a Nazi attack led him to sign the NAZI–SOVIET PACT with HITLER. He was drawn into WORLD WAR II in 1941 when Germany invaded the Soviet Union. After World War II he secured military and political control over the Eastern European countries liberated by the Soviet Union. His repressive rule, which contributed to COLD WAR tensions, ended with his death in 1953. He was criticized by his successor, KHRUSHCHEV, for crimes against the party and the use of the 'cult of personality'. Many of those prosecuted by Stalin were rehabilitated under GORBACHOV.

Stalingrad, Battle of (1942–3), a bitter engagement fought in and around the suburbs of Stalingrad (now Volgograd) between German and Soviet forces in WORLD WAR II (see map, p. 39). Intent on capturing Stalingrad, the German Sixth Army, under General Friedrich von Paulus, met with fierce Soviet resistance. As the bitter winter conditions began to bite, the Soviets counterattacked to the N and S of the city, and trapped nearly 200,000 German troops. Despite attempts to breach the cordon, the ring tightened around the German troops, and on 31 January 1943, von Paulus surrendered. The battle was a major turning-point of the war in the East. See EASTERN FRONT CAMPAIGNS.

Stamford Bridge, Battle of (25 September 1066), English victory over the VIKINGS at Stamford Bridge near York. HAROLD Godwinson defeated a Norwegian invasion under Harold Hardrada, but was killed at the Battle of HASTINGS three weeks later.

Stamp Act (1765), a British taxation measure designed to increase the American contribution to the costs of defending the North American colonies. The Act, which imposed a stamp duty on legal documents and merchandise, provoked widespread opposition. The British government was forced to back down, but continued to insist that it had full power to make laws for the colonies and left a tax on tea as proof as its authority. This was to lead to the BOSTON TEA PARTY and contributed to the outbreak of the American War of INDEPENDENCE.

Stanley, Sir Henry Morton (1841–1904), Anglo-American explorer and journalist. He was sent by the New York Herald to find David LIVINGSTONE, whom he met at Ujiji on Lake Tanganyika (10 November 1871). He later helped the Belgian king LEOPOLD II to establish the Congo Free State.

START, see STRATEGIC ARMS REDUCTION TALKS.

Star Wars, see STRATEGIC DEFENSE INITIATIVE.

States-General or **Estates-General**, the name given to two historical assemblies: **1.** in the UNITED PROVINCES of the Netherlands, a permanent assembly of deputies from the estates of the seven provinces of the Dutch Republic; **2.** in France, the periodic meeting of deputies of the three estates of clergy, nobility and commons, as in 1614 and 1789. The THIRD ESTATE (the commoners) of the States-General declared itself a National Assembly in 1789. Fearing an attack on the Assembly from the French king's forces, the Paris mob seized the Bastile, sparking off the FRENCH REVOLUTION.

states' rights, a US political doctrine upholding the rights of individual states against the central power of the federal government.

Stephen I, St (c. 975–1038), first king of HUNGARY (1001–38). He established the Christian church in his realm and campaigned energetically to convert his subjects.

Stephen of Blois (c. 1096–1154), king of England (1135–54). He seized the crown after the death of his uncle HENRY I, but spent his reign fighting to retain England (more or less successfully) and Normandy (unsuccessfully) against the claims of the Empress MATILDA and her son, the future HENRY II.

Steppes, the grasslands of Eurasia, stretching from the UKRAINE in the W to SW Siberia in the E.

Stern Gang, a Zionist terrorist group, an offshoot of the IRGUN ZVAI LEUMI, dedicated to ousting the British from Palestine in the 1940s. Officially called *Lohamei Heruth Israel* ('Fighters for the Freedom of Israel'), it was led by Avraham Stern until his death in 1942.

Stolypin, Peter Arkadievich (1862–1911), Russian politician. As prime minister (1906–11), he combined a policy of agricultural reform with political repression, ruthlessly punishing activists in the 1905 RUSSIAN REVOLUTION. He was assassinated in 1911.

Stone Age, a division of human PREHISTORY, based on the use of stone materials used for tools. The Stone Age is subdivided into the PALAEOLITHIC ('Old Stone'), MESOLITHIC ('Middle Stone') and NEOLITHIC ('New Stone') Ages.

Stonehenge, a prehistoric ritual site in Wiltshire, England, a circular earth bank with internal stone settings. It was started in the NEOLITHIC period (about 3000 BC). The present monument was built around 1500 BC.

Strategic Arms Limitation Talks (SALT), a series of meetings between the USA and USSR with the aim of limiting the number of nuclear weapons deployed by both sides. In 1972, after three years of negotiation, an ABM (Anti-ballistic missile) Treaty, limiting deployment to two systems only in each superpower homeland, was signed as part of the SALT I package. This was refined at Vladivostok in 1974 to impose 'ceilings' on the number of nuclear delivery vehicles (bombers, intercontinental ballistic missiles and submarines) deployed by each side. The process was taken a stage further by SALT II in 1979, when the ceilings were reduced, but the Russian invasion of Afghanistan in December 1979 prevented ratification by the US Senate. The SALT talks were followed by START in the early 1980s.

Strategic Arms Reduction Talks (START), disarmament negotiations between the USA and USSR during the 1980s aimed at reducing stockpiles of strategic nuclear weapons. The follow-up to SALT, START made slow progress. It was not until the Soviet government became more flexible under Mikhail GORBACHOV – after both sides had begun to update and increase their intermediate-range nuclear systems – that a breakthrough occurred. After lengthy negotiation, both superpowers agreed in December 1987 to abolish land-based INTERMEDIATE NUCLEAR FORCES (INF). The Americans and Soviets, anxious to cut defence spending, continued with START, but little headway was made until July 1991, when a treaty was finally signed in Moscow to cut strategic arsenals to 6000 weapons on each side by 1998. Further cuts were agreed between US President CLINTON and Russia's President Boris YELTSIN in 1993.

Strategic Defense Initiative (SDI, or 'Star Wars'), a space-based US defence system against nuclear attack. Ronald REAGAN announced work had begun on it in 1983. The system was centred upon an elaborate system of laser and charged-particle-beam weapons in space, ready to destroy an incoming Soviet nuclear strike. The project, however, proved ruinously expensive ($16.5 billion by 1990) and less than 100% effective, and was dropped in 1993.

Stresemann, Gustav (1878–1929), German politician. As foreign minister (1923–9) during the WEIMAR Republic, he pursued conciliatory policies towards Germany's former enemies. He accepted the DAWES and YOUNG Plans for reparations and negotiated the Treaties of LOCARNO and Germany's entry into the LEAGUE OF NATIONS.

Stroessner, Alfredo (1912–), president of PARAGUAY (1954–89).

Stuart or **Stewart, House of,** the royal dynasty that ruled in Scotland (1371–1714), and in England from the accession of JAMES I (1603) to the death of Queen ANNE (1714), apart from the period of the COMMONWEALTH and the PROTECTORATE (1649–60). The first Stuart king of Scotland was ROBERT II, a descendant of the hereditary stewards of the kings of Scotland. After 1714, the Old and Young PRETENDERS unsuccessfully maintained the Stuart claim to the thrones of England and Scotland against the House of HANOVER.

Sudan, a republic of NE Africa. N Sudan – once known as NUBIA – was strongly influenced by EGYPT, and was later the seat of the kingdom of Cush (600 BC–AD 350). Medieval Christian kingdoms fell to Muslim invaders from the 13th century. In 1820–1 Sudan was conquered by the Egyptians, who were challenged in the 1880s by an Islamic leader who claimed to be the MAHDI. The Mahdists took Khartoum, killed Sudan's Egyptian-appointed governor, General GORDON (1885), and created a theocratic state. Britain intervened, and – after the FASHODA INCIDENT – Sudan was administered jointly by Britain and Egypt. Nationalism developed strongly after World War I, but independence was only gained in 1956. Sudan remains politically unstable, alternating between civilian and military regimes. The civil war between the Muslim N and the animist-Christian S that began in 1955 remains unresolved. Sudan is increasingly isolated internationally owing to its backing for Iraq and Libya.

Sudetenland, a region of CZECHOSLOVAKIA (now in the Czech Republic), bordering Germany, annexed by HITLER as part of the THIRD REICH in 1938. It was returned to Czechoslovakia in 1945, the POTSDAM Agreement authorizing the expulsion of most of its German-speaking inhabitants. See map, p. 37.

Sueves, a term denoting the German tribes of the Upper Danube: the Alemanni, Marcomanni and Quadi. They entered Gaul in 406, and with the Asding VANDALS set up a kingdom in NW Spain (409) that survived until it was absorbed by the VISIGOTHS in 584.

Suez Canal, an international waterway linking the E Mediterranean to the Red Sea, built through Egyptian territory by the French engineer Ferdinand de Lesseps and opened in 1869. Control of the Canal was shared by Britain and France between 1875 and 1956. NASSER'S nationalization of the Canal in 1956 provoked the SUEZ CRISIS.

Suez Crisis (Oct–Dec 1956), the military confrontation that arose from NASSER'S nationalization of the Anglo-French Suez Canal Company in July 1956. Fearful of losing access to the Suez Canal, Britain and France came to a secret agreement with ISRAEL to attack Egypt. In a short, sharp war the Israeli forces occupied Sinai, while British and French forces attacked the area around the Canal. There was an international outcry, and the USA in particular exerted pressure that led to a withdrawal. A UN peacekeeping force moved into Sinai to keep the two sides apart. The Suez Crisis diminished the role of Britain and France in the Middle East, while Nasser's reputation in the Arab world soared as a result of his defiance of two Western powers.

suffragette, a member of the Women's Social and Political Union, a militant British feminist movement founded by Emmeline PANKHURST in 1903 to campaign for the right of adult women to vote in general elections. They employed militant tactics such as chaining themselves to railings, breaking windows and hunger strikes, which in some cases led to imprisonment. The force-feeding in prison of hunger-striking Suffragettes aroused much criticism. The notorious 'Cat-and-Mouse-Act' (1913) allowed the release of sick suffragettes but made them liable to re-arrest once they had recovered their health. Their militant methods were suspended on the outbreak of World War I. See WOMEN'S SUFFRAGE.

Sufi, a Muslim mystic. From the 12th century Sufis began to be organized into a number of orders (Arabic, *tariqa*), many of which still survive and remain influential.

Suharto (1921–), INDONESIAN soldier and politician, president (1967–). He overthrew SUKARNO in a bloody coup (1967) in which tens of thousands of supposedly Communist sympathizers were killed. His invasion of EAST TIMOR in 1975 has been internationally condemned.

Sui, a Chinese imperial dynasty (AD 589–618) which restored unity to China after years of rule by nomad dynasties. A Turco-Chinese general (Yang Jian) first seized power in the N and then conquered the S, founding the short-lived Sui dynasty.

Sukarno, Achmed (1901–70), Indonesian statesman and nationalist. He declared INDONESIA a republic in 1945 and opposed the return of Dutch colonial power after World War II. He was president until his overthrow and arrest by SUHARTO in 1966.

Suleiman I (the Magnificent; 1494–1566), OTTOMAN sultan (1520–66), whose reign saw a golden age of Ottoman power and grandeur. In three major campaigns against the SAFAVID Persians he annexed Mesopotamia. Suleiman also established Turkish power in Europe to an unprecedented degree, occupying Belgrade in 1521 and defeating Hungary in the Battle of MOHÁCS in 1526. He went on to besiege Vienna in 1529, occupied Transylvania and most of Hungary, which became the warring frontier between Western Christendom and Islam. The capture of Rhodes in 1522 gave the Ottomans an important naval base in the E Mediterranean. The Ottoman fleet enabled the Turks to attack Italy and challenge the Holy Roman Emperor for control of the central and W Mediterranean. In 1551 Tripoli became an Ottoman vassal state. By Suleiman's death, his empire stretched from Central Europe to the Yemen and from present-day Morocco to the Persian Gulf. Suleiman gave his empire greater centralized administrative unity and a system of law; his reign was a time of economic prosperity associated with the development of town life and a flowering of the arts.

Sulla, Lucius Cornelius (c. 138–78 BC), Roman dictator, opponent of MARIUS in the ROMAN CIVIL WARS of the 80s. Both men marched against Rome and massacred their political opponents and in 81 BC Sulla set himself up as dictator. He retired suddenly in 79 BC after failing in his attempts to reform the political system.

sultanate, an institution of government in the Islamic world, prominent since the 11th century, when the SELJUK Turks were granted the title of sultan (in Arabic the word originally meant 'power') by the ABBASID caliph. In effect, though not in theory, the Seljuk sultan exercised secular power, while religious authority was left to the CALIPH. Sultanates arose throughout the Islamic world; the largest and most long-lived was that of the OTTOMANS (late 13th–early 20th centuries).

Sumatra, the westernmost island of INDONESIA.

Sumer, the S part of ancient MESOPOTAMIA, where several city-states had emerged by 3000 BC. Much of the evidence for Sumerian cities comes from the remains of temples. Between 3500 and 3000 BC, buildings in these cities became progressively larger and more elaborate. The best example is the White Temple at URUK. The wheel was invented around the same period. The earliest writing – simple pictures drawn on clay – developed probably because of the need for record keeping in an ever more complex society. Each Sumerian city had a king, whose power was believed to come from the gods. Throughout the so-called Early Dynastic period (c. 2900–2370 BC) the Sumerian rulers fought each other for supremacy over their land. Cities involved in these struggles included Eridu, Kish, Uruk, Lagash, Umma and UR. Sumer was conquered by SARGON of AKKAD c. 2370 BC, but enjoyed a renaissance under a dynasty at Ur c. 2113–2006 BC.

Sung, see SONG.

Sunni, the majority sect within ISLAM, followers of the *sunna* or tradition of the prophet Muhammad. Sunnis regard the first four CALIPHS as legitimate heirs to the Prophet MUHAMMAD, but the minority SHIITES accept only the fourth caliph, ALI, as his true successor.

Sun Yat-sen (Sun Zhong Shan; 1866–1925), Chinese politician. As leader of the KUOMINTANG he overthrew the MANCHU dynasty in 1911 and was briefly president of the republic (1912) before resigning in favour of YUAN SHIKAI. In the period of civil strife following Yuan's death, he led a series of governments controlling small areas of S China. He reorganized the Kuomintang with Russian help and cooperated with the Chinese Communist Party. He is seen as the father of modern China by both Nationalists and Communists.

Suppiluliumas I, HITTITE ruler (c. 1380–1350 BC). A formidable warrior king, he established a strong Hittite empire that reached its greatest extent under his reign. In N Syria the main centres of power were Carchemish and Alalakh. A series of 'vassal treaties' – notably one with UGARIT – institutionalized Hittite control of the region.

Supremacy, Acts of, English parliamentary legislation confirming the supreme authority of HENRY VIII (1534) and ELIZABETH I (1559) over the ANGLICAN Church.

Suriname, a republic of South America. Dutch settlement began in 1602 and the area was confirmed as a Dutch colony in 1667. Suriname has a mixed population, including American Indians, and the descendants of African slaves and of Javanese, Chinese and Indian plantation workers. Since independence in 1975, racial tension has contributed to instability and there have been several coups. Constitutional rule was restored in 1991.

SWAPO (South West African People's Organization), a Namibian political party founded in 1959 to oppose South African rule. With the aid of Angola it began guerrilla attacks on South African forces. The United Nations recognized SWAPO as the legitimate government of NAMIBIA in 1966. In 1990, under its leader Sam NUJOMA, SWAPO won the first elections held there after South African withdrawal.

Swaziland, a kingdom of S Africa. The Swazi kingdom was formed early in the 19th century, and came under British rule in 1904. The country resisted annexation by the BOERS in the 1890s and by SOUTH AFRICA during the colonial period. Following independence (1968), much of the traditional royal authority was restored (1973). A bitter power struggle within the royal family followed the death of King Sobhuza II (1982).

Sweden, a kingdom of N Europe. See panel.

Sweyn Forkbeard (d. 1014), king of DENMARK (987–1014) and father of CNUT. He was involved in several raids on England before attempting its conquest (1013–14). He gained considerable support there, becoming king in 1014 when ETHELRED II fled to Normandy, but died soon afterwards.

Switzerland, a republic of W Central Europe. Switzerland occupies a strategic position, but the Swiss have used their remarkable position to withdraw from, rather than participate in, European power politics. In the 11th century, what is now Switzerland became part of the Holy Roman Empire. In 1291, three local territorial units – the 'Forest Cantons' of Schwyz (which gave its name to the country), Unterwalden and Uri – joined together in a League against the (Austrian) Habsburg Emperors. Other similar cantons joined the infant League throughout the later Middle Ages, and by 1513 the League included 13 cantons and a variety of dependent territories. Intense religious rivalries in the 16th century – with Zürich, Basel, Berne and Schaffhausen becoming Protestant – resulted in a civil war that tested but did not destroy the

League. At the end of the THIRTY YEARS WAR (1648), Switzerland's independence was finally recognized. The French REVOLUTIONARY WARS saw the creation of a Helvetian Republic in 1798, but in 1803 Napoleon dismantled this unitary state and returned the country to a confederation. At the Congress of VIENNA (1815) Swiss neutrality was recognized and the country gained its present boundaries. Continuing tensions in the early 19th century saw attempts by some cantons to secede and set up a new federation (see SONDERBUND), but the compromises of a new constitution in 1848 – which is still the basis of Swiss government – balanced cantonal and central power. As a neutral country Switzerland proved the ideal base for the RED CROSS (1863), the LEAGUE OF NATIONS (1920) and other world organizations, but Switzerland has avoided membership of any body it considers might compromise its neutrality – national referenda voted against Swiss membership of the UN (1986) and of the EEA (the combined trade block to be formed by EFTA and EC countries; 1992).

syndicalism, a movement related to SOCIALISM, advocating the overthrow of CAPITALISM and the ownership of industry by industrial workers. Its ideology was popular up to 1914.

Syracuse, a seaport in Sicily, founded by Greek colonists in the 8th century BC, and absorbed into the Roman Empire in 212 BC. The Athenian expedition to capture it during the PELOPONNESIAN WAR was a military disaster for Athens.

Syria, a republic of SW Asia. Syria was an important part of the HITTITE, ASSYRIAN and ACHAEMENID Persian empires, before being conquered by Alexander the Great (332 BC). From 305 BC Syria was the centre of the Seleucid Empire, and in 64 BC the area became a Roman province based on Antioch. The Byzantine Empire ruled the area (300–634) until the Muslim armies of Khaled ibn al-Walid invaded the country. Most Syrians accepted Islam rapidly. In 661 Mu'awiyya, the founder of the UMAYYAD dynasty, established his capital in Damascus, and the city reached the zenith of its power. When the Umayyads were overthrown by the ABBASID dynasty from Baghdad (750) Damascus's pre-eminence ended. From the 12th to the 14th century parts of coastal Syria were ruled by CRUSADER principalities. The MAMLUKS – originally Turkish slaves – ruled Syria from the 13th century until 1516 when the area was annexed by the (Turkish) OTTOMAN Empire. Ottoman rule was not ended until 1917, when a combined British-Arab army was led into Damascus. In 1920 independence was declared, but the victors of World War I handed Syria to France (1920) as a League of Nations MANDATE. Since independence in 1946 Syria has suffered political instability. The pan-Arab, secular, socialist BA'ATH Party engineered Syria's unsuccessful union with Egypt (1958–61). Syria fought wars with Israel in 1948–49, 1967 and 1973, and in the 1967 ARAB-ISRAELI WAR Israel captured the strategic GOLAN HEIGHTS from Syria. A pragmatic Ba'athist leader Hafiz ASSAD came to power in 1970 and allied Syria to the USSR. Assad's popularity has been challenged by Syria's increasing involvement in LEBANON since 1976 and by SHIITE fundamentalism. After 1989–90, economic pressures lessened Syria's dependence upon the USSR. Syria's participation in the coalition against Iraq (1990–1) gained greater international acceptance for Syria, which had attracted criticism for sympathizing with terrorism.

SWEDEN

10th and 11th centuries: Sweden became Christian; stable monarchy dominated the country through much of the Middle Ages. **1397–1523:** The Danish-dominated Union of KALMAR united the crowns of Sweden, NORWAY and DENMARK. **1523:** Danish rule thrown off during the reign of GUSTAVUS I, who founded the Vasa dynasty and confiscated Church lands, an act that led to the REFORMATION in Sweden. **1560–84:** Sweden gained Estonia from Russia. **1611–32:** Reign of GUSTAVUS ADOLPHUS; Sweden became a major power, intervening on the Protestant side in the THIRTY YEARS WAR and gaining Bremen, Verden and Pomerania. **1654–60:** Charles X scored victories over the Poles and seized S Sweden from the Danes. **1660–1:** Sweden's conquests recognized by its neighbours in the Baltic peace settlement. **1697–1718:** Reign of CHARLES XII. **1700–21:** GREAT NORTHERN WAR; Sweden's defeat led to the loss of its Baltic empire. **From 1721:** Sweden troubled by internal struggles between the monarchy and the aristocracy. **1798–1813:** Sweden involved in the NAPOLEONIC WARS. **1810:** Jean-Baptiste BERNADOTTE was elected crown prince to the childless king. **1814:** Sweden lost Finland and its last possessions S of the Baltic, but Norway united with Sweden. **1818:** Bernadotte succeeded to the throne as Charles XIV. **1905:** The union of Norway and Sweden was dissolved. **After 1932:** Sweden developed a comprehensive WELFARE STATE under SOCIAL DEMOCRATIC governments. **1986:** Assassination of PM Olaf PALME. **1990s:** Economic necessity obliged Sweden to dismantle aspects of its welfare system.

Taft, William Howard (1857–1930), 27th president of the USA (1909–13). A conservative Republican, he sought re-election in 1912, but was well beaten by the Democrat Woodrow WILSON, the Republican vote being split by ROOSEVELT'S decision to run on a PROGRESSIVE Party ticket.

Tahiti, an island of French Polynesia in the S Pacific. Claimed by British and French navigators in the 18th century, Tahiti became a French protectorate in 1842 and a colony in 1880.

Taiping Rebellion (1851–64), a Chinese peasant rebellion. The Taiping ('heavenly peace') Movement took up arms in 1851 and controlled a large part of the S for over a decade, ruling from Nanjing between 1853 and 1864. Under its messianic leader, Hong Xiuquan – who claimed to be the younger brother of Jesus Christ – the movement developed an ideology that mixed peasant egalitarianism with elements of Christianity. The rebellion was brutally suppressed by the QING armies revitalized by Western arms and military advice, and the death toll is estimated to have run into millions.

Taira Kiyamori, military dictator who seized power in JAPAN in the mid-12th century. His successor, Yoritomo, established the KAMAKURA shogunate.

Taiwan, see CHINA, REPUBLIC OF.

Taizong (T'ai-tsung; 596–649), the second TANG emperor of China (627–49). One of the greatest of Chinese emperors, he reformed the administration of the empire, restored the supremacy of the civil service and established the principle of selection for office by examination.

Tajikistan, a republic of Central Asia (see map, p. 43). The Tajiks, an Iranian people, were included in the Persian Empire until the 8th century AD when the Arabs extended their influence over most of the area. From the 10th century, the Tajiks were also subject to Turkic influences from the N. In the 13th century the Tajiks were overrun by the MONGOLS. The area was, in turn, part of the Mongol Empire, the JAGATAI Khanate and the empire of TAMERLANE and his descendants. A period of UZBEK rule ended when the Afghans invaded in the 18th century. In the 19th century most of the Tajiks owed allegiance to the (Uzbek) khan of Bukhara. The area was annexed by tsarist RUSSIA (1860–8). After the RUSSIAN REVOLUTIONS, the area was reoccupied by the Soviet RED ARMY (1920), but Tajik revolts simmered from 1922 to 1931. Tajikistan became a Union Republic within the USSR in 1929, and gained its independence on the dissolution of the Soviet Union in December 1991. Since independence the country has been wracked by civil war between former Communists and Islamic fundamentalists.

Talleyrand-Périgord, Charles Maurice de (1754–1838), French foreign minister (1799–1807 and 1814–15). He negotiated secretly with the allies to depose NAPOLEON I after 1807, and represented France at the Congress of VIENNA.

Tamerlane ('Timur the Lame'; 1336–1405), MONGOL conqueror. Claiming descent from GENGHIS KHAN, he took over the western half of the JAGATAI Khanate in the later 14th century. In virtually every year of his long reign (1369–1405) he added another major city to the list of places he had plundered. These included Delhi, Saray (the capital of the GOLDEN HORDE), Baghdad, Aleppo, Damascus and Bursa (the capital of the Ottoman Sultans of Anatolia). The area he conquered stretched from the Mediterranean to Mongolia, and after 1369 he ruled from his capital in Samarkand. However, he took little interest in administration and his empire began to contract within a few years of his death.

Tamil, a people of S INDIA and SRI LANKA. From the 10th century Tamils from SE India established a substantial presence in the N part of Sri Lanka and soon replaced the native SINHALESE. Tamil–Sinhalese ethnic rivalry led to disturbances in 1958, 1961 and intermittently since 1977. Separatist Tamil guerrillas have been active in N Sri Lanka since 1979.

Tang, a Chinese imperial dynasty (618–907) under which the Chinese empire was extended into Central Asia and Korea. The dynasty was established by TAIZONG, who became its second emperor. Under the Tang, the empire rose to classic perfection and ruled with rigid efficiency from Changan (modern (Xi'an). The dynasty is noted for its technological and artistic achievements, including the invention of printing and manufacture of gunpowder. The fall of the Tang – under pressure from peasant rebellions and nomad incursions on the N frontiers – was followed by half a century of disintegration until the SONG dynasty was established.

Tanganyika, see TANZANIA.

Tannenberg, Battle of, 1. the defeat of the TEUTONIC KNIGHTS by the Poles in 1410. **2.** a series of actions fought in East Prussia (now Poland) between Germany and Russia in August 1914. Two Russian armies advancing towards Königsberg (now Kaliningrad) were respectively defeated and forced to retreat by Generals von HINDENBURG and LUDENDORFF. The Russians never again entered German territory in WORLD WAR I. See map, p. 36.

Tanzania, a republic of E Africa. The coast was explored by Arabs from the 8th century and the Portuguese from the 16th century. ZANZIBAR was an Omani possession from the 18th century, became an independent sultanate in 1856 and then a British protectorate (1890–1963). After independence in 1963 the sultan of Zanzibar was deposed in a radical left-wing coup. The mainland became the colony of German East Africa in 1884, the British trust territory of Tanganyika in 1919 and an independent state in 1961. In 1964 Tanganyika and Zanzibar united to form Tanzania. President Julius NYERERE'S policies of self-reliance and egalitarian socialism were widely admired, but proved difficult to implement and were largely abandoned by the time he retired as president in 1985. In 1992 amendments to the constitution to legalize a multi-party system were presented to the National Assembly.

Taoism, see DAOISM.

Tariq ibn Zaid (fl. 700–12), Berber general who led the first Islamic invasion of Spain. In 711 he crossed from North Africa by way of Gibraltar (*Jabal Tariq*). The country was soon conquered and formed into an Arab province, al-Andalus, with its capital at Córdoba.

Tarquin the Proud, the last of the seven kings of Rome who had begun with ROMULUS. He was expelled in 509 BC when the ROMAN REPUBLIC was set up.

Tartars or **Tatars,** the name given to the westernmost group of nomads of Turkish and MONGOL origin. They moved into the area N of the Black and Caspian Seas with the 13th-century Mongol advance, establishing the Khanate of the GOLDEN HORDE. Most Tartars came under Russian rule in the 16th century, although the Tartar Khanate of the Crimea survived until 1783.

Tasman, Abel (1603–61), Dutch explorer. In 1642 he discovered Tasmania and the south island of New Zealand, and by sailing round Australia proved it to be an island.

Taylor, Zachary (1784–1850), 12th president of the USA (1849–50). A hero of the MEXICAN–AMERICAN WAR, he was nominated by the WHIGS as their presidential candidate in 1848. He opposed concessions to the Southern states on the issue of the extension of slavery to the new states gained from Mexico.

Tecumseh (c. 1768–1813), Shawnee Indian chief who sided with the British in the WAR OF 1812, dying in the Battle of the Thames (1813).

Teheran Conference (28 November–1 December 1943) the first meeting between CHURCHILL, STALIN and F.D. ROOSEVELT during WORLD WAR II. The 'Big Three' discussed the opening of a SECOND FRONT in Western Europe, future Soviet influence in Eastern Europe, and the establishment of the UNITED NATIONS after the war.

Templars or **Knights Templar,** a military and religious order of knights founded c. 1120. The first of the orders established to fight a Christian holy war, they were named after their base in Jerusalem (the Temple of Solomon) and were predominantly French in composition. The Templars grew wealthy from donations of land and became great bankers. But after the fall of Acre they were rich men without a cause. In 1306 Philip IV of France had the Order of the Temple dissolved and profited from its riches.

Temple Mound Culture, see MISSISSIPPI CULTURE.

Tennis Court Oath (20 June 1789), the declaration by commoners (the THIRD ESTATE) of the French STATES GENERAL that they would not disperse until LOUIS XVI had agreed to a written constitution. (They had met in one of the royal tennis courts after they were shut out of their usual meeting place.)

Tenochtitlán, the ancient island capital of the AZTECS, on the site of present-day Mexico City. Its capture by CORTEZ in 1521 led to the capitulation of the Aztec empire.

Teotihuacán, an early temple-city of Meso-America near Mexico City. It exercised a power and influence in the region around AD 500 that was more than purely religious and cultural. It is known that the rulers of the city despatched embassies far afield to enforce the acknowledgement of Teotihuacán's supremacy and the collection of tribute. Teotihuacán was abandoned in the 7th century.

Teresa of Avila (1515–82), Spanish nun and mystic. She reformed the Carmelite order, returning it to older, more austere rules. Her account of her mystical experiences brought her – briefly – before the INQUISITION. She was canonized in 1622.

Terror, Reign of, the period during the FRENCH REVOLUTION, when the CONVENTION pursued a ruthless policy of liquidating all those who were seen as a threat to the regime. In the summer of 1793 the JACOBINS used a revolutionary mob to expel the moderate GIRONDIN deputies from the Convention. Virtually dictatorial powers were assumed by the Committee of Public Safety, of which Maximilien ROBESPIERRE was the most prominent member. The Committee persecuted suspected counter-revolutionaries, and all over France at least 300,000 people were arrested, and of these about 17,000 were guillotined. In the spring of 1794 the Terror intensified. The Committee eliminated its political opponents, including those on the left responsible for a policy of dechristianization. Other victims included the moderate Georges DANTON. Suspects' rights were reduced and no mercy shown to those convicted. Fearing for their own lives, and that Robespierre's power was too great, his enemies had him arrested and executed in July. A new regime, the DIRECTORY, was established and the Terror brought to an end.

Terrorism, violent activity intended to achieve a political objective. In modern parlance the term is generally used to denote acts of terror carried out by clandestine organizations against non-combatant groups to force a national government to accede to a demand. As such it has been used by extremists of both left and right (notably the BAADER-MEINHOF Gang), and by groups representing national minorities (notably the Provisional wing of the IRISH REPUBLICAN ARMY). Political terrorism has been used by totalitarian regimes to liquidate opposition, as under HITLER and STALIN.

Test Acts (1673 and 1678), English legislation making the holding of public office conditional upon a denial of transubstantiation in the mass (as believed by Roman Catholics) and a certificate of attendance at ANGLICAN communion. The Acts were not repealed until 1829.

Tet Offensive (29 January–25 February 1968), a coordinated offensive launched by the North Vietnamese army and the VIET CONG against US, Allied, and South Vietnamese forces during the VIETNAM WAR. Despite the ultimate defeat of the Tet attackers, the scale of the offensive shocked the American public and called into question the ability of the South Vietnamese and their US allies to win the war. Under mounting pressure, US President JOHNSON declined to stand for president in the forthcoming elections, called for peace talks and halted the bombing of North Vietnam.

tetrarchy, the 'rule of four' established by the Roman emperor DIOCLETIAN in the 3rd century. Realizing he could not rule the whole empire on his own, Diocletian chose his colleague, Maximian, to manage the western provinces, while he took charge of the east. Shortly afterwards the two emperors (*Augusti*) each took on an assistant (*Caesar*). The tetrarchy was intended to be a permanent institution, but when Diocletian retired in 305 civil war erupted between the various heirs. CONSTANTINE, son of Maximian's Caesar, was victorious in the west in 312, and in 324 defeated the eastern emperor. He thus reunited the empire under his sole rule, which lasted until his death in 337.

Teutoburger Forest, Battle of the (AD 9), the annihilation of three Roman legions under VARUS by German tribesmen. Their defeat forced the Romans to abandon their plans to extend their rule in Germany E of the Rhine.

Teutonic Knights, a German military and religious order, founded in 1190 in Acre in Palestine. The Order gained ground in N Europe as well as the Levant. After their expulsion by the MAMLUKS in 1268, the Knights of the Teutonic Order returned to their homeland and headed the drive to the E into Slav lands, creating a Baltic empire in what later became Prussia (see map, p. 21). After playing a large part in the warfare and politics of Eastern Europe, they were defeated by the Poles at TANNENBERG in 1410. Thereafter a decline set in, compounded by the secularization of the Order in Prussia in 1525. The Order was dissolved in Germany in 1809.

Tewkesbury, Battle of (4 May 1471), a battle fought during the Wars of the ROSES, in which EDWARD IV defeated the Lancastrian forces of MARGARET of Anjou, wife of HENRY VI. Following the battle Edward was able to re-enter London and resume his reign, which was not seriously challenged thereafter.

Texas, Republic of (1836–45), a short-lived independent republic in the SW USA, established when American settlers in the Mexican province of Texas staged a successful revolt (1835–6). It was extinguished in 1845, when the USA annexed it as a slave state.

Thailand, a kingdom of SE Asia, known before 1939 as Siam. The Thais originated in Yunnan (China) and moved S after the MONGOL destruction of their kingdom, Nanchao (1253). The Thais seized the KHMER (Cambodian) city SUKHOTAI, making it the centre of a new kingdom. After

1350 – based on the city of AYUTTHAYA – Thai rulers consolidated their hold on S Siam and the Malay peninsula. Centuries of warfare with BURMA, LAOS and CAMBODIA did not prevent Siam from becoming the most powerful state in SE Asia, and the adroit diplomacy of its rulers enabled it to remain free of European colonization. Rama I (reigned 1782–1809), founder of the present dynasty, moved the capital to Bangkok. His successors were forced to cede their claims over neighbouring lands to Britain and France. A constitutional monarchy was established by a bloodless coup (1932), whose Westernized leaders (Pibul Songgram and Pridi Phanomyang) struggled for political dominance for the next quarter of a century. During World War II Thailand was forced into an alliance with Japan. Since then Thailand has made a decisive commitment to the US political camp, which has brought major benefits in military and technical aid. Despite continuing army interventions in politics, Thailand has prospered. However, the stability of the country was compromised by the wars in VIETNAM and by the continuing Cambodian conflict (until 1991), as Cambodian refugees and guerrillas remained in Thai border regions. Under a revised constitution (1991) the military-dominated Senate assumed a leading role. Constitutional rule was restored in 1992.

Thatcher, Margaret (1925–), British Conservative politician, prime minister (1979–90). Europe's first woman PM, and a vigorous advocate of the free-market philosophy of the NEW RIGHT, she applied a rigid MONETARIST economic policy, reduced government intervention in industry, curbed trade union power, privatized major industries, cut taxes, and called into question the values of the WELFARE STATE. The defeat of Argentina in the 1982 FALKLANDS WAR secured her an overwhelming victory over Labour in the 1983 election, and the short-lived boom of the late 1980s brought her a third term in 1987. Growing economic problems together with her strident opposition to greater European integration led to her replacement by John MAJOR in November 1990.

Thebes, 1. the most important city of ancient BOEOTIA in central Greece. It gained steadily in power after the PELOPONNESIAN WAR, but was defeated by PHILIP II of Macedon at Chaeronea in 338 BC, and was sacked by ALEXANDER THE GREAT after it had revolted against him in 336. **2.** a city of ancient EGYPT. It became a religious centre during the New Kingdom and included the grandiose temple complex of KARNAK.

Themistocles (c. 523–c. 458 BC), Athenian general and statesman. He was the main driving force behind the development of the Athenian navy and the strategy adopted in 480–79 during the PERSIAN WARS.

Theoderic ('the Great'; c. 450–526), king of the OSTROGOTHS (474–526). He was recognized as king of Italy in 497 and as king of the VISIGOTHS from 511. Ruling in Roman imperial style, he was the most successful barbarian ruler of his era.

Theodosius I (349–95), Roman emperor (378–395), the last to rule over both halves of the ROMAN EMPIRE. Prompted by St Ambrose, Bishop of Milan, Theodosius, a fervent Christian, persecuted heretics and banned pagan worship.

Thera, a small island in the Aegean (now known as Santoríni). An entire section of the island – including the MINOAN site of Akrotiri – was buried under the debris of a gigantic volcanic eruption around 1500–1450 BC.

Thermopylae, Battle of (480 BC), the first land battle of the PERSIAN WARS. The small Greek forces under the Spartan king LEONIDAS held up the invading Persian army at the narrow pass at Thermopylae in central Greece. Phocian guards treacherously revealed to the Persians a mountainous route round the the back, and Leonidas, the Spartans and the Boeotians remained to die heroically, while the rest of the Greeks withdrew.

Thessaly, a region in NE Greece, south of Macedonia. A Thessalian Confederacy had developed by the 6th century BC, but was only briefly a major power in Greece in the mid-4th century, before falling under the domination of Philip II of MACEDON.

Thiers, Louis Adolphe (1797–1877), French politician, first president of the Third Republic (1871–3). As head of the provisional government he negotiated peace with Prussia after the FRANCO-PRUSSIAN WAR and suppressed the Paris COMMUNE.

Third Estate, the class of commoners in a society divided into social groups known as estates (particularly in France before the the FRENCH REVOLUTION). The other estates were the nobility and the clergy. See also STATES-GENERAL.

Third Reich, the name used by the NAZIS to describe the regime they established in GERMANY (1933–45). In Nazi parlance the First Reich was the HOLY ROMAN EMPIRE (962–1806), and the Second Reich the empire founded by BISMARCK after the defeat of France (1871–1918).

Third World, a term, coined in France in the early 1950s, to describe those newly independent states in Central and South America, the Caribbean, most of Africa, Asia excluding Japan and China, and Oceania excluding Australia and New Zealand. Many Third World countries, often referred to as developing countries, are heavily in debt to the developed world, its banking institutions and the INTERNATIONAL MONETARY FUND. These debts involve very large sums, and the interest payments constitute a severe drain on the economies of debtor nations.

Thirteen Colonies, the 13 British colonies of North America that rebelled against Great Britain (1775–83) and surrendered elements of their sovereignty to form the UNITED STATES OF AMERICA: i.e. MASSACHUSETTS, New Hampshire, Rhode Island, Connecticut, NEW YORK, New Jersey, PENNSYLVANIA, Delaware, Maryland, VIRGINIA, North Carolina, South Carolina and Georgia. Of these states only Rhode Island was unrepresented at the Constitutional Convention that met in Philadelphia in 1787. The designation 'Thirteen Colonies' distinguishes them from other New World colonies such as Nova Scotia and Barbados, which remained loyal to the crown during the American War of INDEPENDENCE.

Thirty-Nine Articles, the doctrines of the ANGLICAN Church, drawn up in the 16th century by CRANMER and Ridley. ELIZABETH I re-established the Church of England on the basis of the Thirty-Nine Articles.

Thirty Tyrants, a brutal oligarchy that ruled Athens (404–403 BC) following the Athenian defeat in the PELOPONNESIAN WAR. Spartan-backed and led by CRITIAS, the Thirty

Tyrants ended democracy and began a rule of terror. They were overthrown when Sparta withdrew its support for the unpopular regime, and democracy was restored.

Thirty Years War (1618–48), a complex series of struggles in Europe, sparked off by religious tensions that had built up in western Europe over half a century (see REFORMATION and COUNTER-REFORMATION). The war began with a revolt in BOHEMIA against the anti-Protestant and centralizing policies of the Habsburg emperor FERDINAND II (see Defenestration of PRAGUE). By 1620 the revolt had been crushed. However, the struggle quickly became entangled with wider European conflicts. In 1620, Spain, the ally of the Austrian Habsburgs, occupied the Rhenish Palatinate (in W Germany) whose ruler had led the Bohemian revolt and had subsequently been elected king of Bohemia (Frederick V). The following year, Spain resumed its war with the Dutch (see DUTCH REVOLTS). By 1629 Habsburg power seemed dominant in Germany, and in that year Ferdinand II attempted to reimpose the religious settlement of 1555, thus ending unofficial toleration of Calvinism. Fear of Habsburg and Catholic power led GUSTAVUS ADOLPHUS, Protestant king of Sweden, to invade Germany in 1630. A string of brilliant successes brought most of N Germany under the control of the Swedes and their allies. Only Gustavus' death at the Battle of LÜTZEN in 1632 halted his further progress. However, a subsidy from France and military assistance from German Protestants enabled the Swedes to fight on for financial compensation and territorial concessions in N Germany. The entry of France (1635), the greatest anti-Habsburg power, changed the character of the war into an essentially political struggle. The growing difficulties of both the Spanish and Austrian Habsburgs led in 1648 to the Peace of WESTPHALIA. The struggle between France and Spain went on until 1659, when it was ended by the Treaty of the PYRENEES.

Thrace, a region comprising what is now S Bulgaria and European Turkey. Its Indo-European tribes warred and traded with each other and the Greek cities. Much of Thrace was overcome by PHILIP II of Macedon, and later became part of a Hellenistic kingdom.

Three Emperors' League (German, *Dreikaiserbund*), an alliance between Germany, Austria-Hungary and Russia in 1873. The League was negotiated by BISMARCK with the aim of keeping France isolated. The League collapsed after Austria and Russia clashed over policy in the Balkans, and it was replaced by the DUAL ALLIANCE between Germany and Austria-Hungary in 1879.

Three Kingdoms, a period of Chinese history (AD 220–265) after the fall of the HAN empire, when power was contested by three regional states: Wei in the N, Shu in the W and Wu in the E.

Thule Culture, an INUIT (ESKIMO) culture that flourished early in the first millennium AD.

Thutmose I, pharaoh of EGYPT (c. 1525–1512 BC) and father of HATSHEPSUT. He extended Egyptian rule into parts of NUBIA and Syria. At KARNAK he enlarged the temple of Amun, erecting monumental gateways and the granite obelisks.

Thutmose III, pharaoh of Egypt (c. 1504–1450 BC) and nephew of HATSHEPSUT, with whom he ruled jointly for the first 20 years of his reign. He campaigned in Palestine and Syria and established an Egyptian empire extending from the Euphrates to the Sudan.

Tiahuanaco, the most important temple-city of pre-Columbian (MAYAN) South America, on the shore of Lake Titicaca. It reached the height of its splendour in the first millennium AD. Tiahuanaco was more a religious and social centre of an agricultural people than a political capital.

Tianenmen Square, an open space in central Beijing, CHINA, where over 1000 unarmed supporters of China's pro-democracy movement were massacred by government troops 3–4 June 1989.

Tiberius (42 BC–AD 37), Roman emperor (AD 14–37). He was the stepson of AUGUSTUS, who chose him as successor only after he had run out of alternatives. Tiberius' rule was prudent and cautious, but was marred by treason trials and palace conspiracies and became a reign of terror.

Tiglath-Pileser III, king of ASSYRIA (745–727 BC). After usurping the throne he began the imperial expansion of Assyria. Gradual Assyrian encroachment on Babylonian territory to the S culminated in the conquest of BABYLON in 729 BC. In the W the Syrian states were reconquered and placed under direct Assyrian rule. The ARAMAEAN kingdom of Damascus and outlying parts of Israel were seized and turned into provinces. He also campaigned against URARTU, but it was not eliminated until the reign of SARGON II.

Tigris, the fast-flowing river to the E of the EUPHRATES. Great centres such as Hellenistic Seleucia and Ctesiphon, a capital of the Parthians and Sassanians, were built on its banks.

Tilsit, Treaty of (7 and 9 July 1807), the agreements between France and Russia following NAPOLEON'S defeat of Russia at the Battle of Friedland (June 1807) and of PRUSSIA at JENA. Russia gained much of Poland, while Prussia lost a third of its territory and half its population. Tsar ALEXANDER I promised to mediate between Britain and France and, if unsuccessful, to join an anti-British coalition.

Timur, see TAMERLANE.

Tipu Sultan (1750–99), ruler of the Indian state of MYSORE (1789–99). His attempts to continue the policy of his father, HYDER ALI, in building a powerful and militarily effective state ended in defeat by the British and death in battle at his capital of Seringapatam.

Tirpitz, Alfred von (1849–1930), German admiral, secretary of state for the navy (1897–1916). In 1907 he announced a programme of construction of Dreadnought-class battleships for the High Seas Fleet. The announcement led to a further British order for Dreadnoughts, fuelling the Anglo-German naval race.

Tito (Josip Broz; 1892–1980), Yugoslav guerrilla leader and statesman, prime minister (1945–53), president (1953–80). A Croat, he founded the Yugoslav Communist Party, organizing partisans against occupying German forces (1941–4) in WORLD WAR II. As PM of YUGOSLAVIA he split with Moscow in 1948 and adopted a policy of NON-ALIGNMENT in the COLD WAR. He established a collective government with rotational leadership to succeed him. However, after his death Yugoslavia faltered in nationalist crises that led to the breakup of the country.

Tobruk, siege of (1941–2), German siege of British and Commonwealth troops in the Libyan port of Tobruk in WORLD WAR II. Tobruk surrendered to German and Italian forces in June 1942 but was recaptured by MONTGOMERY in November 1942 following the battle of EL ALAMEIN. See also NORTH AFRICAN CAMPAIGN.

Togo, a republic in W Africa. Colonized by Germany in 1884, Togoland was occupied by Franco-British forces in World War I, after which it was divided between them as trust territories. British Togoland became part of GHANA; the French section gained independence as Togo in 1960, and subsequently relations with Ghana have been strained. Togo has experienced great political instability and several coups. Following anti-government protests, a multi-party system was restored in 1991.

Tojo, Hideki (1884–1948), Japanese general and politician. As prime minister (1941–4), he gave the order to attack PEARL HARBOR, and turned Japan into a virtual military dictatorship. He resigned after repeated Japanese defeats by the USA in the Pacific and was hanged as a war criminal in 1948.

Tokugawa, the last Japanese shogunate (1603–1867), founded by TOKUGAWA IEYESU. The shogunate was built on feudal concepts, but governed as a military bureaucracy. In particular, the DAIMYOS were subject to close supervision from Edo and their local power diminished by longer periods of compulsory residence at the court of the shogun. Loyalty to the regime was further encouraged by excluding foreign influences. Christianity was suppressed, and the only foreign traders permitted were the Dutch, who were restricted to Nagasaki harbour. Hermitically sealed from the outside world, Tokugawa Japan was a stable and, in many ways, a prosperous pre-industrial society. However, the arrival of Commodore PERRY and an American fleet in 1853 destabilized the shogunate world. In 1867–8 a group representing daimyos and imperial courtiers seized power in Kyoto and imposed the MEIJI restoration.

Tokugawa Ieyesu (1542–1616), the founder of the TOKUGAWA shogunate (1603–1867) in JAPAN. Like ODO NOBUNAGA and TOYATOMI HIDEYOSHI before him, he used muskets to fight his way out of the impasse of feudal anarchy and into control of a united Japan. He established a shogunate at Edo (Tokyo) headed by the Tokugawa family. The emperor, with some dignity restored, remained at Kyoto.

Tolpuddle martyrs, the name given to six Dorset farm workers who were transported to Australia in 1834 for administering an illegal oath to establish a TRADE UNION. Their conviction caused considerable protest, and they were eventually pardoned.

Toltecs, a former people of N Mexico. From their headquarters at Tula, they came to dominate a large part of central Mexico between the 10th and 12th centuries. They imposed their rule on the YUCATÁN from their base at Chichén Itzá. Their dominance was established on a more secular basis than other Meso-American peoples. The ruling elite had religious functions, but ruled through the power of a warrior tribe.

Tone, (Theobald) Wolfe (1763–98), Irish Protestant and nationalist. He was joint founder (1791), with the Catholic Lord Edward Fitzgerald, of the Society of United Irishmen, a movement seeking the independence of IRELAND from Britain. He sought French support for an Irish revolt, and was arrested in the abortive rebellion of 1797–8, later committing suicide.

Tonga, a kingdom in the S Pacific. Inhabited by Polynesians for over 3000 years, Tonga has been ruled by kings since the 10th century. European intervention began when Captain COOK visited Tonga (1773–7). Civil war in the first half of the 19th century was ended by King George Tupou I (reigned 1845–93), who reunited Tonga, preserved its independence and gave it a modern constitution. Tonga was a British protectorate from 1900 to 1970, when it became independent.

Topa Inca (d. 1493), the ruler responsible for the expansion of INCA power in the 15th century.

Tordesillas, Treaty of (7 June 1494), an agreement between SPAIN and PORTUGAL dividing between them the new lands discovered by the late 15th-century voyages of exploration. All lands W of an imaginary north-to-south line drawn 370 leagues W of the Azores and Cape Verde Islands were to go to Spain, and all those E of it to Portugal. The result of this was that Portugal acquired BRAZIL, and Spain virtually all the rest of South and Central America, and even parts of North America.

Torquemada, Tomás de (1420–98), the first Grand Inquisitor of the Spanish INQUISITION.

Tory, a British political party. The name was originally applied to those royalists opposed to the WHIGS' attempts to exclude JAMES II from the succession to the English throne after the POPISH PLOT. They were generally supporters of the divine right of kings and sometimes of absolutist theories of government. Hostile to the GLORIOUS REVOLUTION and tainted by JACOBITE associations, they were excluded from power by the monarchs of the House of HANOVER for most of the 18th century. Toryism revived with the Younger PITT in the 1780s, and gained further impetus from opposition to the French Revolution in the 1790s. Under Sir Robert PEEL, the Tory Party developed into the modern CONSERVATIVE Party in the 1830s.

totalitarianism, government by a centralized authoritarian single-party regime that closely regulates all aspects of life, as in HITLER'S Germany or STALIN'S Soviet Union.

Toulouse, Kingdom of, a VISIGOTH kingdom founded in AQUITAINE in 418, the first Germanic kingdom to be established in Roman territory.

Touré, Sékou (1922–84), first president (1958–84) of the Republic of GUINEA. After securing Guinean independence, he continued to serve as president, surviving attempts to overthrow him. On his death the army took control of the country.

Toussaint l'Ouverture (?1744–1803), a former slave and the greatest of the leaders of HAITI'S revolt against the French. He was governor-general of Haiti from 1801, but was betrayed when NAPOLEON I sent troops to restore French control.

Toyatomi Hideyoshi (1536–98), military ruler of JAPAN (1582–98). He consolidated military rule over the whole of Japan and invaded Korea in 1592. His military success rested largely on the use of European firearms.

Trades Union Congress (TUC), a British TRADE UNION organization. It was founded in 1868 by members of 'trades' who established a national congress to secure legal status for unions, which was finally achieved in 1871. The Parliamentary Committee of the TUC lobbied governments in the interest of unions and was transformed into a General Council in 1921. The TUC has had close links with the British LABOUR Party since the early 20th century.

trade unions, organizations of workers formed to promote collective bargaining with employers to secure better wages and improved working conditions. In the early 19th century they were opposed by employers in all of the industrializing countries. In Britain they were prohibited by the COMBINATION ACTS, which were not repealed until 1824–5. Government animosity to trade unions was exemplified by the treatment of the TOLPUDDLE MARTYRS. Attempts were made to build larger, less parochial, unions, including Robert OWEN's Grand National Consolidated Trades Union of 1833–4, but it was not until the greater prosperity of the 1850s and 1860s that 'new model' unionism developed on a national scale, producing the Miners' Association (1841) and the Amalgamated Society of Engineers (1851). However, British trade unions were still not fully legal. The campaigns of the TRADES UNION CONGRESS, established in 1868, secured legal status in 1871. Mass 'new unionism' among unskilled workers developed in the 1880s. The more militant leaders of these unions encouraged political action, and in 1900 joined socialist organizations to form the forerunner of the British LABOUR PARTY. The growth of trade unionism elsewhere in Europe was hampered by legal restrictions. In France many early workers' associations were driven underground. They enjoyed a brief period of legality under Napoleon III from 1868 until 1871, when the repression of the Paris COMMUNE was followed by persecution of socialists and trade unions. The French 'syndicates' finally gained legal protection. German unions revived in the 1860s but remained illegal until BISMARCK's fall from power in 1890. By 1914 the German unions were the most powerful workers' organizations in continental Europe. In America, 'combinations' of workers appeared in the early 19th century but proved small and weak, and it was not until the mid-19th century that American unions began to amalgamate in larger federations, including the National Labor Union, the KNIGHTS OF LABOR, and the AMERICAN FEDERATION OF LABOR. Many of the large US unions were socialist-inspired and proved popular despite the bad publicity caused by anarchist-inspired acts of violence. They reached their peak before 1914 and declined thereafter. All trade-union activity was banned as subversive in Russia throughout the 19th century, and those unions that existed were clandestine. They flourished briefly following the RUSSIAN REVOLUTION of 1905 but were repressed thereafter.

Trafalgar, Battle of (21 October 1805), a naval clash between a combined Franco-Spanish fleet and the British fleet under NELSON off the Spanish port of Cadiz. Nelson's victory ended NAPOLEON's hopes of an invasion of Britain, but he was fatally wounded in the battle. See map, p. 29.

Trajan (AD 53–117), Roman emperor (AD 98–117). His highly stable and successful reign saw the conquest of DACIA and a less successful war against PARTHIA. He also won over the Senate, which regarded him as an ideal emperor.

Transjordan, see JORDAN.

Transoxiana, an area of Central Asia between the Amu Darya and Syr Darya rivers (the ancient Oxus and Jaxartes). Crossed by the SILK ROUTE, it was the place where European/Near Eastern culture met the nomad world of Central Asia.

Transvaal, a province in the NE of the Republic of SOUTH AFRICA, a former independent AFRIKANER (BOER) republic (1852–1900) and British colony (1901–10). Transvaal forms the heartland of South Africa, including the administrative capital Pretoria and gold mining areas around Johannesburg. Boer insistence on Transvaal's independence helped precipitate the two BOER WARS.

Trasimene, Battle of Lake (217 BC), HANNIBAL's defeat of the Romans in central Italy during the Second PUNIC WAR.

Treaty Ports, the Chinese ports opened to Western trade by the 'Unequal Treaties' in the mid-19th century. The treaties were imposed on the Chinese after their defeat by the British in the first OPIUM WAR (1839–42). They regulated trade on European terms (including the import of opium) and secured European control over five 'Treaty Ports'. Further 'Treaty Ports' were conceded to all the Western powers after the second Opium War (1856–60).

Trenchard, Hugh Montague, 1st Viscount (1873–1956), British soldier and airman, and creator of the Royal Air Force (RAF). He became Chief of the Air Staff with the formation of the RAF in 1918. He was a strong advocate of strategic bombing.

Trent, Council of (1545–63), three councils of the Catholic Church held at Trento in N Italy. The council was established to reform the Catholic Church from within in the wake of criticisms made during the REFORMATION. It is seen as marking the beginning of the COUNTER-REFORMATION. The Council made few concessions to Protestant criticisms, but instead restated traditional doctrine regarding the sacraments, the Bible and papal supremacy, making clear the differences between Catholics and Protestants. It declared that Catholics should be better instructed in their faith and that they should attend mass and confession more regularly. In order to ensure that the clergy were better trained, bishops were urged to establish seminaries in their dioceses. The Council's decrees shaped Catholic doctrine and practice until the second Vatican Council in 1962–5.

Trianon, Treaty of (4 June 1920), a treaty between the Allied Powers and the new republic of HUNGARY, part of the PARIS PEACE CONFERENCE after World War I. As one half of the AUSTRO-HUNGARIAN EMPIRE, Hungary was stripped of two-thirds of its territory to help form CZECHOSLOVAKIA, the new state of YUGOSLAVIA and Poland.

tribune, an official representing the PLEBEIANS in ancient Rome.

Trinidad and Tobago, a republic in the E Caribbean. Trinidad was inhabited by Arawak Indians and Tobago by Carib Indians when COLUMBUS discovered them in 1498. Trinidad was neglected by Spain and became British in 1797. Tobago was claimed by the Spanish, Dutch and French before being ceded to Britain in 1802. African slaves were imported to work sugar plantations, but after the abolition of slavery in the 1830s, labourers came from India. The islands merged as a single colony in 1899 and gained independence in 1962. The country – which has been a republic since 1976 – witnessed a Black Power revolt in 1970 and an attempted coup by Islamic fundamentalists in 1990.

Triple Alliance (1882), an alliance between Germany, Austria and Italy. In 1879 Germany and Austria-Hungary signed the DUAL ALLIANCE aimed at mutual protection against France and Russia respectively. Three years later, in response to French expansion in N Africa, Italy joined them to produce the Triple Alliance.

Triple Entente (1907), the alliance between Britain, France and Russia during WORLD WAR I. In 1904 Britain agreed an entente (an 'understanding', short of a formal alliance) with France, opening the way to informal military talks on the containment of Germany. Three years later they signed a further entente with Russia.

triumvirate, a group of three ruling collectively. In ancient ROME the First Triumvirate comprised POMPEY, CAESAR and CRASSUS and was established in 60 BC. It came to an end in 48 BC when Caesar turned on Pompey and Crassus and, after defeating them, became dictator. The Second Triumvirate was established after Caesar's assassination in 44 BC. It comprised Mark ANTONY, OCTAVIAN and LEPIDUS. Lepidus was soon squeezed out of the Triumvirate, and in 31 BC Mark Antony was defeated by Octavian at ACTIUM. Mark Antony's suicide left the empire in the sole hands of Octavian.

Trotsky, Leon (Lev Davidovich Bronstein; 1879–1940), Russian revolutionary. He played a major role in organizing the RUSSIAN REVOLUTION of November 1917, after which he became Commissar for Foreign Affairs (1917–18). As Commissar for War (1918–24) he created the RED ARMY. He lost influence as STALIN'S power increased and was expelled from the Communist Party in 1927. In 1940 he was assassinated in Mexico by a Spanish Communist, probably acting for Stalin.

Troy, an ancient city of NW Asia Minor (see map, p. 11). Excavations carried out by the German archaeologist Heinrich Schliemann between 1870 and 1890, and continued by others since, have revealed evidence of ten cities built on the site between the early Bronze Age and the Roman period. The seventh city, which was probably destroyed by fire in the mid-13th century BC, may be the city whose ten-year siege by the Greeks is described in Homer's *Iliad*.

Troyes, Treaty of (1420), a treaty between England and France. The Treaty temporarily ended the HUNDRED YEARS WAR, the French king CHARLES VI agreeing to name HENRY V as his successor. The Anglo-Burgundian regime took control of Paris and much of N France. However, Henry V died two months before Charles VI.

Trucial States, see UNITED ARAB EMIRATES.

Trudeau, Pierre Elliott (1919–), Canadian Liberal statesman, prime minister (1968–79 and 1980–4). His most significant accomplishment was to take the heat out of QUEBEC'S francophone separatist movement by promoting substantive constitutional reforms. Canada achieved final constitutional independence from the UK parliament during his second period in office.

Trujillo (Molina), Rafael (Léonidas) (1891–1961), dictator of the DOMINICAN REPUBLIC (1930–61). His dictatorship established complete control of all aspects of Dominican life. Isolated by CASTRO'S revolution in Cuba and democratic revolution in Venezuela, he was assassinated in 1961.

Truman, Harry S. (1884–1972), 33rd president of the USA (1945–53). A southern-born 'New Deal' Democrat, Truman succeeded to the presidency when F.D. ROOSEVELT died shortly before the end of World War II. In office he consented to the use of the atomic bomb against Japan and launched the MARSHALL PLAN. In 1947 Truman declared the intention of the USA to resist Communist expansion. This policy, known as the Truman Doctrine, has been pursued by all subsequent US governments, and led the USA to commit itself firmly to Western Europe, Japan and the Republic of Korea.

Tshombe, Moise (1920–69), Congolese politician. Under his 'presidency' the province of Katanga seceded from the newly independent Congo in 1960, during the CONGO CRISIS. Forced into exile in 1963, he was invited back by Congolese president KASAVUBU to take control of central government in 1964. His identification with mining interests and white settlers made him unpopular, and he was dismissed again by Kasavubu. He was forced into exile by MOBUTU'S coup of November 1965.

Tubman, Harriet (c. 1821–1913), black American abolitionist and social reformer. A fugitive slave, she was a leading figure in the informal 'Underground Railroad' network that spirited Southern blacks to freedom before the AMERICAN CIVIL WAR.

Tudor, House of, a royal dynasty that ruled England from the accession of HENRY VII in 1485 to the death of ELIZABETH I in 1603, when the throne passed to JAMES I of the House of STUART.

Tughluqs, a Muslim dynasty ruling the Indian DELHI SULTANATE (1320–1413). Under Muhammad ibn Tughluq (1324–51) they ruled over an empire which comprised almost the entire subcontinent. The empire, however, contracted under his successor, and thereafter N India was divided into a number of small states. The Tughluqs continued to rule until 1413, but their empire had effectively collapsed with the invasion of Delhi by TAMERLANE in 1398.

Tunisia, a country of N Africa. The PHOENICIANS founded CARTHAGE (near Tunis) in the 8th century BC. The Carthaginian empire fell to Rome in the PUNIC WARS. The area passed to the BYZANTINE Empire in AD 533. In 647 an Arab invasion won Tunisia for the Islamic world and for over 900 years the area was disputed by a variety of Muslim dynasties. From 1574 to 1881 Tunisia was part of the (Turkish) OTTOMAN Empire. In 1881 France established a protectorate, although the bey (monarch) remained the nominal ruler. Nationalist sentiments grew in the 20th century. Tunisia was occupied by the Germans (1942–3). Independence was gained under Habib BOURGUIBA in 1956 and the monarchy was abolished (1957). In the late 1980s the regime became increasingly unpopular and intolerant of opposition. Since Bourguiba's deposition by his PM (1988) – because of 'incapacity' – multi-party politics have been permitted.

Tupac Amarú, José Gabriel (1740–81), the leader of the largest Indian rebellion of the colonial period in South America (1780–1), which affected Peru and Bolivia directly and had echoes elsewhere in Spanish America. A descendant of the INCA, he was defeated and executed in May 1781.

Turkestan, an area of S Central Asia dominated since the middle of the 1st millennium by nomads speaking Turkic languages: Kazakh, Kirghiz, Turkmen, Uighur and Uzbek. The area came under Russian and Chinese rule in the 18th and 19th centuries.

Turkey, a country of SE Europe and Asia Minor. See panel.

Turkmenistan, a republic in Central Asia (see map, p. 43). The Turkmens are a nomadic Turkic people who were conquered by the Mongols in the 13th century and were then ruled by the GOLDEN HORDE and the JAGATAI Khanates, before becoming nominally subject to Persia, or the (Uzbek) khans of Khiva and Bukhara. The area came under Russian rule between 1869 and 1881. The Turkmens fiercely resisted the Russians and rose in revolt in 1916. An autonomous Transcaspian government was formed after the RUSSIAN REVOLUTIONS and the area was not brought under Soviet control until the RED ARMY invaded in 1919. The Turkmen territories were reorganized as the Republic of Turkmenistan in 1924 and admitted to the USSR as a full Union Republic in 1925. Independence was declared following the abortive coup by Communist hardliners in Moscow (September 1991) and the republic received international recognition when the USSR was dissolved (December 1991).

Turks, a nomad people of Central Asian, Altaian origins. They periodically dominated surrounding, settled peoples and, from the 11th century, under SELJUK and – later – OTTOMAN leadership, established their power over SW Asia and the Near East, many eventually settling in Anatolia (modern TURKEY).

Tuscany, a former state of central Italy (see maps, pp. 25 and 27). The MEDICI family – who had been leaders of the Florentine republic for most of the Middle Ages – became dukes of FLORENCE in 1531 and grand dukes of Tuscany in 1569. Tuscany passed to the Duke of Lorraine – the husband of MARIA THERESA of Austria – when the Medici became extinct in 1737, was absorbed into the Napoleonic states (1801–14) and was incorporated in the kingdom of ITALY (1860).

Tutankhamun, pharaoh of EGYPT (c. 1361–1352 BC). He is famous for his burial site, discovered by Howard Carter in 1922, but was in fact an insignificant king.

Tyler, John (1790–1862), tenth president of the USA (1841–5). As WHIG vice-president he succeeded to the presidency after the premature death of William Henry HARRISON. His defence of STATES' RIGHTS lost him the support of his cabinet.

Tyler, Wat (d. 1381), English rebel. He emerged as leader of the Kentish insurgents in the PEASANTS' REVOLT in 1381, presenting their demands to RICHARD II at Smithfield. After he was stabbed to death in a quarrel, the rebels dispersed.

Tyndale, William (1494–1535), English Protestant and Bible translator. Exiled in the Habsburg Low Countries, he set up a printing press at Antwerp, producing Protestant literature, including Bibles, for export to England. A victim of CHARLES V's repression of heresy, he was strangled to death at Louvain.

Tyre, a PHOENICIAN city. Loyal to the Persian king, it was besieged for months by ALEXANDER THE GREAT, who captured it after a lengthy siege in 332 BC.

TURKEY

1650 BC: HITTITE empire founded and quickly gained control of all Anatolia (present-day Turkey). **By the 6th century BC:** Persian ACHAEMENID power was expanding into Anatolia. **334 BC:** ALEXANDER THE GREAT crossed into Asia and destroyed the Achaemenid Empire. **From c. 323 BC:** Anatolia was divided into several Hellenistic states. **31 BC:** The ROMAN EMPIRE took control of the area. **AD 330:** Emperor CONSTANTINE established the new city of CONSTANTINOPLE, which became the capital of the BYZANTINE EMPIRE. **11th century:** Muslim SELJUK Turks occupied most of Asia Minor. **13th century:** The Seljuks were replaced by the Ottoman Turks. By the end of the **14th century:** Ottomans had conquered most of the Balkans; Turkey became the centre of the powerful OTTOMAN EMPIRE. **19th century:** Decline of the Ottoman Empire. **1908:** The YOUNG TURK revolt attempted to stop the decline. **1912–13:** Turkish defeat in the BALKAN WARS virtually expelled Turkey from Europe. **1914–18:** Turkey's alliance with Germany in WORLD WAR I ended in defeat and the loss of all non-Turkish areas. **1920:** Treaty of SÈVRES gave parts of the old Ottoman Empire to France and Britain as MANDATES; defeat by Mustafa Kemal (ATATÜRK) of a Greek army that had occupied Izmir (Smyrna). **1922–38:** Turkey transformed into a secular Westernized state. **1923:** Treaty of Lausanne returned Izmir to Turkey; republic of Turkey proclaimed with Atatürk as president. **1952:** Turkey joined NATO. **1960–1:** Military government following coup. **1961–80:** Constitutional rule restored. **1974:** Turkey invaded N CYPRUS, where a Turkish administration was established (1975). **1980-3:** Period of military rule. **Since 1983:** Constitutional rule restored. **1991:** Unrest among Turkey's Kurdish population intensified after exodus of Iraqi Kurds into Turkey.

Tyrol (Tirol), an Alpine province of AUSTRIA. Tyrol was under HABSBURG rule from 1363 until 1918 except during the NAPOLEONIC WARS, when it was ceded to Bavaria (1805–15), causing the Tyrolese to rise in a major revolt (1809). South Tyrol was ceded to Italy in the Treaty of St GERMAIN after World War I. See map, p. 37.

Tyrone, Hugh O'Neill, 2nd Earl of (1540–1616), Ulster chieftain. With O'Donnell he led a major revolt in Ulster against the English crown (1595–1603). Despite early successes and some support from Philip II of Spain, their rebellion was eventually suppressed by a concerted English effort, and Tyrone fled to Spain.

Tz'u-hsi, see CIXI.

U-boat (German, *Unterseeboot*), German submarine used to attack shipping in both World Wars to cut off trade and resources to Britain. Protected convoys of merchantmen were organized in response.

UDI, the Unilateral Declaration of Independence by the white settler government under Ian SMITH in Southern Rhodesia (ZIMBABWE) in 1965.

Uganda, a republic of E Africa. The British protectorate of Uganda – established in 1894 – was built around the powerful African kingdom of Buganda, whose continuing special status contributed to the disunity that has plagued the country since independence in 1962. Dr Milton OBOTE, who suppressed the Buganda monarchy in 1966, was overthrown in a coup by General Idi AMIN in 1971. Amin earned international criticism when political and human rights were curtailed, opponents of the regime were murdered and the Asian population was expelled. The army took over in 1979, supported by Tanzanian troops. Obote was restored but was ousted in a military coup in 1985, since when instability and guerrilla action have continued.

UKRAINE

1st millennium BC: SLAVS from the Carpathians migrated towards the Dnieper Valley. **From the 7th century BC:** Greek colonies flourished on the Crimean coast. **9th century:** Foundation of the state of KIEV RUS. **1237–41:** Kiev was wrecked by the invasion of the TARTARS. **From the mid-13th century:** Other powerful centres grew up in Galicia in the W and the Vladimir area in the NW. **14th century:** These centres came under Polish rule when both Poland and Lithuania extended S and E. **16th century:** Increase in Polish influence in Ukraine following the formal union of Poland and Lithuania (1569); Ukrainians reduced to serfdom. **16th century:** Poland encouraged the foundation in Ukraine of autonomous colonies of COSSACKS to act as buffers against Tartar invasions. **1648–51:** Cossacks challenged the Poles in a rebellion led by Bohdan Khmelnytsky, who requested assistance from the Russian tsar (1652). **1660–7:** Following two Russo-Polish wars Ukraine was partitioned between Poland and Russia. **1672–99:** The OTTOMAN Turks occupied Polish Ukraine. **Early 18th century:** PETER THE GREAT suppressed the autonomy of the Cossacks. **1772:** Galicia in the W annexed by Austria in the first partition of POLAND. **1793:** Russia reunited most of Ukraine under Russian rule in the second partition of Poland. **1878:** Russia banned the use of the Ukrainian language in schools and in print. **1918:** Independence declared in W Ukraine following the RUSSIAN REVOLUTIONS (January); Ukrainian Soviet government proclaimed in Kharkov in the E; Ukraine united with Galicia when Austria-Hungary collapsed (November). **1919–21:** Civil war; Poland invaded Ukraine in pursuit of territorial claims; RED ARMY invaded in support of Kharkov Soviet. **1922:** Ukraine became a Union republic of the USSR after the Red Army prevailed; Lvov district of Galicia remained in Polish hands. **From 1928:** Programme of Russification instituted by STALIN. **1941–5:** Ukraine occupied by Germany during World War II. **1945:** Ukraine enlarged by addition of Lvov (from Poland), Bukovina (from Romania) and Ruthenia (from Czechoslovakia). **1954:** Crimea became part of Ukraine. **1986:** Nuclear accident at Chernobyl; Ukrainian nationalism spurred by perceived Soviet indifference. **1991:** Ukraine declared its independence following abortive coup by hardliners in USSR (August) and gained international recognition when the USSR was dissolved (December). **Since 1991:** Tension with Russia over the status of Crimea and the Black Sea fleet.

Ugarit, an ancient Canaanite city on the N Syrian coast. A trading city, it expanded considerably under the hegemony of MITANNI, but was conquered by the HITTITES in the mid-14th century BC. Much of its wealth came from the copper trade with Cyprus and from metalworking. The city also had close links with the Aegean world.

Uitlanders (Afrikaans, 'outlanders'), the term used for non-Boer immigrants in the TRANSVAAL, who arrived there following the discovery of gold in 1886. See also BOER WARS, JAMESON RAID.

Ukraine, a republic of Eastern Europe. See panel.

Ulbricht, Walter (1893–1973), East German Communist politician. As party leader (1950–71) he implemented a policy of 'sovietization' of East Germany.

Ulm, Battle of (October 1805), NAPOLEON'S defeat of a large Austrian force was followed by the French occupation of Vienna. See NAPOLEONIC WARS and map, p. 29.

Ulster, a former kingdom and province in the N of Ireland. Six of its nine counties (Antrim, Armagh, Down, Fermanagh, Londonderry and Tyrone) fall within NORTHERN IRELAND (which is often referred to as Ulster), while the remaining three (Cavan, Donegal and Monaghan) are in the Republic of IRELAND.

Ulster Unionist Party, a political party supported by Northern Ireland's Protestant majority, dedicated to preserving the Union between Great Britain and NORTHERN IRELAND. It ruled the province from the partition of Ireland in 1922 to the reimposition of direct rule from London in 1972. Since 1969 it has had to contend for the Unionist vote with the Rev. Ian PAISLEY'S more militant Democratic Unionist Party.

Ulster Volunteers, a paramilitary force raised by CARSON in January 1913 to exclude ULSTER from the Third HOME RULE Bill. By 1914 over 100,000 men were under arms, but civil war between Ulster Volunteers and Irish nationalists was averted by the outbreak of World War I.

Umar ibn al-Khattab (c. 581–644), second CALIPH of ISLAM (634–44). Under his rule the Muslim Arab conquest of the Middle East began.

Umayyad, a dynasty of Muslim CALIPHS ruling from Damascus (661–750). A later Umayyad dynasty ruled in Spain (928–1031). The dynasty was founded in 661, when Mu'awiya seized control of the Islamic empire from ALI and moved the capital from Medina to Damascus. Despite sectarian divisions between SHIITE and SUNNI Muslims the Umayyad empire continued to expand, especially into Central Asia and, to the West, along the coast of North Africa and into Spain. The Umayyads, however, proved unpopular and were replaced by the ABBASIDS after revolts.

Union, Acts of, the laws creating the political union of Great Britain and Ireland. An act passed by HENRY VIII in 1536 formally incorporated WALES into the English crown, though the region had been subjugated by England since the late 13th century. The thrones of England and Scotland were united with the accession of JAMES I in 1603. The Act of Union between England and SCOTLAND (1707) abolished the Scottish

Parliament, the Scots henceforth sending MPs and peers to the Westminster PARLIAMENT, but retained the separate Scottish legal system and PRESBYTERIAN Church and allowed Scotland to trade with England's colonies. The United Kingdom of Great Britain and IRELAND was established with the amalgamation of the British and Irish parliaments in 1801. Southern Ireland left the United Kingdom in 1921 (becoming the Irish Free State in 1922), while NORTHERN IRELAND remained part of the UK.

UNITED KINGDOM

From c. 400 BC: Pre-Roman Britain was inhabited by the CELTS. **55–54 BC:** Julius CAESAR invaded Britain. **By AD 43:** Wholesale conquest followed by Romanization of Britain. **5th century:** The Roman province of Britannia – covering the area S of Hadrian's Wall – collapsed. **5th–6th centuries:** The Scots from NE Ireland invaded N Britain. **From 6th century:** WALES was divided into small kingdoms, which by the 12th century had been reduced to Gwynedd (in the N), Powys (centre) and Deheubarth (the S). **5th–7th centuries:** ANGLO-SAXON invasions of Britain; emergence of independent Anglo-Saxon kingdoms, notably MERCIA, NORTHUMBRIA and WESSEX. **597:** Christianity brought to England by St AUGUSTINE of Canterbury. **829:** Wessex became dominant kingdom in England. **843:** State of SCOTLAND founded when the Scots king also became king of the PICTS. **865:** VIKING invasion of Britain – Northumbria, East Anglia and Mercia overwhelmed. **By 896:** ALFRED THE GREAT had ended the Viking threat to Wessex. **By 960:** Alfred's successors had conquered the rest of England, forming one kingdom for the first time. **1066:** NORMAN CONQUEST of England; after defeat at the Battle of HASTINGS England came under the rule of WILLIAM I (the Conqueror). **12th century:** England became the dominant force in an ANGEVIN empire that included much of France. **1171:** HENRY II became overlord of IRELAND. **1215:** King JOHN was forced to sign MAGNA CARTA. **1272–1307:** EDWARD I attempted to dominate Scotland at a time of disputed succession. **1284:** WALES conquered by England despite attempts by LLYWELYN II of Gwynedd to establish an independent Welsh nation. **1295:** Model parliament summoned by EDWARD I. **1314:** English defeat at the Battle of BANNOCKBURN by Scottish forces under ROBERT THE BRUCE; Scottish independence asserted thereafter. **1337–1453:** England waged war to retain its possessions in France in the HUNDRED YEARS WAR. **1348–9:** Nearly a third of the population was killed in the BLACK DEATH. **1381:** Suppression of the PEASANTS REVOLT. **1399:** RICHARD II deposed by Parliament for absolutism. **1455–85:** Wars of the ROSES ended with the establishment of the TUDOR dynasty. **1497:** HENRY VII's suppression of the Yorkist revolts eclipsed the power of the feudal nobility. **1529:** HENRY VIII broke with Rome and became head of the Church of ENGLAND; start of the English REFORMATION. **1536:** UNION of England and Wales. **1547:** Protestant Reformation consolidated under EDWARD VI. **1553:** MARY I attempted to re-Catholicize England. **1558–1603:** Church of England re-established by ELIZABETH I; attempted invasion of England by the SPANISH ARMADA (1588); first attempts at English colonization overseas. **1603:** Scottish and English crowns united on the accession of JAMES I (James VI of Scotland). **1642–9:** ENGLISH CIVIL WAR ended in the defeat of supporters of CHARLES I by Parliament. **1649–60:** Following the execution of CHARLES I England was ruled as a republican COMMONWEALTH dominated by Oliver CROMWELL. **1660:** Restoration of monarchy with the accession of CHARLES II. **1685:** MONMOUTH'S REBELLION. **1688–9:** GLORIOUS REVOLUTION replaced JAMES II with WILLIAM III and MARY II. **18th century:** Colonial wars against the French saw expansion of the BRITISH EMPIRE. **1707:** Act of Union united England and Scotland. **1714:** Accession of the HANOVERIAN dynasty. **1721–42:** Robert WALPOLE – the first 'prime minister' – developed cabinet government. **1745–6:** The last JACOBITE rebellion was put down at the Battle of CULLODEN. **1757:** The English EAST INDIA COMPANY became the dominant trading power in India. **1775–83:** Britain lost its American colonies in the American War of INDEPENDENCE. **1792–1815:** Britain confronted France in the REVOLUTIONARY and NAPOLEONIC WARS, which led to further colonial gains. **1801:** United Kingdom of Britain and Ireland established. **Early 19th century:** The INDUSTRIAL REVOLUTION transformed economic and social life in Britain. **1832:** The First REFORM ACT gave the vote to the middle classes. **1837–1901:** Reign of Queen VICTORIA witnessed the height of British commercial and colonial power; statesman such as PEEL, PALMERSTON, GLADSTONE and DISRAELI dominated the world stage; British Empire included much of Africa, the Indian subcontinent and Australasia. **1846:** Repeal of the CORN LAWS. **1858:** British government took control of India. **1867:** Second Reform Act. **1886:** Gladstone's third administration dominated by the HOME RULE bill for Ireland. **By 1900:** Britain's economic dominance was challenged by the USA and Germany. **1906:** Establishment of the LABOUR Party. **1908–16:** Reforming Liberal government of Herbert ASQUITH. **1914–18:** WORLD WAR I. **1916:** EASTER RISING in Ireland; LLOYD GEORGE replaced Asquith as PM. **1922:** Partition of Ireland. **1931:** Statute of WESTMINSTER confirmed independence of the 'old dominions' of CANADA, AUSTRALIA, NEW ZEALAND and SOUTH AFRICA. **1939–45:** Britain – led by Winston CHURCHILL – played a major role in the defeat of the AXIS powers in WORLD WAR II. **1945–51:** Labour government of Clement ATTLEE established the 'welfare state'. **1947:** Dissolution of British Empire began with the independence of India. **1956:** SUEZ CRISIS. **Since 1969:** Resurgence of terrorism and unrest in NORTHERN IRELAND; British troops sent to keep order. **1973:** UK joined EUROPEAN COMMUNITY. **1979–90:** Right-wing premiership of Margaret THATCHER. **1982:** FALKLANDS WAR. **1990:** Margaret Thatcher replaced as PM by John MAJOR. **1992:** Conservatives won fourth consecutive term in office.

KINGS AND QUEENS
since 1066

(1066–1603 of England, 1603–1707 of England and Scotland, 1707–1801 of Great Britain, from 1801 of the United Kingdom)

Monarch	***Reign***	***House of***
William I	1066–87	Normandy
William II	1087–1100	Normandy
Henry I	1100–35	Normandy
Stephen	1135–41 and 1141–54	Blois
Matilda	1141 (Apr–Nov)	Normandy
Henry II	1154–89	Anjou
Richard I	1189–99	Anjou
John	1199–1216	Anjou
Henry III	1216–72	Plantagenet
Edward I	1272–1307	Plantagenet
Edward II	1307–27	Plantagenet
Edward III	1327–77	Plantagenet
Richard II	1377–99	Plantagenet
Henry IV	1399–1413	Plantagenet
Henry V	1413–22	Plantagenet
Henry VI	1422–61 and 1470–71	Plantagenet
Edward IV	1461–70 and 1471–83	Plantagenet
Edward V	1483 (Apr–Jun)	Plantagenet
Richard III	1483–85	Plantagenet
Henry VII	1485–1509	Tudor
Henry VIII	1509–47	Tudor
Edward VI	1547–53	Tudor
Jane Grey	1553 (July; 9 days)	Grey or Suffolk

Monarch	***Reign***	***House of***
Mary I	1553–58	Tudor
Elizabeth I	1558–1603	Tudor
James I (James VI of Scotland)	1603–25	Stuart
Charles I	1625–49	Stuart
Charles II	1660–85	Stuart

Between 1649 and 1660 England was ruled as a republican Commonwealth.

Monarch	***Reign***	***House of***
James II	1685–88	Stuart
William III (with Mary II	1689–1702 1689–94	Stuart and Orange Stuart and Orange)
Anne	1702–14	Stuart
George I	1714–27	Hanover and Brunswick-Lüneburg
George II	1727–60	Hanover and Brunswick-Lüneburg
George III	1760–1820	Hanover and Brunswick-Lüneburg
George IV	1820–30	Hanover and Brunswick-Lüneburg
William IV	1830–37	Hanover and Brunswick-Lüneburg
Victoria	1837–1901	Hanover and Brunswick-Lüneburg
Edward VII	1901–10	Saxe-Coburg and Gotha
George V	1910–36	Saxe-Coburg and Gotha†
Edward VIII	1936 (Jan–Dec)	Windsor
George VI	1936–52	Windsor
Elizabeth II	1952–	Windsor

† On 17 July 1917 King George V declared by Royal Proclamation that he had changed the name of the royal house to the House of Windsor.

UK PRIME MINISTERS 1721–1994

Prime Minister	Party	In Office
Sir Robert Walpole	Whig	1721–42
Earl of Wilmington	Whig	1742–43
Henry Pelham	Whig	1743–46
Earl of Bath	Whig	1746 (3 days)
Henry Pelham	Whig	1746–54†
Duke of Newcastle	Whig	1754–56
Duke of Devonshire	Whig	1756–57
Earl Waldegrave	Tory	1757 (5 days)
Duke of Newcastle	Whig	1757–62
Earl of Bute	Tory	1762–63
George Grenville	Whig	1763–65
Marquess of Rockingham	Whig	1765–66
Earl of Chatham (Pitt the Elder)	Whig	1766–68
Duke of Grafton	Whig	1768–70
Lord North	Tory	1770–82
Marquess of Rockingham	Whig	1782†
Earl of Shelburne	Whig	1782–83
Duke of Portland	Coalition	1783
William Pitt (the Younger)	Tory	1783–1801
Henry Addington	Tory	1801–04
William Pitt	Tory	1804–06
Lord Grenville	Whig	1806–07
Duke of Portland	Tory	1807–09
Spencer Perceval	Tory	1809–12*
Earl of Liverpool	Tory	1812–27
George Canning	Tory	1827
Viscount Goderich	Tory	1827–28
Duke of Wellington	Tory	1828–30
Earl Grey	Whig	1830–34
Viscount Melbourne	Whig	1834
Duke of Wellington	Tory	1834
Sir Robert Peel	Conservative	1834–35
Viscount Melbourne	Whig	1835–41
Sir Robert Peel	Conservative	1841–46
Lord John Russell	Liberal	1846–52
Earl of Derby	Tory	1852
Lord Aberdeen	Peelite	1852–55
Viscount Palmerston	Liberal	1855–58
Earl of Derby	Conservative	1858–59
Viscount Palmerston	Liberal	1859–65
Lord John Russell	Liberal	1865–66
Earl of Derby	Conservative	1866–68
Benjamin Disraeli	Conservative	1868
William Gladstone	Liberal	1868–74
Benjamin Disraeli	Conservative	1874–80
William Gladstone	Liberal	1880–85
Marquess of Salisbury	Conservative	1885–86
William Gladstone	Liberal	1886
Marquess of Salisbury	Conservative	1886–92
William Gladstone	Liberal	1892–94
Earl of Rosebery	Liberal	1894–95
Marquess of Salisbury	Conservative	1895–1902
Arthur Balfour	Conservative	1902–05
Sir Henry Campbell-Bannerman	Liberal	1905–08
Herbert Asquith	Liberal	1908–16
David Lloyd George	Liberal-led Coalition	1916–22
Andrew Bonar Law	Conservative	1922–23
Stanley Baldwin	Conservative	1923–24
Ramsay MacDonald	Labour	1924 (Jan–Nov)
Stanley Baldwin	Conservative	1924–29
Ramsay MacDonald	Labour	1929–35
Stanley Baldwin	National Government	1935–37
Neville Chamberlain	National Government	1937–40
Winston Churchill	Coalition	1940–45
Clement Attlee	Labour	1945–51
Sir Winston Churchill	Conservative	1951–55
Sir Anthony Eden	Conservative	1955–57
Harold Macmillan	Conservative	1957–63
Sir Alexander Douglas-Home	Conservative	1963–64
Harold Wilson	Labour	1964–70
Edward Heath	Conservative	1970–74
Harold Wilson	Labour	1974–76
James Callaghan	Labour	1976–79
Margaret Thatcher	Conservative	1979–90
John Major	Conservative	1990–

† died in office * assassinated in office

United Arab Emirates, a federation of seven EMIRATES on the Persian Gulf. The Gulf tribes were converted to ISLAM in the 7th century AD. When the Portuguese occupied some ports in the 16th century, the region was prosperous, but economic decline followed, coinciding with the (Turkish) OTTOMAN conquest. A political vacuum in the mid-18th century was filled by the British, who saw the region as a link in the trade route to India. Treaties ('truces') were signed with local rulers during the 19th century, bringing the Trucial States under British protection. In 1958 oil was discovered in Abu Dhabi. When the British withdrew in 1971 the Trucial States formed the United Arab Emirates.

United Arab Republic, the unsuccessful union of EGYPT and SYRIA (1958–61). Syria broke away from the union in 1961 following a military coup.

United Democratic Front (UDF), a non-racial political party of SOUTH AFRICA founded in 1983. It was incorporated into the AFRICAN NATIONAL CONGRESS in 1991.

United Empire Loyalists, the term applied to those Americans who remained loyal to the British crown during the War of INDEPENDENCE and who migrated to CANADA in the wake of their side's military defeat in 1783.

United Kingdom, the union of ENGLAND, SCOTLAND, WALES and NORTHERN IRELAND. See panels, pp. 239, 240 and 241.

United Nations (UN), an international organization formed in 1945 to promote international peace and security. The founders of the UN, who included the United Kingdom, the USA and the USSR, gave the organization three basic purposes: primarily, to maintain international peace and security; secondly, to develop friendly and equal relations among nations; and thirdly, to achieve international cooperation in solving international problems of an economic, social, cultural, or humanitarian character. The UN was given the authority to discuss and to make recommendations for the settlement of disputes, and, if necessary, to order collective measures to enforce the peace. This authority was vested primarily in two of the organizations' principal organs, the GENERAL ASSEMBLY and the SECURITY COUNCIL. The role of the Secretary-General is that of chief administra-

UNITED STATES OF AMERICA

10,000 BC: Likely date for earliest human settlement in America, when descendants of hunters from Siberia moved S. **c. AD 1000:** Possible Viking landings on coast of Maine and at Cape Cod. **1513:** First recorded European landing by the Spaniard Juan Ponce de León in Florida. **1607:** First permanent English settlement made at JAMESTOWN. **1620:** The PILGRIM FATHERS established the colony of Plymouth in MASSACHUSETTS. **1634:** Maryland founded by English Catholics. **1664:** The Dutch settlement on Manhattan Island became known as NEW YORK when it was taken by England. **1682:** English QUAKERS established a settlement in PENNSYLVANIA. **Late 17th century:** Transportation of African slaves to America. **By 1750:** Most of the colonies possessed governors appointed by the British crown. **18th century:** English colonies threatened by French expansion until Britain won mastery of the continent by defeating the French in the SEVEN YEARS WAR (1756–63). **1765:** Imposition of STAMP DUTY on the American colonies. **1773:** The BOSTON TEA PARTY fuelled the flames of revolution. **1775–83:** American War of INDEPENDENCE ended with British recognition of US independence. **1789:** The CONSTITUTION OF THE USA came into force; George WASHINGTON became first US president. **19th century:** America's geographical frontier moved steadily westward; displacement of native NORTH AMERICAN INDIAN peoples. **1803:** America purchased LOUISIANA from the French. **1812–14:** WAR OF 1812 with Britain. **1819:** Spain ceded Florida to the USA. **1820s and 1830s:** Beginnings of industrialization in the NE. **After 1840:** Massive increase in railroad construction. **1830s:** President Andrew JACKSON encouraged a belief in MANIFEST DESTINY. **1845:** Annexation of TEXAS. **1846–8:** The MEXICAN-AMERICAN WAR secured the territories of Arizona, California, part of Colorado and Wyoming, Nevada, Utah and New Mexico. **1854:** KANSAS–NEBRASKA ACT. **1861–5:** The AMERICAN CIVIL WAR ended in victory for the North. **1862:** Emancipation of slaves. **1865:** Assassination of President LINCOLN. **1867:** Alaska purchased from Russia. **1867–8:** Passing of the RECONSTRUCTION ACTS. **1880–1900:** Large-scale immigration to the USA from E and central Europe; emergence of the USA as an industrial giant. **1898:** SPANISH–AMERICAN WAR. **1917–18:** US participation in WORLD WAR I hastened the ALLIED victory. **1919:** Woodrow WILSON'S FOURTEEN POINTS compromised by the postwar settlement. **After 1918:** USA retreated into ISOLATIONISM and protectionism in trade. **1919–33:** PROHIBITION increased activities of criminal gangs. **1929:** Wall Street Crash; start of the DEPRESSION. **1933–9:** President F.D. ROOSEVELT'S NEW DEAL policies brought federal investment and intervention. **1941:** Japanese attack on PEARL HARBOR brought the USA into WORLD WAR II, during which the USA played a decisive role in the European and PACIFIC theatres of war. **1948–52:** MARSHALL PLAN assisted in the rebuilding of Europe. **1950s:** USA confronted the perceived threat of the USSR in the COLD WAR. **1950–3:** US involvement in the KOREAN WAR. **1950s and 1960s:** Martin Luther KING led the CIVIL RIGHTS MOVEMENT. **1954:** US intervention in GUATEMALA. **1958:** US intervention in Lebanon. **1961:** US support for unsuccessful invasion by Cuban exiles at the BAY OF PIGS. **1962:** CUBAN MISSILE CRISIS. **1963:** Assassination of President J.F. KENNEDY. **1964–73:** US involvement in the VIETNAM WAR. **1968:** Assassination of Martin Luther King. **1972:** WATERGATE scandal led to the resignation of President NIXON (1974). **1981–9:** Right-wing presidency of Ronald REAGAN. **1983:** US intervention in GRENADA. **1983–5:** US intervention in LEBANON. **1990–1:** USA led coalition against Saddam Hussein's Iraq in the GULF WAR. **1993:** George BUSH lost presidential election to the Democrat Bill CLINTON.

tor and international mediator. Major UN operations to cope with international crises included military assistance to South KOREA in June 1950, the imposition of diplomatic and economic sanctions against Southern RHODESIA in 1966 and against IRAQ in 1990, an arms embargo against SOUTH AFRICA in 1977, and an arms and economic embargo against SERBIA and Montenegro in 1992. UN peace-keeping forces – which act as buffers between warring states or factions – have been deployed in various combat zones, including CYPRUS, the GOLAN HEIGHTS, the Lebanon, Cambodia and the former Yugoslavia. Many of the UN's efforts to maintain peace have been undermined by deep political divisions, especially those associated with the COLD WAR, but since the lessening of East–West tension in 1991, cooperation has proved easier. Other important organs of the UN include the Economic and Social Council and the International Court of Justice. The WORLD BANK, the INTERNATIONAL MONETARY FUND (IMF) and GATT are also specialized agencies of the UN.

United Provinces of the Netherlands, see DUTCH REPUBLIC and the NETHERLANDS.

United States of America, a republic of North America. See panels.

Ur, a city of ancient SUMER which reached its peak during the third millennium BC. Incursions of Semitic AMORITES from the W, together with famine and loss of provincial support, made Ur vulnerable. In 2006 BC, the Elamites sacked the city and carried off its king, Ibbi-Sin. The city recovered but did not regain its former glory, and was finally abandoned in the 4th century BC. See map, p. 8.

Urartu, a state that flourished in E Anatolia from the 9th to the 7th centuries BC. The kingdom expanded during the period of relative ASSYRIAN weakness following the end of the reign of Shalmaneser III (858–824 BC). For a time Urartu controlled the eastern trade routes and the Syrian vassals, who were important as suppliers of metals and horses from Asia Minor. Urartu finally fell victim to Assyria's imperial expansion during the reign of SARGON II (721–705 BC).

Urban II (c. 1042–99), pope (1088–99). He urged the sending of the First CRUSADE and was also a notable reformer.

UNITED STATES OF AMERICA
Presidents

George Washington	Fed	1789–97
John Adams	Fed	1797–1801
Thomas Jefferson	Dem Rep	1801–09
James Madison	Dem Rep	1809–17
James Monroe	Dem Rep	1817–25
John Quincy Adams	Dem Rep	1825–29
Andrew Jackson	Dem	1829–37
Martin Van Buren	Dem	1837–41
William H. Harrison	Whig	1841
John Tyler	Whig	1841–45
James K. Polk	Dem	1845–49
Zachary Taylor	Whig	1849–50
Millard Fillmore	Whig	1850–53
Franklin Pierce	Dem	1853–57
James Buchanan	Dem	1857–61
Abraham Lincoln (assassinated)	Rep	1861–65
Andrew Johnson	Dem U	1865–69
Ulysses S. Grant (b. Hiram Grant)	Rep	1869–77
Rutherford B. Hayes	Rep	1877–81
James A. Garfield (assassinated)	Rep	1881
Chester A. Arthur	Rep	1881–85
Grover Cleveland	Dem	1885–89
Benjamin Harrison	Rep	1889–93
Grover Cleveland	Dem	1893–97
William McKinley (assassinated)	Rep	1897–1901
Theodore Roosevelt	Rep	1901–09
William H. Taft	Rep	1909–13
Warren Gamaliel Harding	Rep	1921–23
Calvin Coolidge	Rep	1923–29
Herbert C. Hoover	Rep	1929–33
Franklin Delano Roosevelt	Dem	1933–45
Harry S. Truman	Dem	1945–53
Dwight D. Eisenhower	Rep	1953–61
John Fitzgerald Kennedy (assassinated)	Dem	1961–63
Lyndon B. Johnson	Dem	1963–69
Richard M. Nixon	Rep	1969–74
Gerald R. Ford (b. Leslie Lynch King)	Rep	1974–77
Jimmy Carter	Dem	1977–81
Ronald Reagan	Rep	1981–89
George Bush	Rep	1989–93
William J. (Bill) Clinton	Dem	1993–

Key:
Dem = Democrat
Dem Rep = Democratic Republican
Dem U = Democrat (Union)
Fed = Federalist
Rep = Republican

Urnfield cultures, a group of BRONZE AGE cultures originating in E Central Europe in the 2nd millennium BC and spreading across much of the rest of Europe. They were characterized by cemeteries in which the ashes of the dead were buried in urns.

Uruguay, a republic on the E coast of South America. The Spanish landed in Uruguay in 1516, and for much of the colonial era Uruguay was disputed between Spain and Portugal. In 1808 independence was declared from Spain, but Uruguay had to repulse successive Brazilian and Argentinian armies (1811–27) before independence was achieved (1828). Until 1903 Uruguay was ruled by dictators and wracked by civil war. However, prosperity from cattle and wool, and the presidencies of the reformer José Battle (1903–7 and 1911–15), turned Uruguay into a democracy and an advanced welfare state. A military dictatorship held power during the DEPRESSION. By the late 1960s economic problems had ushered in a period of social and political turmoil, and urban guerrillas became active. In 1973 a coup installed a military dictatorship that made Uruguay notorious for abuses of human rights. The country returned to democratic rule in 1985.

Uruk, one of the greatest cities of ancient SUMER. It came under the domination of UR c. 2100 BC, but outlasted that state, surviving into the 3rd century AD. See map, p. 8.

USSR, see SOVIET UNION.

Uthman (c. 574–656), third caliph of ISLAM (644–56). He commissioned scholars to collect the revelations of MUHAMMAD and produced the definitive version of the Qur'an (Koran). Internal division over the distribution of gains from Muslim conquests, together with poor administration, led to a revolt in which he was killed. He was succeeded by ALI.

Utilitarianism, the philosophical belief that the highest good is the greatest happiness of the greatest number of people. Most fully articulated by BENTHAM and later also in a modified form by John Stuart MILL, it greatly influenced 19th-century reform activity.

Utrecht, Peace of (1713), the treaty ending the War of the SPANISH SUCCESSION between LOUIS XIV'S France and the European grand alliance. By the terms of the treaty Philip of Anjou became King PHILIP V of Spain. Austria gained the Spanish Netherlands and became the dominant power in Italy. Britain kept Gibraltar and Minorca, and gained Newfoundland, Hudson Bay and recognition of the Hanoverian succession from France. The Treaty significantly checked French power in Europe, and laid the foundations for Britain's imperial and commercial expansion. See also RASTADT, PEACE OF, and map, p. 27.

Uzbekistan, a republic of Central Asia (see map, p. 43). The region was overrun by the Persians (6th century BC), the Arabs (8th century AD) and the MONGOLS (13th century), before becoming the centre of the empire of TAMERLANE and his descendants, who established their capital at Samarkand. The Uzbek khanates of Bukhara and Khiva were established in the 15th and 16th centuries respectively. Persia ruled part of the area during the 18th century. Tsarist Russia attempted to invade the region in 1717, but gained control only after the khans of Bukhara and Khiva became vassals of the tsar (1868–73). After the RUSSIAN REVOLUTIONS, the Basmachi revolt (1918–22) resisted Soviet rule, but the khans were eventually deposed (1920) and Soviet republics established (1923–4). Uzbekistan was created when the USSR reorganized the boundaries of Soviet Central Asia. Independence was gained following the dissolution of the USSR in December 1991.

Uzbeks, Central Asian nomads of Altaian origins, speaking a Turkic language. They moved S into TRANSOXIANA in the late 15th century and have been the dominant group in the area since.

U Thant (1909–74), Burmese statesman, Secretary-General of the UNITED NATIONS (1961–71).

Valerian (d. AD 260), Roman emperor (253–260). During his reign he renewed the persecution of Christians, but failed to defend the Empire from attacks by the Goths and Sassanian Persians. He was captured by the Persians when they overran Syria in 260.

Valley of the Kings, the desolate valley on the W bank of the Nile near Thebes, where the pharaohs of the ancient Egyptian New Kingdom were buried in rock-cut tombs.

Valois, a dynasty that ruled France from 1328 to 1589. EDWARD III'S decision to dispute the right of Philip of Valois to inherit the CAPETIAN throne precipitated the HUNDRED YEARS WAR, but Philip's descendants retained the crown until HENRY III was stabbed to death in 1589 during the FRENCH WARS OF RELIGION.

Van Buren, Martin (1782–1862), eighth president of the USA (1837–41). His close association with Andrew JACKSON secured him the posts of secretary of state and then vice-president under the latter's presidency, and ensured his own election to the presidency in 1836.

Vandals, a Germanic people who raided Roman provinces in the 3rd and 4th centuries (see map, p. 15.). Under pressure from the HUNS they crossed the Rhine, ravaged Gaul and Spain and under their king, GAISERIC, founded a kingdom in N Africa (429), which was destroyed in 533 by the Byzantines.

Vargas, Getúlio (1885–1954), Brazilian statesman. See BRAZIL.

Varus (d. AD 9), Roman commander. As governor of Syria with responsibility for Judaea, he suppressed the revolt that followed HEROD'S death in 4 BC. However, he is remembered chiefly for his defeat in the Battle of TEUTOBURGER FOREST in AD 9.

Vatican City, a tiny sovereign state that is all that remains of the once extensive PAPAL STATES in Italy. When the French troops protecting the Pope were withdrawn in 1870, Italian forces entered Rome, which became the capital of the new kingdom of Italy. Pope Pius IX (reigned 1846–78) protested at the loss of his temporal power and retreated into the Vatican, from which no Pope emerged until 1929, when the LATERAN TREATIES provided for Italian recognition of the Vatican City as an independent state. Since the 1960s the papacy has again played an important role in international diplomacy, particularly under Popes Paul VI (reigned 1963–78) and JOHN PAUL II (1978–).

Vauban, Sébastien le Prestre de (1633–1707), French military engineer serving under LOUIS XIV. He planned 160 bastion fortresses and conducted some 50 sieges during his long career.

Veneti, an ancient people who settled around the area of modern Venice, later absorbed by the Romans.

Venezuela, a republic of N South America. Venezuela was originally inhabited by Arawak and Carib Indians. Although the first permanent Spanish settlement was established in 1520, Spain did not begin to develop Venezuela until the 17th century. Spanish rule was thrown off following the campaign led by Simon BOLÍVAR. Initially united with Colombia and Ecuador, Venezuela seceded in 1830. Independence was followed by a series of military coups, revolts and dictators, including Juan Vicente Gómez, whose harsh rule lasted from 1909 to 1935. Since General Marcos Peréz Jiménez was overthrown in 1958, Venezuela has been a civilian democracy. There have been two coup attempts in the 1990s, partly as a result of economic uncertainty and austerity.

Venice, a former republican city-state in NE Italy (see maps, pp. 21 and 25); it became a great commercial and maritime power in the later medieval period. By the late 13th century Venetian trading stretched from the Far East to the Atlantic. Venice's only serious rival was GENOA, against which it fought five naval wars in two centuries. The Venetian defeat of Genoa in 1380 eliminated Genoese influence from the E Mediterranean. Venetian power declined from the 16th century, and it came under Austrian control after the French invasion of 1797. Venice was absorbed into the Kingdom of Italy after the AUSTRO-PRUSSIAN WAR of 1866.

Vercingetorix (d. 46 BC), chief of the Arverni, a tribe of central Gaul, and the leader of a great revolt against CAESAR in 52 BC. He was eventually defeated and besieged at Alésia. He was later paraded at Caesar's triumph and executed shortly afterwards.

Verdun, Battle of (21 February–December 1916), a lengthy engagement between French and German forces around the fortress town of Verdun in WORLD WAR I. The German assault on positions around Verdun, intended to 'bleed the French Army white' – thereby leaving the British to face future German attacks alone – led to combined losses of nearly one and a half million men by December 1916. See WESTERN FRONT and map, p. 36.

Verdun, Treaty of (August 843), a treaty between the three grandsons of CHARLEMAGNE. After 13 years of intermittent civil war the three sons of LOUIS I – Lothar, Louis the German and CHARLES THE BALD – agreed to a three-way partition of the Carolingian empire.

Vereeniging, Treaty of (31 May 1902), the treaty ending the Second BOER WAR. The Boers accepted British rule, with a promise of future self-government within a British-dominated federation of South African states.

Versailles, the palace built for LOUIS XIV. The ornate rococo style palace was designed by J.H. Mansart and the extensive formal gardens organized by André Le Nôtre. Louis took up residence there in 1670, and Versailles became the symbol of his absolute rule. The greater nobles were expected to attend the court as a sign of loyalty.

Versailles, Treaty of (June 1919), a treaty between the ALLIED POWERS and Germany, part of the PARIS PEACE CONFERENCE after WORLD WAR I. Under the terms of the Treaty the state of POLAND was created in the E and awarded the 'Danzig Corridor' (a belt of former German land that gave the Poles access to the sea), and the town of DANZIG became a free city administered by the LEAGUE OF NATIONS. Germany also lost N Schleswig to Denmark, and Eupen and Malmedy to Belgium. The provinces of ALSACE and Lorraine were returned to France. The SAARLAND was to be governed by an international commission for 15 years, and the coalmines of the area given to France. The RHINELAND was occupied by Allied troops and a 50-km wide swathe of land E of the Rhine was demilitarized. Control of German colonies were given to the Allies. The size of the German army was limited to 100,000 men, conscription was forbidden, and Germany was banned from possessing tanks, military aircraft and large naval vessels. In addition, heavy REPARATIONS were imposed. The terms of the Treaty were considered harsh, and the unpopularity of the Treaty in Germany and Italy fuelled the rise of Nazism and Fascism in the 1920s and 1930s.

Verwoerd, Hendrik Frensch (1901–66), South African prime minister (1958–66). He was the main architect of APARTHEID, initially as minister of 'Bantu affairs'.

Vespasian (AD 9–79), Roman emperor (69–79). He was commander of the Roman forces against the Jewish revolt at the time of Nero's death. Proclaimed by his army, he emerged as the victor of the ensuing civil wars and established the Flavian dynasty. His largely peaceful reign was marked by financial stringency and administrative efficiency. He was succeeded by his son Titus (ruled 79–81).

Vespucci, Amerigo (1454–1512), Florentine explorer whose published accounts of his voyages to the New World (1499–1500; 1501–2) helped ensure that the new continent was called 'America'.

Vichy Government, the semi-Fascist French government established after the fall of France (July 1940) in WORLD WAR II, named after the town in unoccupied France where it was set up by PÉTAIN. Dominated by LAVAL and Darlan, it was opposed by the FREE FRENCH and by the French Resistance, and collapsed in 1945.

Vicksburg Campaign (1863), a decisive campaign of the AMERICAN CIVIL WAR waged for control of a CONFEDERATE stronghold on the Mississippi River. On 4 July General Ulysses S. GRANT forced its surrender. The defeat split the Confederacy in two and ended any hopes of its diplomatic recognition by Britain.

Victor Emmanuel II (1820–78), king of PIEDMONT and Sardinia (1849–61) and first king of ITALY (1861–78). A key figure of the RISORGIMENTO, he supported his liberal Prime Minister, Camillo di CAVOUR, both in his domestic and his Italian policy.

Victoria (1819–1901), queen of Great Britain and Ireland (1837–1901) and empress of India (1876–1901). The only child of GEORGE III's fourth son, she succeeded WILLIAM IV as the last sovereign of the House of HANOVER and became the longest reigning British monarch. She married her cousin, Albert of Saxe-Coburg Gotha, who exerted considerable influence over her until his death in 1861 – an event from which she never fully recovered. Her popularity was mirrored in her Golden Jubilee (1887), and Diamond Jubilee

(1897) celebrations. Her death in 1901 marked the end of an era in English history. See also UNITED KINGDOM.

Vienna, Congress of (1814–15), the international peace conference held following the defeat of NAPOLEON I. METTERNICH, the dominant figure of the Congress, established as its guiding principle the restoration of the rule of hereditary monarchs. A ring of strong states was established around France, including a new kingdom of the Netherlands and a Prussian presence in the Rhineland. The CONFEDERATION OF THE RHINE was abolished, but security needs meant that not all the small states were restored. Austria kept Venice, and Russia was rewarded by the acquisition of most of Poland. The settlement suppressed much radical and nationalist sentiment in Europe, which was to come to the boil in the REVOLUTIONS OF 1848.

Viet Cong, the name used by its opponents to describe the National Front for the Liberation of South Vietnam, a Communist guerrilla organization active in South Vietnam (1959–75) during the VIETNAM WAR.

Viet Minh, a Vietnamese nationalist guerrilla organization founded by HO CHI MINH in 1941 with the aim of expelling the Japanese and the French from Vietnam. It fought successfully against the French in the FRENCH–INDOCHINA WAR.

VIETNAM

207 BC: Tongking (the N of Vietnam) conquered by a Chinese warlord. **AD 939:** Tongking and ANNAM (the centre of Vietnam) broke free of Chinese rule to establish independent Vietnamese state. **1407–28:** Brief Chinese reconquest of the region. **1471:** Kingdom of CHAMPA overthrown by the Viets of Tongking. **18th century:** Annam chased the last Cham king into Cambodia and took the Mekong delta from the KHMERS. **1802:** Nguyen Anh united Tongking, Annam and Cochin China (the S), and made himself emperor of Vietnam. **From 1860s:** French intervention in the area. **1883:** French established a protectorate in Vietnam. **1887:** The Union of Indochina – including Vietnam, Cambodia and Laos – set up by France. **1930s:** Revolts against French colonial rule. **1940–5:** Vietnam occupied by Japanese during World War II; establishment of the nationalist VIET MINH. **1946–54:** FRENCH–INDOCHINA WAR; Nationalist forces under HO CHI MINH secured Vietnamese independence after defeating the French at DIEN BIEN PHU. **1954:** Vietnam partitioned into a Communist state in the N and a pro-Western state in the S. **From 1959:** War between Communist VIETCONG, supported by the N, and the S Vietnamese government. **1964–73:** US involvement in VIETNAM WAR in support of the S. **1975:** Communist takeover of the S; reunification of Vietnam. **Since 1975:** Large numbers of refugees – the 'Boat People' – have fled Vietnam. **1979:** Border war with China. **1979–89:** Occupation of CAMBODIA by Vietnamese forces. **From 1989–90:** Some pragmatic policies adopted in an attempt to attract Western capital.

Vietnam, a country of SE Asia. See panel.

Vietnam War (1959–75), a war between US-backed South Vietnam and Communist North Vietnam (see map, p. 41). After independence in 1954, VIETNAM was split along the 17th parallel of latitude, with a Communist government in the North and a pro-Western government in the South. The North was intent on reunification under Communist rule, and Communist guerrillas in the South known as VIET CONG (VC) began to mount attacks in rural areas with support from fellow Communists in LAOS and CAMBODIA. The USA, which saw South Vietnam as a bulwark against the spread of Communism in Asia, committed advisers to train the South Vietnamese army. In August 1964, after an alleged North Vietnamese attack on US warships in the Gulf of Tonkin, the US Congress approved an expanded US military commitment to Vietnam. Although the Americans attempted to avoid full-scale commitment of their forces, they were drawn deeper and deeper into the struggle. The Viet Cong's 1968 TET OFFENSIVE, although finally defeated, created a deep sense of shock in the USA. Richard NIXON, who replaced Lyndon JOHNSON as president in 1969, sought to hand responsibility for the war to the South Vietnamese army, so that US troops could withdraw. However, US incursions into neighbouring Cambodia and Laos, culminating in a successful US-backed coup against Prince SIHANOUK of Cambodia, spread the war and left both countries vulnerable to their own indigenous Communist groups. A North Vietnamese invasion of the South in March 1972 was halted by US airpower. After renewed US air attacks on the North, the North Vietnamese agreed to a ceasefire that left their forces in place in South Vietnam. The Americans completed their withdrawal, having lost over 47,000 servicemen in the conflict. Nixon's successor Gerald FORD lacked the political strength to maintain support for the South. The South Vietnamese army collapsed in the face of a North Vietnamese invasion in early 1975, and by April Saigon was in Communist hands. Cambodia and Laos also fell to the Communists in what was a massive defeat for US policy. See also COLD WAR.

Vijayanagar, a former Hindu empire of S INDIA (14th–16th centuries). Named after its capital ('City of Victory'), it was the personal creation of its first ruler, Harihara. It lasted until 1565, when it was finally vanquished by a coalition of neighbouring Muslim rulers.

Vikings (also called the Norsemen), the Danish, Swedish and Norwegian seafarers and traders who raided and settled parts of N and W Europe between the 8th and 11th centuries (see map, p. 18). The Norwegians were active on both shores of the Irish Sea, ultimately settling in E Ireland, W Scotland, the Isle of Man and NW England, as well as the Orkney, Shetland and Faeroe Islands. They also colonized Iceland. It was from there that ERIC THE RED sailed W in c. 986 to discover GREENLAND, where a settlement survived into the 15th century. In around 1000 the Norwegians, under LEIF ERIKSSON, also briefly settled in NE North America, which they called VINLAND (possibly Newfoundland). The Swedes went E into Russia, where they formed the first organized states. Sailing down the great river systems to the Black Sea, they also traded with – and even assaulted – the Byzantine capital, Constantinople.

The Danes directed most of their energies against the ANGLO-SAXON and Frankish kingdoms. By the end of the 9th century the kingdoms of NORTHUMBRIA, East Anglia and MERCIA had been taken over. These Viking kingdoms, in the area known as the DANELAW, were short-lived, but they had an important impact on the culture and language of England. Only WESSEX survived the onslaught, under ALFRED THE GREAT. The Viking attacks were renewed during ETHELRED II's reign. After prolonged resistance the English kingdom finally capitulated to the Danish king, CNUT, in 1016. However, this conquest did not involve a major new settlement of Scandinavians in England. Traditionally drawn as pillagers and pagans, the Vikings were not militantly anti-Christian and by the end of the 11th century had all been converted to Christianity. They also shared many values with societies they attacked in Western Europe and found it easy to stay as settlers.

Villa, Francisco ('Pancho', b. Doroteo Atango; 1878–1920), Mexican revolutionary. A former bandit, he led some of the northern forces in the MEXICAN REVOLUTION from 1911 until his defeat by rivals in 1915. He was assassinated in 1920.

Villafranca di Verona, Treaty of (1859), an agreement concluding the Franco-Piedmontese war against Austria. In the subsequent Peace of Zürich (1859) Austria retained Venetia and ceded Lombardy to France.

Villanovan Culture, an Iron Age culture from which the ETRUSCAN civilization probably developed. It was named after Villanova, a village near Bologna, where the first discoveries of the culture were made in 1853.

villein, a tenant holding property from a manorial lord in medieval Europe. From the 12th to the 15th centuries villeins were regarded as 'unfree' (and thus often called SERFS), on the grounds that they were denied access to the public courts (jurisdiction over the villein belonging to his landlord). See FEUDAL SYSTEM.

Vimy Ridge, Battle of (9 April 1917), a successful attack by Canadian forces on a key German position on high ground N of Arras in WORLD WAR I.

Vinland, the VIKING name for an area of E Canada, possibly N Newfoundland, which was discovered accidentally by Norsemen from Greenland c. 1000.

Virginia, one of the 13 original states of the USA. The 'Old Dominion' dates from the establishment of an English colony at JAMESTOWN in 1607. The original charter of Virginia included most of the SE of what is now the USA in its boundaries. Virginia played a leading role in the American War of INDEPENDENCE and called the first CONTINENTAL CONGRESS. Four of the first five US presidents were Virginians. In the AMERICAN CIVIL WAR, the state was the political centre of the CONFEDERACY, whose capital was Richmond, Virginia.

Virginia Campaigns (1861–5), a series of important operations fought in the E theatre of the AMERICAN CIVIL WAR. Union forces experienced early setbacks, and the effective generalship of Robert E. LEE and 'Stonewall' JACKSON enabled the CONFEDERACY to hold Union forces at bay for much of the war. GRANT's murderous drive towards the Confederate capital in 1864–5 (the Petersburg campaign) ultimately decided the outcome of the conflict in the North's favour.

Virginia Plan, a plan advocating strong federal government for the USA, presented to the Constitutional Convention in 1787. James MADISON had been the major influence in drawing up the Plan, which proposed to invest substantial powers in a stronger federal government made up of a national executive, judiciary and legislature. After much debate the Plan was modified and in its final form was a compromise between the various regional interests in the Convention. Anti-federalists were placated by the passage of a BILL OF RIGHTS.

Visconti, Giangaleazzo (1351–1402), duke of MILAN. He ruled jointly with his uncle until 1385, when he had him put to death. During his personal reign Milan briefly acquired control of most of N and much of central Italy.

Visigoths, the western Goths, a people who migrated to the Danube delta from NE Europe in the 3rd century (see map, p. 15). They defeated and killed the Roman emperor Valens at ADRIANOPLE in 378. Under ALARIC they invaded Italy (401) and sacked Rome (410). In 418 they established a kingdom based on TOULOUSE in S France until expelled by the FRANKS (507). Their kingdom in Spain lasted until the Muslim invasion of 711.

Vitoria, Battle of (21 June 1813), WELLINGTON's final victory in the PENINSULAR WAR, fought in N Spain, ousting the French from the Iberian Peninsula and clearing the way for an allied invasion of S France. See NAPOLEONIC WARS and map, p. 29.

Vittorio Veneto, Battle of (27 October 1918), the final battle on the Italian Front in WORLD WAR I, in which Allied troops defeated weakened Austro-Hungarian forces. Three days later Austria asked for an armistice. See map, p. 36.

vizier, a leading court official in the OTTOMAN Empire. The KÖPRÜLÜ family supplied a series of vigorous and capable grand viziers during the weak reign of Mehmed IV (1648–87). The grand viziers that succeeded them, however, were unable to provide the same energetic leadership. The rapid turnover of grand viziers during the 18th century contributed to the domestic instability of the Ottoman Empire.

Voortrekkers, pioneer AFRIKANER migrants who made the GREAT TREK into the interior from the British-dominated Cape Colony in the 1830s.

Vorster, Balthazar Johannes (1915–1983), South African statesman, prime minister (1966–78). The architect of the state security system, he was forced to resign in the aftermath of the 1976 SOWETO uprising.

Vyshinsky, Andrei (1883–1954), Soviet politician and diplomat, foreign minister (1949–53). As public prosecutor (1935–8) he presided over STALIN's show trials.

V-2, a rocket-powered ballistic missile used by the Germans to bombard London in late WORLD WAR II.

Wagram, Battle of (5/6 July 1809), a victory of NAPOLEON over the Austrians NE of Vienna. The Austrians had sought to exploit his difficulties in the PENINSULAR WAR, but were forced to seek an armistice. See NAPOLEONIC WARS.

Waitangi, Treaty of (1840), a treaty between the British government and New Zealand MAORI chiefs. Britain obtained sovereignty over New Zealand and – in exchange – guaranteed Maori rights over tribal lands. Breaches of the treaty led to intermittent warfare over the next 30 years. See ANGLO-MAORI WARS.

Waldheim, Kurt (1918–), Austrian diplomat and politician, Secretary-General of the United Nations (1972–81), president of Austria (1986–92).

Wales, a principality of the UNITED KINGDOM, in the W of the island of Great Britain. Wales was incorporated into the English crown in 1536.

Walesa, Lech (1943–), Polish politician. Underground trade union organizer in the Gdansk shipyard in the 1970s, he led the wave of strikes in August 1980 that led to the creation of the free trade union SOLIDARITY. He was imprisoned after the declaration of martial law in November 1981. In 1989 he negotiated the historic agreement ending Communist rule in Poland. He became president in 1990.

Wallace, William (c. 1270–1305), the leader of a Scottish revolt against English domination. He defeated the English at Stirling Bridge in 1297, but was himself defeated and captured at Falkirk in 1298 by EDWARD I, who had him executed.

Wallachia, a former principality of SE Europe, now part of ROMANIA (see maps, pp. 27 and 30).

Wallenstein, Albrecht Wenzel Eusebius von (1583–1634), Czech nobleman and general. His ability to raise troops and money was crucial for HABSBURG success in the first half of the THIRTY YEARS WAR. His increasing attempts to build up his own personal power worried the Emperor FERDINAND II, who had him assassinated.

Wall Street Crash (24 October 1929), the collapse of share prices on the New York stock exchange. Before the Crash speculation had increased until the prices paid for shares bore little relation to the economic strength of the companies concerned. As few shares had any real value, the façade of Wall Street soon came crashing down and precipitated panic selling, with nearly 13 million shares passing throught the exchange by the end of 'Black Thursday'. Deep-rooted economic difficulties caused by World War I and its aftermath combined with the Crash to produce the DEPRESSION.

Walpole, Sir Robert (1676–1745), English WHIG politician. As 'Prime Minister' (1721–42), his power was based in part on a system of bribing MPs to ensure the winning of votes in Parliament, and on the support of the crown. Committed to low taxation and a peaceful foreign policy, he refused to enter the War of the POLISH SUCCESSION. His opposition to the War of JENKINS'S EAR contributed to his downfall.

Walsingham, Sir Francis (1530–90), English politician, secretary of state to ELIZABETH I from 1573. A Puritan, he favoured an aggressive anti-Spanish and anti-Catholic foreign policy (in contrast with the moderate CECIL), and exposed a number of plots against Elizabeth, including that of MARY, Queen of Scots.

Warbeck, Perkin (1474–99), a pretender to the English throne. From 1492 onwards he claimed to be Richard of York, the younger of the princes last seen in the Tower of London in 1483 (see EDWARD V). He was captured in 1497 and executed two years later.

war crimes, acts committed in wartime that breach the accepted rules and customs of war. At the NUREMBERG TRIALS, Nazi politicians and soldiers were charged with 'crimes against humanity' and with 'waging aggressive war' by international tribunals from the victorious Allied powers.

warlord, ruler of a region owing his power to the command of military force rather than legitimate civil authority or hereditary right. Warlords were a prominent feature of the history of CHINA in periods of imperial decline.

War of 1812 (1812–14), a conflict between Britain and the USA fought mainly on the US–Canadian border. Aggressive British naval policy and American hopes of conquering Canada led to war between the two countries. Although the British managed a raid on Washington, DC, and the Americans, ably led by General Andrew JACKSON, defeated the redcoats at the Battle of NEW ORLEANS in 1815, the final result was a military stalemate. Nonetheless, the war confirmed American independence and strengthened the forces of American nationalism.

Warring States, a period of Chinese history (481–221 BC) following the end of the ZHOU dynasty, when the country was divided into small kingdoms. The westernmost of the Warring States – the QIN – emerged as the final victor, uniting the country under SHI HUANGDI.

Warsaw Ghetto, a ghetto of 400,000 Jews established during the German occupation of Warsaw. In 1943 its 100,000 survivors staged an uprising against the NAZIS, after which they were put to death.

Warsaw Pact, a military treaty and alliance of the USSR and seven East European countries, signed in May 1955 in response to the establishment of NATO. The signatories were Bulgaria, Czechoslovakia, the German Democratic Republic (East Germany), Hungary, Poland, Romania and the USSR. Albania began to distance itself from the Pact in 1962 and withdrew in 1968. Political changes in Eastern Europe in 1989–90 weakened the Pact, and it was formally disbanded in March 1991.

Warsaw Rising (1944), a Polish insurrection in Warsaw during WORLD WAR II. The uprising was brutally suppressed by the Germans – the advancing Soviet forces outside the city failing to give help to the insurgents. The SS deported Warsaw's inhabitants and razed the city.

Warwick, Richard Neville, Earl of (1428–71), English nobleman active during the Wars of the ROSES. Later known as the 'kingmaker', owing to his prominent role in helping EDWARD IV to win the crown in 1461 and in restoring HENRY VI to the throne in 1470, he was killed at the Battle of Barnet.

Washington Conference (1921–2), an international conference that discussed political tensions in the Far East and naval disarmament. The nine participating countries – including the USA, Britain, France, China and Japan – guaranteed China's independence and territorial integrity. In addition ratios of naval strength were laid down. The ratio of tonnage of capital ships (i.e. battleships and heavy cruisers) was laid down as 5:5:3 between the fleets of the USA, Britain and Japan.

Washington, George (1732–99), first president of the USA (1789–97). A wealthy Virginia slaveholder, he proved an able commander of American forces in the War of INDEPENDENCE. Fearful of social unrest, he was a strong supporter of the federal Constitution and in 1788 was a popular choice for chief executive of the new republic. His presidency saw the growth of the USA's first political parties in the 1790s. As father of his country, Washington was anxious to adopt a neutral stance in politics, but he himself was identified with FEDERALIST policies.

Watergate scandal, a major US political scandal during the 1972 presidential campaign. Five men were caught breaking into the Democratic National Campaign offices in Washington's Watergate hotel. The men, it was discovered, were agents of Republican President NIXON's re-election organization and their aim was to wire-tap Democratic meetings. Attempts by the White House to cover up the affair were exposed by journalists from the *Washington Post.* Irredeemably compromised by his actions, Nixon resigned from office in April 1974 in order to stave off the humiliation of impeachment.

Waterloo, Battle of (18 June 1815), a battle in which British and Prussian forces under WELLINGTON and BLÜCHER defeated NAPOLEON, following the latter's return to France from exile on the island of Elba and invasion of the S Netherlands. Wellington's Allied army took up a strong position S of the Belgian village of Waterloo and held back repeated French assaults until the timely arrival of Blücher's Prussians. In the general Allied advance that followed, the French were routed. Four days later Napoleon abdicated for the second and last time. See map, p. 29.

Wavell, Archibald Percival, lst Earl (1883–1950), British field marshal. He was commander in chief in the Middle East (1940–1) during WORLD WAR II, defeating the Italians in N Africa. As viceroy of INDIA (1944–7) he took part in the negotiations for Indian independence.

Webster, Daniel (1782–1852), US lawyer and politician, a leader of the WHIG Party in the 1830s and 1840s. As secretary of state (1841–3) he negotiated the Maine–New Brunswick border in the Webster–Ashburton Treaty.

Weimar Republic (1919–33), the German republic formed after World War I. Following the SPARTACIST uprising of 1919, a National Constituent Assembly was convened at Weimar to draw up a new democratic constitution. In its early years, the republic came under intense pressure; associated by many Germans with military defeat and with the punitive Treaty of VERSAILLES, it was vilified by extremists of both left and right. If it had not been for individual politicians such as Friedrich Ebert (president 1919–25) and Gustav STRESEMANN, it would probably not have survived the hyperinflation of the early 1920s and occupation of the RUHR by France and Belgium in 1923. The Republic experienced a recovery of sorts after 1923 with the introduction of a new currency – the Reichsmark – and the rescheduling of REPARATIONS repayments under the DAWES Plan. In 1925 a coalition of rightist parties under President von HINDENBURG promised greater political stability. But the onset of the DEPRESSION in 1929 brought a fresh economic crisis, for which many blamed the Weimar Republic. As unemployment increased, so did support for Hitler's NAZI Party, seen by many as the only alternative to Communism. In March 1930 Hindenburg appointed Heinrich Brüning as chancellor and allowed him to rule more and more by decree, according to Article 48 of the Weimar Constitution. This was the beginning of moves away from democracy that culminated in Hindenburg's legal but misguided decision to appoint Adolf HITLER chancellor in January 1933.

Weizmann, Chaim (1874–1952), Polish-born Zionist leader and first President of independent ISRAEL in 1948. He was instrumental in persuading the British government to issue the BALFOUR Declaration in 1917.

welfare state, a system whereby the state protects the social and economic well-being of the population through a variety of measures paid for by general taxation, such as unemployment benefit, old-age pensions and free comprehensive health care. The postwar British welfare state was based on the BEVERIDGE Report, which outlined a social insurance scheme 'from cradle to grave', and was implemented by the LABOUR Party under ATTLEE. Similar systems exist in most West European countries. From the 1980s the system has come under increasing attack from the radical right, which claims that welfare provision fosters a culture of dependency.

Wellington, Arthur Wellesley, 1st Duke of (1769–1852), Anglo-Irish soldier and statesman. Sent to Portugal with English troops to exploit the uprising there against the French in 1809 (see PENINSULAR WAR), he expelled the French from Portugal, and advanced into Spain. Subsequent victories, notably at VITORIA (1813), were followed by his invasion of France. His greatest success was the defeat of NAPOLEON at WATERLOO (1815). An unpopular TORY prime minister (1828–30), he reluctantly abolished the TEST ACTS and vehemently opposed the reform of PARLIAMENT.

Wenceslas (c. 907–29), Christian prince of BOHEMIA killed by his pagan brother Boleslav during the course of a struggle for power. He was subsequently canonized and is regarded as the Czech national saint.

Wessex, the kingdom of the West Saxons, consisting of lands S of the Thames and W as far as Dorset. In the 9th century Wessex, under ALFRED the Great, led the resistance to the VIKINGS, and was able to end the Viking threat to the kingdom by 896. By 960 Alfred's successors had conquered the rest of England, forming one kingdom for the first time. See ANGLO-SAXONS, MERCIA, NORTHUMBRIA.

West Bank, a region of PALESTINE W of the River Jordan, occupied by ISRAEL since 1967. The West Bank was administered by Jordan from 1948 to 1967, when it was lost to Israel in the SIX-DAY WAR. Jordan renounced all legal responsibility for the West Bank (in favour of the PLO) in 1980. The region has been at the heart of Palestinian resistance in the INTIFADA.

Western European Union (WEU), an organization formed on 17 March 1948 with the original intention of collaborating in 'economic, social and cultural matters and for collective self-defence'. These functions have gradually been transferred to the EUROPEAN COMMUNITY, the Council of Europe and NATO. However, in 1984 the WEU was reactivated to improve military cooperation between members and to strengthen their contributions to NATO. Its members are Belgium, France, Germany, Italy, Luxembourg, the Netherlands, Portugal, Spain and the UK.

Western Front, the line of fighting in WORLD WAR I, stretching from the Vosges mountains in the E of France, through Verdun, Amiens and Arras to Ostend on the coast of Belgium (see map, p. 36). In August 1914 German forces swept into Belgium and NE France in accordance with the SCHLIEFFEN PLAN, aiming to take Paris in a huge outflanking movement, but were checked by the French (with British assistance) at the Battle of the MARNE. A German attempt to reach the Channel ports was thwarted in the First Battle of YPRES, after which the rival armies dug in and settled down to trench warfare. British and French soldiers were thwarted in their attempts to liberate NE France and Belgium by mud, barbed wire, machine guns and quick-fire artillery. In 1915 Anglo-French offensives in Champagne (February), Neuve Chapelle (March) and Loos (September) failed to break the deadlock. Poison gas was used by the Germans for the first time on the Western Front in the Second Battle of Ypres (April). The nightmare deepened in 1916; the German attack at VERDUN cost each side about 700,000 men. The British tried to break through on the SOMME and between July and December lost 460,000 men. Things were no better in 1917: a French offensive in Champagne failed in April, while at PASSCHENDAELE in July the British lost a further half a million casualties in the nightmare of mud. The Battle of Cambrai (November 1917) saw the first effective use of massed tanks by the British. Having signed a peace treaty with Russia, in March 1918 Germany was able to launch the LUDENDORFF Offensive, which took them as far as the Marne. However, by the middle of April the Allies had rallied and stopped the advance. In August they moved onto the offensive, using tanks supported by ground-attack aircraft and involving the first of the newly arrived US divisions. By October Germany was exhausted, and an armistice was signed on 11 November, bringing the fighting to an end.

Western Jin, a Chinese dynasty (AD 265–316) founded by Sima Yan, ruler of Wei, the most northerly of the THREE KINGDOMS. It briefly reunited CHINA before losing the N to nomad invaders in 316, surviving in the S (as the Eastern JIN) until 420.

Western Sahara, a disputed territory in NW Africa. The region was a Spanish possession from the 19th century until 1976, when it was divided between MOROCCO and MAURETANIA. Morocco absorbed the Mauretanian sector when Mauretania withdrew (1979). The Polisario liberation movement declared the territory independent. They controlled the E part of Western Sahara and continued guerrilla activity against the Moroccans until informal UN talks between the Sahrawis (the indigenous population) and Morocco began (1988–9). Agreement for a ceasefire and a referendum on the future of the territory was reached (1991), but no date has been fixed for the referendum.

Western Samoa, a state in the S Pacific. Samoa was settled by Polynesians about 300 BC. From the 1870s the USA, UK and Germany became active in Samoa. In 1899 the three rival powers divided the group, giving the western islands to Germany. New Zealand occupied the German islands in 1914, and administered Western Samoa until independence in 1962.

West Germany, see GERMANY.

Westminster, Statute of (1931), British declaration granting self-government and self-determination to all DOMINIONS within the British Commonwealth – Canada, Australia, New Zealand, the Union of South Africa and the Irish Free State. All could now determine their own foreign and economic policies, though the constitutional question of the status of the British crown in the dominions was left unresolved.

Westphalia, Peace of (1648), the agreement ending the THIRTY YEARS WAR, comprising the treaties of Münster (between the United Provinces of the Netherlands and Spain) and Osnabrück (between Sweden, the Holy Roman Emperor and France). The treaties, which represented a blow to HABSBURG imperial ambitions, confirmed Dutch independence, split Germany into over 300 states, and gave territories in Germany to Sweden. They also checked Habsburg ambitions in Germany and gave important territorial gains to BRANDENBURG-Prussia.

Whig, a British political party opposed to the TORIES. The name was originally applied to those who, following the POPISH PLOT, sought to exclude CHARLES II's Catholic brother, later JAMES II, from the succession. Broadly, the Whigs wished to limit the authority of the monarch in accordance with the social contract theories of John LOCKE that triumphed in the GLORIOUS REVOLUTION of 1688–9. They engineered the accession of the House of HANOVER, monopolizing power and office after 1714. Increasingly oligarchical and aristocratic, the movement broke down in the changed social and political conditions of the 19th century, but contributed men and ideas to the new LIBERAL Party.

Whig Party, a US political party active from the late 1830s to the mid-1850s. Led by some of the most famous statesmen in American history (notably Daniel WEBSTER and Henry CLAY), the Whig party campaigned vigorously in favour of economic nationalism, but was eventually destroyed by the sectional tensions of the pre-Civil War period.

Whitby, Synod of, a meeting held at Whitby in NORTHUMBRIA in 664 that effectively brought the CELTIC CHURCH under the control of Rome.

White Mountain, Battle of (1620), an early engagement of the THIRTY YEARS WAR between Duke Maximilian of Bavaria on behalf of the Habsburg emperor FREDERICK II, and the forces of Frederick V, king of Bohemia and Moravia. Frederick's defeat ended hopes of Czech independence and Ferdinand became king of Bohemia.

White Russians, those Russians who fought against and were defeated by the RED ARMY during the RUSSIAN CIVIL WAR following the RUSSIAN REVOLUTION. They were named after the royalist opponents of the French Revolution, who adopted the white flag of the BOURBON dynasty.

Whitlam, (Edward) Gough (1916–), Australian Labor statesman, prime minister (1972–5). Whitlam was controversially dismissed by the governor-general, Sir John Kerr, when he refused to call a general election during a financial crisis.

Wilberforce, William (1759–1833), British politician. The leader of a group of evangelical Christian MPs who championed moral reform at home and abroad, his efforts resulted in the abolition of the slave trade (1807) and of SLAVERY (1833) in Britain and its colonies.

'Wild West', a romantic designation for the final stage of US frontier settlement in the late 19th century. Characterized in the popular mind by gunfighters, golddiggers, cowboys and Indians, the 'Wild West' was a much harsher place than the myth implied, 'colourful' characters such as Billy the Kid and Wyatt Earp being pathological killers, and the 'savage' Native Americans helpless (if sometimes cruel) victims of modern western civilization. Although frontier conditions were certainly fluid, the historical West was the more humdrum (and substantial) creation of farm families and ranchers.

Wilhelm I (1797–1888), king of PRUSSIA (1861–88), emperor of GERMANY (1871–88). He used arms to suppress the REVOLUTION OF 1848 in Baden and was regent for his insane brother FREDERICK WILLIAM IV of Prussia from 1858. He appointed BISMARCK as chancellor in 1862 and thereafter supported his policy of strengthening the power of Prussia. He became the first emperor of the united Germany in 1871.

Wilhelm II (1859–1942), emperor of GERMANY and king of PRUSSIA (1888–1918), a grandson of Queen VICTORIA of Britain. He dropped BISMARCK in 1890, took control of Germany himself and set about strengthening the country's military and naval forces. His aggressive foreign policy led to a breakdown in relations with Britain and France, and his support of AUSTRIA-HUNGARY against Serbia led to the outbreak of WORLD WAR I. He abdicated on Germany's defeat in 1918.

William ('the Lion'; c. 1142–1214), king of Scotland (1165–1214). Invading England in pursuit of his claim to NORTHUMBRIA, he was captured (1174) and forced to cede Edinburgh and other castles. However, RICHARD I allowed him to buy them back in 1189.

William I ('the Conqueror'; 1028–87), the first Norman king of England (1066–87). He claimed that he had been made heir to the English throne by his cousin, EDWARD the Confessor. However, when Edward died in 1066 HAROLD Godwinson was crowned king by the English. To secure the English throne William sailed to England and defeated Harold in the Battle of HASTINGS. During the NORMAN CONQUEST William replaced the English ruling classes with Norman-French nobility, introduced Norman architecture, and embarked on an inventory of English property in the DOMESDAY BOOK.

William I ('the Silent'; 1533–84), Lutheran Prince of ORANGE and Count of Nassau, founding father of the UNITED PROVINCES of the Netherlands. As provincial governor of Holland, Zeeland and Utrecht he opposed the centralizing absolutism and strongly Catholic policies of PHILIP II in the 1560s. After the arrival of Spanish troops under ALBA in 1567, he became a key figure in the first phase of the DUTCH REVOLTS, negotiating military and financial help from abroad, while the rebels offered resistance to the Spanish. He briefly succeeded in uniting the Calvinist northern provinces and the Catholic south (the Pacification of Ghent; 1576), but could not prevent the permanent division of the northern and southern provinces (1579). He was assassinated by a Catholic fanatic in 1584.

William II (Rufus; c.1056–1100), king of England (1087–99). He suppressed baronial revolts and consolidated the NORMAN CONQUEST. His premature death, which has led to fanciful theories, was probably a hunting accident.

William III (1650–1702), king of England (1689–1702) with his wife MARY II following the GLORIOUS REVOLUTION. He was also effective ruler of the United Provinces of the Netherlands (1672–1702). His victory at the Battle of the BOYNE ensured the triumph of British rule and the Protestant ascendancy in Ireland.

William IV (1765–1837), king of Great Britain and Ireland and dependencies overseas, and king of HANOVER (1830–7). The third son of GEORGE III, he succeeded his childless brother GEORGE IV.

Wilson, Harold James (1916–), British LABOUR prime minister (1964–70 and 1974–6). He succeeded GAITSKELL as Labour leader, defeating Alec Douglas-HOME in the 1964 election. In his first period in office he faced balance-of-payments and sterling crises, but his administration passed some important reforming legislation, notably the introduction of comprehensive education, and changes in the laws on homosexuality, divorce and abortion. He was defeated in the 1970 election by Edward HEATH. His last minority administration confirmed Britain's membership of the EUROPEAN COMMUNITY after a referendum. He was succeeded as Labour leader and PM by James CALLAGHAN.

Wilson, Woodrow (1856–1924), 28th president of the USA (1913–21). He won the watershed election of 1912 as a reform-minded Democrat, taking the USA into WORLD WAR I on the side of the Allies and masterminding the creation of the LEAGUE OF NATIONS. A moralist in politics, he outlined his programme for a peaceful postwar world order in the FOURTEEN POINTS. ISOLATIONISTS in the US Senate dealt him a massive blow by rejecting American entry into the League in 1920.

Windsor, House of, the dynastic name adopted by the British royal family in 1917, when GEORGE V dropped all his German titles – derived from the marriage of VICTORIA to Prince Albert of Saxe-Coburg-Gotha – because of World War I.

witchcraft, the use of supernatural powers – supposedly acquired through a pact with the devil – for evil purposes. It was first declared a heresy by Pope INNOCENT III in 1484. The religious struggles of the REFORMATION stimulated even further the obsession with witchcraft, and between 1580 and 1650 the number of witch trials rocketed throughout Western Europe. Both Roman Catholic and Protestant theologians identified witchcraft with active heresy. The witch craze died down in Western Europe after 1650.

Wolsey, Thomas (1473–1530), English cardinal and Lord Chancellor. He served as HENRY VIII's chief minister until discredited by his failure to secure from Pope Clement VII the king's divorce from CATHERINE of Aragon.

women's liberation, a movement campaigning to improve the status of women in society that emerged in the 1960s and early 1970s. The movement was much influenced by radical student politics in North America and Western Europe. Key texts for the movement were *The Feminine Mystique* (1963) by Betty Friedan (1921–) and *The Female Eunuch* (1970) by Germaine Greer (1939–), which presented feminist critiques of women's subordinate position in society, revealing the difficulty for women of entering the world of public and political affairs and the male-dominated sectors of business, industry and banking. In terms of organization, the women's movement has never been a unified whole, but rather a network of separate campaigns and interest groups. Methods have varied from political lobbying to mass demonstrations and there has been much emphasis on the need for women to work together in separate, women-only groups. The contemporary women's movement has emphasized issues of childcare, sexuality, male violence and the role of men and women in the home. Division has surfaced since the early 1970s between those who are most concerned with gaining equal rights, those who adopt a 'radical' stance and argue for women's separation from men in political and sexual ways (often adopting lesbianism as a political statement), and those who link feminist aims with other objectives such as socialism.

women's suffrage, the right of women to vote in elections. The cause of women's suffrage was taken up by 19th-century feminists, and – most famously – by the British SUFFRAGETTES in the early 20th century. Some countries gave the vote to women at the turn of the century – New Zealand (1893), Australia (1902) and Finland (1906). However, it required the impact of the work that many women did in WORLD WAR I, taking over from the men at the Front, to secure the vote for most women in the West. Female suffrage came to Denmark in 1915, the Soviet Union in 1917, Britain, Germany and Poland in 1918, the Netherlands in 1919, Canada in 1920, the USA in 1920 and Ireland in 1922. Women in France, Italy and Eastern Europe had to wait until the 1940s to win the vote. In Britain women aged 30 and over were granted the vote in 1918; in 1928 this was extended to women aged 21 and over.

World Bank (International Bank for Reconstruction and Development), a specialized agency of the UNITED NATIONS set up in 1945 to aid development – particularly in poorer member-countries – through capital investment. However, interest on loans to THIRD WORLD countries have led to debts that have caused strains on already weak economies.

World Health Organization (WHO), a specialized agency of the UNITED NATIONS, established in 1945 with the aim of promoting the attainment by all peoples of the highest possible standards of health.

World War I (1914–18), the war fought between the ALLIES (principally Britain, France, Russia and the USA after 1917) and the CENTRAL POWERS (principally Germany, Austria-Hungary and Turkey; see map, p. 36). Its origins lay in European territorial and political rivalries, and in nationalist agitation in the BALKANS. Germany, allied to Austria-Hungary since 1879 and Italy since 1882, feared an attack from France and Russia (allied since 1894), yet threatened expansion against either or both. Britain viewed German industrial development, naval expansion and colonial ambitions with distrust, and since 1904 had been associated with Germany's rivals. When the Austrian heir Archduke FRANZ FERDINAND was assassinated, the Austrians blamed Serbia and threatened war. The Serbs appealed for help to their fellow Slavs in Russia who mobilized their vast army. Fearing an attack, Germany put into action the SCHLIEFFEN PLAN and declared war on both Russia and France. As German troops crossed into neutral Belgium as a preliminary to their attack on France, Britain (which had guaranteed Belgian independence) declared war on Germany. Fighting on the WESTERN FRONT was characterized by the attritional deadlock of trench warfare. The latter emerged because of new weapons that gave the advantage to the defender, and produced appalling casualties. In the E the Russians advanced into East Prussia in August 1914, but were defeated at TANNENBERG. Further S, however, the Russians pushed the Austrians back into Galicia, necessitating a German reinforcement to prevent defeat. By Christmas 1914 Germany was fighting a war on two fronts. In 1915, as casualties mounted alarmingly, the nature of the war changed, forcing all the major combatants to raise large armies and to mobilize their societies to produce new armaments. Anglo-French offensives failed to break the deadlock on the Western Front, while on the Eastern Front the situation, although more fluid, similarly denied victory to either side. Instead the war expanded. In October 1914 Turkey declared war on the Allies, and in May 1915 Italy – in return for Allied promises of territorial gains from Austria-Hungary – declared war on the Central Powers. In mid-1915 the Germans forced the Russians back through Poland, taking pressure off Germany's E border, and in October Bulgaria joined the Central Powers. Only in Serbia was a decisive campaign fought: by December 1915 the country had been conquered by the Central Powers. The year 1916 saw the attritional slaughter of the Battles of VERDUN and the SOMME on the Western Front, and the nightmare continued at PASSCHENDAELE in 1917. Only on the Austrian–Italian front was there a break in the stalemate, with the defeat of the Italians at CAPORETTO. In these circumstances efforts were made to find alternatives to trench deadlock. In April 1915, in an attempt to open up the southern flank of the Central Powers, the Allies launched a seaborne attack on the GALLIPOLI peninsula. It failed, however, as did a similar campaign in Mesopotamia in April 1916. Only later was success achieved in Mesopotamia and Palestine when a British advance against the Turks was aided by an Arab revolt (1917). Naval campaigns were rare, the only major engagement, at JUTLAND, resulted in stalemate. Britain, however, was successful in imposing a naval blockade on Germany. The German U-boat (submarine) offensive caused heavy British losses, but in 1915 the German U-boat attack on the liner LUSITANIA, with American passengers on board, propelled the Americans into the war. By the end of 1917 the balance of power between the two sides had shifted. In late 1917 Russia dissolved into revolutionary chaos and exited the war in March 1918 after signing the Treaty of BREST-LITOVSK with Germany. This enabled the Germans to concentrate their forces in the West for a major assault on the British and French. However, the initial success of the German offensive of March 1918 was followed by a successful Allied counterattack. Elsewhere, the Central Powers began to crumble, first in the Middle East, then in Italy, where the Austro-Hungarians were defeated at VITTORIO VENETO and forced to seek terms. By November the Germans were isolated and the Allies closing in, and after the German Kaiser WILHELM II fled to Holland an armistic was arranged. At 11 am on 11 November 1918 the fighting ceased. Peace terms were agreed at the VERSAILLES Peace Settlement.

World War II (1939–45), the war fought between the ALLIES (principally the UK, the British Commonwealth, the USSR and the USA from 1941) and the AXIS powers (principally Germany, Italy from 1940 to 1943, and Japan from 1941; see map, p. 39). Its principal causes were the failure of the VERSAILLES Peace Settlement to provide for international security after WORLD WAR I and the territorial ambitions of NAZI Germany under HITLER. The West's policy of APPEASEMENT failed to contain the expansionist aims of Nazi Germany, and on 1 September Germany invaded Poland in pursuance of its territorial demands. Britain and France declared war on Germany on 3 September. After the phase known as the PHONEY WAR, Hitler turned towards the West. In early April 1940 German forces invaded Denmark and Norway and then used BLITZKRIEG tactics to attack the Netherlands, Belgium and France. Anglo-French forces moved into Belgium, but soon found themselves trapped on the coast and were obliged to retreat to DUNKIRK. After the French surrender of 22 June the N part of France was placed under German occupation, while the rest of the country was administered by the pro-German VICHY government. A German U-boat campaign against British shipping began to take its toll. The Germans tried to destroy the RAF as a preliminary to an invasion of the British Isles, but were defeated in the Battle of BRITAIN. The Germans then switched to attacks on London and other cities in the BLITZ. Italy entered the war in June 1940, seizing Somaliland and invading Egypt. The British counterattacked successfully in E Libya in December 1940, but were pushed back by German forces under ROMMEL (see NORTH AFRICAN CAMPAIGNS). In the Mediterranean the Germans overran Yugoslavia, Greece and Crete (April–May 1941). British fortunes were at a low ebb, boosted only by the LEND-LEASE policy of the USA. The war escalated on 22 June 1941 when Hitler's forces attacked the USSR, bringing the Soviets into the war, and creating an EASTERN FRONT. On 7 December 1941 the war spread to the Pacific when the Japanese bombed the US Pacific fleet at PEARL HARBOR, bringing the USA into the war (see PACIFIC CAMPAIGNS). Concerted strategies were agreed between the Allies, with the defeat of Germany given priority. In North Africa the tide turned for the Allies at EL ALAMEIN. German forces were pushed out of North African by May 1943. In July 1943 Sicily was invaded, and in September, southern Italy (see ITALIAN CAMPAIGN). On the Eastern Front the decisive battles of STALINGRAD and KURSK turned the tide against Germany. On 6 June 1944 – D-DAY – the Allies invaded N France in the NORMANDY LANDINGS, marking the beginning of 'Operation Overlord', the liberation of NORTHWEST EUROPE. From now the end came swiftly for Germany. Attacked from the air by fleets of Anglo-US bombers, its cities lay in ruins and, despite a desperate German counterattack through the ARDENNES in December 1944, the Allies closed in. In the E the Russians drove from Warsaw to Berlin; in the W the Anglo-Americans crossed the Rhine and reached the River Elbe; in Italy the Germans were pushed over the Alps. Hitler committed suicide in late April 1945 and Berlin fell to the Soviets in early May. On 8 May Germany surrendered unconditionally. The Japanese surrendered on 15 August, the Americans having brought the Pacific War to an end with the use of atomic bombs at HIROSHIMA and NAGASAKI. The dead in World War II have been estimated at 15 million military and as many as 35 million civilians. The USA and USSR emerged from the war as the world's two superpowers. See also YALTA and POTSDAM CONFERENCES.

Worms, Diet of (1521), a meeting of the DIET of the HOLY ROMAN EMPIRE, at which LUTHER defended his teachings in the presence of the Emperor CHARLES V. Having heard Luther, the Diet condemned his teaching.

Wounded Knee, massacre of (1890), the last major 'battle' of America's Indian Wars, fought in South Dakota. US 7th cavalry gunned down some 200 SIOUX men, women and children who were resisting attempts to disarm them.

Wyclif, John (?1330–84), English theological reformer. He based his criticism of the established Church on a study of scripture, rejecting the authority of the papacy and the doctrine of transubstantiation in the Eucharist. His followers – insultingly known as LOLLARDS – stressed the importance of individual action for salvation, in contrast to the Church's emphasis on the mediatory role of the priesthood. His writings influenced the Bohemian reformer, Jan HUS.

Xenophon (c. 435–354 BC), Greek soldier, who led 10,000 Greek mercenaries in a heroic retreat during a civil war in the Persian Empire. He recounted this exploit in his great work, the *Anabasis*.

Xerxes I (c. 519–465 BC), king of Persia (486–465 BC) and son of DARIUS I. He crushed a rebellion in Egypt shortly after his accession and three years later put down a revolt in Babylon. He reversed the Persian tradition of tolerance, ignoring local traditions and pursuing ruthless policies after his victories. In 480 BC he invaded the Greek mainland at the head of a large army, reviving the PERSIAN WARS. After initial successes, the campaign foundered with defeats at SALAMIS and PLATAEA. By that time he had returned to Persia, leaving his general Mardonius in charge. The rest of his reign was spent attending to his building programme at Persepolis and dealing with harem intrigues, which were to lead to his assassination in 465.

Xhosa, a cattle-farming people of S Africa. The eastward push of British settlers from the early 19th century led to wars in 1834–5, 1846–53 and 1877–9. Today the Xhosa live mainly in the BANTUSTANS of the Transkei and the Ciskei.

Xia, traditionally the first dynasty to rule China (c. 21st–16th centuries BC).

Yalta Conference (4–11 February 1945), the second meeting of the 'Big Three' Allied leaders at which STALIN, CHURCHILL and ROOSEVELT discussed the final stages of WORLD WAR II and the postwar division of Europe. It was implicitly agreed that the USSR should maintain its influence in Eastern Europe, and that Germany should be partitioned. The Conference also agreed on the establishment of the UNITED NATIONS.

Yamashita, Tomoyuki (1885–1946), Japanese general known as the 'Tiger of Malaya'. He commanded the forces that overran Malaya (1941–2) and Singapore (1942) in the PACIFIC CAMPAIGNS of WORLD WAR II. He was defeated in the Philippines in the campaign against the Americans (1944–5) and was later executed for war crimes.

Yeltsin, Boris Nikolayevich (1931–), the dominant statesman of post-Communist Russia. An outspoken critic of

GORBACHOV from the late 1980s, he was president of the Russian Federation 1990–1, led the opposition to the Soviet coup of August 1991, and became president of the newly independent Russian federation when the Soviet Union collapsed in December 1991. He was instrumental in the establishment of the COMMONWEALTH OF INDEPENDENT STATES, and introduced price deregulation and privatization. Faced with severe economic problems, political wrangles with parliament and constitutional crises, he has had to rely in part on the support and financial aid from the West to maintain his position.

Yemen, a country of SW Asia. From the 8th to the 1st century BC the N was the home of the Sabaeans. In AD 628 the area became Islamic. The OTTOMAN Turks first occupied the area in 1517 and were not finally expelled from the N until 1911, when Imam Yahya secured Yemen's independence. Britain took ADEN as a staging post to India (1839) and gradually established a protectorate over the S. In 1963 an armed rebellion began against British rule in the S which gained independence in 1967 after a civil war between rival liberation movements. A republican revolution broke out in the N in 1962, and from 1963 until 1970 a civil war was fought, with President NASSER's Egypt supporting the victorious republicans and Saudi Arabia supporting the royalists. Relations between North Yemen and Marxist South Yemen were difficult. The collapse of South Yemen's Communist trading partners (1989–90) undermined the country's weak economy, and the two countries merged in May 1990.

Yom Kippur War, the name given by the Israelis to the 1973 ARAB–ISRAELI WAR. Following the failure of diplomatic overtures aimed at recovering territory lost in the SIX DAY WAR, Egypt and Syria mounted major attacks on Israel, under cover of the Jewish religious holiday Yom Kippur. Despite being caught by war on two fronts, the Israelis defeated Egypt and Syria after 19 days of hard fighting. At one point the war threatened to escalate when a US nuclear alert was triggered by apparent Soviet moves to commit troops to support Egypt and Syria.

Yongle (1359–1424), MING emperor of CHINA (1403–24) and son of HONGWU. He extended the Chinese empire with campaigns in Central Asia and Annam (modern Vietnam), and sent out the voyages of discovery of ZHENG HE.

York, Richard, 3rd Duke of (1411–60), heir to the throne of England until 1453. He claimed the throne in 1460, in opposition to HENRY VI of the house of LANCASTER. Despite his death at the battle of Wakefield (1460), and the YORKIST defeat at the second battle of St Albans (1461) during the Wars of the ROSES, Richard's son gained the throne as EDWARD IV shortly afterwards.

Yorkist, the dynastic name given to the English kings from EDWARD IV to RICHARD III, descendants of Richard, 3rd Duke of YORK. In 1460 Richard claimed their right to the throne in opposition to the LANCASTRIAN HENRY VI; in consequence they became one of the two warring parties in the Wars of the ROSES.

Yorktown, Battle of (1781), the final battle of the American War of INDEPENDENCE. When a British army under CORNWALLIS found itself besieged by George WASHINGTON at Yorkstown in 1781, a French fleet in Chesapeake Bay cut off its only avenue of escape. Cornwallis surrendered on 19 October. The battle turned out to be the decisive engagement of the war, and two years later Britain recognized American independence.

Yoruba, a people living in the SW of modern NIGERIA; the focus of early cultures such as Ife and the development of kingship and urbanism in W Africa. The Yoruba kingdom of Oyo was a major force in 18th-century W Africa. They lived in symbiosis with the coastal traders, supplying them with gold and slaves to work the plantations of the Americas in exchange for textiles, iron goods and guns.

Young Italy, an Italian nationalist organization founded during the RISORGIMENTO. A radical democratic sect led by Giuseppe MAZZINI, it generated a few abortive uprisings, but was more successful in spreading patriotic feeling among future leaders, such as GARIBALDI.

Young Plan (1929), a plan for German REPARATIONS payments after WORLD WAR I. Devised by a committee under US financier Owen D. Young, it replaced the DAWES Plan.

Young Turks, OTTOMAN patriots dedicated to the Westernization of Turkey, who forced constitutional change in 1908 by allying themselves to elements of the Turkish army. In 1909 they forced Sultan ABDUL HAMID II to abdicate in favour of his son and effectively seized power.

Ypres, Battles of, three battles fought on a salient in the British line near the Belgian town of Ypres in WORLD WAR I. The first (October 1914) defeated the German attempt to reach the Channel ports. The second (April–May 1915) saw the first use of poison gas on the WESTERN FRONT. The third (July–November 1917) is better known as PASSCHENDAELE. See map p. 36.

Yuan, the MONGOL dynasty (1271–1368) established in CHINA by KUBLAI KHAN (see map, p. 19). Kublai ruled China in the traditional imperial fashion, as did his successors. The system worked well under Kublai, but under less brilliant successors and long minorities, Mongol control over China began to disintegrate. By the mid-14th century, nationalist rebellion was being raised in the provinces. A rebel army took the southern capital of Nanjing in 1356 and gradually extended its power over China until the Mongols fled from Beijing in 1368. They were succeeded by the MING dynasty.

Yuan Shikai (Yuan Shih-k'ai; 1859–1916), Chinese soldier and politician. He became president of the new Chinese republic in 1912 after the fall of the QING dynasty, but his suppression of Sun Yat-sen's KUOMINTANG and submissive attitude to an increasingly expansionist Japan provoked further unrest. China was left divided between rival WARLORDS after his death.

Yucatán, a tropical lowland peninsula of E Mexico, a major centre of pre-Columbian Meso-American civilization, particularly at the height of MAYA culture (AD 300–900). It was later dominated by the TOLTECS and AZTECS.

Yugoslavia, a country of SE Europe. See panel.

Zaire, a republic of central Africa. The African Luba and Kuba kingdoms flourished from the 16th to the 18th centuries. The region was ravaged by the slave trade, and in 1885 became the personal possession of King LEOPOLD II of the Belgians. It finally achieved independence in 1960, but was plunged immediately into the CONGO CRISIS. Colonel MOBUTU twice intervened in the troubled affairs of the Congo and in 1965 made himself head of state. He renamed the country Zaire, gradually restored the authority of the central government, and introduced a one-party state (1967). Mobutu's strong rule has attracted international criticism. Following unrest in the early 1990s, some reforms were made and a national conference was summoned to bring democracy to Zaire (1991). In 1992–3 conflicts developed between the national conference and the PM on the one hand and President Mobutu on the other. Sections of the army became disaffected and law and order has broken down in parts of the country.

YUGOSLAVIA

6th and 7th centuries AD: The SLAV ancestors of the Serbs arrived in the W Balkans creating a large kingdom. **14th century:** Slav kingdom destroyed by OTTOMAN conquest in the Battle of Kosovo (1369). **1516–1851:** Autonomous MONTENEGRO ruled by independent prince-bishops. **1804–13:** The Serbs, led by KARAGEORGE, rose against Turkish rule. **1815:** Under Miloś OBRENOVIĆ, the Serbs rose again and became an autonomous principality; Serbia destabilized by rivalry between the Karageorge and Obrenović dynasties thereafter. **1878:** Both SERBIA and Montenegro were recognized as independent at the Congress of BERLIN. **By the early 20th century:** Growing nationalist feeling in CROATIA, which looked increasingly to Serbia to create a South ('Yugo') Slav state. **1912–13:** BALKAN WARS; Serbia acquired MACEDONIA. **1914:** Assassination of the Habsburg heir by a Serb student gave Austria an excuse to quash Serbian independence, leading to the outbreak of World War I. **1914–18:** WORLD WAR I; Serbia and Montenegro overrun by (Habsburg) Austro-Hungarian Empire. **1918:** Serbia and Montenegro united with BOSNIA, CROATIA and SLOVENIA to form the Kingdom of Serbs, Croats and Slovenes (renamed Yugoslavia in 1929); the new state, wracked by nationalist tensions, was run as a highly centralized 'Greater Serbia' in the interwar period. **1941:** Yugoslavia attacked and dismembered by NAZI Germany. **1934:** King Alexander murdered by Croat separatists. **1941–5:** Yugoslavs fought the Nazis and each other; Communist partisans, led by Josip TITO, emerged victorious. **1945:** Yugoslavia re-formed on Soviet lines, with Tito as president. **1948:** Yugoslavia expelled from the Soviet bloc. **1980:** Death of Tito. **After 1980:** Rise of local nationalism; Serbia suppressed Albanian nationalists in Kosovo province. **1990:** Free elections held throughout Yugoslavia. **1991:** SLOVENIA and CROATIA seceded; Serb-dominated Yugoslav federal forces conducted a short and unsuccessful campaign against Slovenia, but occupied one-third of Croatia. **1992:** BOSNIA-HERZEGOVINA and MACEDONIA declared independence; Yugoslavia reduced to a small Serb-dominated state consisting of Serbia and Montenegro; Serbia intervened in Bosnian civil war; international sanctions against Serbia and Montenegro crippled the Yugoslav economy, leading to hyperinflation.

Zama, Battle of (202 BC), the defeat of HANNIBAL by SCIPIO AFRICANUS in N Africa, ending the Second PUNIC WAR.

Zambia, a republic of central Africa. The area was brought under the control of the British South Africa Company of Cecil RHODES in the 1890s. In 1924 Britain took over the administration from the Company, but development of the colony (named Northern Rhodesia) was initially slow. Skilled mining jobs were reserved for white immigrants, and, fearing increased discrimination, Africans opposed inclusion in the Central African Federation – with Nyasaland (Malawi) and Southern Rhodesia (Zimbabwe) – in 1953. Against strong opposition from white settlers Kenneth KAUNDA led Zambia to independence in 1964. He ruled the country as a one-party state from 1973 to 1990, when he was defeated in free elections.

Zanzibar, see TANZANIA.

Zapata, Emiliano (1879–1919), an agrarian rebel and guerrilla leader during the MEXICAN REVOLUTION. He dominated the sugar-growing state of Morelos from 1911 until his assassination in 1919.

Zealots, a militant Jewish sect involved in the anti-Roman revolt of AD 66. They were besieged by the Romans at MASADA. See also ISRAEL.

zeppelin, a generic term for German airships, principally in WORLD WAR I, named after their designer Graf Ferdinand von Zeppelin.

Zheng He (Cheng Ho; died c. 1433), Chinese admiral and explorer. A eunuch of the court of Emperor YONGLE, he took Chinese fleets to explore the old trade routes to the Spice Islands, Arabia and Africa between 1405 and 1433, when an inward-looking Chinese government decided against further exploration. The abandonment of exploration by the Chinese left the field to European explorers. See map, p. 24.

Zhivkov, Todor (1911–), Bulgarian Communist politician, First Secretary of the Communist Party (1954–89), prime minister (1962–71), president (1971–89). A hardliner, he was replaced as party leader by reformers in 1989.

Zhou, the second historical Chinese dynasty (1122–256 BC). Moving in from the W, the rulers of the Zhou displaced the SHANG as overlords of the Chinese heartland c. 1000 BC. The Zhou expanded their hegemony N as far as Manchuria and S over the Yangtze basin. Within those boundaries, advances in agriculture (irrigation) and technology (iron-working) made it possible to support powerful local rulers, their courts and warriors. As the centuries passed, power devolved to these smaller states, which eventually – from the mid-5th century BC – became the WARRING STATES. At the courts of Zhou China, the essentials of Chinese views on the good society were developed, particularly by the administrator-philosopher KONGFUZI.

Zhou Enlai (Chou En-lai; 1898–1976), Chinese Communist politician, prime minister (1949–76), foreign minister (1949–58). A founder member of the Chinese Communist

Party, in 1949 he became the first PM of the People's Republic. He exercised a moderating influence on extremist elements during the CULTURAL REVOLUTION. The best-known and best-regarded of China's leaders on the international stage, he played a major role in the Sino–US détente of the early 1970s.

Zhukov, Georgi Konstantinovich (1896–1974), Soviet field marshal. The architect of the Soviet Union's campaigns in WORLD WAR II, he defeated the Germans at STALINGRAD, lifted the siege of LENINGRAD, and led the final assault on Germany and capture of Berlin.

Zia ul-Haq, Mohammed (1924–88), Pakistani soldier and politician. He overthrew Z.A. BHUTTO in a coup (1977). As president of PAKISTAN from 1978 he banned political parties, introduced an Islamic legal code, and played the role of US surrogate in the Afghan civil war. He died in an air crash in 1988, while still in office.

Zimbabwe, a republic of S central Africa. The region was the location of the ancient Zimbabwe kingdom. The area was gradually penetrated by British and Boer hunters, missionaries and prospectors from the 1830s, and was occupied by the British South Africa Company of Cecil RHODES in the 1890s. The highlands of what became Southern Rhodesia were settled by white farmers, who deprived Africans of land and reduced them to a cheap labour force. Britain took over the administration from the Company in 1923 and granted self-government to the white colonists. Immigration from Britain and South Africa increased after World War II, but the whites remained outnumbered by the Africans by more than 20 to 1. Racial discrimination stimulated African nationalism, initially led by Joshua Nkomo (1917–). When the short-lived CENTRAL AFRICAN FEDERATION of South Rhodesia, North Rhodesia (Zambia) and Nyasaland (Malawi) was dissolved (1963), Britain refused the white South Rhodesian administration independence without progress to majority rule. The white government led by Ian SMITH (1919–) unilaterally declared independence in 1965, renaming the country Rhodesia. Internal opposition was crushed and international economic sanctions were overcome, but guerrilla wars, mounted by African nationalists during the 1970s, became increasingly effective. In 1979 Smith had to accept majority rule, but the constitution he introduced was unacceptable either to the Zimbabwe African People's Union (ZAPU) of Joshua Nkomo or to the Zimbabwe African National Union (ZANU) of Robert MUGABE. All parties agreed to the brief reimposition of British rule to achieve a settlement. ZANU under Mugabe took the country to independence in 1980. In 1987 ZANU and ZAPU finally agreed to unite, effectively introducing a one-party state, though proposals for an official one-party system have been shelved.

Zimbabwe, Great, an ancient palace-city of SE Africa. The existing palace was built by rulers of the local SHONA people in the 14th and 15th centuries AD. The power and wealth of its rulers had its roots in their control over the supply of local gold to the E coast of Africa and its Arab traders.

Zimmermann note (January 1917), a secret telegram from German foreign minister Alfred Zimmermann to the German minister in Mexico City, stating that should the USA join the ALLIES, Germany would help Mexico to recover Texas, New Mexico and Arizona (lost to the USA in 1848). Revelation of the telegram accelerated the decline of US-German relations which led to US entry into WORLD WAR I on 6 April.

Zinoviev, Grigory Yevseyevich (1883–1936), Soviet politician. A letter allegedly written by Zinoviev urging British Communists to revolt may have contributed to the LABOUR government's defeat in the 1924 general election.

Zionism, the Jewish national liberation movement, founded in the 1890s by Theodor HERZL. It was dedicated to the creation of a national home for the Jews, free from the ANTI-SEMITISM rife in parts of Europe. It became the political creed of the Jewish settlers in Palestine and the driving force behind the creation of ISRAEL in 1948.

Zizka, John (?1370–1424), Bohemian priest and soldier who led the HUSSITE rebellion. Influenced by Jan HUS, he led the Hussites in their defeat of the crusaders from Germany, Austria and Hungary.

Zog I (Ahmed Zogu; 1895–1961), king of ALBANIA (1928–39). He dominated the interwar politics of Albania, becoming first president (1925–8) and then king. He fled to Britain when MUSSOLINI invaded in 1939, and formally abdicated in 1946.

Zollverein (German, 'customs union'), a customs union abolishing economic barriers between the various German states in 1834. The union established PRUSSIA's economic domination of the GERMAN CONFEDERATION and isolated protectionist Austria. The union was accompanied by practical measures to bring currencies into line and construct a transport infrastructure of roads and railways.

Zoroastrianism, the religion of the ancient Iranians and their rulers, particularly the SASSANIANS. It was the Persian state religion from the 6th century BC to the 6th century AD, but after ISLAM spread to Iran, the Zoroastrians were persecuted and retreated to the cities of Yazd and Kerman. In the 10th century AD, some fled to India. Today Bombay is the centre for these exiled Zoroastrians, known as Parsis.

Zulus, a BANTU people of SE Africa (modern NATAL). They became the dominant military force in the area under the leadership of Shaka (1818–28). Zulu expansion – to secure grazing land for their cattle – precipitated the migration of surrounding peoples. They remained powerful until defeated by Britain in the Zulu War (1879). Zululand was annexed by Britain in 1894. Today the Zulus live mainly in the BANTUSTAN of Kwazulu. Chief BUTHELEZI leads the Inkatha cultural movement for Zulu revival.

Zuni, a native North American people of the Southwest, living in New Mexico.

Zwingli, Ulrich (1484–1531), the leader of the REFORMATION in Switzerland. He broke with LUTHER over differences between them on the nature of the Eucharist. Whereas Luther sometimes allowed what the Bible did not reject, Zwingli would only permit what it specifically mentioned. The Zwinglian church therefore tended to be simpler, and a more radical break with past practice, than the Lutheran. After his death in battle against the Swiss Catholic cantons, the leadership of the Swiss Reformation passed to CALVIN.